The Princeton Review

PrincetonReview.com

THE BEST 172 LAW SCHOOLS

2010 EDITION

Eric Owens, Esq., John Owens, Esq., Julie Doherty, and The Staff of The Princeton Review

Random House, Inc.
New York

The Princeton Review, Inc.
2315 Broadway
New York, NY 10024
E-mail: bookeditor@review.com

ISBN: 978-0-375-42958-3

VP, Publisher: Robert Franek
AVP, Production: Scott Harris
Senior Production Editor: M. Tighe Wall
Content Manager: David Soto
Editors: Seamus Mullarkey and Laura Braswell

Printed in the United States of America on partially recycled paper.

9 8 7 6 5 4 3 2 1

2010 Edition

ACKNOWLEDGMENTS

Eric Owens would like to say, "Thank you, John Katzman, for pretty much everything."

Thanks also to Laura Braswell for the support and guidance on this book and many others and to Bob Spruill for his LSAT expertise.

In addition, many thanks should go to David Soto and Ben Zelevansky for spearheading the law school data collection efforts. Their survey, along with the support and assistance of Andrea Kornstein, allowed for the completion of a totally cohesive stat-packed guide.

A special thanks must go to our production team: Scott Harris and M. Tighe Wall. Your commitment, flexibility, and attention to detail are always appreciated in both perfect and crunch times.

—Eric Owens

I'd like to send my thanks:

To Eric Owens, my quasi-cousin, who kept me in mind for this project.

To my editors at The Princeton Review, who trusted me (and the other Eric Owens) enough to give me the chance.

To my family and friends, who support me in the things I do.

To the law students who took the time to complete the law student survey.

—John Owens

I would like to thank my parents, Brucine and Francis Doherty, the staff of The Princeton Review, and Arturo Meade.

—Julie Doherty

CONTENTS

PREFACE

Welcome to *The Best 172 Law Schools*, The Princeton Review's truly indispensable guide for anyone thinking about entering the law school fray. This is not simply a reprint of the garden-variety fluff in each law school's admissions booklet. We have attempted to provide a significant amount of essential information from a vast array of sources to give you a complete, accurate, and easily digestible snapshot of the best law schools in the country. Here you'll find a wealth of practical advice on admissions, taking and acing the Law School Admissions Test (LSAT), choosing the right school, and doing well once you're there. You'll also find all the information you need on schools' bar exam pass rates, ethnic group and gender breakdown percentages, tuition, average starting salaries of graduates, and much more. For 172 ABA-approved law schools, you'll find descriptive profiles of the student experience based on the opinions of the only true law school experts: current law school students. Indeed, with this handy reference, you should be able to narrow your choices from the few hundred law schools in North America to a handful in no time at all.

Never trust any single source of information too much, though—not even us. Take advantage of all the resources available to you, including friends, family members, the Internet, and your local library. Obviously, the more you explore all the options available to you, the better decision you'll make. We hope you will be happy wherever you end up and that this guide will be helpful in your search to find the best law school for you.

Best of luck!

So Much More Online!

MORE GUIDANCE...

- Find the school that best fits your needs, from part-time options to specialized programs.

- Learn about raising test scores, finding an internship, and planning out your career after you graduate.

- Get the inside scoop of scholarships and financial aid.

MORE INFORMATION...

- Read articles on what it's really like to be in grad school.

- Learn what students have to say in detailed profiles for hundreds of colleges covering everything from administration to student diversity on campus.

- Compare Top 10 ranking lists regarding Quality of Professors, Classroom Experience, Career Prospects, Competitive Students, Quality of Life, and tons more!

MORE GOOD STUFF . . .

- Discover other Princeton Review titles that will help you take your career in a new direction or ace that next big exam.

- Discuss issues with your peers on our discussion board.

- Find answers to any of your grad school questions, and much, much more!

ALL ABOUT LAW SCHOOL

CHAPTER 1
So You Want to Go to Law School

Congrats! Law school is a tremendous intellectual challenge and an amazing experience. It can be confusing and occasionally traumatic—especially during the crucial first year—but the cryptic ritual of legal education will make you a significantly better thinker, a consummate reader, and a far more mature person over the course of three years.

The application process is rigorous, but it's not impossible. Here's our advice.

WHAT MAKES A COMPETITIVE APPLICANT?
It depends. One of the great things about law schools in the United States is that there are a lot of them, and standards for admission run the gamut from appallingly difficult to not very hard at all.

Let's just say, for example, you have your heart set on Yale Law School, arguably the finest law school in all the land. Let's also say you have stellar academic credentials: a 3.45 GPA and an LSAT score in the 99th percentile of everyone who takes it. With these heady numbers, you've got a whopping 2 percent chance of getting into Yale, at best. However, with the same 3.45 GPA and LSAT score in the 99th percentile, you are pretty much a lock at legal powerhouses like Duke University School of Law and Boston College Law School. With significantly lower numbers—say, a 3.02 GPA and an LSAT score in the 81st percentile—you stand a mediocre chance of getting into top-flight law schools like Case Western or Indiana. With a little bit of luck, these numbers might land you a spot at George Washington or UCLA.

> **Fascinating Acronyms**
>
> **LSAC:** Law School Admission Council, headquartered in beautiful Newtown, Pennsylvania
>
> **LSAT:** Law School Admissions Test
>
> **LSDAS:** Law School Data Assembly Service
>
> **ABA:** American Bar Association

This is good news. The even better news is that there are several totally respectable law schools out there that will let you in with a 2.5 GPA and an LSAT of 148 (which is about the 36th percentile). If you end up in the top 10 percent of your class at one of these schools and have even a shred of interviewing skill, you'll get a job that is just as prestigious and pays just as much money as the jobs garnered by Yale grads. Notice the important catch here, however: You *must* graduate in the top 10 percent of your class at so-called "lesser" schools, while almost every Yale Law grad who wants a high-paying job can land one.

Ultimately, there's a law school out there for you. If you want to get into a "top-flight" or "pretty good" school, you're in for some fairly stiff competition. Unfortunately, it doesn't help that the law school admissions process is somewhat formulaic; your LSAT score and your GPA are vastly more important to the process than anything else about you. If your application ends up in the "maybe" pile, your recommendations, your major, the reputation of your college alma mater, a well-written and nongeneric essay, and various other factors will play a larger role in determining your fate.

THE ADMISSIONS INDEX
The first thing most law schools will look at when evaluating your application is your "index." It's a number (which varies from school to school) made up of a weighted combination of your undergraduate GPA and LSAT score. In virtually every case, the LSAT is weighted more heavily than the GPA.

While the process differs from school to school, it is generally the case that your index will put you into one of three piles:

(Probably) Accepted. A select few applicants with high LSAT scores and stellar GPAs are admitted pretty much automatically. If your index is very, very strong compared with the school's median or target number, you're as good as in, unless you are a convicted felon or you wrote your personal statement in crayon.

(Probably) Rejected. If your index is very weak compared with the school's median or target number, you are probably going to be rejected without much ado. When Admissions Officers read weaker applications (yes, at almost every school every application is read) they will be looking for something so outstanding or unique that it makes them willing to take a chance. Factors that can help include ethnic background, where you are from, or very impressive work or life experience. That said, don't hold your breath because not many people in this category are going to make the cut.

Well...Maybe. The majority of applicants fall in the middle; their index number is right around the median or target index number. People in this category have decent enough LSAT scores and GPAs for the school, but not high enough for automatic admission. Why do most people fall into this category? For the most part, people apply to schools they think they have at least a shot of getting into based on their grades and LSAT scores; Yale doesn't see very many applicants who got a 140 on the LSAT. What will determine the fate of those whose applications hang in the balance? One thing law schools often look at is the competitiveness of your undergraduate program. On the one hand, someone with a 3.3 GPA in an easy major from a school where everybody graduates with a 3.3 or higher will face an uphill battle. On the other hand, someone with the same GPA in a difficult major from a school that has a reputation for being stingy with A's is in better shape. Admissions Officers will also pore over the rest of your application—personal statement, letters of recommendation, resume, etc.—for reasons to admit you, reject you, or put you on their waiting lists.

ARE YOU MORE THAN YOUR LSAT SCORE?

Aside from LSAT scores and GPAs, what do law schools consider when deciding who's in and who's out? It's the eternal question. On the one hand, we should relieve you hidebound cynics of the notion that they care about nothing else. On the other hand, if you harbor fantasies that a stunning application can overcome truly substandard scores and grades, you should realize that such hopes are unrealistic.

Nonquantitative factors are particularly important at law schools that receive applications from thousands of numerically qualified applicants. A "top 10" law school that receives 10 or 15 applications for every spot in its first-year class has no choice but to "look beyond the numbers," as admissions folks are fond of saying. Such a school will almost surely have to turn away hundreds of applicants with near-perfect LSAT scores and college grades, and those applicants who get past the initial cut will be subjected to real scrutiny.

Less competitive schools are just as concerned, in their own way, with "human criteria" as are the Harvards and Stanfords of the world. They are on the lookout for capable people who have relatively unimpressive GPAs and LSAT scores. The importance of the application is greatly magnified for these students, who must demonstrate their probable success in law school in other ways.

CAN PHYSICS MAJORS GO TO LAW SCHOOL?

"What about my major?" is one of the more popular questions we hear when it comes to law school admissions. The conventional answer to this question goes something like, "There is no prescribed, pre-law curriculum, but you should seek a broad and challenging liberal arts education, etc."

Translation: It really doesn't matter what you major in. Obviously, a major in aviation or hotel and restaurant management is not exactly ideal, but please—we beg you!—don't feel restricted to a few majors simply because you want to attend law school. This is especially true if those particular majors do not interest you. Comparative literature? Fine. American studies? Go to town. Physics? No problem whatsoever. You get the idea.

Think about it. Because most would-be law students end up majoring in the *same* few fields (e.g., political science and philosophy), their applications all look the *same* to the folks in law school Admissions Offices. You want to stand out, which is why it is a good idea to major in something *different*. Ultimately, you should major in whatever appeals to you. Of course, if you want to major in political science or philosophy (or you already have), well, that's fine too.

DOES GRAD SCHOOL COUNT?

Your grades in graduate school will not be included in the calculation of your GPA (only the UGPA, the undergraduate grade point average, is reported to the schools) but will be taken into account separately by an Admissions Committee if you make them available. Reporting grad school grades would be to your advantage, particularly if they are better than your college grades. Admissions Committees are likely to take this as a sign of maturation.

ADVICE FOR THE "NONTRADITIONAL" APPLICANT

The term "nontraditional" is, of course, used to describe applicants who are a few years or many years older than run-of-the-mill law school applicants.

In a nutshell, there's no time like the present to start law school. While it's true that most law students are in their early to mid-20s, if you aren't, don't think for a minute that your age will keep you from getting in and having a great experience. Applicants for full-time and part-time slots at U.S. law schools range in ages from 21 to 71 and include every age in between. Some of these older applicants always intended to go to law school and simply postponed it to work, travel, or start a family. Other older applicants never seriously considered law school until after they were immersed in other occupations.

Part-time attendance is especially worth checking into if you've been out of college for a few years. Also, dozens of law schools offer evening programs—particularly in urban centers.

MINORITY LAW SCHOOL APPLICANTS

Things are definitely looking up. According to figures published by the American Bar Association's Committee on Legal Education, in 1978 more than 90 percent of the law students in the ABA's 167 schools were white. In recent years, however, the number of non-whites enrolled in law school has nearly doubled, from about 10 percent to more than 20 percent. Taking an even longer view, figures have tripled since 1972, when minority enrollment was only 6.6 percent. These days, the American Bar Association and the legal profession in general seem pretty committed to seeking and admitting applicants who are members of historically underrepresented minority groups.

WOMEN IN LAW SCHOOL

During the past decade, the number of female lawyers has escalated rapidly, and women undeniably have become more visible in the uppermost echelons of the field. According to statistics compiled by the American Bar Association (ABA), more than 17.9 percent of all law firm partners are women, and women make up more than 30 percent of all lawyers.

More and more women are going to law school as well. At a solid majority of the ABA-approved law schools in the United States, the percentage of women in the student population is 49 percent, and women make up more than half of the students at a handful of schools.

Gender discrimination certainly lingers here and there, though. You might want to check certain statistics on the law schools you are interested in, such as the percentage of women on Law Review and the percentage of female professors who are tenured or on track to be tenured. (Nationally, 36 percent of all full law school professors are women, and 27 percent of tenured faculty are women.) Also, visit each law school and talk with female students and female professors about how women are treated at that particular school. Finally, see if the school has published any gender studies about itself. If it has, you obviously ought to check those out, too.

Waiting Lists

If a law school puts you on its waiting list, it means you may be admitted depending on how many of the applicants they've already admitted decide to go to another school. Most schools rank students on their waiting list; they'll probably tell you where you stand if you give them a call. Also, note that schools routinely admit students from their waiting lists in late August. If you are on a school's waiting list and you really, really want to go there, keep your options at least partially open. You just might be admitted in the middle of first-year orientation.

Engineering and Math Majors Make Great Law Students

A disproportionate number of law students with backgrounds in the so-called "hard sciences" (math, physics, engineering, etc.) make very high grades in law school, probably because they are trained to think methodically and efficiently about isolated problems (which is what law students are supposed to do on exams).

CHAPTER 2
CHOOSING A LAW SCHOOL

There are some key things you should consider before randomly selecting schools from around the country or just submitting your application to somebody else's list of the Top 10 law schools.

LOCATION

It's a big deal. If you were born and raised in the state of New Mexico, care deeply about the "Land of Enchantment," wish to practice law there, and want to be the governor someday, then your best bet is to go to the University of New Mexico. A school's reputation is usually greater on its home turf than anywhere else (except for some of the larger-than-life schools, like Harvard and Yale). Also, most law schools tend to teach law that is specific to the statutes of the states in which they are located. Knowledge of the eccentricities of state law will help you immensely three years down the road when it comes time to pass the bar exam. Even further, the Career Services Office at your school will be strongly connected to the local legal industry. As a purely practical matter, it will be much easier to find a job and get to interviews in Boston, for example, if you live there. Still another reason to consider geographical location is the simple fact that you'll put down professional and social roots and get to know many really great people throughout your law school career. Leaving them won't be any fun. Finally, starting with geographic limitations is the easiest way to reduce your number of potential schools dramatically.

SPECIALIZATION

Word has it that specialization is the trend of the future. General practitioners in law are becoming less common, so it makes sense to let future lawyers begin to specialize in school. At certain schools, you may receive your JD with an official emphasis in, say, taxation. Specialization is a particularly big deal at smaller or newer schools whose graduates cannot simply get by on their school's reputation. Just between us, it's kind of hard to specialize in anything at most law schools because every graduate has to take this huge exam—the bar—that tests about a dozen topics. Most of your course selections will (and should) be geared toward passing the bar, which leaves precious few hours for specialization. You'll almost certainly specialize, but it's not something to worry about until you actually look for a job. All of that said, if you already know what kind of law you want to specialize in, you're in good shape. Many schools offer certain specialties because of their locations. If you are very interested in environmental law, you'd be better off going to Vermont Law School or Lewis and Clark's Northwestern School of Law than to Brooklyn Law School. Similarly, if you want to work with children as an attorney, check out Loyola University Chicago's Child Law Center. So look at what you want to do in addition to where you want to do it.

JOINT-DEGREE PROGRAMS

In addition to offering specialized areas of study, many law schools have instituted formal dual-degree programs. These schools, nearly all of which are directly affiliated with a parent institution, offer students the opportunity to pursue a JD while also working toward some other degree. Although the JD/MBA combination is the most popular joint-degree sought, many universities offer a JD program combined with degrees in everything from public policy to public administration to social work. In today's perpetually competitive legal market, dual degrees may make some students more marketable for certain positions. However, don't sign up for a dual-degree program on a whim—they require a serious amount of work and often a serious amount of tuition.

Dean's List

According to a letter signed by just about every dean of every ABA-approved law school in the country, the following are the factors you should consider when choosing a law school:

- *Breadth and support of alumni network*
- *Breadth of curriculum*
- *Clinical programs*
- *Collaborative research opportunities with faculty*
- *Commitment to innovative technology*
- *Cost*
- *Externship options*
- *Faculty accessibility*
- *Intensity of writing instruction*
- *Interdisciplinary programs*
- *International programming*
- *Law library strengths and services*
- *Loan repayment assistance for low-income lawyers*
- *Location*
- *Part-time enrollment options*
- *Public interest programs*
- *Quality of teaching*
- *Racial and gender diversity within the faculty and student body*
- *Religious affiliation*
- *Size of first-year classes*
- *Skills instruction*
- *Specialized areas of faculty expertise*

YOUR CHANCE OF ACCEPTANCE

Who knows how law schools end up with their reputations? Everything else being equal, you really do want to go a to a well-respected school. It will enhance your employment opportunities tremendously. Remember, whoever you are and whatever your background, your best bet is to select a couple of "reach" schools, a couple of schools at which you've got a good shot at being accepted, and a couple of "safety" schools where you are virtually assured acceptance. Remember also that being realistic about your chances will save you from unnecessary emotional letdowns. Getting in mostly boils down to numbers. Look at the acceptance rates and the average LSATs and GPAs of incoming classes at various schools to assess how you stack up.

The Dreaded Bar Exam

Once you graduate, most states require you to take a bar exam before you can practice law. Some state bar exams are really, really hard; New York's and California's are examples. If you don't want to take a bar exam, consider a law school in beautiful Wisconsin. Anyone who graduates from a state-certified Wisconsin law school does not need to take the state bar exam to practice law in the Badger State, as long as they are approved by the Board of Bar Examiners.

PERSONAL APPEAL

A student at a prominent law school in the Pacific Northwest once described his law school to us as "a combination wood-grain bomb shelter and Ewok village." Another student at a Northeastern law school told us her law school was fine except for its "ski-slope classrooms" and "East German Functionalist" architecture. While the curricula at various law schools are pretty much the same, the weather, the surrounding neighborhoods, the nightlife, and the character of the student populations are startlingly different. An important part of any graduate program is enjoying those moments in life when you're not studying. If you aren't comfortable in the environment you choose, it's likely to be reflected in the quality of work you do and your attitude. Before you make a $10,000 to $80,000 investment in any law school, you really ought to check it out in person. While you are there, talk to students and faculty. Walk around. Kick the tires. *Then* make a decision.

EMPLOYMENT PROSPECTS

Where do alumni work? How much money do they make? What percentage of graduates is employed within nine months of graduation? How many major law firms interview on campus? These are massively important questions, and you owe it to yourself to look into the answers before choosing a school.

YOUR VALUES

It is important that you be honest about defining your criteria for judging law schools. What do you want out of a law school? Clout? A high salary? A hopping social life? To live in a certain city? To avoid being in debt up to your eyeballs? A non-competitive atmosphere? Think about it.

MAKE A LIST

Using these criteria (and others you find relevant), develop a list of prospective schools. Ideally, you'll find this book useful in creating the list. Assign a level to each new school you add (something like *reach*, *good shot*, and *safety*).

Did You Know?

According to the people who take the LSAT, the average applicant applies to four or more law schools.

At your *reach* schools, the average LSAT scores and GPAs of incoming students should be higher than yours. These are law schools that will probably not accept you based on your numbers alone. In order to get in, you'll need to wow them with everything else (e.g., personal statement, stellar recommendations, work experience).

Your *good shot* schools should be the schools you like that accept students with about the same LSAT scores and GPA as yours. Combined with a strong and *cohesive* application, you've got a decent shot at getting into these schools.

At your *safety* schools, the average LSAT scores and GPAs of current students should be below yours. These schools should accept you pretty painlessly if there are no major blemishes on your application (e.g., a serious run-in with the law).

CHAPTER 3
APPLYING TO LAW SCHOOL

Our advice: Start early. The LSAT alone can easily consume 80 or more hours of prep time, and completing a single application form might take as much as 30 hours if you take great care with the essay questions. Don't sabotage your efforts through last-minute sloppiness or by allowing this already-annoying process to become a gigantic burden.

WHEN TO APPLY

Yale Law School's absolute final due date is February 1, but Loyola University—Chicago's School of Law will accept your application up to April 1. There is no regular pattern. However, the longer you wait to apply to a school, regardless of its deadline, the worse your chances of getting into that school may be. No efficient Admissions Staff is going to wait to receive all the applications before starting to make their selections.

If you're reading this in December and hope to get into a law school for next fall but haven't done anything about it, you're in big trouble. If you've got an LSAT score you are happy with, you are in less trouble. However, your applications will get to the law schools after the optimum time and, let's face it, they may appear a little rushed. The best time to think about applying is early in the year. Methodically take care of one thing at a time, and *finish by December*.

Early Admissions Options. A few schools have Early Admissions options (for instance, New York University's Early Admission deadline is on or about October 15), so you may know by December if you've been accepted. Early Admission is a good idea for a few reasons. It can give you an indication of what your chances are at other schools. It can relieve the stress of waiting until April to see where you'll be spending the next three years of your life. Also, it's better to get wait listed in December than in April (or whenever you would be notified for regular admission); if there is a "tie" among applicants on the waiting list, they'll probably admit whoever applied first. Of course, not every school's Early Admission option is the same (and many schools don't even have one), so do your research.

Rolling Admissions. Many law schools evaluate applications and notify applicants of admission decisions continuously over the course of several months (ordinarily from late fall to midsummer). Obviously, if you apply to one of these schools, it is vital that you apply as early as possible because there will be more spots available at the beginning of the process.

Applying Online. Almost all law schools allow applicants to submit applications online. The LSAC online service (LSAC.org) has a searchable database and applications to ABA-approved schools.

LAW SCHOOL ADMISSIONS COUNCIL: THE LAW SCHOOL APPLICATION MAFIA

In addition to single-handedly creating and administering the LSAT, an organization called the Law School Admissions Council (LSAC) maintains the communication between you and virtually every law school in the United States. It runs the Law School Data Assembly Service (LSDAS), which provides information (in a standard format) on applicants to the law schools. They—not you—send your grades, your LSAT score, and plenty of other information about you to the schools. You'll send only your actual applications directly to the law schools themselves. Oh, by the way, the fee for this service is $121 of your hard-earned money plus $12 (or more) every time you want LSDAS to send a report about you to an additional law school.

THE BIG HURDLES IN THE APPLICATION PROCESS: A BRIEF OVERVIEW

Take the LSAT. The Law School Admission Test is a roughly three-and-a-half-hour multiple-choice test used by law schools to help them select candidates. The LSAT is given in February, June, October (or, occasionally, late September), and December of each year. It's divided into five multiple-choice sections and one writing sample. All ABA-approved and most non-ABA-approved law schools in the United States and Canada require an LSAT score from each and every applicant.

Register for LSDAS. You can register for the Law School Data Assembly Service at the same time you register to take the LSAT; all necessary forms are contained in the *LSAT and LSDAS Registration Information Book* (hence the name). It can also be done, of course, online.

Get applications from six or seven schools. Why so many? Because it's better to be safe than sorry. As early as July, select a couple of *reach* schools, a couple of schools to which you've got a good shot at being accepted, and a couple of *safety* schools to which you are virtually assured of acceptance. Your safety school—if you were being realistic—will probably accept you pretty quickly. It may take a while to get a final decision from the other schools, but you won't be totally panicked because you'll know your safety school is there for you. If, for whatever reason, your grades or LSAT score is extremely low, you should apply to several safety schools. Most schools won't post online applications until mid-September at the earliest. Still, it is a good idea to familiarize yourself with the previous year's applications as soon as possible, as law schools tend not to radically alter components of their applications from one year to the next.

Write your personal statement. With any luck, you'll only have to write one personal statement. Many, many schools will simply ask you the same basic question: "Why do you want to obtain a law degree?" However, just in case you need to write several personal statements and essays, you need to select your schools fairly early.

Obtain two or three recommendations. Some schools will ask for two recommendations, both of which must be academic. Others want more than two recommendations and want at least one to be from someone who knows you outside traditional academic circles. As part of your LSDAS file, the LSAC will accept up to three letters of recommendation on your behalf, and they will send them to all the schools to which you apply. This is one of the few redeeming qualities of the LSAC. The last thing the writers of your recommendations are going to want to do is sign, package, and send copies of their letters all over the continent.

Update/create your resume. Most law school applicants ask that you submit a resume. Make sure yours is up to date and suitable for submission to an academic institution. Put your academic credentials and experience first—no matter what they are. This is just a supplement to the rest of the material; it's probably the simplest part of the application process.

Get your academic transcripts sent to LSDAS. When you subscribe to LSDAS, you must request that the Registrar at every undergraduate, graduate, and professional school you ever attended send an official transcript to Law Services. Don't even think about sending your own transcripts anywhere; these people don't trust you any farther than they can throw you. *Make these requests in August.* If you're applying Early Decision, start requesting transcripts as early as May. Law schools require complete files before making their decisions, and LSDAS won't send your information to the law schools without your transcripts. Undergraduate institutions can and will screw up and delay the transcript process—even when you go there personally and pay them to provide your records. Give yourself some time to fix problems should they arise.

Write any necessary addenda. An addendum is a brief explanatory letter written to explain or support a "deficient" portion of your application. If your personal and academic life has been fairly smooth, you won't need to include any addenda with your application. If, however, you were ever on academic probation, arrested, or if you have a low GPA, you may need to write one. Other legitimate addenda topics are a low/discrepant LSAT score, DUI/DWI suspensions, or any time gap in your academic or professional career.

An addendum is absolutely not the place to go off on a rant about the fundamental unfairness of the LSAT or how that evil campus security officer was only out to get you when you got arrested. If, for example, you have taken the LSAT two or three times and simply did not do very well, even after spending time and money preparing with a test prep company or a private tutor, simply tell the Admissions Committee that you worked diligently to achieve a high score. Say you explored all possibilities to help you achieve that goal. Whatever the case, lay out the facts, but let them draw their own conclusions. Be brief and balanced. Be fair. Do not go into unneccessary detail. Explain the problem and state what you did about it. This is no time to whine.

Send in your seat deposit. Once you are accepted at a particular school, that school will ask you to put at least some money down to hold your place in that year's class. A typical fee runs $200 or more. This amount will be credited to your first-term tuition once you actually register for classes.

Do any other stuff. You may find that there are other steps you must take during the law school application process. You may request a fee waiver, for example. Also make sure to get a copy of the LSAC's *LSAT/LSDAS Registration and Information Book*, which is unquestionably the most useful tool in applying to law school. It has the forms you'll need, a sample LSAT, admissions information, the current Law Forum schedule, and sample application schedules.

The Princeton Review	LAW SCHOOL APPLICATION CHECKLIST (suitable for framing)
January	• **Take a practice LSAT.** Do it at a library or wherever you won't be interrupted. Also, take it all at once.
February	• **Investigate LSAT prep courses.** If you don't take one with The Princeton Review, do *something*. Just as with any test, you'll get a higher score on this one if you prepare for it first.
March	• **Obtain an *LSAT/LSDAS Registration and Information Book*.** The books are generally published in March of each year. You can get one at any law school, by calling the LSAC at 215-968-1001, or by stopping by The Princeton Review office nearest you. You can also download one in PDF format at www.lsac.org.
April	• **Register for the June LSAT.** • **Begin an LSAT prep course.** At the very, very least, use some books or software.
May	• **Continue your LSAT prep.**
June	• **Take the LSAT.** If you take the test twice, many schools will average them. Your best bet is to take it once, do exceedingly well, and get it out of your hair forever.
July	• **Register for LSDAS.** • **Research law schools.**
August	• **Obtain law school applications.** You can call or write, but the easiest and cheapest way to get applications is via the Internet. This is, of course, only necessary if you plan to send in paper applications. Go to www.lsac.org to access and submit online applications. • **Get your undergraduate transcripts sent to LSDAS.** Make sure to contact the registrar at each undergraduate institution you attended.
September	• **Write your personal statements.** Proofread them. Edit them. Edit them again. Have someone else look them over for all the mistakes you missed. • **Update your resume,** or create a resume if you don't have one. • **Get your recommendations in order.** You want your professors to submit recommendations exactly when you send your applications (in October and November).
October	• **Complete and send early decision applications.**
November	• **Complete and send all regular applications.**
December	• **Chill.** • **Buy holiday gifts.** • **Make plans for New Year's.**

CHAPTER 4
THE LSAT

As you may know, we at The Princeton Review are pretty skeptical of most of the standardized tests out there. They make us a lot of money, of course, and we like that, but they are hideously poor indicators of anything besides how well you do on that particular standardized test. They are certainly not intelligence tests. The LSAT is no exception. It is designed to keep you out of law school, not facilitate your entrance into it. For no good reason we can think of, this 125-question test is *the single most important factor in all of law school admissions*, and, at least for the foreseeable future, we're all stuck with it.

Unfortunately, with the possible exception of the MCAT (for medical school), the LSAT is the toughest of all the standardized tests. Only 24 to 26 of the 125 questions have a "correct" answer (Logic Games), as opposed to Arguments and Reading Comprehension, for which you must choose the elusive "best" answer. As ridiculous as they are, the GMAT, GRE, SAT, MCAT, and ACT at least have large chunks of math or science on them. There are verifiably correct answers on these tests, and occasionally you even have to know something to get the right answers. *Only the LSAT requires almost no specific knowledge of anything whatsoever, which is precisely what makes it so difficult.* The only infallible way to study for the LSAT is to study the LSAT itself. The good news is that *anybody* can get significantly better at the LSAT by working diligently at it. In fact, your score will increase exponentially directly in proportion to the amount of time and work you put into preparing for it.

HOW IMPORTANT IS THE LSAT?

The LSAT figures very prominently in your law school application, especially if you've been out of school for a few years. Some law schools won't even look at your application unless you achieve a certain score on your LSAT. Most top law schools average multiple LSAT scores, so you should aim to take it only once. By the way, each score you receive is valid for five years after you take the test.

LSAT STRUCTURE

Section Type	Sections	Questions Per Section	Time Per Section
Logical Reasoning (Arguments)	2	24–26 2 sections, about 25 questions each	35 minute sections
Analytical Reasoning (Games)	1	24–26	35 minutes
Reading Comprehension	1	27–28	35 minutes
Experimental	1	24–26	35 minutes
Writing Sample	1	1	35 minutes

Each test has approximately 125 questions. Neither the Experimental section nor the Writing Sample counts toward your score. The multiple-choice sections may be given in any order, but the Writing Sample is always administered last. The Experimental section can be any of the three types of multiple-choice sections and is used by the test writers to test out new questions on your time and at your expense.

The Writing Sample is not scored, and unlikely to be read by anyone other than you. However, the law schools to which you apply will receive a copy of your writing sample, so you should definitely do it. A blank page would stand out like a sore thumb, and you wouldn't want the Admissions Office to think you were some kind of revolutionary.

WHAT'S ON THE LSAT, EXACTLY?

We asked the experts in the LSAT Course Division of The Princeton Review for the lowdown on the various sections of the LSAT. Here's what they had to say.

Registering for the LSAT

You can register for the LSAT by mail, over the phone, or online. To register by mail, you will need a copy of the Registration and Information Bulletin, which you may request from Law Services or pick up from your pre-law advisor. You may also register for the LSAT online at www.lsac.org. The LSAT fee is currently a whopping $132; if you're late, it's an extra $66. To avoid late fees, mail your registration form at least six weeks — six weeks — before the test. Also, by registering early, you are more likely to be assigned your first choice of test center. You can reach the Law School Admissions Council at

Phone: 215-968-1001

www.lsac.org

lsacinfo@lsac.org

Analytical Reasoning: If you've ever worked logic problems in puzzle books, then you're already somewhat familiar with the Analytical Reasoning section of the LSAT. The situations behind these problems—often called "games" or "logic games"—are common ones: deciding in what order to interview candidates, or assigning employees to teams, or arranging dinner guests around a table. The arrangement of "players" in these games is governed by a set of rules you must follow in answering the questions. Each Analytical Reasoning section is made up of four games, with five to seven questions each. Questions may ask you to find out what *must* be true under the rules or what *could* be true under the rules; they may add a new condition that applies to just that question; or they may ask you to count the number of possible arrangements under the stated conditions. These questions are difficult mostly because of the time constraints under which they must be worked; very few test-takers find themselves able to complete 24 questions on this section in the time allotted.

Logical Reasoning: Because there are two scored sections of them, Logical Reasoning questions on the LSAT are the most important to your score. Each Logical Reasoning—sometimes called "arguments"—question is made up of a short paragraph, often written to make a persuasive point. These small arguments are usually written to contain a flaw—some error of reasoning or unwarranted assumption that you must identify to answer the question successfully. Questions may ask you to draw conclusions from the stated information, to weaken or strengthen the argument, to identify its underlying assumptions, or to identify its logical structure or method. There are most often a total of 50 or 51 argument questions between the two sections—roughly half of the scored questions on the LSAT.

As of June 2007 a modification, called Comparative Reading, appears as one of the four sets in the LSAT Reading Comprehension section. In general, Comparative Reading questions are similar to traditional Reading Comprehension questions, except that Comparative Reading questions are based on two shorter passages that together are roughly the same length as one Reading Comprehension passage. A few of the questions that follow a Comparative Reading passage pair might concern only one of the two passages, but most questions will be about both passages and how they relate to each other. Also, since June 2007, test-takers no longer are randomly assigned one of two different kinds of writing prompt—decision or argument—for the writing sample. All test-takers will be assigned a decision prompt. The Writing Sample will continue to be unscored.

We strongly recommend that you prep for this test. Although we provide the best prep for the LSAT, you certainly don't have to take The Princeton Review's course (or buy our book, *Cracking the LSAT*, or sign up for our awesome distance learning course), as much as we'd obviously like it. There are plenty of books, software products, courses, and tutors out there. The people who make the LSAT will gleefully sell you plenty of practice tests as well. The key is to find the best program for you. Your first step should be taking a free full-length practice LSAT given under realistic testing conditions (we offer them across the country), so you can gauge where you stand and how much you need to improve your LSAT score. Whatever your course of action, however, make sure you remain committed to it, so you can be as prepared as possible when you take the actual test.

WHEN SHOULD YOU TAKE THE LSAT?

Here is a quick summary of test dates along with some factors to consider for each.

JUNE

The June administration is the only time the test is given on a Monday afternoon. If you have trouble functioning at the ordinary 8:00 A.M. start time, June may be a good option. Furthermore, taking the LSAT in June frees up your summer and fall to research schools and complete applications. However, if you are still in college, you'll have to balance LSAT preparation with academic course work and, in some cases, final exams. Check your exam schedules before deciding on a June LSAT test date.

OCTOBER/SEPTEMBER

The October test date (which is sometimes in late September) will allow you to prepare for the LSAT during the summer. This is an attractive option if you are a college student with some free time on your hands. Once you've taken the LSAT, you can spend the remainder of the fall completing your applications.

DECEMBER

December is the last LSAT administration that most competitive law schools will accept. If disaster strikes and you get a flat tire on test day, you may end up waiting another year to begin law school. December test-takers also must balance their time between preparing for the LSAT and completing law school applications. Doing so can make for a hectic fall, especially if you're still in college. You should also remember that, while a law school may accept December LSAT scores, taking the test in December could affect your chances of admission. Many law schools use a rolling admissions system, which means that they begin making admissions decisions as early as mid-October and continue to do so until the application deadline. Applying late in this cycle could mean that fewer spots are available. Check with your potential law schools to find out their specific policies.

FEBRUARY

If you want to begin law school in the following fall, the February LSAT will be too late for most law schools. However, if you don't plan to begin law school until the *next* academic year, you can give yourself a head start on the entire admissions process by taking the LSAT in February, then spending your summer researching schools and your fall completing applications.

UPCOMING LSAT TEST DATES		
TEST DATE	**Registration Deadline**	**Late Registration Ends**
September 26, 2009*	August 25, 2009	August 26–September 4, 2009
December 5, 2009*	November 3, 2009	November 4–November 13, 2009
February 6, 2010*	January 5, 2010	January 6–January 15, 2010

* The test is available the following Monday for those who cannot take a Saturday exam for religious purposes.

HOW IS THE LSAT SCORED?

LSAT scores currently range from 120 to 180. Why that range? We have no idea. The table on page 16 indicates the percentile rating of the corresponding LSAT scores between 141 and 180. This varies slightly from test to test.

Your raw score (the number of questions you answer correctly) doesn't always produce the same scaled score as previous LSATs. What actually happens is that your raw score is compared with that of everyone else who took the test on the same date you did. The LSAC looks at the scales from every other LSAT given in the past three years and "normalizes" the current scale so that it doesn't deviate widely from those scaled scores in the past.

LSAT Score	Percent Below	LSAT Score	Percent Below
180	99.9	160	82.2
179	99.9	159	79.1
178	99.9	158	76.5
177	99.8	157	72.6
176	99.7	156	68.7
175	99.6	155	65.7
174	99.5	154	61.5
173	99.3	153	57.3
172	99.0	152	53.2
171	98.5	151	49.1
170	98.1	150	44.9
169	97.5	149	41.0
168	96.7	148	37.0
167	95.7	147	33.4
166	94.6	146	29.6
165	93.2	145	26.4
164	91.4	144	23.3
163	89.7	143	20.2
162	87.3	142	17.7
161	84.9	141	15.2

A GOOD LSAT SCORE

A good score on the LSAT is the score that gets you into the law school you want to attend. Remember that a large part of the admissions game is the formula of your UGPA (undergraduate grade point average) multiplied by your LSAT score. Chances are, you are at a point in life where your UGPA is pretty much fixed (if you're reading this early in your college career, start getting very good grades pronto), so the only piece of the formula you can have an impact on is your LSAT score. We cannot emphasize enough the notion that you must prepare for this test.

A LITTLE IMPROVEMENT GOES A LONG WAY

A student who scores a 154 is in the 62nd percentile of all LSAT-takers. If that student's score was 161, however, that same student would jump to the 85th percentile. Depending upon your score, a 7-point improvement can increase your ranking by more than 25 percentile points.

COMPETITIVE LSAT SCORES AROUND THE UNITED STATES

The range of LSAT scores from the 25th to 75th percentile of incoming full-time students at U.S. law schools is pretty broad. Here is a sampling.

Law School	Score 25 to 75 percentile
Widener University, School of Law, Harrisburg	150–154
Gonzaga University, School of Law	153–156
Rutgers University Newark, School of Law	155–161
University of Pittsburgh, School of Law	157–161
University of Arizon, College of Law	159–164
Temple University, James E. Beasley School of Law	159–164
University of Florida, Levin College of Law	158–163
University of Tennessee, College of Law	154–161
Case Western Reserve University, School of Law	156–160
University of Alabama, School of Law	160–165
Southern Methodist University, School of Law	157–165
Loyola University Chicago, School of Law	160–163
University of San Diego, School of Law	160–164
Emory University, School of Law	164–166
The College of William & Mary, Law School	160–166
George Washington University, Law School	162–168
University of California Berkeley, School of Law	150–180
Georgetown University, Law Center	166–170
Stanford University, School of Law	168–172
University of Chicago, Law School	169–173
Yale University, Yale Law School	169–177

PREPARING FOR THE LSAT

No matter who you are—whether you graduated *magna cum laude* from Cornell University or you're on academic probation at Cornell College—the first thing you need to do is order a recent LSAT. One comes free with every *Official LSAT Registration Booklet*. Once you get the test, take it, but not casually over the course of two weeks. Bribe someone to be your proctor. Have them administer the test to you under strict time conditions. Follow the test booklet instructions exactly, and do it right. Your goal is to simulate an actual testing experience as much as possible. When you finish, score the test honestly. Don't give yourself a few extra points because "you'll do better on test day." The score on this practice test will provide a baseline for mapping your test preparation strategy.

If your practice LSAT score is already at a point where you've got a very high-percentage shot of getting accepted to the law school of your choice, chances are you don't need much preparation. Order a half dozen or so of the most recent LSATs from LSAC and work through them over the course of a few months, making sure you understand why you are making specific mistakes. If your college or university offers a free or very cheap prep course, consider taking it to get more tips on the test. Many of these courses are taught by pre-law advisors who will speak very intelligently about the test and are committed to helping you get the best score you can.

If, after you take a practice LSAT, your score is not what you want or need it to be, you are definitely not alone. Many academically strong candidates go into the LSAT cold because they assume that the LSAT is no more difficult than or about the same as their college courses. Frankly, many students are surprised at how poorly they do the first time they take a dry run. Think about it this way: It's better to be surprised sitting at home with a practice test than while taking the test for real.

If you've taken a practice LSAT under exam conditions and it's, say, 10 or 15 points below where you want it to be, you should probably consult an expert. Test preparation companies spend quite a bit of money and time poring over the tests and measuring their students' improvement. We sure do. Ask around. Assess your financial situation. Talk to other people who have improved their LSAT scores and duplicate their strategies.

Whatever you decide to do, make sure you are practicing with real LSAT questions and you take full-length practice tests under realistic testing conditions—again and again and again.

SOME ESSENTIAL, DOWN-AND-DIRTY LSAT TIPS

Slow down. Way down. The slower you go, the better you'll do. It's that simple. Any function you perform, from basic motor skills to complex intellectual problems, will be affected by the rate at which you perform that function. This goes for everything from cleaning fish to taking the LSAT. You can get 25 questions wrong and still get a scaled score of 160, which is a very good score (it's in the 84th percentile). You can get at least six questions wrong per section or, even better, you can ignore the two or three most convoluted questions per section, *still* get a few more questions wrong, and you'll get an excellent overall score. Your best strategy is to find the particular working speed at which you will get the most questions correct.

There is no penalty for guessing. If you don't have time to finish the exam, it's imperative that you leave yourself at least 30 seconds at the end of each section in which to grab free points by bubbling in some answer to every question before time is called. Pick a letter of the day—like B—don't bubble in randomly. If you guess totally randomly, you might get every single guess right. Of course, you may also get struck by lightning in the middle of the test. The odds are about the same. *You are far more likely to miss every question if you guess without a plan.* However, if you stick with the same letter each time you guess, you will definitely be right once in a while. It's a conservative approach, but it is also your best bet for guaranteed points, which is what you want. By guessing the same letter pretty much every time as time runs out, you can pick up anywhere from two to four raw points per section. Be careful about waiting until the very last second to start filling in randomly, though, because proctors occasionally cheat students out of the last few seconds of a section.

Use process of elimination all the time. This is absolutely huge. On 75 percent of the LSAT (all the Logical Reasoning and Reading Comprehension questions), you are *not* looking for the *right* answer, only the *best* answer. It says so right there in the instructions. Eliminating even one answer choice increases your chances of getting the question right by 20 to 25 percent. If you can cross off two or three answer choices, you are really in business. Also, very rarely will you find an answer choice that is flawless on the LSAT. Instead, you'll find four answer choices that are definitely wrong and one that is the least of five evils. You should constantly look for reasons to get rid of answer choices so you can eliminate them. This strategy will increase your odds of getting the question right, and you'll be a happier and more successful standardized test-taker. We swear.

Attack! Attack! Attack! Read the test with an antagonistic, critical eye; look for holes and gaps in the reasoning of arguments and in the answer choices. Many LSAT questions revolve around what is wrong with a particular line of reasoning. The more adept you become at identifying what is wrong with a problem before going to the answer choices, the more successful you'll be.

Write all over your test booklet. Actively engage the exam, and put your thoughts on paper. Circle words. *Physically cross out wrong answer choices you have eliminated.* Draw complete and exact diagrams for the logic games. Use the diagrams you draw.

Do the questions in whatever order you wish. Just because a logic game question is first doesn't mean you should do it first. There is *no order of difficulty* on the LSAT—unlike some other standardized tests—so you should hunt down and destroy those questions at which you are personally best. If you are doing a Reading Comprehension question, for example, or tackling an argument, and you don't know what the hell is going on, then cross off whatever you can, guess, and move on. If you have no idea how to solve a particular logic game, don't focus your energy there. Find a game you can do and milk it for points. Your mission is to gain points wherever you can. By the way, if a particular section is really throwing you, it's probably because it is the dastardly Experimental section (which is often kind of sloppy and, thankfully, does not count toward your score).

CHAPTER 5
WRITING A GREAT PERSONAL STATEMENT

There is no way to avoid writing the dreaded personal statement. You'll probably need to write only one personal statement, and it will probably address the most commonly asked question: "Why do you want to obtain a law degree?" This question, in one form or another, appears on virtually every law school application and often represents your only opportunity to string more than two sentences together. Besides your grades and your LSAT score, it is the most important part of your law school application. Your answer should be about two pages long, and it should amount to something significantly more profound than "A six-figure salary really appeals to me," or "I watch *Law & Order* every night."

Unlike your application to undergraduate programs, the personal statement on a law school application is not the time to discuss what your trip to Europe meant to you, describe your wacky chemistry teacher, or try your hand at verse. It's a fine line. While you want to stand out, you definitely don't want to be *overly* creative here. You want to be unique, but you don't want to come across as a weirdo or a loose cannon. You want to present yourself as intelligent, professional, mature, persuasive, and concise because these are the qualities law schools seek in applicants.

THE BASICS

Here are the essentials of writing essays and personal statements.

Find your own unique angle. The admissions people read tons of really boring essays about "how great I am" and how "I think there should be justice for everyone." If you must explain why you want to obtain a law degree, strive to find an angle that is interesting and unique to you. If what you write *isn't* interesting to you, we promise that it won't be remotely interesting to an Admissions Officer. Also, in addition to being more effective, an interesting essay will be far more enjoyable to write.

In general, avoid generalities. Again, Admissions Officers have to read an unbelievable number of boring essays. You will find it harder to be boring if you write about particulars. It's the details that stick in a reader's mind.

Good writing is easily understood. You want to get your point across, not bury it in words. Don't talk in circles. Your prose should be clear and direct. If an Admissions Officer has to struggle to figure out what you are trying to say, you'll be in trouble. Also, legal writing courses make up a significant part of most law school curricula; if you can show that you have good writing skills, you have a serious edge.

Buy and read *The Elements of Style* by William Strunk Jr. and E. B. White. We can't recommend it enough. In fact, we're surprised you don't have it already. This little book is a required investment for any writer (and, believe us, you'll be doing plenty of writing as a law student and a practicing attorney). You will refer to it forever, and if you do what it says, your writing will definitely improve.

Have three or four people read your personal statement and critique it. If your personal statement contains misspellings and grammatical errors, Admissions Officers will conclude not only that you don't know how to write but also that you aren't shrewd enough to get help. What's worse, the more time you spend with a piece of your own writing, the less likely you are to spot any errors. You get tunnel vision. Ask friends, boyfriends, girlfriends, professors, brothers, sisters—somebody—to read your essay and comment on it. Use a computer with a spellchecker. *Be especially careful about punctuation!* Another tip: Read your personal statement aloud to yourself or someone else. You will catch mistakes and awkward phrases that would have gotten past you otherwise because they sounded correct in your head.

Don't repeat information from other parts of your application. It's a waste of time and space.

Stick to the length that is requested. It's only common courtesy.

Maintain the proper tone. Your essay should be memorable, without being outrageous and easy to read, without being too formal or sloppy. When in doubt, err on the formal side.

Being funny is much harder than you think. An applicant who can make an Admissions Officer laugh never gets lost in the shuffle. The clever part of the personal statement is passéd around and read aloud. Everyone smiles and the Admissions Staff can't bear to toss your application into the "reject" pile. But beware! Most people think they're funny, but only a few are able to pull it off in this context. Obviously, stay away from one-liners, limericks, and anything remotely off-color.

WHY DO YOU WANT TO GO TO LAW SCHOOL?

Writing about yourself often proves to be surprisingly difficult. It's certainly no cakewalk explaining who you are and why you want to go to law school, and presenting your lifetime of experiences in a mere two pages. On the bright side, the personal statement is the only element of your application over which you have total control. It's a tremendous opportunity to make a great first impression as long as you avoid the urge to communicate your entire genetic blueprint. Your goal should be much more modest.

Websites about Getting into Law School

www.PrincetonReview.com

You can access tons of information about law school and the LSAT at our site.

www.lsac.org

This site is home to the people who bring you the LSAT and the LSDAS application processing service.

DON'T GET CARRIED AWAY

Although some law schools set no limit on the length of the personal statement, you shouldn't take their bait. You can be certain that your statement will be at least glanced at in its entirety, but Admissions Officers are human, and their massive workload at admissions time has an understandable impact on their attention spans. You should limit yourself to two or three typed, double-spaced pages. Does this make your job any easier? Not at all. In fact, practical constraints on the length of your essay demand a higher degree of efficiency and precision. A two-page limit allows for absolutely no fluff.

MAKE YOURSELF STAND OUT

We know you know this, but you will be competing against thousands of well-qualified applicants for admission to just about any law school. Consequently, your primary task in writing your application is to separate yourself from the crowd. Particularly if you are applying directly from college or if you have been out of school for a very short time, you must do your best to ensure that the Admissions Committee cannot categorize you too broadly. Admissions Committees will see innumerable applications from bright 22-year-olds with good grades. Your essay presents an opportunity to put those grades in context, to define and differentiate yourself.

WHAT MAKES A GOOD PERSONAL STATEMENT?

Like any good writing, your law school application should be clear, concise, and candid. The first two of these attributes, clarity and conciseness, are usually the result of a lot of reading, rereading, and rewriting. Without question, repeated critical revision by yourself and others is the surest way to trim and tune your prose. The third quality, candor, is the product of proper motivation. Honesty cannot be superimposed after the fact; your writing must be candid from the outset.

In writing your personal statement for law school applications, pay particularly close attention to the way your essay is structured and the fundamental message it communicates. Admissions Committees will read your essay two ways: as a product of your handiwork and as a product of your mind. Don't underestimate the importance of either perspective. A well-crafted essay will impress any Admissions Officer, but if it does not illuminate, you will not be remembered. You will not stand out. Conversely, a thoughtful essay that offers true insight will stand out unmistakably, but if it is not readable, it will not receive serious consideration.

THINGS TO AVOID IN YOUR PERSONAL STATEMENT

"MY LSAT SCORE ISN'T GREAT, BUT I'M JUST NOT A GOOD TEST-TAKER."

If you have a low LSAT score, avoid directly discussing it like the plague in your personal statement. Law school is a test-rich environment. In fact, grades in most law-school courses are determined by a single exam at the semester's end, and as a law student, you'll spend your Novembers and Aprils in a study carrel, completely removed from society. Saying that you are not good at tests will do little to convince an Admissions Committee that you've got the ability to succeed in law school once accepted.

Consider also that a low LSAT score speaks for itself—all too eloquently. It doesn't need you to speak for it too. The LSAT may be a flawed test, but don't go arguing the merits of the test to Admissions Officers, because ordinarily it is the primary factor they use to make admissions decisions. We feel for you, but you'd be barking up the wrong tree. The attitude of most law school Admissions Departments is that while the LSAT may be imperfect, it is equally imperfect for all applicants. Apart from extraordinary claims of serious illness on test day, few explanations for poor performance on the LSAT will mean much to the people who read your application.

About the only situation in which a discussion of your LSAT score is necessary is if you have two (or more) LSAT scores and one is significantly better than another. If you did much better in your second sitting than in your first, or vice versa, a brief explanation couldn't hurt. However, your explanation may mean little to the committee, which may have its own hard-and-fast rules for interpreting multiple LSAT scores. Even in this scenario, however, you should avoid bringing up the LSAT in the personal statement. *Save it for an addendum.*

The obvious and preferable alternative to an explicit discussion of a weak LSAT score would be to focus on what you *are* good at. If you really are bad at standardized tests, you must be better at something else, or you wouldn't have gotten as far as you have. If you think you are a marvelous researcher, say so. If you are a wonderful writer, show it. Let your essay implicitly draw attention away from your weak points by focusing on your strengths. There is no way to convince an Admissions Committee that they should overlook your LSAT score. You may, however, present compelling reasons for them to look beyond it.

"MY COLLEGE GRADES WEREN'T THAT HIGH, BUT . . ."

This issue is a bit more complicated than the low LSAT score. Law school Admissions Committees will be more willing to listen to your interpretation of your college performance but only within limits. Keep in mind that law schools require official transcripts for a reason. Members of the Admissions Committee will be aware of your academic credentials before ever getting to your essay. As with low LSAT scores, your safest course of action is to *explain low grades in addendum.*

If your grades are unimpressive, you should offer the Admissions Committee something else by which to judge your abilities. Again, the best argument for looking past your college grades is evidence of achievement in another area, whether in your LSAT score, your extracurricular activities, your overcoming economic hardship as an undergraduate, or your career accomplishments.

"I'VE ALWAYS WANTED TO BE A LAWYER."

Sure you have. Many applicants seem to feel the need to point out that they really, really want to become attorneys. You will do yourself a great service by avoiding such throwaway lines. They'll do nothing for your essay but water it down. Do not convince yourself in a moment of desperation that claiming to have known that the law was your calling since age six (when—let's be honest—you really wanted to be a firefighter) will somehow move your application to the top of the pile. The Admissions Committee is not interested in how much you want to practice law. They want to know *why*.

"I WANT TO BECOME A LAWYER TO FIGHT INJUSTICE."

No matter how deeply you feel about battling social inequity, between us, writing it down makes you sound like a superhero on a soapbox. Moreover, though some people really do want to fight injustice, way down in the cockles of their hearts, most applicants are motivated to attend law school by less altruistic desires. Among the nearly one million practicing lawyers in the United States, there are relatively few who actually earn a living defending the indigent or protecting civil rights. Tremendously dedicated attorneys who work for peanuts and take charity cases are few and far between. We're not saying you don't want to be one of them; we're merely saying that people in law school admissions won't *believe* you want to be one of them. They'll take your professed altruistic ambitions (and those of the hundreds of other personal statements identical to yours) with a (huge) grain of salt.

If you can, in good conscience, say that you are committed to a career in the public interest, show the committee something tangible on your application and in your essay that will allow them to see your statements as more than mere assertions. If however, you cannot show that you are already a veteran in the good fight, don't claim to be. Law school Admissions Committees certainly do not regard the legal profession as a saints versus sinners proposition, and neither should you. Do not be afraid of appearing morally moderate. If the truth is that you want the guarantee of the relatively good jobs a law degree practically ensures, be forthright. Nothing is as impressive to the reader of a personal statement as the ring of truth, and what's wrong with wanting a good job, anyway?

CHAPTER 6
RECOMMENDATIONS

The law schools to which you apply will require two or three letters of recommendation in support of your application. Some schools will allow you to submit as many letters as you like. Others make it clear that any more than the minimum number of letters of recommendation is unwelcome. If you've ever applied to a private school (or perhaps a small public school) then you know the drill.

Unlike the evaluation forms for some colleges and graduate programs, however, law school recommendation forms tend toward absolute minimalism. All but a few recommendation forms for law school applications ask a single, open-ended question. It usually goes something like, "What information about this applicant is relevant that is not to be found in other sources?" The generic quality of the forms from various law schools may be both a blessing and a curse. On the one hand, it makes it possible for those writing your recommendations to write a single letter that will suffice for all the applications you submit. This convenience will make everybody much happier. On the other hand, if a free-form recommendation is to make a positive impression on an Admissions Committee, it must convey real knowledge about you.

WHOM TO ASK

Your letters of recommendation should come from people who know you well enough to offer a truly informed assessment of your abilities. Think carefully before choosing them to do this favor for you, but, as a general rule, pick respectable people whom you've known for a long time. If the writers of your recommendations know you well and understand the broader experience that has brought you to your decision to attend law school, they will be able to write a letter that is specific enough to do you some good. You also want people who can and are willing to contribute to an integrated, cohesive application.

The application materials from most law schools suggest that your letters should come, whenever possible, from people in academic settings. Some schools want at least two recommendations, both of which must be academic. Others explicitly request that the letters come from someone who has known you in a professional setting, especially if you've been out of school for a while.

HELP YOUR RECOMMENDATION WRITERS HELP YOU

Here, in essence, is the simple secret to great recommendations: Make sure the writers of your recommendations know you, your academic and professional goals, and the overall message you are trying to convey in your application. The best recommendations will fit neatly with the picture you present of yourself in your own essay, even when they make no specific reference to the issues your essay addresses. An effective law school application will present to the Admissions Committee a cohesive picture, not a montage. A great way to point your recommendation writers in the right direction and maximize their abilities to contribute to your overall cause is to provide them with copies of your personal statement. Don't be bashful about amiably communicating a few "talking points" that don't appear in your personal statement, as well.

ACADEMIC REFERENCES

Most applicants will (and should) seek recommendations from current or former professors. The academic environment in law school is extremely rigorous. Admissions Committees will be looking for assurance that you will be able not just to survive but to excel. A strong recommendation from a college professor is a valuable corroboration of your ability to succeed in law school.

You want nothing less than stellar academic recommendations. While a perfunctory, lukewarm recommendation is unlikely to damage your overall application, it will obviously do nothing to bolster it. Your best bet is to choose at least one professor from your major field. An enthusiastic endorsement from such a

---

Helpful Websites

www.findlaw.com

This site is the mother lode of free information about law, law schools, and legal careers.

www.ilrg.com

Mother lode honorable mention.

www.hg.org/students.html

Another honorable mention.

www.jurist.law.pitt.edu

The University of Pittsburgh School of Law's splendid "Legal News and Research" website offers a wealth of useful information.

professor will be taken as a sign that you are an excellent student. Second—and we hope that this goes without saying—you should choose professors who do not immediately associate your name with the letter C.

Specifics are of particular interest to Admissions Officers when they evaluate your recommendations. If a professor can make *specific* reference to a particular project you completed, or at least make substantive reference to your work in a particular course, the recommendation will be strengthened considerably. Make it your responsibility to enable your professors to provide specifics. Drop hints, or just lay it out for them. You might, for example, make available a paper you wrote for them of which you are particularly proud. Or you might just chat with the professor for a while to jog those dormant memories. You might feel uncomfortable tooting your own horn, but it's for the best. Unless your professors are well enough acquainted with you to be able to offer a very personal assessment of your potential, they will greatly appreciate a tangible reminder of your abilities on which to base their recommendation.

ESCAPING THE WOODWORK

If you managed to get through college without any professors noticing you, it's not the end of the world. Professors are quite talented at writing recommendations for students they barely know. Most consider it part of their job. Even seemingly unapproachable academic titans will usually be happy to dash off a quick letter for a mere student. However, these same obliging professors are masters of a sort of opaque prose style that screams to an Admissions Officer, "I really have no idea what to say about this kid who is, in fact, a near-total stranger to me!" Although an Admissions Committee will not outrightly dismiss such a recommendation, it's really not going to help you much.

REELING IN THE YEARS

Obviously, the longer it has been since you graduated, the tougher it is to obtain academic recommendations. However, if you've held on to your old papers, you may still be able to rekindle an old professor's memory of your genius by sending a decent paper or two along with your request for a recommendation (and, of course, a copy of your personal statement). You want to provide specifics in any way you can.

NON-ACADEMIC REFERENCES

Getting the mayor, a senator, or the CEO of your company to write a recommendation helps only if you have a personal and professional connection with that person. Remember, you want the writers of your recommendations to provide specifics about your actual accomplishments. If you're having trouble finding academic recommendations, choose people from your workplace, from the community, or from any other area of your life that is important to you. If at all possible, talk to your boss or a supervisor from a previous job who knows you well (and, of course, likes you).

SEND A THANK-YOU NOTE

Always a good idea. It should be short and handwritten. Use a blue pen so the recipient knows for sure that your note is no cheap copy. As with any good thank-you note and any good recommendation, mention a specific. (Send a thank-you note if you have an interview at a law school, too.)

CHAPTER 7
REAL-LIFE WORK EXPERIENCE AND COMMUNITY SERVICE

WORK EXPERIENCE IN COLLEGE

Most law school applications will ask you to list any part-time jobs you held while you were in college and how many hours per week you worked. If you had to (or chose to) work your way through your undergraduate years, this should come as good news. A great number of law schools make it clear that they take your work commitments as a college student into consideration when evaluating your undergraduate GPA.

WORK EXPERIENCE IN REAL LIFE

All law school applications will ask you about your work experience beyond college. They will give you three or four lines on which to list such experience. Some schools will invite you to submit a resume. If you have a very good one, you should really milk this opportunity for all it's worth. Even if you don't have a marvelous resume, these few lines on the application and your resume are the only opportunities you'll have to discuss your post-college experience meaningfully—unless you choose to discuss professional experience in your personal statement as well.

The kind of job you've had is not as important as you might think. What interests the Admissions Committee is what you've made of that job and what it has made of you. Whatever your job was or is, you want to offer credible evidence of your competence. For example, mention in your personal statement your job advancement or any increase in your responsibility. Most important, though, remember your overriding goal of cohesive presentation—you want to show off your professional experience within the context of your decision to attend law school. This does not mean that you need to offer geometric proof of how your experience in the workplace has led you inexorably to a career in law. You need only explain truthfully how this experience influenced you and how it fits nicely into your thinking about law school.

COMMUNITY SERVICE

An overwhelming majority of law schools single out community involvement as one of several influential factors in their admissions decisions. Law schools would like to admit applicants who show a long-standing commitment to something other than their own advancement.

It is certainly understandable that law schools would wish to determine the level of such commitment before admitting an applicant, particularly since so few law students go on to practice public interest law. Be forewarned, however, that nothing—*nothing*—is so obviously bogus as an insincere statement of a commitment to public interest issues. It just reeks. Admissions Committees are well aware that very few people take the time out of their lives to become involved significantly in their communities. If you aren't one of them, trying to fake it can only hurt you.

CHAPTER 8

INTERVIEWS

The odds are very good that you will never have to sit through an interview in the law school admissions process. Admissions Offices just aren't very keen on them. They do happen occasionally, however, and if you are faced with one, here are a few tips.

Be prepared. Interviews do make impressions. Some students are admitted simply because they had great interviews; less often, students are rejected because they bombed. Being prepared is the smartest thing you can do.

Don't ask questions that are answered in the brochures you got in the mail. You have to read those brochures—at breakfast before the interview would be an ideal time.

If there is a popular conception of the school (e.g., Harvard is overly competitive), don't ask about it. Your interviewer will have been through the same song and dance too many times. While you don't want to seem off the wall by asking bizarre questions, you don't want to sound exactly like every other boring applicant before you.

Look good, feel good. Wear nice clothes. If you aren't sure what to wear, *ask the Admissions Staff*. Get a respectable haircut. Don't chew gum. Clean your fingernails. Brush your teeth. Wash behind your ears. You can go back to being a slob as soon as they admit you.

Don't worry about time. Students sometimes are told that the sign of a good interview is that it lasts longer than the time allowed for it. Forget about this. Don't worry if your interview lasts exactly as long as the assistant said it would. Don't try to stretch out the end of your interview by suddenly becoming long-winded or asking questions you don't care about.

CHAPTER 9
MONEY MATTERS

Law school is a cash cow for colleges and universities everywhere and, especially at a private school, you are going to be gouged for a pretty obscene wad of cash over the next three years. Take Thomas M. Cooley Law School, where tuition is about $39,000 a year. If you are planning to eat, live somewhere, buy books, and (maybe) have health insurance, you are looking at about $56,000 per year. Multiply that by three years of law school and you get $168,000. Now faint. Correct for inflation (USC certainly will), add things like computers and other miscellany, and you can easily spend $175,000 to earn a degree. Assume that you have to borrow every penny of that $165,000. Multiply it by 8 percent through 10 years (a common assumption of law school applicants is that they will be able to pay all their debt back in 10 years or less). Your monthly payments will be about $2,123.

On the bright side, while law school is certainly an expensive proposition, the financial rewards of practicing can be immensely lucrative. You won't be forced into bankruptcy if you finance it properly. There are tried-and-true ways to reduce your initial costs, finance the costs on the horizon, and manage the debt with which you'll leave school—all without ever having to ask, "Have you been in a serious accident recently?" in a television commercial.

LAW SCHOOL ON THE CHEAP

Private schools aren't the only law schools, and you don't have to come out of law school saddled with tens of thousands of dollars of debt. Many state schools have reputations that equal or surpass some of the top private ones. It might be worth your while to spend a year establishing residency in a state with one or more good public law schools. Here's an idea: Pack up your belongings and move to a cool place like Minneapolis, Seattle, Berkeley, Austin, or Boulder. Spend a year living there. Wait tables, hang out, listen to music, walk the Earth, write the great American novel, and *then* study law.

COMPARISON SHOPPING

Here are the full-time tuition costs at law schools around the country. The two schools listed for each state are randomly paired schools in the same region (one public and one private) and are provided to help you get a feel of what law school costs are going to run you. Those schools that have the same tuition in both columns are private law schools.

Law School	In-State	Out-of-State
University of Florida, Levin College of Law	$10,814	$10,814
University of Miami, School of Law	$37,418	$37,418
Indiana University–Bloomington, School of Law	$19,125	$36,510
University of Notre Dame, Law School	$37,190	$37,190
The University of Tennessee, College of Law	$10,272	$27,192
Vanderbilt University, Law School	$41,850	$41,850
The University of Iowa, College of Law	$16,758	$33,526
Drake University, Law School	$28,850	$28,850
Louisiana State University, Law Center	$10,722	$19,818
Tulane University, Law School	$35,500	$35,500
University of California, Hastings College of Law	$28,864	$40,089
University of San Francisco, School of Law	$35,800	$35,800
The University of Texas at Austin, School of Law	$23,998	$39,642
Baylor University, School of Law	$34,524	$34,524
University of Illinois, College of Law	$18,102	$29,100
Northwestern University, School of Law	$45,062	$45,062
University of Pittsburgh, School of Law	$23,432	$31,576
University of Oregon, School of Law	$18,954	$23,994
Lewis & Clark College, Northwestern School of Law	$30,436	$30,436

LOAN REPAYMENT ASSISTANCE PROGRAMS

If you are burdened with loans, we've got more bad news. The National Association of Law Placement (NALP) shows that while salaries for law school graduates who land jobs at the big, glamorous firms have skyrocketed in the past few years, salaries of less than $85,000 are more common than salaries of $100,000 to $130,000 for the general run of law school grads. There are, however, a growing number of law schools and other sources willing to pay your loans for you through loan forgiveness programs in return for your commitment to work in public interest law.

While doing a tour of duty in public service law will put off dreams of working at a big firm or becoming the next Mark Geragos, the benefits of these programs are undeniable. Here's how just about all of them work. You commit to working for a qualified public service or public interest job. As long as your gross income does not exceed the prevailing public service salary, the programs will pay off a good percentage of your debt. Eligible loans are typically any educational debt financed through your law school, which really excludes only loan sharks and credit-card debts.

The Skinny on Loan Repayment Assistance Programs

For a comprehensive listing of assistance programs and for other loan-forgiveness information, call Equal Justice Works at 202-466-3686, or look them up on the Web at www.napil.org.

MAXIMIZE YOUR AID

A simple but oft-forgotten piece of wisdom: If you don't ask, you usually don't get. Be firm when trying to get merit money from your school. Some schools have reserves of cash that go unused. Try simply asking for more financial aid. The better your grades, of course, the more likely schools are to crack open their safe of financial goodies for you. Unfortunately, grants aren't as prevalent for law students as for undergrads. Scholarships are not nearly as widely available either. To get a general idea of availability of aid at a law school, contact the Financial Aid Office.

PARENTAL CONTRIBUTION?!

If you are operating under the assumption that, as a tax-paying grownup who has been out of school for a number of years, you will be recognized as the self-supporting adult you are, you could be in for a surprise. Veterans of financial aid battles will not be surprised to hear that even law school Financial Aid Offices have a difficult time recognizing when apron strings have legitimately been cut. Schools may try to take into account your parents' income in determining your eligibility for financial aid, regardless of your age or tax status. Policies vary widely. Be sure to ask the schools you are considering exactly what their policies are regarding financial independence for the purposes of financial aid.

BORROWING MONEY

It's an amusingly simple process, and several companies are in the business of lending large chunks of cash specifically to law students. Your law school Financial Aid Office can tell you how to reach them. You should explore more than one option and shop around for the lowest fees and rates.

WHO'S ELIGIBLE?

Anyone with reasonably good credit, regardless of financial need, can borrow enough money to finance law school. If you have financial need, you will probably be eligible for some types of financial aid if you meet the following basic qualifications:

- You are a United States citizen or a permanent U.S. resident.

- You are registered for Selective Service if you are a male, or you have the documentation to prove that you are exempt.

- You are not in default on student loans already.

- You don't have a horrendous credit history.

- You haven't been busted for certain drug-related crimes, including possession.

Let the Law School Pick Up the Tab for Phone Calls Whenever Possible

Many schools have free telephone numbers that they don't like to publish in books like this one. If the number we have listed for a particular law school is not an 800 number, it doesn't necessarily mean that you have to pay every time you call the school. Check out the school's website, or ask for the 800 number when you call the first time.

WHAT TYPES OF LOANS ARE AVAILABLE?

There are three basic types of loans: federal, private, and institutional.

Federal

The federal government funds federal loan programs. Federal loans, particularly the Stafford Loan, are usually the first resort for borrowers. Most federal loans are need-based, but some higher-interest loans are available regardless of financial circumstances.

TABLE OF LOANS			
NAME OF LOAN	**SOURCE**	**ELIGIBILITY**	**MAXIMUM ALLOCATION**
Federal Stafford (Subsidized) Student Loan http://studentaid.ed.gov/ students/publications/ student_guide/index.html	Federal, administered by participating lender	Demonstrated financial need	$8,500/year. The maximum aggregate total for subsidized loans is $65,500. The maximum aggregate total includes any Stafford loans received for undergraduate study.
Unsubsidized Stafford Student Loan http://studentaid.ed.gov/ students/publications/ student_guide/index.html	Federal, administered by participating lender	Not need-based	The total Stafford loan limit is $20,500, including Unsubsidized loans and Subsidized loans not to exceed $8,500. The maximum aggregate total of Stafford loans is $138,500, including Unsubsidized loans and Subsidized loans not to exceed $65,500.*
Health Professions Student Loan/Primary Care Loan (HPSL) Contact school for more information	Federal, administered by school	Exceptional financial need; commitment to primary care	For first- and second-year students, the maximum allocation is the cost of attendance (including tuition, educational expenses, and reasonable living expenses). Third- and fourth-year students may receive allocations beyond this amount.
Perkins Loan (formerly NDSL) Contact school for more information	Federal, administered by school	Demonstrated financial need	$6,000/year, with aggregate of $40,000. Aggregate amount includes undergraduate loans.
Alternative Loan Program (ALP) www.aamc.org/programs/ medloans	AAMC, administered under MEDLOANS division of AAMC	Not need-based	Cost of attendance minus other aid received. Aggregate: $250,000 (total educational indebtedness from all sources).

*Students pursuing certain health professions and enrolled in programs accredited by the appropriate approved accreditation agency are eligible to receive increased amounts of Unsubsidized Stafford loans. If a student is granted the maximum additional allocation, the maximum aggregate total will be $189,500. This number includes all undergraduate and graduate Subsidized and Unsubsidized Stafford loans. See "Increased Eligibility for Health Professions Students" in the Federal Student Aid Handbook for details and updates.

Private

Private loans are funded by banks, foundations, corporations, and other associations. A number of private loans are targeted to aid particular segments of the population. You may have to do some investigating to identify private loans for which you might qualify. As always, contact your law school's Financial Aid Office to learn more.

Institutional

The amount of loan money available and the method by which it is disbursed vary greatly from one school to another. Private schools, especially those that are older and more established, tend to have larger endowments and can offer more assistance. To find out about the resources available at a particular school, refer to its catalog or contact—you guessed it—the Financial Aid Office.

TABLE OF LOANS (continued)			
REPAYMENT AND DEFERRAL OPTIONS	**INTEREST RATE**	**PROS**	**CONS**
10–30 years to repay. Begin repayment 6 months after graduation. Forbearance possible for up to 3 years of residency training.	Variable 4% loan disbursement fee. Capped at *8.25%.	Most common medical school loan. Interest is paid by the government during school. Once you get a loan, later loans are at the same rate.	None
10–30 years to repay. Interest begins to accrue from day loan is disbursed; you can pay the interest or have it capitalized (added to principal). Begin repayment 6 months after graduation. Forbearance possible for up to 3 years of residency training.	Variable 4% loan disbursement fee. Capped at *8.25%.	Not need-based.	Interest is not paid by the government while you're in school.
10 years to repay, beginning 1 year after graduation. Deferrable during residency and under special circumstances.	Fixed, 5%.	Fixed, relatively low interest rate.	Very limited availability.
10 years to repay. Begin repayment 9 months after graduation. Can be deferred for 2 years during residency.	Fixed, 5%.	Fixed, relatively low interest rate.	Low maximum allocation.
Standard: 20 years of interest and principal payments. Alternative: 3 years of interest only and 17 years of interest and principal. Repayment generally begins 3–4 years after graduation, depending on length of residency.	Prime rate plus 1.25%; variable, adjusted monthly. (While in school, prime rate plus 0%. Variable, adjusted monthly.)	High maximum allocation; not need-based.	"Loan of last resort." High interest rate.

*Check http://studentaid.ed.gov/students/publications/student_guide/index.html

CHAPTER 10
LAW SCHOOL 101

IS IT REALLY THAT BAD?

The first semester of law school has the well-deserved reputation of being among the greatest challenges to your intellect and stamina that you'll ever face. It requires tons and tons of work and, in many ways, it's an exercise in intellectual survival. Just as the gung-ho army recruit must survive boot camp, so, too, must the bright-eyed law student endure the humbling effects of the first year.

Though complex and difficult, the subject matter in first-year law school courses is probably no more inherently difficult than what is taught in other graduate or professional schools. The particular, private terror that is shared by roughly 40,000 1Ls every year stems more from law school's peculiar *style*. The method of instruction unapologetically punishes students who would prefer to learn passively.

THE FIRST-YEAR CURRICULUM

The first-year curriculum in the law school you attend will almost certainly be composed of a combination of the following courses:

TORTS

The word comes from the Middle French for *injury*. The Latin root of the word means *twisted*. Torts are wrongful acts, excluding breaches of contract, over which you can sue people. They include battery, assault, false imprisonment, and intentional infliction of emotional distress. Torts can range from the predictable to the bizarre, from "Dog Bites Man" to "Man Bites Dog" and everything in between. The study of torts mostly involves reading cases to discern the legal rationale behind decisions pertaining to the extent of, and limits on, the civil liability of one party for harm done to another.

CONTRACTS

They may seem fairly self-explanatory, but contractual relationships are varied and complicated, as two semesters of contracts will teach you. Again, through the study of past court cases, you will follow the largely unwritten law governing the system of conditions and obligations a contract represents, as well as the legal remedies available when contracts are breached.

CIVIL PROCEDURE

Civil procedure is the study of how you get things done in civil (as opposed to criminal) court. "Civ Pro" is the study of the often dizzyingly complex rules that govern not only who can sue whom, but also how, when, and where they can do it. This is not merely a study of legal protocol, for issues of process have a significant indirect effect on the substance of the law. Rules of civil procedure govern the conduct of both the courtroom trial and the steps that might precede it: obtaining information (discovery), making your case (pleading), pre-trial motions, and so on.

PROPERTY

You may never own a piece of land, but your life will inevitably and constantly be affected by property laws. Anyone interested in achieving an understanding of broader policy issues will appreciate the significance of this material. Many property courses will emphasize the transfer of property and, to varying degrees, economic analysis of property law.

CRIMINAL LAW

Even if you become a criminal prosecutor or defender, you will probably never run into most of the crimes to which you will be exposed in this course. Can someone who shoots the dead body of a person he believes to be alive be charged with attempted murder? What if they were both on drugs or had really rough childhoods? Also, you'll love the convoluted exam questions in which someone will invariably go on a nutty crime spree.

CONSTITUTIONAL LAW

"Con Law" is the closest thing to a normal class you will take in your first year. It emphasizes issues of government structure (e.g., federal power versus state power) and individual rights (e.g., personal liberties, freedom of expression, property protection). You'll spend a great deal of time studying the limits on the lawmaking power of Congress as well.

LEGAL METHODS

One of the few twentieth-century improvements on the traditional first-year curriculum that has taken hold nearly everywhere, this course travels under various aliases, such as Legal Research and Writing or Elements of the Law. In recent years, increased recognition of the importance of legal writing skills has led more than half of the U.S. law schools to require or offer a writing course after the first year. This class will be your smallest, and possibly your only, refuge from the Socratic Method. Methods courses are often taught by junior faculty and attorneys in need of extra cash and are designed to help you acquire fundamental skills in legal research, analysis, and writing. The methods course may be the least frightening you face, but it can easily consume an enormous amount of time. This is a common lament, particularly at schools where very few credits are awarded for it.

In addition to these course requirements, many law schools require 1Ls to participate in a moot-court exercise. As part of this exercise, students—sometimes working in pairs or even small groups—must prepare briefs and oral arguments for a mock trial (usually appellate). This requirement is often tied in with the methods course so that those briefs and oral arguments will be well researched—and graded.

THE CASE METHOD

In the majority of your law school courses, and probably in all of your first-year courses, your only texts will be things called casebooks. The case method eschews explanation and encourages exploration. In a course that relies entirely on the casebook, you will never come across a printed list of "laws." Instead, you will learn that in many areas of law there is no such thing as a static set of rules, but only a constantly evolving system of principles. You are expected to understand the principles of law—in all of its layers and ambiguities—through a critical examination of a series of cases that were decided according to such principles. You will often feel utterly lost, groping for answers to unarticulated questions. This is not only normal but also intended.

In practical terms, the case method works like this: For every class meeting, you will be assigned a number of cases to read from your casebook, which is a collection of (extremely edited) written judicial decisions in actual court cases. The names won't even have been changed to protect the innocent. The cases are the written judicial opinions rendered in court cases that were decided at the appeals or Supreme Court level. (Written opinions are not generally rendered in lower courts.)

Your casebook will contain no instructions and little to no explanation. Your assignments will be to simply read the cases and be in a position to answer questions based on them. There will be no written homework assignments, just cases, cases, and more cases.

You will write, for your own benefit, summaries—or briefs—of these cases. Briefs are your attempts to summarize the issues and laws around which a particular case revolves. *By briefing, you figure out what the law is.* The idea is that, over the course of a semester, you will try to integrate the content of your case briefs and your notes from in-class lectures, discussions, or dialogues into some kind of cohesive whole.

Tips for Classroom Success

- Be alert. Review material immediately before class so that it is fresh in your memory. Then review your notes from class later the same day and the week's worth of notes at the end of each week.

- Remember that there are few correct answers. The goal of a law school class is generally to analyze, understand, and attempt to resolve issues or problems.

- Learn to state and explain legal rules and principles with accuracy.

- Don't want to focus on minutiae from cases or class discussions; always try to figure out what the law is.

- Accept the ambiguity in legal analysis and class discussion; classes are intended to be thought provoking, perplexing, and difficult.

- No one class session will make or break you. Keep in mind how each class fits within the course overall.

- Write down the law. Don't write down what other students say. Concentrate your notes on the professor's hypotheticals and emphases in class.

- Review the table of contents in the casebook. This is a simple but effective way of keeping yourself in touch with where the class is at any given time.

- If you don't use a laptop, don't sit next to someone who does. The constant tapping on the keys will drive you crazy, and you may get a sense that they are writing down more than you (which is probably not true).

- Don't record classes. There are better uses of your time than to spend hours listening to the comments of students who were just as confused as you were when you first dealt with the material in class.

THE SOCRATIC METHOD

As unfamiliar as the case method will be to most 1Ls, the real source of anxiety is the way in which the professors present it. Socratic instruction entails directed questioning and limited lecturing. Generally, the Socratic professor invites a student to attempt a cogent summary of a case assigned for that day's class. Hopefully, it won't be you (but someday it will be). Regardless of the accuracy and thoroughness of your initial response, the professor then grills you on details overlooked or issues unresolved. Then, the professor will change the facts of the actual case at hand into a hypothetical case that may or may not have demanded a different decision by the court.

The overall goal of the Socratic method is to forcibly improve your critical reasoning skills. If you are reasonably well prepared, thinking about all these questions will force you beyond the immediately apparent issues in a given case to consider its broader implications. The dialogue between the effective Socratic instructor and the victim of the moment will also force nonparticipating students to question their underlying assumptions of the case under discussion.

WHAT IS CLINICAL LEGAL EDUCATION?

The latest so-called innovation in legal education is ironic in that it's a return to the old emphasis on practical experience. Hands-on training in the practical skills of lawyering now travels under the name "Clinical Legal Education."

HOW IT WORKS

Generally, a clinical course focuses on developing practical lawyering skills. "Clinic" means exactly what you would expect: a working law office where second- and third-year law students counsel clients and serve human beings. (A very limited number of law schools allow first-year students to participate in legal clinics.)

> **Watch The Paper Chase.** *Twice.*
> *This movie is the only one ever produced about law school that comes close to depicting the real thing. Watch it before you go to orientation. Watch it again on Thanksgiving break, and laugh when you can identify prototypes of your classmates.*

In states that grant upper-level law students a limited right to represent clients in court, students in a law school's clinic might actually follow cases through to their resolution. Some schools have a single on-site clinic that operates something like a general law practice, dealing with cases ranging from petty crime to landlord-tenant disputes. At schools that have dedicated the most resources to their clinical programs, numerous specialized clinics deal with narrowly defined areas of law, such as employment discrimination. The opportunities to participate in such live-action programs, however, are limited.

OTHER OPTIONS

Clinical legal education is much more expensive than traditional instruction, which means that few law schools can accommodate more than a small percentage of their students in clinical programs. If that's the case, check out external clinical placements and simulated clinical courses. In a clinical externship, you might work with a real firm or public agency several hours a week and meet with a faculty advisor only occasionally. Though students who participate in these programs are unpaid, they will ordinarily receive academic credit. Also, placements are chosen quite carefully to ensure that you don't become a gopher.

There are also simulated clinical courses. In one of these, you'll perform all of the duties that a student in a live-action clinic would, but your clients are imaginary.

CHAPTER 11
HOW TO EXCEL AT ANY LAW SCHOOL

Preparation for law school is something you should take very seriously. Law school will be one of the most interesting and rewarding experiences of your life, but it's also an important and costly investment. Your academic performance in law school will influence your career for years to come. Consider the following facts when thinking about how important it is to prepare for law school:

- The average full-time law student spends more than $125,000 to attend law school.

- The average law student graduates with more than $80,000 of debt.

- The median income for law school graduates in both public and private practice is only about $60,000.

As you can see, most law students cannot afford to be mediocre. Money isn't everything, but when you're strapped with close to six figures of debt, money concerns will weigh heavily on your career choices. Even if money is not a concern for you, your academic performance in law school will profoundly affect your employment options after graduation and, ultimately, your legal career. Consider these additional facts

- Students who excel in law school may have opportunities to earn up to $135,000 plus bonuses right out of law school.

- Only law students who excel academically have opportunities to obtain prestigious judicial clerkships, teaching positions, and distinguished government jobs.

As you can see, law students who achieve academic success enjoy better career options and have a greater ability to escape the crushing debt of law school. The point is obvious: Your chances of achieving your goals—no matter what you want to do with your career—are far better if you succeed academically.

Now comes the hard part: How do you achieve academic success? You are going to get plenty of advice about how to excel in law school—much of it unsolicited. You certainly don't need any from us. We strongly advise, however, that you pay close attention to what Don Macaulay, the president of Law Preview, has to say about surviving and thriving as a law student. Macaulay, like all the founders of Law Preview, graduated at the top of his law school class and worked at a top law firm before he began developing and administering Law Preview's law school prep course in 1998.

All B-pluses put you in the top quarter at most schools and in the top fifth at many.

While there are many resources that claim to provide a recipe for success in law school, Law Preview is the best of the lot. They have retained some of the most talented legal scholars in the country to lecture during their week-long sessions, and they deliver what they promise—a methodology for attacking and conquering the law school experience.

We asked Macaulay a few questions to which we thought prospective law students might like to know the answers:

It is often said that the first year of law school is the most important year. Is this true and, if so, why?

It is true. Academic success during the first year of law school can advance a successful legal career unlike success in any other year because many of the top legal employers start recruiting so early that your first-year grades are all they will see. Most prestigious law firms hire their permanent attorneys from among the ranks of the firm's "summer associates"—usually second-year law students who work for the firm during the summer between the second and third years of law school. Summer associates are generally hired during the fall semester of the second year, a time when only the first year grades are available. A student who does well during the first year, lands a desirable summer associate position, and then impresses his or her employer, is well on his or her way to a secure legal job regardless of his or her academic performance after the first year.

In addition, first-year grades often bear heavily upon a student's eligibility for law review and other prestigious scholastic activities, including other law journals and moot court. These credentials are considered the most significant signs of law school achievement, often even more than a high grade point average. Many of the top legal employers in the private and the public sectors seek out young lawyers with these credentials, and some employers will not even interview candidates who lack these honors, even after a few years of experience. As a result, a solid performance during the first year of law school can have a serious impact upon your professional opportunities available after graduation.

How does law school differ from what students experienced as undergraduates?

Many students, especially those who enjoyed academic success in college, presume that law school will be a mere continuation of their undergraduate experience, and that, by implementing those skills that brought them success in college, they will enjoy similar success in law school. This couldn't be further from the truth. Once law school begins, students often find themselves thrown into deep water. They are handed an anchor in the form of a casebook (they are told it's a life preserver), and they are expected to sink or swim. While almost nobody sinks in law school anymore, most spend all of their first year just trying to keep their heads above water. In reality, virtually every student who is admitted into law school possesses the intelligence and work ethic needed to graduate. But in spite of having the tools needed to survive the experience, very few possess the know-how to truly excel and make Law Review at their schools.

> **Websites About Doing Well in Law School**
> **www.lawpreview.com**
> Law Preview is an intensive week-long seminar designed to help you conquer law school. Learn why hundreds of students have made Law Preview their first step to Law Review.
> **www.LawBooksForLess.com**
> LawBooksForLess.com is the best place to purchase casebooks and legal study aids, cheap!

What makes the law school experience unique is its method of instruction and its system of grading. Most professors rely on the case method as a means for illustrating legal rules and doctrines encountered in a particular area of the law. With the case method, students are asked to read a particular case or, in some instances, several cases, that the professor will use to lead a classroom discussion illustrating a particular rule of law. The assigned readings come from casebooks, which are compilations of cases for each area of law. The cases are usually edited to illustrate distinct legal rules, often with very little commentary or enlightenment by the casebook editor. The casebooks often lack anything more than a general structure, and law professors often contribute little to the limited structure. Students are asked to read and analyze hundreds of cases in a vacuum. Since each assigned case typically builds upon a legal rule illustrated in a previous case, it isn't until the end of the semester or, for some classes, the end of the year, that students begin to form an understanding of how these rules interrelate.

One of the objectives of Law Preview's law school prep course is to help students to understand the big picture before they begin their classes. We hire some of the most talented law professors from around the country to provide previews of the core first-year law school courses: Civil Procedure, Constitutional Law, Contracts, Criminal Law, Property, and Torts. During their lectures, our professors provide students with a roadmap for each subject by discussing the law's development, legal doctrines, and recurring themes and policies that students will encounter throughout the course. By providing entering law students with a conceptual framework for the material they will study, Law Preview eliminates the frustration that most of them will encounter when reading and analyzing case law in a vacuum.

What is the best way to prepare for law school, and when should you start?

When preparing for law school, students should focus on two interrelated tasks: 1) developing a strategy for academic success, and 2) preparing mentally for the awesome task ahead. The primary objective for most law students is to achieve the highest grades possible, and a well-defined strategy for success will help you direct your efforts most efficiently and effectively toward that goal. You must not begin law school equipped solely with some vague notion of hard work. Success requires a concrete plan that includes developing a reliable routine for classroom preparation, a proficient method of outlining, and a calculated strategy for test-taking. The further you progress in law school without such a plan, the more time and energy you will waste struggling through your immense work-load without moving discernibly closer to achieving academic success.

You must also become mentally prepared to handle the rigors of law school. Law school can be extremely discouraging because students receive very little feedback during the school year. Classes are usually graded solely based on final exam scores. Midterm exams and graded papers are uncommon, and classroom participation is often the only way for students to ascertain if they understand the material and are employing effective study methods. As a result, a winning attitude is critical to success in law school. Faith in yourself will help you continue to make the personal sacrifices during the first year that you need to make to succeed in law school, even when the rewards are not immediately apparent.

Incoming law students should begin preparing for law school during the summertime prior to first year, and preparation exercises should be aimed at gaining a general understanding of what law school is all about. A solid understanding of what you are expected to learn during the first year will give you the information you need to develop both your strategy for success and the confidence you need to succeed. There are several books on the market that can help in this regard, but those students who are best prepared often attend Law Preview's one-week intensive preparatory course specifically designed to teach beginning law students the strategies for academic success.

What factors contribute to academic success in law school?

Academic success means one thing in law school—exam success. The grades that you receive, particularly during the first year, will be determined almost exclusively by the scores you receive on your final exams. Occasionally, a professor may add a few points for class participation, but that is rare. In most classes, your final exam will consist of a three- or four-hour written examination at the end of the semester or—if the course is two semesters long—at the end of the year. The amount of material you must master for each final exam will simply dwarf that of any undergraduate exam you have ever taken. The hope that you can "cram" a semester's worth of information into a one-week reading period is pure fantasy and one that will surely lead to disappointing grades. The focus of your efforts from day one should be success on your final exams. Don't get bogged down in class preparation or in perfecting a course outline if it will not result in some discernible improvement in your exam performance. All of your efforts should be directed at improving your exam performance in some way. It's as simple as that.

What skills are typically tested on law school exams?

Law school exams usually test three different skills: 1) the ability to accurately identify legal issues, 2) the ability to recall the relevant law with speed, and 3) the ability to apply the law to the facts efficiently and skillfully. The proper approach for developing these skills differs, depending on the substantive area of law in question and whether your exam is open book or closed book.

Identifying legal issues is commonly known as issue spotting. On most of your exams, you will be given complex, hypothetical fact patterns. From the facts you are given, you must identify the particular legal issues that need to be addressed. This is a difficult skill to perfect and can only be developed through practice. The best way to develop issue-spotting skills is by taking practice exams. For each of your classes, during the first half of the semester, you should collect all of the available exams that were given by your professor in the past. Take all of these exams under simulated exam conditions—find an open classroom, get some blue books, time yourself, and take the exams with friends so that you can review them afterward. It is also helpful for you to practice any legal problems you were given during the semester. Issue spotting is an important skill for all lawyers to develop. Lawyers utilize this skill on a daily basis when they listen to their clients' stories and are asked to point out places where legal issues might arise.

The ability to recall the law with speed is also very important and frequently tested. On all of your exams, you will be given a series of legal problems, and for each problem you will usually be required to provide the relevant substantive law and apply it to the facts of the problem. Your ability to recall the law with speed is critical because, in most classes, you will be under time constraints to answer all of the problems. The faster you recall the law, the more problems you will complete and the more time you will have to spend on demonstrating your analytical skills. For courses with closed-book exams, this means straight memorization or the use of memory recall devices, such as mnemonics. Do not be passive about learning the law—repeatedly reviewing your outline is not enough. You must actively learn the law by studying definitions and using memory-assistance devices like flash cards. When you have become exceedingly familiar with your flash cards, rewrite them so as to test your memory in different words. This is particularly critical for courses such as torts and criminal law where you must learn a series of definitions with multiple elements. For courses with open-book exams, this means developing an index for your outline that will enable you to locate the relevant law quickly. Create a cover page for your outline that lists the page number for each substantive subtopic. This will help you get there without any undue delay.

Books About Doing Well in Law School:
Getting to Maybe: How to Excel on Law School Exams, *Professors Jeremy Paul and Michael Fischl*
This book is excellent! While many books and professors may preach "IRAC"—Issue, Rule, Application, Conclusion—as a way of structuring exam answers, Getting to Maybe rightly points out that such advice does not help students correctly identify legal issues or master the intricacies of legal analysis.

Law School Confidential: A Complete Guide to the Law School Experience (Second Edition), *Robert H. Miller, Esq.*
Robert H. Miller, a former federal judicial clerk, Law Review editor, and graduate of University of Pennsylvania Law School, covers every aspect of the law school experience in thoughtful detail. Whether you are a college student just starting to think about law school, a student in the midst of law school applications, or someone who has already been admitted, Law School Confidential is a book you should not be without. An extensive new chapter is devoted to an exclusive one-on-one interview with Dean of Admissions Richard Geiger of the Cornell Law School, wherein closely guarded secrets of the increasingly competitive admissions process are discussed openly for the first time anywhere. In another chapter, Miller goes one-on-one with the hiring partners of two prestigious U.S. law firms about how to succeed in the hiring process, and what it takes to make it to partnership.

The final skill you need to develop is the ability to apply the law to the facts efficiently and skillfully. On your exams, once you have correctly identified the relevant issue and stated the relevant law, you must engage in a discussion of how the law applies to the facts that have been given. The ability to engage in such a discussion is best developed by taking practice exams. When you are practicing this skill, you should focus on efficiency. Try to focus on the essential facts, and do not engage in irrelevant discussions that will waste your energy and your professor's time.

Any final comments for our audience of aspiring law students?

The study of law is a wonderful and noble pursuit, one that I thoroughly enjoyed. Law school is not easy, however, and proper preparation can give you a firm foundation for success. I invite you to visit our website (LawPreview.com) and contact us with any questions (888-PREP-YOU).

CHAPTER 12
CAREER MATTERS

Okay, it's a long time away, but you really ought to be thinking about your professional career beyond law school from day one, especially if your goal is to practice with a major law firm. What stands between you and a job as an associate, the entry-level position at one of these firms, is a three-stage evaluation: first, a review of your resume, including your grades and work experience; second, an on-campus interview; and last, one or more call-back interviews at the firm's offices. It's a fairly intimidating ordeal, but there are a few ways to reduce the anxiety and enhance your chances of landing a great job.

YOUR RESUME

The first thing recruiters tend to notice after your name is the name of the law school you attend. Tacky, but true. Perhaps the greatest misconception among law students, however, is that hiring decisions are based largely upon your school's prestige. All those rankings perpetuate this myth. To be sure, there are a handful of schools with reputations above all others, and students who excel at these schools are in great demand. But you are equally well situated, if not better off, applying from the top of your class at a strong, less prestigious law school class than from the bottom half of a Top Ten law school class.

FIRST-YEAR GRADES ARE THE WHOLE ENCHILADA

Fair or not, the first year of law school will unduly influence your legal future. It's vital that you hit the ground running because law school grades are *the* critical factor in recruitment. An even harsher reality is that *first-year grades are by far the most critical in the hiring process*. Decisions about who gets which plum summer jobs are generally handed down before students take a single second-year exam. Consequently, you're left with exactly *no* time to adjust to law school life and little chance to improve your transcript if you don't come out on top as a first-year student.

WORK EXPERIENCE

If you're applying to law school right out of college, chances are your most significant work experience has been a summer job. Recruiters don't expect you to have spent these months writing Supreme Court decisions. They are generally satisfied if you show that you have worked diligently and seriously at each opportunity. Students who took a year or more off after college obviously have more opportunities to impress but also more of a burden to demonstrate diligence and seriousness.

Work experience in the legal industry—clerkships and paralegal jobs for instance—can be excellent sources of professional development. They are fairly common positions among job applicants, though, so don't feel you have to pursue one of these routes just to show your commitment to the law. You'll make a better impression by working in an industry in which you'd like to specialize (e.g., a prospective securities lawyer summering with an investment bank).

Making Law Review

Every law school has an academic periodical called Law Review, produced and edited by law students. It contains articles about various aspects of law—mostly written by professors. While some schools sponsor more than one Law Review, there is generally one that is more prestigious than all the others. In order to "make" Law Review, you will have to finish the all-important first year at (or very, very near) the top of your class or write an article that will be judged by the existing members of the Law Review. You might have to do both. Making Law Review is probably the easiest way to guarantee yourself a job at a blue-chip firm, working for a judge, or in academia. In all honesty, it is a credential you will proudly carry for the rest of your life.

A Couple Good Books

If you are thinking about law school, here are a few books you might find interesting:

The Princeton Review's Law School Essays That Made a Difference
Check out successful essays written for an assortment of selective schools.

Jeff Deaver, The Complete Law School Companion: How to Excel at America's Most Demanding Post-Graduate Curriculum
This straightforward law school survival guide gives excellent advice on how to brief cases, sample briefs, survive class, and plenty more.

THE INTERVIEWS

There are as many right approaches to an interview as there are interviewers. That observation provides little comfort, of course, especially if you're counting on a good interview to make up for whatever deficiencies there are on your resume. Think about the purpose of the initial 30-minute interview you are likely to have: it provides a rough sketch of not only your future office personality but also your demeanor under stress. The characteristics you demonstrate and the *impression* you give are more important than anything you say. Composure, confidence, maturity, articulation, and an ability to develop rapport are characteristics recruiters are looking for. Give them what they want.

CHAPTER 13
HOW TO USE THIS BOOK

It's pretty simple.

The first part of this book provides a wealth of indispensable information covering everything you need to know about selecting and getting into the law school of your choice. There is also a great deal about what to expect from law school and how to do well. You name it—taking the LSAT, choosing the best school for you, writing a great personal statement, interviewing, paying for it—it's all in the first part.

The second part is the real meat and potatoes of *The Best 172 Law Schools*. It contains portraits of 172 law schools across the United States and Canada. Each school has one of two possible types of entries. The first type of entry is a two-page descriptive profile. It contains data The Princeton Review has collected directly from law school administrators and textual descriptions of the school we have written based on our surveys of current law students. The second type of entry is a data listing, which includes all the same data that appears in the sidebars of the descriptive profiles but does not have the student survey-driven descriptive paragraphs. For an explanation of why all schools do not appear with descriptive profiles, turn to page 59. As is customary with school guidebooks, all data, with the exception of tuition (which should be for the current year if the school reported it by our deadline), reflects figures for the academic year prior to publication unless otherwise noted on the pages. Since law school demographics vary significantly from one institution to another and some schools report data more thoroughly than others, some entries will not include all the individual data described below.

The third part of the book hosts the "School Says . . ." profiles. The "School Says . . ." profiles give extended descriptions of admissions processes, curricula, internship opportunities, and much more. This is your chance to get even more in-depth information on programs that interest you. These schools have paid us a small fee for the chance to tell you more about themselves, and the editorial responsibility is solely that of the law school. We think you'll find these profiles add lots to your picture of a school.

WHAT'S IN THE PROFILES: DATA

The Heading: The first thing you will see for each profile is (obviously) the school's name. On the facing page, you'll find the school's snail mail address, telephone number, fax number, e-mail address, and website. You can find the name of the Admissions Office contact person in the heading, too.

INSTITUTIONAL INFORMATION

Public/Private: Indicates whether a school is state-supported or funded by private means.

Affiliation: If the school is affiliated with a particular religion, you'll find that information here.

Student/Faculty Ratio: The ratio of law students to full-time faculty.

% Faculty Part-time: The percentage of faculty who are part-time.

% Faculty Female: The percentage of faculty who are women.

% Faculty Minority : The percentage of people who teach at the law school who are also members of minority groups.

Total Faculty: The total number of faculty members at the law school.

> *Yet Another Good Book:*
> **One L: The Turbulent True Story of a First Year at Harvard Law School,** *Scott Turow*
> *This law school primer is equal parts illuminating and harrowing.*

SURVEY SAYS

The Survey Says list appears in the sidebar of each law school's two-page descriptive profile, and up to three Survey Says items will appear on each list. As the name suggests, these items communicate results of our law student surveys. There are 10 possible Survey Says items, each explained below. Of these 10, the 3 items that appear are those about which student respondents demonstrated the greatest degree of consensus. Survey Says items represent the agreement among students only at *that particular law school* and are not relative to how students at other law schools feel about that particular Survey Says item.

Liberal students: Students report that their fellow law students lean to the left politically.

Conservative students: Students report that their fellow law students lean to the right politically.

Students love Hometown, State: Students are pleased with the location of their law school.

Good social life: Students report a lively social life at the law school.

Students never sleep: Students report a low average number of hours of sleep each night. Little sleep in law school is often an indication of extra-long hours of study on a daily basis.

Heavy use of Socratic Method: Students report that their professors primarily employ the traditional Socratic Method in the classroom.

Beautiful campus: Students report that their law school campus is practical and beautiful.

Great research resources: Students report that the library, computer databases, and other research tools are good.

Great judicial externship/internship/clerkship opportunities: Students rate these opportunities as excellent.

Diverse opinions in classrooms: Students agree that differing points of view are tolerated in the classroom.

STUDENTS

Enrollment of Law School: The total number of students enrolled in the law school.

% Male/Female: The percentage of full-time students with an X and a Y chromosome and the percentage of students with two X chromosomes, respectively.

% Out-of-state: The percentage of full-time students who are out-of-state.

% Full-time: The percentage of students who attend the school on a full-time basis.

% Minority: The percentage of full-time students who represent minority groups.

% International: The percentage of students who hail from foreign soil.

# of Countries Represented: The number of different foreign countries from which the current student body hails.

Average Age of Entering Class: On the whole, how old the 1Ls are.

ACADEMICS

Academic Experience Rating: The quality of the learning environment, on a scale of 60 to 99. The rating incorporates the Admissions Selectivity Rating and the average responses of law students at the school to several questions on our law student survey. In addition to the Admissions Selectivity Rating, factors considered include how students rate the quality of teaching and the accessibility of their professors, the school's research resources, the range of available courses, the balance of legal theory and practical lawyering skills stressed in the curriculum, the tolerance for diverse opinions in the classroom, and how intellectually challenging the course work is. This individual rating places each law school on a continuum for purposes of comparing all law schools within this edition only. If a law school receives a "low" Academic Experience Rating, it doesn't mean that the

---

Law School Fun Fact

The least litigated amendment in the Bill of Rights is the Third Amendment, which prohibits the quartering of soldiers in private homes without consent of the owner.

---

school provides a bad academic experience for its students. It simply means that the school scored lower than other schools in our computations based on the criteria outlined above. Because this rating incorporates law student opinion data, only those law schools that appear in the section with the descriptive profiles based on student surveys receive an Academic Experience Rating.

Professors Interesting Rating: Based on law student opinion. We asked law students to rate the quality of teaching at their law schools on a scale from 60 to 99. Because this rating incorporates law student opinion data, only those law schools that appear in the section with the descriptive profiles receive a Professors Interesting Rating.

Professors Accessible Rating: Based on law student opinion. We asked law students to rate how accessible the law faculty members at their schools are on a scale from 60 to 99. Because this rating incorporates law student opinion data, only those law schools that appear in the section with the descriptive profiles receive a Professors Accessible Rating.

Hours of Study Per Day: From our student survey. The average number of hours students at the school report studying each day.

Academic Specialties: Different areas of law and academic programs on which the school prides itself.

Advanced Degrees Offered: Degrees available through the law school and the length of the program.

Combined Degrees Offered: Programs at this school involving the law school and some other college or degree program within the larger university, and how long it will take you to complete the joint program.

Grading System: Scoring system used by the law school. (Appears in the data listings section only.)

Academic Requirements: Most law schools require their students to complete some courses and/or programs that go beyond traditional legal theory, whether to broaden their understanding of and experience with the law or to develop important practical lawyering skills.

Clinical Program Required? Indicates whether clinical programs are required to complete the core curriculum.

Clinical Program Description: Programs designed to give students hands-on training and experience in the practice of some area of law. (Appears in the data listings section only.)

Legal Writing Course Requirement? Tells you whether there is a required course in legal writing.

Legal Writing Description: A description of any course work, required or optional, designed specifically to develop legal writing skills vital to the practice of law. (Appears in the data listings section only.)

Legal Methods Course Requirements? Indicates whether there is a mandatory curriculum component to cover legal methods.

Legal Methods Description: A description of any course work, required or optional, designed specifically to develop the skills vital to legal analysis. (Appears in the data listings section only.)

Legal Research Course Requirements? If a school requires course work specifically to develop legal research skills, this field will tell you.

Legal Research Description: A description of any course work, required or optional, designed specifically to develop legal research skills vital to the practice of law. (Appears in the data listings section only.)

Moot Court Requirement? Indicates whether participation in a moot court program is mandatory.

Moot Court Description: This will describe any moot court program, mandatory or optional, designed to develop skills in legal research, writing, and oral argument. (Appears in the data listings section only.)

Public Interest Law Requirement? If a school requires participation on a public interest law project, we'll let you know here.

Public Interest Law Description: Programs designed to expose students to the public interest law field through clinical work, volunteer opportunities, or specialized course work. (Appears in the data listings section only.)

Academic Journals: This field will list any academic journals offered at the school. (Appears in the data listings section only.)

ADMISSIONS INFORMATION

Admissions Selectivity Rating: How competitive admission is at the law school, on a scale of 60 to 99. Several factors determine this rating, including LSAT scores and the average undergraduate GPA of entering 1L students, the percentage of applicants accepted, and the percentage of accepted applicants who enrolled in the law school. We collect this information through a survey that law school administrators completed for the Fall 2009 entering class. This individual rating places each law school on a continuum for purposes of comparing all law schools within this edition only. All law schools that appear in this edition of the guide, whether in the section with the descriptive profiles based on student surveys or in the section with school-reported statistics only, receive an Admissions Selectivity Rating. If a law school has a relatively low Admissions Selectivity Rating, it doesn't necessarily mean that it's easy to gain admission to the law school. (It's not easy to get into any ABA-approved law schools, really.) It simply means that the school scored lower relative to other schools in our computations based on the criteria outlined in the previous page.

# of Applications Received: The number of people who applied to the law school's full-time JD program.

# of Applicants Accepted: The number of people who were admitted to the school's full-time class.

# of Acceptees Attending: The number of those admitted who chose to attend the school full-time.

Average LSAT/LSAT Range: Indicates the average LSAT score of incoming 1Ls, as reported by the school. The range is the 25th to 75th percentiles of 1Ls.

Average Undergrad GPA: It's usually on a 4.0 scale.

Application Fee: How much it costs to apply to the school.

> **Law School Trivia**
>
> The guarantee that each state must have an equal number of votes in the United States Senate is the only provision in the Constitution of 1787 that cannot be amended.

Regular Application Deadline and "Rolling": Many law schools evaluate applications and notify applicants of admission decisions on a continuous, rolling basis over the course of several months (ordinarily from late fall to midsummer). Obviously, if you apply to one of these schools, you want to apply early because there will be more places available at the beginning of the process.

Regular Notification? The official date by or on which a law school will release a decision for an applicant who applied using the regular admission route.

Early Application Program? Whether the law school has an early application program. If you are accepted to an Early Decision program, you are obligated to attend that law school. If you are accepted under an Early Action program, you have no obligation to attend. You just get to know earlier whether you got in.

Early Application Deadline: The official date by which the law school must receive your application if you want to be considered for its early application program.

Early Application Notification: The official date on which a law school will release a decision for an applicant who applied using the early application route.

Transfer Students Accepted? Whether transfer students from other schools are considered for admission.

Evening Division Offered? Whether the school offers an evening program in addition to its full-time regular program. Evening division programs are almost always part-time and require four years of study (instead of three) to complete.

Part-time Accepted? Whether part-time students may enroll in the JD program on a basis other than the standard full-time.

LSDAS Accepted? "Yes" indicates that the school utilizes the Law School Data Assembly Service.

Applicants Also Look At: The law schools to which applicants to this school also apply. It's important. It's a reliable indicator of the overall academic quality of the applicant pool.

RESEARCH FACILITIES (APPEARS IN THE DATA LISTINGS SECTION ONLY)

Research Resources Available: Online retrieval resources, subscription services, libraries, and databases available for legal research.

% of JD Classrooms Wired: The percentage of dedicated law school classrooms wired for laptops and Internet access.

Computer Labs: The number of rooms full of computers that you can use free.

School-Supported Research Centers: Indicates whether the school has on-campus, internally supported research centers.

INTERNATIONAL STUDENTS

TOEFL Required/Recommended of International Students? Indicates whether or not international students must take the TOEFL, or Test of English as a Foreign Language, to be admitted to the school.

Minimum TOEFL: Minimum score (paper and computer) an international student must earn on the TOEFL to be admitted.

FINANCIAL FACTS

Annual Tuition (Residents/Nonresidents): What it costs to go to school for an academic year. For state schools, both in-state and out-of-state tuition is listed.

Books and Supplies: Indicates how much students can expect to shell out for textbooks and other assorted supplies during the academic year.

Fees Per Credit (Residents/Nonresidents): That mysterious extra money you are required to pay the law school in addition to tuition and everything else, on a per-credit basis. If in-state and out-of-state students are charged differently, both amounts are listed.

Tuition Per Credit (Residents/Nonresidents): Dollar amount charged per credit hour. For state schools, both in-state and out-of-state amounts are listed when they differ.

Room and Board (On-/Off-campus): This is the school's estimate of what it costs to buy meals and to pay for decent living quarters for the academic year. Where available, on- and off-campus rates are listed.

Financial Aid Application Deadline: The last day on which students can turn in their applications for monetary assistance.

% First-Year Students Receiving Some Sort of Aid: The percentage of new JD students who receive monetary assistance.

% Receiving Some Sort of Aid: The percentage of all the students at the school presently accumulating a staggering debt.

% of Aid That Is Merit-Based: The percentage of aid not based on financial need.

% Receiving Scholarships: The percentage of students at the school who received some sort of "free money" award. This figure can include grants as well.

Average Grant: Average financial aid amount awarded to students that does not have to be paid back. This figure can include scholarships as well.

Average Loan: Average amount of loan dollars accrued by students for the year.

Average Total Aid Package: How much aid each student at the school receives on average for the year.

Average Debt: The amount of debt—or, in legal lingo, arrears—you'll likely be saddled with by the time you graduate.

EMPLOYMENT INFORMATION

Career Rating: How well the law school prepares its students for a successful career in law, on a scale of 60 to 99. The rating incorporates school-reported data and the average responses of law students at the school to a few questions on our law student survey. We ask law schools for the average starting salaries of graduating students, the percentage of graduating students who find employment after graduation, and the percentage of students who pass the bar exam the first time they take it. We ask students about how much the law program encourages practical experience; the opportunities for externships, internships, and clerkships; and how prepared to practice law they will feel after graduating. If a school receives a "low" Career Rating, it doesn't necessarily mean that the career prospects for graduates are bad; it simply means that the school scored lower relative to how other schools scored based on the criteria outlined above. Because this rating incorporates law student opinion data, only those law schools that appear in the section with the descriptive profiles receive a Career Rating.

Rate of Placement (nine months out): Percent of graduates who secured employment within nine months of graduating from law school.

Average Starting Salary: The average amount of money graduates of this law school make the first year out of school.

State for Bar Exam: The state for which most students from the school will take the bar exam.

Pass Rate for First-Time Bar: After three years, the percentage of students who passed the bar exam the first time they took it. It's a crucial statistic. You *don't* want to fail your state's bar.

Employers Who Frequently Hire Grads: Firms where past grads have had success finding jobs.

Prominent Alumni: Those who made it . . . *big*.

Grads Employed by Field: The percentage of students in the most recent graduating class who have obtained jobs in a particular field.

Academia: The percentage of graduates who got jobs at law schools, universities, and think tanks.

Business/Industry: The percentage of graduates who got jobs working in business, corporations, consulting, and so on. These jobs are sometimes law-related and sometimes not.

Government: Uncle Sam needs lawyers like you wouldn't even believe.

Judicial Clerkships: The percentage of graduates who got jobs doing research for judges.

Military: The percentage of lawyers who work to represent the Armed Forces in all kinds of legal matters, like Tom Cruise in *A Few Good Men*.

Private Practice: The percentage of graduates who got jobs in traditional law firms of various sizes or "put out a shingle" for themselves as sole practitioners.

Public Interest: The percentage of (mostly) altruistic graduates who got jobs providing legal assistance to people who couldn't afford it otherwise.

NOTA BENE

If a 60* appears for any of a law school's ratings, it means that the school's administrators did not report by our deadline all of the statistics that rating incorporates.

Please note that we target each law school for resurveying at least every other year, which means we rewrite each law school's descriptive profile at least every other year, too. Student surveys captured via our online survey (http://survey.review.com) are considered current for the purposes of our own rating, rankings, and Survey Says items for two years.

WHAT'S IN THE PROFILES: DESCRIPTIVE TEXT

Academics, Life, and Getting In Sections: The text of the descriptive profiles is broken out into three sections: Academics, Life, and Getting In. The Academics and Life sections of each descriptive profile are driven by the student survey responses collected from current law students at the school, and the quotations sprinkled throughout each of these sections come directly from the written comments students provided us with on their surveys. In the Academics section, we often discuss professors and their teaching methods, the workload, special clinical programs, the efficiency of the administration, and the helpfulness of the library staff. In the Life section, we often discuss how academically competitive the student body is, how (and if) students separate into cliques, clubs, or organizations students often join, and the amenities of the town in which the school is located. We don't follow a cookie-cutter formula when writing these profiles. Instead we rely on students' responses to the open-ended questions on our student survey and analysis of their aggregate responses to our multiple choice questions to determine each profile's major "theme." The information in the Getting In section is based on the data we collect from law school administrators and our own additional research.

DECODING DEGREES

Many law schools offer joint- or combined-degree programs with other departments (or sometimes even with other schools) that you can earn along with your Juris Doctor. You'll find the abbreviations for these degrees in the individual school profiles, but we thought we'd give you a little help in figuring out exactly what they are.

AMBA	Accounting Master of Business		MEM	Master of Environmental Management
BCL	Bachelor of Civil Law		MFA	Master of Fine Arts
DJUR	Doctor of Jurisprudence		MHA	Master of Health Administration
DL	Doctor of Law		MHSA	Master of Health Services Administration
EdD	Doctor of Education		MIA	Master of International Affairs
HRIR	Human Resources and Industrial Relations		MIB	Master of International Business
IMBA	International Master of Business Administration		MIP	Master of Intellectual Property
JD	Juris Doctor		MIR	Master of Industrial Relations
JSD	Doctor of Juridical Science		MILR	Master of Industrial and Labor Relations
JSM	Master of the Science of Law		MJ	Master of Jurisprudence
LLB	Bachelor of Law		MJS	Master of Juridical Study (not a JD)
LLCM	Master of Comparative Law (for international students)		MLIR	Master of Labor and Industrial Relations
LLM	Master of Law		MLIS	Master of Library and Information Sciences
MA	Master of Arts		MLS	Master of Library Science
MAcc	Master of Accounting		MMA	Master of Marine Affairs
MALD	Master of Arts in Law and Diplomacy		MOB	Master of Organizational Behavior
MAM	Master of Arts Management		MPA	Master of Public Administration
MM	Master of Management		MPAFF	Master of Public Affairs
MANM	Master of Nonprofit Management		MPH	Master of Public Health
MAPA	Master of Public Administration		MPP	Master of Public Planning or Master of Public Policy
MAUA	Master of Arts in Urban Affairs		MPPA	Master of Public Policy
MBA	Master of Business Administration		MPPS	Master of Public Policy Sciences
MCJ	Master of Criminal Justice		MPS	Master of Professional Studies in Law
MCL	Master of Comparative Law		MRP	Master of Regional Planning
MCP	Master of Community Planning		MS	Master of Science
MCRP	Master of City and Regional Planning		MSEL	Master of Studies in Environmental Law
MDiv	Master of Divinity		MSES	Master of Science in Environmental Science
ME	Master of Engineering or Master of Education		MSF	Master of Science in Finance
MEd	Master of Education		MSFS	Master of Science in Foreign Service
MED	Master of Environmental Design		MSI	Master of Science in Information

MSIA	Master of Science in Industrial Administration
MSIE	Master of Science in International Economics
MSJ	Master of Science in Journalism
MSPH	Master of Science in Public Health
MSW	Master of Social Welfare or Master of Social Work
MT	Master of Taxation
MTS	Master of Theological Studies
MUP	Master of Urban Planning
MUPD	Master of Urban Planning and Development
MURP	Master of Urban and Regional Planning
PharmD	Doctor of Pharmacy
PhD	Doctor of Philosophy
REES	Russian and Eastern European Studies Certificate
SJD	Doctor of Juridical Science
DVM	Doctor of Veterinary Medicine
MALIR	Master of Arts in Labor and Industrial Relations

LAW SCHOOLS RANKED BY CATEGORY

ABOUT OUR LAW SCHOOL RANKINGS

On the following few pages, you will find 11 top 10 lists of ABA-approved law schools ranked according to various metrics. It must be noted, however, that none of these lists purports to rank the law schools by their overall quality. Nor should any combination of the categories we've chosen be construed as representing the raw ingredients for such a ranking. We have made no attempt to gauge the *prestige* of these schools, and we wonder whether we could accurately do so even if we tried. What we have done, however, is presented a number of lists using information from two very large databases—one of statistical information collected from law schools and another of subjective data gathered via our survey of more than 18,000 law students at 172 ABA-approved law schools. We target each law school's student body for resurveying at least every other year. This means that schools'student opinion data is considered current for the book's rankings and descriptive profiles for two years.

Ten of the ranking lists are based partly or wholly on opinions collected through our law student survey. The only schools that may appear in these lists are the 172 ABA-approved law schools from which we were able to collect a sufficient number of student surveys to accurately represent the student experience in our various ratings and descriptive profiles.

One of the rankings, Toughest to Get Into, incorporates *only* admissions statistics reported to us by the law schools. Therefore, any ABA-approved law school appearing in this edition of the guide, whether we collected student surveys from it or not, may appear on this list.

New to our rankings this year is out Best Classroom experience list, based on student assessment of professors' teaching abilities, balance of theory and practical skills in the curricula, tolerance for differing opinions in class discussion, and classroom facilities.

Under the title of each list is an explanation of the criteria on which the ranking is based. For explanations of many of the individual rankings components, go back to page 46–47.

It's worth repeating: There is no one best law school in America, but there is a best law school for you. By using these rankings in conjunction with the descriptive profiles and data listings of the schools in this book, we hope that you will begin to identify the attributes of a law school that are important to you, as well as the law schools that can best help you to achieve your personal and professional goals.

The schools in each category appear in descending order.

TOUGHEST TO GET INTO

BASED ON THE ADMISSIONS SELECTIVITY RATING (SEE PAGE 47 FOR EXPLANATION)

1. Yale University
2. Harvard University
3. Stanford University
4. University of California—Berkeley
5. Columbia University
6. University of Pennsylvania
7. Northwestern University
8. University of Virginia
9. University of Chicago
10. University of Michigan

BEST PROFESSORS

BASED ON THE PROFESSORS INTERESTING AND PROFESSORS ACCESSIBLE RATINGS (SEE PAGE 47 FOR EXPLANATIONS)

1. University of Chicago
2. University of Virginia
3. Boston University
4. Stanford University
5. Boston College
6. Pepperdine University
7. Chapman University
8. Washington and Lee University
9. Wake Forest University
10. City University of New York—Queens College

MOST COMPETITIVE STUDENTS

BASED ON LAW STUDENT ASSESSMENTS OF: THE NUMBER OF HOURS THEY SPEND STUDYING OUTSIDE OF CLASS EACH DAY, THE NUMBER OF HOURS THEY THINK THEIR FELLOW LAW STUDENTS SPEND STUDYING OUTSIDE OF CLASS EACH DAY, THE DEGREE OF COMPETITIVENESS AMONG LAW STUDENTS AT THEIR SCHOOL, AND THE AVERAGE NUMBER OF HOURS THEY SLEEP EACH NIGHT

1. Baylor University
2. Ohio Northern University
3. Brigham Young University
4. Thomas M. Cooley Law School
5. St. Thomas University
6. Campbell University
7. Whittier College
8. Syracuse University
9. Albany Law School
10. University of California, Hastings College of Law

BEST CAREER PROSPECTS

BASED ON THE CAREER RATING (SEE PAGE 49 FOR EXPLANATION)

1. Northwestern University
2. University of Pennsylvania
3. University of Michigan
4. University of Chicago
5. Stanford University
6. Boston University
7. Boston College
8. Harvard University
9. New York University
10. Georgetown University

BEST CLASSROOM EXPERIENCE

BASED ON STUDENT ASSESSMENT OF PROFESSORS' TEACHING ABILITIES, BALANCE OF
THEORY AND PRACTICAL SKILLS IN THE CURRICULA, TOLERANCE FOR DIFFERING OPINIONS
IN CLASS DISCUSSION, AND CLASSROOM FACILITIES

1. The University of Texas at Austin
2. Chapman University
3. Stanford University
4. University of Virginia
5. Loyola Marymount University
6. Vanderbilt University
7. Duke University
8. University of Chicago
9. George Washington University
10. Northwestern University

MOST CONSERVATIVE STUDENTS

BASED ON STUDENT ASSESSMENT OF THE POLITICAL BENT OF THE STUDENT BODY AT LARGE

1. Brigham Young University
2. Regent University
3. George Mason University
4. University of Notre Dame
5. Ave Maria
6. Louisiana State University
7. Texas Tech
8. University of Alabama
9. Campbell University
10. The University of Mississippi

MOST LIBERAL STUDENTS

BASED ON STUDENT ASSESSMENT OF THE POLITICAL BENT OF THE STUDENT BODY AT LARGE

1. City University of New York—Queens College
2. Northeastern University
3. Lewis & Clark College
4. American University
5. New York University
6. University of Oregon
7. University of California—Berkeley
8. University of Wisconsin
9. Rutgers, The State University of New Jersey—Newark
10. Vermont Law School

BEST ENVIRONMENT FOR MINORITY STUDENTS

BASED ON THE PERCENTAGE OF THE STUDENT BODY THAT IS FROM UNDERREPRESENTED
MINORITIES AND STUDENT ASSESSMENT OF WHETHER ALL STUDENTS RECEIVE EQUAL
TREATMENT BY FELLOW STUDENTS AND THE FACULTY, REGARDLESS OF ETHNICITY

1. University of Hawaii at Manoa
2. Northeastern University
3. Florida International University
4. University of Nevada—Las Vegas
5. St. Thomas University
6. Loyola Marymount University
7. Santa Clara University
8. University of Southern California
9. Southern University
10. American University

MOST DIVERSE FACULTY

BASED ON THE PERCENTAGE OF THE LAW SCHOOL FACULTY THAT IS FROM A MINORITY GROUP AND STUDENT ASSESSMENT OF WHETHER THE FACULTY MAKES UP A BROADLY DIVERSE GROUP OF INDIVIDUALS

1. Florida International University
2. Temple University
3. North Carolina Central University
4. Southern University
5. University of Hawaii at Manoa
6. University of the District of Columbia
7. City University of New York—Queens College
8. Phoenix School of Law
9. University of California—Davis
10. University of New Mexico

BEST QUALITY OF LIFE

BASED ON STUDENT ASSESSMENT OF: WHETHER THERE IS A STRONG SENSE OF COMMUNITY AT THE SCHOOL, HOW AESTHETICALLY PLEASING THE LAW SCHOOL IS, THE LOCATION OF THE LAW SCHOOL, THE QUALITY OF THE SOCIAL LIFE, CLASSROOM FACILITIES, AND THE LIBRARY STAFF

1. University of Virginia
2. Stanford University
3. Chapman University
4. University of St.Thomas
5. University of Colorado
6. Vanderbilt University
7. New York University
8. University of Oregon
9. Northwestern University
10. George Washington University

MOST CHOSEN BY OLDER STUDENTS

BASED ON THE AVERAGE AGE OF ENTRY OF LAW SCHOOL STUDENTS AND STUDENT REPORTS OF HOW MANY YEARS THEY SPENT OUT OF COLLEGE BEFORE ENROLLING IN LAW SCHOOL

1. City University of New York—Queens College
2. University of Hawaii at Manoa
3. University of Maine
4. Seattle University
5. University of the District of Columbia
6. University of New Mexico
7. Lewis & Clark College
8. Georgia State University
9. University of Arizona
10. William Mitchell College of Law

LAW SCHOOL DESCRIPTIVE PROFILES

In this section you will find the two page descriptive profile of each of the 172 ABA-approved law schools. As there are currently a total of 200 ABA-approved law schools in the country, there are obviously many law schools not appearing in this section; those schools appear in the following section, Law School Data Listings.

In order for a law school to appear in this section, we had to collect the opinions of a sufficient number of current law students at that school to fairly and responsibly represent the general law student experience there. Our descriptive profiles are driven primarily by 1) comments law students provide in response to open-ended questions on our student survey, and 2) our own statistical analysis of student responses to the many multiple-choice questions on the survey. While many law students complete a survey unsolicited by us at http://survey.review.com, in the vast majority of cases we rely on law school administrators to get the word out about our survey to their students. In an ideal scenario, the law school administration e-mails a Princeton Review–authored e-mail to all law students with an embedded link to our survey website (again, http://survey.review.com). If for some reason there are restrictions that prevent the administration from contacting the entire law student body on behalf of an outside party, they often help us find other ways to notify students that we are seeking their opinions, like advertising in law student publications or posting on law student community websites or electronic mailing lists. In almost all cases, when the administration is cooperative, we are able to collect opinions from a sufficient number of students to produce an accurate descriptive profile and ratings of its law school.

There is a group of law school administrators, however, that doesn't agree with the notion that the opinions of current law students presented in descriptive profile and rankings formats are useful to prospective law school students trying to choose the right schools to apply to and attend. Administrators at the 23 ABA-approved law schools not appearing in this section are a part of this group. They either ignored our multiple attempts to contact them to request their assistance in notifying their students about our survey, or they simply refused to work with us at all. While we would like to be able to write a descriptive profile on each of these 23 schools anyway, we won't do so with minimal law student opinion. So if you are a prospective law school student and would like to read the opinions of current law students about your dream school(s), contact the missing school(s) and communicate this desire to them. (We include contact information in each of the data listings.) If you are a current law student at one of the 23 ABA-approved law schools not profiled in this section, please don't send us angry letters; instead, go to http://survey.review.com, complete a survey about your school, and tell all of your fellow students to do the same. If we collect enough current student opinion on your school in the coming year, we'll include a descriptive profile in the next edition of the guide.

SPECIAL NOTE ON THE TEXT OF EACH DESCRIPTIVE PROFILE

The Academics and Life sections of each descriptive profile are driven by the student opinions collected from current law students at the school, and the quotations sprinkled throughout each of these sections comes directly from the written comments with which students provided us on their surveys. The Getting In section is based on the data we collect from law school administrators and our own additional research. Every law school with a descriptive profile has its students resurveyed and its profile rewritten at least every other year.

SPECIAL NOTE ON THE SIDEBAR STATISTICS

Explanations of what each field of data signifies may be found in the How to Use This Book section, which begins on page 45.

ALBANY LAW SCHOOL

Academics

Albany Law School "is the oldest independent law school in the nation" with "relatively small classes" and "great course offerings." The "very strong government law and administrative law program" is particularly noteworthy. "Hands down," though, Albany's best feature is its "field placement program." Again and again, students tell us that their school is "famed for its practical side." "The lack of nearby competing law schools," "Albany Law's geographic location," and a "deluge of internship opportunities" make it "all but a forgone conclusion that every student" will have "real-world experience." The school has a "monopoly" on "amazing juridical or state government internship opportunities." "I clerked at both the Attorney General's Office and the United States Attorney's Office," brags a 3L. "Needless to say, I learned more than I ever could in a classroom setting."

There are some "dud professors," but "By and large, the faculty here is excellent" and "excited about teaching." A few "legendary" professors are "heavyweights" who "have played instrumental roles in drafting and interpreting the laws." "We have some of the most respected practitioners in the state of New York," emphasizes one student. Though some "Socratic professors scare you into learning the material," all faculty members are "very accessible" and "really get to know their students."

"Discontent expressed about the administration has decreased in the past few years," one student notes. These days, the "extremely involved and helpful" administration "goes out of its way to ensure that every student is accommodated," and an "open-door policy" reigns supreme. You can't please everybody, though. Some students now complain that administrators "like to hold hands and coddle." Also, "Tuition has been raised at an incredible rate." "No one is happy to be racking up this much debt," gripes a 3L. "To find an unfriendly face and an attitude greeting you at the door doesn't make handing over your first two years' salary... any easier."

The "helpful" Career Center works "tirelessly" and manages "time and again to deliver jobs to students." Some find that "if you are in the middle or bottom of the class, it is difficult to find a job," but this is clearly offset by Albany's reported graduate employment rate of 96 percent. That said, one student explains that "if you want a high paying, sexy job after you graduate, you have to do very well." Those who do excel find their hard work's reward "with some major law firms, especially in New York City."

The facilities, though "improving every day," are "serviceable but not amazing." The "beautiful Gothic building" offers "plenty of quiet spaces to study." "We have a decent library," says a 2L. It's "like a home away from home, except with less comfortable chairs." "The library staff is phenomenal," too. Students appreciate the "wireless" classrooms but find that some older classrooms "are freezing when they should be warm and warm when they should be cooler."

GAIL BENSEN, DIRECTOR OF ADMISSIONS
80 NEW SCOTLAND AVENUE, ALBANY, NY 12208
TEL: 518-445-2326 FAX: 518-445-2369
EMAIL: ADMISSIONS@ALBANYLAW.EDU • WEBSITE: WWW.ALBANYLAW.EDU

Life

The student population tends to be on the younger side but "The community embraces nontraditional students" as well. "The political atmosphere here is undoubtedly liberal," reports one student. "As with any other school," though, "you will find your (usually drunken) jocks, mouthy liberals, angry conservatives, slackers, overachievers, nice people, unfriendly people, over-competitive people, and those who just really don't care." One student notes that "when you have a school filled with people who want to argue for the rest of their lives, there is bound to be conflict. Every time a new issue arises at the law school, it's fought over the e-mail listserv, with every student feeling the need to weigh in on the issue."

Differences of opinions aside, "The community is tight-knit and people genuinely care about each other." "The student body is a great reason to come here, and often parties and socializes together," claims another. However, there are those who "concentrate themselves in small social cliques" exclusively. Extracurricular activities are plentiful with "many clubs and community events which most students get involved in. There are also a lot of receptions and free food and drinks." "There are always things to do on a Friday night." To the disappointment of students, the administration "no longer tolerates" on-campus "beer bashes."

The surrounding community of Albany is chock-full of "beautiful old buildings," and its "Gray winter months are great for studying indoors." "There is some nice off-campus housing if you look in the right places. The on-campus housing is okay, but it is much like a dorm," says one lodger. Most agree that "parking is a tremendous problem." This "might seem trite," admits one student, "but you try parking a mile away and walking through a 20-degree Albany winter at 7:30 A.M. to get to class."

Getting In

Students at the 25th percentile admitted into Albany Law School post an average LSAT score of 152 and GPAs of 2.9. Those students admitted at the 75th percentile have average LSAT scores of 156 and GPAs of 3.56.

Clinical program required	No
Legal writing course requirement	Yes
Legal methods course requirement	Yes
Legal research course requirement	Yes
Moot court requirement	No
Public interest law requirement	No

ADMISSIONS

Selectivity Rating	**73**
# applications received	2,332
# applicants accepted	1,010
# acceptees attending	255
Average LSAT	154
LSAT Range	152–156
Average undergrad GPA	3.27
Application fee	$60
Regular application	Rolling, up to 3/15
Regular notification	Rolling
Early application program	No
Transfer students accepted	Yes
Evening division offered	No
Part-time accepted	No
LSDAS accepted	Yes

Applicants Also Look At
Syracuse University, American University, SUNY at Buffalo, University of Miami, Pace University

International Students

TOEFL required of international students	Yes
Minimum TOEFL (paper/computer)	600/250

FINANCIAL FACTS

Annual tuition	$38,900
Books and supplies	$1,100
Fees	$150
Tuition per credit	$1,345
Room & board (off-campus)	$10,100
% first-year students receiving some sort of aid	89.7
% receiving some sort of aid	92.5
% of aid that is merit based	94.6
% receiving scholarships	31.5
Average grant	$16,537
Average loan	$25,615
Average total aid package	$33,848
Average debt	$105,996

EMPLOYMENT INFORMATION

		Grads Employed by Field (%)
Career Rating	**76**	Academic (3)
Rate of placement (nine months out)	97	Business/Industry (20)
Average starting salary	$70,414	Government (18)
State for bar exam	NY	Judicial Clerkships (9)
Pass rate for first-time bar	78	Military (1)

Employers Who Frequently Hire Grads
Private law firms, government agencies, high-tech industry and coporations.

Private Practice (44)
Public Interest (5)

Prominent Alumni
Thomas Vilsack, U.S. Secretary of Agriculture; Richard D. Parsons, Chairman of Citigroup; Andrew Cuomo, New York State Attorney General; David Beier, VP of Global Government Affairs of Amgen.

AMERICAN UNIVERSITY
WASHINGTON COLLEGE OF LAW

INSTITUTIONAL INFORMATION

Public/private	Private
Student-faculty ratio	14:1
% faculty part-time	59
% faculty female	39
% faculty minority	17
Total faculty	214

SURVEY SAYS...

Diverse opinions accepted
in classrooms
Abundant externship/internship/
clerkship opportunities
Liberal students

STUDENTS

Enrollment of law school	1,461
% male/female	44/56
% full-time	84.5
% minority	35
% international	2
# of countries represented	29
Average age of entering class	24

ACADEMICS

Academic Experience Rating	**85**
Profs interesting rating	81
Profs accessible rating	78
Hours of study per day	4.49

Academic Specialties

Commercial law, corporation securities, environmental law, government
services, human rights, international
law, intellectual property law

Advanced Degrees Offered

LL.M., International Legal Studies,
12–18 months; LL.M., Law and
Government, 12 months; S.JD, 3–4
years.

Combined Degrees Offered

International Dual J.D. Program,
JD/MBA, JD/MA International
Affairs, JD/MS Justice, JD/MPA,
JD/MPP, all 3.5–4 year programs.
LLM/MBA,LLM/MPA, LLM/MPP, all
2–3 years;

Clinical program required	No
Legal writing course requirement	Yes

Academics

American University's Washington College of Law is an "amazing place" for "public interest law." Students appreciate the "full-tuition scholarship" offered to "10 students every year with a dedicated commitment to social justice work." Adding to the school's civic focus, the issue of international human rights "seems to pervade nearly everything the school does." Also, "The range of courses relating to governmental ideas cannot be matched." "If you have any interest in government, come to this law school," says one student. Along with "an abundance" of "research opportunities," several "excellent study abroad opportunities," and "great clinical programs" are lauded with praise. "The opportunities for internships and externships" in the District of Columbia's courts, government agencies, and nonprofit sector "far exceed those offered by law schools in any other city."

Students note that "teachers really run the gamut" and "Some are very eccentric," but many reports echo the opinion of one student, who says, "Overall I have really liked most of my teachers and feel I have gotten a really good education." An "an amazing open-door policy" permeates WCL. There are many "captivating," "extraordinary teachers" who are "very good at relating their subject matter to social-justice issues." This faculty includes "attorneys on famous cases, a Supreme Court clerk, Ivy League grads, prominent scholars, and even a Jeopardy contestant." Professors here are also "astoundingly liberal." "My professors range between gay-rights-feminist activists and critical-race-theorist-anti-death-penalty activists," comments a 2L. "God help you if you say in Con Law that Roe v. Wade was a poorly reasoned decision," adds a 3L. "The liberal orthodoxy is downright oppressive (and I'm a liberal)."

Though "far from first-rate," WCL's facilities "are more than sufficient." A student explains, "We're starting to outgrow our building, so sometimes space is tight." The "cramped" library is "often crowded and loud." The e-mail program "could be more sophisticated" and "wireless Internet is intermittent, at best." However, "the library and some other offices have received makeovers lately," and the "clean and large" classrooms offer "plenty of space, as well as sufficient electrical outlets to accommodate the many laptops that students have."

All in all, "The school functions fairly smoothly." The administration is "very student-focused" though also "Byzantine" at times. The financial aid staff could stand "to improve communication." The Office of Career Development gets mixed reviews. "Perhaps the top third get interviews" at "midsize firms" in "the Mid-Atlantic region." "About the top 15 percent of students have a chance of being selected for on-campus interviews with the major international law firms," says a student. Another notes, "While George Washington is proclaimed to be so much better, every job I've had has been with GW students, so I have no idea what they are doing that we aren't."

Life

WCL is "pretty big." There is "a diverse student body" here "with differing nationalities, opinions, and goals." "There is really every kind of person at WCL, for better or worse," remarks a 2L. "I think generally for the better." Many students "have spent a year or two between law school (or more) doing really fascinating things with their lives." These "extremely intelligent" students "are still idealistic and strive to make the law a better profession and our society a better society." "A lot of students are very politically active." Several "used to work on the Hill." There is "a slight hippy streak," and "Everyone has a cause." Some lament that the "incredibly liberal" students are so "vocal about it" as "The aura of political correctness can be a bit suffocating at times."

AKIRA SHIROMA, ASSISSTANT DEAN OF ADMISSIONS AND FINANCIAL AID
4801 MASSACHUSETTS AVENUE, NW, WASHINGTON, DC 20016
TEL: 202-274-4101 FAX: 202-274-4107
EMAIL: WCLADMIT@WCL.AMERICAN.EDU • WEBSITE: WWW.WCL.AMERICAN.EDU

Academically, though "somewhat of a competitive edge" is "lurking underneath," the atmosphere "isn't hyper-competitive." In fact, WCL is a "very friendly place" full of "genuinely nice people." There is "lots of sharing of notes and outlines." "There is an incredible sense of camaraderie," reports one student. Students are also "incredibly involved with the community." There is an "array" of guest lectures and symposia "every day" and "more academic activities than you could ever attend." "I have had many opportunities to meet students at American through clubs, activities, and community service projects," beams a 3L.

Students think that "it's great that [the school] is in DC" but say that "for being in DC," WCL "has a terrible location." Getting to and from campus can be "difficult" and "time consuming," meaning at times "It very much feels like a commuter school." In addition, students report that "no taxi cabs pass by the school when you're in a pinch." The closest subway station "is slightly over a mile away (though "There is a free shuttle that goes directly to the law school)." Parking remains "an ongoing struggle," especially for 1Ls. (For 2Ls and 3Ls, there is "a garage underneath the building"). On the bright side, "There are a lot of ways to cheat the system" if you drive. "Everyone has all the nooks and crannies figured out."

Getting In

Admitted students at the 25th percentile have LSAT scores of 160 and GPAs of about 3.14. Admitted students at the 75th percentile have LSAT scores of 163 and GPAs of 3.60. WCL says that it considers your highest score if you take the LSAT more than once.

Legal methods	
course requirement	No
Legal research	
course requirement	Yes
Moot court requirement	No
Public interest	
law requirement	No

ADMISSIONS

Selectivity Rating	**89**
# applications received	7,512
# applicants accepted	1561
# acceptees attending	381
Average LSAT	162
LSAT Range	160–163
Average undergrad GPA	3.41
Application fee	$70
Regular application	Rolling, up to 3/1
Regular notification	Rolling
Early application program	Yes
Early application deadline	11/13
Early application notification	12/20
Transfer students accepted	Yes
Evening division offered	Yes
Part-time accepted	Yes
LSDAS accepted	Yes

Applicants Also Look At

The Catholic University of America, Boston University, George Mason University, Fordham University, The George Washington University, University of Maryland—Baltimore, Georgetown University

FINANCIAL FACTS

Annual tuition	$38,652
Books and supplies	$6,569
Fees	$750
Tuition per credit	$1,431
Room & board	$13,948
Financial aid application deadline	3/1
% first-year students receiving some sort of aid	84
% receiving some sort of aid	89
% of aid that is merit based	9
% receiving scholarships	25
Average grant	$14,483
Average loan	$42,120
Average total aid package	$50,626
Average debt	$112,276

EMPLOYMENT INFORMATION

Career Rating	**84**
Rate of placement (nine months out)	95
Average starting salary	$92,000
State for bar exam	MD, NY
Pass rate for first-time bar	83

Employers Who Frequently Hire Grads

Akin Gump Strauss Hauer & Feld LLP; Arent Fox PLLC; Arnold & Porter LLP; Bingham McCutchen LLP; Cadwalader, Wickersham & Taft LLP.

Prominent Alumni

Robert F. Pence, president, Pence Friedel Developers; Tom Goldstein, Partner, Akin Group; The Honorable Gerald B. Lee, Judge, U.S. District Court, Eastern Division of Virginia; Pamela Deese, Partner, Arent Fox; Betty Southland Murphy, Partner, Baker & Hostetler

Grads Employed by Field (%)

Academic (1)
Business/Industry (12)
Government (14)
Judicial Clerkships (12)
Military (1)
Private Practice (50)
Public Interest (10)

APPALACHIAN SCHOOL OF LAW

INSTITUTIONAL INFORMATION

Public/private	Private
Student-faculty ratio	20:1
% faculty female	45
% faculty minority	20
Total faculty	20

SURVEY SAYS...

Diverse opinions accepted
in classrooms
Great research resources
Great library staff
Students never sleep

STUDENTS

Enrollment of law school	364
% male/female	62/38
% full-time	98
% minority	9

ACADEMICS

Academic Experience Rating	**61**
Profs interesting rating	63
Profs accessible rating	65

Academic Specialties

Alternate Dispute Resolution

Advanced Degrees Offered

Juris Doctor, 3 years

Clinical program required	Yes
Legal writing	
course requirement	Yes
Legal methods	
course requirement	Yes
Legal research	
course requirement	Yes
Moot court requirement	Yes

Academics

The Appalachian School of Law is a young, private institution, organized in 1994 and given full accreditation from the American Bar Association in 2006. The traditional-looking campus is very beautiful and the library is "new." Wireless Internet access is available and, in recent years, "The technology aspect of the Law School has shown a significant improvement."

Students report that "trial advocacy training," "moot court programs," and other "practical courses" are "first rate" at ASL. The mock trial team "has trounced big names" in national competitions. "The law school's emphasis on practical legal skills has thoroughly prepared me for everyday situations in the general practice of law," says a 3L. "I will graduate and know what to do in a courtroom besides espouse constitutional theory with opposing counsel at lunch." Appalachian also "distinguishes itself from the majority of other law schools by requiring 150 hours of community service." A summer externship is also "required of all first-year students." "The community-service requirement promotes student involvement in law school organizations, benefits the community, and strengthens the reputations of both ASL and the legal profession in general," explains one student. "The summer externship program provides all rising 2Ls with the opportunity to apply the knowledge they gained from first-year classes to real-life situations." There is also a "mandatory alternative dispute resolution requirement," though the school seems keener on this than the students.

The "knowledgeable" and "very approachable" professors here are "down-to-earth people who have a wide variety of legal experience" and "extensive practical and theoretical knowledge of the subjects they teach." Their dedication means that "they are exceptionally concerned with bar passage" and always "available outside of the classroom." "My experience at the Appalachian School of Law has been nothing short of exceptional," confides one student. "The teachers love interacting with the students and are our greatest cheerleaders, mentors, and leaders." "Faculty turnover" has been a problem, though. The "remote location" is "not the most appealing place" for academics to "hang their hats for the long term." However, "The town and area are progressing."

Students tell us that "the greatest strength" of their law school is its "concern and respect for students as individuals." "The administration, faculty, staff, and students have created a community where you can receive an excellent legal education in the midst of the natural beauty of the Appalachian Mountains," explains one student. However, there is a "communication gap between students and administration," meaning that "it often takes days to cut through whatever hidden red tape or underlying ineptness or unwillingness exists." "The administration is very unpredictable" as well. "I realize every new school needs to work out its quirks, but ASL especially needs to do so," gripes one student. Career Services could stand to be "more active," and there seems to be a revolving door regarding deans. "The school appears to promote diversity among our deans with the tenure running about a dean a year," observes a wry 2L.

Life

Grundy is a "small community" located near the convergence of Virginia, Kentucky, and West Virginia. "You can't go to the grocery store without seeing another law student." "The remote location of the school" helps to make "studying is [the] number-one priority." One student explains, "There's nothing to do but study in Grundy, so I went from a below-average college student to above average," adds a proud 3L. "I will

NANCY PRUITT, ADMISSIONS COUNSELORS
P.O. BOX 2825, GRUNDY, VA 24614
TEL: 276-935-4349 FAX: 276-935-8261
EMAIL: ASLINFO@ASL.EDU • WEBSITE: WWW.ASL.EDU

probably graduate with honors. I'm not so sure that's [because] of the law school itself . . . [or] the general area."

Town-gown relations are strained. "There is some resentment from locals toward law students and vice versa," most agree. "The rugged, desolate terrain" and "isolation" lead students to say that "Appalachian could benefit from more things to do in Grundy outside of law school activities." Students lament that "there isn't a bar or club in the town" where they could "relieve stress and get a drink." (In fact, there is "no liquor by the drink in the county.") "The three-screen movie theater is the most diversion many will get," says one student. That said, people here take a DIY approach to entertainment and "typically find or make [their] own fun to blow off the steam and stress of law school." "A culture of frugal bacchanalia persists in the form of student-hosted house parties." When cabin fever sets in, students take "sojourns" to the nearest bigger cities, "both of which are over the mountains and about 45 minutes away."

Not surprisingly, "You definitely develop a sense of family with the law school students and faculty." "The law students are a very tight-knit group," though beware as "gossip flourishes" and "Everyone's life is an open book." "With scant few exceptions, the student body is Caucasian." Most students would like to see "diversity promoted" at ALS, feeling that "out in town" "underlying discrimination" exists "based on race, sexual orientation, socioeconomic status, and even geographic origin."

Getting In

Appalachian Law School's admitted students at the 25th percentile have LSAT scores of 146 and GPAs of 2.60. Admitted students at the 75th percentile have LSAT scores of 152 and GPAs of 3.30.

ADMISSIONS

Selectivity Rating	**63**
# applications received	990
% applicants accepted	46
% acceptees attending	32
Average LSAT	148
LSAT Range	146–152
Average undergrad GPA	2.8
Application fee	$50
Regular application	Rolling
Regular notification	Rolling
Early application program	No
Transfer students accepted	Yes
Evening division offered	No
Part-time accepted	No
LSDAS accepted	Yes

FINANCIAL FACTS

Annual tuition	$26,500
Books and supplies	$2,500
Room & board (off-campus)	$12,295
% receiving some sort of aid	64
Average grant	$6,468
Average loan	$21,372

EMPLOYMENT INFORMATION

Career Rating	**61**	**Grads Employed by Field (%)**
Average starting salary	$45,000	Business/Industry (11)
State for bar exam	VA, TN, KY, NC, WV	Judicial Clerkships (19)
Pass rate for first-time bar	52	Private Practice (69)

ARIZONA STATE UNIVERSITY
SANDRA DAY O'CONNOR COLLEGE OF LAW

Academics

Arizona State University's Sandra Day O'Connor College of Law "is a serious and challenging school" where "The tuition is cheap" and "There are a ton of pro-bono and clinical opportunities." "Students can gain practical experience in most any arena they plan on entering upon graduation." Over 150 students receive academic credit for participating in externships each year. "Our externship coordinator is great at finding positions for us in the legal community," commends a 2L. Pro-bono work isn't mandatory, "but almost all of the students participate" in order to "start getting practical experience outside of the classroom." "The school offers a broad range of electives and particularly strong offerings" in intellectual property and technology law, and the nationally recognized Indian Legal Program helps train Native American lawyers and furthers an understanding of the distinctions between the legal systems of Indian Nations and the United States. The cutting-edge Center for Law, Science, and Technology "offers a core of dedicated and professional professors" and sponsors speakers drawn from across the country.

The biggest beef among students here is the "terribly one-sided and unreachable" administration "The administration at every school I've ever been familiar with is crappy," says a well-traveled 2L "ASU is no exception." This sentiment may be shifting however with the welcome of a changing administration including a Dean who has pledged to make student accessibility one of his top priorities. Further, ASU's "supportive," "truly motivated," and generally "world-class" professors give students "the opportunity to appreciate the nuances of the law." ASU's faculty has "a real talent and passion for teaching." Sandra Day O'Connor herself teaches courses here "and is a frequent visitor to the school." Outside the classroom, "it is obvious that nearly all of the professors genuinely care about the students' well-being." "Most professors maintain an open-door policy for questions, comments, laments, or coffee."

Students are seriously split regarding their employment prospects. Many students emphasize ASU's "quasi-monopoly" on "one of the hottest job markets" and say "A large number of employers recruit here." "If you plan to practice in Phoenix, ASU provides a good connection to the local legal community," counsels a 3L. "However, there's very little opportunity to work outside of Arizona. Very few out-of-state firms recruit here and a degree from ASU does not travel well." "Phoenix is a small legal market," cautions another student, and "Opportunities for employment in the private sector, especially larger private firms, are limited."

Many of the law school's facilities have "seen better days." There is an "overwhelming sense of Arizona off-pink décor," classrooms are "simply dated," and "The layout of some of the classrooms is flat-out strange." On the upside, the school has recently renovated and redecorated, and "There is fancy-schmancy technology in nearly all the classrooms." Wireless access is great, and the law library is "state-of-the-art." Student say the library staff is "excellent and a very valuable resource." Also, "There is natural light coming through multiple large windows in the library, which makes it easier to stay awake and to concentrate on studying."

SHELLI SOTO, ASSOCIATE DEAN FOR ADMISSIONS AND FINANCIAL AID
1100 S. MCALLISTER AVE., PO BOX 877906, TEMPE, AZ 85287-7906
TEL: 480-965-1474 FAX: 480-727-7930
EMAIL: LAW.ADMISSIONS@ASU.EDU • WEBSITE: WWW.LAW.ASU.EDU

Life

Life here is "pretty laid-back." "The school is not very competitive" and even "somewhat lackadaisical." ASU is home to one of the largest groups of Native American law students in the nation and "There is a good blend of recent college grads and people who have been in the workforce, which brings a good range of opinions to class discussions." "There is also a good blend of out-of-state and in-state students," many of whom are married. "Students seem to genuinely like each other," though they can be "rather cliquish." "People are very social, and the size of the school is big enough that we aren't too into each other's business and small enough that it's easy to get to know a lot of people," explains a 1L.

ASU is "a bit of a commuter school, so it's important to live close by to avoid a lengthy commute and to be socially available." "Largely as a result of the commute, the student body is fairly apathetic when it comes to getting involved in organizations." Those who do decide to get involved enjoy "plenty of opportunity for leadership positions in some great activities." While Arizona State has a world-famous reputation as an undergraduate party school, some students tell us that the social scene for law students "is very lame." Others disagree. "The [law] students know how to have a good time," declares one happy soul. "There is a lot of involvement in intramurals, going out drinking after a particularly rough late-afternoon class, and partying on the weekends."

ASU's location—"minutes away from downtown Phoenix"—is "desirable," though "The beautiful weather can be a terrible distraction." "There's sunshine almost year-round," says one student. "If you have to spend all your time reading, you might as well be doing it by the pool."

Getting In

Admission to ASU's College of Law is competitive. Admitted students at the 25th percentile have LSAT scores of 155 and GPAs of 3.3. Admitted students at the 75th percentile have LSAT scores of 162 and GPAs of 3.8.

Legal methods course requirement	Yes
Legal research course requirement	Yes
Moot court requirement	Yes
Public interest law requirement	No

ADMISSIONS

Selectivity Rating	**84**
# applications received	2,736
# applicants accepted	757
# acceptees attending	181
Average LSAT	159
LSAT Range	156–162
Average undergrad GPA	3.54
Application fee	$50
Regular application	Rolling, up to 2/1
Regular notification	Rolling
Early application program	Yes
Early application deadline	11/1
Early application notification	1/31
Transfer students accepted	Yes
Evening division offered	No
Part-time accepted	No
LSDAS accepted	Yes

Applicants Also Look At
University of Southern California, University of Arizona, University of Colorado at Boulder, University of Denver, University of Utah, University of California—Los Angeles

International Students

TOEFL required of international students	Yes
Minimum TOEFL (paper/computer/web)	550/213/80

FINANCIAL FACTS

Annual tuition (in-state/out-of-state)	$16,040/$28,604
Books and supplies	$2,180
Fees	$254
Room & board	$9,970
Financial aid application deadline	3/1
% first-year students receiving some sort of aid	81
% receiving some sort of aid	93
% of aid that is merit based	15
% receiving scholarships	50
Average grant	$7,557
Average loan	$24,557
Average total aid package	$25,636
Average debt	$67,441

EMPLOYMENT INFORMATION

Career Rating	81
Rate of placement (nine months out)	95
Average starting salary	$93,727
State for bar exam	AZ
Pass rate for first-time bar	84

Employers Who Frequently Hire Grads
Snell & Wilmer; Perkins Coie; Bryan Cave; Gammage & Birnham; Lewis and Roca; Fennemore Craig; Jennings, Strouss & Salmon; Gallagher & Kennedy.

Prominent Alumni
Dan Burk, Oppenheimer Wolff & Donnelly Professor, UMinn Law; Ruth McGregor, Chief Justice, Arizona State Supreme Court.

Grads Employed by Field (%)
Academic (2)
Business/Industry (11)
Government (18)
Judicial Clerkships (8)
Private Practice (55)
Public Interest (8)

AVE MARIA SCHOOL OF LAW

Academics

If you are looking for "a challenging, rigorous education" in "a supportive, collegial environment," consider Ave Maria School of Law. This "unique" and "familial" bastion of legal education opened its doors in the Fall of 2000 thanks largely to the extraordinarily Catholic-oriented philanthropy of Tom Monaghan, the founder of Domino's Pizza. "Natural law theory, moral reasoning, [and Catholicism] pervade the school," as does a strong "commitment to training lawyers who will work for justice." One student explains, "The school does not dwell on policy and theory, but rather teaches the meat and potatoes, black-letter law that you should have a great grounding in to be successful upon graduation." In keeping with its religious foundation, "Every class is begun with prayer, usually the Lord's Prayer or Hail Mary."

Students tell us that Ave Maria is "intellectually rigorous [and] first-class in every aspect." Students also say the school's "Professors honestly love us and want us to do well." "They challenge students, but are respectful," says one student. "They are always available and extremely helpful inside and outside of the classroom." But their dedication doesn't end in the classroom: "They show up at student barbeques and picnics, care about our families, and are always 100 percent available," students boast. The "incredibly professional" administration is "prone to micromanaging" but otherwise "runs the school like clockwork [and] will bend over backward to help you." Ave is "really generous too." Full and nearly full scholarships absolutely abound.

Ave Maria's facilities are "spectacular." Students report that "you can always plug into an Internet port (they deliberately hard-wired everywhere for a better connection) and you also can always plug in your laptop to save precious batteries." One student swears, "It's the nicest law school facility I've seen." Everybody loves the "beautiful" library, where "the fusion of traditional resources and computer technology is wonderfully accomplished." Also (and this is a massive plus), "The library staff lets you eat, drink, and talk in the main reading room!" Students vigorously complain about the lack of parking though.

As a new law school, Ave Maria does have some disadvantages. Piquing the interest of law firms can be difficult. "It is difficult to attract employers when I must introduce, not only myself, but also my school," one student says. Ave Maria offers "widely available" externships and internships, but "There could be a stronger emphasis on the practical." Students feel "The school should increase its faculty so that further course offerings may be had." Overall, however, students are happy, and they are confident that the bells and whistles are just around the corner. In the meantime, Ave Maria boasts the highest bar passage rate in Michigan for "three of the last four years" and "an uncommon *esprit de corps.*" One student asserts, "It is a place where students who have a passion for the law have the opportunity to let that passion flourish."

Life

The atmosphere at this little law school is "competitive without being too stressful." Camaraderie is strong, and "People genuinely try to help each other." One student expounds, "The students at Ave Maria are extremely competitive; however, they are highly cooperative. Perhaps this is oxymoronic to the rest of the legal profession, but it is nonetheless true."

RACHELE CONNER, DIRECTOR OF ADMISSIONS
3475 PLYMOUTH ROAD, ANN ARBOR, MI 48105
TEL: 734-827-8063 FAX: 734-622-0123
EMAIL: INFO@AVEMARIALAW.EDU • WEBSITE: WWW.AVEMARIALAW.EDU

Ave Maria is home to "the kindest people on the planet." The "genuine" students at Ave Maria "place a strong interest on family priorities." One student says, "Ave is a great school for married students and parents. The school goes out of its way to support and involve families." Students feel that "the downside of our law school is the lack of diversity." Although they do say that "the school is actively working to recruit minorities and people with different life experiences," for the time being Ave Maria "basically [consists of] Catholic, conservative, White males."

Not surprisingly, "Many activities surround the Catholic faith" at Ave Maria. This strongly Catholic sentiment has advantages and drawbacks. On the plus side, "There is a pervasive sense that each student is important as a person," both in class and in social settings. Also, if following "the teachings of the Catholic Church" is important to you, you will have oodles of support. While Ave Maria is a bit too "right-wing" for some students' tastes, other students are not bothered. "It gets awkward once in a while, but on the whole I'm getting a high-quality legal education in a great setting among truly concerned people." "Nobody dislikes anybody here, even when they disagree fundamentally about things like abortion, gay rights, or Catholicism," asserts one student. As one student puts it, "It might well be [conservative], but reasonableness and intellectualism are what's demanded, not being conservative."

Getting In

Admitted students at the 25th percentile had an LSAT score of 147 and a grade point average of 3.17. Admitted students at the 75th percentile have an LSAT score of 155 and a GPA of 3.61. Of those accepted, 25 percent scored in the top 13 percent on the LSAT.

ADMISSIONS

Selectivity Rating	**67**
# applications received	1,543
% applicants accepted	51
% acceptees attending	16
Average LSAT	152
LSAT Range	147–155
Average undergrad GPA	3.17
Application fee	$50
Regular application	Rolling, up to 7/1
Regular notification	Rolling
Early application program	No
Transfer students accepted	Yes
Evening division offered	No
Part-time accepted	No
LSDAS accepted	Yes

Applicants Also Look At

Michigan State University, University of Denver, Barry University, University of Detroit—Mercy, St. Thomas University, Thomas M. Cooley Law School, Loyola University—Chicago

International Students

TOEFL required of international students	Yes
Minimum TOEFL (paper/computer)	600/250

FINANCIAL FACTS

Annual tuition	$31,862
Books and supplies	$900
Fees	$440
Room & board (off-campus)	$13,131
Financial aid application deadline	6/1
% first-year students receiving some sort of aid	88
% receiving some sort of aid	91
% of aid that is merit based	29
% receiving scholarships	62
Average grant	$19,016
Average loan	$29,309
Average total aid package	$47,935
Average debt	$79,211

EMPLOYMENT INFORMATION

Career Rating	**80**	**Grads Employed by Field (%)**
Rate of placement (nine months out)	79	Academic (8)
State for bar exam	MI, IL, NY, NJ, FL	Business/Industry (9)
Pass rate for first-time bar	75	Government (19)
Employers Who Frequently Hire Grads		Judicial Clerkships (11)
Federal, State, and Trial Court Judges;		Military (5)
United States Military (JAG), The Federal		Private Practice (40)
Government, Butzel Long, P.C.		Public Interest (8)

BAYLOR UNIVERSITY
SCHOOL OF LAW

Academics

While Baylor's Baptist ties show in its efforts to produce lawyers that are both "ethical and public-serving," it is predominantly a school that "teaches to the bar" and does it well. "It's a huge strength," says a 2L. "If you keep up with the work for class and put in the effort to prepare, you are almost guaranteed to pass the bar on your first try." In fact, Baylor's first-time bar-passage rate is an impressive 98 percent, according to the university. The school embraces a "practical approach" and is thorough in teaching students all the essentials of practicing law. "Other schools teach you about the law and leave it up to firms to make you a lawyer," a 3L reports. "But at Baylor you really become one before you have 'JD' at the end of your name." Skills are imparted via a "practice makes perfect" philosophy, which is exemplified by the school's Practice Court Program for 3Ls. "After going through Practice Court, I don't know how any new lawyer who hasn't gone through that process would ever know where to begin in the courtroom; I feel well prepared to be a trial lawyer," a program veteran notes. "Even if you don't become a litigator, it will help you communicate and be confident in your lawyering skills," another adds.

Students here describe their professors as "drill instructors" who "are not afraid to push students to realize their full potential." A 3L explains: "They aren't afraid of calling on you in Practice Court when you have a trial that afternoon, and then kicking you out because you aren't prepared and assigning you a memo due the next day." While tough, most students recognize that professors here "are some of the brightest in their fields" and are "interested in every student learning the material." "You can almost always find your professors in their offices, and they're always willing to help, even with problems outside of their particular classes," a 1L reports. Students also avow that Baylor "has the finest facilities in Texas—not just for a law school, but for any educational institution." "The classrooms and the library are fabulous and are equipped with the latest technology," a 2L brags. "I can get on LexisNexis or Westlaw right in class to get an exact quote from a case as the professor is quoting it."

The school's quarter system—students start in either the spring, summer, or fall quarter—allows for smaller classes and uniformity in the academic experience, as every student takes a given course with the same instructor. Many here, however, warn that a "drawback of the quarter system is that there's never any letup on work; students are seemingly always preparing for exams." "Whereas most schools only have finals twice a year, we have them three times," a 1L gripes. Still, most here are buoyed by a belief that "few schools in the nation train their students better."

BECKY BECK-CHOLLETT, ASSISTANT DEAN OF ADMISSIONS
ONE BEAR PLACE #97288, WACO, TX 76798
TEL: 254-710-1911 FAX: 254-710-2316
EMAIL: BECKY_BECK@BAYLOR.EDU • WEBSITE: LAW.BAYLOR.EDU

Life

"We have fun during the first month of the quarter, but after that we pretty much just hit the books," a 1L writes. While some say that Baylor's heavy workload fosters an "unparalleled sense of camaraderie between the students," others perceive "intense competition" over grades simmering just below the surface. "I work part-time in the library and I know firsthand that students at Baylor do hide books," a 2L reports. (Whether this undercurrent of tension dissipates with the new grading system is to be determined.) At least on the surface, however, students say their peers are "very friendly," and many at the school "compare it to the high school experience" as "The student body of about 400 is smaller than most people's graduating classes." Students report little diversity on campus but state that "no one should confuse the religiosity and famously conservative mindset of Baylor undergrad with Baylor Law School. As an attendee of both and a liberal, I can say that the liberal-to-conservative ratio at the law school is probably 40:60, compared to probably 25:75 at the undergrad [school]."

Students say hometown Waco offers "very few distractions." "There are really only three bars that students frequent," a 3L writes. "Scruffy's is the dive bar. Crickets is the college bar. Treff's is somewhere in between." Some find the positive in this, such as a 2L that admits "There isn't much to distract me from studying." Take heart, though, since "Even though Waco seems like it's in the middle of nowhere, the city lies in between the great cities of Dallas and Austin, so when law school stress starts to get to you, hop on the interstate and get away."

Getting In

Prospective students apply to the quarter in which they wish to enroll. The fall quarter is the most competitive, with a median GPA and LSAT of 3.75 and 162, respectively. Students who apply to and are admitted to multiple quarters choose the one they most want to attend. Those rejected from the fall quarter are often encouraged to apply to another quarter.

ADMISSIONS

Selectivity Rating	85
# applications received	2,212
# applicants accepted	776
# acceptees attending	81
Average LSAT	162
LSAT Range	161–164
Average undergrad GPA	3.68
Application fee	$40
Regular application	Rolling
Regular notification	Rolling
Early application program	Yes
Early application deadline	11/1
Early application notification	3/1
Transfer students accepted	Yes
Evening division offered	No
Part-time accepted	No
LSDAS accepted	Yes

Applicants Also Look At
University of Texas at Austin, University of Houston, Northwestern University, Texas Tech University, Duke University, Southern Methodist University, Emory University, University of Notre Dame, Pepperdine University, Washington and Lee University

International Students
TOEFL recommended
of international students   Yes

FINANCIAL FACTS

Annual tuition	$34,524
Books and supplies	$6,898
Fees	$1,556
Room & board (on/off-campus)	$9,237/$6,898
Financial aid application deadline	2/15
% first-year students receiving some sort of aid	96
% receiving some sort of aid	91.7
% of aid that is merit based	28.5
% receiving scholarships	80
Average grant	$15,646
Average loan	$30,818
Average total aid package	$39,865
Average debt	$88,681

EMPLOYMENT INFORMATION

Career Rating	**89**
Rate of placement (nine months out)	98
Average starting salary	$79,363
State for bar exam	TX
Pass rate for first-time bar	98

Employers Who Frequently Hire Grads
Akin Gump; DLA Piper; Thompson & Knight; Strasburger & Price; Baker Botts; Haynes & Boone; Bracewell & Giuliani; Jackson Walker; Fulbright & Jaworski; Andrews & Kurth; Winstead; Hunton & Williams; Locke Lord Bissell & Liddell.

Prominent Alumni
Leon Jaworski, Special Prosecutor for the Watergate trials; William Sessions, Former FBI Director.

Grads Employed by Field (%)
Academic (2)
Judicial Clerkships (10)
Private Practice (65)
Public Interest (1)
Business (10)
Government (12)

BOSTON COLLEGE
LAW SCHOOL

INSTITUTIONAL INFORMATION

Public/private	Private
Affiliation	Roman Catholic
Student-faculty ratio	12:1
% faculty part-time	54
% faculty female	41
% faculty minority	10
Total faculty	114

SURVEY SAYS...

Great research resources
Great library staff

STUDENTS

Enrollment of law school	815
% male/female	49/51
% out-of-state	70
% full-time	100
% minority	22
% international	2
# of countries represented	4
Average age of entering class	24

ACADEMICS

Academic Experience Rating	**94**
Profs interesting rating	89
Profs accessible rating	91
Hours of study per day	4.33

Academic Specialties

Civil procedure, commercial law, constitutional law, corporation securities, criminal law, environmental law, human rights, international law, labor law, legal history, legal philosophy, property, taxation, intellectual property law, business law

Advanced Degrees Offered

Juris Doctor, 3 years; LLM, 1 year

Combined Degrees Offered

JD/MBA, 4 years; JD/MSW, 4 years; JD/M.Ed., 3 years; JD/MA Philosophy, 3.5 years

Clinical program required	No
Legal writing course requirement	Yes
Legal methods course requirement	Yes

Academics

Boston College law students may "work really, really hard," but what the majority here find most remarkable about the school is how "interesting and enjoyable" it is. "So many people describe law school as being a bitter pill that one has to swallow in order to become an attorney," a 2L writes. "That's just not the case at Boston College." It's the people that make BC Law special, and professors are "truly extraordinary in their capacities as teachers, mentors, and friends." Faculty members here are at the "top of their field" and "challenge their students to think critically without subjecting [them] to cruel and unusual punishment." While some of the "Visiting professors are hard to follow," instructors "are always well-prepared for class and dedicated to their students." Reinforcing this dedication is the retreat held each year, lead by "approximately five faculty [members] and five students," . . . "that aims to help students discern their vocation in the law."

The "interesting, intellectual, and fun" students are another part of BC's appeal. Law schools are frequently places where egos run rampant, but BC students compliment their peers by calling them "highly normal" and "willing to help." While students would like to see more ethnic, geographic, and religious diversity on campus, there is "a high level of respect" among all in the BC community, and both faculty members and fellow students are "willing to use their personal contacts" to help advance a student's career. "Last year I was able to help two classmates get summer jobs," a 2L reports. Throw in "several events on campus with alumni and Boston attorneys," and students say you can "get a position at a top law firm with relative ease," though the employees in the Career Services Office often "seem limited in their knowledge of job markets to those in [the] major cities of the Northeast and Mid-Atlantic."

While the administration here is sometimes "disorganized" and has, in the past, created "difficult scheduling conflicts for students," others find it "approachable, flexible, and student oriented." By all accounts, the school is "incredibly accommodating to people with family commitments, children, and disabilities." "I have had friends that have had personal problems [and] illness, and the staff has been very helpful and understanding in allowing for help and guidance during difficult times and providing . . . things like make-up exams," a 1L writes. The school is less flexible, however, when it comes to what many students believe to be its "overly conservative" policies.

On the academic front, BC's legal writing program is "one of the best in the country" and "great for learning to write legal briefs." In addition, its "1L class introducing lawyering and ethics helps pull together the various stages of a trial which helped me through my various internships. The course allowed me to ask questions about the legal process in a safe environment instead of learning it through 'sink or swim later.'" Students do, however, call for "more concentrations outside of general corporate and public interest. Other big law schools are committing themselves to advancing IP studies or other 'hot' issues." While "Some of the older sections of the law school show their age," BC's "Classroom and research facilities are beautiful and brand new," and the "awe-inspiring" library particularly boasts "a legion" of "technologically savvy" "research librarians who are always more than willing to help with a particular problem. Many of them teach one-credit classes on legal research which students often take advantage of." A 1L sums up the BC experience: "Where else would your research librarian tell you to call her up over the summer if you have a research issue you need help with?"

RITA JONES, ASSISTANT DEAN OF ADMISSIONS AND FINANCIAL AID
885 CENTRE STREET, NEWTON, MA 02459
TEL: 617-552-4351 FAX: 617-552-2917
EMAIL: BCLAWADM@BC.EDU • WEBSITE: WWW.BC.EDU/LAW

Life

The Law Students Association (LSA) "sponsors monthly 'Bar Reviews' at Boston and Cambridge bars, as well as special events such as a fall Harbor Cruise, Halloween Party, and Spring Gala." The LSA has "also begun adding events for the incoming 1L class, such as a reception on Main Campus, a Duck Tour, and tailgating before home football games." As this just scratches the surface of student programming, it's not surprising that "people develop very strong friendships during their time here." Some go as far as to call BC "the Disneyland of law schools." When considering BC's social scene, however, its "massive workload" should not be overlooked.

The school is located "about a mile and a half down the road from BC's main campus, out in the suburb of Newton." While Newton is "a beautiful town," public transportation isn't easily accessible, which makes "the law school is somewhat isolated." Still, most BC law students choose to live in Boston, as there is no housing for law students on the Newton campus, and Newton itself is outside the budget of most students. Much to the chagrin of BC law students, however, there are "three freshman dorms" for undergraduate students on the Newton campus. While the law library "is off-limits for frosh, and the security people do a good job enforcing that," it "closes before midnight." A "cafeteria-type room [is] open all night," but "It is sometimes overridden with freshmen" who "are not particularly respectful of the peace and quiet needed to study late."

Getting In

Only about one in five applicants is admitted to BC Law, but the school offers prospective students some nice options. Through the school's early notification plan, you can submit your application by November 1 and receive a decision by December 15. You may also reactivate an application submitted in the previous year by submitting a new application form, personal statement, LSDAS report, and application fee.

Legal research course requirement	Yes
Moot court requirement	No
Public interest law requirement	No

ADMISSIONS

Selectivity Rating	92
# applications received	6,609
% applicants accepted	20
% acceptees attending	22
Average LSAT	164
LSAT Range	162–165
Average undergrad GPA	3.64
Application fee	$75
Regular application	Rolling, up to 3/1
Regular notification	Rolling
Early application program	Yes
Early application deadline	11/1
Early application notification	12/15
Transfer students accepted	Yes
Evening division offered	No
Part-time accepted	No
LSDAS accepted	Yes

Applicants Also Look At

Harvard University, American University, Columbia University, University of California—Berkeley, University of California—Los Angeles, New York University, Boston University, University of Virginia, Fordham University

International Students

| TOEFL required of international students | Yes |
| Minimum TOEFL (paper/computer) | 600/250 |

FINANCIAL FACTS

Annual tuition	$38,340
Books and supplies	$1,000
Fees	$366
Room & board (off-campus)	$17,390
Financial aid application deadline	3/15
% first-year students receiving some sort of aid	95
% receiving some sort of aid	87
% of aid that is merit based	23
% receiving scholarships	47
Average grant	$16,514
Average loan	$31,946
Average total aid package	$45,538
Average debt	$100,715

EMPLOYMENT INFORMATION

Career Rating	97
Rate of placement (nine months out)	97
Average starting salary	$124,025
State for bar exam	MA
Pass rate for first-time bar	96

Employers Who Frequently Hire Grads

Most of our graduates join private practices initially or after clerkships. The majority of these graduates join large law firms. No one firm hires a majority of our students.

Prominent Alumni

John Kerry, U.S. Senator/Democratic Nominee for President; Debra Yang, former United States Attorney, CA.

Grads Employed by Field (%)

Private practice (67)
Judicial clerkship (13)
Government (6)
Business/Industry (5)
Academic (4)
Public interest (3)
Military (2)

BOSTON UNIVERSITY
SCHOOL OF LAW

INSTITUTIONAL INFORMATION

Public/private	Private
Student-faculty ratio	12:1
% faculty part-time	46
% faculty female	25
% faculty minority	9
Total faculty	106

SURVEY SAYS...

Diverse opinions accepted
in classrooms

STUDENTS

Enrollment of law school	826
% male/female	50/50
% full-time	100
% minority	21
% international	3
# of countries represented	14
Average age of entering class	24

ACADEMICS

Academic Experience Rating	**96**
Profs interesting rating	98
Profs accessible rating	98
Hours of study per day	4.94

Academic Specialties

Corporate/business law, international law, intellectual property law, health care, litigation and dispute resolution

Advanced Degrees Offered

LL.M Taxation, one year full-time, up to 4 years part-time; LL.M Banking and Financial Law, 1 year full-time, up to 3 years part-time; LL.M American Law, 1 year full-time; LL.M Intellectual Property Law, 1 year full-time.

Combined Degrees Offered

JD/MBA, JD/MBA Health Care Management, JD/MA International Relations, JD/MS Mass Communication, JD/MA Preservation Studies, JD/MPH Public Health, JD/MA Philosophy, JD/LLM in taxation, JD/LLM in Banking; JD/LM in European Law; all except the Philosophy program and the JD/LLM in European Law (3 years) are 3 1/2 to 4.5 year programs.

Academics

The Boston University School of Law boasts "an incredibly open and welcoming learning environment" along with "many dual-degree options." The writing program and mandatory first-year moot court program are "very strong." "I don't think there is a law school in the country that could possibly be better than BU for the overall law school experience," adds a 2L.

BU's "incredibly personable" professors "love to teach." "They encourage debate and [a] thorough understanding of the material," explains one student. They "put 150 percent into every single class" and in return "expect a lot out of you which makes you work harder." Their "quirky teaching styles...make even tedious subjects interesting," leading one professor to "sing to us about restitution to the tune of 'SexyBack' by Justin Timberlake," says an impressed 1L. Not surprisingly, the faculty is "very approachable outside of the classroom," and students find it "very refreshing to have such a small-school feel at such a large university."

The "dedicated" and "very responsive" administration "constantly" solicits feedback and "doesn't pull any punches." Deans are "genuine" and "willing to speak with students about any issue." The Career Development Office is "well organized" and "friendly." Whatever career you want, "There is someone who can point you in the right direction." "The best firms from New York and Boston" interview here, as do firms across the country "A number of students" secure "big law" jobs. "Even students who don't finish in the top third" after the first year "have excellent chances of being recruited by the top firms in the Northeast." "There is a strong sense of commitment" to public interest law as well.

The "aging building" is BU's one big drawback, and most students agree that it "isn't exactly up to par with its very high academic excellence." The good news is that there have been "many improvements to the Law Tower." The "small" library is "old" yet "lacks the classic law-library feel." The "newly renovated" classrooms are "modern" but "nothing that'll blow you away." That said, there is "wireless Internet throughout" and "The chairs are very comfortable," not to mention the "fantastic" views of the city "from the tower." Despite the building's aesthetic issues, most students agree that "at the end of the day, would you rather have a nice library that you'll never use or would you rather have outstanding, engaging, entertaining professors who bring the law alive?"

Life

"Considering that everyone is brilliant and comes from great undergrads, the school has a surprisingly congenial atmosphere," observes a 1L. Students are mostly "willing to help each other" and "Everyone shares outlines." Nevertheless, there are some "hyper-competitive" types "trying to prove that their application was the one that Harvard inadvertently rejected."

BOSTON UNIVERSITY SCHOOL OF LAW, OFFICE OF ADMISSIONS
765 COMMONWEALTH AVENUE, BOSTON, MA 02215
TEL: 617-353-3100 FAX: 617-353-0578
EMAIL: BULAWADM@BU.EDU • WEBSITE: WWW.BU.EDU/LAW

Having "a great time out in the city" is easy. "There's never a lack of things to do to avoid doing work," says one student. "You would have to be a social pariah not to enjoy the social life." Those that "thought partying was done when law school started" are pleasantly surprised to find otherwise. "There's this little hole-in-the wall bar across the street called the Dugout" that "is absolutely infamous at BU," particularly when final exams end. The location "right along the Charles River" is tremendous. It's easy to "grab a meal at someplace local," and "There's lots to do right in the area." Fenway Park is "five-minute walk." On the other hand, "Housing is horrible for what you pay."

BU "attracts a group of people from different walks of life." "There are people who just graduated college, but there are also people who are quite a few years out." "Members of the student body can be a little odd," though "Politically, there is a good mix." There are "quite a few international students" as well. "There are a lot of gay students, and the faculty is very receptive" to their concerns. It's all shapes and sizes on campus with "plenty of Northeastern preppies," "snappy, funky dressers," "bikers and punk rockers," and other "loads of quirky characters." Some think BU "could do more to encourage racial diversity." Other students point out that BU is very integrated ethnically: "Everyone forms one big multicolored bundle of love." "I have never had so many multiracial friends in my life," proclaims a 2L. "Really, you should see us in a bar, it's like the beginning of a bad joke: 'So a Chinese guy, an Indian, a Jew, and an Italian exchange student are sitting in a bar...'"

Getting In

Academic credentials of incoming students are very high. BU's admitted students at the 25th percentile have LSAT scores of 163 and GPAs of 3.48. Admitted students at the 75th percentile have LSAT scores of 166 and GPAs of 3.82.

Clinical program required	No
Legal writing course requirement	Yes
Legal methods course requirement	No
Legal research course requirement	Yes
Moot court requirement	Yes
Public interest law requirement	No

ADMISSIONS

Selectivity Rating	**91**
# applications received	5,907
% applicants accepted	29
% acceptees attending	16
Average LSAT	165
LSAT Range	148–174
Average undergrad GPA	3.68
Application fee	$75
Regular application	Rolling, up to 3/1
Regular notification	Rolling
Early application program	No
Transfer students accepted	Yes
Evening division offered	No
Part-time accepted	No
LSDAS accepted	Yes

Applicants Also Look At
Columbia University, New York University, University of Pennsylvania, Boston College

International Students

TOEFL required of international students	Yes
Minimum TOEFL (paper/computer)	600/250

FINANCIAL FACTS

Annual tuition	$38,816
Books and supplies	$1,374
Fees	$842
Room & board (off-campus)	$11,808
% first-year students receiving some sort of aid	84
% receiving some sort of aid	83
% of aid that is merit based	4
% receiving scholarships	60
Average grant	$17,400
Average loan	$34,440
Average total aid package	$37,900
Average debt	$91,000

EMPLOYMENT INFORMATION

Career Rating	**98**	**Grads Employed by Field (%)**
Rate of placement (nine months out)	99	Academic (7)
Average starting salary	$138,000	Business/Industry (5)
State for bar exam	MA, NY, CA, NJ, IL	Government (6)
Pass rate for first-time bar	94	Judicial Clerkships (6)
Prominent Alumni		Private Practice (70)
		Public Interest (6)

Prominent Alumni
Judd Gregg, U.S. Senator New Hampshire; William S. Cohen, Former Secretary of Defense; David Kelley, Executive Producer; Gary F. Locke, Hon. Sandra L. Lynch, Judge, U.S. Court of Appeals, First Circuit; Martha Coakley, Massachusetts Attorney general; Michael Fricklas, Executive Vice President, General Counsel & Secretary, Viacom Inc.; Peter McCausland, Chairman & CEO of Airgas, Inc.

BRIGHAM YOUNG UNIVERSITY
J. REUBEN CLARK LAW SCHOOL

INSTITUTIONAL INFORMATION

Public/private	Private
Affiliation	Church of Jesus Christ of Latter Day Saints
Student-faculty ratio	18:1
% faculty part-time	65
% faculty female	22
% faculty minority	6
Total faculty	76

SURVEY SAYS...

Great research resources
Great library staff
Conservative students

STUDENTS

Enrollment of law school	462
% male/female	64/36
% full-time	100
% minority	17
# of countries represented	12
Average age of entering class	26

ACADEMICS

Academic Experience Rating	**96**
Profs interesting rating	97
Profs accessible rating	93
Hours of study per day	5.42

Advanced Degrees Offered

International Comparative Law, one school year

Combined Degrees Offered

JD/MBA, JD/MPA, JD/MAcc, JD/MOB, JD/MEd (education), each 4 years; JD/EdD (education), 5 years.

Clinical program required	No
Legal writing course requirement	Yes
Legal methods course requirement	No
Legal research course requirement	Yes
Moot court requirement	Yes
Public interest law requirement	No

Academics

Brigham Young University's J. Rueben Clark Law School prides itself on "an uplifting, enriching atmosphere" where "very high moral/ethical standards" "are taught as an integral part of law." Opportunities for international externships abound. There are also "some good opportunities" if you are "interested in Federal Indian Law." Most importantly, though, "you can't beat the price." "Tuition is ridiculously inexpensive" and, "at the same time," BYU Law provides "one of the greatest legal educations in the nation." Generous scholarships are just gravy.

BYU Law's vast resources are "well within the grasp of every student." "Everyone at the school wants you to succeed," and there is seemingly unlimited money to present papers, travel for trial and appellate advocacy competitions, and participate in anything that could benefit the school. BYU's "brilliant and inspiring" professors are "captivating teachers" who are "far too qualified to be teaching law school but eager to give back." In class, professors "keep it interesting" and "use the Socratic Method really well." Discussion is lively. Outside of class, they are "approachable" and "genuinely care." An "open-door policy reigns supreme." Administrators are "mostly very available" as well. The writing program is either "intense" or "could be a little more vigorous," depending on whom you ask. If they could change one thing, students say "some courses" need to be available more often.

The "amazing" Career Services Office "gets things done." Upon graduation, few students have any problems finding employment. "I am in the lower half of the class and I still expect to make $70,000 starting out," claims a 2L. BYU Law's "connections to alumni and supporters throughout the country and the world" are very useful in this regard. "Pick the city where you want to live," explains another 2L, "and there will be lawyers with BYU connections who are willing to get you an interview."

The law school building "was built in the 1970s" when "large concrete slabs" were all the rage. It's "not very pretty" and "does not have enough windows." Inside, though, "The facilities are fabulous." The library is "state-of-the-art" (despite some "really uncomfortable" chairs). "I am amazed at how many hours the library is open, and equally amazed at how large the library staff is," applauds a 2L. Also, "Each law student has an individual carrel in the law library" with "three drawers, two cabinets that lock, an Ethernet connection, and three electrical outlets." You even get a lamp. Technology, wireless Internet, and tech support are "top of the line" as well.

Life

BYU Law's affiliation with the Church of Jesus Christ of Latter-day Saints adds "an important spiritual component." "Many students read the Bible on a daily basis and openly talk about religion in the halls, classroom, and in their academic papers." BYU Law can seem "extremely homogeneous" but, "If you are comfortable in that environment, it's perfect." Students tell us that BYU is "doable for a non-Mormon," too, particularly "considering the price tag." "Take it from a non-member when I say that attending J. Reuben Clark Law School is well worth the sacrifice in giving up Friday night cocktail mixers in favor of Friday family barbeques," promises a 1L. "If nothing else, I guarantee a once-in-a-lifetime experience with enough bizarre situations to warrant a fabulous book in the future."

GaeLynn Kuchar, Director of Admissions
340 JRCB, Brigham Young University Law School, Provo, UT 84602
Tel: 801-422-4277 Fax: 801-422-0389
Email: kucharg@law.byu.edu • Website: www.law.byu.edu

The thing to understand is that BYU is "very conservative." An honor code includes "dress and grooming standards" as well as a total ban on alcohol, drugs, and tobacco. No tea or coffee, either. "The strongest drink you will find at the BYU Law School is orange-flavored Metamucil." Single students "spend a lot of time together" but "If you're on the hunt for men and you're not Mormon, good luck." "Many students are married" with children. There are "all kinds of accommodations for families" including a trick-or-treat day through the study carrels. "Yeah," emphasizes one happy student, "it's that good."

BYU Law is "one of the most competitive schools in the country." It's "not an in-your-face type of competitiveness"; "No one would ever sabotage you, and notes are widely circulated." Instead, students here "will simply outwork you." "Everyone works ridiculously hard," says one student. "Everybody reads all their cases all the time." It's not uncommon to see "the library parking lot full on a Saturday morning at 8:00 A.M." "The students are machines." Despite the "exceptional" competitiveness, BYU is also very friendly. With a class size of roughly 150, "It is hard not to get to know your peers." "There is a real sense of community at the law school," relates a 1L. "The informal sense of friendship is profound and hard to explain, but I trust the other students to be looking out for me and they expect the same from me. It is a great atmosphere in which to study."

When, at last, students relax, BYU Law "has a ton of clubs" for "just about anything." "The clubs end up being social clubs with fun activities and dinners and other social events." Lectures and "fabulous intramural programs" are plentiful as well. Winters "get a little cold" but "You couldn't ask for a more beautiful setting." The campus is "within an hour" of world-class ski resorts and "outdoor adventures" galore. "Housing is crazy affordable" too. Basically, "If you don't mind driving 25 minutes to Salt Lake for the partying and clubbing that doesn't happen in Provo, then really there's nothing missing."

Getting In

Admitted students at the 25th percentile have LSAT scores of 161 and GPAs of about 3.5. Admitted students at the 75th percentile have LSAT scores of 166 and GPAs of better than 3.8. When you apply, you have to establish by way of a letter of recommendation that you will live in accordance with BYU's Honor Code. If you take the LSAT more than once, BYU Law will consider your highest score.

ADMISSIONS

Selectivity Rating	**93**
# applications received	790
% applicants accepted	31
% acceptees attending	61
Average LSAT	164
LSAT Range	161–166
Average undergrad GPA	3.63
Application fee	$50
Regular application	Rolling, up to 3/1
Regular notification	Rolling
Early application program	No
Transfer students accepted	Yes
Evening division offered	No
Part-time accepted	No
LSDAS accepted	Yes

Applicants Also Look At
University of Texas at Austin, University of Southern California, University of Utah, Loyola Marymount University, Georgetown University

International Students
Minimum TOEFL
(paper/computer/web) 590/243/96

FINANCIAL FACTS

Annual tuition	$9,240
Books and supplies	$1,760
Room & board	$6,550
% first-year students receiving some sort of aid	86
% receiving some sort of aid	78
% of aid that is merit based	33
% receiving scholarships	50
Average grant	$2,300
Average loan	$13,400
Average debt	$41,000

EMPLOYMENT INFORMATION

Career Rating	**89**
Rate of placement (nine months out)	98.7
Average starting salary	$97,386
State for bar exam	UT, CA, NV, AZ, TX
Pass rate for first-time bar	94

Employers Who Frequently Hire Grads
Allen Matkins; Alverson Taylor; Ascione Heideman; Baker & McKenzie; Ballard Spahr; Bryan Cave; Carlsmith Ball; Christensen & Jensen.

Prominent Alumni
Steve Young, former quarterback, San Francisco 49ers; Dee V. Benson, Senior Judge, Federal District Court, Utah; Chris Cannon, Congressman.

Grads Employed by Field (%)
Academic (1)
Business/Industry (13)
Government (9)
Judicial clerkships (12)
Military (1)
Other (1)
Private practice (52)
Public Interest (1)

BROOKLYN LAW SCHOOL

INSTITUTIONAL INFORMATION

Public/private	Private
Student-faculty ratio	19:1
% faculty part-time	48.7
% faculty female	36
% faculty minority	10
Total faculty	150

SURVEY SAYS...

Abundant externship/internship/
clerkship opportunities
Liberal students
Students love Brooklyn, NY

STUDENTS

Enrollment of law school	1,490
% male/female	51/49
% out-of-state	45
% full-time	81
% minority	26
# of countries represented	34
Average age of entering class	24

ACADEMICS

Academic Experience Rating	**82**
Profs interesting rating	77
Profs accessible rating	72
Hours of study per day	4.19

Academic Specialties

Business organizations law, civil practice & litigation, clinics, commercial transactions law, constitutional law & theory, criminal law, family law, health law, LP, media and information law, international business law, international & comparative law, labor & employment law, legal theory & jurisprudence, legal writing & research, property, public interest law, real estate & environmental law, regulatory law and policy, taxation, trusts & estates.

Advanced Degrees Offered

JD, 3 years FT; 4 years PT

Combined Degrees Offered

JD/MA Political Science, JD/MS City and Regional Planning, JD/MBA, JD/MS Library/Information Science, JD/M Urban Planning; 4–6 Years

Clinical program required	No
Legal writing course requirement	Yes

Academics

Large and private Brooklyn Law School offers a "broad range of classes," "four scholarly journals," five joint degree programs, and a moot court program that successfully does battle around the country. The legal writing program is reportedly "invaluable" as well. "We do so well at all the competitions because we are taught how to write great briefs and how to advocate well," boasts a 3L. There's "a very strong public interest community." A vast array of clinical programs includes bankruptcy, immigration, securities law, criminal defense, and mediation. There is also a "strong emphasis on" and an "excellent selection of" internships and externships all over New York City. "The practical experience you can get at BLS is amazing."

A nice combination of "young superstars and ancient pillars" comprises the faculty at Brooklyn Law. A few of the pillars are "out of touch" and "appear to not care whether or not they teach the students anything." Most professors, however, are "committed to teaching, enthusiastic," and "very accessible." "They have a unique ability to connect with students, offer valuable insight, and genuinely give the impression that they enjoy doing what they do." Concrete and practical application of the law is big here, too. "All of my professors have tried to incorporate real-world lawyering into the curriculum, rather than sticking solely to the case law," relates a happy 2L. Not everyone is satisfied with the administration but the majority of students call it "competent and efficient." "Everything is run pretty well," most students say. "The financial aid office has been fantastic in helping me navigate the winding path of financing a legal education," notes a 3L.

Some students call the Career Center "hit or miss." "The administration appears too focused on the top of the class, largely pushing clerkships and big law as the best opportunities," complains a 3L. Others think that Career Services should do nothing less and declare that employment prospects for newly-minted grads are excellent. They point to a "strong alumni network" that is "always eager to assist Brooklyn students." "Most people who do well have no problem finding competitive jobs," says a 2L. The fact that some of the best firms in the country are "only a subway ride away" certainly doesn't hurt. BLS also provides ample help for students who would rather not work in the private sector. "My expectations of Brooklyn Law School's commitment to assisting students interested in public interest accomplish their dreams have been exceeded," gushes a 3L.

Students are divided in their view of the facilities. "The school's appearance is pretty nice," devotees say. Research facilities are "entirely adequate." "BLS offers several different places for individual as well as group studying on campus." Classrooms are "fairly comfortable." Critics contend that "the classrooms and bathrooms need a serious upgrade." And they hate the chairs. "Whoever chose them must have a great core or an extremely flexible back," speculates a 2L. Detractors also say that the design of the campus is deficient. "The school is comprised of only two buildings yet somehow still manages to be a maze," gripes a frequently lost 1L.

Life

Diversity "in terms of race, ethnicity, and interests" is "thriving" among the "hardworking and intelligent" students here. You'll probably be able to find whatever scene you are after. There's "frat culture spilling out from students who attended straight from undergrad." There's also a strong contingent of slightly older people who have taken some time off and have been living in New York for awhile. A lot of the people here

HENRY W. HAVERSTICK III, DEAN OF ADMISSIONS AND FINANCIAL AID
250 JORALEMON STREET, BROOKLYN, NY 11201
TEL: 718-780-7906 FAX: 718-780-0395
EMAIL: ADMITQ@BROOKLAW.EDU • WEBSITE: WWW.BROOKLAW.EDU

"already have lives and friends" and "have their own things going on." At the same time, "there's a great sense of community," especially for students who live in campus housing.

Academically, "BLS is known for having a particularly harsh curve first year that is a humbling experience for some 1Ls." Nevertheless, students assure us that "there is a spirit of cooperation and unity that creates a very supportive environment." "Students tend to get along and help each other more than compete." Outside the classroom, the school sponsors "tons of" lectures and "student groups are very active." A few students contend that "the location of the school within Brooklyn is terrible" but most call surrounding Brooklyn Heights "a great neighborhood." "You have more courts within two blocks than you could ever visit, must less intern with." "Shops and restaurants dot tree-lined Montague Street on the way to the Brooklyn Heights Promenade (with the best view of Manhattan)," says a 2L. "The rest of the neighborhood consists of well-kept historic brownstones. It's just a great place to wander around." And, of course, the Big Apple offers a never-ending array of activities and nightlife.

Getting In

Admitted students at the 25th percentile have LSAT scores around 159 or so and GPAs of about 3.2. Admitted students at the 75th percentile have LSAT scores of 164 or so and GPAs of around 3.6.

Legal methods course requirement	Yes
Legal research course requirement	Yes
Moot court requirement	Yes
Public interest law requirement	No

ADMISSIONS

Selectivity Rating	**87**
# applications received	4,860
# applicants accepted	1,525
# acceptees attending	493
Average LSAT	162
LSAT Range	159–164
Average undergrad GPA	3.39
Regular application	Rolling, up to 8/15
Regular notification	Rolling
Early application program	Yes
Early application deadline	12/1
Early application notification	12/31
Transfer students accepted	Yes
Evening division offered	Yes
Part-time accepted	Yes
LSDAS accepted	Yes

Applicants Also Look At
Boston University, Yeshiva University, Boston College, Fordham University, The George Washington University

International Students

TOEFL required of international students	No
TOEFL recommended of international students	Yes
Minimum TOEFL (paper/computer/web)	600/250/100

FINANCIAL FACTS

Annual tuition	$42,024
Books and supplies	$1,177
Fees	$326
Fees per credit	$326
Tuition per credit	$1,500
Room & board (off-campus)	$20,829
Financial aid application deadline	4/30
% first-year students receiving some sort of aid	74
% receiving some sort of aid	62
% of aid that is merit based	68
% receiving scholarships	51
Average grant	$20,113
Average loan	$33,800
Average total aid package	$39,100
Average debt	$93,672

EMPLOYMENT INFORMATION

Career Rating	**85**
Rate of placement (nine months out)	92.2
Average starting salary	$97,291
State for bar exam	NY
Pass rate for first-time bar	92

Employers Who Frequently Hire Grads
Cahill Gordon; Fried, Frank, Harris, Shriver & Jacobson; Proskauer Rose; NYC Law Department; Skadden, Arps, Slate, Meagher & Flom; Sidley Austin; O'Melveny& Meyers.

Prominent Alumni
David Dinkins, former Mayor, City of New York; Stephen J. Dannhauser, Chairman, Weil Gotshal & Manges LLP.

Grads Employed by Field (%)
Academic (1)
Law Firms (57)
Corporations (12)
Government (18)
Judicial Clerkship (6)
Public Interest (6)

CAMPBELL UNIVERSITY
NORMAN ADRIAN WIGGINS SCHOOL OF LAW

INSTITUTIONAL INFORMATION

Public/private	Private
Affiliation	Baptist
Student-faculty ratio	15:1
% faculty part-time	17
% faculty female	56
% faculty minority	12
Total faculty	189

SURVEY SAYS...

Heavy use of Socratic Method
Diverse opinions accepted in classrooms
Great research resources
Great library staff
Conservative students

STUDENTS

Enrollment of law school	361
% male/female	53/47
% full-time	100
% minority	8
Average age of entering class	34

ACADEMICS

Academic Experience Rating	81
Profs interesting rating	83
Profs accessible rating	87
Hours of study per day	5.7

Academic Specialties
Tracks in Business/Transactions and Trial & Appellate Advocacy.

Advanced Degrees Offered
JD, 3 years

Combined Degrees Offered
JD, MBA

Clinical program required	No
Legal writing course requirement	Yes
Legal methods course requirement	Yes
Legal research course requirement	Yes
Moot court requirement	Yes
Public interest law requirement	No

Academics

Soon to be making the move to Raleigh, NC, the Norman Adrian Wiggins School of Law at Campbell University is leaving behind its "old and dilapidated" building in Buies Creek for some shiny new digs. Students expect the proximity to the state capital's law offices and courthouses will be the cherry on the top of an already solid law school experience. A small private school that is steadily building a name for itself through its practical approach to instruction and the high standards placed on the students, Campbell boasts the state's top bar passage rate, and "as a bit of an under-dog in a state filled with several well-known law schools, Campbell students benefit from having something to prove." The school encourages self-discipline and "real knowledge"; all 1L exams are completely closed book, which forces the student to really know the material and be able to apply it. By the time students graduate, they will already have had the experience of trying their first case, of working through discovery issues and traps through its Pre-Trial litigation program, and many will have tried another case with a simulated appeals process through Campbell's Advanced Trial Ad program. Students "are able to make those mistakes that attorneys make when they first start practicing on imaginary clients and get instantaneous feedback on how to prevent it the next time."

Don't come to Campbell Law if you like to cut corners. The professors "demand that every student come to every class prepared to discuss and analyze all assignments." Most professors employ the Socratic Method, so you'll only be able to breathe easy if you've read and actually thought about the assignment for that day. Trial Advocacy is a central focus at the school, and Campbell teaches each student to "think on their feet" by religiously employing this method. "Quite a few of our administrators and faculty are Campbell alum, so they know that students can hack it." "I have professors who were taught by some of my other professors," says a 1L. Professors "refuse to let up the pressure the second and third years," and this shows in the school's excellent bar passage rate. The professors actively encourage students to seek them out to discuss anything and everything, creating an atmosphere in which students are challenged and "removing students that are not likely to succeed as lawyers." The small class sizes (around 30–45 people) are "less intimidating and prevent you from getting lost in a sea of people." There are more than a few complaints about the somewhat byzantine grading system in respect to its diminishing effect on grades (and in turn, job prospects). Career services also leaves something to be desired, and many believe that the school needs to "increase its out-of-state exposure to widen the scope of job opportunities for its students," as well as offer more resources to those not in the top 10% of the class. The accessibility of administration is "unparalleled," though. "I have no difficulty in approaching any of my instructors, or even wandering into the Dean's suite," says a student.

LEWIS HUTCHISON, ASSISTANT DEAN FOR ADMISSIONS
POST OFFICE BOX 158, 113 MAIN STREET, BUIES CREEK, NC 27506
TEL: 910-893-1754 FAX: 910-893-1780
EMAIL: ADMISSIONS@LAW.CAMPBELL.EDU • WEBSITE: WWW.LAW.CAMPBELL.EDU

Life

"With approximately 350 students total, we spend A LOT of time together," says a student. This fosters a strong sense of camaraderie and trust, and purses and laptops are left about freely without worry. Buies Creek isn't exactly a hub of entertainment. "We do like to say 'At Campbell we make our own fun,'" says a student of the current offerings. "I do believe that the quirks stemming from the current local, rural community which make Campbell what it is, will travel to Raleigh with the law school. The place will not change, just the address," says another. While Campbell is exploring its range in diversity, there is still quite a bit of room for improvement, and the student body is "relatively small and homogenous." The student body wants all of its members to succeed, which "creates a very stimulating academic environment"; everyone wants to do as well as they can, but "not at the expense of other students."

Getting In

Accepted students to the class entering had a median GPA of 3.19 and a median LSAT score of 155. (Note that median and average LSAT scores can differ significantly.) In addition to common law school application requirements, Campbell does what few other law schools do: Prior to admission, students may also complete a personal interview with the law school faculty. Invitations to interview are based on a student's application.

ADMISSIONS

Selectivity Rating	79
# applications received	1,220
# applicants accepted	346
# acceptees attending	148
Average LSAT	155
LSAT Range	152–157
Average undergrad GPA	3.3
Application fee	$50
Regular application	Rolling
Regular notification	Rolling
Early application program	No
Transfer students accepted	Yes
Evening division offered	No
Part-time accepted	No
LSDAS accepted	Yes

Applicants Also Look At

University of South Carolina, University of North Carolina at Chapel Hill, Regent University, Wake Forest University, North Carolina Central University, Samford University, Appalachian

International Students

TOEFL recommended of international students	Yes

FINANCIAL FACTS

Annual tuition	$28,520
Books and supplies	$1,500
Fees	$252
Room & board (on/off-campus)	$10,749/$13,063
Financial aid application deadline	3/15
% receiving some sort of aid	89
% receiving scholarships	49
Average grant	$7,450
Average loan	$41,000
Average debt	$85,015

EMPLOYMENT INFORMATION

Career Rating	70
Average starting salary	$55,000
State for bar exam	NC, SC, VA, MD, UT
Pass rate for first-time bar	95

Employers Who Frequently Hire Grads
small to medium size private firms

Prominent Alumni
Elaine Marshall, North Carolina Secretary of State; John Tyson, Judge, North Carolina Court of Appeals; Richard Thigpen, General Counsel, Carolina Panthers NFL Franchise.

Grads Employed by Field (%)
Business/Industry (9)
Government (11)
Judicial Clerkships (5)
Private Practice (70)
Public Interest (5)

CAPITAL UNIVERSITY
LAW SCHOOL

INSTITUTIONAL INFORMATION

Public/private	Private
Affiliation	Lutheran
Student-faculty ratio	23:1
% faculty part-time	36
% faculty female	21
% faculty minority	14
Total faculty	29

SURVEY SAYS...

Diverse opinions accepted
in classrooms
Great research resources
Abundant externship/internship/clerk-
ship opportunities
Students love Columbus, OH

STUDENTS

Enrollment of law school	683
% male/female	54/46
% out-of-state	27
% full-time	61
% minority	9
# of countries represented	9
Average age of entering class	25

ACADEMICS

Academic Experience Rating	**68**
Profs interesting rating	70
Profs accessible rating	72
Hours of study per day	4.31

Academic Specialties

Corporation securities, environmental law, government services, international law, labor law, taxation, dispute resolution, children and family
law, environmental

Advanced Degrees Offered

LL.M in Taxation, 1–6 years; LL.M
in Business, 1–6 years; LL.M in
Business & Taxation, 1–6 years; MT,
1–6 years.

Combined Degrees Offered

JD/MBA, 3.5–6 years; JD/MSN,
3.5–6 years; JD/MSA, 3.5–4 years;
JD/MTS, 4–6 years

Clinical program required	No
Legal writing	
course requirement	Yes

Academics

Capital University Law School "in the heart of downtown" Columbus, Ohio "is a great place to study law," particularly if you seek a balance between "legal theory and actual practice." The "broad range of courses" here emphasizes "practical lawyering skills." "The legal writing program is awesome," says one student. A wealth of externships, internships, and clerkships offers "the best hands-on experience possible." The law school is "only a few short blocks from the Ohio Supreme Court" and is "nestled within two miles" of a bevy of other state and federal courthouses and agencies. Capital has "outstanding" part-time and evening programs and "All of the offices are open longer hours to accommodate this group of students." The "highly reputable" National Center for Adoption Law and Policy "offers a great way to gain expertise" and "get connected with family-law attorneys." Another plus is an Advanced Bar Studies course "designed to prepare 3Ls for taking the bar." It seems to be working. "We are ecstatic about our third-in-the-state passage rate this year," raves a 3L. Employment prospects are also good. Capital is "respected in the Columbus legal community" and has "a strong reputation with local government and private firms for producing students with strong research and writing skills and good practical knowledge." When "Many loyal alumni practice locally," it goes to say that students find plenty to keep them in Columbus and at Capital.

"With very few exceptions, the teaching faculty is top-notch as communicators and mentors." There is also "an excellent base of adjunct professors who are practitioners by day." Capital's "devoted, highly prepared, [and] usually pretty easygoing" professors "make an effort to stay easily accessible." "So far, minus one pompous and unhelpful professor, my experience with Capital's faculty has been amazing," comments a 1L. "Most professors emphasize the real-world aspects of the curriculum as well as what is required to perform well on the bar exam." Some professors "could make class more interesting," though. Also, be warned: "There is no grade inflation here." Something like "four to eight percent of students in first-year classes" receive an A. The "median grade" is more like a "B-minus." "When someone gets an A at Capital, it should be an unambiguous signal to an employer that the person is highly qualified in the subject matter," explains a student.

The "approachable" administration is "improving every year" and "open to criticisms and suggestions." The "Registrar, Career Services staff, and even the security guards are incredibly friendly and helpful." "Not a lot of people fall through the cracks." Organization can be "very lackluster sometimes," though. There are "small mix-ups (e.g., a classroom for the class not being large enough to accommodate all the students)," and the "terrible" scheduling process is "tiresome."

Capital's "aesthetically boring" facilities are "pretty much completely modern." So "don't be fooled by the gray, outdated exterior." Classrooms are "all equipped with state-of-the-art technology." "The wireless Internet throughout the school is wonderful," claims one student. The library "needs improvement" though and "The building is a maze." Also, some areas get "a little crowded with everyone's books and laptops."

Life

There is both "a strong sense of camaraderie" and "a somewhat competitive atmosphere" here. Capital is "small" and "very family-oriented." "Everyone is friendly and willing to help out," says one student. Competition for coveted A's can be stiff, though.

Linda J. Mihely, Assistant Dean of Admissions and Financial Aid
303 E. Broad Street, Columbus, OH 43215-3200
Tel: 614-236-6310 Fax: 614-236-6972
Email: admissions@law.capital.edu • Website: www.law.capital.edu

"It is best not to mention grades except among close friends." "There seems to be a sort of divide among students at the law school." "Day and evening students don't interact much at all," and most agree that "the day program is much more competitive." "The evening program is much more relaxed in class" because "Most people have very busy lives outside of school." "Evening students are a different breed," explains one student. "I can honestly report that studying law with people whose resumes are already filled with diverse experience has been very rewarding."

"Students here are generally pretty vocal about issues that matter to them." Ethnically, "Students are mainly White," but "There is a great minority community." You'll find a very high number of "nontraditional law students" here and a "wide range in age" and "professions." "Some spend their days talking about drinking and parties, while other more serious students spend their days studying," observes a 2L. "It is quite obvious which students are fresh out of undergrad."

There are "lots of student organizations" and "ways to get involved." "Community-service projects are everywhere," and "The main law fraternities are very active." Capital sponsors "planned social hours" and "a lot of events and different opportunities for students to get to know each other." "It is very easy to find a group of people with similar interests both in and out of the legal field." Students give the city of Columbus reasonably high marks. "It's not San Francisco or Boston," but "There are usually student-group sponsored happy hours at various bars downtown" and "social nights in and around Columbus at other bars." "Often after classes are over on Friday or after a midterm, an impromptu group will just go out somewhere."

Getting In

Admitted students at the 25th percentile here have LSAT scores of about 150 and GPAs hovering just around 3.0. Admitted students at the 75th percentile have LSAT scores of 156 and GPAs of approximately 3.5.

Legal methods course requirement	Yes
Legal research course requirement	Yes
Moot court requirement	No
Public interest law requirement	No

ADMISSIONS

Selectivity Rating	73
# applications received	1,575
% applicants accepted	40
% acceptees attending	41
Average LSAT	153
LSAT Range	151–156
Average undergrad GPA	3.21
Application fee	$40
Regular application	Rolling, up to 5/1
Regular notification	Rolling
Early application program	No
Transfer students accepted	Yes
Evening division offered	Yes
Part-time accepted	Yes
LSDAS accepted	Yes

Applicants Also Look At
The University of Akron, Cleveland State University, University of Dayton, University of Toledo, Ohio Northern University, Thomas M. Cooley Law School, Florida Costal School of Law

International Students

TOEFL required of international students	Yes

FINANCIAL FACTS

Annual tuition	$24,795
Books and supplies	$898
Fees per credit	$855
Tuition per credit	$855
Room & board (off-campus)	$10,580
Financial aid application deadline	4/1
% first-year students receiving some sort of aid	94
% receiving some sort of aid	93
% of aid that is merit based	40
% receiving scholarships	40
Average grant	$8,000
Average loan	$23,570
Average total aid package	$28,737
Average debt	$70,806

EMPLOYMENT INFORMATION

Career Rating	**76**	**Grads Employed by Field (%)**
Rate of placement (nine months out)	95	Academic (4)
Average starting salary	$59,849	Business/Industry (19)
State for bar exam	OH	Government (21)
Pass rate for first-time bar	87	Judicial Clerkships (3)

Employers Who Frequently Hire Grads
Military (1)
Law firms, government agencies, business and corporate employers
Private Practice (46)
Public Interest (6)

Prominent Alumni
David Tannenbaum, Partner, Fulbright Jaworski; Deborah Pryce, U.S. Congresswoman; Paul McNulty, Deputy Attorney General, U.S. Dept. of Justice; Robert Schottenstein, Chairman, CEO, and President of M/I Homes, Inc.

CASE WESTERN RESERVE UNIVERSITY
SCHOOL OF LAW

Academics

Case Western Reserve University School of Law is a dynamic institution emphasizing technology and "practical lawyering skills." Numerous cutting-edge academic centers on campus offer instruction in a wide range of unique legal niches, including regulatory law and law and medicine. According to many students, the crown jewel among these centers is the International Law Center. The international law program is "one of the best in the entire country." Students participate in "research for the government's cases against Guantanamo Bay inmates" and do research for the international courts for Rwanda, Cambodia, Sierra Leone, and the former Yugoslavia. Concentration programs include law and technology, litigation, and health law. Dual-degree programs include a JD/MD and a JD/Master's in social work. Also, "If you're interested in community-service and public interest work, you have more options than you'd ever have time to pursue."

"Professors are excellent" at Case Law. They are "intelligent, dedicated, and experienced" and "They all seem to love teaching and love the law." Courses are generally "lively and interesting." "Many members of the faculty are younger and they bring energy and enthusiasm to the classroom along with pedagogical methods that keep pace with modern technology." "They have an amazing knack for generating excitement out of mundane material," raves a 2L. "I will enroll in any course that these professors teach, simply because they are so passionate and challenging." The "interesting" adjuncts are "almost always great" as well, "and often come from elite firms." "One adjunct professor, who teaches law of the music industry, won a Grammy." Outside of class, professors are "quite accessible and willing to grab a drink with you." The administration is "amazingly accessible" as well.

On the career front, students are mostly satisfied with the Career Services Office. The school's location in one of the nation's top 10 legal markets certainly doesn't hurt. "Case has a strong reputation," and "Students who do exceptionally well academically do not have much of a problem" getting "an incredibly high-paying job" in any number of major cities across the country. Case Law's reputation "does not extend greatly to the coasts," though. "Finding employment outside of the Midwest region has been a problem for some students," and "It can be very difficult" for less-than-stellar students to find work, particularly outside the surrounding area.

The "aesthetically pleasing" law school facility is situated between an art museum, a botanical garden, and "the beautiful $25 million dollar Geary-designed business school." "The area is beautiful and a pleasure to relax in after the stresses of law school." "The library staff is excellent and always more than happy to help." Recent renovations "have made the library a great place to study," and there are plenty of "private cubicles with comfortable desks and chairs." The main university library is nearby as well and "open 24 hours," which is "a very important plus." "The classrooms are pretty standard," but they are generously outfitted with wireless access and ample power sources for laptops. However, "The wireless Internet often quits working in class, although that is sometimes for the best," admits a 3L. Also, "The building is always freezing cold regardless of the season, but no one seems to know why."

Life

"There is a fair amount of race, gender, and social diversity" at Case Law. The majority of students in each class hail from "states other than Ohio," and many "don't plan to

ELAINE GREAVES, ASSISTANT DEAN FOR ADMISSIONS
11075 EAST BOULEVARD, CLEVELAND, OH 44106
TEL: 800-756-0036 FAX: 216-368-1042
EMAIL: LAWADMISSIONS@CASE.EDU • WEBSITE: WWW.LAW.CASE.EDU

stay" after graduation. Some students are competitive, but there are "very few overly competitive students." "Everyone is extremely helpful and people in the same class pass around outlines." "Although students at Case are competitive, there is a real sense of community here. Students help each other and don't try to undermine their classmates to get ahead." "There is a feeling of community where we all want to be successful and are proud of being Case Law students, and in that sense we compete together against the rest of the legal world."

Socially, "There is a decent sense of community." "You can make your life as social as you want." Students call the "extremely active" Student Bar Association "the best SBA anywhere." Receptions, speakers, and happy hours are frequent. "Every Thursday, you can go to the bars and see people at school on a social level and it's very laid-back," explains a 1L.

Of their environs, students say "The campus is beautiful," located in walking distance from a beautiful orchestra hall, art museum, botanical garden, and planetarium, and only 15 minutes from the bars, restaurants, and theaters of downtown Cleveland. Much of the rest of the Queen City is "less attractive" but, as one student notes, this feature makes it "a great place to study." "Coming to Case, I was most concerned about living in Cleveland—the 'mistake on the lake'—where even the river caught fire," confides a 3L. "But really, it's not a bad place to spend three years."

Getting In

Admitted students at the 25th percentile have LSAT scores of approximately 156 and GPAs around 3.28. Admitted students at the 75th percentile have LSAT scores of 161 and GPAs in the 3.68 range.

EMPLOYMENT INFORMATION	
Career Rating 73	**Grads Employed by Field (%)**
Rate of placement (nine months out) 95.6	Academic (2)
Average starting salary $77,360	Private Practice (48)
State for bar exam OH, NY, CA, IL, PA	Business Industry (17)
Employers Who Frequently Hire Grads	Government (14)
Large law firms in major U.S. cities,	Judicial Clerk (5)
including Cleveland, New York, Chicago,	Public Interest (11)
Los Angeles, Washington DC, and Boston.	Academic (2)
Prominent Alumni	Military (3)
Barry M. Meyer, Chairman and CEO,	
Warner Bros. Entertainment; Fred Gray,	
Legendary civil rights attorney for Rosa	
Parks and Martin Luther King, Jr.;	
Catherine M. Kilbane, Sr. VP and General	
Counsel, American Greetings; Richard	
North Patterson, Author; Geralyn Presti,	
Sr. VP and General Counsel, Forest City	
Enterprises, Inc.	

Legal methods course requirement	Yes
Legal research course requirement	Yes
Moot court requirement	No
Public interest law requirement	No

ADMISSIONS

Selectivity Rating	**81**
# applications received	2,112
% applicants accepted	38
% acceptees attending	25
Average LSAT	158
LSAT Range	156–160
Average undergrad GPA	3.5
Application fee	$40
Regular application	Rolling, up to 4/2
Regular notification	Rolling
Early application program	Yes
Early application deadline	11/15
Early application notification	12/20
Transfer students accepted	Yes
Evening division offered	No
Part-time accepted	Yes
LSDAS accepted	Yes

International Students

TOEFL recommended of international students	Yes

FINANCIAL FACTS

Annual tuition	$36,150
Books and supplies	$2,620
Fees	$524
Fees per credit	$524
Tuition per credit	$1,507
Room & board	$13,790
Financial aid application deadline	5/1
% first-year students receiving some sort of aid	92
% receiving some sort of aid	90
% of aid that is merit based	99.5
% receiving scholarships	49
Average grant	$11,333
Average loan	$45,000
Average total aid package	$53,000
Average debt	$86,000

THE CATHOLIC UNIVERSITY OF AMERICA

COLUMBUS SCHOOL OF LAW

INSTITUTIONAL INFORMATION

Public/private	Private
Affiliation	Roman Catholic
Student-faculty ratio	16:1
% faculty part-time	64
% faculty female	27
% faculty minority	16
Total faculty	136

SURVEY SAYS...

Diverse opinions accepted
in classrooms
Great research resources
Great library staff
Beautiful campus

STUDENTS

Enrollment of law school	950
% male/female	47/53
% full-time	73
% minority	18
Average age of entering class	25

ACADEMICS

Academic Experience Rating	**81**
Profs interesting rating	78
Profs accessible rating	77
Hours of study per day	4.06

Academic Specialties

Corporation securities, international law, communications, law and public policy

Advanced Degrees Offered

JD, 3 years FT or 4 years PT

Combined Degrees Offered

JD/MA programs in accounting, canon law, history, philosophy, psychology, politics, library science, economics, and social work, 3–4 years.

Clinical program required	No
Legal writing	
course requirement	No
Legal methods	
course requirement	Yes
Legal research	
course requirement	No
Moot court requirement	No

Academics

Students who come to Catholic University's Columbus School of Law in Washington, D.C., shouldn't be surprised to learn that Catholic University's religious affiliation is right in the name. However, though a majority of the student body self-identifies as Catholic, many students "are actually quite liberal, as is the faculty." There is still a "heavy emphasis on public service and public interest" and there is a university wide Catholic "speaker policy"—"only 'Catholic' speakers are allowed, i.e. no pro-choice and no pro-gay"—but overall, it is" a very diverse group in terms of beliefs and political leanings, which, being in D.C., creates a very stimulating environment."

The law school provides excellent specialization opportunities; including six institutions and special programs which allow students who qualify to concentrate in a chosen area of law. Among these, the Center for Law, Philosophy & Culture and the related journal "provide a swath of events for students interested in a theoretical approach to the law," and the Institutes program is great for those who "have a good idea of what area of law we wish to focus on in practice or are simply interested in and enjoy; the program requirements are rigorous and clearly defined and well suited for focusing on the particular program areas."

Some evening students, feel that their program is "poorly administered," especially considering that they "are held to the exact same standards as day students." Many complain about the lack of forethought put into the planning of classes in regard to their needs and the communication skills of the administration, among other things. "We are made aware of school-related obligations and news through a last-minute and piecemeal communication process—more often than not, we have to dig to find out information we need," says a student. Many (but not all) full-time students log similar complaints regarding the administration's way of doing things, particularly the incredibly clunky scheduling of classes. "It is near-impossible to have days off to accommodate intern/externships." There are also grumblings about course offerings: "There are LOTS of students going into intellectual property, [but there are] very few classes," says one student. One student also says that the school is "not as 'on top of' up-and-coming areas of law as they could be," says another.

Luckily, the faculty "more than compensates for any shortfall" in the administration. Though there are definitely some bad apples, "most professors are more than willing to help with any request—be it classroom or employment related." "Professors often treat us as colleagues, and there is a mutual respect inside and outside the classroom," says a student. They are "brilliant, accomplished, but also approachable and genuinely care about the students." Another thing the school has going for it is "location, location, location." There are "numerous opportunities to gain practical experience in the legal epicenter that is Washington, D.C.," and that location allows the school to draw professors with "high-powered experience and strong connections." "The stuff happening in town is relevant to what you're studying in class," says a 1L. Facilities here are also "top-notch"—not only are they visually appealing, but "they provide all the required technological advances required by a student in today's world."

Life

This bunch is a convivial crew who are instilled with the knowledge that "the people in our classes are going to be our colleagues when we are done with school, so everyone is willing to work together if someone needs help." Though some concede that the school is "full of amazing students who perhaps didn't get into their first choice," students still work hard, and "the environment amongst students is about as positive as a system based on pure academic competition can be." Again, there is a split between evening and day students, but as there isn't much overlap, tension is kept at a minimum. The average student here is "smart, conscientious, and fun," and "it seems like there are no 'bad apples'" in this "supportive and positive environment."

As far as student social life goes, there are plenty of opportunities for extracurricular involvement, both social and academic: clubs, organizations, social events/parties, moot court, journal, trial advocacy. "Although I do not have a social life, it is of my own doing as the school provides the opportunity for a vast number of happy hours both on and off campus as well as larger events," confesses a 2L. Though the D.C. neighborhood isn't the best, "campus security drives SUVs and has big guns," and "the entire law school is self-contained, with "everything from the classrooms, to the library, prof's offices, and cafeteria…all in one gorgeous building made of marble and limestone."

Getting In

Catholic often faces strict competition from Georgetown and GW for students that want to get a law degree in the D.C. area, so typical admissions stats aren't as high. Full-time enrolled students for the most recent class have an LSAT score of 156 at the 25th percentile and a GPA of roughly 3.09. Enrolled students at the 75th percentile have an LSAT score of 160 and a GPA of 3.57. Students in the evening division have slightly lower grades and LSAT scores on average, yet all possess relevant professional experience.

ADMISSIONS

Selectivity Rating	80
# applications received	2,679
% applicants accepted	33
% acceptees attending	19
Average LSAT	158
LSAT Range	156–160
Average undergrad GPA	3.3
Application fee	$65
Regular application	Rolling, up to 3/1
Regular notification	Rolling
Early application program	Yes
Early application deadline	11/1
Early application notification	12/15
Transfer students accepted	Yes
Evening division offered	Yes
Part-time accepted	Yes
LSDAS accepted	Yes

International Students

TOEFL required of international students	Yes

FINANCIAL FACTS

Annual tuition	$33,230
Books and supplies	$1,500
Fees	$1,175
Tuition per credit	$1,215
Room & board (off-campus)	$14,600
Financial aid application deadline	7/15
% first-year students receiving some sort of aid	87
% receiving some sort of aid	90
% of aid that is merit based	34
% receiving scholarships	31
Average grant	$11,397
Average loan	$39,080
Average total aid package	$43,375
Average debt	$92,000

EMPLOYMENT INFORMATION

Career Rating	71
Rate of placement (nine months out)	91
Average starting salary	$64,000
State for bar exam	MD, VA, PA, NY, NJ

Employers Who Frequently Hire Grads
Akin, Gump, Strauss, Hauer and Feld; Clifford Chance; Jones Day; U.S. Department of Justice.

Grads Employed by Field (%)
Business/Industry (24)
Government (27)
Judicial Clerkships (11)
Private Practice (34)
Public Interest (3)
Other (1)

CHAPMAN UNIVERSITY
SCHOOL OF LAW

INSTITUTIONAL INFORMATION

Public/private	Private
Affiliation	Disciples of Christ
Student-faculty ratio	10:1
% faculty part-time	45
% faculty female	20
% faculty minority	8
Total faculty	99

SURVEY SAYS...

Diverse opinions accepted
in classrooms
Beautiful campus
Students love Orange, CA

STUDENTS

Enrollment of law school	560
% male/female	53/47
% out-of-state	18
% full-time	94.2
% minority	17
% international	.01
# of countries represented	2
Average age of entering class	25

ACADEMICS

Academic Experience Rating	**93**
Profs interesting rating	93
Profs accessible rating	98
Hours of study per day	4.49

Academic Specialties

Environmental law, international law, property, taxation, advocacy and dispute resolution, enterntainment law

Advanced Degrees Offered

JD, 3 years; LLM Tax, 1 year; LLM Prosecutorial Science, 1 year; General LLM

Combined Degrees Offered

JD/MBA, 4 years; JD/MFA 4 years

Clinical program required	No
Legal writing	
course requirement	Yes
Legal methods	
course requirement	Yes
Legal research	
course requirement	Yes

Academics

"There is a certain youthful exuberance about the place" that instills "a great sense of pride" in Chapman University School of Law students. Administrators here are "constantly working" "to raise the reputation of the school" and to "help [students] get jobs and have successful careers." They're also "incredibly receptive to student ideas. When we ask for things, they happen," a 1L reports. One example is Chapman's brand-new entertainment law certificate program, which incorporates "courses from [its] prestigious School of Film." Students are even more upbeat regarding Chapman's professors, who boast tremendous real-world experience: "I took civil procedure from a professor that was one of the attorneys in the Exxon Valdez litigation; my constitutional law professor clerked for Justice Thomas and is on a first-name basis with Justice Scalia; my criminal law professor's prior career was defending death-row candidates; and my evidence professor was an Assistant U.S. Attorney for a number of years," a 2L brags. While "Being taught by prestigious and experienced professors would be great on its own," professors here don't rest on their laurels, staying "in touch with their students, encouraging[ing] feedback, and [remaining] very accessible for class-related discussions as well as life advice." All "keep open office hours, and even the busiest are keen to make appointments with interested students. It is great to know that some of the most knowledgeable people in the country in various areas of the law are merely a flight of stairs away," a 2L writes. It also doesn't hurt that they "give career advice and provide contacts."

If Chapman students can't get enough of their professors, clinics provide them the opportunity to get hands-on experience in a specific area of the law under the supervision of a faculty member. Many students flock to the entertainment and tax law clinic; Chapman is "the only school in the area" to offer such a program. Regarding his constitutional jurisprudence clinic, a 2L tells us he is learning "the legal and constitutional implications of current situations (the NSA surveillance program was one of our topics). I also helped to prepare congressional testimony, amicus briefs, and other legal memoranda under the guidance of one of the country's more recognized constitutional scholars. While I don't doubt that there are institutions throughout the country with professors as knowledgeable and experienced...I highly doubt that any other school offers students the chance to interact and participate with those top scholars in the actual representation of clients in cases of particular constitutional import. I certainly don't know of many 2L students whose work is cited by the Senate Judiciary Committee!" In the area of academic support, a 1L writes: "All of my professors have been willing to meet with students to review exams and assignments, some even scheduling weeks of extended office hours to accommodate everyone and even holding meetings to conduct review problem sessions." In addition, many "successful upperclassmen run small study groups."

"Everyone takes pride" in the "immaculate" law building, which features a "polished marble" lobby and classrooms designed "with acoustics in mind." In addition, "Each classroom is equipped with a computer for the instructor, a projector, [a] document camera, [a] microphone, and a number of other gadgets... There are power outlets everywhere and wireless Internet access is ubiquitous," though "ubiquitous" may mean "doesn't work in a few key rooms and certain places in the library." Students' biggest complaint remains that "people outside of Orange County have never heard of us, and that can make getting a job difficult." While some here suggest "more marketing" to boost the school's profile, a sanguine 2L asserts that as students here "graduate and disseminate into the legal community, Chapman's name grows," adding, "It is already very well-respected within Orange County and is quickly gaining prominence in Los Angeles

Tracy Simmons, Assistant Dean of Admissions and Financial Aid
One University Drive, Orange, CA 92866
Tel: 714-628-2500 Fax: 714-628-2501
Email: lawadm@chapman.edu • Website: www.chapman.edu/law

and San Diego. I feel that it is only a matter of time before Chapman's reputation matches the education it provides."

Life

Chapman students argue that the school's location in Orange—right in the middle of Orange County, California—"can't be beat." "It's 80 degrees in February, and you're only 20 minutes from the beach," a 1L writes. In the midst of the Southern California sun, students report, "Even though we are all enduring law school, everyone is quite pleasant and fun to be around." Students are "concerned about class rankings and job opportunities," but are still "very willing to assist each other with the material." A 2L explains, "Everyone wants to do well, but not at the expense of others. People are willing to share notes, books, space at a table in the library—[it's] a very cooperative environment that allows students to focus on their studies." Though some complain that "after the first year, [students] really still only socialize within their 1L track," most here don't seem to mind. "The environment is a bit high school–ish, but in a fun way," a 2L reports. "Everyone enjoys the daily gossip." "We all hang out on the weekends and after school," a 1L adds. It should be noted that "diversity is well accepted" at Chapman, though a "more diverse student body" is called for.

Getting In

Chapman requires that all applicants apply online via the Law School Admission Council's website. As admissions decisions here are not driven by a mathematical index, care should be given to "soft factors," such as letters of recommendation and the personal statement. For the accepted class of 2008, students reported a median undergraduate GPA of 3.44 and a median LSAT of 158.

Moot court requirement	No
Public interest law requirement	No

ADMISSIONS

Selectivity Rating	**85**
# applications received	2,483
% applicants accepted	24
% acceptees attending	33
Average LSAT	158
LSAT Range	155–159
Average undergrad GPA	3.44
Application fee	$65
Regular application	Rolling, up to 4/15
Regular notification	Rolling
Early application deadline	No
Early application program	No
Transfer students accepted	Yes
Evening division offered	No
Part-time accepted	Yes
LSDAS accepted	Yes

Applicants Also Look At

University of Southern California; University of California—Los Angeles; Arizona State University; University of the Pacific; University of California, Davis; University of LaVerne; Golden Gate University; Loyola Marymount University; University of Miami

International Students

TOEFL required of international students	Yes
Minimum TOEFL (paper/computer/internet)	600/250/100

FINANCIAL FACTS

Annual tuition	$37,950
Books and supplies	$1,500
Fees	$331
Tuition per credit	$1,260
Room & board	$15,300
Financial aid application deadline	3/2
% first-year students receiving some sort of aid	95
% receiving some sort of aid	92
% of aid that is merit based	23
% receiving scholarships	45
Average grant	$24,106
Average loan	$40,258
Average total aid package	$48,748
Average debt	$102,914

EMPLOYMENT INFORMATION

Career Rating	**88**
Rate of placement (nine months out)	92.6
State for bar exam	CA
Pass rate for first-time bar	77

Employers Who Frequently Hire Grads
O'Melveny & Myers; Orange County District Attorney; Orange County Public Defender; United States District Courts; Knobbe Martens; Riverside DA; Bonne Bridges Mueller O'Keefe and Nichols; Bremer Whyte; Rutan & Tucker; Jones Day; Deloitte; Walsworth, Franklin, Bevins & McCall; Koeller, Nebeken, Carlson & Haluck

Prominent Alumni
Catherine Parsons, Associate, Rutan & Tucker; Jody Linneman, Assistant Vice President, Counsel Pacific Life Insurance, Co.; Nikole Kingston; O'Melreny & Myers.

Grads Employed by Field (%)
Public Interest (2)

CHARLESTON SCHOOL OF LAW*

INSTITUTIONAL INFORMATION

Public/private	Private

SURVEY SAYS...

Diverse opinions accepted in classrooms
Students love Charleston, SC

STUDENTS

% male/female	53/47
% out-of-state	37
Average age of entering class	23

ACADEMICS

Academic Experience Rating	**82**
Profs interesting rating	83
Profs accesible rating	89
Clinical program required	No
Legal writing course requirement	Yes
Legal methods course requirement	No
Legal research course requirement	Yes
Moot court requirement	No
Public interest law requirement	Yes

Academics

Students are thrilled to have gotten in at the ground floor of Charleston School of Law, which recently received provisional approval from the ABA. For Charleston, this has meant that "everyone is invested in the success of the school, and their number one mission is the well-being and success of the students." The CSOL community is new but eager. "Everyone is determined to build a nationally recognized program," says a 1L. The opportunities for internships and externships in the local legal community are plentiful, and the atmosphere collegiate, with "a very personal feel." "I honestly think that you could take any dean, and they could put a name to every students face and tell you about that person, i.e., where he is from, where he went to school, etc.," says a 2L. Indeed, students credit the "wonderful administrative staff" with their recent jump in reputation, and love the fact that "the school actually listens to the students when the students want a change." "It is still learning and adapting to the students, which is helpful," says a 1L.

Oddly, the school is split up among several different buildings, some of which have other businesses in them, such as Bell South. Facilities are still top notch, however, and the school spares little expense when providing students with resources (the "most up-to-date technology is being used in every classroom"), but "the law school still needs to acquire more space, preferably near the main building," and preferably in the library, where there "is very limited individual study space/cubbies." Since this is a private school, the tuition can be a bit expensive relative to a state school such as the University of South Carolina, but one of the main benefits of the school is "location, location, location... Charleston, SC is truly an amazing city."

The professors here are real people that mix in their practical legal experience when teaching a class, making them "very approachable and genuinely concerned about [students'] success." The teachers "could not be more willing to work with the students—whether in class or out." Most of the professors "have a nice combination of academic and practical knowledge." There are complaints that there isn't enough tenured faculty, which creates a reliance on adjuncts, and the Socratic Method isn't used very often here, so lectures can be a bit dull and "student participation is negligible"; students also wish there were more specialization options, but there are excellent pro bono, maritime law, and real estate programs and a public service emphasis. "We are slowly growing and this process continues with each year that passes," says a student.

* Provisionally approved by the ABA.

Life

Everyone in the country loves Charleston for its southern charm and beauty, so it's no surprise that students do, too. "It's Charleston, SC... if you've ever been, you understand," says one simply. Other than the parking situation at the school, "Charleston is a wonderful place to live." The school community is very tightly knit; students frequently find time to interact outside of school, and "there is no shortage of things to do in the area." "I have to leave thirty minutes earlier to get to class on time because everyone is so friendly and wants to talk," says a 2L. In fact, there are almost too many social and/or extracurricular groups/organizations for such a young school. "Some people look at our brochure and wonder 'When do they study the law?'" says a student. There's no backstabbing, and the administration encourages a sense of camaraderie and cooperation, so "most students are willing to share their notes and answer questions about the material." Though there can be a bit of competition, it "is more intrinsic, more concerned with self-improvement, rather than 'beating' your classmates." "The biggest issue we have is racing to sign up for seats when we have really excellent speakers coming," says a student. As a brand spanking new school, there's "zero diversity" here, but this can change as the school's reputation and history grows. "The old boy southern network is in full effect here," says a student. However, "there is a surprising diversity of minds and opinions."

Getting In

The Charleston School of Law is still pretty new and only recently received its provisional accreditation from the ABA, so numbers and selectivity rates have yet to reflect this stronger reputation. For the time being, admission is relatively easy, with about a third of applicants gaining acceptance to the entering class of 2010, but as word about the school gets out, standards will get tougher. At the moment, students with a solid B average and a 155 on the LSATs should have no problem getting in.

ADMISSIONS

Selectivity Rating	**78**
# applications received	870
# applicants accepted	298
# acceptees attending	134
Average LSAT	155
LSAT Range	153–157
Average undergrad GPA	3.2
Application fee	$50
Regular application	3/1
Regular notification	4/15
Rolling notification	Yes
Early application program	No
Transfer students accepted	Yes
Evening division offered	Yes
Part-time accepted	Yes
LSDAS accepted	Yes

International Students

TOEFL required	
of international students	Yes
TOEFL recommended	
of international students	Yes

FINANCIAL FACTS

Annual tuition	$29,648

CITY UNIVERSITY OF NEW YORK
SCHOOL OF LAW AT QUEENS COLLEGE

Academics

Designed to be the anti-law school, the incredibly affordable, CUNY—Queens is "full of school spirit, clinical training, and no page ripping out of library books." Working under the mission "law in the service of human needs," the school is "genuinely committed to the struggle for justice," and tends to attract a different type of law student; unlike a lot of New York law schools, the vast majority of the "dedicated" and "idealistic" students here go on to careers in public interest. This mission creates a law school experience like no other-students are encouraging to one another and help each other to thrive, and everyone involved with the school wishes success on each new class. "Put it this way, I have a number of my professors' cell phone numbers, I call them by their first names, and our janitors come to our graduation because they are proud of us," says a 3L.

The curriculum here provides a well-rounded education of law and case-teaching method, along with policy and legal theory, enabling students to do more progressive work in the legal field. There is no grading curve, classes stress doctrinal work and advocacy, seminars teach practical skills with lawyering, and the research requirements prepare students for internships/careers. Legal clinics offer myriad of practical experience, particularly in the third year. Professors are "diverse, engaged and receptive to students," and many "have amazing histories of advocacy work," with backgrounds in feminist organizing work, gay rights, environmental justice, reproductive rights and "everything else fun and liberal." There can be a touch of disorganization and bureaucracy in the administration, but it's kept to a minimum, and administrators "can be great if you find them on a good day." The law school building is actually an old middle school in a somewhat remote part of New York City, so the "facilities definitely leave something to be desired" (though there are plans for a future relocation), but all classrooms are equipped with at least one computer and a SmartBoard for easy note taking, and outside of the classroom, discussions are continued "on the course websites that each professor dedicate to maintain."

In the end, it's the complete commitment from faculty, staff, and students to the school's mission that wins students over, and the comfortable, supportive environment created when surrounded by people with similar motives. "No one here is trying to be an ambulance chaser or a barracuda or any of the other stereotypes of lawyers. Everyone here is genuinely interested in being a champion for a cause and the cause is people who genuinely need the law on their side," says a proud student.

Yvonne Cherena-Pacheco, Asst. Dean for Enrollment Mgmt & Dir. of Admiss'ns
65-21 Main Street, Flushing, NY 11367-1358
Tel: 718-340-4210 Fax: 718-340-4435
Email: admissions@mail.law.cuny.edu • Website: www.law.cuny.edu

Life

Most who attend school here have been out of undergrad for quite awhile and have a wide variety of experience working for non-profit organizations and activist jobs, so they come to school with a clear idea of the type of public interest law they want to practice. This results in an "incredibly collaborative learning environment" and students want to see each other succeed. In fact, they're downright rabid about the fact that competition does not exist at CUNY: "I had computer problems during midterms and finals my first semester, and people were practically throwing their outlines at me so I would do well!" says a student. Since a lot of people commute and there is no out-of-state housing, it "sometimes feels hard to get everyone together," but "small class sizes make it easier to make 'school friends.'" and people "definitely coalesce around local bars to celebrate midterms, finals and anything in between." There are many student clubs and events, even if students are often too exhausted to take part in them. Though the location in New York City is always a plus and the nearby Flushing cuisine is delicious and authentic, the school itself is a full 15-minute bus ride from the closest subway, so the commute can be trying for some students.

Although the school is very liberal in its ideology, when it comes to conversation and debate, "no one is shunned because they aren't of a certain persuasion." This liberalism also translates to action, and "everything gets heated up, from new list-servs, banning Coke products, and scheduling of classes and finals." Still, everyone here gets along really well and is "like a family," but just like in a family, "any drama is magnified because of the school's small size."

Getting In

CUNY evaluates prospective students based on their demonstrated abilities and intellectual capacity to complete a rigorous legal program, using test scores, previous academic records, and, where applicable, post-college work experience. In addition to these factors, CUNY seeks students who can bring diversity of background and experience to the campus and who express a specific interest in and affinity for the values of the program. Finally, CUNY favors New York residents or students with a particular interest in serving the New York community.

EMPLOYMENT INFORMATION

Career Rating	**72**
Rate of placement (nine months out)	84
Average starting salary	$53,524
State for bar exam	NY
Pass rate for first-time bar	82

Employers Who Frequently Hire Grads

District Attorney Offices (NYC—Bronx, Manhattan & Queens); Legal Aid Society (NYC); Legal Services Offices (NYC); Nassau County Attorney's Office.

Prominent Alumni

Katherine Gallagher, Staff Attorney at the Center for Constitutional Rights and International Human Rights Law; Sanja Zgonjanin, Law Clerk U.S. Court of Appeals 2nd Circuit Judge Peter Wall.

Grads Employed by Field (%)

Business/Industry (7)
Government (17)
Judicial Clerkships (18)
Private Practice (21)
Public Interest (35)
Other (0)
Academic (2)

ADMISSIONS

Selectivity Rating	**76**
# applications received	2,206
% applicants accepted	578
% acceptees attending	129
Average LSAT	153
LSAT Range	151–155
Average undergrad GPA	3.23
Application fee	$50
Regular application	3/16
Regular notification	6/16
Early application program	No
Transfer students accepted	Yes
Evening division offered	No
Part-time accepted	No
LSDAS accepted	Yes

Applicants Also Look At

American University, Seattle University, Northeastern University, University of the District of Columbia

International Students

TOEFL recommended of international students	Yes

FINANCIAL FACTS

Annual tuition (in-state/ out-of-state)	$8,900/$14,800
Books and supplies	$1,712
Fees	$312
Tuition per credit (in-state/ out-of-state)	$370/$620
Room & board (off-campus)	$14,893
Financial aid application deadline	5/1
% first-year students receiving some sort of aid	79
% receiving some sort of aid	82
% of aid that is merit based	18
% receiving scholarships	56
Average grant	$5,000
Average loan	$27,604
Average total aid package	$31,693
Average debt	$66,142

CLEVELAND STATE UNIVERSITY
CLEVELAND-MARSHALL COLLEGE OF LAW

Academics

Students agree that the universally well-regarded law school at Cleveland State University "is the sort of school that lets students know they matter." The "responsive" administration "works very hard to ensure that students make it through school and find jobs afterwards" and does so at roughly half the price of other institutions, offering "great bang for the buck." Though many would like to see Cleveland-Marshall's reputation expand outside northeast Ohio, a second-year student testifies, "While I was interviewing for summer positions many interviewers told me that they liked Cleveland-Marshall students because we write well and work hard to prove ourselves."

At Cleveland-Marshall, the "very approachable" professors are "understanding of the first-year experience" and "treat you like a colleague rather than an interruption." Students say "one particular professor will go to the lounge after class and allow students to ask in-depth questions they may have, as well as engage in a longer dialogue about legal issues of note." As one 3L claims, "These individuals are the school's most valuable asset." Cleveland-Marshall's "very experienced" faculty has extremely strong ties to the local community, and students claim that their involvement "helps the overall reputation of the school in the local area," adding to the school's cachet during the job hunt (the "huge alumni network" doesn't hurt, either). "If you want to stay in Cleveland after graduation, this is the best choice for a legal education."

Though there's great praise for the new law library and its "wall of windows where you can read and look outside to remember what it was like to have a life before law school," the law building as a whole receives lukewarm reviews, with students describing some of the older classrooms as "unchanged since the 1970s" and "resembling prison cells." Recent renovations, however, include tech-enhanced classrooms, moot court room, new law clinics and meeting space. While most students agree that the library's staff is "particularly helpful with research assignments," there are some gripes about the support staff, which students describe as "overworked, underpaid, and uninterested in helping students."

Complaints about the workload of a first-year law student are nothing new, but the unique setup of the first year curriculum at Cleveland-Marshall seems to lend itself to a particularly "brutal second semester." One student claims that the schedule "essentially 'forces' you to become a night student, or at least take a few classes at night." Some claim that it "takes forever to get through the requirements and bar courses," leaving little time for outside academic interests. However, the school's Moot Court Program is "exceptional," and its "great writing program" and "emphasis on practical (as opposed to theoretical) approaches to studying the law" are major advantages. One first-year student sums up a common sentiment: "I often feel like I am getting a better education than my friends who are paying twice as much money to study at a neighboring private law school."

Life

Cleveland-Marshall's "racially diverse, culturally diverse, and socioeconomically diverse" group of people is "vibrant" and "friendly." Since the school is located in downtown Cleveland, "Parking is a nightmare," and though the law school building isn't winning any architecture awards, construction is underway to make it "more open and attractive," as well as to add a "great new student lounge." Though "local Bar Associations provide excellent resources and young adult socials," students complain that the school empties out on weekends. Cleveland-Marshall's large percentage of non-traditional students—many who come from Cleveland and its surrounding areas—help contribute to the ghost town effect.

Other students feel that "the part-time...and full-time students have a separate community" on campus. While "the evening program is just as challenging as the day program," one student tells us "part-timers are not treated the same as full-time day students. I switched to day this year, and the difference is obvious. Faculty, administration, and Career Services absolutely cater to the full-timers." Differences aside, many students are pleased to find a lack of the competitiveness inherent among so many law schools; "Most students know one another" and "support each other." As one first-year student puts it, "Sometimes things are like high school, but ultimately that is not a bad thing, unless you make it such. We have lockers, you wait for girls to go to the bathroom before lunch, and there can be rumors, but take it all in stride, know your goals, and you should be fine."

Getting In

Getting into Cleveland-Marshall, while far from being a given, is slightly easier than average. While there are no cutoff numbers, last year's admitted students at the 25th percentile had an LSAT score of 153 and an average GPA of 3.08, while admitted students at the 75th percentile had an LSAT score of 157 and a GPA of 3.68. The school also stresses the importance of personal statements in the admissions process.

EMPLOYMENT INFORMATION

Career Rating	80
Rate of placement (nine months out)	89.5
Average starting salary	$81,823
State for bar exam	OH, NY, MD, MA, FL
Pass rate for first-time bar	90%

Employers Who Frequently Hire Grads

Jones Day; Baker & Hostetler; Thompson, Hine; Squire, Sanders & Dempsey; Calfee, Halter & Griswold; Arter & Hadden; Ernst & Young; Benesch, Friedlander.

Prominent Alumni

Tim Russert, The late Sr. VP, NBC News and moderator of; Hon. Louis Stokes, U.S. House of Representatives, Rtd.

Grads Employed by Field (%)

Law Firms (61)
Business (17)
Government (16)
Academic (3)
Judicial Clerkship (2)
Public Interest (1)

Legal methods	
course requirement	No
Legal research	
course requirement	Yes
Moot court requirement	No
Public interest	
law requirement	No

ADMISSIONS

Selectivity Rating	79
# applications received	1,768
# applicants accepted	621
# acceptees attending	211
Average LSAT	156
LSAT Range	153–157
Average undergrad GPA	3.38
Regular application	Rolling, up to 5/1
Regular notification	Rolling
Early application program	No
Transfer students accepted	Yes
Evening division offered	Yes
Part-time accepted	Yes
LSDAS accepted	Yes

Applicants Also Look At

The Ohio State University–Columbus, The University of Akron, Case Western Reserve University, University of Dayton

International Students

TOEFL required	
of international students	Yes
Minimum TOEFL	
(paper/computer/web)	600/250/100

FINANCIAL FACTS

Annual tuition (in-state/ out-of-state)	$16,478/$22,608
Books and supplies	$1,500
Fees	$25
Fees per credit	$25
Tuition per credit (in-state/out-of-state)	$634/$870
Room & board	$13,000
Financial aid application deadline	5/1
% first-year students receiving some sort of aid	90
% receiving some sort of aid	95
% of aid that is merit based	90
% receiving scholarships	40
Average grant	$6,457
Average loan	$24,070
Average total aid package	$24,906
Average debt	$59,458

THE COLLEGE OF WILLIAM & MARY
MARSHALL-WYTHE LAW SCHOOL

INSTITUTIONAL INFORMATION

Public/private	Public
Student-faculty ratio	14:1
% faculty part-time	54
% faculty female	32
% faculty minority	9
Total faculty	81

SURVEY SAYS...
Diverse opinions accepted
in classrooms
Great library staff
Abundant externship/internship/
clerkship opportunities

STUDENTS

Enrollment of law school	626
% male/female	51/49
% out-of-state	53
% full-time	100
% minority	16
# of countries represented	7
Average age of entering class	24

ACADEMICS

Academic Experience Rating	**89**
Profs interesting rating	89
Profs accessible rating	88
Hours of study per day	4.42

Academic Specialties
Civil procedure, commercial law,
constitutional law, corporation securities, criminal law, environmental
law, human rights, international law,
labor law, legal history, property,
intellectual property law

Advanced Degrees Offered
JD, 3 years; LL.M. in the American
Legal System, 1 year

Combined Degrees Offered
JD/Master of Public Policy, 4 years;
JD/Master of Business
Administration, 4 years; JD/Master
of Arts in American Studies, 4 years

Clinical program required	No
Legal writing	
course requirement	Yes
Legal methods	
course requirement	Yes

Academics

Professors at the The College of William & Mary's Marshall-Wythe School of Law are "breathtakingly prepared, experienced, and—most importantly—focused on teaching." They want students "to learn the material and how to effectively express ideas, without having to feel stupid." "Class discussions range from the slightly dull to the side-splittingly funny," and the faculty "does an excellent job of emphasizing both ethics and the greater role that lawyers play in society." "The school's greatest strength is its dedication to graduating not merely lawyers, but citizen-lawyers," relates a 3L, "Attorneys who are not only competent but also of the highest ethical and moral character." "Most professors know every single student by first name," and "They are always willing to meet with students, offer letters of recommendation, or give advice." W&M's administration is "very helpful and organized" as well. Deans are "approachable" and "extremely accessible." "First-year students have a social with the dean before classes even begin," explains a 1L. "Everyone learns your name and greets you in the halls. I've never experienced anything else quite like it."

The "outstanding" Office of Career Services "has helped many students to get summer jobs [that] often lead to permanent employment." "W&M is the type of school that'll allow you to find the job you want, where you want, if you're willing to work for it." Washington, D.C. and New York City "are the most popular markets," but the staff "works really hard to help you to find jobs wherever you want to go." "Upon graduating from William & Mary, I'll be working in my dream job in Texas, an opportunity I would not have had at a more regional school," enthuses one satisfied customer.

There is "a lot of practical training in written and oral advocacy" here. The unique and time-consuming Legal Skills Program combines legal research, writing, and ethics into a "valuable" two-year program. Groups of about 16 students are organized into mock law firms, which take mock clients through all stages of a trial—from initial contact to appeals. Over 50 percent of the students here receive (often substantial) scholarships or fellowships. About the only complaint we hear concerns the limited clinical program, which "needs to expand and improve."

"William & Mary has recently witnessed a facilities renaissance, with renovated classrooms, an expanded new library, and a more attractive lobby, main hallway, and front entranceway." Nevertheless, "The law school building is certainly not elaborate or first-class." "There isn't a whole lot within a short distance, so if you're used to being 15 minutes from a city, it might not be the place for you." Despite these shortcomings, students here are overwhelmingly satisfied. "I believe that William & Mary is truly the most unique of law schools," attests a 1L. "Any school can profess to have a collegial student body, to have accessible professors, and to provide the most enriching legal education. William & Mary has delivered on each and every one of its promises, and has exceeded my expectations for what the law school experience could offer."

Life

While the student body is predominantly white, "There is a large group of minority students" at William & Mary. The "extremely intelligent and hardworking" students here "really are friendly and don't take themselves too seriously." "Most every student who decides to attend William & Mary Law School raves about the friendly and supportive atmosphere." They also applaud the Honor Code. "We take an oath to not lie, cheat, or steal," explains a 3L, "and students really do abide by it. I can leave my laptop,

FAYE SHEALY, ASSOCIATE DEAN
WILLIAM & MARY LAW SCHOOL, OFFICE OF ADMISSION, PO BOX 8795, WILLIAMSBURG, VA 23187-8795
TEL: 757-221-3785 FAX: 757-221-3261
EMAIL: LAWADM@WM.EDU • WEBSITE: LAW.WM.EDU

books, purse—everything—in the lobby, the lounge, or the library, and go to lunch. I know, without doubt, that it will all be there when I return."

W&M is "fairly small," "so students get to know each other very well." "There are social cliques, for sure," says a 2L. "But every person gets a chance to make friends." "Like most law schools, William & Mary can be a bit like high school at times, with the gossip mill running full tilt." With few bars in town," social outlets are somewhat limited, catalyzing drama." "The social life is surprisingly booming," though. "Fun is there if you wish to have it."

"William & Mary is located in one of the most historical and beautiful areas of United States: Colonial Williamsburg." "If you love history, you couldn't get any better." "It's a great source of pride to be able to say George Wythe, Thomas Jefferson, and John Marshall taught, walked, or slept here," relates one student. Other students observe that "Williamsburg is a great town in which to go to graduate school "because there are "no distractions." This might be an exaggeration, as Busch Gardens is nearby, "as well as plenty of nice parks, recreation centers, and shopping." There are "a lot of outdoorsy things to do" as well.

Getting In

Admitted students at the 25th percentile have LSAT scores of 164 and GPAs around 3.5. Admitted students at the 75th percentile have LSAT scores of 169 and GPAs just above 3.8. If you take the LSAT more than once, W&M "will evaluate the LSAT portion of the application by looking to the highest reported score."

Legal research course requirement	Yes
Moot court requirement	No
Public interest law requirement	No

ADMISSIONS

Selectivity Rating	**88**
# applications received	4,585
% applicants accepted	25
% acceptees attending	19
Average LSAT	162
LSAT Range	160–166
Average undergrad GPA	3.56
Application fee	$50
Regular application	Rolling, up to 3/1
Regular notification	3/30
Early application program	No
Transfer students accepted	Yes
Evening division offered	No
Part-time accepted	No
LSDAS accepted	Yes

Applicants Also Look At
University of Virginia, The George Washington University, Georgetown University

FINANCIAL FACTS

Annual tuition (in-state/ out-of-state)	$15,902/$25,892
Books and supplies	$1,200
Fees (in-state/ out-of-state)	$4,244/$4,454
Room & board	$5,909
Financial aid application deadline	2/15
% first-year students receiving some sort of aid	95
% receiving some sort of aid	92
% of aid that is merit based	75
% receiving scholarships	64
Average grant	$6,405
Average loan	$25,061
Average total aid package	$31,563
Average debt	$76,600

EMPLOYMENT INFORMATION

Career Rating	**88**	**Grads Employed by Field (%)**
Rate of placement (nine months out)	97	Private Practice (61)
Average starting salary	$101,352	Judicial Clerkships (13)
State for bar exam	VA, CA, MD, NY, TX	Government (8)
Pass rate for first-time bar	89	Business/Industry (65)
		Military (7)
		Public Interest (5)

COLUMBIA UNIVERSITY
SCHOOL OF LAW

INSTITUTIONAL INFORMATION

Public/private	Private
Student-faculty ratio	10:1
% faculty part-time	41
% faculty female	31
% faculty minority	12
Total faculty	198

SURVEY SAYS...

Diverse opinions accepted
in classrooms
Great research resources
Abundant externship/internship/
clerkship opportunities
Students love New York, NY

STUDENTS

Enrollment of law school	1,229
% male/female	55/45
% full-time	100
% minority	30
% international	7
# of countries represented	44
Average age of entering class	24

ACADEMICS

Academic Experience Rating	91
Profs interesting rating	81
Profs accessible rating	68
Hours of study per day	4.11

Academic Specialties

Civil procedure, commercial law, constitutional law, corporation securities, criminal law, environmental law, government services, human rights, international law, labor law, legal history, legal philosophy, property, taxation, intellectual property law

Advanced Degrees Offered

LL.M., one year; JSD, two semesters in residence and a dissertation.

Combined Degrees Offered

JD/Ph.D., 7 years; JD/MA, 4 years; JD/MBA, 3 or 4 years; JD/MFA (Arts Administration), 4 years; JD/MS Urban Planning, 4 years; JD/MS Social Work, 4 years; JD/MS Journalism, 3.5 years; JD/MIA in International Affairs, 4 years; JD/MPA in Public Administration with Columbia, 4 years

Academics

There is a "focus on international law," "a moot court requirement for 1Ls," and "a nice blend of theory and practice" at Columbia Law School, "although the school tilts [more] towards the theory." "The theoretical focus of the faculty is a good thing," explains one student. "We'll have plenty of time to learn practical job skills, but this is the only time many of us will have the leisure to study theoretical issues in the law." The recently revamped legal writing curriculum is "more than sufficient," and "No law school in America has access to more prestigious practitioners." "Leading lawyers teach practical courses, and clinics get access to all types of activities," applauds one 3L. "Couple that with a top-notch reputation, and you have the best law school in the world."

The "eclectic" faculty at Columbia is "an incredible array of superstars," and otherwise "really talented, motivated, interested, and interesting people." There are "a lot of young, dynamic, and engaging professors," and most "seem to consider their students their primary concern." "Even those who are fiercely Socratic and would grill students in class are quite friendly outside of it." Professors are "respectful of differing political views." There is a "willingness to openly discuss" gender and race issues in class "in a way that is nonprejudicial but still acknowledges and values differences."

The "ineffective" and "very bureaucratic" administration at CLS is "positively frustrating." "They treat you like a walking dollar sign and nothing more," charges one annoyed student. "Signing up for classes is too hard." "Student Services has cultivated an amazing air of indifference and sometimes disdain for students." "The only way I got the Housing Office to tell me I had an apartment the day before moving was to sic a law school dean on them," claims a student.

Career prospects are dreamy. "A Columbia degree opens countless doors." "The 'big law' opportunities couldn't be better." "If you come here, you will get a job," agrees a confident 1L, "no matter how well or poorly you do." "Law firms around the country are banging down my door and begging me to work at their firm for six-figure salaries," says another student. "It's unbelievable how mediocre you can be at Columbia and yet have any law firm job in the country." There is "a stellar Public Interest Office" as well, and "small pockets of students" are "extraordinarily dedicated to public interest and other alternative legal careers."

The "overly modern" law school facilities are "highly functional," but "ugly, especially in comparison to the undergrad campus." On the outside, the building is "a postmodern mistake." Inside, the "elegant, sleek" classrooms are "equipped with the latest technology." The "soulless and depressing" library is "not very comfortable." "The research librarians are gods," though, and students "have access to resources most people don't even know exist."

Life

"It turns out that (almost) everybody here gets a B or B-plus." "Even a B reflects a lot of hard work." "Everyone is competitive," but at the same time, "People are happy to share notes." "Although there is a small public interest community, it is dwarfed by the majority of students who want nothing more than high-paying big-firm jobs." "Most people are only passing through on their way to a six- or seven-figure salary."

NKONYE IWEREBON, DEAN OF ADMISSIONS
435 WEST 116TH STREET, BOX A-3, NEW YORK, NY 10027
TEL: 212-854-2670 FAX: 212-854-1109
EMAIL: ADMISSIONS@LAW.COLUMBIA.EDU • WEBSITE: WWW.LAW.COLUMBIA.EDU

Some of these "future corporate lawyers" are "spoiled rich brats" who "do nothing but party." Others are "awkward and dull" types who "only see the outside of the library when they close it for breaks." But, "for the number of inflated egos, advanced degrees, and native New Yorkers in the law school, it is a remarkably collegial place," observes a 1L. "There is a lot of camaraderie" but the location in New York City makes it "much harder to build a community of people." "Students who are involved, engaged, and active tend to be very involved, very engaged, and very active (and thus, very stressed out), while the majority of students mostly do class work and keep their eyes on their future employment." "It is also extremely easy to become socially isolated if you are from a working-class family and attended a public university for undergrad."

Hometown New York City "is a huge asset." "You have to like urban environments," advises a 2L, "but if you are a city person, the location can't be beat. It is a great combination of a traditional campus and a big-city school." There is "substantial subsidization of housing" (once you wade through the red tape of the Housing Office), for which students are grateful. "You cannot find cheaper space in all of Manhattan." The number of events, debates, speeches, receptions and other social opportunities is "mind-boggling." "Naturally everyone's out in the city a lot."

Getting In

Good luck. Admitted students at the 25th percentile have LSAT scores of 169 and GPAs of just over 3.5. Admitted students at the 75th percentile have LSAT scores of 174 and GPAs of around 3.8. If you take the LSAT more than once, Columbia will consider all of your scores.

Clinical program required	No
Legal writing course requirement	Yes
Legal methods course requirement	Yes
Legal research course requirement	Yes
Moot court requirement	Yes
Public interest law requirement	Yes

ADMISSIONS

Selectivity Rating	**98**
# applications received	8,020
% applicants accepted	15
% acceptees attending	32
Average LSAT	170
LSAT Range	168–173
Average undergrad GPA	3.64
Application fee	$70
Regular application	Rolling, up to 2/15
Regular notification	Rolling
Early application program	Yes
Early application deadline	11/15
Early application notification	1/1
Transfer students accepted	Yes
Evening division offered	No
Part-time accepted	No
LSDAS accepted	Yes

Applicants Also Look At
Harvard University, Yale University, New York University

FINANCIAL FACTS

Annual tuition	$38,120
Books and supplies	$950
Fees	$1,052
Fees per credit	$1,906
Room & board (on-campus)	$16,951
Financial aid application deadline	3/1
% first-year students receiving some sort of aid	79
% receiving some sort of aid	84
% of aid that is merit based	35
% receiving scholarships	38
Average grant	$15,069
Average loan	$37,730
Average total aid package	$37,070
Average debt	$98,675

EMPLOYMENT INFORMATION

Career Rating	**94**
Rate of placement (nine months out)	99
Average starting salary	$145,000
State for bar exam	NY, NJ, CA, FL
Pass rate for first-time bar	90

Employers Who Frequently Hire Grads
Large international corporate law firms, federal judges, federal government agencies, and public interest organizations.

Prominent Alumni
Ruth Bader Ginsburg, Justice/U.S. Supreme Court; George Pataki, Governor/New York State; Franklin D. Roosevelt, former President of U.S.

Grads Employed by Field (%)
Academic (1)
Business/Industry (3)
Government (2)
Judicial Clerkships (9)
Private Practice (79)
Public Interest (6)

CORNELL UNIVERSITY
LAW SCHOOL

Academics

Cornell University is a small school with a big name. Thanks to this favorable combination, Cornell students enjoy a world-class education in the context of a personal, student-oriented environment. Across the board, "The professors at Cornell are top scholars in their respective fields" whose "prodigious academic accomplishments" are a significant asset to the classroom experience. What's more, most professors "are witty and make the classes worth getting up early for." Despite their impressive names and backgrounds, Cornell professors invest a lot of time and energy into their roles as teachers and mentors. A 2L insists, "The faculty is focused on teaching, not only publishing, and are clearly the greatest asset at Cornell Law School."

While Cornell boasts the high level of scholarship one would expect to find at a top school, "The close relationship between faculty and students is what sets Cornell apart from its peers." There are few lecture halls at Cornell, and "Small class sizes allow professors to really get to know students." Outside of class, professors are available for academic assistance, mentorship, and advice. "It is an honor to have classes and discussions with my professors. I have never had anyone here meet my questions without enthusiasm or support," gushes one student. Don't mistake kindness for laxness. Cornell is tough, and students caution that "professors drive us hard." In fact, students are constantly scrambling to keep up with the demands of their educations. A 2L recalls that "Last year, I definitely spent more than nine hours a day studying outside of class."

It is unanimously agreed that "Cornell's strength is in its size," but there's a flip side to that coin, for students point out that Cornell's course offerings are narrower than they would likely be if the school were larger. In addition, since "The faculty is too small, we end up with way too many visiting professors." Still, for many students "small seminars with current topics make up for an otherwise small range of classes." In addition, Cornell provides a number of first-rate programs and opportunities within the law school and the greater university. In particular, many students mention the school's excellent international law program: "If you're interested in international law with a European focus, this is the place to be," advises one student. "The school is also adding to its international program by offering new classes in Asian law (e.g., Japanese law)." On top of that, Cornell students say they really benefit from their affiliation with the greater university. For example, "Cornell has a wide range of non–law school classes" for which law students are able to sign up. "A small community within a large university means that professors and students aren't stretched too thin, but we have ample opportunity for a broad curriculum if we try hard enough," is how one student puts it.

When it comes to the administration, students report that "Cornell is run like a well-oiled machine . . . everything is done quickly and efficiently." Another major benefit to a Cornell education is that the school enjoys "name recognition in NYC," and as a result, "Across the board, Cornell graduates seem to get the very best jobs." Students say that "Cornell's career office is amazing—knowledgeable, accessible, and well connected. I have absolutely no complaints. I just got my dream job for the summer—and most of my classmates will say the same thing." Some students would, however, like to see more connections in public interest firms, as well as outside of New York.

Life

Cornell attracts ambitious, interesting, and accomplished students who "come from all walks of life and experience." For at least one student, "My classmates are the most uni-

SARAH LEVY, ASSISTANT DIRECTOR OF ADMISSIONS
226 MYEARON TAYLOR HALL, ITHACA, NY 14853-4901
TEL: 607-255-5141 FAX: 607-255-7193
EMAIL: LAWADMIT@POSTOFFICE.LAW.CORNELL.EDU • WEBSITE: WWW.LAWSCHOOL.CORNELL.EDU

formly intelligent and ambitious group of which I've ever been a member." Despite their personal accomplishments and drive, "Students are cooperative. Everyone feels they are in this together and there is no point in trying to knock one another down."

The campus vibe is friendly and social, and "The very active student organizations provide numerous non-academic opportunities." That's good, since "Students here are uniformly amiable and like spending time together" even to the exclusion of other members of the Cornell community; "The majority of law students socialize only with other law students," reports one student.

Consider yourself warned: "People are warm; weather is cold" in Ithaca, NY. Indeed, if there is one resounding complaint among Cornell students, it is that "Ithaca is an isolated college town." Students joke that the best way to improve the atmosphere at Cornell would be to "put the whole school in a bio-dome and turn up the heat and sunshine." However, one student aptly adds, "Everyone knew that before they came here. [There is] not much night life to speak of, but that's not what I am here for." Students make the best of the situation, however, informing us that "Cornell is beautiful [and] it's a great place to study for the lack of distraction."

Getting In

Admissions to Cornell is highly competitive. The Admissions Committee weighs all aspects of an applicant's background, including extracurricular and community activities, graduate work, LSAT scores, letters of recommendation, and undergraduate transcripts. Applicants are also encouraged to submit a separate document that details how their ethnic, cultural, or linguistic background will contribute to the diversity of the school community.

Public interest law requirement	No

ADMISSIONS

Selectivity Rating	**95**
# applications received	4,172
% applicants accepted	23
% acceptees attending	20
Average LSAT	167
LSAT Range	165–168
Average undergrad GPA	3.7
Application fee	$70
Regular application	Rolling, up to 2/1
Regular notification	Rolling
Early application program	No
Transfer students accepted	Yes
Evening division offered	No
Part-time accepted	No
LSDAS accepted	Yes

FINANCIAL FACTS

Annual tuition	$40,580
Books and supplies	$850
Room & board	$10,300
Financial aid application deadline	3/15
% receiving some sort of aid	80
% receiving scholarships	50

EMPLOYMENT INFORMATION

Career Rating	**93**	**Grads Employed by Field (%)**
Rate of placement (nine months out)	99	Academic (4)
Average starting salary	$125,000	Business/Industry (3)
State for bar exam	NY	Government (2)
Pass rate for first-time bar	94	Judicial Clerkships (9)
		Private Practice (72)
		Public Interest (2)
		Other (1)

CREIGHTON UNIVERSITY
SCHOOL OF LAW

Academics

Small Creighton University School of Law boasts a "solid reputation" "in the Midwest" and a "strong" alumni network. Students note that "the practical experience that you receive at Creighton is beyond comparison." "The practical aspects of the legal profession are stressed in every class" so that Creighton's graduates "can be effective in the legal world from the start." "A variety of trial practice courses" is available. Nebraska's Supreme Court "holds a session at the law school" each year for students to observe. Justice Clarence Thomas has co-taught a "truly remarkable" Supreme Court Seminar here. There is "a required moot court competition in the second year," and many students "participate in traveling moot court and trial teams." "Look at the results for any of the trial competitions in the nation, and you will find Creighton University near the top," guarantees a 3L. "Creighton is the place for you" if you are "interested in becoming a trial lawyer." Creighton also offers "a broad range of classes" (though it "could offer a broader selection of class times"). Some students confide that the legal writing program "isn't the greatest."

Expect "a great deal of hard work." "The teachers are hard; the reading is difficult," says one student. But take heart in the "wonderful and insightful" faculty. The vast majority of professors are "outstanding," "incredibly dedicated," and "capable teachers" who are "well-versed in all of their subjects." They "display a true passion for the subjects they teach, and that passion seems infectious." "Creighton professors really care that students learn the law and understand how to apply it." Here, the "very accessible" faculty "know you by name." "Professors are involved in the student organizations and often attend the student activities." "'Faculty row'" provides an all-access pass to law students. "The school's open-door policy really is an open-door policy," adds a student. "Your tuition dollars definitely buy you the right to extract knowledge from the professors."

The "very genuine and welcoming" administrators are "exceptionally devoted to catering to their students' needs." "They really care about the students as individuals" and "You're treated like a person, not just a number." Career Services is more of a mixed bag. Some students tell us that "opportunities for Creighton grads upon graduation seem excellent." "Everyone I know is employed," says one student. "Some have judicial clerkships; some are working for large corporations; and many are working for large firms." Other students complain that Career Services "is very unhelpful" and say that there is "almost no recognition outside of Omaha, especially out west."

Most students agree that the facilities "need to be updated." The building "was built in the 1970s and could use a makeover," says one student. "Some of the classrooms have been updated but the rest of them badly need renovating." The "somewhat drab" and "windowless" "main teaching halls" are "out of date." Also, "Some of the classrooms only have a few electrical outlets, which makes using a laptop difficult." On the plus side, "very reliable" wireless Internet "is available throughout the law school." Also, the "new and beautiful" library is "phenomenal."

ANDREA D. BASHARA, ASSISTANT DEAN
2500 CALIFORNIA PLAZA, OMAHA, NE 68178
TEL: 402-280-2586 FAX: 402-280-3161
EMAIL: LAWADMIT@CREIGHTON.EDU • WEBSITE: LAW.CREIGHTON.EDU

Life

Let's face it: Nebraska is "a very homogeneous state." Ethnic diversity is largely "non-existent" at Creighton. Students say the population is "mostly upper-middle-class White students." Geographically, many states are represented, though "Most students are from the Midwest—Nebraska and Iowa mostly." Students "range from ultra-competitive and pretentious all the way down to careless and unkempt." Politics aren't much of a big deal here. "The students are a lot less politically active than I anticipated," professes a 2L.

"Small class sizes help you have more individual contact with your teachers," explains one student. Thanks to this, "You get to really know all of your classmates" as well. Life at Creighton is "competitive," but "It's a very positive environment." "The students want to do well but not at the expense of others," says one student. Most happily report that "students are generally cooperative and easy to get along with." "Most people here are extremely friendly" as "that good old Midwestern hospitality" pervades, meaning that "everyone really gets along quite well." However, some note that social life can tend to have "many cliques," making it a bit "like going back to high school again."

Creighton students are a hardworking crowd, but "opportunities to be involved" socially are ample. "There is always something going on" and "almost everyone is always busy." "There are several student groups to get involved in" and "multiple out-of-school functions, which large portions of the student body attend." The Student Bar Association holds a solid number of "drink fests." Creighton's "gorgeous urban campus" in "downtown Omaha" provides "a pleasant metropolitan setting." "Creighton is not located in the best part of Omaha" and students note that "you have to be careful...off campus." However, students are confident that this will be a thing of the past as "the school and city are making great efforts to improve the area."

Getting In

Creighton's admitted students at the 25th percentile have LSAT scores of 151 and GPAs of 3.17. Admitted students at the 75th percentile have LSAT scores of 156 and GPAs of 3.67.

Moot court requirement	Yes
Public interest law requirement	No

ADMISSIONS

Selectivity Rating	71
# applications received	1,092
# applicants accepted	622
# acceptees attending	159
Average LSAT	154
LSAT Range	151–156
Average undergrad GPA	3.43
Application fee	$45
Regular application	Rolling, up to 5/1
Regular notification	Rolling
Early application program	No
Transfer students accepted	Yes
Evening division offered	No
Part-time accepted	Yes
LSDAS accepted	Yes

Applicants Also Look At
University of Nebraska—Lincoln, Saint Louis University, Drake University

International Students

TOEFL recommended of international students	Yes

FINANCIAL FACTS

Annual tuition	$27,042
Books and supplies	$3,055
Fees	$1,290
Fees per credit	$24
Tuition per credit	$900
Room & board	$13,500
Financial aid application deadline	7/1
% first-year students receiving some sort of aid	94
% receiving some sort of aid	96
% of aid that is merit based	13
% receiving scholarships	51
Average grant	$9,752
Average loan	$38,045
Average total aid package	$40,319
Average debt	$99,045

EMPLOYMENT INFORMATION

Career Rating	74
Rate of placement (nine months out)	89.04
Average starting salary	$60,000
State for bar exam	NE, IA, AZ, CO, TX
Pass rate for first-time bar	91

Employers Who Frequently Hire Grads
Kutak Rock; Stinson, Morrison, & Hecker; Blackwell, Sanders, Peper, & Martin; Shughart, Thompson, & Kilroy; McGrath & North; Fraser & Stryker; Baird & Holm; Koley & Jessen.

Prominent Alumni
Michael O. Johanns, United States Senator; Brig. Gen. David G. Ehrhart, Assistant Judge Advocate General for Military Law.

Grads Employed by Field (%)
Private Practice (51)
Business/Industry (19)
Government (22)
Judicial Clerkships (5)
Public Interest (1)
Military (3)

DePaul University
College of Law

Academics

The College of Law at DePaul University is home to a slew of highly respected professors and satisfied students. "Every time I tell someone I go to DePaul they perk up," says one student. With six law schools located in Chicago, "There is a lot of concern among the students regarding summer employment positions and finding permanent positions upon completion of school" (though the same could be said of law school students in many big cities), and therefore many are thrilled with the "alumni connections" provided by the school. One student explains, "DePaul has a great reputation for being a law family. With all the time I spend at the law school, they really are!"

DePaul's "amazing" faculty "truly represent a global viewpoint," and many are "distinguished practitioners within the Chicago legal community." "Most of the professors love their job, and it shows," explains one student, and this is evidenced by their accessibility outside of the classroom. A large number of students speak highly of the vastly differing instruction methods used by DePaul teachers, and cite these "very different teaching styles and personalities" as a unique academic resource, though the rule of thumb that "you'll always have one you don't like" seems to ring true here. Even with such a diverse range of techniques, one thing is always clear: DePaul's "inspiring" professors are "dedicated to making sure the students grasp the relevant concepts and material." As one 1L puts it, "No one is out to embarrass us, though that doesn't mean we aren't challenged!"

The administration also receives widespread praise for being "extremely helpful and always available" and "taking the time out to make sure that students' concerns are answered," as well as keeping students up to date on "all academic support program activities at the school and at other local schools." Many students also mentioned the "very hands-on" Admissions Office, which even employs student help "to give a unique perspective to potential and incoming students." Student input is valued very highly in other areas of DePaul life; the "wonderful professor review" at the end of each semester is taken very seriously, and helps keep the faculty at the top of their game.

Since the facilities "are subject to the limitations of a high-rise in downtown Chicago," the law school building "can be a little bit cramped at times," and the "terrible" classrooms are "not spacious" and "can be depressing to be in." "It's a confusing building. After four months, I still can't find certain places," says one exasperated 1L. Many complaints are also directed at the Career Services Office and the "frustrating" legal writing program, which needs "more exact instruction" and offers "little-to-zero appropriate feedback" from which "students are able to learn from their mistakes." It's a tough legal environment, to be sure, but one 3L seems to sum up the sentiments of his peers when he says: "If I did it over again, I wouldn't change anything."

Life

Students speak fondly of each other and claim not to have noticed any undue competitive streak amongst their classmates. "You won't find anyone hiding books in the library so only they have access to it," says one. Though there is "a helpful, polite competitiveness" amongst the student body, it's "more of a fun competition between classmates." People "freely share outlines with one another," "post jokes, helpful study aids they have found, etc. on the section blackboard," and "It is noticeable that everyone cares about each other and has a genuine desire to support and encourage each other." Students find it easy to make friends; one first-year student "likes to think it is because...DePaul attracts

MICHAEL S. BURNS, ASSOCIATE DEAN & DIRECTOR OF ADMISSION
25 EAST JACKSON BOULEVARD, CHICAGO, IL 60604
TEL: 312-362-6831 FAX: 312-362-5280
EMAIL: LAWINFO@DEPAUL.EDU • WEBSITE: WWW.LAW.DEPAUL.EDU

a certain type of student." "The school is committed to diversity and maintains its goal," making for a solid group of people committed to their studies and to helping each other do well.

"As an urban school, there's not a lot of hanging out after class, though most of us do end up at local bars at some point or other throughout the week," says a 1L. The school itself is located "close to both federal and county courthouses" as well as "a variety of social activities such as the art institute and millennium park." As one student declares, "Everything is here...[and there is] lots of opportunity to do stuff while going to school." The school's unbeatable location combined with students' contentment with the academics creates a "colloquial atmosphere," and "Everyone in a section becomes almost like a family." Luckily there are "only a few who think that they are god's gift to lawyering."

Getting In

Students admitted for the class of 2011 at the 25th percentile had an LSAT score of 158 and an average GPA of 3.4, while admitted students at the 75th percentile had an LSAT score of 162 and a GPA of 3.62. Like many schools, DePaul offers rolling admissions, but first-year students may only be admitted for the fall semester.

Clinical program required	No
Legal writing course requirement	Yes
Legal methods course requirement	No
Legal research course requirement	Yes
Moot court requirement	No
Public interest law requirement	No

ADMISSIONS

Selectivity Rating	83
# applications received	4,346
# applicants accepted	1,476
# acceptees attending	233
Average LSAT	161
LSAT Range	158–162
Average undergrad GPA	3.4
Application fee	$60
Regular application	Rolling, up to 3/1
Regular notification	Rolling
Early application program	No
Transfer students accepted	Yes
Evening division offered	Yes
Part-time accepted	Yes
LSDAS accepted	Yes

Applicants Also Look At
University of Illinois at Urbana-Champaign, Illinois Institute of Technology

International Students

TOEFL required of international students	Yes
Minimum TOEFL (paper/computer)	600/250

FINANCIAL FACTS

Annual tuition	$35,400
Books and supplies	$1,280
Fees	$441
Fees per credit	$100
Tuition per credit	$1,160
Room & board	$20,975
Financial aid application deadline	4/1
% first-year students receiving some sort of aid	96
% receiving some sort of aid	94
% of aid that is merit based	16
% receiving scholarships	62
Average grant	$12,216
Average loan	$38,710
Average total aid package	$43,148
Average debt	$104,459

EMPLOYMENT INFORMATION

Career Rating	78
Rate of placement (nine months out)	95
Average starting salary	$75,331
State for bar exam	IL, CA, NY, MO, WI
Pass rate for first-time bar	92

Employers Who Frequently Hire Grads
Bell Boyd & Lloyd; Chapman and Cutler; Hinshaw & Culbertson; Kirkland & Ellis; Vedder Price; Winston & Strawn; Cook County State's Attorney's Office.

Prominent Alumni
Richard M. Daley, Mayor, City of Chicago; Benjamin Hooks, Former Exec Dir NAACP; 2007 Pres. Medal of Freedom; Frank Clark, President, ComEd.

Grads Employed by Field (%)
Judicial Clerkships (1)
Private Practice (62)
Business/Industry (19)
Government (12)
Public Interest (5)
Academic (2)
Military (1)

DRAKE UNIVERSITY
LAW SCHOOL

INSTITUTIONAL INFORMATION

Public/private	Private
Student-faculty ratio	13:1
% faculty part-time	40
% faculty female	35
% faculty minority	13
Total faculty	51

SURVEY SAYS...

Diverse opinions accepted in classrooms
Great research resources
Great library staff
Abundant externship/internship/clerkship opportunities

STUDENTS

Enrollment of law school	445
% male/female	58/42
% out-of-state	40
% full-time	98
% minority	12
# of countries represented	3
Average age of entering class	24

ACADEMICS

Academic Experience Rating	**76**
Profs interesting rating	77
Profs accessible rating	82
Hours of study per day	4.01

Academic Specialties

Constitutional law, international law, intellectual property law, agricultural law, legislative practice, litigation and dispute resolution, health law

Advanced Degrees Offered

JD, 3 years

Combined Degrees Offered

JD/MBA; JD/MPA; JD/PharmD; JD/MA Poli. Sci.; JD/MS Ag. Econ.; JD/MSW

Clinical program required	No
Legal writing course requirement	Yes
Legal methods course requirement	Yes
Legal research course requirement	Yes

Academics

Drake University's Law School "prides itself on educating practical lawyers," through an approach which contented students say offers "the perfect balance of academic tradition and excellence." Much of Drake's teaching methodology "is focused on effective lawyering" instead of law theory. A second-year student sums up Drake's unique approach eloquently: "Other schools graduate theoretically sound students of the law; Drake graduates lawyers."

Most of Drake's faculty members have worked within their respective fields, which is "readily apparent in their pragmatic approach to teaching." Students cite professors' practical experience and open-door policies as two of the school's greatest strengths. Students "spend a lot of time learning how to do research, how to write, and how to convey ideas in the best manner possible"—a simple enough course of study that often gets needlessly complicated at other law schools. "The professors are truly concerned that you not only know the material for an exam but that you comprehend the material for your career," says one 2L. They also take the time to "get to know students on a first-name basis as well as [learn about] our interests both in and out of the classroom." A first-year student even tells of a torts professor who "brought in all kinds of canned and boxed food for the kids who couldn't make it home for Thanksgiving. This was of course to prevent them from having a lonely Thanksgiving dinner of Beef-a-roni like he had to do as a 1L!"

Drake's "knowledgeable and experienced" administrators are "unbelievably accessible" and "always stop to say hello." However, some students claim that they can be "frequently rigid about course offerings and credits," and wish there was more flexibility allowed in the adding and dropping of courses. The first-year curriculum is known for its intensity and its "huge emphasis on writing," but many students cite visits from Supreme Court Justices and Drake's "one-of-a-kind" trial practicum program (which allows students to observe an actual trial at the school's legal clinic) as first-year high points. Drake also recently "totally reinvented" its Career Development Department, which now sets up on-campus interviews with recruiters from several top firms in the surrounding area. As a result, job opportunities are "much more available [now] than in the past," though some still think the school could stand to benefit from "greater exposure outside of the Midwest job market."

Though Drake's campus "is functional but definitely not overly aesthetically pleasing," the school's "expansive" facilities received universal commendations for being "state of the art, fully electronic, with wireless network access campus wide," and for having a "good variance on classroom size that allows for small classes and survey courses." The library is "impressive in resources"—one student calls it the "highlight of the school"—and the school's location in the capital city of Des Moines "presents many opportunities for networking and clerkships."

Life

"Relations amongst students are what make Drake." The "collegial environment" provides a "helpful and healthy place to study and learn." "Cutthroat, competition-type behavior is virtually unheard of"—"There is always someone who will send notes if you miss a class." The school's "supportive" atmosphere is palpable from day one: "On our first day of orientation, instead of telling us to look to our right and our left and that at least one of us would be gone by graduation, the dean told us that these individuals would one day be our colleagues," says a first-year student.

KARA BLANCHARD, DIRECTOR OF ADMISSIONS AND FINANCIAL AID
2507 UNIVERSITY AVENUE, DES MOINES, IA 50311
TEL: 515-271-2782 FAX: 515-271-1990
EMAIL: LAWADMIT@DRAKE.EDU • WEBSITE: WWW.LAW.DRAKE.EDU

Moot court requirement	Yes
Public interest law requirement	No

ADMISSIONS

Selectivity Rating	**74**
# applications received	1,172
% applicants accepted	48
% acceptees attending	29
Average LSAT	155
LSAT Range	153–157
Average undergrad GPA	3.4
Application fee	$50
Regular application	Rolling
Regular notification	Rolling
Early application program	No
Transfer students accepted	Yes
Evening division offered	No
Part-time accepted	Yes
LSDAS accepted	Yes

Applicants Also Look At
Marquette University, DePaul University, Creighton University, University of Iowa, Hamline University

International Students

TOEFL required of international students	Yes
Minimum TOEFL (paper/computer/web)	560/220/80

FINANCIAL FACTS

Annual tuition	$28,850
Books and supplies	$1,300
Fees	$436
Tuition per credit	$1,000
Room & board (off-campus)	$15,400
Financial aid application deadline	3/1
% first-year students receiving some sort of aid	98
% receiving some sort of aid	98
% receiving scholarships	60
Average grant	$13,675
Average loan	$28,846
Average total aid package	$42,500
Average debt	$82,380

With all of the classes located in one building (which is connected to the library) "It is very convenient to study between classes without losing a lot of time trekking around campus." The small size of the school "allows students to get to know one another well," and "It is not uncommon to be friendly with everyone in the law school." Fortunately, life at Drake isn't all work and no play. Aside from the "plethora of organizations to join," there is an official social event once a week where the majority of students "get together and enjoy each other's company outside of the law school," as well as "a popular law school fraternity that provides additional social opportunities for students." Concerned about the Des Moines winters? Take your cues from one third-year student who says, "If you haven't been to Iowa, you're missing out; where else can it be 50 degrees one day and negative 10 the next!"

Getting In

Though the admit rate at Drake is higher than at most law schools, the significant number of enrolled out-of-staters in a relatively sparsely populated state is a testament to Iowa's increasing popularity (and increasing selectivity). Last year's admitted students at the 25th percentile had an LSAT score of 154 and an average GPA of 3.1, while admitted students at the 75th percentile had an LSAT score of 157 and a GPA of 3.6. Though admission decisions are made on a rolling basis, applicants are strongly encouraged to submit application materials early.

EMPLOYMENT INFORMATION

Career Rating	**78**	**Grads Employed by Field (%)**
Rate of placement (nine months out)	93.8	Business/Industry (22)
Average starting salary	$61,381	Government (11)
State for bar exam	IA	Military (1)
Pass rate for first-time bar	90	

Prominent Alumni
Dwight D. Opperman, CEO Publishing Company; Chief Justice Marcia Ternus, Iowa Supreme Court; Robert Ray, Former Governor; Terry Branstad, Former Governor; General Russell Davis, Head of U.S. National Guard.

DUKE UNIVERSITY
SCHOOL OF LAW

INSTITUTIONAL INFORMATION

Public/private	Private
Student-faculty ratio	12:1
% faculty part-time	33
% faculty female	41
% faculty minority	4
Total faculty	92

SURVEY SAYS...

Diverse opinions accepted in classrooms
Great research resources
Abundant externship/internship/ clerkship opportunities

STUDENTS

% full-time	100
Average age of entering class	25

ACADEMICS

Academic Experience Rating	**94**
Profs interesting rating	87
Profs accessible rating	93
Hours of study per day	3.77

Academic Specialties
no formal specializations; see below for areas of significant strength.

Advanced Degrees Offered
JD 3 years; LL.M 1 year, for international students only; SJD 1 year, for international students only

Combined Degrees Offered
JD/LLM in International & Comparative Law, 3.5 years; JD/MA, 3.5 years in Art History, Cultural Anthropology, East Asian Studies, Economics, Engineering Management, English, Environmental Science and Policy, History, Humanities, Literature, Philosophy, Political Science, Religion, Romance Studies, Sociology; JD/MS, 3.5 years in Biomedical Engineering, Electrical and Computer Engineering, Mechanical Engineering; JD/MBA, JD/MPP, JD/MEM, JD/MTS, 4 years

Clinical program required	No
Legal writing course requirement	Yes

Academics

The highly regarded School of Law at Duke University provides an "extremely unique academic environment" in which the students unquestionably "get [their] money's worth." The small size of the law school "allows for a great deal of interaction with faculty and a small community feel." Students also speak of the benefits of "not being pegged as a 'New York' school or a 'California' school." This allows them to "go anywhere for jobs." Under the instructional guidance of a "wide array of legal rock stars," Duke's graduates become a part of an "incredible network of successful individuals." With fewer than 200 students per class and no plans to expand, the school's small size also makes grads "a novelty in the legal market," though some students speak of a lack of assistance for those who want to pursue nontraditional legal careers or jobs at smaller firms.

"Accessible" seems to be the foremost trait of the knowledgeable faculty at Duke Law School. "I think most of my classmates, including myself, have been to at least one of our professors' homes for dinner," says one 2L. Though many students wish for "a more diverse faculty," students across the board rave about professors' open-door policies and "special interest in helping you succeed." Instructors "are proud to be a part of the Duke community," and it shows in their teaching. "My constitutional law professor from last year is now the advisor on my independent study, and he treats me like I'm a client—he always e-mails me back within a few hours, which is nuts since he always happens to be arguing in front of the Supreme Court!" Though the first year of classes follow the typical curriculum for beginning law students, 2Ls and 3Ls "have the opportunity to take a broad a range of classes." Duke also offers a wide variety of solid clinics, pro bono opportunities, and a lunchtime speaker series "full of notable speakers flying in to talk."

There is a great deal of warmth for those who run the school itself, and their devotion to the school's message of learning does not go unnoticed. "Our [former] dean and her husband [also a professor at the law school] gave $100,000 of their own money to start a Loan Repayment Assistance Program endowment," offers a 3L as evidence. Student satisfaction "appears to be the highest priority of the administration," and administrators solicit student input "in everything from website design to selecting a new dean to shaping admissions policies." The administration's receptiveness "to student-initiated change" gives students "a real sense of ownership" in the school.

"If law school is the smart person's incubator, then I am happily incubated," says one 2L, happily describing the law school's facilities. The "beautiful" law building was just redone last year and includes state-of-the-art classrooms equipped with wireless Internet and personal power plug-ins, and this technology is "seamlessly integrated into the teaching and learning," making the building a "very comfortable place to spend time."

Life

Surprisingly for a law school of Duke's caliber, the level of competition among students is minimal: "I expected law school to be cutthroat and somewhat evil, to be honest. It's the exact opposite here," attests a second-year student. "We joke amongst ourselves regularly about how we must be the 'Kumbaya' law school." This "fosters a tremendous sense of community throughout the school," and "No one even thinks of being a psycho and hiding books." One student speculates on the reasoning behind this "collegial" and "supportive" environment: "We all know there are enough employers coming to hire us that we do not need to employ cutthroat tactics to steal jobs from our

WILLIAM J. HOYE, ASSOCIATE DEAN FOR ADMISSIONS AND STUDENT AFFAIRS
PO BOX 90393, DURHAM, NC 27708-0393
TEL: 919-613-7020 FAX: 919-613-7257
EMAIL: ADMISSIONS@LAW.DUKE.EDU • WEBSITE: ADMISSIONS.LAW.DUKE.EDU

peers." However, the competitiveness inherent in students at a top-tier law school "is brought out on the softball field and in the bowling alley (we have the largest bowling league in North Carolina)."

Duke's location in Durham plays a key role in fostering the sense of community that its "down-to-earth" and "diversified" students applaud. "The lives of both students and faculty at Duke Law revolve around the law school—it is not like schools in major cities where people show up, come to class, and go home, never to see each other again," says a 2L. This "fun-loving" bunch "likes to go out, party, and have a good time," and the low cost of living means they can afford the "great restaurants, bars, arts, and nightlife" of the town, as well as those in nearby Raleigh. Taking all things into account, Duke is "a very pleasant place to go to school."

Getting In

Duke's 23 percent acceptance rate may be somewhat higher than expected for a top-tier law school that makes no bones about the fact that it wants only the best, most ambitious students. Students enrolling for the class of 2011 at the 25th percentile had an LSAT score of 165 and an average GPA of 3.55, while admitted students at the 75th percentile had an LSAT score of 170 and a GPA of 3.85. Be sure to complete the optional essay, and know that applications received earlier in the admissions process are at a distinct advantage.

Legal methods course requirement	Yes
Legal research course requirement	Yes
Moot court requirement	Yes
Public interest law requirement	No

ADMISSIONS

Selectivity Rating	**94**
# applications received	6,069
% applicants accepted	25
% acceptees attending	13
Average LSAT	169
LSAT Range	165–170
Average undergrad GPA	3.74
Application fee	$70
Regular application	Rolling
Regular notification	Rolling
Early application program	No
Transfer students accepted	Yes
Evening division offered	No
Part-time accepted	No
LSDAS accepted	Yes

International Students

TOEFL required of international students	Yes
Minimum TOEFL (paper)	600

FINANCIAL FACTS

Annual tuition	$39,960
Books and supplies	$1,140
Room & board (off-campus)	$9,180
Financial aid application deadline	3/15

EMPLOYMENT INFORMATION

Career Rating		**93**
State for bar exam	NY, NC, CA, MD, VA	
Pass rate for first-time bar		90

Grads Employed by Field (%)
Business/Industry (4)
Government (2)
Judicial clerkships (14)
Military (1)
Private practice (77)
Public Interest (2)

EMORY UNIVERSITY
SCHOOL OF LAW

INSTITUTIONAL INFORMATION

Public/private	Private
Affiliation	Methodist
Student-faculty ratio	11:1
% faculty part-time	42
% faculty female	38
% faculty minority	22
Total faculty	104

SURVEY SAYS...

Diverse opinions accepted
in classrooms
Great research resources
Great library staff
Abundant externship/internship/
clerkship opportunities
Students love Atlanta, GA

STUDENTS

Enrollment of law school	697
% male/female	52/48
% out-of-state	55
% full-time	100
% minority	28
% international	4
# of countries represented	23
Average age of entering class	24

ACADEMICS

Academic Experience Rating	92
Profs interesting rating	89
Profs accessible rating	82
Hours of study per day	4.51

Academic Specialties

Corporation securities, environmental law, human rights, international law, intellectual property law, health law, trial practice, law & religion, business law, comparative law, legal theory

Advanced Degrees Offered

LL.M., 1 year

Combined Degrees Offered

JD/MBA, 4 years; JD/MTS, 4 years; JD/MDIV, 5 years; JD/MPH, 3.5 years; JD/REES, 3 years; JD/PhD Religion, 7 years; JD/MA Judaic Studies, 4 years.

Academics

Emory University School of Law offers "an extremely strong brand name" that "allows for amazing networking opportunities and instant recognition." "Emory has wonderful connections in the city of Atlanta" and "opportunities to practice law in field placements and other internships" are "diverse." Emory students are "routinely" placed "with the Georgia Supreme Court, the U.S. Attorney's Office, the Eleventh Circuit Court of Appeals," and "major Atlanta-based corporations." A 3L explains, "If you are interested in intellectual property, Emory has a program that works with Georgia Tech to give you real experience." "If you are into criminal justice, Emory works with the Georgia Innocence Projects." The Turner Environmental Clinic and the Barton Child Law and Policy Clinic are "active and renowned." The "joint-degree program with the theology school" is "a very unique and prolific source of scholarship on a range of issues at the nexus of law and religion." Emory's "Feminist and Legal Theory project" garners more raves.

Professors here are described as "world class." "Emory Law's faculty is one of the best kept secrets of any top 30 law school," asserts one student. "They have a great sense of humor and seem to genuinely enjoy teaching." "The professors go the extra mile in terms of helping students network for clerkships and jobs with top firms." This "brilliant," "engaging," and "very dynamic" faculty "includes a couple of the world's foremost human rights scholars (one of whom is the preeminent scholar in Islamic law)." Students are split on Emory's administration. One faction says that the "friendly, approachable, and straightforward" administration is "on the ball" and "willing to listen to student concerns." Others say that those in the administration "take themselves too seriously." "The administration at Emory Law is herding cats with a spatula," offers one student. "They are attempting an impossible task in the manner least likely to succeed."

Career prospects for Emory Law grads "abound" in Atlanta and "The Emory degree also carries significant weight outside of Atlanta, especially along the entire East Coast." "The Emory degree has legs," affirms a 2L. "It can take you places. I'm going to Washington, DC to work with a great firm. I had offers as far away as Houston, and I'm not near the top 10 percent." "I haven't known people to have significant trouble getting jobs in the Northeast or elsewhere," adds another 2L. Nevertheless, "many students complain" that Career Services is Emory's "biggest weakness."

"The library is beautiful, but the classroom building needs a facelift," says one student. Emory's "stale," "bland," facilities are "uninspiring." "The classrooms are in dire need of some sprucing up," speculates a 2L. "White walls and windowless classrooms give the school an institutional feel." "It seems every year they paint the building, but students are not fooled." "The technology sucks," too, though the "law library is amazingly nice." It's "bright and open with lots of tables and study carrels." An insider's tip: "The trek to the undergraduate library, surprisingly, is worth it if you want quiet study."

Life

Students say "Emory draws an interesting mix of folks from both North and South (though not as many from the West)." "Long Island kids" and "conservative Southerners" create a "strange dichotomy" and an "extremely dynamic student body." There are students fresh out of college and those who "took some time off and are coming in with families or significant others." Politically, there is a "liberal bent," but you will find "various" viewpoints. Emory's "ambitious" students are "impossibly smart" and "focused." Many

LYNELL A. CADRAY, ASSISTANT DEAN FOR ADMISSION
1301 CLIFTON ROAD, ATLANTA, GA 30322-2770
TEL: 404-727-6801 FAX: 404-727-2477
EMAIL: LAWINFO@LAW.EMORY.EDU • WEBSITE: WWW.LAW.EMORY.EDU

are "outgoing" and "sociable." Others "stay hidden behind the books the whole semester and you don't even know they are there until they win many of the high-paying jobs." As good as Emory is, "not everyone is thrilled" to be here. "Some think they should be elsewhere" and "have a chip on their shoulder." But as one student explains, "Overall, the quality of students here is very high, and the reputation of the school will only continue to improve."

"Classes are small, so there is a strong sense of community." Emory can be "moderately competitive," though. "Some students are just downright nasty to each other," claims a 3L. "During first year, it is a very stressful environment." That said, most of the students are "congenial, helpful, and fun to go out with."

Social life at Emory is just swell. There is "an amazing Barrister's Ball" and "The Harvest Moon Ball Halloween party is a howling good time year after year." "We have weekly 'Bar Reviews' around Atlanta," explains one student. "Each Thursday we have a keg in 'Bacardi Plaza' (our atrium)." Atlanta is "an exciting place" and "a great city for 20-somethings." It's "the economic hub of the South," but at the same time it's "very affordable for students." "Having moved here from New York City, I'm shocked at how much Atlanta has to offer and how easy it is to get off campus and get lost in a genuinely cool city," declares a happy 1L.

Getting In

Emory Law receives more than 4,200 applications. The admitted students at the 25th percentile have LSAT scores of roughly 164 and GPAs of roughly 3.3. Admitted students at the 75th percentile have LSAT scores of about 166 and GPAs of about 3.6. Emory says that it will average scores if you take the LSAT more than once.

EMPLOYMENT INFORMATION

Career Rating	92	**Grads Employed by Field (%)**
Rate of placement (nine months out)	88.02	Business/Industry (7)
Average starting salary	$109,502	Government (10)
State for bar exam	GA	Judicial clerkships (13)
Pass rate for first-time bar	91.73	Private practice (65)
Prominent Alumni		Public Interest (4)
Hon. Sanford Bishop, U.S. Congressman;		Academic (1)

Hon. Leah Sears, Chief Justice, Georgia Supreme Court; Hon. Sam A. Nunn, U.S. Senator (ret.), CEO Nuclear Threat Initiative; Raymond McDaniel, CEO, Moody's Investor Services; C.

Clinical program required	No
Legal writing course requirement	Yes
Legal methods course requirement	Yes
Legal research course requirement	Yes
Moot court requirement	No
Public interest law requirement	No

ADMISSIONS

Selectivity Rating	**90**
# applications received	4,209
% applicants accepted	24
% acceptees attending	23
Average LSAT	164
LSAT Range	164–166
Average undergrad GPA	3.54
Application fee	$70
Regular application	Rolling, up to 3/1
Regular notification	Rolling
Early application program	No
Transfer students accepted	Yes
Evening division offered	No
Part-time accepted	No
LSDAS accepted	Yes

Applicants Also Look At
Boston University, Duke University, Vanderbilt University, Boston College, Fordham University, The George Washington University, Georgetown University

International Students

TOEFL required of international students	Yes
Minimum TOEFL (paper/computer)	600/250

FINANCIAL FACTS

Annual tuition	$39,300
Books and supplies	$6,056
Fees	$476
Room & board	$18,167
Financial aid application deadline	3/1
% first-year students receiving some sort of aid	95
% receiving some sort of aid	87
% of aid that is merit based	26
% receiving scholarships	39
Average grant	$19,247
Average loan	$38,100
Average total aid package	$42,110
Average debt	$109,475

FAULKNER UNIVERSITY*
THOMAS GOODE JONES SCHOOL OF LAW

INSTITUTIONAL INFORMATION

Public/private	Private
Student-faculty ratio	10:1
% faculty female	35
% faculty minority	12
Total faculty	26

SURVEY SAYS...

Heavy use of Socratic Method
Diverse opinions accepted
in classrooms
Great research resources
Great library staff

STUDENTS

Enrollment of law school	304
% male/female	62/38
% full-time	87
% minority	13
Average age of entering class	25

ACADEMICS

Academic Experience Rating	**72**
Profs interesting rating	84
Profs accessible rating	88
Hours of study per day	4.4

Academic Specialties

Civil procedure, commercial law, constitutional law, corporation securities, criminal law, environmental law, government services, human rights, international law, labor law, legal history, legal philosophy, property, taxation, intellectual property law, alternative dispute resolution

Clinical program required	No
Legal writing course requirement	Yes
Legal methods course requirement	No
Legal research course requirement	Yes
Moot court requirement	Yes
Public interest law requirement	No

Academics

Faulkner University's Jones School of Law in Montgomery, Alabama is "a Church of Christ–affiliated school" with "a non-intimidating environment." According to students here, it's "the best-kept secret in Alabama." The "bar-passage rate is very high;" in fact, students report that Faulkner has had "the highest bar-passage rate in the state of Alabama." "The trial advocacy program is top-notch." "The faculty and administration actually care about you as a person" and "make sure you have practical knowledge for the real world." Many appreciate that professors "treat them like a friend and not a subordinate." Some feel that Jones "could benefit from a broader curriculum." While the "small" campus can mean fewer opportunities, many students find that "the resources of the law school are growing everyday."

The many "very knowledgeable" and "distinguished" professors here "truly are a hidden gem." Their ranks include "some of the most experienced legal minds anywhere." They also "possess a great deal of real-world experience" and "give practical lessons about real-life lawyering." The faculty is pretty big on the "Socratic Method." A student explains that his torts professor "writes everyone's name on a playing card. Before class he draws three cards, and the three people have a roundtable discussion presenting the cases that were assigned. It is by far the most memorable first-year experience." "Small class sizes" "allow for greater participation" and "You are able to get to know your professors better." The intimacy "strongly encourages differing viewpoints and class discussion" as well. Professors here "truly care about your success and take an interest in your life outside of the classroom." "The amount of time each professor is willing to dedicate to each student never fails to impress me," agrees another student. "They genuinely want each student to succeed."

The "professional looking" facilities (featuring "marble and mahogany throughout") are "outstanding." There is also "Internet access throughout the school." "Every classroom is equipped with plenty of electrical outlets," notes one student. Nevertheless, an "increase in building size" would be good. Classrooms can "sometimes" get "very hot". "Regulate the temperature in the classrooms," urges a 1L. Most students would also like to see the library "open later hours."

The well-liked administration here is "always available and extremely helpful" It's worth noting that the Jones School of Law is currently provisionally approved by the American Bar Association. Provisional approval is an intermediate step between full approval and no approval. For students here, it basically means that they can take any bar exam in any state when they graduate just like graduates of all ABA-approved law schools."

* Provisionally approved by the ABA.

ANDREW R. MATHEWS, ASSISTANT DEAN FOR STUDENT SERVICES
5345 ATLANTA HIGHWAY, MONTGOMERY, AL 36109
TEL: 334-386-7210 FAX: 334-386-7908
EMAIL: LAW@FAULKNER.EDU • WEBSITE: WWW.FAULKNER.EDU/LAW

Life

"There is a definite sense of community" since "Everyone knows everyone," but students insist that "that's a plus." At the same time, "There is a competitive environment, but that's what the real world is like." "We are all in this struggle together, and we help each other to survive," explains a 3L. "This includes saving someone who is drowning in class when briefing a case or forming study groups for exams." Faulkner University is definitively "Christian oriented," and overall, it's "a very conservative campus." The law school is "extremely conservative" as well, but people who aren't on the political right feel welcome here. "Even though I am very liberal and a bit outside the norm, the faculty and staff do not attempt to curtail my individuality," comments a 3L. "I do not hesitate to be vocal in my opinions and viewpoints (both in and out of class) and have never had any repercussions."

Ethnic diversity "leaves a lot to be desired." However, students do say that their peers "come from all strata of society and bring varying perspectives based upon their personal, professional and educational experiences." "There are people that are directly out of college as well as people that have been out of undergrad for 15 to 20 years," explains one student.

Outside of class, there are "seminars, speakers," and "even school parties," but students feel "There should be a few more social opportunities, especially on the weekends." Many students are active in church. "I play basketball with friends," says an athletic 2L. "We also play flag football and get together for poker and other events to take our minds off school."

Getting In

Admitted students at the 25th percentile have LSAT scores of 147 and GPAs of 2.79. Admitted students at the 75th percentile have LSAT scores of 153 and GPAs of 3.28. If you take the LSAT more than once, Faulkner will use your highest score.

ADMISSIONS

Selectivity Rating	**64**
# applications received	589
# applicants accepted	323
# acceptees attending	126
Average LSAT	150
LSAT Range	147–153
Average undergrad GPA	3.03
Application fee	$30
Regular application	Rolling, up to 6/15
Regular notification	Rolling
Early application program	No
Transfer students accepted	Yes
Evening division offered	No
Part-time accepted	No
LSDAS accepted	Yes

FINANCIAL FACTS

Annual tuition	$30,500
Books and supplies	$3,000
Fees	$370
Room & board (off-campus)	$12,000
Financial aid application deadline	7/15

EMPLOYMENT INFORMATION

Career Rating	**91**
Rate of placement (nine months out)	90
State for bar exam	AL, GA, FL, MS, TN
Pass rate for first-time bar	94

Prominent Alumni
Greg Allen, Partner of Beasley, Allen, et.al.; Patricia Smith, Associate Justice, Alabama Supreme Court; Ernestine Sapp, Partner of Gray, Langford, Sapp, et.al.; Bobby Bright, U.S. Congressman.

Grads Employed by Field (%)
Academic (2)
Business/Industry (7)
Government (11)
Judicial Clerkships (7)
Private Practice (71)
Public Interest (2)

FLORIDA INTERNATIONAL UNIVERSITY
COLLEGE OF LAW

INSTITUTIONAL INFORMATION

Public/private	Public
Student-faculty ratio	15:7
% faculty part-time	5
% faculty female	44
% faculty minority	53
Total faculty	36

SURVEY SAYS...

Diverse opinions accepted
in classrooms
Great research resources
Great library staff
Beautiful campus

STUDENTS

Enrollment of law school	542
% male/female	54/46
% out-of-state	5
% full-time	69
% minority	53
# of countries represented	24
Average age of entering class	25

ACADEMICS

Academic Experience Rating	**85**
Profs interesting rating	89
Profs accessible rating	76

Academic Specialties
international law, legal skills and
values

Combined Degrees Offered
JD/MSW (Master of Social Work),
4.5 years; JD/MPA (Master of Public
Administration), 3.5 years;
JD/MIB(Master of International
Business), 3.5 years; JD/MSPsych
(Master of Science in Psychology),
4 years; JD/MALACS(Master of
Latin America and Caribbean
Studies), 3.5 years; JD/MBA
(Master of Business
Administration), 4 years; JD/MSCS
(Master of Science in Criminal
Justice), 3 1/2 years.

Clinical program required	No
Legal writing	
course requirement	Yes

Academics

Florida International University College of Law is very new as far as law schools go. The first graduating class left for the real world in 2005, and the school received full accreditation from the American Bar Association in 2006. Students assure us that the future is bright, though, and they say that FIU has a lot to offer. There is an "excellent legal writing program." The moot court teams have enjoyed some success in regional and national competitions. Also, the four clinical programs here include an immigration and human rights clinic which allows students to represent real clients in political asylum and other immigration cases. Cost is another perk. This place is reportedly "one of the best deals in town financially," particularly for residents of the Sunshine State. "FIU's reasonable tuition allowed me to graduate with very little debt," a 3L says. "I couldn't be happier with my legal education." However, the "international focus in the curriculum" is probably the most unique feature here. True to its name, FIU tries to devote some time to global issues in every course. Additionally, first-year students must take an introductory course that covers international law and comparative law. There's an upper-level international law requirement, too, and students are able to choose from a fairly broad array of specialized electives to fulfill it.

"Classes sizes are not large" here. "The professors know your name," a 1L says, "which I feel is important." "The faculty is generally young, bright, and energetic." "They are all brilliant and come from a wide range of backgrounds," a 3L declares. Professors are "always available to meet outside of class," too. They "are very open to mentoring young (and old) law students." In the classroom, though, professors at FIU are either "inspiring" or "terrible." "There has been no middle ground," says a 2L. A few FIU students describe the administration as "very weak" and "unwilling to compromise." One student calls the mandatory attendance policy "strict and sometimes insulting." However, most students tell us that management is "awesome" and "extremely student-friendly." The staff "maintains an open door policy," they say. The dean is "easily approachable" and "always seen interacting with the students."

Florida International's location is helpful for students looking to network and gain practical experience. In additional to the "multitude of Miami firms" nearby, Florida's Third District Court of Appeals is "directly behind the school." The school has managed to build a decent local reputation in a short time as well. Several large firms participate in on-campus interviews. However, only graduates at the very top of the class are able to secure those really high-paying gigs and some students argue that Career Planning and Placement "could do a better job of getting students jobs." Also, the school remains very regional. Its good name doesn't really travel very well beyond the Florida state line. "It would help to get the word out there to the legal community so that more recruiters come to FIU," a 1L suggests.

The "brand new" law school itself is "beautiful." You would be hard pressed to find a spiffier building. It's "completely wireless," and students have access to "the latest technology." "The classrooms are state-of-the-art" and in "great shape." Research facilities are "fantastic." The library is "very conducive to studying." Nearly all here agree that "it's a pleasure to have such a great environment in which to learn and work."

ALMA O. MIRÓ, DIRECTOR OF ADMISSIONS AND FINANCIAL AID
FIU COLLEGE OF LAW, OFFICE OF ADMISSIONS AND FINANCIAL AID, RDB 1055, MIAMI, FL 33199
TEL: 305-348-8006 FAX: 305-348-2965
EMAIL: LAWADMIT@FIU.EDU • WEBSITE: LAW.FIU.EDU

Life

There is "a strong presence" of Latino students in particular, but you'll find people of every "race, nationality, and age" on campus. Students come from a wide range of backgrounds. "My colleagues at FIU make it a much broader experience," a 1L says. "Although there is an underlying competitiveness," a 3L explains, "the students generally get along great and really pull for each other." They help each other out, too, but "within limits."

The student population at FIU is "fairly small." Students are "close to each other" and the social environment outside of class is "very friendly." "There are student organizations for just about every interest you can think of," one student says. The "happy hour every week" is "well attended." The law school is "a bit far from the city," but the nightlife in and around Miami is unparalleled. Students boast that this "culture-filled" area is a "great" place to spend three years studying law.

Getting In

FIU Law is small and its acceptance rate is low, but the raw numbers of admitted applicants are on the lower side. Admitted students at the 25th percentile have LSAT scores in the low 150s and GPAs right at 3.0. Admitted students at the 75th percentile have LSAT scores in the mid 150s and GPAs a little over 3.6.

Legal methods	
course requirement	Yes
Legal research	
course requirement	Yes
Moot court requirement	No
Public interest	
law requirement	Yes

ADMISSIONS
Selectivity Rating	**78**
# applications received	2,507
# applicants accepted	651
# acceptees attending	211
Average LSAT	154
LSAT Range	152–156
Average undergrad GPA	3.34
Application fee	$20
Regular application	Rolling, up to 5/1
Regular notification	Rolling
Early application program	No
Transfer students accepted	Yes
Evening division offered	Yes
Part-time accepted	Yes
LSDAS accepted	Yes

Applicants Also Look At
Florida State University, University of Florida, Nova Southeastern University, University of Miami, St. Thomas University

International Students
TOEFL required	
of international students	Yes
Minimum TOEFL	
(paper/computer/web)	550/213/80

FINANCIAL FACTS
Annual tuition (in-state/ out-of-state)	$10,826/$25,070
Books and supplies	$2,480
Fees	$340
Tuition per credit (in-state/ out-of-state)	$350/$809
Room & board (on/off-campus)	$11,120/$16,532
Financial aid application deadline	3/1
% first-year students receiving some sort of aid	89
% receiving some sort of aid	87
% of aid that is merit based	14
% receiving scholarships	34
Average grant	$6,360
Average loan	$22,748
Average total aid package	$23,433

EMPLOYMENT INFORMATION

Career Rating	72	Grads Employed by Field (%)
Rate of placement (nine months out)	90	Business/Industry (15)
Average starting salary	$63,681	Government (17)
State for bar exam	FL	Judicial Clerkships (5)
Pass rate for first-time bar	79	Private Practice (51)

Employers Who Frequently Hire Grads
Dade County State Attorney's Office; Astigarraga Davis; Holland and Knight; Greenberg Traurig; Squire Sanders and Dempsey; Dade County Public Defende.

Prominent Alumni
Doug Giuliano, Associate Attorney, Astigarraga Davis; Mauricio Rivero, Associate Attorney, Holland and Knight.

Public Interest (9)

FLORIDA STATE UNIVERSITY
COLLEGE OF LAW

INSTITUTIONAL INFORMATION

Public/private	Public
Student-faculty ratio	15:1
% faculty part-time	36
% faculty female	39
% faculty minority	13
Total faculty	75

SURVEY SAYS...

Diverse opinions accepted
in classrooms
Great library staff

STUDENTS

Enrollment of law school	771
% male/female	59/41
% out-of-state	13
% full-time	100
% minority	16
% international	5
# of countries represented	10
Average age of entering class	23

ACADEMICS

Academic Experience Rating	**87**
Profs interesting rating	86
Profs accessible rating	89
Hours of study per day	3.75

Academic Specialties

Environmental law, international
law, business law & economics

Advanced Degrees Offered

JD, LLM

Combined Degrees Offered

JD/MBA, JD/MS URP, JD/MS IA,
JD/MS (economics), JD/MPA,
JD/MS SW, JD/MS LIS, 4 years

Clinical program required	No
Legal writing	
course requirement	Yes
Legal methods	
course requirement	Yes
Legal research	
course requirement	Yes
Moot court requirement	No
Public interest	
law requirement	Yes

Academics

The law school at Florida State University, a relatively small program "hidden within the confines of a major public university," is considered by many happy students to be "the best-kept secret in Florida legal education opportunities." Not only is their satisfaction level high, but the price is right, too. "If all goes well, I will be working after graduation at a firm with lawyers from the top 14 schools, but the difference in my student loan payments will allow me to buy that new BMW instead of pay back Harvard! " exclaims one second-year student.

In contrast to many of the horror stories spouted by shell-shocked students at other law schools, Florida State Law's 1L survivors have nothing but praise for their trial-by-fire year. "All of the first-year teachers are memorable and qualified, and seem genuinely interested in making sure that students adjust," says one 2L. "One first-year contracts teacher went as far as starting a fantasy NASCAR league amongst students." Another says, "I loved the first-year required curriculum. Now that I can pick and choose my classes/externships, I feel pleasantly overwhelmed with all the choices." Maybe it's the result of starting off on the right foot, but students remain pleased as punch with the faculty right up through graduation. Speaking of "approachable" teachers who "are readily available to lend their expertise to a student's scholarship in a particular field" and who "even roam the halls looking for pick-up interaction with students," students say selflessness is evident in all aspects of instruction. "Classroom teaching seems just as important—if not more so—than producing scholarly articles," says a 2L.

Students also sing the praises of Florida State Law's "extremely eager" staff, who they see as being "fully committed to making students' three years of law school a memorable experience." "There is not a single person in the leadership of this school who I could not approach at any time," avers one. Career Services is lauded for encouraging employers to "interview more than the top 10 percent of the class," and the job situation is helped by "fantastic" alumni who believe in the "kinship that is felt by being a Florida State Seminole."

No one can argue that Florida State Law's location—"in the capital, across the street from the First District Court of Appeal and a block away from the State Supreme Court"—is ideal for a student of the law looking for practical experience on "a law clerk's playground." "By being so close to the capitol I was able to have two former state senators on my list of references," says one graduating student. However, such hotspots have their downsides; as one student puts it, "It doesn't take a math major to discover that 750 vehicles can't park in 50 spaces." Facilities get average reviews, and some students would like to see "more classrooms." A newly renovated student lounge was unveiled earlier this year. The school has funded such renovations in recent years, demonstrating "a true sense of investment in the student body and in the success of the law school, and planning money has been appropriated for the law school to annex the 50,000-square-foot courthouse across the street."

JENNIFER L. KESSINGER, DIRECTOR OF ADMISSIONS AND RECORDS
425 WEST JEFFERSON STREET, TALLAHASSEE, FL 32306-1601
TEL: 850-644-3787 FAX: 850-644-7284
EMAIL: ADMISSIONS@LAW.FSU.EDU • WEBSITE: WWW.LAW.FSU.EDU

Life

"Balanced" is a word that comes up a lot when Florida State Law students describe various aspects of their lives. The small size of the law school helps foster a "tight-knit" "sense of community that is pronounced," but avoids "being so small that you are singled out." Political persuasions seem to run middle of the road, or, as one second-year student puts it, "If you're from one of the more liberal areas of the country, Florida State Law students will seem very conservative. Native Floridians tell me that the school is considered 'liberal.'" While most students cop to some level of contest among their peers, they say almost all are "willing to share outlines and their previous experiences with the exams of various professors." Students waver on whether or not the academics are as challenging as those at some other schools, but the general consensus seems to be that the age-old adage "work hard and play hard" is in top form here.

Special events such as lectures and networking opportunities are available for students to participate in on a regular basis thanks to an "extremely active group of student organizations." Socials "are usually once a week and have pretty high attendance." The beautiful Floridian weather means there's much fun to be had outdoors, including involvement in the "law school golf association" and the "club for University of Florida students/fans called the LitiGators!" Florida State Law is "generally a fun place to work and study every day. Well, as much as law school can be 'fun,'" sums up one student.

Getting In

The actual admissions rate runs about average here, but the freshman profile runs a bit higher than one would expect for a state school. Students admitted had an LSAT score of 160 and an average GPA of 3.5. The school does not offer a part-time or evening program, but it does accept a few highly qualified transfer students from other ABA-accredited law schools, and those lucky few must be in the top third of their class.

ADMISSIONS

Selectivity Rating	82
# applications received	3,013
% applicants accepted	33
% acceptees attending	26
Average LSAT	159
LSAT Range	157–161
Average undergrad GPA	3.54
Application fee	$30
Regular application	Rolling, up to 4/1
Regular notification	Rolling
Early application program	No
Transfer students accepted	Yes
Evening division offered	No
Part-time accepted	No
LSDAS accepted	Yes

Applicants Also Look At

American University, University of Georgia, Duke University, Tulane University, University of Florida, Emory University, Stetson University

International Students

TOEFL required of international students	Yes
Minimum TOEFL (paper/computer/web)	600/250/100

FINANCIAL FACTS

Annual tuition (in-state/ out-of-state)	$10,664/$10,664
Books and supplies	$2,250
Fees (in-state/ out-of-state)	$1,688/$21,700
Room & board	$10,000
% first-year students receiving some sort of aid	88
% receiving some sort of aid	85
% receiving scholarships	38
Average grant	$3,865
Average loan	$18,672
Average total aid package	$23,577
Average debt	$54,784

EMPLOYMENT INFORMATION

Career Rating	68
Rate of placement (nine months out)	98
Average starting salary	$66,315
State for bar exam	FL, GA, TX, CA, NY
Pass rate for first-time bar	87

Employers Who Frequently Hire Grads
Akerman Senterfitt; Alston & Bird LLP; Arnstein & Lehr LLP; Balch & Bingham; Broad & Cassel; Carlton Fields, P.A.; Foley & Lardner; Gray Robinson.

Prominent Alumni
The Honorable Mel R. Martinez, United States Senate; Justice Rick Polston, Florida Supreme Court; Jeffrey A. Stoops, SBA Communications Corp.

Grads Employed by Field (%)
Academic (1)
Business/Industry (9)
Government (23)
Judicial clerkships (2)
Military (2)
Private practice (51)
Public Interest (9)

FORDHAM UNIVERSITY
SCHOOL OF LAW

INSTITUTIONAL INFORMATION

Public/private	Private
Affiliation	Roman Catholic
Student-faculty ratio	15:1
% faculty part-time	63
% faculty female	34
% faculty minority	12
Total faculty	244

SURVEY SAYS...

Diverse opinions accepted
in classrooms
Abundant externship/internship/
clerkship opportunities
Students love New York, NY

STUDENTS

Enrollment of law school	1,484
% male/female	53/47
% out-of-state	36
% full-time	79
% minority	24
% international	2
# of countries represented	13
Average age of entering class	24

ACADEMICS

Academic Experience Rating	**93**
Profs interesting rating	89
Profs accessible rating	81
Hours of study per day	3.68

Academic Specialties

Civil procedure, commercial law, constitutional law, corporation securities, criminal law, environmental law, government services, human rights, international law, labor law, legal history, legal philosophy, property, taxation, intellectual property law

Advanced Degrees Offered

JD, 3 years; LLM, 1 year

Combined Degrees Offered

JD/MBA with Fordham Grad School of Business (4 years full-time); JD/MSW with Fordham Grad School of Social Work (4 years full-time).

Clinical program required	No
Legal writing course requirement	Yes

Academics

"Ridiculously underrated" Fordham Law School is "well respected in the New York City area" and it boasts an "incredibly strong" and "exceedingly loyal" alumni network. While Fordham's main campus is located in the depths of the Bronx, the Law School is situated "steps from Central Park and a stone's throw from many of the top law firms in the world." "All the big law firms you hear about are right outside our doorstep in Midtown," enthuses a 2L. Most agree that "employment prospects are incredible," but a few students call the Career Planning Center "terrible." "I cannot imagine that any law school could create a more efficient, comprehensive, and successful environment for job placement," says one happy student. "They knock themselves out to help students who may not be at the top of the class," adds a 3L.

Academically, "if you're interested in corporate law, you have plenty of opportunities to take really amazing classes." "The public interest program is strong" as well. There are also "valuable opportunities for internships and externships" and important people actually read the Fordham Law Review, one of the most cited law journals in the country. The "really accessible" faculty here is "a good mix of practitioners and academics." "Fordham gets great adjuncts from a variety of practice and business areas." "It seems that every teacher I've had is famous for something," notes a 2L. Students tell us that most professors are "lively, entertaining, and supportive," though some are "highly mediocre," and even "God awful." "There have been professors I enjoyed more than others," says a 2L, "but overall they all know what they're talking about."

Student opinion concerning the top brass is divided. Some students call management "very good." "The administration is an incredibly impressive yet down-to-earth group of people who genuinely care about making Fordham a comfortable place," they say. Others contend that "the administration is a mess." "They will help you when it is convenient for them but will not go out of their way," complains a 3L. The registrar's office is generally "in shambles" and "they seem to schedule all the good classes at the same exact time."

Students at Fordham don't have much in the way of praise for their "really crappy" facilities. The good news is that the current building is "slated for replacement." In the meantime, though, it's a "drab," "giant concrete cinderblock" that is "totally overcrowded" and "outdated (and not in a pretty, vintage-y way)." It's "severely lacking in light, seating, temperature, and overall comfort." "Classrooms are cramped and some are rather rundown." "The entire school is wireless," but "there is always something wrong" with the connection and "everything computer-related is just a bit clunky." However, "research facilities are great" and you'll find a decent number of "comfy" chairs in the library. "But good luck getting a space to study in the library come finals time," says a 2L.

JOHN CHALMERS, ASSISTANT DEAN OF ADMISSIONS
33 WEST 60TH STREET, NINTH FLOOR, NEW YORK, NY 10023
TEL: 212-636-6810 FAX: 212-636-7984
EMAIL: LAWADMISSIONS@LAW.FORDHAM.EDU • WEBSITE: LAW.FORDHAM.EDU

Life

The "very diverse" student body at Fordham Law School reflects its urban environs. Minority enrollment is excellent and the evening program attracts a slew of older students who have professional experience in a variety of fields. You might find some "reprehensible people with no social skills" here, but most students are "people who you actually want to hang out with." "The students at Fordham tend to have a really work-hard mentality because we are not NYU or Columbia and still compete for the same jobs," explains a 2L. Nevertheless, first-year sections are "intimate" and students describe the atmosphere here as "a pleasant paradise of cooperation and friendliness." "Our classes are curved (even our 15-person legal writing courses)," explains a 1L. "So you cannot avoid competitiveness entirely, but it is not prevalent." "Each student is willing to help the next," claims another 1L, "keeping competitiveness at a minimum."

Students brag that Fordham's Manhattan location "can't be beat." It's "really nice to be in school in the middle of New York City." School-sponsored social activities are plentiful, especially for first-year students. "There are lots of opportunities to get involved in the community socially, especially if you like to drink." However, "Fordham has less of a feeling of a social community than some other schools." "Not every personality will survive here," warns a 2L. "This is not the type of school where you can show up and expect it to create your entire social life. Many, if not most, students have lives outside of school."

Getting In

Though it's unlikely that Fordham will ever surpass its Manhattan neighbors Columbia or New York University in terms of academic reputation, it's still one of the very best law schools in the country. The acceptance rate here is about 20 percent and admission is highly competitive. Admitted students at the 25th percentile have LSAT scores around 163 and GPAs of just over 3.4. Admitted students at the 75th percentile have LSAT scores of 167 or so and GPAs of around 3.7.

Legal methods	
course requirement	Yes
Legal research	
course requirement	Yes
Moot court requirement	No
Public interest	
law requirement	No

ADMISSIONS

Selectivity Rating	**94**
# applications received	6,812
% applicants accepted	24
% acceptees attending	31
Average LSAT	166
LSAT Range	163–167
Average undergrad GPA	3.66
Application fee	$70
Regular application	Rolling, up to 3/1
Regular notification	Rolling
Early application program	No
Transfer students accepted	Yes
Evening division offered	Yes
Part-time accepted	Yes
LSDAS accepted	Yes

Applicants Also Look At
Columbia University, New York University, Yeshiva University, Boston College, The George Washington University, Georgetown University, Brooklyn Law School

FINANCIAL FACTS

Annual tuition	$38,900
Books and supplies	$1,400
Fees	$550
Tuition per credit	$1,620
Room & board	$16,260
Financial aid application deadline	4/1
% first-year students receiving some sort of aid	82
% receiving some sort of aid	76
% of aid that is merit based	19
% receiving scholarships	33
Average grant	$12,085
Average loan	$42,399
Average total aid package	$45,168
Average debt	$100,554

EMPLOYMENT INFORMATION

		Grads Employed by Field (%)	
Career Rating	**95**	Academic	(1)
Rate of placement (nine months out)	98	Business/Industry	(9)
Average starting salary	$125,806	Government	(7)
State for bar exam	NY, CA, NJ, DC, FL	Judicial Clerkships	(6)
Pass rate for first-time bar	89	Private Practice	(69)
		Public Interest	(5)

Employers Who Frequently Hire Grads
Firms including Cahill Gordon & Reindel; Cravath, Swaine & Moore; Davis Polk & Wardwell; Dewey & LeBouef; Hughes Hubbard & Reed.

Prominent Alumni
Christopher Cuomo, Co-anchor, Good Morning America; Geraldine A. Ferraro, First female vice-presidential candidate.

Franklin Pierce Law Center

Franklin Pierce Law Center

Franklin Pierce Law Center

INSTITUTIONAL INFORMATION

Public/private	Private
Student-faculty ratio	13:1
% faculty part-time	46
% faculty female	36
% faculty minority	5
Total faculty	58

SURVEY SAYS...

Diverse opinions accepted
in classrooms
Great research resources
Great library staff
Abundant externship/internship/
clerkship opportunities

STUDENTS

Enrollment of law school	427
% male/female	62/38
% out-of-state	87
% full-time	99
% minority	17
% international	4
# of countries represented	15
Average age of entering class	27

ACADEMICS

Academic Experience Rating	**73**
Profs interesting rating	76
Profs accessible rating	82
Hours of study per day	5.3

Academic Specialties

Commercial law, criminal law, human rights, intellectual property law, International Criminal Law and Justice

Advanced Degrees Offered

LL.M, 1 year; Master of Intellectual Property, Commerce & Technology (MIPCT), 1 year

Combined Degrees Offered

JD/MIPCT, 3 years

Clinical program required	No
Legal writing	
course requirement	Yes
Legal methods	
course requirement	Yes
Legal research	
course requirement	Yes

Academics

As the only law school in the small state (and capital city) of New Hampshire, Franklin Pierce Law Center is able to give its students direct access to a wide range of activities in the legal profession. A "close-knit" school of just over 400 students, the environment invariably "develops a strong, healthy and a memorable relationship with faculty and administrative staff." Though it might seem like just another small school at first glance (and students all grouse about the lack of name recognition for the school), all the resources are there, teaching-wise and experience-wise, and so that "if you avail yourself of those opportunities you are in for rousing discussions and thought provoking conversations."

FPLC is best known for its program in Intellectual Property, which is one of the best in the country; the school recently added a large section to the IP library with study areas for students (along with major renovations to other parts of the facilities), and there are "unparalleled connections" in IP and Patent Law. Though most students do choose to attend FLPC for these studies, those that don't wish there were "more diverse classes" and more attention paid to them on the part of the Career Center. There is also a healthy Public Interest Coalition that hosts an annual auction, raising money to fund 10–15 national and international public interest fellowships. With a great emphasis on its "exceptional" externship program, the "knowledgeable, engaging, and personable" professors "really want you to develop as a legal professional" and are eager to impart their wisdom, making sure that the curriculum stresses practice instead of just theory (FLPC is "not as Socratic as in other schools"). "Their focus is more on making us excellent attorneys who can interact well with clients than on making us memorize antebellum decisions that no longer apply," says a 1L. Not only are they completely accessible in their offices and by e-mail, but are "frequently hanging out with students in the cafeteria, hallways and library. Not only do they know your name, they also know your story." There are often night classes with adjunct professors, as well, many of whom are still working in the fields they are teaching. The administration is generally well-received by students, especially as changes have occurred in recent years, but the registrar's office is "out to lunch most of the time."

Though "the grading system would make a statistician weep," FLPC is the first school in the nation to enact a specific program where upon completion, students automatically pass the bar; the Webster Scholar Program works to prepare students to be client-ready, and it "is highly-esteemed by attorneys in the area." The school's relationship with the New Hampshire court system allows three students to extern at the State Supreme Court each semester, and many more extern in the superior court system, and there are an impressive six different clinics in which students represent indigent clients

KATIE McDONALD, ASSISTANT DEAN FOR ADMISSIONS
TWO WHITE STREET, CONCORD, NH 03301
TEL: 603-228-9217 FAX: 603-228-1074
EMAIL: ADMISSIONS@PIERCELAW.EDU • WEBSITE: WWW.PIERCELAW.EDU

Life

Unfortunately, Concord, New Hampshire isn't the most exciting place to live, but "it's the perfect opportunity to form a strong social circle" and students make the most of it, taking advantage of the myriad outdoor activities and the hour-long commute to Boston. "If you are an outdoorsy type of person, New Hampshire is a paradise," says a student. On the plus side, it's a "short commute and low to no crime to worry about." Pierce Law attracts students who often are later in life and have spouses/children, and the married students "quite frequently get together and have very good camaraderie"; "students that don't have families become close and spend a lot of time together doing things other than studying." Lots of students live in apartments in nearby houses and "have little problem meeting others." The school fosters an environment of cooperation among students, though "it is competitive, but not cut-throat"; "Most people leave their laptops in the library and they are left alone." Backstabbing would be difficult, as the small size of the school means "you can study with these people for finals and party with them after finals are over," and "anything said or done most likely will be said/heard to all." As a result of the close quarters, the "social life is great," and there are a few bars in town, so "on any given weekend night, you will see half of your class at one of them." There are a decent number of student organizations, and even though they tend to be fairly small, several put on "very good events." The school is somewhat limited in facilities, in that there is no student center, no gym, no showers, and "high school-style lockers."

Getting In

Pierce Law's Intellectual Property program is a huge draw to attract students from all over the country, so residence is irrelevant and acceptance is fairly easy; around one out of every two students gets in. A B-average and a decent LSAT score should do the trick numerically, but beyond that, Pierce Law has a very small admissions department that carefully reviews applications to make sure that the student will bring add perspective and ambition to the mix.

Moot court requirement	Yes
Public interest law requirement	No

ADMISSIONS

Selectivity Rating	**71**
# applications received	1,447
% applicants accepted	49
% acceptees attending	22
Average LSAT	154
LSAT Range	150–156
Average undergrad GPA	3.2
Application fee	$55
Regular application	Rolling, up to 4/1
Regular notification	Rolling
Early application program	No
Transfer students accepted	Yes
Evening division offered	No
Part-time accepted	No
LSDAS accepted	Yes

Applicants Also Look At
Syracuse University, Suffolk University, Quinnipiac University, Western New England College, Albany Law School of Union University, New England Law|Boston, Roger Williams University

International Students

TOEFL required of international students	Yes
Minimum TOEFL (paper/computer)	600/250

FINANCIAL FACTS

Annual tuition	$29,000
Books and supplies	$1,000
Fees	$50
Room & board (off-campus)	$9,220
% first-year students receiving some sort of aid	92
% receiving some sort of aid	97
% of aid that is merit based	63
% receiving scholarships	72
Average grant	$8,600
Average loan	$32,440
Average total aid package	$37,274
Average debt	$93,476

EMPLOYMENT INFORMATION

		Grads Employed by Field (%)
Career Rating	**82**	Academic (8)
Rate of placement (nine months out)	92	Business/Industry (23)
Average starting salary	$85,000	Government (9)
State for bar exam	MA, NH, NY, DC, CA	Judicial Clerkships (6)
Pass rate for first-time bar	84	Private Practice (49)

Employers Who Frequently Hire Grads
Connecticut Superior Court Fenwick & West, Palo Alto, Calif. Fitzpatrick, Cella Harper & Cinto, New York Kirkpatrick Gates.

Prominent Alumni
Hon. Samuel Der-Yeghiayan, U.S. District Court for Northern Illinois; Hon. Timothy Ryan, U.S. House of Representatives; Douglas Wood, Esq., Partner, Reed Smith.

Grads Employed by Field (%)
Public Interest (4)
Other (1)

GEORGE MASON UNIVERSITY
SCHOOL OF LAW

INSTITUTIONAL INFORMATION

Public/private	Public
Student-faculty ratio	16:1
% faculty part-time	73
% faculty female	25
% faculty minority	7
Total faculty	168

SURVEY SAYS...
Conservative students
Students love Arlington, VA

STUDENTS

Enrollment of law school	751
% male/female	62/38
% full-time	62
% minority	14
% international	2
Average age of entering class	25

ACADEMICS

Academic Experience Rating	**83**
Profs interesting rating	73
Profs accessible rating	66
Hours of study per day	4.33

Academic Specialties
Civil procedure, corporation securities, criminal law, government services, international business law, legal philosophy, taxation, intellectual property law, technology law, regulatory law, law & economics, international and homeland security

Advanced Degrees Offered
LL.M.

Combined Degrees Offered
JD/MA or PhD in Economics; JD/MPP.

Clinical program required	No
Legal writing	
course requirement	Yes
Legal methods	
course requirement	No
Legal research	
course requirement	Yes
Moot court requirement	Yes
Public interest	
law requirement	No

Academics

George Mason University School of Law has "a very strong reputation in the surrounding area," and "It's got to be one of the best bangs for your buck in the country." A "robust legal clinic program" provides "clinics for almost everything you can imagine." GMU's location "on the outskirts of Washington, DC" means that "there is a plethora" of judicial internships and work opportunities within the federal government. A host of specialization programs includes intellectual property, technology law, and international business law. Probably the most unique feature here is the ubiquitous emphasis on the nexus between law and economics. "The law and economics approach pervades the curriculum" and "teaches you as much about how the world operates as it does about the law." "It's like getting two degrees for the price of one," says a satisfied 3L. However, "the extent of the econ bent" is the bane of some students. "If you want to focus on something else, you have to pick your classes very carefully," notes a critic. The "arduous," four-semester legal writing program requires an enormous investment of time and is "by far the biggest complaint" among students. Students also tell us that "there's a mandatory attendance requirements" (as per ABA regulations), and they warn that "the curve at Mason is tough."

GMU's "supportive" and "incredibly dedicated faculty" is full of "intelligent, witty," and approachable professors. "They are always happy to discuss career plans and even send your resume to their friends," beams a 2L. "Some professors are so brilliant that they can't teach," but most "engage the students" and "keep class lively." "Older teachers are more likely to adhere to the Socratic Method, whereas classes with younger teachers are more relaxed and laid-back." "Lots of classes are taught by adjuncts" (including a "large number of judges") who are able to offer "practical, job-related advice." GMU has a reputation as a "right-of-center" law school. For many students, "the collection of so many conservative and libertarian geniuses among the faculty is wondrous and nearly incomparable." "A strong argument from any perspective is always welcome," though. "I am a liberal in a school whose administration and faculty lean toward the conservative or libertarian side," counsels a 3L. "While I sometimes find myself at odds with their beliefs, I love the academic challenge they provide and have always felt accepted in the community."

Career Services on campus "will go to great lengths to try and assist you in finding a job." "Each year, more and more prestigious law firms and government agencies recruit" at Mason. Also, "Alumni are extremely interested in helping current students meet their career goals." "My class has graduates heading to top 10 firms in the most competitive legal markets," boasts a 3L.

"Technology resources are top of the line," but the facilities at GMU aren't great. In the past, students have noted that though the building is "new and shiny on the outside," once you walk through the door the interior is "generally unattractive," and the buildings "cold, stark and lack windows." Fortunately, the school has recently completed interior renovations which receive compliments. The elevators and the lack of parking are another source of vexation. Classrooms have poor acoustics "so it's often hard to hear," and they "are too small."

ALISON PRICE, SR. ASSOCIATE DEAN AND DIRECTOR OF ADMISSIONS
3301 FAIRFAX DRIVE, ARLINGTON, VA 22201
TEL: 703-993-8010 FAX: 703-993-8088
EMAIL: APRICE1@GMU.EDU • WEBSITE: WWW.LAW.GMU.EDU

Life

Many students come to Mason "for the school's conservative reputation." Others "come for the cheap tuition." The student population is especially diverse "in terms of work and practical experience." Also, "All kinds of perspectives and political backgrounds are apparent." "The student body is hardly monolithic," explains a 3L. "Students are older" on the whole. "There is a noticeable chasm in social interaction between the straight-out-of-college group and the students who have worked for a few years." Competition for grades is minimal among these "unusually motivated and down-to-earth students." (The evening section is "less competitive than the day sections.") "There are only about 5 or 10 people who are hyper-competitive gunner types." "Except for the total spazzes and the slackers, the majority of us just want to get through it," confesses a 3L.

Some students complain that "there is absolutely no sense of community at Mason, mainly because everyone works at least 20 hours per week and only comes to campus for class." Some say their classmates "seem too busy to enjoy themselves." "Students may try to tell themselves that the social void thing is normal, but it's simply not," says a 2L. Other students perceive that "there's a wealth of school-sponsored social activities" and that GMU's location "in the heart of" suburban Virginia "provides unparalleled social and cultural opportunities." "We have an abundance of student groups with something for everyone—from the GMU Sports Club, to the Jewish Law Student Association, to ACLU, to the Mason Republicans," declares a 1L. "There are hermits and partiers," adds another student, "so you can always find a quiet evening out with friends, or a drunken evening stumbling through the bar-laden streets." "There is a large faction, myself included, who enthusiastically immerse ourselves in the culture and nightlife of DC and Northern Virginia," says a fun-loving 2L. "Thursday nights you'll find some of us having dollar beers and tacos at the Mexican restaurant up the road, and you might run into another group of Masonites at two-dollar mug night at Whitlow's in Clarendon."

Getting In

At George Mason, admitted students at the 25th percentile have LSAT scores in the range of 160 and GPAs in the range of 3.1 or so. Admitted students at the 75th percentile have LSAT scores of about 166 and GPAs of roughly 3.78.

EMPLOYMENT INFORMATION

Career Rating	86
Rate of placement (nine months out)	99
Average starting salary	$83,871
State for bar exam	VA, MD, DC, CA, NY

Employers Who Frequently Hire Grads
Hunton & Williams; Finnegan, Henderson, Farabow, Garrett & Dunner, L.L.P.; Pillsbury Winthrop Shaw Pittman; Paul, Hastings, Janofsky & Walker, L.L.P.

Prominent Alumni
Richard Young, U.S. District Court Judge; Kathleen Casey, Commissioner, Securities and Exchange Commission; Paul Misener, VP of Global Policy for Amazon.com.

Grads Employed by Field (%)
Academic (3)
Business/Industry (14)
Government (22)
Judicial Clerkships (12)
Military (3)
Private Practice (41)
Public Interest (5)

ADMISSIONS

Selectivity Rating	91
# applications received	5,024
% applicants accepted	20
% acceptees attending	18
Average LSAT	164
LSAT Range	160–166
Average undergrad GPA	3.6
Application fee	$35
Regular application	Rolling, up to 4/1
Regular notification	Rolling
Early application program	Yes
Early application deadline	12/15
Early application notification	1/15
Transfer students accepted	Yes
Evening division offered	Yes
Part-time accepted	Yes
LSDAS accepted	Yes

Applicants Also Look At
American University, The Catholic University of America, The George Washington University, University of Maryland, Baltimore, The College of William & Mary in Virginia, Georgetown University

International Students

TOEFL required of international students	Yes
Minimum TOEFL (paper/computer)	600/250

FINANCIAL FACTS

Annual tuition (in-state/ out-of-state)	$18,200/$31,864
Books and supplies	$1,000
Tuition per credit (in-state/out-of-state)	$546/$947
Room & board (off-campus)	$20,228
Financial aid application deadline	3/1
% first-year students receiving some sort of aid	90
% receiving some sort of aid	90
% of aid that is merit based	3
% receiving scholarships	9
Average grant	$8,270
Average loan	$28,424
Average total aid package	$29,084
Average debt	$35,041

THE GEORGE WASHINGTON UNIVERSITY
LAW SCHOOL

Academics

The caliber of the "limitless" resources available to a George Washington University law student are outstanding, and the location cannot be beat; its various connections to federal agencies, lobbyists, firms, and judges in the area make it easy to find some area of law that will interest any student, as well as allowing for a wealth of outside placement and internship possibilities. "I have enough room in my schedule to go hear oral arguments at the Supreme Court or the Federal Circuit Court," says a student. "Nearly everyone I know has had the opportunity to intern in the federal or DC courts or some federal agency," says another. Even if students aren't happy with the Career Development office (and many outside of the top 15% are not), there's the matter of the upstanding reputation with employers. "People that don't get jobs that attend GW either (1) didn't try hard enough to diversify where they were applying (particularly, geographically—people seem to forget there are jobs outside DC, NY and the coasts), or (2) aren't trying hard enough period," says a 3L. Add to that stellar academics, and this "close knit, high energy" school is definitely on the move, though the price tag can be steep. The somewhat high enrollment means "at times it feels a bit crowded" at GW, but the law school complex is very big, and the school has done a good job of expanding spaces, having recently developed a café for students and enlarging student conference spaces. In addition to the excellent law library, at one's fingertips on any given day there are lectures, panels, and workshops.

The Student Bar Association is one of the best in the nation, which is a reflection of the close relationship between the students and the administration, who "make a clear effort to engage students on the decisions of the law school." GW Law's Dean is a "terrific fundraiser and cheerleader," and even normally teaches a 1L Criminal Law class. The emphasis placed upon the teaching abilities is reflected in the inclusion of a student panel on the Faculty Appointments Committee, where students' views as reflected in their reports to the faculty are "given serious consideration during the appointment process." It shows, too, as the professors at GW are first-rate; there are "so many 'must-takes' here that you are guaranteed a great professor (at least by reputation) for each major doctrinal course." Indeed, GW Law professors are well-known locally and nationally, and "it's not unusual to attend a professor's class, and then later see him or her on the television that evening." These superstars are approachable as well, and "you would be hard-pressed to go to a student function and not find a friendly face from the faculty and staff enjoying time away from the formal school setting and lending their wisdom and wit to the outside student life." Classes mix theory and practice, placing an emphasis on didactic ability, and "there can be a little tough love involved" if needed. Each lecture "is an experience," and while the Socratic Method is used, it is used "very gently, and tends to create more of an open discussion format than a fear-invoking grilling process." However, students would like to see their torts class expanded to two semesters. The student culture and atmosphere at GW Law rounds out the experience, as "people actually like each other and enjoy a good conversation, whether studying or not."

ANNE M. RICHARD, ASSOCIATE DEAN FOR ADMISSIONS & FIN. AID
700 20TH STREET, NW, WASHINGTON, DC 20052
TEL: 202-994-7230 FAX: 202-994-3597
EMAIL: JDADMIT@LAW.GWU.EDU • WEBSITE: WWW.LAW.GWU.EDU

Life

As a large law school, "there is a group (or clique) for everyone," and while "most law students are naturally Type A," the school is not competitive, possibly because most students have a job when graduating. There is a genuine atmosphere of camaraderie, where "students are colleagues not just in the classroom, but in the outside world as well." Only a few blocks from the National Mall and a short walk to Georgetown and Dupont Circle, GW has the perfect location for social, career, and academic needs of students. It "is expensive to live here," but "the benefits far outweigh the costs." Students are all business for the most part in the classroom, but "relaxed and laidback outside of it," and most "tend to be social and well-adjusted." The school is a social paradise, with "beautiful people, 200-student ski trip, weekly special events at local bars, formal dances at luxury hotels, intra-class dating, and everything other extra-curricular activity necessary for keeping your sanity in law school is provided for in healthy amounts." Despite the more visible liberal element at the school, "liberals and conservatives, atheists, Jews, Mormons, the occasional Evangelical, and kids of all different backgrounds and ethnicities get together and enjoy each others' company on a regular basis." Tons of student groups help bring together the already diverse student body, and a huge percentage attend SBA events like the Halloween party and Barrister's Ball.

Getting In

Admission to George Washington is highly competitive. It's not quite as hard to get in as it is at its crosstown rival, Georgetown, but it's close. You should have an LSAT score at or above the 90th percentile and an A-minus average to be seriously considered.

Legal methods course requirement	Yes
Legal research course requirement	Yes
Moot court requirement	No
Public interest law requirement	No

ADMISSIONS

Selectivity Rating	96
# applications received	8,225
% applicants accepted	22
% acceptees attending	21
Average LSAT	167
LSAT Range	162–168
Average undergrad GPA	3.75
Application fee	$80
Regular application	Rolling, up to 3/1
Regular notification	Rolling
Early application program	Yes
Early application deadline	12/15
Early application notification	1/15
Transfer students accepted	Yes
Evening division offered	Yes
Part-time accepted	Yes
LSDAS accepted	Yes

Applicants Also Look At
University of Texas at Austin, University of Southern California, American University, Columbia University, University of Michigan—Ann Arbor, Northwestern University, University of California—Los Angeles, New York University, Georgetown University

FINANCIAL FACTS

Annual tuition	$40,100
Books and supplies	$1,185
Tuition per credit	$1,432
Room & board	$13,600
% first-year students receiving some sort of aid	85
% receiving some sort of aid	87
% of aid that is merit based	48
% receiving scholarships	47
Average grant	$13,000
Average loan	$35,000
Average total aid package	$35,000
Average debt	$107,000

EMPLOYMENT INFORMATION

Career Rating	96
Rate of placement (nine months out)	95
Average starting salary	$136,643
State for bar exam	NY
Pass rate for first-time bar	94

Employers Who Frequently Hire Grads
Department of Justice; Howrey Simon; Finnegan, Henderson et.al.; Akin, Gump, et.al.; Shearman & Sterling; Arnold & Porter; Wiley, Rein & Fielding; Arent Fox; Dickstein, Shapiro, Morin & Oshinsky; various government agencies.

Grads Employed by Field (%)
Academic (1)
Business/Industry (5)
Government (12)
Judicial Clerkships (10)
Military (1)
Private Practice (65)
Public Interest (4)
Other (1)

GEORGETOWN UNIVERSITY
LAW CENTER

INSTITUTIONAL INFORMATION

Public/private	Private
Affiliation	Roman Catholic
Student-faculty ratio	12:1
% faculty female	34
% faculty minority	10
Total faculty	252

SURVEY SAYS...

Great research resources
Great library staff
Abundant externship/internship/
clerkship opportunities

STUDENTS

Enrollment of law school	2,005
% male/female	51/49
% full-time	78
% minority	27
% international	8
Average age of entering class	25

ACADEMICS

Academic Experience Rating	**97**
Profs interesting rating	89
Profs accessible rating	79
Hours of study per day	4.78

Academic Specialties

Civil procedure, commercial law, constitutional law, corporation securities, criminal law, environmental law, government services, human rights, international law, labor law, legal history, legal philosophy, property, taxation, intellectual property law, Alternative dispute resolution, clinical legal studies, national security law and global health law.

Advanced Degrees Offered

SJD, 2–4 years; LLM taxation, LLM securities and financial regulation, LLM international business and economic law, LLM global health law, LLM individualized, all 1 year full-time or 2–3 years part-time; LLM general studies & LLM international legal studies, 1 year; 2 Year LLM in same substantive areas.

Academics

The Law Center at Georgetown University is "the perfect blend of old-school intellectualism, [and] modern pragmatism." The school's location in the heart of Capitol Hill means that "connections to political and judicial institutions abound." Frequent visitors to the law school include high-ranking government officials, legal scholars, and interest group leaders who pop on over after work to chat due to the school's location "right smack in the hub of Washington activity." In addition, "About 70 percent of the cases that go before the Supreme Court have had one of the arguing attorneys go through a practice run at Georgetown Law." Students can sign up to watch before observing the actual trial, providing "an unparalleled source of training for any legal student." "It's like going to a concert in undergrad, but now we go to watch the justices do their thing," says a first-year student.

Many professors are considered to be "masters of their fields," which "can at first be intimidating," but then "They will insist that you call them by their first name" and "You will find yourself wanting to hang out during their office hours." First-year classes tend to be big, but even in the larger lecture courses, the instructors are "are able to facilitate great conversation and debate." In the smaller classes, the "genius of conversational teaching is fully developed," and an ongoing orientation program offers first-year students lessons on how to take notes, study for exams, and develop other study skills. The Law Center's unique alternative First-Year Curriculum B concentrates on making law school applicable to the legal world, and focuses heavily on jurisprudence and historical context, combining Torts and Contracts into one year-long class. Though many claim that the curve makes things unduly difficult and "Expectations and academic rigor are high," students' stress levels remain low, in large part due to the "warm and approachable" faculty, some of whom "even offer to meet with students they don't have in class." The Law Center is also heralded for its teachings in international law, its wide variety of course offerings "in just about any theoretical or practical area you can imagine," and for having one of the best clinical programs in the country, with twelve clinics providing enough variety to satisfy even the most obscure of interests. "There simply isn't that permeating fear of failure here because our attention, as students, is constantly pushed toward a focus on all of the incredible things that we can do with our knowledge and skills," explains a first-year student.

Students at the Law Center universally agree that its "Bureaucracy is navigable," and "The administration is always open to hearing student ideas on how to improve" one observes. "Doors are open and e-mails are returned really quickly." Students say Washington, DC is "the perfect place to get any type of internship." As one 1L puts it, "There's nothing better than studying law where it is made." The Career Center is "unbelievable"; each student is assigned a counselor who "basically acts as your life coach and gives you all the tools and advice you need." The law building is within walking distance of the Supreme Court, Congress, embassies, NGOs, the Smithsonian museums, administrative agencies, and dozens of public interest organizations. It boasts a "brand-new gym" and "two beautiful law libraries" with lots of group study rooms.

ANDREW P. CORNBLATT, DEAN OF ADMISSIONS
600 NEW JERSEY AVENUE, NW, ROOM 589, WASHINGTON, DC 20001
TEL: 202-662-9010 FAX: 202-662-9439
EMAIL: ADMIS@LAW.GEORGETOWN.EDU • WEBSITE: WWW.LAW.GEORGETOWN.EDU

Life

"It is great that we have our own campus, apart from the undergrad and other graduate institutions, because a complete sense of community is fostered," claims one happy student. Despite the school's large size, the division of first-year students into smaller 100–120 person sections helps create a more intimate atmosphere from which students benefit. Students socialize frequently within their own sections, though "The intra-section drama gets tired pretty quickly." There are tons of social, political, ethnic, and religious groups on campus, and myriad extracurricular activities are available. "Bar reviews" are held at different bars throughout the city and "keg on the quad" on some Wednesday nights provides students with free beer and food. "The amount of school-sponsored boozing that goes on is mind boggling," attests a graduating student. Without a doubt, the group at GULC is a social bunch who "love to spend time together both in and outside class." The level of competition at the school is low, and students are "respectful of each other" and "extremely friendly across the board." "Everyone wants to do well, but we act cooperatively to reach that goal." Plus, it's Washington, DC, and "You can't go wrong living here."

Getting In

One of the most highly regarded law schools in the nation, the Law Center receives the most applications out of any law school, and the numbers for those that they do admit certainly are impressive: Recently admitted students at the 25th percentile had an LSAT score of 167 and an average GPA of 3.4, while admitted students at the 75th percentile had an LSAT score of 171 and a GPA of 3.8. Georgetown also offers early decision programs.

Combined Degrees Offered

JD/MBA; JD/MPH; JD/MPP; JD/MSFS; JD/PhD Government; JD/PhD or MA Philosophy; JD/MSPS; JD/MAAS; JD/MAGES; JD/MALAS; JD/MAREES; JD/MASS; JD/LLM taxation

Clinical program required	No
Legal writing course requirement	Yes
Legal methods course requirement	Yes
Legal research course requirement	Yes
Moot court requirement	No
Public interest law requirement	No

ADMISSIONS

Selectivity Rating	**96**
# applications received	10,688
% applicants accepted	24
% acceptees attending	23
Average LSAT	169
LSAT Range	166–170
Average undergrad GPA	3.65
Application fee	$80
Regular application	Rolling, up to 2/1
Regular notification	Rolling
Early application program	Yes
Early application deadline	11/1
Early application notification	12/15
Transfer students accepted	Yes
Evening division offered	Yes
Part-time accepted	Yes
LSDAS accepted	Yes

FINANCIAL FACTS

Annual tuition	$42,065
Books and supplies	$1,000
Tuition per credit	$1,545
Room & board	$20,235
Financial aid application deadline	3/1
% first-year students receiving some sort of aid	89
% receiving some sort of aid	88
% receiving scholarships	33
Average grant	$16,236
Average loan	$43,132
Average total aid package	$49,016
Average debt	$115,420

EMPLOYMENT INFORMATION

Career Rating	**96**	**Grads Employed by Field (%)**
Rate of placement (nine months out)	97	Academic (1)
Average starting salary	$160,000	Business/Industry (5)
State for bar exam	NY, MD	Government (6)
Pass rate for first-time bar	92	Judicial Clerkships (8)
Prominent Alumni		Private Practice (74)
The Honorable George J. Mitchell, U.S.		Public Interest (5)
Middle East Envoy; Regina M. Pisa,		
Managing Partner, Goodwin Proctor; U.S.		
Senator Patrick J. Leahy, Chairman of		
Senate Judiciary Committee; Marc H.		
Morial, President and CEO, National Urban		
League.		

GEORGIA STATE UNIVERSITY
COLLEGE OF LAW

INSTITUTIONAL INFORMATION
Public/private	Public
Student-faculty ratio	16:1
% faculty part-time	26
% faculty female	38
% faculty minority	18
Total faculty	72

SURVEY SAYS...
Diverse opinions accepted
in classrooms
Great library staff
Abundant externship/internship/clerk-
ship opportunities
Students love Atlanta, GA

STUDENTS
Enrollment of law school	663
% male/female	50/50
% out-of-state	13
% full-time	68
% minority	19
% international	3
# of countries represented	8
Average age of entering class	27

ACADEMICS
Academic Experience Rating	**82**
Profs interesting rating	78
Profs accessible rating	65
Hours of study per day	3.76

Academic Specialties
Civil procedure, commercial law,
corporation securities, criminal law,
environmental law, human rights,
international law, taxation, intellectual property law

Combined Degrees Offered
JD/MBA, 4 years; JD/MPA, 4 years;
JD/MA Philosophy, 4 years:
JD/MCRP, 4 years; JD/MHA, 4
years; JD/MSHA, 4 years

Clinical program required	No
Legal writing course requirement	Yes
Legal methods course requirement	No
Legal research course requirement	Yes

Academics

The College of Law at Georgia State University receives solid reviews from students who appreciate the "quality, affordable legal education" they're receiving in the state's capital. Indeed, praise of the school's bargain tuition is sung from the rooftops; one practical 3L says, "It made no sense to go to a law school with a $35,000 a year tuition." Georgia State students get a "great caliber" of teachers, many of whom "have recently come from practicing or are still practicing, and thus are able to give...great insight into what it's 'really like' out there in the legal profession." This practical experience is a perfect complement to the grounded atmosphere of GSU, where students are more trained to become attorneys than to theorize about the law.

Multiple kudos go out to Georgia State's part-time program, which "allows not only for nontraditional students to obtain a law degree while potentially working full-time and/or caring for a family, but makes these night classes available for anyone who wishes to take them, allowing full- and part-time students to mingle." The school's significant nontraditional student body appreciates this flexibility, as many of them come from the working world and would not be able to attend law school otherwise. There are a few gripes from day students that the scheduling of professors and classes can seem "heavily weighted towards evening classes." Others with more adaptable schedules believe it "gives us the opportunity to learn from adjuncts who practice during the day and teach at night." "The faculty is nothing less than outstanding," proclaims one student.

Although the Urban Life Building in which the College of Law is located "is sometimes more 'urban' than 'life'" with some "security/theft issues," the school's "surprisingly pleasant" downtown Atlanta location provides a plentiful and "amazingly diverse selection of externship opportunities." Though "Everyone agrees that we need a new building" (there are plans for it down the road) and many speak of the depressing aspects of having almost all of their 1L classes in the same two auditoriums, the "high level of technology" in the current classrooms help diminish some of the building's downsides.

One major point of contention amongst GSUers is that the College of Law "has no set curve for non-required classes, meaning the curve in one corporations class could be a 90 while another corporations class could be an 81. This necessitates either willful indifference or the careful selection of classes so as to manipulate your GPA—a difficult choice even for the most ideal among us." This also puts GSU students "at a significant disadvantage in the competition for employment," and it doesn't help that the "Career Services Office is considerably below par." Luckily, "the Federal Reserve, the Eleventh Circuit, the State Capitol, and most large law firms in the South" are all located very close to GSU (some within walking distance).

DR. CHERYL JESTER-GEORGE, DIRECTOR OF ADMISSIONS
PO BOX 4049, ATLANTA, GA 30302-4049
TEL: 404-413-9200 FAX: 404-413-9203
EMAIL: ADMISSIONS@GSULAW.GSU.EDU • WEBSITE: LAW.GSU.EDU

Life

The "mature, unpretentious, hardworking, and real-world savvy" students at the College of Law often bring "more than a couple years of impressive life experience with them into the classroom," making class discussions "interesting and relevant." "We have students who used to be doctors, researchers, police officers, engineers, business owners, stay-at-home moms (and dads), teachers, etc.," explains one 3L. "There do not seem to be too many people who came to school because they had nothing else to do." Even though there is a large part-time student population and diverse ages represented on campus, students still claim to "spend a considerable amount of social time together." In fact, students agree that a sense of camaraderie pervades the campus. As one states, "I have never...felt the razor's edge of cutthroat competitiveness."

Concerning hometown Atlanta, a graduating student suggests that incoming first-years "get used to the idea of a homeless person snoozing in the library cubicle next to you! What can I say—it's not Emory. But you're not paying the Emory price tag either, so something has to give." The fact that "most people commute" and the impression that the law building "seems a little shunted off to a random corner" does "deter the school from ever really attaining a campus-like feel." Fortunately there is a way to combat any unwelcome feelings of isolation: "Joining student activities are a great way to meet people at GSU."

Getting In

Georgia State cops to the fact that both the LSAT and GPA are significant factors in its admissions decision, though personal statements and letters of recommendation do play a role. Recently admitted students at the 25th percentile had an LSAT score of 157 and an average GPA of 3.1, while admitted students at the 75th percentile had an LSAT score of 160 and a GPA of 3.6. For prospective students who have taken the LSAT more than once, all scores will be reviewed.

Moot court requirement	No
Public interest law requirement	No

ADMISSIONS

Selectivity Rating	**87**
# applications received	2,690
% applicants accepted	21
% acceptees attending	38
Average LSAT	159
LSAT Range	157–161
Average undergrad GPA	3.33
Application fee	$50
Regular application	Rolling, up to 3/15
Regular notification	Rolling
Early application program	No
Transfer students accepted	Yes
Evening division offered	Yes
Part-time accepted	Yes
LSDAS accepted	Yes

Applicants Also Look At

University of Georgia, Mercer University, University of Florida, Emory University

International Students

TOEFL recommended of international students	Yes
Minimum TOEFL (web)	680

FINANCIAL FACTS

Annual tuition (in-state/ out-of-state)	$9,360/$29,016
Books and supplies	$950
Fees (in-state/ out-of-state)	$390/$1,290
Fees per credit	$657
Tuition per credit (in-state/out-of-state)	$390/$1,290
Room & board (on/off-campus)	$12,796/$12,986
Financial aid application deadline	4/1
% first-year students receiving some sort of aid	65
% receiving some sort of aid	70
% of aid that is merit based	7
% receiving scholarships	10
Average grant	$5,542
Average loan	$19,951
Average total aid package	$15,341
Average debt	$45,326

EMPLOYMENT INFORMATION

Career Rating	**78**	**Grads Employed by Field (%)**
Rate of placement (nine months out)	93	Academic (4)
Average starting salary	$79,003	Business/Industry (17)
State for bar exam	GA	Government (10)
Pass rate for first-time bar	95	Judicial Clerkships (3)
Prominent Alumni		Military (2)
Glenn Richardson, Speaker of the House,		Private Practice (57)
Ga General Assembly; Ms. Evelyn Ann		Public Interest (6)
Ashley, Partner, Founder/Red Hot Law		
Group of Ashley LLC A; Ms.Mary M.		
Brockington, Attorney, Partner/Holland and		
Knight; Mr. Larry McKenzie Dingle,		
Attorney/Wilson Brock and Irby.		

GONZAGA UNIVERSITY
SCHOOL OF LAW

INSTITUTIONAL INFORMATION

Public/private	Private
Affiliation	Roman Catholic
Student-faculty ratio	15:1
% faculty part-time	46
% faculty female	39
% faculty minority	4
Total faculty	67

SURVEY SAYS...

Diverse opinions accepted
in classrooms
Great research resources
Great library staff
Beautiful campus

STUDENTS

Enrollment of law school	549
% male/female	59/41
% out-of-state	60
% full-time	99
% minority	7
Average age of entering class	24

ACADEMICS

Academic Experience Rating	**73**
Profs interesting rating	66
Profs accessible rating	85
Hours of study per day	5.17

Academic Specialties
Business law, fedearal Indian law, public interest law

Advanced Degrees Offered
None

Combined Degrees Offered
JD/MBA, JD/MAcc, JD/MSW; 3 to 4 years.

Clinical program required	Yes
Legal writing	
course requirement	Yes
Legal methods	
course requirement	Yes
Legal research	
course requirement	Yes
Moot court requirement	No
Public interest	
law requirement	Yes

Academics

Relatively small Gonzaga University School of Law has quite a lot to offer. The Jesuit influence is notable in Gonzaga's "great tradition of public service," and the school offers great respect and support to those pursuing a career in public interest (all students must perform 30 documented public service hours to get a diploma). Another perk is the "fabulous legal research and writing program," which "provides an excellent understanding of how to effectively and efficiently explain complex legal issues." "A strong externship program" "provides real-world experience," and the "on-site" University Legal Assistance Clinic gives students "real-life experience while under the supervision of attorneys."

Academically, "It really seems that the professors and administration want you to succeed." The "very driven and dedicated" administration is "open and accessible." "The administration has been very helpful and friendly to even my most idiotic of questions," confides a 1L. The "collegial, approachable, [and] enthusiastic" professors maintain "an open-door policy" and "will find time to meet with you if their office hours don't work." "It is nice to be at a school where the faculty knows you by name and truly cares about your academic success," says a 2L. In class, a few professors are "absolutely horrible," but most are "absolutely incredible." Professors tend to have "unique backgrounds" and "relevant, real-world experience." "While the majority of the faculty is relatively young in comparison to other institutions," Gonzaga's professors "all have very strong backgrounds in their respective subject areas," which gives students "an opportunity to learn what the real practice of law is like."

Gonzaga has "many ties to the local community." "The lawyers in town are practically all from GU and participate in the events here often," notes a 2L. One contingent of students says that "Career Services works very hard to help you find work" and "aggressively" offers assistance with resumes, networking, and job opportunities. "Several times a year, Career Services will bring in attorneys from various fields and give students free pizza while the practitioners talk about their particular area of expertise and how to get into it." The pro-Career Services faction also says that "opportunities to practice in big cities are increasing" for Gonzaga students. "I know plenty of students who are getting into big firms," declares a 2L. However, another group of students says that "Career Services needs a lot of help" because "Too many students are worried about finding jobs in desirable locations." "If you want to practice in eastern Washington, Gonzaga is a great school," acknowledges one student. "If you want to practice in civilization, going to Gonzaga puts you at a great disadvantage."

Gonzaga's "brand-new" facility "sits right next to the Spokane River," affording "beautiful views." The building itself "has limited space for students to gather or study" but it's "almost in the very center of the city," so "commuting every morning is a breeze." "Modern technology" is everywhere and "very reliable" wireless Internet access is available "throughout." The "excellent" library boasts a "helpful staff" and "a large selection of resources." "Only a few" of the classrooms "are less than ideal, and this is only the case when larger classes are held in those particular rooms."

Life

There isn't "very much" ethnic diversity here. "See the handful of minority students in admissions brochures and [the] DVD?" asks a 2L. "They're the only ones." "The Catholic and Mormon students create a fairly conservative atmosphere" but there is more than enough political diversity to go around, with both liberals and conservative abounding.

SUSAN LEE, DIRECTOR OF ADMISSIONS
P. O. BOX 3528, 721 N. CINCINNATI STREET, SPOKANE, WA 99220-3528
TEL: 800-793-1710 FAX: 509-313-3697
EMAIL: ADMISSIONS@LAWSCHOOL.GONZAGA.EDU • WEBSITE: WWW.LAW.GONZAGA.EDU

"The mandatory curve creates a very competitive environment, particularly among first-year students." "Students get especially competitive around finals." "For the most part," though, "fellow students are more than willing to lend a helping hand when you are lost." "It's not nearly as competitive as I expected it to be," emphasizes a 1L. The Student Bar Association routinely "provides review sessions for each first-year class and for each professor." During these sessions, "Students can ask questions in an environment that is less intimidating than the classroom."

"There are tons of opportunities to get involved" in extracurricular activities. Student organizations cover "almost every issue," and "Their participation in the law school community is prominent." "Like any smaller school, Gonzaga has its cliques," but overall "The sense of community is amazing." "We go to Gonzaga basketball games, run along the Spokane River, or just get together to watch football," says a 2L. "Spokane's small-town nature, the relatively small student body, and the fact that almost all the students are from elsewhere means that there is a tendency for the students to become very close," explains another student. Far and away, the "boring," "blue-collar" town of Spokane is the most griped-about aspect of life here. The cost of living is low, but students end most compliments there. "Spokane is one step above purgatory," reflects one student, "but it is not a very big step." On the bright side, "Glacier National Park, Banff, Seattle, Northern Idaho, and lower British Columbia are all within a few hours' drive." "There are awesome outdoor activities nearby" as well. "There's rock climbing and mountain biking" as well as "plenty of smooth asphalt for road cyclists." "Tons of great ski areas and golf courses" are nearby and "dirt cheap."

Getting In

Gonzaga's admitted students at the 25th percentile have LSAT scores in the range of 153 and GPAs hovering around 3.0. Admitted students at the 75th percentile have LSAT scores of about 157 and GPAs of about 3.6.

EMPLOYMENT INFORMATION

Career Rating	**72**	**Grads Employed by Field (%)**
Rate of placement (nine months out)	93	Academic (1)
Average starting salary	$67,189	Business/Industry (14)
State for bar exam	WA	Government (17)
Pass rate for first-time bar	75	Judicial Clerkships (13)

Employers Who Frequently Hire Grads

Military (2)

Various law firms; various local and state government entities, including military; various corporate entities.

Private Practice (47)

Public Interest (6)

Prominent Alumni

Christine Gregoire, Governor, State of Washington; Barbara Madsen, Justice, Washington Supreme Court; Catherine Cortez Masto, Attorney General of State of Nevada; Paul Luvera, Plantiffs Attorney, lead in tobacco litigation; Christopher J. Dietzen, Justice, Minnesota State Supreme Court.

ADMISSIONS

Selectivity Rating	**76**
# applications received	1,536
# applicants accepted	661
# acceptees attending	182
Average LSAT	155
LSAT Range	153–156
Average undergrad GPA	3.41
Application fee	$50
Regular application	Rolling, up to 4/15
Regular notification	Rolling
Early application program	No
Transfer students accepted	Yes
Evening division offered	No
Part-time accepted	Yes
LSDAS accepted	Yes

Applicants Also Look At

University of Denver, Seattle University, Arizona State University—Main Campus, University of Oregon, University of the Pacific, University of Idaho, Golden Gate University, University of San Francisco, Santa Clara University, University of Washington, Lewis & Clark College, Willamette University

International Students

TOEFL required of international students	Yes
Minimum TOEFL (paper/computer)	600/100

FINANCIAL FACTS

Annual tuition	$30,120
Books and supplies	$1,000
Fees	$130
Tuition per credit	$1,004
Room & board (off-campus)	$8,775
Financial aid application deadline	2/1
% first-year students receiving some sort of aid	100
% receiving some sort of aid	100
% of aid that is merit based	25
% receiving scholarships	84
Average grant	$11,000
Average loan	$31,576
Average total aid package	$44,654
Average debt	$91,984

HAMLINE UNIVERSITY
SCHOOL OF LAW

INSTITUTIONAL INFORMATION

Public/private	Private
Student-faculty ratio	15:1
% faculty part-time	0
% faculty female	58
% faculty minority	19
Total faculty	36

SURVEY SAYS...

Diverse opinions accepted
in classrooms
Great research resources

STUDENTS

Enrollment of law school	716
% male/female	46/54
% out-of-state	45
% full-time	71
% minority	13
Average age of entering class	25

ACADEMICS

Academic Experience Rating	**70**
Profs interesting rating	73
Profs accessible rating	85
Hours of study per day	4.78

Academic Specialties

Commercial law, criminal law, government services, international law, labor law, property, intellectual property law, health law, dispute resolution

Advanced Degrees Offered

JD, 3 years; LL.M., 1 year

Combined Degrees Offered

JD/MAPA (Masters of Public Administration), 4 years; JD/MANM (Masters-Nonprofit Mgmt), 4 years; JD/MAOL (Masters Arts in Organizational Leadership), 4 years; JD/MBA, 4 years, JD-MFA (Masters of Fine Arts—Creative Writing)

Clinical program required	No
Legal writing course requirement	Yes
Legal methods course requirement	Yes

Academics

Hamline University's School of Law is a relatively new program that focuses on giving its legal education curriculum a family feel. Those studying within Hamline's confines speak warmly of their teachers, a "combination of full-time faculty and adjuncts" who "provide a good balance of theory and practice." This "accessible" group is "committed to student learning" and even goes as far "as giving out their home phone numbers and encouraging students to call" in order to make sure that students properly grasp the material. The majority of Hamline's "liberal" professors "don't use the Socratic Method after first year," which students say is a nice reprieve. As an added bonus, "Many of Hamline's professors have worked prior to teaching," which "brings great real-world experience to the classroom."

Located in St. Paul, Minnesota, school officials run the school with a heartland touch. The administration is "always open to hear concerns," creating a "supportive environment" that encourages "connections with the broader community." A third-year student offers an example of the administration's focus on community: "When I deployed to Afghanistan midway through the second semester of my first year, the administration bent over backwards to ensure that my slot remained open and my scholarship was put into a holding status. The faculty and students maintained contact with me during the next 24 months, sending me care packages and e-mails." This sense of devotion to the student body is complimented by Hamline's "strong" Career Services Office, which "is helpful in all different types of legal career paths (and quite a few grads go public interest or nonpracticing)." The school's concentration on real-world experience also plays a key role in both developing grads who entered law school fresh out of college, as well as helping educate the nontraditional students who are coming from outside careers. Hamline's diverse clinical programs offer students the chance to clerk for a judge, do public interest law, corporate law, or work for the DA, all of which is done for credit during the semester.

Though it's not winning any prizes, the law building is described by students as "not bad," though some think it could benefit from more quiet locations for studying, and the law library is "more than adequate." Hamline's new Health Law Institute wins raves merely for "(preparing) its students for an area that will require attorney assistance long into the future," and the Alternative Dispute Resolution Program offers a unique specialization not found at many other schools. The unusual (and popular) part-time weekend program is especially tailored to nontraditional working students, which "allows students juggling families and/or jobs [to have] some flexibility." However, for weekday students, "Registration is tough when there is only one section of every class, even popular ones like Evidence or Corporations (that is, unless as a weekday student you want to go to a weekend class on Sunday morning)." Still, second- and third-year law students are given the opportunity to self-schedule finals, and the "quality of the legal education is competitive with the other area schools." One third-year student proclaims, "If you want a rigorous environment, but don't want to have to watch your back for three years, Hamline is for you."

ROBIN INGLI, DIRECTOR OF ADMISSIONS
1536 HEWITT AVENUE, ST. PAUL, MN 55104-1284
TEL: 800-388-3688 FAX: 651-523-3064
EMAIL: LAWADM@GW.HAMLINE.EDU • WEBSITE: WWW.HAMLINE.EDU/LAW

Life

Students at the School of Law mention the word "community", and they mention it often. This group "is quite diverse in terms of race, geographic background, politics, sexual orientation, age, and careers before law school," and this diversity "adds a nice dynamic to classroom discussions." "Hamline certainly operates like a family, but it's really two families: the weekend students and the day students," says one student, to a chorus of agreement. "Weekend program students are a different breed," says one 2L. "We already have careers for the most part." Some claim that this difference in background and priorities adds flavor to the student body's eclectic mix. Though Bar Review on Thursday nights is a good social opportunity to mingle with classmates at local bars, the weekenders are "more likely to socialize while we are studying, or to meet for a nice, more formal dinner—or meet at McDonald's with [their] kids." Still, "everyone gets along and cares about one another" which makes Hamline "a far cry from the dog-eat-dog world of law school." "There are many different student organizations that are perfect for networking, support, or simply to build friendships," says a second-year student. Apropos of nothing, "As far as mid-life crises go, law school is cheaper than fast cars and fast women," says a 3L.

Getting In

With an admit rate of nearly 50 percent, no one would ever accuse Hamline of closing its doors to qualified students. The school's rolling admissions policy allows students to submit an application up until the July prior to the fall in which they would enter (though the preferred deadline is April 1). The average LSAT for last year's admitted students was 153.

Legal research	
course requirement	Yes
Moot court requirement	No
Public interest	
law requirement	Yes
ADMISSIONS	
Selectivity Rating	**71**
# applications received	1,219
% applicants accepted	46
% acceptees attending	28
Average LSAT	153
LSAT Range	150–158
Average undergrad GPA	3.34
Application fee	$50
Regular application	Rolling, up to 4/1
Regular notification	Rolling
Early application program	No
Transfer students accepted	Yes
Evening division offered	Yes
Part-time accepted	Yes
LSDAS accepted	Yes

Applicants Also Look At

University of Wisconsin—Madison, University of Denver, University of Minnesota—Twin Cities, Drake University, Marquette University, St. Thomas University, William Mitchell College of Law

International Students

TOEFL required	
of international students	Yes
Minimum TOEFL (web)	100

FINANCIAL FACTS

Annual tuition	$30,068
Books and supplies	$1,500
Fees	$400
Room & board	
(on/off-campus)	$11,019/$14,621
Financial aid application	
deadline	4/1
% first-year students	
receiving some sort of aid	95
% receiving some sort of aid	88
% of aid that is merit based	98
% receiving scholarships	42
Average grant	$21,200
Average loan	$286,320
Average debt	$85,896

EMPLOYMENT INFORMATION

Career Rating	68	Grads Employed by Field (%)
Rate of placement (nine months out)	95	Academic (1)
Average starting salary	$52,000	Business/Industry (27)
State for bar exam	MN, WI, IL, NY, WA	Government (9)
Pass rate for first-time bar	92	Judicial Clerkships (15)
		Private Practice (41)
		Public Interest (7)

HARVARD UNIVERSITY
HARVARD LAW SCHOOL

INSTITUTIONAL INFORMATION

Public/private	Private
Student-faculty ratio	10:1
% faculty part-time	21
% faculty female	48
% faculty minority	11
Total faculty	260

SURVEY SAYS...

Great research resources
Great library staff
Abundant externship/internship/
clerkship opportunities

STUDENTS

Enrollment of law school	1,900
% full-time	100
Average age of entering class	24

ACADEMICS

Academic Experience Rating	**92**
Profs interesting rating	79
Profs accessible rating	61
Hours of study per day	3.67

Academic Specialties

Civil procedure, commercial law, constitutional law, corporation securities, criminal law, environmental law, government services, human rights, international law, labor law, legal history, legal philosophy, property, taxation, intellectual property law

Advanced Degrees Offered

LL.M. (Master of Laws), 1 year; S.JD, (Doctor of Judicial Science(SJD))

Combined Degrees Offered

JD/LL.M.(with Cambridge University),JD/MBA, JD/MPP, JD/MPP/ID, JD/Ph.D, JD/MA, JD/MALD, JD/Ed.M, JD/M.Div, JD/MPH, JD/MUP, JD/MPA

Clinical program required	No
Legal writing	
course requirement	Yes
Legal methods	
course requirement	Yes

Academics

Welcome to Harvard Law School, where "the resources—financial and material—are ridiculous." "Everything you need is right at your fingertips," says one student. "It's like having a remote control for your legal education." There is a "tremendous variety of courses" along with an "amazing" alumni network ("Chief Justice Roberts, President Barack Obama, and Elle Woods . . . "). The perennial complaint here is the lack of "practical emphasis." "We need a stronger legal writing curriculum," gripes a 3L. Many worry that the first year of classes have "little or no bearing on actual law practice," and Harvard is currently at the forefront of law schools looking to overhaul their first-year curriculum to include a wider range of classes. Other students disagree, though, citing the "incredible" clinical programs. "Nothing could prepare me better for a career in litigation than the real experience I am getting in litigation," explains a 2L.

The "fabulous" professors "range from amazing scholars and teachers to true nuts who probably couldn't find employment outside of academia." "I'm being taught contracts by one of the most prominent contracts theorists in the world and a former Solicitor General," brags a 1L. "You can't really beat that." "The breadth of knowledge of the professors, along with their professional experience, continually amazes me," adds another 1L. "There is a lot to be said for simply having the ability to interact with a large number of the country's greatest legal minds." However, some find certain professors "arrogant" and "aloof." This means that the faculty can be "somewhat inaccessible." "There's an intimidation factor in approaching some profs," and others "are just too busy to pin down."

The "very responsive" administration is "concerned about student issues." Dean Kagan "rocks." "If we need it, we get it," claims a 3L. "The administration spoils us ridiculously, all in the name of making students happy." At times, though, "This school is too big" and "feels like a factory, albeit one that pumps out very smart and well-qualified products."

"The career counseling services are pretty good," says one student. Not that they really need to be since "The Harvard name will take you anywhere in the world." "As one professor told us last year, '80 percent of what Harvard will do for you it did on the day you were accepted.'" "If you have a pulse and you graduate from HLS, you can get an excellent job," promises one student, adding that "it will probably be at the highest possible level in whatever city you work." One truly spectacular feature of Harvard Law is the "generous financial support for students working in the public interest during and after law school." There is an "excellent loan repayment program" if you want to do "public interest, government, or low-income work."

The facilities here "are almost all recently renovated." "The only buildings that are truly ugly are the dorms," which are "supposed to be magnificent examples of Bauhaus architecture." Most classrooms "are beautiful and intimate" and have plenty of "high-tech additions." Wireless access is good, but there are "too few outlets for laptops." Students love that the "library has every book ever imagined." This comes as no surprise as it's the biggest academic law library in the world.

Life

Students find that "everyone is extraordinarily talented" at Harvard. "Accomplished, hardworking, [and] unnervingly bright" are just a few ways to describe these future lawyers. "Sitting in class, you can look around and realize these are the brightest people of our generation," says a 2L, "and 75 percent of the learning here is from engaging your classmates and friends." "The kids here tend to be serious and a bit socially awkward," though. Despite "stereotypes" claiming "They're not the nicest group of people," many note "how friendly, cooperative, and even fun the vast majority of Harvard's students are."

Harvard can be "competitive." Some students are "obsessed with prestige." However, "The Harvard Law depicted in *The Paper Chase* is dead, and in its place is a much more collegial, respectful place." "Approximately the top 10 or 20 percent of students are intensely competitive," one student explains. "Everyone else is content getting a top-firm job...and is hardly competitive at all."

"The school is a bit large," and "There is a thriving social atmosphere." "Dean Kagan's metaphor of HLS as the New York City of law schools is remarkably accurate," says one student. "Having so many students here provides for a tremendous wealth of student organizations, activities, clubs, and events." "Funding for all sorts of student projects" makes it "very easy to put together amazing extracurricular experiences that are fantastic skill and resume builders." "From BLSA to the Federalist Society, the California Club to the Shooting Club," "There is a lot going on, always." "We have free coffee morning and night, a law school ice rink in the winter, and sand volleyball courts in the fall and spring," says a 2L. "The gym is brand new and insanely good." There are even "free professional massages during finals." Ultimately, "It all makes for a highly caffeinated, active, and involved community."

Getting In

When students arrive at law school to hear the dean say—"The competition is over. You've won."—it's safe to say that getting in wasn't what most would call slightly difficult. Admitted students at the 25th percentile have LSAT scores of 170 and GPAs of about 3.75. Admitted students at the 75th percentile have LSAT scores of 176 and GPAs of about 3.95. (Note that Harvard looks at all LSAT scores in their contexts.)

Legal research course requirement	Yes
Moot court requirement	Yes
Public interest law requirement	Yes

ADMISSIONS

Selectivity Rating	99
# applications received	7,099
% applicants accepted	12
% acceptees attending	68
Average LSAT	173
LSAT Range	170–176
Average undergrad GPA	3.88
Application fee	$85
Regular application	Rolling, up to 2/1
Regular notification	Rolling
Early application program	No
Transfer students accepted	Yes
Evening division offered	No
Part-time accepted	No
LSDAS accepted	Yes

Applicants Also Look At
Yale University, Columbia University, New York University, Samford University

FINANCIAL FACTS

Annual tuition	$41,500
Books and supplies	$1,100
Fees	$2,830
Room & board	$19,770
% first-year students receiving some sort of aid	78
% receiving some sort of aid	80
% receiving scholarships	41
Average grant	$18,193
Average loan	$41,938
Average total aid package	$51,373
Average debt	$105,494

EMPLOYMENT INFORMATION

Career Rating	95	**Grads Employed by Field (%)**
Rate of placement (nine months out)	99	Academic (1)
State for bar exam	NY, MA	Business/Industry (4)
Pass rate for first-time bar	98	Government (4)
Employers Who Frequently Hire Grads		Judicial Clerkships (19)
Major national law firms, federal & state		Private Practice (66)
governments, investment banks, consulting firms, law schools.		Public Interest (6)

HOFSTRA UNIVERSITY
SCHOOL OF LAW

INSTITUTIONAL INFORMATION

Public/private	Private
Student-faculty ratio	15:1
% faculty part-time	44
% faculty female	33
% faculty minority	23
Total faculty	108

SURVEY SAYS...
Diverse opinions accepted
in classrooms
Great research resources
Great library staff

STUDENTS

Enrollment of law school	1,108
% male/female	50/50
% out-of-state	29.8
% full-time	75.99
% minority	36
% international	2
# of countries represented	14
Average age of entering class	24

ACADEMICS

Academic Experience Rating	**70**
Profs interesting rating	69
Profs accessible rating	64
Hours of study per day	4.58

Academic Specialties
Civil procedure, commercial law, constitutional law, corporation securities, criminal law, environmental law, government services, human rights, international law, labor law, property, taxation, intellectual property law, family law, trial advocacy, international law, health law

Advanced Degrees Offered
JD: Full-time, 3 years, part-time four years. LL.M.: Full-time one year, part-time two years.

Combined Degrees Offered
JD/MBA: four years

Clinical program required	No
Legal writing	
course requirement	Yes
Legal methods	
course requirement	Yes

Academics

Haven't heard of Hofstra Law School? Your loss. The mid-sized Long Island school has been kicking around since 1970, and though it is not as well-known as some of its longer-standing compadres, it happily eschews the burden of carrying on tradition in favor of looking forward to what's to come for its graduates and the law in general. "Instead of hiring teachers only for what they've done, [the school] looks beyond to what the teachers will do for the school," says a 3L.

In keeping with its progressive vision, the school pays the most attention to those who will be bringing its name out into the world—the students. The law school has an official dean's hour once a month, where students can meet with the newly installed dean directly, and students enthusiastically agree that she "really listens to the wants of the students" and is "charting what appears to be a proper course" for the school. "All you have to do is speak with [the administration], and they'll consider your requests," says a 3L. This active consideration makes you "constantly feel as though you're in the midst of something new and exciting, and that you can have a voice in the school," says another student. Students also applaud the school's organization in regards to their academic careers, because "what is expected of you is clearly stated, and the tools of success are laid out very well."

Evaluations of the Hofstra faculty are a series of peaks and valleys; while students are extraordinarily happy with most of their teachers, there are some whose teaching abilities (or even knowledge of their course's subject matter) draw much ire, with no middle ground in between. "There are really no 'okay' professors. I have had great teachers and horrible professors," says a 2L. The exodus of professors to other law schools is a problem for many students, who often find their favorite professors here one day and gone the next. Still, all levels are devoted to their role as educators, and "gear their teaching to the pace of the class and relate the subject to current events." One student offers an example from a contracts class: "The teacher had an optional extra hour of class one day to discuss the sub prime meltdown and what factors led to it."

Though facilities and computer labs are large enough and "are in excellent condition, with modern equipment," some students wish the outside façade matched the beauty of Hofstra's campus, which is accredited by the American Association of Botanical Gardens and Arboreta. Research resources are in adequate supply (the library always remains open), and the combination of a solid Career Services department and the school's proximity to New York City's major courts and internships are a major reason that 95% of graduates are employed within 6 months of graduation, 70% of which are in Manhattan. The school also offers several clinics and skills courses "which allow for students to get practical experience well before graduating," and the school is very encouraging of students understanding their own limits. "You can be on a journal, moot court, etc.—as much as you can handle," says a student.

Life

Students refer to the utter lack of a competitive streak at Hofstra, aside from two little blips each academic year. "Finals week is cut-throat; you have no friends, and everyone is trying to trip you. But during the year everyone is nice to you and helps you out a lot," says a 1L. "I like being able to trust that my classmate is giving me correct information if I'm unsure about something," adds one. "Everyone gets along very well for the most part," especially in regards to academics, but "a lot of people form cliques," which makes it "very much like a grown-up version of high school."

JOHN CHALMERS, ASSISTANT DEAN FOR ENROLLMENT MANAGEMENT
121 HOFSTRA UNIVERSITY, HEMPSTEAD, NY 11549
TEL: 516-463-5916 FAX: 516-463-6264
EMAIL: LAWADMISSIONS@HOFSTRA.EDU • WEBSITE: LAW.HOFSTRA.EDU

There are plenty of activities and opportunities to socialize, and "students do bar events occasionally, and the organizations host different events as well." Though Hempstead itself is far from thriving (phrases kicked around include "quite unpleasant" and "pretty dismal"), Manhattan is only 25 miles away, and the school provides free busing to nearby train stations, which students happily take advantage of as "an invaluable resource of jobs and experiences." However, for those who do drive to school, "finding parking here is like a winning the Mega Millions. Impossible," says one student, echoing the sentiments of the large segment of Long Island residents who commute to classes each day. It is "very easy" to get caught up in the social aspect of the school, because there are graduate dorms on campus and the bars are all walking distance from the law school, but students make sure to take advantage of their options. "I like that in a couple hours I can either be in the middle of big city life or somewhere with a small-town feel.

Getting In

The school has a considerable part-time population, which typically raises the average age of an entering student, but at 24, Hofstra's average age remains pretty low. Considering the school's relatively quiet reputation, the school receives a surprising number of applicants for its 366 full- and part-time spots, most likely due to the number of local residents that apply. Like most schools, there isn't a set requirement for LSAT or GPA, but full-time students for the most recent entering class had a 25th percentile LSAT score of 154 and a 75th percentile score of 159.

Legal research course requirement	Yes
Moot court requirement	Yes
Public interest law requirement	No

ADMISSIONS

Selectivity Rating	**76**
# applications received	4,249
# applicants accepted	1,620
% acceptees attending	249
Average LSAT	156
LSAT Range	154–159
Average undergrad GPA	3.19
Application fee	$75
Regular application	Rolling, up to 4/15
Regular notification	Rolling
Early application program	Yes
Early application deadline	11/15
Early application notification	12/21
Transfer students accepted	Yes
Evening division offered	No
Part-time accepted	Yes
LSDAS accepted	Yes

Applicants Also Look At

Seton Hall University, Yeshiva University, Fordham University, Pace University, Rutgers University—Newark, St. John's University, Touro College, Brooklyn Law School, CUNY Law School at Queens College, University of Miami, Villanova University

International Students

TOEFL required of international students	No
TOEFL recommended of international students	No

FINANCIAL FACTS

Annual tuition	$39,014
Books and supplies	$1,400
Fees	$626
Tuition per credit	$1,320
Room & board (on/off-campus)	$15,516/$13,948
Financial aid application deadline	4/15
% first-year students receiving some sort of aid	92
% receiving some sort of aid	90
% of aid that is merit based	97
% receiving scholarships	49
Average grant	$16,958
Average loan	$37,292
Average total aid package	$43,019
Average debt	$110,602

EMPLOYMENT INFORMATION

Career Rating	**83**
Rate of placement (nine months out)	95.33
Average starting salary	$96,170
State for bar exam	NY
Pass rate for first-time bar	86.45

Employers Who Frequently Hire Grads

Certilman, Balin, Adler & Hyman; Davis, Polk & Wardwell; Debevoise & Plimpton; Dewey & LeBouef; Fried, Frank, Harris, Shriver & Jacobson; Holland & Knight; Milbank, Tweed, Hadley & McCloy; Paul; Hastings; Joanofsky & Walker; Shearman & Sterling; Skadden; Arps; Slate, Meagher & Flomm; Stroock & Stroock & Lavan; Sullivan & Cromwell; White & Case.

Prominent Alumni

David A. Paterson, Governor of New York; Hon. Maryanne Trump Barry, Judge, U.S. Ct of Appeals for the Third Circuit.

Grads Employed by Field (%)

Law firm (48)
Judicial Clerkship (6)
Government (13)
Public Interest (3)
Business (25)

Illinois Institute of Technology

Chicago-Kent College of Law

Academics

If you're looking to "feel both challenged and encouraged to learn" rather than "beaten down by the stereotypical combination of sadistic professors and hyper-competitive classmates," then you might want to try Chicago-Kent College of Law which works to create a scholarly community under the auspices of a science and engineering heavyweight. Placed "just high enough in the rankings to attract talented students who aren't arrogant, but not too high so that the professors are attracted for research rather than teaching," the school makes it clear up front that the experience "will be competitive," while also stressing "how important it is to not dwell on grades and rank even though they're important."

Known for its "intense" and "well-recognized" legal writing program (one of the few three-year programs in the country), students at Chicago-Kent must endure "several hellish weeks each semester" so that they can say, "The memo [I] did in the first three weeks of school is the equivalent of another school's 1L final project." "Every attorney I've worked with in the past three years has commented on the strength of my legal writing skills," boasts one third-year student. Other tough aspects of the school's curriculum include its grading curve, which gives transfer students an unfair advantage "because their GPA is not deflated by the first-year curve" and results in the school awarding more scholarships than students can retain "due to the academic standards that must be maintained." Many also cite the Intellectual Property Program and the variety of in-house clinics (in which students work with actual clients for credit) as strengths.

As one would expect judging from its parent institution, Chicago-Kent's "top-notch" classrooms are "enabled with the best educational technology," including myriad outlets, and the entire campus is blanketed with wireless Internet (some even claim the technology "outranks" the institute itself). The comprehensive library provides plenty of study space, and is run by a "knowledgeable" staff that is "willing to assist you with any issues." Chicago-Kent's location in the West Loop "is crucial to practical experience" and "maximizes chances for great externships," though summer jobs "aren't all that easy to come by with the competition of Northwestern, University of Chicago, U of I, and Michigan so close by."

Despite a large contingent of part-time faculty in the upper-level courses, professors at Chicago-Kent are "passionately engaged in the subject matter" and "totally committed to the students as well as to their research." They "work hard to encourage you and support you outside of the classroom," and are particularly good at "treating the students as adults and expecting them to perform at a higher level," according to a first-year student. Though they're not without complaints, most here say that the administration is "very accommodating [of] students' needs," and "are always quick to reply to questions." The general opinion of the Career Services Office is one of mild discontent, and a large number of students wish the school could "expand its ability to place students in the legal workplace nationwide" having noticed that most of the "prestigious" law firms only hire the top 10 percent of Chicago-Kent students. "For some reason, I say we are associated with IIT and people outside of the legal community think I am going to truck driving school," complains a 3L. After three years at Chicago-Kent, one student can safely say that "students are happy, teachers want to teach, and learning is fun, yet also difficult."

NICOLE VILCHES, ASSISTANT DEAN FOR ADMISSIONS
565 WEST ADAMS STREET, CHICAGO, IL 60661
TEL: 312-906-5020 FAX: 312-906-5274
EMAIL: ADMIT@KENTLAW.EDU • WEBSITE: WWW.KENTLAW.EDU

Life

Numerous clubs and organizations "for everything you can imagine" mean that "there is a constant flow of speakers and programs for students to attend that cover all areas of the law." After a hard day of classes and legal writing boot camp, students look forward to the Student Bar Association's monthly "Kent Nights," for which the SBA rents out a different downtown bar for a "really great way to get noses out of books and make the student body relax with each other to have a good time." The student body at Chicago-Kent is a friendly bunch, and while there is a "subtle" competitive streak throughout the years, most agree that "there is definitely a friendly, helpful attitude that prevails among students here," especially between the different sections of 1Ls. "I love being surrounded by individuals who allow me to have intelligent and insightful discussions about current issues or about what we are discussing in classes," says one student. However, a definite divide exists between day and evening students, with evening students complaining that most of the extracurricular activities are "pretty much unavailable to the evening students due to the timing of special events." While it's true that students live scattered all throughout the Chicago area, preventing some from attending certain events, others see it as a plus: "Most students will spend the better part of their day interacting with each other, instead of simply coming to class and then going home," explains a third-year student.

Getting In

Though admissions are on a rolling basis, Chicago-Kent's binding Early Decision Program is somewhat unique in the field of law school admissions. Recently enrolled students at the 25th percentile had an LSAT score of 158 and an average GPA of 3.3, while enrolled students at the 75th percentile had an LSAT score of 163 and a GPA of 3.8.

Legal methods	
course requirement	No
Legal research	
course requirement	Yes
Moot court requirement	Yes
Public interest	
law requirement	No

ADMISSIONS

Selectivity Rating	**84**
# applications received	3,056
# applicants accepted	1,059
# acceptees attending	234
Average LSAT	161
LSAT Range	158–163
Average undergrad GPA	3.53
Application fee	$60
Regular application	Rolling, up to 7/1
Regular notification	Rolling
Early application program	Yes
Early application deadline	11/1
Early application notification	12/15
Transfer students accepted	Yes
Evening division offered	Yes
Part-time accepted	Yes
LSDAS accepted	Yes

Applicants Also Look At

University of Illinois at Urbana-Champaign, American University, Northwestern University, The George Washington University, DePaul University, John Marshall Law School, Loyola University—Chicago

FINANCIAL FACTS

Annual tuition	$35,416
Books and supplies	$1,000
Fees	$894
Tuition per credit	$1,135
Room & board	
(on/off-campus)	$8,867/$14,247
% first-year students	
receiving some sort of aid	95
% receiving some sort of aid	92
% of aid that is merit based	28
% receiving scholarships	62
Average grant	$16,647
Average loan	$33,119
Average total aid package	$40,397
Average debt	$92,898

EMPLOYMENT INFORMATION

		Grads Employed by Field (%)
Career Rating	**84**	
Rate of placement (nine months out)	90	Academic (2)
Average starting salary	$90,077	Business/Industry (17)
State for bar exam	IL	Judicial Clerkships (5)
Pass rate for first-time bar	96	Private Practice (55)

Employers Who Frequently Hire Grads

Public Interest (8)

Approximately 55 employers conduct on-campus interviews. Hundreds of additional employers request resume collection or direct contact from students, hire students through consortium job fairs, and post open job listings with the career services office.

Prominent Alumni

The Honorable Ilana Diamond Rovner, U.S. Court of Appeals for the 7th Circuit.

INDIANA UNIVERSITY—BLOOMINGTON
MAURER SCHOOL OF LAW

INSTITUTIONAL INFORMATION

Public/private	Public
Student-faculty ratio	10:1
% faculty part-time	5
% faculty female	37
% faculty minority	15
Total faculty	65

SURVEY SAYS...

Great research resources
Great library staff

STUDENTS

Enrollment of law school	613
% male/female	58/42
% out-of-state	57
% full-time	100
% minority	18
# of countries represented	2
Average age of entering class	23

ACADEMICS

Academic Experience Rating	**90**
Profs interesting rating	85
Profs accessible rating	79
Hours of study per day	4.62

Academic Specialties

Civil procedure, commercial law, constitutional law, corporation securities, criminal law, environmental law, government services, human rights, international law, labor law, legal history, legal philosophy, property, taxation, intellectual property law, telecommunications, trial and appellate advocacy

Advanced Degrees Offered

SJD; LLM; LLM practicum; MCL.

Combined Degrees Offered

JD; JD/MBA; JD/MBAA; JD/MPA; JD/MSES; JD/MPA; JD/MA; JD/MA or MS; JD/MS; JD/PHD.

Clinical program required	Yes
Legal writing course requirement	Yes
Legal methods course requirement	No
Legal research course requirement	Yes

Academics

Students at the Indiana University Maurer School of Law enjoy "first-rate resources and education" at "an excellent value." The law school boasts no fewer than 19 clinical programs and projects including a community legal clinic, an entrepreneurship law clinic, and an inmate legal assistance project. Externship programs include the Washington Public Interest Program, which allows 3Ls to earn credit for public interest internships with government agencies and nonprofits in Washington, DC. Students can study abroad in Florence, Barcelona, Beijing, Auckland, and a host of other international cities. Several interesting dual-degree programs and a bevy of specialization programs in taxation, international and comparative law, and intellectual property round out IU's "excellent" academic options.

The "extremely knowledgeable and accessible" faculty at IU "is really impressive." "When you go to class, you get the sense that your professors want to be in the classroom, and that makes engaging yourself in the material much easier," says a 2L. "There's a nice balance between professors who try to scare the pants off of you and the ones who really encourage you to take risks and push yourself, even if you turn out to be wrong." Even "boring" professors "really have a lot of important things to say." Outside the classroom, professors "participate in the law school social events" and "will go to great lengths to help students publish, research, and get placed" in jobs.

IU's administration "is genuinely concerned about students as individuals," and its "helpful and nice" Financial Aid Office "is the best in the country." Though in the past students have noted that "Career Services, while improving, has a long way to go," the Office of Career and Professional Development has since created an alternative career series, lunch-with-a-lawyer programs, and two alumni career service committees as well as expanded off campus interviews, hired new staff and hosted alumni sponsored Welcome-to-the-City events in key cities around the country. Many students tell us that the Office of Career and Professional Development "does all it can to assist students in obtaining jobs." "I think they're great," declares a 1L. "They're not going to get a job for you, but they'll do pretty much everything else." "If you are near the top of the class," "You'll have the Indy firms drooling all over you" and you won't have a problem working at "any of the best firms in Chicago" "or even Washington, D.C."

Everyone here agrees that the campus surrounding the law school is "beautiful." Classrooms once described as "uncomfortable," have been recently renovated. "The entire building has wireless Internet" and "there are electrical outlets at each seat." The gem of IU is the law library, which students claim is "without equal in the world, in part because of its staff." "With large windows that look out on the forest in the middle of campus, it's easy to forget that you're in the middle of a Big Ten school."

Life

IU's Midwestern location helps encourage a collegial attitude that frowns on aggressive competition." Students "simply do not let the abstract, competitive nature of the grading system affect their outward nature or the way they see their classmates." "If there is a more laid-back group of students at any law school in the country, I'd like to see it," challenges a 2L. "Students find their groups and comfort zones relatively quickly." Smaller class sizes "contribute to some minor drama at times," but students "get to know each other better and have a closer relationship with the faculty." "You can learn as much law as well here as at Harvard or Yale," promises a 3L. "But you will pay less, will see people being nicer to each other, and don't have to live in a grungy New England city."

FRANK MOTLEY, ASSISTANT DEAN OF ADMISSIONS
211 SOUTH INDIANA AVENUE, BLOOMINGTON, IN 47405-1001
TEL: 812-855-4765 FAX: 812-855-1967
EMAIL: LAWADMIS@INDIANA.EDU • WEBSITE: WWW.LAW.INDIANA.EDU

The law school is "settled into a big university" "far away from the real world" in "one of the greatest college towns in America." "The school is great for young undergraduates who appreciate a small-town environment." "Moving from a city to the boonies is still taking some getting used to," says one urbanite, "but the school offers some phenomenal cultural opportunities." There are "at least 30 ethnically diverse restaurants within a three-minute walk from the law school." Students here "work hard," but "There is great balance between the social life and the academic life." "The fitness and recreation facilities are superb" and "There are law school teams for intramurals." The Law and Drama Society "puts on a play in the school's moot court room." "The annual Women's Law Caucus Auction" is a big hit, as is an annual basketball game in IU's beloved Assembly Hall which pits students against professors. Mostly, though, "The social environment is aimed at those who like to go out and party." "We're very social, very involved, and very fun," boasts a 2L. "The school is the focal point around which life spins, but there's always something to do, somewhere to go, someone to talk to." "There are after-hours activities sponsored by the school or a student group almost each week, and if there's nothing going on students will always congregate somewhere to have fun."

Getting In

Admitted students at the 25th percentile have LSAT scores of about 156 and GPAs hovering around 3.39. Admitted students at the 75th percentile have LSAT scores of approximately 165 and GPAs of approximately 3.85.

EMPLOYMENT INFORMATION

Career Rating	**85**
Rate of placement (nine months out)	95.8
Average starting salary	$90,000
State for bar exam	IN, IL, NY, CA, OH
Pass rate for first-time bar	92

Employers Who Frequently Hire Grads
Arnola & Porter; Baker & Daniels; Winston & Strawn; Ice Miller; Jones Day; Kirkland & Ellis; Mayer Brown; U.S. Dept. of Justice; U.S. Federal Circuit & District Courts.

Prominent Alumni
Shirley Abrahamson, Chief Justice, Wisconsin Supreme Court; Lee Hamilton, Former Congressman; Justices Michael Kanno and John Tinder, 7th Circuit Court of Appeals; Michael Maurer, Entrepreneur & Philanthropist; Bruce McLean, Chairman, Akin Group.

Grads Employed by Field (%)
Academic (4)
Business/Industry (16)
Government (14)
Judicial Clerkships (11)
Military (3)
Private Practice (46)
Public Interest (6)

Moot court requirement	No
Public interest law requirement	No

ADMISSIONS

Selectivity Rating	**92**
# applications received	2,384
# applicants accepted	597
# acceptees attending	205
Average LSAT	161
LSAT Range	156–165
Average undergrad GPA	3.6
Application fee	$35
Regular application	Rolling, up to 8/1
Early application program	Yes
Early application deadline	11/15
Early application notification	12/15
Transfer students accepted	Yes
Evening division offered	No
Part-time accepted	No
LSDAS accepted	Yes

Applicants Also Look At
University of Texas at Austin, University of Illinois at Urbana-Champaign, University of Michigan–Ann Arbor, Emory University, University of Notre Dame, George Washington University, University of Wisconsin at Madison, College of William and Mary, Washington University, University of Minnesota—Twin Cities, The Ohio State University—Columbuse

International Students

TOEFL required of international students	Yes
Minimum TOEFL (paper/computer)	600/250

FINANCIAL FACTS

Annual tuition (in-state/out-of-state)	$19,125/$36,510
Books and supplies	$1,714
Fees	$863
Room & board	$9,257
Financial aid application deadline	4/1
% first-year students receiving some sort of aid	94
% receiving some sort of aid	95
% of aid that is merit based	80
% receiving scholarships	77
Average grant	$9,294
Average loan	$32,482
Average total aid package	$38,655
Average debt	$93,800

INDIANA UNIVERSITY—INDIANAPOLIS

SCHOOL OF LAW

INSTITUTIONAL INFORMATION

Public/private	Public
Student-faculty ratio	15:1
% faculty part-time	51
% faculty female	42
% faculty minority	9
Total faculty	95

SURVEY SAYS...

Great research resources
Beautiful campus
Students love Indianapolis, IN

STUDENTS

Enrollment of law school	953
% male/female	55/45
% out-of-state	23
% full-time	67
% minority	13
% international	2
# of countries represented	13
Average age of entering class	26

ACADEMICS

Academic Experience Rating	**72**
Profs interesting rating	68
Profs accessible rating	63
Hours of study per day	4.25

Academic Specialties

Constitutional law, criminal law, government services, human rights law, international law, taxation, health law

Advanced Degrees Offered

S.JD, LL.M.

Combined Degrees Offered

JD/MPA, 4 years; JD/MBA, 4 years; JD/MHA, 4 years; JD/MPH, 4 years; JD/M. Phil, 4 years; JD/MLS, 4 years; JD/MSW, 4 years

Clinical program required	No
Legal writing course requirement	Yes
Legal methods course requirement	Yes
Legal research course requirement	Yes
Moot court requirement	No

Academics

Despite being the lesser known of the two IU law schools (the other one is in Bloomington), the School of Law at Indiana University—Indianapolis still manages to carve out a well-regarded nook in the legal education world. Professors get solid reviews for their overall accessibility and for doing "a good job of engaging students in class discussions." "Besides ensuring academic success, faculty members take the initiative to help students find their niche in the legal community. There have been examples of professors reaching out to their contacts to obtain experiences for students," attests a 3L. IU-Indy's semester rotation system alternates the classes in IU's day and evening curriculum so that evening students learn from the same professors as do the day students, offering a good example of how the staff at IU—Indy "understands what [you're] taking on as [an] evening student." Students point out that the range of course selection and the legal writing program could use some work; many report of a muddled and unnecessarily lengthy legal writing program, which one student says "may as well be an upper-level foreign language [course] for me."

The "extremely student-friendly" administration is appreciated by most students, although there are detractors who claim that they are made to feel like "a tuition cow" and that "constant poor planning and communication cause a lot of unnecessary heartache for the students." However, for the most part, students are satisfied. "It is never a problem to schedule a meeting to sit down with the dean," says one. "Between the administration and the student groups, it seems that there's always some sort of activity being planned for us," backs up another. Office of Professional Development does its part for students as well; some would like to see more "firms from out of town" recruiting on campus, but others say that the office "has been helpful in reminding students that there are plenty of other wonderful jobs in small- to medium-sized firms, government jobs, as well as a myriad of other opportunities (all the while reminding us that those positions pay well too)."

With easy access to computer labs, advanced technology in all of the classrooms, wireless Internet, and many academic offerings available online (including online meetings with professors and remote speakers), the law school "promotes an environment that utilizes today's technology." The "spacious" and "bright" law building "is small enough to find someone easily but large enough to get away from the chit-chat and find a quiet place to study alone." "There is never a day that I dread being in the building, and that is a big deal considering how much time I spend in it!" chirps a first-year student. As an added benefit, the law school's location in Indianapolis ("for all intents and purposes, the center of the legal universe in Indiana") provides students access to many state and local resources for gaining practical experience, and IU-Indy "holds favorable rapport with all the largest firms in town." As the sole law school located in the state capital, networking opportunities are plentiful, and IU-Indy students "have a monopoly on available externships with government agencies and large corporations." "A student can take an externship in state government and walk there from class," says one.

PATRICIA KINNEY, DIRECTOR FOR ADMISSIONS
530 WEST NEW YORK STREET, INDIANAPOLIS, IN 46202-3225
TEL: 317-274-2459 FAX: 317-278-4780
EMAIL: LAWADMIT@IUPUI.EDU • WEBSITE: WWW.INDYLAW.INDIANA.EDU

Life

Students at IU—Indy are a pleasant enough group, and "It's very easy to make new friends thanks to the various social activities, networking events, and classes" on campus. Though the social circuit seems to be less thriving for evening students, it's often due to outside responsibilities; as one night student puts it, "Anyone who complains about lack of social scene simply isn't trying to make friends or get out, because there is plenty to do if you're open to it." A large number of students speak of a need for more diversity within the student body, an issue the school has been trying to combat in recent years. Unfortunately, "Indiana still has a 'good ole boy' mentality present in many places," says a third-year. There is a certain amount of competitiveness "in the sense of not revealing grades or performance," but overall, students help foster an encouraging environment.

Without campus housing and with a large part-time, evening student contingent, IU—Indy is considered a commuter school, and people tend to scatter after classes end. Social life is "based strictly on friendship and/or social club membership." A 2L warns: "It is not the kind of school where all 100 people in your section will go grab a beer after class. It is a place where you can develop 10–20 really strong friendships." Once you do find these friendships, they are "great opportunities for leisure activities" both inside and outside of the school, as "Indianapolis is a cheap city." Be forewarned, however: "Parking is horrendous."

Getting In

When evaluating applicants for admission, Indy first looks at undergraduate GPA and LSAT scores, but also takes into account letters of recommendation. For applicants taking the LSAT more than once, the school will look at the best score. Applicants who are not admitted during the regular admissions cycle are considered for Indy's special summer program, meant for 30–40 students who the school feels can benefit from a rigorous, individualized summer course.

Public interest law requirement	No

ADMISSIONS

Selectivity Rating	**77**
# applications received	1,662
# applicants accepted	646
# acceptees attending	285
Average LSAT	155
LSAT Range	152–158
Average undergrad GPA	3.4
Application fee	$50
Regular application	Rolling, up to 3/1
Regular notification	Rolling
Early application program	Yes
Early application deadline	11/15
Early application notification	12/31
Transfer students accepted	Yes
Evening division offered	Yes
Part-time accepted	Yes
LSDAS accepted	Yes

International Students

TOEFL required of international students	Yes
Minimum TOEFL (paper/internet)	550/79

FINANCIAL FACTS

Annual tuition (in-state/ out-of-state)	$16,083/$35,520
Books and supplies	$1,600
Fees	$1,176
Tuition per credit (in-state/out-of-state)	$518/$1,145
Room & board	$21,124
% first-year students receiving some sort of aid	48
% receiving some sort of aid	82
% of aid that is merit based	30
% receiving scholarships	47
Average grant	$5,000
Average loan	$17,965
Average total aid package	$20,500
Average debt	$51,676

EMPLOYMENT INFORMATION

Career Rating	75	Grads Employed by Field (%)	
Rate of placement (nine months out)	96	Academic (2)	
Average starting salary	$75,000	Business/Industry (16)	
State for bar exam	IN	Government (25)	
Pass rate for first-time bar	85	Judicial Clerkships (2)	
Prominent Alumni		Military (1)	
John Pistole, Deputy Director of the FBI;		Private Practice (47)	
Ellen Engleman, Chairman of the National		Public Interest (2)	
Transportation Safety Bd; Mark Roesler,		Other (1)	
President & CEO, CMG Worldwide, Inc.;			
Alan Cohen, Chairman, President & CEO,			
The Finish Line Inc.			

THE JOHN MARSHALL LAW SCHOOL

Academics

The John Marshall Law School is an independent bastion of legal education that offers day and evening programs as well as both fall and spring admission. John Marshall is pretty large as far as law schools go and it "places a huge emphasis on real-world practice." Students report that they are "ready to hit the ground running even as clerks and interns." The "unparalleled" writing program "creates students who can file complaints and briefs immediately, with little or no additional training." The trial advocacy program is "outstanding" as well. "When you graduate from John Marshall, you are ready to work in a courtroom," a 2L says. John Marshall also offers specialized programs and joint JD/LLM programs in a host of areas including emplyee benefits, information technology and privacy law, international business and trade law, real estate law, intellectual property law, and tax law. "Students are encouraged to find a specific field of interest and are given every opportunity to become experts" in that field.

"The school's faculty is comprised mostly of professors who have accumulated years of experience," a 2L explains. "Their experiences and knowledge give a true and practical look at the actual practice of law." Students boast that John Marshall's "accessible" faculty is comprised of "the best professors, judges, and lawyers in Chicago." It's also worth noting that the hardcore, old-school Socratic Method is very much alive and well at John Marshall. A few professors are "very hard to comprehend" and "not good teachers," though. Opinion concerning the administration is split. One faction of students calls management "extremely helpful." "There seems to be a genuine interest in the needs of the students," they say. Other students aren't so happy. "The deans never get anything done," a 3L says. "They're like the Queen of England; there for show and to wave their hand."

About 10 percent of each graduating class is able to obtain the really plum jobs at big firms. Most students tell us they are satisfied with their career prospects. "The connections that John Marshall has to the Chicago area are incredible," a 1L says. "It is very easy to connect with other John Marshall alumni, who are very willing to meet with and help you." A 3L adds, "John Marshall has done everything possible to put its graduates in a position of getting a job." Some students aren't as pleased, though. "I have had little help from the staff at the Career Services office," a 2L gripes. "Every time I have asked for assistance, they have merely told me where to look. I really could have figured that out for myself."

John Marshall is located in the middle of Chicago's South Loop "in the heart of the legal community" and "close to all the action." The United States District Court of Appeals for the Seventh Circuit is across the street. The Chicago Bar Association is "right next door." As for the actual law school facilities, "the buildings are old Chicago architectural mainstays" and "they've got charm." "The place needs a little sprucing up," though. It "doesn't offer many perks you see on other campuses." "The classrooms that are newer are very good." On the other hand, some classrooms are "a couple decades behind." Students also complain that John Marshall is generally "overcrowded." "Elevators are hard to come by" and "it's slightly hard to get around."

WILLIAM B. POWERS, ASSOCIATE DEAN FOR ADMISSION & STUDENT AFFAIRS
315 SOUTH PLYMOUTH COURT, CHICAGO, IL 60604
TEL: 800-537-4280 FAX: 312-427-5136
EMAIL: ADMISSION@JMLS.EDU • WEBSITE: WWW.JMLS.EDU

Life

The student population at John Marshall is pretty diverse, ethnically and just about every other way. Some students tell us that the academic atmosphere is cordial. "We help each other, share outlines, and study in groups," a 2L says. However, the prevailing opinion seems to be that John Marshall is home to "a very competitive environment which rewards achievement." "One thing that sets John Marshall apart is that they give people who would otherwise not get to go to law school a chance," a 2L explains. "That leads to a large number of people failing out the first year." "After first semester things became much more competitive among people in my section," another 2L recalls.

The South Loop is not conducive to an active social life. It's not unsafe or anything, it's just very commercial and kind of dead after business hours. Nevertheless, students here say that it's "very easy to find friends here" and they promise that they are a "very nice, normal bunch." "People are split into those active in school activities, such as trial teams, versus those who choose to work outside of school." "The social aspect really depends on the individual," a 1L says. "Some prefer to get in, do the work, and get out. Others prefer to socialize. There is something for everyone." If you want to get involved, "there are plenty of school-sponsored social events." "We have over 50 student organizations to choose from so that everyone can find their niche," a 3L notes. "Being a joiner at John Marshall is easy and doesn't feel corny like it did in undergrad."

Getting In

Admitted students at the 25th percentile have LSAT scores in the mid 150s and GPAs around 3.02. Admitted students at the 75th percentile have LSAT scores in the high 150s and GPAs in the 3.5 range.

Legal writing	
course requirement	Yes
Legal methods	
course requirement	Yes
Legal research	
course requirement	Yes
Moot court requirement	No
Public interest	
law requirement	No

ADMISSIONS

Selectivity Rating	**75**
# applications received	3,084
% applicants accepted	40
% acceptees attending	45
Average LSAT	154
LSAT Range	151–156
Average undergrad GPA	3.18
Application fee	$60
Regular application	Rolling,
	up to 8/1
Regular notification	Rolling
Early application program	No
Transfer students accepted	Yes
Evening division offered	Yes
Part-time accepted	Yes
LSDAS accepted	Yes

Applicants Also Look At

Illinois Institute of Technology, DePaul University, Loyola University—Chicago

International Students

TOEFL required	
of international students	Yes
Minimum TOEFL (paper)	600

FINANCIAL FACTS

Annual tuition	$35,090
Books and supplies	$2,162
Fees	$100
Tuition per credit	$1,210
Room & board	
(off-campus)	$24,058
% first-year students	
receiving some sort of aid	90
% receiving some sort of aid	90
% of aid that is merit based	95
% receiving scholarships	35
Average grant	$6,500
Average loan	$20,000
Average total aid package	$20,500
Average debt	$105,889

EMPLOYMENT INFORMATION

		Grads Employed by Field (%)
Career Rating	**76**	Academic (3)
Rate of placement (nine months out)	89.1	Business/Industry (23)
Average starting salary	$78,494	Government (14)
State for bar exam	IL	Judicial Clerkships (2)
Pass rate for first-time bar	89.1	Military (1)

Employers Who Frequently Hire Grads

Private Practice (55)
Public Interest (2)

Mayer Brown; DLA Piper; Cook County State's Attorneys Office; City of Chicago Law Department; Vedder Price.

Prominent Alumni

Mark Pedowitz, Senior Advisor to the Office of the Co-Chairman ABC Entertainment Group; Bill Daley, Former U.S. Secty of Commerce, Now Vice Chairman JP Morgan Chase.

LEWIS & CLARK COLLEGE
LEWIS & CLARK LAW SCHOOL

INSTITUTIONAL INFORMATION

Public/private	Private
Student-faculty ratio	10:1
% faculty part-time	47
% faculty female	38
% faculty minority	8
Total faculty	85

SURVEY SAYS...
Great research resources
Liberal students

STUDENTS

Enrollment of law school	716
% male/female	53/47
% out-of-state	62
% full-time	77
% minority	18.9
% international	2
# of countries represented	8
Average age of entering class	26

ACADEMICS

Academic Experience Rating	**84**
Profs interesting rating	80
Profs accessible rating	81
Hours of study per day	4.23

Academic Specialties
Commercial law, constitutional law, corporation securities, criminal law, environmental law, government services, international law, labor law, property, taxation, intellectual property law, animal law

Advanced Degrees Offered
LL.M./Environmental & Natural Resources, 12–18 months

Combined Degrees Offered
LL.M in Environmental & Natural Resources Law/JD, 3–3.5 years

Clinical program required	No
Legal writing course requirement	Yes
Legal methods course requirement	Yes
Legal research course requirement	Yes
Moot court requirement	Yes

Academics

Students who take the legal plunge at Lewis & Clark Law School in beautiful Portland, Oregon, enjoy professors who are "uniformly excellent and approachable for discussion about class topics and other issues striking your fancy." The small size of the law school allows for an extremely personalized educational experience, and students benefit from this cozy setup on multiple levels, "from an academic perspective as well as from a functional perspective." "I have been lucky enough to develop solid mentor relationships with specific professors that were particularly inspirational," says a second-year student. Practically everyone involved in running the school, from the dean to the cafeteria staff, "seem to truly like each other," and the well-regarded faculty is given an "unusual amount of influence in the way that the school is run, and [in the] school's policies."

Lewis & Clark Law School has a relatively small course load of required classes and offers a night program, bringing a large contingent of older and more experienced students to the classrooms which "adds a valuable, practical dimension to the learning experience." As one would expect from such an environmentally conscious institution, programs such as environmental and natural resources law and animal law are "unparalleled." No matter what their specialization, the faculty is considered to be "inspirational and knowledgeable enough to stimulate thinking beyond what's required by the curriculum," and the school's size "allows for an ideal student/teacher ratio that goes further to foster a highly effective teaching environment."

Lewis & Clark's National Crime Victim Law Institute (NCVLI) is another source of pride for the school, "leading the way in an emerging field of law."

Administrators are friendly, accessible, "always willing to help out a student," and they keep the law school "running very smoothly." The research librarians are cited for being "very knowledgeable," and the Career Services Department also does its part to make sure students' needs are met, though some would like to see more non-metro area firms on campus. For students who are interested in staying in the area after graduation, there is "heavy support and involvement from the Portland legal community," and for others, "alumni are distributed all around the world."

Since the school and its student body are known for being nature-friendly, it follows that the buildings on campus are all "green" and "tucked into a forested state park." This is nice, students say, because "When you are facing the gut-wrenching pain of law school, a 'walk in the park' goes a long way." Students are quite pleased with the library and the newer building, Wood Hall, but many are clamoring for an update of the other facilities. Portland is universally beloved as "a great place to live," though students say the parking situation could stand some improvements. A graduating student sums up life at the law school this way: "The professors are passionate about what they teach, and the students actually want to help each other get ahead in school. And where else do you get to study while in an overly large tree-house?"

TRACY SULLIVAN, ASSOCIATE DIRECTOR OF ADMISSIONS
LEWIS & CLARK LAW SCHOOL, 10015 SW TERWILLIGER BOULEVARD, PORTLAND, OR 97219
TEL: 503-768-6613 FAX: 503-768-6793
EMAIL: LAWADMSS@LCLARK.EDU • WEBSITE: LAW.LCLARK.EDU

Life

No one would argue that "the school could definitely use a little diversity"; "liberal" describes the majority of those enrolled at Lewis & Clark, and as one 3L warns, "If you are conservative, religious, or a meat-eating capitalist, be prepared." Fortunately, the laid-back nature of the majority of the student body means that there is "a complete void of competition"; absolutely "No one participates in the awful game of one-upmanship or cutthroat competition," and "The students are genuinely interested in helping and supporting each other." The day and night students don't often interact outside of class, but this doesn't seem to be a source of much tension. There are plenty of clubs in which they can relate if they so choose, and students here "are spoiled with the number of lunchtime events," including speakers and panels. "Everyone is accepted for who they are," coos a 2L. A second-year student puts it in another way: "Good people go here."

Getting In

Gaining admission to Lewis & Clark isn't very difficult; the typical student has been in the work force for several years, which plays into the amount of weight placed on various admissions factors. GPA will factor in more heavily for recent grads, and applicants should make sure their letters of recommendation come from the appropriate sources (professors or employers). Recently admitted students at the 25th percentile had an LSAT score of 157 and an average GPA of 3.14, while admitted students at the 75th percentile had an LSAT score of 163 and a GPA of 3.67.

Public interest	
law requirement	No

ADMISSIONS

Selectivity Rating	**83**
# applications received	2,845
% applicants accepted	37
% acceptees attending	21
Average LSAT	161
LSAT Range	163–157
Average undergrad GPA	3.49
Application fee	$50
Regular application	Rolling, up to 8/1
Regular notification	Rolling
Early application program	No
Transfer students accepted	Yes
Evening division offered	Yes
Part-time accepted	Yes
LSDAS accepted	Yes

Applicants Also Look At

American University, University of Colorado at Boulder, University of Denver, Seattle University, University of California—Berkeley, University of California—Los Angeles, University of Oregon, The George Washington University, University of San Francisco, Santa Clara University, University of Washington

International Students

TOEFL recommended	
of international students	Yes
Minimum TOEFL	
(paper/computer)	600/250

FINANCIAL FACTS

Annual tuition	$30,436
Books and supplies	$1,050
Fees	$50
Fees per credit	$50
Tuition per credit	$22,826
Room & board	
(off-campus)	$16,092
Financial aid application	
deadline	3/1
% first-year students	
receiving some sort of aid	96
% receiving some sort of aid	94
% of aid that is merit based	100
% receiving scholarships	50
Average grant	$8,508
Average loan	$47,578
Average total aid package	$47,578
Average debt	$94,081

EMPLOYMENT INFORMATION

		Grads Employed by Field (%)
Career Rating	**72**	Business/Industry (20)
Rate of placement (nine months out)	92.6	Judicial Clerkships (6)
Average starting salary	$67,834	Public Interest (11)
State for bar exam	OR, WA	
Pass rate for first-time bar	79	

Employers Who Frequently Hire Grads
Numerous small and medium-sized firms; State Government (Oregon, Washington, Idaho, Alaska); Multnomah, Washington, and Clackamas Counties.

Prominent Alumni
Earl Blumenauer, U.S. Representative; Phil Schrilio, Assistant to the President for Legislative Affairs.

LOUISIANA STATE UNIVERSITY
PAUL M. HEBERT LAW CENTER

INSTITUTIONAL INFORMATION

Public/private	Public
Student-faculty ratio	16:1
% faculty part-time	53
% faculty female	19
% faculty minority	6
Total faculty	90

SURVEY SAYS...
Great research resources

STUDENTS

Enrollment of law school	577
% male/female	52/48
% out-of-state	18
% full-time	98
% minority	8
# of countries represented	11

ACADEMICS

Academic Experience Rating	**78**
Profs interesting rating	79
Profs accessible rating	76
Hours of study per day	3.41

Academic Specialties
Civil procedure, commercial law, constitutional law, corporation securities, criminal law, environmental law, government services, human rights, international law, labor law, legal history, legal philosophy, property, taxation, intellectual property law

Advanced Degrees Offered
Master of Laws (LL.M), 1 year; Master of Civil Law (M.C.L.), 1 year.

Combined Degrees Offered
Masters in Public in Administrations/JD, 3 years; JD/MBA, 4 years; JD/Masters of Mass Communication, 4 years.

Clinical program required	No
Legal writing course requirement	Yes
Legal methods course requirement	Yes

Academics

Often referred to as "LSU Junior High Law," due to its "rigorously enforced attendance policy," the Paul M. Hebert Law Center at Louisiana State University is "undeniably one-of-a-kind in America," according to the students in attendance. Much is made of the grueling 97-hour course load that students must endure in order to graduate (more than at most other law schools), and students definitely feel the burden of the extra work, because it forces them to place an "extremely strong focus on studying." The administration is "very strong" and many of them, including the chancellor, teach classes at the law center, they are "well known by the students and are extremely accessible," in recognition of the fact that "the student-teacher relationship extends beyond the classroom."

The thing that stands out most about the LSU Law Center is its curriculum. Students complete classes "in both common law and civil law studies," which means all graduating students are granted a Diploma in Civil Law as well as the traditional Juris Doctorate, making them "marketable worldwide," a distinction that LSU students hold dear. "Knowledge of the civil law is an invaluable resource as the world continues to become a global market. We have some of the preeminent civil law scholars from around the world on the faculty of LSU Law," says one enthused 2L. Or, as a third-year student simply puts it, "We get two degrees! That makes us twice as good as everyone else." However, for many students not looking to practice international law or become law professors, there is a strong desire for a wider breadth of courses and specializations. This contingent believes that there's "way too much emphasis on a few fields of law and next to nothing in many other fields" and that "almost nothing practical is offered." "If you do not intend to practice in Louisiana, do not attend this school," warns a graduating student.

Luckily, there are all-around raves to be heard about the facilities and the "superior" technology found within its walls, including an "excellent" library as well as "well-maintained" classrooms. With the main LSU campus right next door, one can "look out the window of a classroom across to the parade ground." Faculty come from all corners of the United States, which "provides students with a wealth of diverse experiences and knowledge." "It's nice to be taught by the godfather of all Louisiana tort law, who is forever bringing his infinite theoretical knowledge to practical application, thereby showing us 'where our Porsche is parked,'" says a suitably impressed 1L. With some top names in legal education taking the podium, it's nice to see "The faculty truly engage their students" and heartening to know that professors "actually want their students to learn and enjoy doing it."

Career Services is not without its detractors, with more than a few gripes concerning the lack of encouragement or education about clerkships. "There is a lack of organized career counseling to guide the disillusioned and the misguided," claims a 2L in crisis. But a second-year student assures us: "After two years at LSU Law, I can truly say that I am impressed with the administration and faculty, assured about the quality of my legal education, and prepared to practice in the legal profession."

Life

"While the overall student body may be slightly conservative, there is certainly an

MICHELE FORBES, DIRECTOR OF STUDENT AFFAIRS AND REGISTRAR
202 LAW CENTER, BATON ROUGE, LA 70803
TEL: 225-578-8646 FAX: 225-578-8647
EMAIL: ADMISSIONS@LAW.LSU.EDU • WEBSITE: WWW.LAW.LSU.EDU

equally present liberal segment," states a student. "Both views are equally accepted on campus and in the classroom." Others may disagree on the use of the qualifier "slightly," but overall, students on campus seem to get along. Most point out that there's a tension amongst competing students, especially among those at the top of the class, but no one would ever call it cutthroat. "They're still law students after all, but with a more normal human-being swagger," reasons a first-year student.

As for social outlets, "There is something for everyone, whether it be political organizations, SBA, practice area interest organizations, the LSU Law Football Club, intramurals, or occasional Law School Socials," with a healthy amount of drinking thrown in. Even more importantly, "If there isn't something out there the school is receptive and encourages you to create an organization to satisfy that need." Many are of the opinion that the sense of community is not as strong for "outsiders"—students who are not from Baton Rouge and/or did not attend LSU as an undergraduate—but agree that for the most part, "The social atmosphere is great at LSU. Lifelong friends are made and kept."

Getting In

Naturally GPA and LSAT scores play a huge role in LSU's admissions decisions, but the Admissions Office encourages applicants to submit other information that would help them evaluate the applicant's aptitude for the study of law, including evidence of personal leadership, professional and/or military service, and resumes. The committee also asks that all applicants be of "good moral character."

Legal research	
course requirement	Yes
Moot court requirement	No
Public interest	
law requirement	No

ADMISSIONS

Selectivity Rating	**80**
# applications received	1,299
# applicants accepted	499
# acceptees attending	211
Average LSAT	156
LSAT Range	154–159
Average undergrad GPA	3.51
Application fee	$25
Regular application	Rolling,
	up to 5/1
Regular notification	Rolling
Early application program	No
Transfer students accepted	Yes
Evening division offered	No
Part-time accepted	No
LSDAS accepted	Yes

Applicants Also Look At
Tulane University, Loyola University—New Orleans, University of Mississippi

FINANCIAL FACTS

Annual tuition (in-state/	
out-of-state)	$10,722/$19,818
Books and supplies	$1,500
Fees	$1,421
Tuition per credit	
(in-state/out-of-state)	$447/$826
Room & board	
(on/off-campus)	$10,332/$12,022
Financial aid application	
deadline	4/20
% first-year students	
receiving some sort of aid	76
% receiving some sort of aid	88
% of aid that is merit based	7
% receiving scholarships	15
Average grant	$7,280
Average loan	$23,660
Average total aid package	$18,330
Average debt	$59,218

EMPLOYMENT INFORMATION

Career Rating	**71**	**Grads Employed by Field (%)**
Rate of placement (nine months out)	92	Academic (2)
Average starting salary	$63,401	Business/Industry (11)
State for bar exam	LA	Government (12)
Pass rate for first-time bar	77	Judicial Clerkships (18)
Employers Who Frequently Hire Grads		Military (2)
Adams & Reese; Baker & Hostetler;		Private Practice (52)
Breazeale Sachse & Wilson; Phelps		Public Interest (3)
Dunbar; McGinchey Stafford; Taylor Porter		
Brooks & Phillips; Stone Pigman; Vinson		
& Elkins; Chaffe McCall Phillips Toler &		
Sarpy; Cook Yancey King & Galloway;		
Correro Fishman Haygood Phelps Weiss		

LOYOLA MARYMOUNT UNIVERSITY
LOYOLA LAW SCHOOL

INSTITUTIONAL INFORMATION

Public/private	Private
% faculty part-time	41
% faculty female	38
% faculty minority	17
Total faculty	133

SURVEY SAYS...

Diverse opinions accepted
in classrooms
Great research resources
Great library staff

STUDENTS

Enrollment of law school	1,287
% male/female	50/50
% full-time	77
% minority	42
Average age of entering class	25

ACADEMICS

Academic Experience Rating	**95**
Profs interesting rating	95
Profs accessible rating	95
Hours of study per day	4.12

Academic Specialties

Civil procedure, commercial law, constitutional law, corporation securities, criminal law, environmental law, government services, human rights, international law, labor law, legal history, legal philosophy, property, taxation, intellectual property law, entertainment law, mediation, cancer rights law

Advanced Degrees Offered

LLM in Taxation full-time 1 year, part-time 3 years; JD/LLM in Taxation 3 years

Combined Degrees Offered

JD/MBA, 4 years.

Clinical program required	No
Legal writing course requirement	Yes
Legal methods course requirement	Yes
Legal research course requirement	Yes

Academics

Loyola Law School (affiliated with Loyola Marymount University, or the "mothership") is "an understated gem" in downtown Los Angeles that "seeks to create top lawyers who use the profession for the betterment of society and [to] give back to [the] legal community." It's a generally happy place that quite simply seeks to make good lawyers, send them out to the world, and repeat; all the people associated with the school, from students to staff, are accordingly pleasant and uncomplicated, if not a little resentful of the relative anonymity as compared to the other law schools in the area. As one 1L puts it, "Masochists would be disappointed at Loyola. For legal torture, look elsewhere in Los Angeles."

Professors are "smart [and] demanding yet understanding of the pressures of a first-year law student." They are of "the highest caliber" and "set the bar high, but [they] give you all of the tools to use at your discretion to meet that bar." Classes are "lively and enjoyable," and teachers keep their doors open for whatever's troubling the masses. "Every professor I have had seems to truly care about the success of their students, both inside and outside the classroom," says a student.

The curriculum itself offers "a strong foundation in legal theory but also the practical skills necessary to excel in the workplace," including a comprehensive legal research and writing program. There are a "broad range of specialists within a variety of fields" to help students narrow down their field of focus, and many "solid opportunities for public interest law," as well as "a tremendous trial advocacy program, moot court, and three law reviews." However, all of this opportunity comes at a truly private school price, and financial aid is not easy as easy to come by as most students would like. "A break in $40k tuition payments would be nice. For a school that boasts itself on public interest, taking out well over $100k in tuition loans doesn't exactly amend itself to accepting a $50k per year public interest job," says a 3L. Graduates of LLS mainly practice in California and L.A., so the school enjoys a much greater reputation within the state than it does nationally, and for those who do stay nearby (very much the majority), the alumni networking opportunities are strong.

As for the administrators, most here have little to no problems with the administration, which "not only talks the talk, but walks the walk." That is, aside from the Registrar's office, which "is like talking to a brick wall. They need to listen and think about what you are saying before they respond with the scripted answer." The law school has its own "cozy" and completely separate campus from Loyola Marymount, so there are "no undergrads taking up the library study rooms." The school operates a shuttle, which takes students to the financial district and the new L.A. Live entertainment complex every 15 minutes, which means that "courts, law firms, and our city's phenomenal entertainment are basically our campus."

Life

As expected, happy students make for a happy campus. Competition is at a low here; notes and outlines "are regularly shared," and "there has not been one hint of dirty competition at all." "I can't imagine a better atmosphere considering the pressures of first year. The 2Ls and 3Ls have been amazingly supportive too," says one first-year. Even outside of the classroom, everyone is "peculiarly friendly"—one student was "caught off guard by how helpful everybody was." There is always something new and exciting going on, from "bowling to benefit the public interest law foundation, to lunches with European patent scholars, to social outings at hot bars and clubs around town." Panel lunches with industry

JANNELL LUNDY ROBERTS, ASSISTANT DEAN OF ADMISSIONS
919 ALBANY STREET, LOS ANGELES, CA 90015
TEL: 213-736-1074 FAX: 213-736-6523
EMAIL: ADMISSIONS@LLS.EDU • WEBSITE: WWW.LLS.EDU

leaders are well-attended at Loyola, and "you could probably go to a meeting and eat for free every day if you wanted," but unfortunately, the school's food itself is not as big a hit: "The food, it is bad."

One of the reasons the lunch hour is so heavily trafficked is the high number of commuters who go to school here, which limits after-class time as an option and means that "developing a large social network isn't as easy as it might be if everyone lived right next to campus" (where everyone also agrees that it'd "be nice if we had a gym"). However, the SBA and student organizations "do a good job of scheduling social activities to bring students closer," and this social bunch obliges for the most part. Though no one is a huge fan of downtown L.A., it is undergoing a massive revitalization effort, and everyone admits that it is "incredibly convenient."

Getting In

To be considered for admission to Loyola Law School, students must submit undergraduate transcripts, LSAT scores, and a personal statement. Students also must submit at least one and up to three letters of recommendation, of which at least one should be from an academic source.

Moot court requirement	No
Public interest law requirement	Yes

ADMISSIONS

Selectivity Rating	**87**
# applications received	4,617
% applicants accepted	32
% acceptees attending	22
Average LSAT	162
LSAT Range	159–163
Average undergrad GPA	3.45
Application fee	$65
Regular application	Rolling, up to 2/2
Regular notification	Rolling
Early application program	No
Transfer students accepted	Yes
Evening division offered	Yes
Part-time accepted	Yes
LSDAS accepted	Yes

Applicants Also Look At

University of California—Davis; University of San Francisco; Santa Clara University; Pepperdine University; University of San Diego; University of California—Hastings

FINANCIAL FACTS

Annual tuition	$37,890
Books and supplies	$1,050
Fees	$560
Fees per credit	$21
Tuition per credit	$1,230
Room & board (off-campus)	$15,526
Financial aid application deadline	3/15
Average debt	$109,649

EMPLOYMENT INFORMATION

Career Rating	**83**
Rate of placement (nine months out)	96
Average starting salary	$103,021
State for bar exam	CA
Pass rate for first-time bar	78

Employers Who Frequently Hire Grads
O'Melveny & Myers; Los Angeles Dist. Atty.; Paul Hastings; Jones, Day, Reavis & Pogue; Sheppard, Mullin, Richter & Hampton; Irell & Manella.

Prominent Alumni
Gloria Allred, Trial Attorney; Johnnie Cochran, Trial Attorney; Larry Feldman, Trial Attorney; Mark Geragos, Trial Attorney; Robert Shapiro, Trial Attorney.

Grads Employed by Field (%)
Academic (3)
Business/Industry (17)
Government (5)
Judicial Clerkships (2)
Private Practice (63)
Public Interest (10)

LOYOLA UNIVERSITY—CHICAGO
SCHOOL OF LAW

INSTITUTIONAL INFORMATION

Public/private	Private
Affiliation	Roman Catholic
Student-faculty ratio	15:1
% faculty part-time	64
% faculty female	47
% faculty minority	5
Total faculty	166

SURVEY SAYS...

Diverse opinions accepted
in classrooms
Great library staff
Students love Chicago, IL

STUDENTS

Enrollment of law school	887
% male/female	48/52
% full-time	72
% minority	17
# of countries represented	15
Average age of entering class	24

ACADEMICS

Academic Experience Rating	**79**
Profs interesting rating	81
Profs accessible rating	73
Hours of study per day	3.6

Academic Specialties

Corporation securities, criminal law,
international law, labor law, taxation,
intellectual property law, child & family law, health law, international law

Advanced Degrees Offered

MJ Health Law, MJ Child Law, MJ
Business Law, 22 semester hours;
LLM Health Law, LLM Child Law,
LLM Tax Law, 24 semester hours;
SJD Health Law, D.Law in Health
Law, two years full-time.

Combined Degrees Offered

JD/MBA, JD/MSW, JD/MA Political
Science, 4 years.

Clinical program required	No
Legal writing course requirement	Yes
Legal methods course requirement	No

Academics

"A phenomenal health law program" and an "incredibly strong" tax program are academic standouts at this Jesuit-affiliated law school in downtown Chicago. This is also "one of the few schools that has specific elder law classes." This makes sense, as one of the hallmarks of a Jesuit education is an "emphasis on public service." In addition, the school has a highly touted "trial advocacy program that allows a select number of students" to train with "the best trial lawyers in Chicago." A sizable evening program "draws unusually diverse and gifted students" who are mostly "working professionals" from the City of Chicago and its environs.

The "first rate" professors not only "have excellent resumes (Harvard, Yale, Chicago . . . DC clerkships, former assistant attorney generals, current judges, etc.)" but "Unlike many professors with sexy resumes they can actually teach!" They also are "easily accessible and always willing to answer any question." "They seem to put students above all else," explains one student. If that's not enough, they are also personable outside of the school setting: "One even invited an entire 1L section to his house for Thanksgiving dinner!" The few complaints there are about faculty center on "older or tenured professors" whose "level of interest or enthusiasm seems nonexistent."

Students have mixed feelings about the administration. Some believe it is "disorganized," pointing out that the "Computer technology is a decade behind the times." Others counter that Dean Yellen, who began his tenure in 2005, "is really turning Loyola around." These students argue that the "quality of new educators has drastically improved, the administration is much more helpful and friendly, and the facilities have come out of the dark ages, specifically with adding wireless Internet to the law building and giving some students the option of taking their exams online."

"Overall Loyola is a solid school with a good reputation in the Midwest," says one student. Graduates find themselves in good company as the State's Attorney General and Chief Justice of the Illinois Supreme Court are alumni of Loyola. Many students claim that, thanks to the "loyal, prestigious, and well-organized alumni," it is possible to find Loyola grads "in the best law firms in the country."

Life

Students agree that "Loyola is located in the heart of the best part of Chicago." There are "so many different activities one could do around campus" and "as it's near downtown," there's "wonderful nightlife [and] shopping." The school itself offers "many opportunities for students to socialize out of class" while also promoting good causes. For example, "The Student Bar Association hosts weekly bar nights and other special events like the Barrister's Ball and the No Talent Show" with the proceeds of the latter going to help support "abandoned children."

Temperamentally, "The Loyola law student community is extremely cooperative, with students sharing notes and outlines constantly." "Students are generally friendly," and "None of the horror stories you hear about law school are true at Loyola." Though some feel like they are "in high school," most students report "a great atmosphere" full of people who embrace Loyola's "spirit of service." Politically, "The school tends to attract a lot of Midwesterners with a slight liberal bent" and "no die-hard Bill O'Reilly fans."

OFFICE OF ADMISSION AND FINANCIAL ASSISTANCE
25 EAST PEARSON SUITE 1440, CHICAGO, IL 60611
TEL: 312-915-7170 FAX: 312-915-7906
EMAIL: LAW-ADMISSIONS@LUC.EDU • WEBSITE: WWW.LUC.EDU/SCHOOLS/LAW

There seems to be a bit of a split between the way full-time and evening division students view each other, which is typical at most law schools that offer part-time study options. Full-time day students are younger and allegedly more "cutthroat" than evening students, who "all are a little older, have families, kids, jobs, etc. and...are just trying to make it through law school." But let's just say that these views reside in the eye of the beholder.

Minuses in terms of student life include the fact that "parking is terrible and validations can still be pricey." However there is always Chicago's famed L-train service; though some students feel "Public transit is undesirable."

Getting In

About one in four applicants is accepted to Loyola Chicago. Typical students who are accepted and enroll here have an A-minus/B-plus undergraduate GPA and an LSAT score in the 80th to 90th percentile. Loyola is somewhat unique in that it at least says that applicants' personal statements and letters of recommendation are more important selection criteria than LSAT scores. Applicants to the evening division will face a slightly less rigorous bar to admission.

Legal research course requirement	Yes
Moot court requirement	Yes
Public interest law requirement	No

ADMISSIONS

Selectivity Rating	84
# applications received	4,313
# applicants accepted	1,356
# acceptees attending	275
Average LSAT	162
LSAT Range	160–163
Average undergrad GPA	3.56
Application fee	$50
Regular application	Rolling
Regular notification	Rolling
Early application program	No
Transfer students accepted	Yes
Evening division offered	Yes
Part-time accepted	Yes
LSDAS accepted	Yes

Applicants Also Look At

University of Illinois at Urbana-Champaign, American University, Northwestern University, Boston University, Illinois Institute of Technology, The George Washington University, DePaul University

International Students

| TOEFL required of international students | Yes |
| Minimum TOEFL (paper/computer) | 650/280 |

FINANCIAL FACTS

Annual tuition	$36,290
Books and supplies	$1,200
Fees	$260
Fees per credit	$120
Tuition per credit	$1,205
Room & board	$13,200
Financial aid application deadline	3/1
% first-year students receiving some sort of aid	85
% receiving some sort of aid	85
% of aid that is merit based	46
% receiving scholarships	66
Average grant	$10,930
Average loan	$30,000
Average total aid package	$47,773
Average debt	$90,718

EMPLOYMENT INFORMATION

Career Rating	74
Rate of placement (nine months out)	90
Average starting salary	$75,000
State for bar exam	IL, MO, NY, DC, MI
Pass rate for first-time bar	95

Prominent Alumni

Lisa Madigan, Attorney General—IL; Henry Hyde, U.S. Senator; Philip Corboy, Attorney-personal injury; Jeff Jacobs, former President—Harpo Entertainment; Mary Ann McMorrow, Chief Justice—IL Supreme Court.

Grads Employed by Field (%)

Academic (1)
Business/Industry (18)
Government (14)
Judicial Clerkships (4)
Military (1)
Private Practice (56)
Public Interest (6)

LOYOLA UNIVERSITY—NEW ORLEANS
SCHOOL OF LAW

INSTITUTIONAL INFORMATION

Public/private	Private
Affiliation	Roman Catholic
Student-faculty ratio	17:1
% faculty part-time	33
% faculty female	34
% faculty minority	21
Total faculty	68

SURVEY SAYS...

Diverse opinions accepted in classrooms
Students love New Orleans, LA

STUDENTS

Enrollment of law school	844
% male/female	50/50
% out-of-state	40
% full-time	78
% minority	32
# of countries represented	5
Average age of entering class	25

ACADEMICS

Academic Experience Rating	**67**
Profs interesting rating	72
Profs accessible rating	69
Hours of study per day	4.35

Academic Specialties

Environmental law, international law, taxation, pubic interest law

Advanced Degrees Offered

LLM in United States Law for international students, 24 credit hours

Combined Degrees Offered

JD/MBA, JD/Masters of Religious Studies, JD/Masters of Communications, JD/Masters of Public Administration, JD/Masters of Urban and Regional Planning. All combined degree programs add an additional year to the JD program.

Clinical program required	No
Legal writing course requirement	Yes
Legal methods course requirement	Yes
Legal research course requirement	Yes

Academics

At Loyola University—New Orleans, School of Law, students are divided on their opinions of nearly everything. "The professors are wonderful resources and teachers of the material we're required to know for the Louisiana and any other common law bar," states one, speaking for a large segment of the population. "They balance stuffy case law with real-world experience, providing the best of both worlds and preparing us for our careers." Another voice representing the (not as widely held) counterpoint says: "I would not take a future class from most of the professors whose classes I took." Perhaps this middle-of-the-road 2L has it right when she observes, "It definitely matters what professors you take at Loyola because while some are great, others seem to know very little about what they are teaching." More than a few students speculate about racial preferences at Loyola, citing administrators who give "extra help to minorities in instruction [private and prior to law school orientation], scholarship, and rate of acceptance," though the administration claims this is untrue. "Merit takes the back seat at Loyola when making admittance and scholarship decisions," opines a student.

The school itself is undergoing a lot of construction (now in its final stages) due to Hurricane Katrina, and though complaints about the noise abound, students know that the new wing will "help the law school in its mission to serve the New Orleans area." Indeed, though New Orleans was hit hard by Katrina, every single student agrees that the administration exhibited nothing but grace under pressure. A second-year student tells of officials' devotion to the school: "The dean evacuated to Houston and without access to any files, Loyola e-mail, or the Loyola server, arranged for us to have a full curriculum at University of Houston's Law School. Professors and faculty who had lost their homes came and taught us—many commuting each week from Baton Rouge or from wherever their families had evacuated." Now back up and running and open for business, Loyola University—New Orleans is able to help the needy with "free legal advice through clinics which [also] allow students hands-on experience" and helps them fulfill their pro bono requirement, one register of the school's commitment to public interest.

In terms of Loyola's academic offerings, students especially commend the moot court, certificate, and legal research and writing programs for being "very practical," though many wish for more diversity in the classes that are offered. "Regular availability of courses on specific areas of law, such as education, health, and employment law would broaden the course offerings for upperclassmen," says one student. Financial aid services receive a universal thumbs-down, as does the parking situation on campus, though the school hired an additional person to help in the Financial Aid Department, which is expected to dramatically increase the response time in the office. The vast majority of students at Loyola are thrilled with the school's Career Services Office ("amazing in helping to revise resumes and in finding job placement") and the ensuing employment opportunities available to them in New Orleans

K. MICHELE ALLISON-DAVIS, DEAN OF ADMISSIONS
7214 SAINT CHARLES AVENUE, BOX 904, NEW ORLEANS, LA 70118
TEL: 504-861-5575 FAX: 504-861-5772
EMAIL: LADMIT@LOYNO.EDU • WEBSITE: LAW.LOYNO.EDU

Life

"Come on now, it's New Orleans..." As one can imagine, the social life here in the home of Mardi Gras is "booming." "A lot of the diverse student population are frequent visitors to local bars, mostly in the French Quarter," says one booster, and "There is always something to do or someone to hang out with," including a fair number of school-sponsored events. "At times the students seem judgmental," but "Once you get to know your classmates you find that they are, for the most part, enjoyable to be around." "Loyola is a small school so there is definitely a lot of gossiping," and as in high school, the student body can be "very cliquey in the sense that a huge number of people are locals who have known each other awhile, thus out-of-staters may feel out of place at first." There also exists a social rift "between common law and civil law students." As is their custom, students are also divided about the level of competitiveness running throughout the school. Opinions range from "cutthroat" to "We help each other as much as possible with things like informing each other of assignments and getting notes to people who were not able to make it to class." One thing is for certain, though: "New Orleans attracts a wide variety of people and takes a special kind of person to live here and enjoy it."

Getting In

At a nearly 60 percent acceptance rate, admission to Loyola University—New Orleans isn't all that difficult, though this rate is a direct result of the decrease in applications received since Hurricane Katrina, and is expected to fall as the school returns to its pre-storm state. The school prefers applicants to apply using the online application, with a priority application deadline of February 1. Though letters of recommendation are not required, they are encouraged, and the school also recommends that all applicants have an LSAT score no lower than 154 and a minimum GPA of 3.3.

Moot court requirement	Yes
Public interest law requirement	Yes

ADMISSIONS

Selectivity Rating	**71**
# applications received	1,453
% applicants accepted	48
% acceptees attending	29
Average LSAT	153
LSAT Range	149–156
Average undergrad GPA	3.33
Application fee	$40
Regular application	Rolling, up to 7/15
Regular notification	Rolling
Early application program	No
Transfer students accepted	Yes
Evening division offered	Yes
Part-time accepted	Yes
LSDAS accepted	Yes

Applicants Also Look At

Louisiana State University, Tulane University, University of Miami, Mississippi College, St. Thomas University, Stetson University, New England Law|Boston, New York Law School, Florida Costal School of Law

International Students

TOEFL recommended of international students	Yes
Minimum TOEFL (paper/computer)	580/237

FINANCIAL FACTS

Annual tuition	$32,395
Books and supplies	$1,500
Fees	$1,026
Fees per credit	$1,026
Tuition per credit	$1,045
Room & board	$18,250
% first-year students receiving some sort of aid	70
% receiving some sort of aid	68
% of aid that is merit based	32
% receiving scholarships	46
Average grant	$14,000
Average loan	$24,000
Average total aid package	$49,740
Average debt	$84,155

EMPLOYMENT INFORMATION

Career Rating	**84**
Rate of placement (nine months out)	94
State for bar exam	LA, TX, FL, GA, MS
Pass rate for first-time bar	74

Employers Who Frequently Hire Grads
private firms, the judiciary, and government agencies

Prominent Alumni
Pascal Calogero, Chief Justice, Louisiana Supreme Court; Moon Landrieu, Secretary of HUD, Mayor of New Orleans, etc.; Carl Stewart, U.S.Court of Appeals, 5th Circuit; Theodore M. Frois, General Counsel, Exxon Mobil International.

Grads Employed by Field (%)
Business/Industry (12)
Government (9)
Judicial Clerkships (11)
Private Practice (61)
Public Interest (6)

MARQUETTE UNIVERSITY
LAW SCHOOL

INSTITUTIONAL INFORMATION

Public/private	Private
Affiliation	Roman Catholic
Student-faculty ratio	17:1
% faculty part-time	25
% faculty female	42
% faculty minority	13
Total faculty	43

SURVEY SAYS...

Diverse opinions accepted
in classrooms
Great library staff
Abundant externship/internship/
clerkship opportunities

STUDENTS

Enrollment of law school	748
% male/female	58/42
% full-time	75
% minority	13
Average age of entering class	25

ACADEMICS

Academic Experience Rating	**81**
Profs interesting rating	81
Profs accessible rating	86
Hours of study per day	4.57

Academic Specialties

Civil procedure, commercial law, constitutional law, corporation securities, criminal law, environmental law, international law, labor law, legal history, property, taxation, intellectual property law, sports law, dispute resolution

Combined Degrees Offered

JD/MBA, JD/MBA Sports Business, JD/MA Political Science, JD/MA International Relations, JD/MA Philosophy, JD/MA in History of Philosophy, JD/MA Bioethics, all 4 year programs. Students may also earn the JD/Certificate in Dispute Resolution in 3 years.

Clinical program required	No
Legal writing course requirement	Yes

Academics

The Law School at Wisconsin's Marquette University is filled with "students who are interested in each other's success" and "who [make] every day worth going." The school places "a huge emphasis" on the fact that students will be future colleagues and encourages them to begin showing that respect during their schooling. This trickles not only down but up, with "the staff, faculty, and students [having] formed such a cohesive unit." The school's administration is incredibly helpful (and, "oddly enough, entertaining"), and "even if you're not talking to the right person, they'll get you there."

Though "the current law library is a dungeon, and the law building itself is dated," the school will be opening a brand new law building in 2010 that students expect will propel them into the next stratosphere of legal education awesomeness. "Watch out when that happens because people will be falling over one another to come here," warns one. As a 1L, all of your courses are picked for you (which can be "a scheduling nightmare" but means "there is no trouble getting into required courses"), but beyond the first year, the school "offers courses in a wide variety of specializations," and class sizes are smaller. "Dean Kearney wants to make sure we learn the law, not the latest in pop sociology," says a student.

The legal writing program is "a real super star in this school. In clerkship after clerkship, the research and writing skills I gained in class have been complimented," says a student. Sports Law is also a program of note at Marquette. The professors are "very knowledgeable, thought-provoking, and engaging," and, to top that off, "unforgettably intelligent and witty." Most come to the school from strong legal careers and top universities, yet "allow students room to debate legal issues in a cordial, professional manner." "It is amazing how a two-second question might turn into an hour discussion outside of class," says a 2L.

The school's "flexible evening program" is "very accommodating to part-time students," offering many night classes that accommodate "full-time work schedules and family lives." The combination of the school's career services center and the location in Milwaukee provides "many opportunities to obtain practical experience through internships and clinic work in the legal community," so that students can get practical experience from day one. As if all of this isn't enough, Marquette keeps making life better even after graduation—the school is also one of two in Wisconsin that offers a state bar exam exemption, meaning students who have graduated from the law school can start practicing law in the state without taking the nationwide test. "My overall experience has blown away the expectations I had when I decided to come here," says a student.

Life

Milwaukee "is all about having fun," which contributes to the communal sense of spirit here, and though the surrounding neighborhoods "are not great," the "campus is good." The school "is not very diverse in faculty or student body," and due to the large part-time program, there is "a broad age range among students" and many people who commute with families, so there's a bit of a divide between these students and the younger ones. Still, everyone is open to meeting new people at Marquette, though "students can be a little cliquey." There are scheduled social events throughout the year, such as the student-faculty basketball game, "Malpractice Ball, Brewers games, Bucks games, and various NCAA Division I sports [games]," and students can play intramural sports or go to the rec center in their free time. Thursday night is Bar Review, "where most stu-

Sean Reilly, Assistant Dean for Admissions
Sensenbrenner Hall, Room 116, P.O. Box 1881, Milwaukee, WI 53201-1881
Tel: 414-288-6767 Fax: 414-288-0676
Email: LAW.ADMISSION@MARQUETTE.EDU • Website: LAW.MARQUETTE.EDU

dents go out to the same bar and blow off steam" and "relax and get ready to study for the weekend."

Law students certainly aren't held back by any sort of cut-throat competitive streak. "I feel like I'm in the 3rd round of 'American Idol.' Everyone is watching their own back, and everyone else's," says a student. "I broke my leg and had to miss two days. I had four sets of notes for each class in my e-mail inbox without soliciting them from anybody," says a 2L. The relatively small community can also lead to "a high school-like feeling—everyone knows everyone else, who they are, and likely some detail of their life. Depending on what a person wants, that could be a good or bad thing."

Getting In

Admission is significantly less competitive than at UW. (Marquette admits at almost twice the rate of UW.) The law school employs a modified rolling admissions process, with the admissions committee typically beginning its evaluations in December. As is the case in all rolling admissions systems, there are more spaces available sooner rather than later—especially if you think you may be a borderline candidate quantitatively. An undergraduate GPA of B+ and an LSAT score in the high 150s would make you solidly competitive for admission at Marquette.

Legal methods	
course requirement	No
Legal research	
course requirement	Yes
Moot court requirement	No
Public interest	
law requirement	No

ADMISSIONS

Selectivity Rating	**77**
# applications received	2,187
# applicants accepted	835
# acceptees attending	225
Average LSAT	154
LSAT Range	155–159
Average undergrad GPA	3.4
Application fee	$50
Regular application	Rolling, up to 4/1
Regular notification	Rolling
Early application program	No
Transfer students accepted	Yes
Evening division offered	Yes
Part-time accepted	Yes
LSDAS accepted	Yes

Applicants Also Look At

University of Wisconsin—Madison, Illinois Institute of Technology, DePaul University, John Marshall Law School, Loyola University—Chicago

International Students

TOEFL required	
of international students	Yes
Minimum TOEFL	
(paper/computer)	600/250

FINANCIAL FACTS

Annual tuition	$32,410
Books and supplies	$1,200
Tuition per credit	$1,295
Room & board	
(off-campus)	$12,670
Financial aid application	
deadline	3/1
% receiving scholarships	40
Average grant	$7,000
Average debt	$90,928

EMPLOYMENT INFORMATION

Career Rating	**79**	**Grads Employed by Field (%)**
Rate of placement (nine months out)	93	Academic (3)
Average starting salary	$68,386	Business/Industry (14
State for bar exam	FL, TX, IL, MN,	Government (9)
	NY, WI, NC, CA, VA	Judicial Clerkships (4)
Pass rate for first-time bar	97	Military (1)
Employers Who Frequently Hire Grads		Private Practice (64)
Quarles & Brady; Godfrey & Kahn; Foley &		Public Interest (5)
Lardner; Whyte Hirschboeck Dudek; von		
Briesen & Roper; Reinhart Boerner Van		
Dueren; Davis & Kuelthau.		
Prominent Alumni		
Hon. Diane Sykes, U.S. Court of Appeals		
Judge; Hon. Terence Evans, U.S. Court of		
Appeals Judge; Hon. John Coffey, U.S.		
Court of Appeals Judge.		

MERCER UNIVERSITY
WALTER F. GEORGE SCHOOL OF LAW

INSTITUTIONAL INFORMATION

Public/private	Private
Affiliation	Baptist
Student-faculty ratio	13:1
% faculty part-time	30
% faculty female	33
% faculty minority	9
Total faculty	54

SURVEY SAYS...

Diverse opinions accepted
in classrooms
Great research resources
Great library staff

STUDENTS

Enrollment of law school	443
% male/female	57/43
% out-of-state	32
% full-time	100
% minority	17
# of countries represented	4
Average age of entering class	25

ACADEMICS

Academic Experience Rating	**89**
Profs interesting rating	91
Profs accessible rating	99
Hours of study per day	5.14

Academic Specialties

Civil procedure, commercial law, constitutional law, corporation securities, criminal law, environmental law, international law, labor law, legal history, taxation, intellectual property law, legal writing certificate program, Internet law, trial advocacy, professionalism/ethics

Advanced Degrees Offered

JD, 3 years.

Combined Degrees Offered

JD/MBA, 3 to 4 years.

Clinical program required	No
Legal writing course requirement	Yes
Legal methods course requirement	Yes
Legal research course requirement	Yes

Academics

In Mercer, students find an institution that "rejects the 'survival of the fittest' mentality of most law schools," adopting instead a "no man left behind" approach. "Every single person—librarians, professors, classmates, and even the sweet lady in the bookstore—is there to help you if you need it," a 1L reports. "I remember once I had to give a presentation in class, and I didn't know how to work the projection equipment—a member of the janitorial crew stopped by and showed me how," a 2L adds. This "encouraging environment" reportedly "takes a huge burden...off the shoulders of incoming law students" and allows them to focus on actually learning the law. Mercer starts 1Ls off with its "Intro to Law class, a one-week sample course designed to introduce new students to the foreign world of case opinions and IRAC," which, according to one 1L, "made a world of difference on the first day of 'real' classes, as I knew what to expect." Throughout students' time here, they receive "great practical skills instruction," which includes an "unbeatable" legal writing program; "Mercer students and graduates have notably superior writing skills, and employers know this," a 3L asserts. With "a bar-passage rate of 95.8 percent," one might assume that its all practical skills all the time at Mercer, but the school also places an "emphasis on legal theory." In fact, a sanguine 1L boasts that Mercer offers "the best blend of theory [and] practice of law in the country."

The school is committed to producing lawyers who demonstrate "compassion for the client," and this goal is reinforced by professors who are accessible and "seem to really care about the student." Students agree that "at any given time, you can pop in on a professor"—one "literally unhinged the door to his office"—or "call [him or her] at home." "Not once have I ever been turned down," a 2L writes. Most Mercer professors are also engaging instructors, who "keep classroom discussions lively" and even—gasp—"make the law fun." "In evidence class, we get to run through mock trials, employing all of the objections," explains a 2L. Things are so chummy here that a 1L writes, "Sometimes I fear that the personal nature of the legal education at Mercer may not adequately prepare students for the harshness of the legal profession."

The physical plant is "one of the oldest buildings in Macon" and features an "awe-inspiring" façade. Mercer "has done an excellent job" of "installing adequate access to electronic resources not only in the library and computer labs, but also in the individual classrooms." "Nearly every classroom seat is hard-wired for power and Internet for our school-issued laptops, and we're completing a new wireless Internet system," reports a 1L.

Students' biggest wish is the expansion of Mercer's "recruiting and reputation" beyond "Georgia and its neighboring states." However, student opinion is split on whether change is indeed on its way. For some, "The administration is extremely responsive to student needs" and displays "a positive attitude toward helping students thrive in the academic setting." Others find the deans "willing to listen to student input about things, but rarely take the initiative to improve the marketability of the students." "They want the students to propose why another journal is needed when we only have one, and employers basically require one to be on a journal." A 1L hypothesizes that "the location is what hinders [Mercer] from breaking into the top 50 law schools. If we moved it to Atlanta, it would provide those internships [and] externships that we lack."

MARILYN E. SUTTON, ASST. DEAN OF ADMISSIONS AND FINANCIAL AID
1021 GEORGIA AVENUE, MACON, GA 31207
TEL: 478-301-2605 FAX: 478-301-2989
EMAIL: MARTIN_SV@MERCER.EDU • WEBSITE: WWW.LAW.MERCER.EDU

Life

"Walking in the first day of your 1L year can be very intimidating, but any apprehensions I had about starting law school were eased when I met the people that would go through the 'torture' with me," a student recalls. By all accounts, "Students feel not like competitors but colleagues." "Exam time is weird when you realize the same people you've been with all semester are the ones you're competing with for grades," a 1L writes. "Despite a slightly more conservative bent" on campus—many are "married" or "engaged"—"all races, genders, and lifestyles are accepted without any hesitation." Not surprisingly, "the single kids" here are more socially active "than the ones who are spoken for." Students generally find that although "Macon has a lot of history, beautiful architecture, and solid infrastructure," "The population is rapidly moving elsewhere," leaving a lack of things to do off campus. Some note that due to the town's small amount of "growth and development" the level of "crime (although not generally violent)" has started to rise. "There isn't a whole lot to do in Macon," a 1L reports. "But it's okay because when you're studying on a Friday night (which happens) you [won't] feel like you're missing out on much."

Getting In

Accepted applicants have average undergrad GPAs of 3.45 and LSAT scores of 156. Applicants to Mercer are automatically considered for a variety of scholarships. Additionally, they may apply for Mercer's George W. Woodruff Scholarship which is a full tuition scholarship plus a $5,000 per year stipend. The deadline is February 1.

Moot court requirement	Yes
Public interest law requirement	No

ADMISSIONS

Selectivity Rating	**78**
# applications received	1,314
% applicants accepted	37
% acceptees attending	31
Average LSAT	155
LSAT Range	153–157
Average undergrad GPA	3.43
Application fee	$50
Regular application	Rolling, up to 3/15
Regular notification	Rolling
Early application program	No
Transfer students accepted	Yes
Evening division offered	No
Part-time accepted	No
LSDAS accepted	Yes

Applicants Also Look At

Florida State University, University of Georgia, University of South Carolina, The University of Alabama, University of Tennessee—Knoxville, University of Florida, Emory University, Georgia State University, University of Miami, University of Mississippi, Samford University, Stetson University

International Students

TOEFL recommended of international students	Yes
Minimum TOEFL (paper/computer/web)	600/250/100

FINANCIAL FACTS

Annual tuition	$32,990
Books and supplies	$1,100
Fees	$200
Room & board	$13,900
Financial aid application deadline	4/1
% first-year students receiving some sort of aid	93
% receiving some sort of aid	89
% of aid that is merit based	17
% receiving scholarships	29
Average grant	$21,021
Average loan	$34,833
Average total aid package	$39,275
Average debt	$97,050

EMPLOYMENT INFORMATION

Career Rating	**77**	**Grads Employed by Field (%)**
Rate of placement (nine months out)	86.9	Academic (1)
Average starting salary	$71,906	Business/Industry (3)
State for bar exam	GA, FL, NC, SC, TN	Government (6)
Pass rate for first-time bar	95.8	Judicial clerkships (12)

Employers Who Frequently Hire Grads

King & Spalding, Atlanta, GA; Holland & Knight, Atlanta, GA; Troutman Sanders, Atlanta, GA; McKenna, Long, and Aldridge, Atlanta, GA.

Military (3)
Private practice (66)
Public Interest (9)

Prominent Alumni

Griffin Bell, Former Attorney General; Cathy Cox, Former Secretary of State, Ga.; John Oxendine, Insurance Commissioner, Ga.; Hugh Thompson, Ga. Supreme Court.

MICHIGAN STATE UNIVERSITY
COLLEGE OF LAW

INSTITUTIONAL INFORMATION

Public/private	Private
Student-faculty ratio	20:1
% faculty part-time	68
% faculty female	58
% faculty minority	16
Total faculty	100

SURVEY SAYS...

Diverse opinions accepted
in classrooms
Great research resources
Great library staff

STUDENTS

Enrollment of law school	910
% male/female	58/42
% out-of-state	36
% full-time	76
% minority	16
% international	6
# of countries represented	14
Average age of entering class	24

ACADEMICS

Academic Experience Rating	**78**
Profs interesting rating	80
Profs accessible rating	80
Hours of study per day	5.04

Academic Specialties

Constitutional law, corporation
securities, criminal law, environmental law, government services,
international law, taxation, intellectual property law, indigenous law,
trial pracitce, family law, health law,
alternative dispute resolution

Advanced Degrees Offered

LLM, 1 year; MJ, 1 year.

Combined Degrees Offered

JD/MBA, 4 years; JD/MS, 4 years
(Various Fields); JD/MA, 4 years
(Various Fields)

Clinical program required	No
Legal writing	
course requirement	Yes
Legal methods	
course requirement	No

Academics

Michigan State University College of Law is "a private law school on a public univer-sity campus" that offers "generous scholarships." The facilities here are reportedly among the best you'll find anywhere. They are "gorgeous, sophisticated, professional, and laden with the latest technology." "Wireless accessibility is a given." Classrooms are "designed with laptops in mind" and otherwise "state of the art." "Moot court facilities are second to none." "The librarians are very helpful" and the library is spacious. It still "gets crowded," though. "It is an open and unrestricted library and, as a result, under-grad use is very heavy," warns a 2L. "This makes it difficult to find the quiet study atmosphere you need." Some students also complain that class sizes are "too large."

Despite a few "old, lazy profs," students are generally pleased with the "very pas-sionate and knowledgeable" faculty at MSU Law. "Some are more theoretical and aca-demic," explains one student. "Others are more concerned with giving you the tools you will need to pass the bar and function as a legal professional." Professors here "never humiliate anyone yet they remain firm while applying the Socratic Method" and they are "very accessible." "Running into a professor and asking a quick question" is quite com-mon. "They are always there," observes a 1L, "just walking the halls, sitting in the lobby, or in the coffee shop." Administrators are not as visible but many students tell us that they are "helpful and available" and "constantly updating programs." Others are tired of "re-filing important forms over and over" and argue that management is "definitely a problem."

The legal writing program here is "exceptional" and MSU Law offers a wealth of opportunities to specialize. "There are journals in medicine and law, entertainment law, international law, gender law, and animal law." There are certificate programs in indige-nous law, trial practice, and child advocacy. "The JD/MBA program is a great bargain for business-minded law students." Real-world skills are fairly easy to acquire. "The clinics are amazing." The moot court competition team is "very good and prestigious." Also, MSU Law's proximity to the state capital allows students "to gain practical experience easily." "Expansive" opportunities for judicial externships and internships with various agencies are just a short drive away.

About half of all newly-minted MSU Law graduates find jobs in Michigan. The other half end up fleeing the state. Part of the reason is that Michigan is saddled with a "ridicu-lously terrible economy." "It is going to be tough to find jobs in this state when we grad-uate," advises a 1L, "and the jobs that do exist probably won't pay as well as those jobs that could be found in places like Chicago." Many who take part in this mass exodus find that they have an easier time finding jobs in other states as MSU Law grads. "It's not a big-name school that will impress employers," says a 2L. "Oddly enough, the farther away from Michigan you go, the better the school sounds just because of the name recog-nition through NCAA sports." Thanks to the glory of the Spartans, MSU Law grads are able to land jobs all over the country.

Charles Roboski, Assistant Dean, Admissions and Financial Aid
230 Law College Building, East Lansing, MI 48824-1300
Tel: (517) 432-0222 Fax: (517) 432-0098
Email: admiss@law.msu.edu • Website: www.law.msu.edu

Life

Students at MSU Law describe themselves as "engaging and ambitious." Some tell us that the academic atmosphere as "pleasantly laidback" and "very collegial." They say that their peers "take on the 'get-through-this-together' mentality." Others suggest that there is "plenty" of "intense" competition and note that "the aura of panic around exam time is palpable."

Just about everyone says that the law school community here is fabulous outside of class. "There is a diverse group of students so, no matter who you are, you should be able to find good friends," promises a 3L. "A vibrant spectrum of social life is available if you choose to partake in it, at a risk to your own grades, depending on how social you choose to be." "There are numerous academic organizations for all areas of law, strong journals and moot court teams, and social organizations." "There are great social events put on by the SBA" as well. Also, "going to a Big Ten school really has its benefits" and the association with a "gigantic" state school "provides a wealth of social activities on the side." East Lansing is an affordable college town that offers "plenty to do on the weekends." "Many students immerse themselves in MSU athletics, with over one-fifth of the students buying season tickets in the law student sections at football and hockey games."

Getting In

The acceptance rate here has varied in recent years, but it is usually pretty high. Admitted students at the 25th percentile have LSAT scores in the middle 150s and GPAs in the 3.3 range. Admitted students at the 75th percentile have LSAT scores around 160 and an approximate GPA of 3.5.

Legal research course requirement	Yes
Moot court requirement	No
Public interest law requirement	No

ADMISSIONS

Selectivity Rating	**73**
# applications received	1,999
% applicants accepted	55
% acceptees attending	28
Average LSAT	156
LSAT Range	154–159
Average undergrad GPA	3.4
Application fee	$60
Regular application	Rolling, up to 4/30
Regular notification	Rolling
Early application program	No
Transfer students accepted	Yes
Evening division offered	Yes
Part-time accepted	Yes
LSDAS accepted	Yes

Applicants Also Look At

University of Michigan—Ann Arbor, Wayne State University, Indiana University—Purdue University Indianapolis, Illinois Institute of Technology, Hofstra University, Cleveland State University, DePaul University, Loyola University—Chicago, Florida Costal School of Law

International Students

TOEFL required of international students	Yes
Minimum TOEFL (paper/computer)	600/250

FINANCIAL FACTS

Annual tuition	$31,552
Books and supplies	$1,344
Fees	$226
Tuition per credit	$1,088
Room & board	$10,344
Financial aid application deadline	4/1
% first-year students receiving some sort of aid	85
% receiving some sort of aid	85
% of aid that is merit based	80
% receiving scholarships	34
Average grant	$20,304
Average loan	$21,427
Average total aid package	$39,811
Average debt	$73,201

EMPLOYMENT INFORMATION

Career Rating	**76**
Rate of placement (nine months out)	91
Average starting salary	$65,000
State for bar exam	MI, IL, OH, CA, NY
Pass rate for first-time bar	90

Prominent Alumni

Dennis Archer, Leadership; Geoffrey Fieger, Trial Lawyer; Marrianne Battani, U.S. District; Clif Haley, Corporate Law; Bernard Friedman, U.S. District.

Grads Employed by Field (%)

Academic (3)
Business/Industry (16)
Government (14)
Judicial Clerkships (8)
Military (1)
Private Practice (48)
Public Interest (5)
Other (5)

MISSISSIPPI COLLEGE
SCHOOL OF LAW

INSTITUTIONAL INFORMATION

Public/private	Private
Affiliation	Southern Baptist
% faculty part-time	57
% faculty female	23
% faculty minority	9
Total faculty	56

SURVEY SAYS...

Diverse opinions accepted
in classrooms
Great research resources
Great library staff
Abundant externship/internship/clerk-
ship opportunities

STUDENTS

Enrollment of law school	538
% male/female	58/42
% out-of-state	54
% full-time	100
% minority	9
# of countries represented	1
Average age of entering class	26

ACADEMICS

Academic Experience Rating	**72**
Profs interesting rating	83
Profs accessible rating	89
Hours of study per day	3.74

Academic Specialties

Certificate Program in Civil Law
Studies

Advanced Degrees Offered

JD, 3 years.

Combined Degrees Offered

JD/MBA; JD, 3 years; MBA, 1 year

Clinical program required	No
Legal writing	
course requirement	Yes
Legal methods	
course requirement	No
Legal research	
course requirement	Yes
Moot court requirement	Yes
Public interest	
law requirement	No

Academics

Mississippi College School of Law "really places an emphasis on practical lawyering" "in addition to the theory of the law." Students offer high praise for MC Law's moot court teams, which are "annually competitive on a national level." Practice rounds for national competition teams "are often coached or judged by sitting Federal Court Judges and State Supreme Court Justices." The "most distinctive feature" is "the visibility and availability of the administration." The dean is "highly committed," reportedly going so far as to occasionally mow the campus lawn. Administrators, professors, staff, security, and "even the custodians" are "very personable and friendly." "Every day you can find the deans and the professors sitting and chatting with the students in the common areas of the school or dropping by the classrooms." "Having come to MCSOL from another institution, I was amazed by the accessibility of professors and genuine interest in the progress of their students," elaborates a 3L. "It is not uncommon for professors to remain 30 to 45 minutes after class answering individual students' questions. This was virtually unheard of at the other institution I attended." "Their doors are always open to us," adds a 1L. "If an office door is closed, there is usually a student already in there." The "knowledgeable, caring, [and] highly motivated" professors are "very effective as instructors." "Their methods of teaching vary from the harsh Socratic Method to a friendlier, more accommodating style." "I like the diversity," observes a 1L. "Some are extremely serious while some make the class more fun."

The "very nice" facilities are "equipped with state-of-the-art technology," including "technology-friendly" classrooms. The three-story law library "is a scene from the 1970s," but it "contains most likely all the legal research materials a student could want or need" and "many private study rooms." If only the school would "invest in chairs that support the lumbar region."

Student opinion regarding the writing program is more mixed. Some say it is "strong"; others call it "pathetic." The bar-passage rate—while quite high—is typically lower than the state average, which irks some students. Also, students tell us they'd like to see "more specialization options." (There is a Louisiana Civil Law Certificate program for students who want to practice in Louisiana, but that's about it.)

Mississippi College is one of only two law schools in the Magnolia State and the "only law school in Mississippi located in a major metro area (where jobs can easily be found)." The campus is located "in the heart of Mississippi's capital city, two blocks from the state capitol and Supreme Court buildings and three blocks from the federal court house." Students have access to "very choice and prestigious" externships. Clerking is easy because the neighborhood is crawling with "judges, legislators, and the top state and regional law firms." A tremendous point of pride here is that MC Law is in the top 15 percent nationally in job placement. Career Services works "tirelessly" to give students networking opportunities, "so that even the students who are fighting to improve their grades have one foot in the door somewhere." "This regional school is trying to develop the first-rate regional reputation it deserves," explains one student. "I can think of no improvements besides the fact that our school gets no national recognition."

ASSISTANT DEAN PATRICIA H. EVANS, DEAN OF ADMISSIONS
151 EAST GRIFFITH STREET, JACKSON, MS 39201
TEL: 601-925-7152 FAX: 601-925-7166
EMAIL: HWEAVER@MC.EDU • WEBSITE: WWW.LAW.MC.EDU

Life

Ethnically, Mississippi College is home to a pretty "a homogenous environment." Many students are graduates of Mississippi State or Ole Miss. "When I arrived from out of state," says a 2L, "I felt as if everyone already knew each other because the majority of my class attended one of those schools." Politically, it's more diverse. "The student body is about 50 percent liberal and 50 percent conservative." Students can be "competitive when it comes to grades" and "There are a few students who have the cutthroat mentality." Mostly, though, "MCSOL is a very strong community." Students are "very sociable" and "easy to talk to." The 2Ls and 3Ls "are helpful with guidance and assistance" and "make you feel like a junior colleague, not a rookie."

Social life can be "a bit cliquish" but a "family-type environment" tends to triumph on campus. "The students seem to generally have a good time." "The prevailing social scene at MCSOL is a continuation of most SEC undergrad scenes, just a little more grown up." "There are clubs and organizations for every interest and many school-wide activities in which to participate." "Golf tournaments, bowling tournaments, tennis tournaments, charity auctions, Halloween parties, and barrister's balls are all annual events."

The "conservative and slow" surrounding city of Jackson "is an extremely affordable place to live." "Rent is low, groceries are inexpensive, and social events are easy to afford." It's "a great town for married couples." As a bonus, "contrary to popular belief, neither Mississippi nor its capital city is a haven for...narrow-minded people." However, "The social scene in Jackson is terrible." "There's very little to do, and the city itself is unattractive at best," says one student. "The downtown area has not been preserved at all, so now it's one big blight."

Getting In

At Mississippi College, admitted students at the 25th percentile have LSAT scores in the range of 149 and GPAs hovering around 3.0. Admitted students at the 75th percentile have LSAT scores of about 153 and GPAs of about 3.5.

ADMISSIONS

Selectivity Rating	64
# applications received	1,153
% applicants accepted	54
% acceptees attending	32
Average LSAT	150
LSAT Range	148–153
Average undergrad GPA	3.2
Regular application	Rolling, up to 6/1
Regular notification	Rolling
Early application program	No
Transfer students accepted	Yes
Evening division offered	No
Part-time accepted	Yes
LSDAS accepted	Yes

Applicants Also Look At
Louisiana State University, The University of Alabama, University of Tennessee—Knoxville, University of Mississippi, Samford University

FINANCIAL FACTS

Annual tuition	$23,850
Books and supplies	$1,100
Fees	$1,270
Tuition per credit	$795
Room & board (off-campus)	$10,125
Financial aid application deadline	7/1
% first-year students receiving some sort of aid	85
% receiving some sort of aid	83
% of aid that is merit based	21
% receiving scholarships	32
Average grant	$12,000
Average loan	$32,000
Average total aid package	$35,000
Average debt	$81,000

EMPLOYMENT INFORMATION

Career Rating	75
Rate of placement (nine months out)	90
Average starting salary	$57,548
State for bar exam	MS, TN, AL
Pass rate for first-time bar	88

Employers Who Frequently Hire Grads
International Law Firms; Multi-state Law Firms; Mississippi Law Firms; State Government; Federal Government; Business; U.S. Military

Prominent Alumni
Sharion Aycock, Federal District Judge; Mike Parker, Federal Magistrate Judge; Linda Anderson, Federal Magistrate Judge.

Grads Employed by Field (%)
Academic (1)
Business/Industry (13)
Government (8)
Judicial Clerkships (13)
Military (3)
Private Practice (60)
Public Interest (2)

NEW ENGLAND LAW|BOSTON

Academics

Students agree that "New England Law is the true Boston gem." Many also note that it's only a matter of time until "New England Law is formally considered a top-tier law school in this nation" and in turn "recognized for the quality institution it is." Everyone, including "students, faculty, and Boston's legal community already know this," but many find it "too bad many outside Massachusetts do not." Such comments reflect the scrappy, going-it-together attitude shared by faculty, students and administration alike. "The professors," for example, "recognize that New England Law is not a first-tier school and thus focus very much on preparing students for the legal profession and passing the bar," which students do on their first try at an impressive rate. Another bonus is the lack of "academic snobbery, and minimal competition between students."

Many students claims New England Law's "greatest strength" is "the practical experience that a student gains from interaction with the adjunct faculty." Students say that the "clinical program is amazing." The school's location provides for easy "access to Boston professionals" and allows for students "to get some real-world practice in before graduation."

The faculty "contains the entire spectrum of the legal community, from New England Law grads to Harvard grads." Overall, they "are accessible, qualified, and have excellent practical and conceptual grasp of the subject material," and they spread the love; full-time day students aren't the only ones who get professors' attention. Students are "amazed at how willing the professors are to stay a couple hours after evening classes end, and even to come in on Saturdays to conduct a review session."

Students are also pleased to report that "The school's administration is very organized," "very accessible," and "responds to student concerns in a timely manner." Folks are "really helpful if you have a problem, especially Financial Aid and the Registrar." The administration makes a point of being proactive. Its recent renovation of the library, for example, has been well received by students, who describe the new look as "modern and elegant." In addition, over the past few years "The school has completely revamped New England Law's technology. Not only is New England Law technologically up-to-date with their Wi-Fi and online services, but their facilities are modern, clean, and laptop friendly."

Life

"New England Law is not as well known as the other law schools in the area, and the professors and students know that," explains one student. Therefore, "Students here are some [of] the hardest-working students in Boston, and rightly so—they face pretty tough competition for law jobs compared to other schools in the area." Contrary to what might be expected in such circumstances, "There is not the highly competitive, cutthroat attitude among the students here" normally associated with law schools that have lots of students vying for few select jobs. New students are often surprised by the "camaraderie" and "helpfulness" "exhibited by the students." That said, socially the school can be "cliquish" and reminds more than a few students of "high school." They note that "rumors fly quickly and everyone wants to know everyone else's business." "Everyone knows everyone" here, but they remain a "generally friendly lot." Politically, "students are extremely liberal. Everyone here wants to eventually take down big business, big oil, [and] Wal-Mart."

MICHELLE L'ETOILE, DIRECTOR OF ADMISSIONS
154 STUART STREET, BOSTON, MA 02116
TEL: 617-422-7210 FAX: 617-422-7201
EMAIL: ADMIT@NESL.EDU • WEBSITE: WWW.NESL.EDU

Being located right in "the heart of Boston," students find themselves "minutes away from everything," and note that the campus is "very accessible from all areas by the T system." Drivers will be happy to note that it is also "conveniently located near parking facilities," though these are in one of the "lesser" (though safe in the daytime) neighborhoods in Boston. One student mentions that "it is a good idea to walk with a friend to the garage—especially at night."

"There are constantly social events at nearby places to give students a break from law." "One bar across the street is practically all New England Law students" and the "food court across the street is loaded with students studying and socializing." In addition to this, the school plans "several social events at the beginning of the year [so they can] meet everyone." The school also offers "many panels of lawyers" who "come in to speak about various legal professions to help students better assess which field of law they might want to pursue."

Getting In

Getting in to New England Law may be easier than getting into than some other Boston-area law schools, but this by no means makes admission a cakewalk. Successful applicants have a B/B+ undergraduate academic record and LSAT scores in the low 150s. As is the case at most law schools offering both day and night courses, acceptance to the part-time evening division is slightly easier to achieve than acceptance to the full-time day division.

ADMISSIONS

Selectivity Rating	**67**
# applications received	2,524
# applicants accepted	1,333
# acceptees attending	260
Average LSAT	152
LSAT Range	151–155
Average undergrad GPA	3.23
Application fee	$65
Regular application	Rolling, up to 3/15
Regular notification	Rolling
Early application program	No
Transfer students accepted	Yes
Evening division offered	Yes
Part-time accepted	Yes
LSDAS accepted	Yes

Applicants Also Look At
Northeastern University, Hofstra University, Suffolk University, Western New England College, New York Law School

International Students
TOEFL required
of international students   Yes
Minimum TOEFL
(paper/computer/web) 600/250/100

FINANCIAL FACTS

Annual tuition	$33,500
Books and supplies	$1,250
Fees	$80
Tuition per credit	$1,400
Room & board (off-campus)	$16,650
Financial aid application deadline	4/9
% first-year students receiving some sort of aid	91
% receiving some sort of aid	88
% of aid that is merit based	78
% receiving scholarships	45
Average grant	$9,253
Average loan	$34,920
Average total aid package	$38,130
Average debt	$90,466

EMPLOYMENT INFORMATION

Career Rating	**73**	**Grads Employed by Field (%)**
Rate of placement (nine months out)	90	Academic (4)
Average starting salary	$59,458	Business/Industry (25)
State for bar exam	MA, NY, CT, PA, NJ	Government (14)
Pass rate for first-time bar	90.3	Judicial Clerkships (13)
Prominent Alumni		Private Practice (37)
Leonard P. Zakim, NE Anti-Defamation		Public Interest (2)
Leag., namesake, Boston bridge; The		Other (6)
Honorable Susan J. Crawford, Chief		
Justice, U.S. Ct of Appeals for Armed		
Forces; The Honorable John R. Simpson,		
Frmr Head of the U.S. Secret Service		

NEW YORK LAW SCHOOL

INSTITUTIONAL INFORMATION

Public/private	Private
Student-faculty ratio	22:1
% faculty part-time	52
% faculty female	33
% faculty minority	11
Total faculty	169

SURVEY SAYS...

Diverse opinions accepted
in classrooms
Liberal students
Students love New York, NY

STUDENTS

Enrollment of law school	1,596
% male/female	49/51
% full-time	75
% minority	22
# of countries represented	28
Average age of entering class	25

ACADEMICS

Academic Experience Rating	**74**
Profs interesting rating	82
Profs accessible rating	70
Hours of study per day	4.39

Academic Specialties

Civil procedure, commercial law, constitutional law, corporation securities, criminal law, environmental law, government services, human rights, international law, labor law, legal history, legal philosophy, property, taxation, intellectual property law, legal profession/ethics, real estate law, information law, financial services law

Advanced Degrees Offered

JD;. LLM; MA and certificate program in Mental Disablity Law.

Combined Degrees Offered

JD/MBA w/ Baruch College; JD/LLM in Tax and JD/LLM in Real Estate

Clinical program required	No
Legal writing	
course requirement	Yes
Legal methods	
course requirement	Yes

Academics

Private, "obscenely underrated" New York Law School in lower Manhattan is a hothouse for hands-on preparation that "focuses on training successful lawyers" who are "ready to make an impact on the legal profession" the day they pass the bar exam. The emphasis here is on practical courses, and there are "many opportunities to take part in real lawyering while you are still in law school." "The clinics are exceptional and a great experience." Externships and courses that simulate real legal work abound. With a host of academic centers and more than 250 elective classes available in a ton of different specialized areas of law, it's very easy to tailor pretty much any program you want. Students tell us that "NYLS has the best location in New York City" as well. "Geographic proximity" to courts, government agencies, banks, securities exchanges, and law firms provides hundreds of opportunities to gain experience as a law student.

The NYLS faculty is "very accomplished" and "well versed." In terms of teaching, there are "a few mediocre professors," but "most bring a passion about the subject they teach, making class time fly by." "In almost every class, I have been instructed by either a nationally known expert or someone with fantastic real-world legal experience," beams a 2L. "Hardly any of the professors are purely academics." Some students are critical of the administration, calling it "unavailable and hostile to criticism." However, most students are happy with the top brass. Management is "present and very accessible to students," they say, and "very responsive to students' needs." Probably the biggest grievance among students here is the fact that classes are "seriously overcrowded." "There are too many students," protests a 3L. The "awful" writing program also comes in for some derision. Unhappy students call it "arbitrary and too narrowly focused."

Opinions concerning employment prospects are mixed. Some of the future lawyers here say that "career opportunities for students outside the top tier seem to be few and far between." "Getting into prestigious law firms is extremely difficult, and recruitment at NY Law is terrible." Other students have much more positive reviews. "If you're at the top of your class," they say, "it's not difficult to get a big firm job here in NYC." Students also point to the "huge network of practicing alumni" currently practicing around the Big Apple in government, public interest, and firms of all sizes.

Many of the facilities on this tiny campus here are excellent. The gleaming, new building is "an impressive space" that is "aesthetically pleasing" and, by all accounts, "very high tech" and otherwise "state of the art." It's chock full of "brand new classrooms, lounges," and study rooms. There's a new library as well. The older buildings, on the other hand, are "held together in some places literally by duct tape." "The school should be a commercial for the many uses of duct tape," suggests a 3L.

Life

NYLS is home to "a very attractive student body," and the students here don't mind telling you so. The population is laudably diverse as well. Traditionally underrepresented minorities account for about a third of the students. Geographic diversity is abundant. People come here from all over the country and all over the world. Age also varies considerably. Many students are straight out of undergrad or just a year or two removed from college. Many others are significantly older career changers. At the end of the day, though, there are two kinds of students: "those that are from the NYC area those that are not."

Some students tell us that the academic atmosphere is "competitive but not brutal." Others maintain that competition doesn't' really exist at all. "People are more than willing to share notes, outlines and briefs," they say. "I was very surprised at how coopera-tive students are to each other," relates a 1L. Outside of class, "student groups are plen-tiful, and there are many leadership opportunities for students." Opinions about the social scene vary widely. Some students see a considerable amount of cohesiveness. "Since New York Law School is not attached to a larger undergraduate institution, we are a more close-knit community," relates a happy 1L, "like a large extended family." "It's a good time," adds a 3L. Others suggest that students are very disjointed. "I would not say that there is a strong New York Law School social scene per se," reflects a 2L. "School spirit, community, and social life at the school should be improved." Either way, no one could doubt that there is plenty for everyone to do. NYLS is located in the hip, trendy (and expensive) neighborhood of Tribeca. The nightlife of Greenwich Village and Soho is right next door, and all of Manhattan is easily accessible by subway.

Getting In

Admitted students at the 25th percentile have LSAT scores in the low 150s and GPAs around 3.0. Admitted students at the 75th percentile have LSAT scores of 157 or so and GPAs of around 3.3.

Legal research course requirement	Yes
Moot court requirement	No
Public interest law requirement	No

ADMISSIONS

Selectivity Rating	**72**
# applications received	5,606
# applicants accepted	2,410
# acceptees attending	565
Average LSAT	154
LSAT Range	151–157
Average undergrad GPA	3.29
Application fee	$65
Regular application	Rolling, up to 4/1
Regular notification	Rolling
Early application program	No
Transfer students accepted	Yes
Evening division offered	Yes
Part-time accepted	Yes
LSDAS accepted	Yes

Applicants Also Look At
New York University, Seton Hall University, Yeshiva University, Fordham University, Hofstra University, Pace University, Rutgers University—Newark, St. John's University, Albany Law School of Union University, Brooklyn Law School

International Students
TOEFL recommended of international students	Yes
Minimum TOEFL (paper/computer/web)	600/250/100

FINANCIAL FACTS

Annual tuition	$42,500
Books and supplies	$1,100
Fees	$1,100
Room & board	$19,824
Financial aid application deadline	4/1
% first-year students receiving some sort of aid	91
% receiving some sort of aid	89
% of aid that is merit based	11
% receiving scholarships	35
Average grant	$11,000
Average loan	$41,800
Average total aid package	$52,800
Average debt	$125,286

EMPLOYMENT INFORMATION

Career Rating	**85**	**Grads Employed by Field (%)**	
Rate of placement (nine months out)	92	Academic (2)	
Average starting salary	$85,000	Business/Industry (22)	
State for bar exam	NY, NJ, CT	Government (13)	
Pass rate for first-time bar	93	Judicial Clerkships (3)	
Employers Who Frequently Hire Grads		Private Practice (48)	
Private Practice; Business & Industry;		Public Interest (5)	
Government; Public Interest		Other (6)	
Prominent Alumni			
John Marshall Harlan, U.S. Supreme Court Justice 1955-1971; Wallace Stevens, Pulitzer Prize-winning poet; David Kelley '86, U.S. Attorney for the Southern District of New York.			

NEW YORK UNIVERSITY
SCHOOL OF LAW

INSTITUTIONAL INFORMATION

Public/private	Private
Student-faculty ratio	10:1
% faculty part-time	34
% faculty female	30
% faculty minority	19
Total faculty	231

SURVEY SAYS...
Great research resources
Students love New York, NY

STUDENTS

Enrollment of law school	1,423
% male/female	54/46
% full-time	100
% minority	22
% international	3
# of countries represented	
Average age of entering class	24

ACADEMICS

Academic Experience Rating	**97**
Profs interesting rating	91
Profs accessible rating	78
Hours of study per day	3.98

Academic Specialties
Civil procedure, commercial law, constitutional law, corporation securities, criminal law, environmental law, human rights, international law, labor law, legal history, legal philosophy, property, taxation, intellectual property law, clinical programs, public interest, trade regulations

Advanced Degrees Offered
LLM, JSD

Combined Degrees Offered
JD/LLM, JD/MBA, JD/MPA, JD/MUP, JD/MSW, JD/MA, JD/PhD, JD/JD (Osgoode)

Clinical program required	No
Legal writing course requirement	Yes
Legal methods course requirement	Yes
Legal research course requirement	Yes

Academics

New York University School of Law is "a lot more practical than theoretical" and it "has more money than it knows what to do with." As a result, the number of programs, colloquia, institutes, and centers are stunning. The "enormous" and "outstanding" clinical program allows tons of students to work with real clients. Public interest law opportunities are profuse. In the Prisoners Rights and Education Project, for example, participating students teach legal research skills to inmates in local prisons. Students here also heap praise on the legal writing program here. "All assignments are given within a particular client context," a 2L explains, "and we are required to practice not only legal research and writing but to engage in other lawyering activities like negotiations, client counseling, mediations, etc."

The faculty here is "world renowned" because, quite frankly, "NYU has no qualms about poaching the best talent" from other law schools. "Professors have a very broad and diverse range of academic and work experience." They're "accessible and really seem to care about the students." Teaching ability tends to vary, though. Some professors "can single-handedly engender student interest in their subjects and captivate an entire class for two hours." Conversely, "Others have the opposite effect, turning off students to otherwise interesting topics." The deans of the law school are "proactive and helpful," but dealing with the administration of the wider university is often "a bureaucratic nightmare." Also, "NYU is pretty large" and many students tell us that "class sizes could be smaller." Registration is a headache, too, and it can be "difficult to get into the classes you want."

NYU "lags behind the Ivies in placing students in clerkships and academic positions," but students generally "have little trouble getting a job at a large law firm with top-of-the-market compensation." "You can pick the firms," a 2L promises. "The firms don't pick you. That is an important distinction." Public interest law and government work are also very big. "There is no law school out there that better prepares its graduates for a career in the public sector," boasts a 2L. "One of the best loan repayment programs available in the country" certainly makes working for less money a plausible alternative.

For the most part, NYU's facilities are "modern" and "outstanding." "One building is brand new and the other has been renovated in the past few years." Some chairs are notably "uncomfortable," though, and "whoever designed the classrooms obviously never walked through them with a backpack." Additionally, the library, one student adds, "could use more space."

Life

Ethnic diversity is a point of pride here. "In fact, the administration never shuts up about it." Politically, liberalism definitely reigns supreme but there's also "a sizable minority of moderates (who qualify as conservatives at NYU)." Students describe themselves as "very interesting," "incredibly intelligent," and "pretty nerdy." A few students call the academic atmosphere "highly competitive." "Even when people realize they will have jobs," they assert, "the competition then becomes about law firms." However, the majority tell us that "the vibe is laidback and collaborative." "The program itself creates neither competition nor tension," they say. "Are some students chronic worry-mongers and stress-ogres who fret and fume?" asks a 2L. "Yes. But do they set the tone for the rest of us? No." "There is a big push to share outlines; study groups are a big thing; and people are more than willing to tell you what to expect from a professor," a 3L says.

NYU is, of course, located "in the heart of a world-class city." "If you're looking for a bucolic, cloistered academic experience, this isn't it." The surrounding neighborhood is "wonderful" and "eclectic." It's also "ridiculously expensive." NYU does offer apartment-style dorms but they are also pricey and "not that great." Consequently, a lot of students choose to live in Brooklyn, where housing is cheaper and there is "some separation from campus life." "The Village rocks," a 2L says. "But I'd still recommend living off-campus. Otherwise, you tend to form this bubble of about 10 blocks around the school and you never leave it." Social life here takes many forms. Some students "go out partying from Thursday through Saturday." Others do nothing but study. "There's a good mix of recent college grads who want law school to be College Part II in terms of social life, but then there are plenty of people who are a few years out of school and live off-campus and don't think keg parties are the most fun way to socialize anymore."

Getting In

As you would expect at one of the most prestigious law schools in the country, admission standards are very high here. Admitted students at the 25th percentile have LSAT scores in the high 160s and GPAs around 3.5. Admitted students at the 75th percentile have LSAT scores in the low 170s and GPAs in the 3.8 range.

Moot court requirement	No
Public interest law requirement	No

ADMISSIONS

Selectivity Rating	**97**
# applications received	7,095
# applicants accepted	1,628
# acceptees attending	448
Average LSAT	170
LSAT Range	169–173
Average undergrad GPA	3.65
Application fee	$75
Regular application	Rolling, up to 2/1
Regular notification	4/30
Early application program	Yes
Early application deadline	11/15
Early application notification	12/31
Transfer students accepted	Yes
Evening division offered	No
Part-time accepted	No
LSDAS accepted	Yes

FINANCIAL FACTS

Annual tuition	$42,890
Books and supplies	$1,100
Fees	$1,357
Room & board	$20,579
Financial aid application deadline	4/15
Average grant	$15,000
Average debt	$115,575

EMPLOYMENT INFORMATION

Career Rating	**99**
Rate of placement (nine months out)	99.79
Average starting salary	$160,000
State for bar exam	NY
Pass rate for first-time bar	95.79

Employers Who Frequently Hire Grads
Private law firms, public interest organizations, government agencies, corporations, and public accounting firms.

Grads Employed by Field (%)
Business/Industry (2)
Government (3)
Judicial Clerkships (8)
Private Practice (79)
Public Interest (8)

NORTH CAROLINA CENTRAL UNIVERSITY

SCHOOL OF LAW

INSTITUTIONAL INFORMATION

Public/private	Public
Student-faculty ratio	18:1
% faculty part-time	47
% faculty female	62
% faculty minority	58
Total faculty	45

SURVEY SAYS...

Diverse opinions accepted
in classrooms
Great research resources
Liberal students

STUDENTS

Enrollment of law school	644
% male/female	39/61
% out-of-state	32
% full-time	81
% minority	59
% international	17
Average age of entering class	27

ACADEMICS

Academic Experience Rating	**76**
Profs interesting rating	86
Profs accessible rating	83
Hours of study per day	5.2

Academic Specialties

Taxation, intellectual property law,
dispute resolution, civil rights

Advanced Degrees Offered

JD Day Program, 3 years; JD
Evening Program, 4 years

Combined Degrees Offered

JD/M.B.A., 4 years; JD/M.L.S.,
4 years

Clinical program required	No
Legal writing	
course requirement	Yes
Legal methods	
course requirement	Yes
Legal research	
course requirement	Yes
Moot court requirement	No
Public interest	
law requirement	No

Academics

"I rave about my law school," gloats a 3L at the North Carolina Central University School of Law. By all accounts, NCCU is a "great value." It's unquestionably possible to graduate from here with little or no debt. The renovated law school building feels "very new" and it's "always well kept." The facilities are state-of-the-art" and "extremely high-tech." "Practical training is strongly encouraged" and readily available. "NCCU has sub-stantial opportunities for practical legal experience outside the classroom," explains a 1L. "Excellent" clinics, pro bono opportunities, externship programs, and hands-on skills courses provide real world experience galore. "The variety of clinics" (18 in all) includes criminal litigation, juvenile law, and a small business clinic—just to name a few. There's also a standard JD/MBA program, a JD/MLS program (for future law librarians), and a unique Biotechnology and Pharmaceutical Law Institute, where you can engross your-self in the labyrinth of prescription drug regulation. It's also worth noting that students here have easy access to the state and federal courts in the nearby state capital, Raleigh.

Inside the classroom, the "passionate, knowledgeable," and "very dedicated" faculty brings plenty of "real world" know-how. At least for the most part, professors are also "very clear in explaining concepts." "The teachers are really encouraging, and they want to see each student succeed." "Motivation, guidance, and encouragement" are ample. "Faculty accessibility" is another huge plus. "They are tough but there for you in many ways." Faculty members are "very responsive" and "always available and willing to help" if you stay after class or stop by their offices.

Some students call NCCU "the total package" and wouldn't change a thing. Others, however, see areas that could be better. While some students tell us that management is "organized" and "always helpful," for example, others complain, "the customer service skills of the administration are lacking." "I get better service at Wendy's," quips a 3L. Also, despite the fact that a loyal alumni base works "to ensure that you have an opportunity to practice," some students say that Career Services "and other support services" could use "an overhaul." A broader selection of electives would be another improvement. "We could offer a wider variety of classes in more concentrated areas," suggests a 3L.

Life

NCCU began in 1939 as North Carolina's only law school for African Americans. Today, it's quite a diverse bastion of legal education, ethnically and otherwise. "Students come from all over the country and all over the world." Ages run the gamut from stu-dents straight out of undergrad to those in their fifties who are training for a second (or third) career. "Different perspectives on life and law" are abundant. "Many schools claim to be diverse and accepting of diversity," observes one 3L. "Yet my school proves it every day. We are a family. It includes the good, the bad, and ugly."

SANDRA BROWN BECHTOLD, DIRECTOR OF ENROLLMENT MANAGEMENT
640 NELSON STREET, DURHAM, NC 27707
TEL: 919-530-5243 FAX: 919-530-7981
EMAIL: SBROWNB@NCCU.EDU • WEBSITE: WWW.NCCU.EDU/LAW

NCCU's relatively small size lends an intimacy that you just won't find at larger schools. First-year sections are particularly cozy, and the atmosphere for all students is "very friendly." "We are a strong, supportive community," explains a 3L. "We help each other out and truly want each other to succeed." "Upperclassmen are mentors for new law students," and they offer advice "on a daily basis and on a variety of subjects and experiences." Nevertheless, and all of this social comfort notwithstanding, students are often competing for just a few precious A's. "The curve of our grading system can be devastating to a GPA," cautions a 2L," but it does force students to work their hardest to achieve good grades."

Students here are very satisfied with their lives outside of law school. The campus has some problems with crime" but students stress that safety isn't much of an issue at all. Durham is a growing and revitalizing city that offers a low cost of living, some 40 annual festivals, and unbeatable medical facilities. With about 15,000 students in town (at NCCU and at nearby Duke University), there are certainly plenty of lively social options. If you prefer laid-back ones, you can find those, too. An array of outdoorsy activities is available in every direction as well.

Gettin In

Though the acceptance rate at NCCU is low, you don't necessarily need outstanding grades and test scores to get admitted. Admitted students at the 25th percentile have LSAT scores of 144 or so and their undergraduate GPA is right around 3.0. Admitted students at the 75th percentile typically have LSAT scores around 150 and GPAs in B+ to A–territory.

ADMISSIONS

Selectivity Rating	**70**
# applications received	2,148
% applicants accepted	408
% acceptees attending	185
Average LSAT	146
LSAT Range	144–149
Average undergrad GPA	3.23
Application fee	$40
Regular application	Rolling, up to 3/31
Regular notification	Rolling
Early application program	No
Transfer students accepted	Yes
Evening division offered	Yes
Part-time accepted	Yes
LSDAS accepted	Yes

Applicants Also Look At

University of North Carolina at Chapel Hill, Thomas M. Cooley Law School

International Students

TOEFL required of international students	Yes

FINANCIAL FACTS

Annual tuition (in-state/out-of-state)	$4,667/$16,837
Books and supplies	$2,000
Fees	$2,025
Room & board (on/off-campus)	$8,174/$10,450
Financial aid application deadline	6/1
% first-year students receiving some sort of aid	97
% receiving some sort of aid	98
% of aid that is merit based	22
% receiving scholarships	62
Average grant	$3,400
Average loan	$22,500
Average total aid package	$26,000
Average debt	$55,500

EMPLOYMENT INFORMATION

Career Rating	**74**
Rate of placement (nine months out)	77
State for bar exam	NC, VA, SC, GA, MD
Pass rate for first-time bar	79

Employers Who Frequently Hire Grads

Public Defender and District Attorney Offices NC Department of Justice Legal Aid of NC

Prominent Alumni

Gov. Michael Easley, Governor, NC; G. K. Butterfield, U.S. House of Rep.; Willie Gary, Private Practice.

Grads Employed by Field (%)

Business/Industry (12)
Government (19)
Judicial Clerkships (4)
Private Practice (50)
Public Interest (11)
Other (4)

NORTHEASTERN UNIVERSITY
SCHOOL OF LAW

INSTITUTIONAL INFORMATION

Public/private	Private
Student-faculty ratio	17:1
% faculty part-time	54
% faculty female	42
% faculty minority	16
Total faculty	85

SURVEY SAYS...

Abundant externship/internship/
clerkship opportunities
Liberal students
Students love Boston, MA

STUDENTS

Enrollment of law school	615
% male/female	43/57
% full-time	100
% minority	27.6
Average age of entering class	25

ACADEMICS

Academic Experience Rating	77
Profs interesting rating	86
Profs accessible rating	80
Hours of study per day	3.77

Academic Specialties

Civil procedure, commercial law, constitutional law, corporation securities, criminal law, environmental law, human rights, international law, labor law, property, taxation, intellectual property law

Combined Degrees Offered

JD/MBA, 45 months; JD/MBA/MS in accountancy, 45 Months; JD/MPH, 42 Months; JD/LPS, 45 Months; JD/MA in Sustainable International Development, 45 Months; JD/MELP Environmental Law and Policy, 33 Months.

Clinical program required	No
Legal writing course requirement	Yes
Legal methods course requirement	Yes
Legal research course requirement	Yes
Moot court requirement	No

Academics

A "commitment to progressive lawyering and the co-op internship model" are the hallmarks of Northeastern University School of Law. Northeastern is "a truly unique school," firmly "grounded in experiential learning." Students here appreciate the "lack of formal grades (students are evaluated in 2–3 paragraph blurbs instead), and a refusal to rank students above each other." Thanks to this "lack of competition," students feel more comfortable to "reach out to each other to prepare for exams and research papers, offering support, sharing outlines and giving advice." On the contrary, while "The school has a great reputation in the Boston legal market," some students grumble that employment prospects in other cities seem dim because "No one wants to read a huge packet of written evaluations." Most don't find this to be too much of a problem though since "Northeastern's co-op program has direct connections with hundreds of employers all across the country," resulting in plenty of "legal internships" that often turn into "job offers."

Students say their "amazing" professors are "super-approachable" experts in their fields who "take the time to care about you and challenge you." Faculty members also "really take the time to write personalized evaluations for each student." Northeastern's administration either "welcomes student voices and opinions [or has] very little commitment to the overall health and well-being of law students," depending on whom you ask.

In the Fall of 2008, Northeastern University School of Law opened its completely renovated Dockser Hall, adjacent to the law school's existing Knowles Center, a state-of-the-art building that includes a moot courtroom, classrooms, seminar rooms, offices and lounge areas and ample space for the law school's clinical program.

It is no doubt that Northeastern's crown jewel is its hands-on Cooperative Legal Education Program. After completing a mostly traditional 1L curriculum, 2Ls and 3Ls rotate every three months between working as full-time, paid legal interns and attending classes. Each student completes "four three-month internships during our three years of law school." This valuable program "is a fantastic opportunity to get twice as much hands-on experience as you would get at other schools," and "means each student has the opportunity to explore areas of interest and make contacts in those fields." One 2L declares, "After next summer I will have completed three internships, one with a judge, one with in-house counsel at a large computer company, and one with a large law firm." Another student adds, "If you want real-world legal experience and to be four internships ahead of all of the other graduating law students, Northeastern is ideal."

Life

"The unique grading system provides for [an] extremely cooperative atmosphere." One student notes, "There is not an overwhelming sense of competition that stifles your ability to concentrate on functioning and thinking like a lawyer." Another explains, "Northeastern isn't a place for people who think of the whole world as a set of adversarial relationships. Students here love to help each other, and there is an honest desire among students and faculty for everyone to do well."

MEREDITH CURTIN SIEGEL, ASSISTANT DEAN AND DIRECTOR OF ADMISSIONS
400 HUNTINGTON AVENUE, BOSTON, MA 02115
TEL: 617-373-2395 FAX: 617-373-8865
EMAIL: LAWADMISSIONS@NEU.EDU • WEBSITE: WWW.SLAW.NEU.EDU

Many agree that Northeastern students are "good, solid, friendly people who are a pleasure to be around." "The level of diversity, activism, and intelligence at this school is simply amazing," says one student. However many find that "the school is diverse in every way except ethnically." Others note that while "there are some conservative and libertarian types, we are very liberal here." "The more progressive students essentially dominate the school," explains one student.

Socially, "The school seems to be pretty cliquish—it's actually frighteningly like being in high school." One student notes, "A majority of the students seem to have taken a year or more to work between undergrad and law school, and the student body is more mature, socially and politically aware, and motivated as a result." That said, the "older" student population can "hurt the dating life of the single students on the prowl" as "most are married." Northeastern can be "a bit of a commuter law school." Geographically speaking, "The community ultimately revolves around e-mail exchanges because half the school at any time is somewhere else in the country." On the plus side, "Boston is a fantastic place to live," and the campus "is within walking distance or a T ride away from" live music, all manner of sports, fabulous food, and "everything exciting in town."

Getting In

Thanks to the public-interest bent, Northeastern's student body is in some ways self selecting. For the most recent class, admitted students at the 25th percentile had an LSAT score of 159 and a GPA of 3.1. Admitted students at the 75th percentile had an LSAT score of 163 and a GPA of 3.58. Keep in mind it's full-time or nothing at Northeastern. The nature of the co-op program makes it next to impossible to accommodate part-time or evening students.

Public interest law requirement	Yes

ADMISSIONS

Selectivity Rating	**83**
# applications received	3,237
# applicants accepted	1,110
# acceptees attending	198
Average LSAT	161
LSAT Range	154–162
Average undergrad GPA	3.44
Application fee	$75
Regular application	Rolling, up to 3/1
Regular notification	Rolling
Early application program	Yes
Early application deadline	11/15
Early application notification	1/15
Transfer students accepted	Yes
Evening division offered	No
Part-time accepted	No
LSDAS accepted	Yes

Applicants Also Look At
American University, Boston University, Boston College, Fordham University, The George Washington University, Suffolk University, New England Law|Boston

International Students
TOEFL required of international students	Yes
Minimum TOEFL (paper/computer)	600/250

FINANCIAL FACTS

Annual tuition	$38,400
Books and supplies	$3,589
Fees	$114
Room & board	$17,400
Financial aid application deadline	2/15
% first-year students receiving some sort of aid	95
% receiving some sort of aid	90
% of aid that is merit based	62
% receiving scholarships	77
Average grant	$9,039
Average loan	$38,200
Average total aid package	$45,664
Average debt	$102,355

EMPLOYMENT INFORMATION

		Grads Employed by Field (%)
Career Rating	**79**	Academic (3)
Rate of placement (nine months out)	92	Business/Industry (26)
Average starting salary	$76,000	Government (8)
State for bar exam	MA	Judicial Clerkships (13)
Pass rate for first-time bar	93	Private Practice (34)

Employers Who Frequently Hire Grads
Committee for Public Counsel Services (Public Defender); Equal Justice Works Fellowships; Suffolk County District Attorney's Offices; Mintz, Levin, Cohn, Ferris, Glovsky & Popeo; Greater Boston Legal Services; U. S. Department of Labor; Morgan, Brown & Joy.

Private Practice (34)
Public Interest (16)

NORTHERN ILLINOIS UNIVERSITY
COLLEGE OF LAW

INSTITUTIONAL INFORMATION

Public/private	Public
Student-faculty ratio	8:1
% faculty part-time	11
% faculty female	40
% faculty minority	20
Total faculty	36

SURVEY SAYS...

Diverse opinions accepted
in classrooms
Great research resources
Great library staff
Students never sleep

STUDENTS

Enrollment of law school	297
% male/female	52/48
% full-time	97
% minority	25
Average age of entering class	24

ACADEMICS

Academic Experience Rating	**64**
Profs interesting rating	63
Profs accessible rating	73
Hours of study per day	3.58

Academic Specialties

Lawyering Skills Training

Combined Degrees Offered

JD/MBA and JD/MPA. Other dual degrees can be structured for students admitted to other graduate programs. Normally these programs are completed in 4–5 years.

Clinical program required	No
Legal writing	
course requirement	Yes
Legal methods	
course requirement	No
Legal research	
course requirement	Yes
Moot court requirement	Yes
Public interest	
law requirement	No

Academics

As the only public school found within the environs of the greater Chicago area, NIUers are released into Illinois' sea of graduating law students equipped with a solid education at a fraction of the price. Known for its commitment to fostering a sense of community and responsibility and pointing its students in the direction of public service jobs, NIU places a high value on pro bono work and makes a number of "public interest stipends" available to its students each summer. The school "has placed a special emphasis on diversity, both amongst its faculty and its student body," and it shows in the number of "divergent viewpoints" that are represented both in and out of the classroom.

Professors are themselves one source of these divergent viewpoints, with many students claiming that "some of the professors are amazing while others clearly enjoy the benefits of tenure." While the vast majority of professors "are well above average" and "do a very good job," offering students a high level of approachability, many students claim to have had a few instructors who were below par. "Simply reciting material straight from the textbook is not teaching," observes a first-year student. For the most part, however, students are happy with the quality of teaching at NIU, and say that the school is very good at balancing theory with practice. "A number of the professors go out of their way to expand on topics illustrated in the text and to relate their real-world experiences to the matters at hand. The professors as a group make themselves accessible to students who have issues that need to be discussed," affirms a student. "The faculty and administration practically begs students to come in and talk to them." Other students would like to see a broader spectrum of courses offered; says a 1L, "This semester I was forced to take a number of classes that I didn't have any interest in, solely to keep myself on pace for graduation."

As for facilities, one student informs us that "the school has chosen to update a number of its classrooms with modern technology." There's an all-around chorus of complaints for the law school building itself and the library, both of which "suffer from a chronic case of tiredness and 1970s décor," but students recognize that rehabilitation is on the way. One of the greatest resources offered to NIU students, many of whom are older, is the Career Opportunities Office, which "will definitively help you get started towards your career." Though some students speak of the disadvantages facing NIU grads—particularly the distance of the school from Chicago proper—who are not in the top three or four people in the class but who are looking to get into "big law," others are reassured by the Career Opportunities Office's strong networking prospects, which complement the school's well-established and reputable clinic and externship programs. "We have a lock on many state attorney and public defenders offices now, and an incredible number of alumni in the judiciary. If you want to be a government trial lawyer in Illinois, this is definitely the school to go to." As an exiting student avers, "The price was right, and if you are willing to do the work you can get a good education."

BERTRAND J. SIMPSON, JR. ESQ., DIRECTOR OF ADMISSION & FINANCIAL AID
SWEN PARSON HALL-COLLEGE OF LAW-ROOM 151, DE KALB, IL 60115
TEL: 815-753-8595 FAX: 815-753-5680
EMAIL: LAWADM@NIU.EDU • WEBSITE: LAW.NIU.EDU

Life

With a strong contingent of older, "second-career" individuals, "a high bar for maturity and professionalism within the student body" tends to be set on campus. Students are friendly enough, but hometown Dekalb can be a "pretty desolate place to kids accustomed to the party life of Champaign-Urbana, Bloomington-Normal, or other major college towns." Dekalb is "without much of the nightlife and amenities that students were accustomed to having from their undergrad experience." There are two fraternities on campus (one is "clearly the party frat, and the other is the academic frat"), and there are a number of student groups which students can join, though "a few struggle to survive" due to lack of participation. As for competition among students, a second-year student assures us that "the shark-eat-shark mentality of other law schools would not be tolerated here." "For one thing, the student body is too small, and we all know each other too well. For another, there's just more a sense of being practical and real-world here; we're 'type A' people, surely, but we've also mellowed with more life experience than your average law student straight out of undergrad."

Getting In

Northern Illinois encourages students to submit their application early, though they do accept applications after the suggested priority deadline of May 15. Recently admitted students at the 25th percentile had an LSAT score of 152 and an average GPA of 3.0, while students at the 75th percentile had an LSAT score of 158 and a GPA of 3.6.

ADMISSIONS

Selectivity Rating	**75**
# applications received	1,146
# applicants accepted	476
# acceptees attending	97
Average LSAT	154
LSAT Range	151–157
Average undergrad GPA	3.41
Application fee	$50
Regular application	Rolling, up to 5/15
Regular notification	Rolling
Early application program	No
Evening division offered	No
Part-time accepted	Yes
LSDAS accepted	Yes

International Students

TOEFL required of international students	Yes
Minimum TOEFL (computer/web)	550/250

FINANCIAL FACTS

Annual tuition (in-state/ out-of-state)	$11,592/$23,184
Books and supplies	$1,500
Fees	$2,392
Room & board	$9,344
Financial aid application deadline	3/1
% first-year students receiving some sort of aid	92
% receiving some sort of aid	87
% receiving scholarships	21
Average grant	$10,584
Average loan	$18,500
Average total aid package	$25,500
Average debt	$49,507

EMPLOYMENT INFORMATION

Career Rating	**75**
Rate of placement (nine months out)	90
Average starting salary	$50,500
State for bar exam	IL
Pass rate for first-time bar	95

Employers Who Frequently Hire Grads
State's Attorneys, Public Defenders, Illinois Appellate Defender, Illinois House of Representatives, Private Firms

Prominent Alumni
Kathleen Zellner, won reversals of seven murder convictions by DNA; Cheryl Niro, Top 10 Female IL Lawyers & former Pres. of ISBA.

Grads Employed by Field (%)
Academic (2)
Business/Industry (12)
Government (16)
Military (4)
Private Practice (58)
Public Interest (8)

NORTHWESTERN UNIVERSITY
SCHOOL OF LAW

INSTITUTIONAL INFORMATION

Public/private	Private
Student-faculty ratio	10:1
% faculty part-time	38
% faculty female	38
% faculty minority	8
Total faculty	168

SURVEY SAYS...

Diverse opinions accepted
in classrooms
Abundant externship/internship/
clerkship opportunities
Students love Chicago, IL

STUDENTS

Enrollment of law school	694
% male/female	56/44
% full-time	100
% minority	38
% international	6
# of countries represented	33
Average age of entering class	26

ACADEMICS

Academic Experience Rating	**97**
Profs interesting rating	88
Profs accessible rating	85
Hours of study per day	4.6

Academic Specialties

corporation securities, human
rights, international law, taxation,
business enterprise, law and social
policy, civil litigation, dispute
resolution

Advanced Degrees Offered

JD, 3 years; LLM, 1 year; SJD, 5
years; LLM in taxation, 1 year; LLM
in human rights, 1 year; JD for
international lawyers, 2 years;
Accelerated JD, 2 years.

Combined Degrees Offered

JD/MBA, 3 years; JD/PhD, 6 years;
JD/MA, 4 years; JD/LLM
International Human Rights, 4
years; JD/LLM Tax, 4 years;
LLM/certificate in management
(Kellogg), 1 year.

Academics

Located "in the heart of Chicago," Northwestern University School of Law has a first-rate "national reputation" for "developing practical skills" and offering "world-class" clinics that give students "unbelievable" opportunities to work on "real cases." Many here agree that "it's hard to imagine getting a better mix of academic rigor and practical job training anywhere else." Other highlights at NU include study abroad programs all over the world, a highly touted JD/MBA program, and lots of "self-scheduled exams." One demerit is the "legal writing program" that students wish was "a pass/fail class" due to the "incredible amount of work" it requires.

Northwestern's "brilliant" and "very friendly" faculty is made up of "nationally and internationally renowned scholars" who have "a great sense of humor." Students have "an unparalleled opportunity to learn from the best, starting right at the beginning." "My classes and instruction have ranged from very good to simply outstanding," relates a 2L. "I'd go so far to say that my Constitutional Law class was one of the most intellectually stimulating courses I've encountered." Professors are "accessible" and "The professors seem to really enjoy talking to students outside of class." "It is not uncommon for them to stop me in the hallway and chat about a class topic, my journal comment, or even college football," explains a student. For the most part the administration is "receptive to student concerns" and "always approachable." "Everything goes pretty smoothly," and the atmosphere is "not very bureaucratic," though some note that "change is very slow to come" in regards to "accommodation for disabilities."

Students happily report that "if you do even moderately well in your 1L classes at Northwestern, you're going to have legal employers knocking down your door." "You'd be hard-pressed to find someone coming out of NU to a less-than-excellent job." "Most of us start out at big firms," adds a 1L. "The Chicago firms just love NU students." However, some students complain that "there should be a greater emphasis on public interest career choices" as "Not everybody wants to go to a big law firm upon graduation."

The architecture here is "nice, consisting of both old, more traditional buildings, and a newer building." "A quiet atmosphere prevails" and the "gorgeous" library overlooks Lake Michigan. Also, trust us: Lincoln Hall is exactly what a law school classroom should look like. While "good," the classrooms could use some "updating," and "There aren't enough areas to study." Also, "lighting conditions" in the library are "bad," and though "Wireless Internet continues to improve," it can still be "insufficient and annoying."

Life

"Northwestern places a huge emphasis on admitting students who have a couple years of work experience after undergrad, and it makes a huge difference," says one student. These future lawyers "come from a variety of backgrounds and offer amazing insights into a range of issues." They "are grounded and have balanced lives." "People have a better sense of the world around them and the realities of life beyond a classroom," observes a 2L. "This keeps the drama to a minimum and also assembles a group of people who've done some pretty interesting things—minor league ball, the military, symphonic bassoon, and so on." "There seems to be the misconception that the students at Northwestern are really old," clarifies another student. "For most students it is only about two years before we come to law school."

DON REBSTOCK, ASSOCIATE DEAN OF ENROLLMENT
357 EAST CHICAGO AVENUE, CHICAGO, IL 60611
TEL: 312-503-8465 FAX: 312-503-0178
EMAIL: ADMISSIONS@LAW.NORTHWESTERN.EDU • WEBSITE: WWW.LAW.NORTHWESTERN.EDU

"Class sizes are small" and "The school goes to great lengths to create and foster a sense of community among the students." In this "collegial" atmosphere, students are "intelligent, friendly, [and] laid-back." "There are not too many gunners," reports one student. "We're smart, personable people who mix well socially while doing topnotch legal work," says a 2L. However, some students project an "'I-don't-study-at-all' attitude in the middle of the semester, trying to throw others off base. Then, suddenly, the same person who 'never studies' has a 150-page annotated outline with hyperlinks to all of its sections and subsections."

Outside of class, Northwestern is "a very fun place to attend school." "The school sponsors many events for students every week" and there are "free lunches almost every day" along with "random social events put on by the many, many student organizations." "Lunchtime speakers, panels, and club meetings provide great opportunities to explore different facets of the law school experience and the legal profession without taking up too much time." In addition, "Chicago is a great city" with "a great mix of...hustle and bustle and Midwestern friendliness"—all of which starts right "next door" to campus with "Michigan Avenue's Magnificent Mile."

Getting In

Northwestern claims to be the only law school in the country that strongly encourages all applicants to interview as a part of the admissions process. Understandably, knowing this, it behooves you to show up for an interview if you apply. With or without an interview, though, admission is unusually competitive. Admitted students at the 25th percentile have LSAT scores of 166 and GPAs of about 3.4. Admitted students at the 75th percentile have LSAT scores of 172 and GPAs of about 3.8.

Clinical program required	No
Legal writing course requirement	Yes
Legal methods course requirement	No
Legal research course requirement	Yes
Moot court requirement	Yes
Public interest law requirement	No

ADMISSIONS

Selectivity Rating	**97**
# applications received	4,868
% applicants accepted	18
% acceptees attending	28
Average LSAT	170
LSAT Range	166–172
Average undergrad GPA	3.7
Application fee	$100
Regular application	Rolling, up to 2/15
Regular notification	Rolling
Early application program	Yes
Early application deadline	12/1
Early application notification	12/31
Transfer students accepted	Yes
Evening division offered	No
Part-time accepted	No
LSDAS accepted	Yes

Applicants Also Look At
Harvard University, Columbia University, University of Michigan—Ann Arbor, New York University, University of Chicago

FINANCIAL FACTS

Annual tuition	$45,062
Books and supplies	$8,828
Fees	$270
Tuition per credit	$2,253
Room & board	$12,376
Financial aid application deadline	3/1
% first-year students receiving some sort of aid	85
% receiving some sort of aid	85
% of aid that is merit based	50
% receiving scholarships	35
Average grant	$22,500
Average debt	$122,197

EMPLOYMENT INFORMATION

Career Rating	**99**	**Grads Employed by Field (%)**
Rate of placement (nine months out)	99	Academic (3)
Average starting salary	$160,000	Business/Industry (4)
State for bar exam	IL	Government (2)
Pass rate for first-time bar	95	Judicial Clerkships (12)

Employers Who Frequently Hire Grads

Private Practice (74)

Public Interest (5)

Kirkland & Ellis; Mayer Brown; Foley & Lardner; McDermott, Will & Emery; Sidley Austin; Latham & Watkins; Skadden, Arps, Slate, Meagher & Flom; Cleary Gottlieb.

Prominent Alumni

John Paul Stevens, Supreme Court Justice; Arthur Goldberg, Former Supreme Court Justice; Dawn Clark Netsch, 1st Female Gubernatorial Candidate in Illinois.

NOVA SOUTHEASTERN UNIVERSITY
SHEPARD BROAD LAW CENTER

INSTITUTIONAL INFORMATION

Public/private	Private
Student-faculty ratio	15:1
% faculty part-time	38
% faculty female	41
% faculty minority	21
Total faculty	107

SURVEY SAYS...

Diverse opinions accepted
in classrooms
Good social life

STUDENTS

Enrollment of law school	1,000
% male/female	46/54
% full-time	83
% minority	26
% international	4
# of countries represented	14
Average age of entering class	26

ACADEMICS

Academic Experience Rating	**61**
Profs interesting rating	63
Profs accessible rating	62
Hours of study per day	3.55

Academic Specialties

Civil procedure, commercial law, constitutional law, corporation securities, criminal law, environmental law, government services, human rights, international law, labor law, legal history, property, taxation, family law

Combined Degrees Offered

JD/MBA; JD/MS, Psychology; JD/MS, Dispute Resolution; JD/MS, Computer; JD/MURP

Clinical program required	No
Legal writing	
course requirement	Yes
Legal methods	
course requirement	No
Legal research	
course requirement	Yes
Moot court requirement	Yes

Academics

At Nova Southeastern University's Shepard Broad Law Center, students are given the unbeatable opportunity to receive a practical law experience while being surrounded by the beautiful beaches and perfect weather of southern Florida. NSU's unique dual-degree law programs in Venice and Barcelona are extremely popular, and offer students the opportunity to study both the common law system in the United States and the civil law systems of Italy or Spain. It's this sort of range of exposure that makes Nova "a great place for students with an aptitude for law who are unsure about the area of law in which they want to practice," though some students express a desire for specialized classes in fields such as constitutional law and trial advocacy. The school places a high importance on practical experience, to the point that all third-year law students are guaranteed a place in one of the clinics.

The professors at NSU get mostly positive but still mixed reviews: "Some professors are incredible, and some make you wonder how they ever got offered a job in the first place." Despite the occasional bad apple, students don't hesitate to give props to the number of "accessible" and "knowledgeable" teachers who are "very open to classroom participation." "While [the professors are] not the most esteemed in the world, they are very hardworking and usually willing to help you out in any way they can," says a graduating student.

Students' satisfaction levels with the administration are "lukewarm," and many criticize the administration's requirement that all students "take a Bar Review class that does not count for credit." However, some students point out that this could be due to the fact that the administration has been "working in reaction mode to the very low bar-passage rates at the school." A third-year student claims that this "'experimentation' with programs to help that problem has not been fun for the gerbils/students." Career Services fares a bit better in students' esteem; "The [school's] reputation among south Florida judges and attorneys is strong" and the networking prospects in Broward County are great. However, a good number of students speak of a need for "more national recognition for students who leave south Florida" to practice.

As for facilities and technology, "The buildings and campus are beautiful, and I couldn't imagine a better location," gushes a third-year student. Those who call the Nova law building home are nothing short of effusive about the excellent wireless coverage that is integrated into all classrooms and course work (including the ability to watch lectures online), a boon which one student claims "makes it very easy to do all of my work on campus between classes and in the library." This accessibility can have its negative aspects as well; "95 percent of students in class are surfing the Net or IM-ing the entire time. There is very little student participation in class discussions as a result," says a 3L.

BETH HALL, ASSISTANT DEAN FOR ADMISSIONS
3305 COLLEGE AVENUE, FORT LAUDERDALE, FL 33314
TEL: 954-262-6117 FAX: 954-262-3844
EMAIL: ADMISSION@NSU.LAW.NOVA.EDU • WEBSITE: WWW.NSULAW.NOVA.EDU

Life

When "Campus is a picture-perfect tropical paradise" located near the beaches of Fort Lauderdale, one does not find many complaints about the quality of life. "What other school allows for beach cleanups, trips to the Everglades, and socials on South Beach and in downtown Ft. Lauderdale?" asks a first-year student. With such idyllic surroundings, it's no wonder that "student life at school is very social." Competition levels are minimal—in fact, a few students suspect that their classmates are merely "looking for a piece of paper that says JD"—but on the upside, this does mean that "there is no internal bickering and fighting to be number one." Student organizations abound, but these organizations are usually run by a dedicated handful of people with little help or participation from other members and students, who tend to be "apathetic when it comes to extracurricular activities." "There are a lot of active clubs on campus for every ideology, ethnic group, or however else you might classify yourself," says a 3L, including numerous American Law Associations (Caribbean Law Student Association, Italian-American Law Student Association, Celtic-American Law Society, etc.). The Goodwin Speaker series also brings several notable speakers to the campus every year.

Getting In

Though the admit rate may seem to run about average, this is more a result of self-selection than it is the result of a particularly tough admissions process, as gaining admission to Nova is not exceptionally difficult for qualified students. Recently admitted students at the 25th percentile had an LSAT score of 148 and an average GPA of 2.8, while admitted students at the 75th percentile had an LSAT score of 152 and a GPA of 3.3. For students who don't meet Nova's standards for admission, the school's AAMPLE summer conditional program provides students with low LSAT scores the opportunity to attend law school.

Public interest law requirement	No

ADMISSIONS

Selectivity Rating	**68**
# applications received	2,512
% applicants accepted	41
% acceptees attending	36
Average LSAT	149
LSAT Range	147–152
Average undergrad GPA	3.27
Application fee	$50
Regular application	Rolling, up to 4/1
Regular notification	Rolling
Early application program	No
Transfer students accepted	Yes
Evening division offered	Yes
Part-time accepted	Yes
LSDAS accepted	Yes

Applicants Also Look At
Florida State University, University of Florida, University of Miami, St. Thomas University, Stetson University, Florida Costal School of Law

International Students

TOEFL required of international students	Yes
Minimum TOEFL (computer/web)	600/250

FINANCIAL FACTS

Annual tuition	$29,972
Books and supplies	$2,800
Fees	$500
Room & board (on/off-campus)	$13,040/$14,940
Financial aid application deadline	4/15
% first-year students receiving some sort of aid	90
% receiving some sort of aid	86
% of aid that is merit based	8
% receiving scholarships	8
Average grant	$17,157
Average loan	$34,882
Average total aid package	$37,596
Average debt	$96,329

EMPLOYMENT INFORMATION

		Grads Employed by Field (%)	
Career Rating	**70**	Academic	(1)
Rate of placement (nine months out)	81.57	Business/Industry	(15)
Average starting salary	$59,167	Government	(16)
State for bar exam	FL, NY	Judicial clerkships	(3)
Pass rate for first-time bar	85.8	Private practice	(58)

Employers Who Frequently Hire Grads
Private law firms, local and state agencies, state attorney's offices, public defender offices

Prominent Alumni
Melanie G. May, Appeals Court Judge; Rob Brzezinski, VP football operations, Minnesota Vikings; Ellyn Setnor Bogdanoff, FLA House of Representative; Rex Ford, U.S. Immigration Judge.

OHIO NORTHERN UNIVERSITY
CLAUDE W. PETTIT COLLEGE OF LAW

INSTITUTIONAL INFORMATION

Public/private	Private
Affiliation	Methodist
Student-faculty ratio	10:1
% faculty part-time	0
% faculty female	40
% faculty minority	15
Total faculty	30

SURVEY SAYS...

Diverse opinions accepted
in classrooms
Great library staff

STUDENTS

Enrollment of law school	320
% male/female	51/49
% out-of-state	60
% full-time	100
% minority	15
# of countries represented	8
Average age of entering class	25

ACADEMICS

Academic Experience Rating	**71**
Profs interesting rating	79
Profs accessible rating	88
Hours of study per day	4.97

Academic Specialties

Civil procedure, commercial law, constitutional law, corporation securities, criminal law, environmental law, human rights, international law, labor law, legal history, legal philosophy, property, taxation, intellectual property law, capital punishment

Advanced Degrees Offered

JD, 3 years.

Clinical program required	No
Legal writing course requirement	Yes
Legal methods course requirement	Yes
Legal research course requirement	Yes
Moot court requirement	No
Public interest law requirement	No

Academics

Ohio Northern University's Claude W. Pettit College of Law is a "remotely located" bastion of legal education that offers "small" classes and "substantial scholarships." The unique "summer starter program" here is also notable. It's designed for students with LSAT scores in the mid 140s and GPAs over 3.5. Students at ONU report that they receive oodles of "personalized attention." "The individualized attention offered by the professors at ONU is outstanding," gushes a 3L. Students call the "experienced, knowledgeable, open, friendly," and generally "wonderful" faculty "the shining star of the school." They "really do care about the students and their success" and they "go out of their way to help the students and to make themselves available" "One-on-one meetings" with professors are common. ONU's "very attentive" administrators "genuinely care for the students" as well and "and they actually get to know you as individuals." The deans' office doors are "always open."

ONU's moot court teams are first rate and ONU's clinics and externships provide "excellent practical educational experiences." "Every law student at ONU has the chance to gain legal experience." Students involved in the ONU Legal Clinic represent more than 200 clients each year. The Innocence Project allows participating students to represent criminal defendants when DNA evidence compellingly demonstrates their innocence. "Opportunities include everything from working in the local prosecutor's office to helping out at the Ohio Supreme Court to carrying out bankruptcy proceedings at the bankruptcy clinic," explains one happy student. The range of clinical offerings is pretty narrow, though, and "for most you have to drive out of town." There aren't tons of courses available, either. "I would like to see a broader selection of classes that are offered every semester," suggests a 2L. Many students also "would like to see the school add more specializations."

ONU isn't a pipeline to very many huge firms but career prospects are reportedly pretty decent. Over 100 legal employers interview law students here each year and, despite the fact that "no one has heard of ONU outside Ohio," graduates frequently get hired outside the state and around the country. However, some students call Career Services "pretty weak."

The facilities at Ohio Northern definitely will not blow you away. "The building is laid out rather strangely and appointed even worse," gripes a 2L. "The classrooms are dull and boring." Otherwise, while "there is nothing horribly wrong with" the law school, students tell us that it feel more than a little uninspiring. "The campus is completely wireless," though, and "there are electrical outlets in every classroom for every seat." Research facilities are "nothing spectacular" and "the library staff is outstanding," but "the library could be much bigger."

Linda K. English, Assistant Dean and Director of Law Admissions
Ohio Northern University, Pettit College, Ada, OH 45810-1599
Tel: 877-452-9668 Fax: 419-772-3042
Email: law-admissions@onu.edu • Website: www.law.onu.edu

Life

Students here can't stress enough that the "microscopically small" surrounding town of Ada, Ohio is located squarely "in the middle of nowhere." "It's not the most ideal town for people that want something besides law school," cautions a 2L. There is "absolutely zero" to do "as far as cultural activities without traveling a couple of hours." Some students used to more vibrant environments reportedly feel like "they've somehow landed in a living hell." Other students call our attention to the "low cost of living" and note that "there are very few distractions," which is a blessing for "people who have problems saying no to temptation." Without question, "Ohio Northern's location is very conducive to studying and learning because there is nothing else to do in Ada."

According to many students, the academic atmosphere at Ohio Northern is "mostly congenial." "There's a great community in terms of helping one another out," they say. Other students here assert that "the level of competition is astounding." Students tend to agree that the atmosphere beyond grades and coursework is pretty good. The campus is pleasant. There are several "active student organizations" and "there are plenty of activities sponsored by groups in the law school to get involved with." "ONU has a very strong sense of community," says a 3L. "There are few students from even classes above or below me who I do not know. This is probably the strongest asset of our school." However, there is "a lot of gossip" and, occasionally, "high school-like drama." Roughly two-thirds of the students here come from outside of Ohio, however ethnic diversity is relatively modest and the overall diversity of the student body is not fabulous. ONU "doesn't mirror an urban environment's makeup because it isn't an urban environment."

Getting In

On one hand, the acceptance rate here isn't exceptionally high. On the other hand, the grades and LSAT score of admitted students aren't spectacular. Admitted students at the 25th percentile have LSAT scores of about 150 and GPAs in the 3.0 range. Admitted students at the 75th percentile have LSAT scores in the mid 150s and GPAs of roughly 3.6. If you take the LSAT multiple times, ONU will look at your highest score.

ADMISSIONS

Selectivity Rating	**72**
# applications received	1,424
# applicants accepted	35
# acceptees attending	120
Average LSAT	153
LSAT Range	150–155
Average undergrad GPA	3.35
Application fee	$40
Regular application	Rolling
Regular notification	Rolling
Early application program	No
Transfer students accepted	Yes
Evening division offered	No
Part-time accepted	No
LSDAS accepted	Yes

Applicants Also Look At
Duquesne, University of Dayton, Capital University, University of Toledo

International Students
TOEFL required	
of international students	Yes
Minimum TOEFL (paper)	550

FINANCIAL FACTS

Annual tuition	$26,500
Books and supplies	$900
Fees	$270
Room & board	
(on/off-campus)	$11,237/$12,137
Financial aid application	
deadline	4/6
% first-year students	
receiving some sort of aid	97
% receiving some sort of aid	97
% of aid that is merit based	23
% receiving scholarships	51
Average grant	$16,390
Average loan	$25,140
Average total aid package	$31,023
Average debt	$74,380

EMPLOYMENT INFORMATION

Career Rating	**64**
Rate of placement (nine months out)	95
Average starting salary	$50,000
State for bar exam	OH, FL, PA, NC, MD
Pass rate for first-time bar	78

Prominent Alumni
Michael DeWine, U.S. Senator; Gregory Frost, U.S. District Judge Southern Ohio; Benjamin Brafman, Senior Partner at Brafman & Ross, New York City; Greg Miller, U.S. Attorney for Northwest Florida.

Grads Employed by Field (%)
Academic (3)
Business/Industry (11)
Government (13)
Judicial Clerkships (2)
Military (12)
Private Practice (54)
Public Interest (4)
Other (1)

THE OHIO STATE UNIVERSITY
MICHAEL E. MORITZ COLLEGE OF LAW

INSTITUTIONAL INFORMATION

Public/private	Public
Student-faculty ratio	13:1
% faculty part-time	18
% faculty female	33
% faculty minority	25
Total faculty	77

SURVEY SAYS...

Diverse opinions accepted
in classrooms
Great research resources

STUDENTS

Enrollment of law school	675
% male/female	57/43
% out-of-state	33
% full-time	100
% minority	23
% international	2
# of countries represented	6
Average age of entering class	23

ACADEMICS

Academic Experience Rating	**86**
Profs interesting rating	83
Profs accessible rating	81
Hours of study per day	4.13

Academic Specialties

Civil procedure, commercial law, constitutional law, criminal law, government services, international law, labor law, property, taxation, intellectual property law, alternative dispute resolution

Advanced Degrees Offered

Masters in the Study of Law, 1 Year; LL.M. International Students, 1 Year

Combined Degrees Offered

JD/MBA, 4 years, JD/MHA, 4 years; JD/MPA, 4 years, JD/over 80 different individually designed, 4–5 years

Clinical program required	No
Legal writing course requirement	Yes
Legal methods course requirement	No
Legal research course requirement	Yes

Academics

The Ohio State University Moritz College of Law manages to create a small college feel in an often chaotic large university setting, all while providing access to the resources of the state capital. "Being the top in Ohio dominates the local market," and with out-of-state students eligible to become Ohio residents and receive in-state tuition throughout their second and third years, the public school price here is certainly right for students (even with the recent tuition increases). Unfortunately, the career services office tends to focus on the top 10% of the class, leaving some students with a sour taste in their mouth. "Moritz has been an excellent investment for me; I'll leave school with five-figure debt and start a job with a six-figure salary. However, I doubt my classmates who've secured jobs with salaries lower than their amount of debt—or who haven't landed jobs at all—feel the same way," says a student. Moritz students express great dislike toward the forced curve grading system and a somewhat lax exam policy that allows "unscrupulous or undeserving students to gain extra time on exams, resulting in higher grades," an issue that when brought up with the administration, resulted in a "stonewalling of the students." The administration can also be "disorganized," but students still manage to find a "collegial environment and unwavering support," and the school is a place that "supports ideas and innovation, and it has the resources and faculty to support any endeavor."

The criminal law, alternative dispute resolution, and legal writing programs here are outstanding, but the school definitely "needs to put more emphasis on the bar exam and practical lawyering skills" as well as the business/finance curriculum, which is "pitifully underdeveloped." Professors tend to lean toward the theoretical aspects of law here and some have "positively byzantine specialties," many of which are "out of touch with the school's atmosphere and the state job market." "Despite the fact that a majority of students from this school will in some way deal in business/commercial law, the faculty's group-think seems to believe that their greatest duty is to ensure that we will all be civil-rights lawyers," says a student. Still, students are overall pleased with the caliber of the faculty here, though this almost always is accompanied by the caveat of "with some notable exceptions." They are "extremely knowledgeable, outgoing, and interested in catering to student needs," and "almost uniformly all liberal." This leftist slant is actually a sore spot with many Moritz students, who find that conservative issues are outright ignored, and the school needs to work on "addressing current legal issues even if they might be politically unpopular." Small class sizes mean students get plenty of personal attention, and clinic classes have two teachers and only fifteen students, allowing for plenty of direct contact with teachers. "I have had the opportunity to meet and work on a one-on-one basis with the Dean," attests a 3L.

JIMMI NICHOLSON, ASSISTANT DIRECTOR
104 DRINKO HALL, 55 WEST 12TH AVENUE, COLUMBUS, OH 43210
TEL: 614-292-8810 FAX: 614-292-1492
EMAIL: LAWADMIT@OSU.EDU • WEBSITE: MORITZLAW.OSU.EDU

Life

Columbus is a great town "with anything you could want," though the actual location of the school within the city "is not ideal, but it has been improving." The actual facilities also need improvement, as "parts of the building are showing age." Many students come here straight out of undergrad and live "in dorm-like housing virtually next door to the school," so there can be a collegiate feel to the atmosphere, and older students are few and far between. Likewise, social life "does tend to revolve around bars," but other opportunities are available, and the SBA does a good job of furthering student interests. As this is Buckeye country, football is huge here. "I've never been anywhere that is like Columbus for OSU sports. OSU football is more popular around the city than professional sports are just about anywhere in the nation," says a student. Small classes and the clinical programs "are great for building student relationships." Moritz students are "mildly competitive," particularly during the 1L year, but "it's really up to the individual here—you either get swallowed by the competition or you stay away from it." Much like the faculty, the school is pretty liberal, and conservatives don't always feel welcome. Some think that the law school focuses too much time and effort on recruiting, getting careers for, and satisfying minorities (including a special lounge/office area) "at the expense of the rest of students."

Getting In

Ohio State University admits students who have demonstrated ability to succeed in a rigorous legal program. In particular, the admissions committee carefully evaluates a student's undergraduate record, examining grades, grade trends, rigor of the course work and major curriculum, reputation of the undergraduate institution, and recommendations from academic faculty.

Moot court requirement	Yes
Public interest law requirement	No

ADMISSIONS

Selectivity Rating	**88**
# applications received	2,320
% applicants accepted	29
% acceptees attending	30
Average LSAT	162
LSAT Range	158–164
Average undergrad GPA	3.61
Application fee	$60
Regular application	Rolling, up to 3/15
Regular notification	Rolling
Early application program	Yes
Early application deadline	11/14
Early application notification	12/20
Transfer students accepted	Yes
Evening division offered	No
Part-time accepted	No
LSDAS accepted	Yes

Applicants Also Look At

American University, University of Cincinnati, Case Western Reserve University, The George Washington University, Capital University, Georgetown University

International Students

TOEFL required of international students	Yes
Minimum TOEFL (paper/computer)	600/260

FINANCIAL FACTS

Annual tuition (in-state/ out-of-state)	$19,232/$34,516
Books and supplies	$3,500
Fees	$1,435
Room & board	$14,000
Financial aid application deadline	3/1
% receiving some sort of aid	83
% of aid that is merit based	70
% receiving scholarships	64
Average grant	$4,300
Average loan	$22,559
Average total aid package	$5,981
Average debt	$53,525

EMPLOYMENT INFORMATION

Career Rating	**78**	**Grads Employed by Field (%)**
Rate of placement (nine months out)	99	Academic (2)
Average starting salary	$71,530	Business/Industry (15)
State for bar exam	OH, DC, NC, IL, CA	Government (16)
Pass rate for first-time bar	88	Judicial Clerkships (14)
Prominent Alumni		Military (3)
Jack Creighton, Former CEO Weyerhauser		Private Practice (42)
Corp. and United Airlines; John Garland,		Public Interest (8)
President Central State University; Erin		
Moriarity, 48 Hours/CBS News Journalist;		
Karen Sarjeant, V.P. Legal Services Corp.;		
George Voinovich, Senator.		

OKLAHOMA CITY UNIVERSITY
SCHOOL OF LAW

Academics

A first-year at Oklahoma City University School of Law writes, "I was nervous about going to a school that did not have a better academic reputation on the national level, but quickly I realized that OCU Law is very competitive with respect to its curriculum and professors." In particular, "If you are going to practice in Oklahoma, OCU Law has a stellar reputation within the community and surrounding states." Students interested in dispute resolution and Native American law find top programs that are backed by "an unmatched Legal Research and Writing Department." Some students, particularly those in the part-time evening program, complain about sparse course options. Furthermore, a few gripe that "the first three semesters are largely mandatory courses." That said, "The school is working on obtaining adjunct professors to teach some of the more popular courses requested by the students," and students are optimistic about having a wider range of course options in the future.

The professors at OCU "range from the typical Ivy-League eggheads to those who worked their way through law school." Students value the "intellectual energy" and practical experiences of their instructors, most of whom can "make even the driest theoretical concept interesting." Take the property professor who "got on top of a desk and shouted, 'Never, never, never change a legal description of a property!'" Professors toss around "fun terms, like 'playground justice,'" and come up with "offbeat hypos that really stick in your memory." A 1L writes, "The classroom environment is open. Free discussions, dissenting opinions, and intellectual dialogues between students are welcomed." Above all, the faculty show they care. "We actually had a professor e-mail 1Ls on driving techniques in the snow because he knew that many of us had never been in those conditions." But don't mistake kind-hearted professors for pushovers. Small classes mean there's nowhere to hide when the Socratic grilling gets going, and "high grades must be truly earned."

When it comes to the administration, "The doors are open at every level." The school's "personal touch" means that faculty and administration members "remember your name even when you are not one of those students who is president of almost every organization." The monthly Dean's Forum "allows students to have lunch with the dean and discuss any matter freely and openly."

While the law library—described as "amazing on the outside, but run-down on the inside"—could use some updating, students write that "the beautiful, historic atmosphere of the building makes the somewhat outdated technology more bearable." Although they've seen some upgrades in recent years, some students find themselves "studying at Starbucks, OU Law School, or the public library, simply because [OCU] facilities aren't comfortable in many ways."

Job placement worries keep some OCU students up at night. Competition with University of Oklahoma grads makes launching a career a difficult task for OCU grads. Some like to fault the "unhelpful" career placement staff, which needs "to do a better job of promoting us to the judges." Students can keep their chins up, though, since there are many factors that mediate this bleak picture. Because the school is located just five minutes from the state capitol building, it remains "very connected to the government and local business." Students are able to build personal networks over their three years, thanks to the "high priority placed on community involvement through internships, externships, and volunteer opportunities." Students can also tap into the "very large and loyal alumni base in Oklahoma" once they've graduated.

BERNARD M. JONES, ESQ., ASSISTANT DEAN FOR ADMISSIONS
2501 N BLACKWELDER, OKLAHOMA CITY, OK 73106-1493
TEL: 405-208-5354 FAX: 405-208-5814
EMAIL: LAWQUESTIONS@OKCU.EDU • WEBSITE: WWW.OKCU.EDU/LAW

Life

Law students at OCU refuse to give up their social lives just because they're pending professionals. "People here party more than the students at my undergraduate institution," admits one student, but this is sometimes to the chagrin of the studious types. The class size is "small enough to make it possible to be friends with your entire cohort"; there are a "plethora [of] clubs for everyone's tastes;" and the student body "organizes numerous activities for the whole school or just your class." "If you want to engage in any type of social activity, there is always something going on." As a result, "lots of people find great friends and relationships." The varied student body includes people of all ages, many of whom come from outside of Oklahoma; this diversity fosters "a welcoming and rich environment," according to a nontraditional student.

The convivial social environment carries over to the academic realm, in which students collaborate rather than compete with one another. "Even though we are pitted against each other in the curve, it is not cutthroat here," writes a 3L. The overriding "atmosphere of teamwork and togetherness" keeps morale high and study groups well attended. The campus may be "a beautiful oasis" in the middle of a "rough" neighborhood, but the cost of living is low, and the friendly campus security force "will always walk you to your vehicle without complaint, or even give you a ride to your off-campus apartment."

Getting In

OCU will accept applications until August 1, but nearly all applications are submitted by April 1. Requisite admissions criteria include LSAT scores, undergraduate GPA, personal statement, resumé, and letters of recommendation. If you are looking to study law in Oklahoma, then Oklahoma City University, like the University of Tulsa, is a good back-up law school to the University of Oklahoma. It's also a good alternative to Texas schools like Southern Methodist University, Texas Tech University, and Texas Wesleyan University.

ADMISSIONS

Selectivity Rating	62
# applications received	1,201
# applicants accepted	782
# acceptees attending	241
Average LSAT	150
LSAT Range	147–153
Average undergrad GPA	3.21
Application fee	$50
Regular application	Rolling, up to 8/1
Regular notification	Rolling
Early application program	No
Transfer students accepted	Yes
Evening division offered	Yes
Part-time accepted	Yes
LSDAS accepted	Yes

Applicants Also Look At

University of Oklahoma, University of Tulsa, St. Mary's University, Texas Wesleyan University, Texas Southern University, South Texas College of Law, Thomas M. Cooley Law School, Florida Costal School of Law, Appalachian

International Students

TOEFL required of international students	Yes
Minimum TOEFL (paper/computer/web)	600/220/100

FINANCIAL FACTS

Annual tuition	$29,550
Books and supplies	$1,800
Fees	$1,705
Tuition per credit	$975
Room & board	$8,350
Financial aid application deadline	3/1
% first-year students receiving some sort of aid	93
% receiving some sort of aid	91
% of aid that is merit based	24
% receiving scholarships	33
Average grant	$14,866
Average loan	$38,349
Average total aid package	$39,404
Average debt	$108,743

EMPLOYMENT INFORMATION

Career Rating	69
Rate of placement (nine months out)	91
Average starting salary	$55,014
State for bar exam	OK, TX, IL, UT, MO
Pass rate for first-time bar	74

Prominent Alumni
Reta Strubhar, First Woman on Oklahoma Court of Criminal Appeals; Andrew Benton, President, Pepperdine University; Nona Lee, VP and General Counsel, Arizona Diamondbacks; Mickey Edwards, Lecturer, Woodrow Wilson School, Princeton Univers; Marian P. Opala, Justice, Oklahoma Supreme Court.

Grads Employed by Field (%)
Academic (1)
Business/Industry (18)
Government (12)
Judicial clerkships (2)
Military (4)
Private practice (56)
Public Interest (7)

PACE UNIVERSITY
SCHOOL OF LAW

INSTITUTIONAL INFORMATION

Public/private	Private
Student-faculty ratio	16:1
% faculty female	40
% faculty minority	10
Total faculty	50

SURVEY SAYS...

Diverse opinions accepted in classrooms

STUDENTS

Enrollment of law school	779
% male/female	46/54
% full-time	70
% minority	17
% international	2
# of countries represented	12
Average age of entering class	24

ACADEMICS

Academic Experience Rating	**70**
Profs interesting rating	74
Profs accessible rating	79
Hours of study per day	4.6

Academic Specialties

Civil procedure, commercial law, constitutional law, corporation securities, criminal law, environmental law, government services, human rights, international law, labor law, legal history, property, taxation, intellectual property law, health law & policy, climate change, public interest and advocacy, real estate, land use law

Advanced Degrees Offered

S.JD in Environmental Law; LL.M. in Environmental Law; LL.M. in Comparative Legal Studies; LL.M. in Real Estate Law

Combined Degrees Offered

JD/M.B.A.; JD/M.P.A.; JD/M.E.M.; JD/M.S.; JD/M.A.

Clinical program required	No
Legal writing course requirement	Yes
Legal methods course requirement	Yes

Academics

While not small by law school standards, Pace has an intimate vibe: "I know the names of probably 75 percent of the students in my graduating class," a 2L reports. This feeling extends to interactions with faculty and staff members, who maintain "an open-door policy" and "are always willing and available to help." "The school's administration . . . [has] always made me feel as if I was a customer of great importance and not just 'another student,'" a 3L writes. The school is currently in the process of updating its facilities: "More consistent wireless Internet access" is one serious need being addressed and students report that much of the campus "is looking pretty darn good," though there are "some portions that are either lagging behind" or "still a little 'classic.'" In addition to being "extremely knowledgeable in the subject areas in which they teach," professors here "really care whether you understand the concept or not." Upperclassmen supply their expertise through the Dean's Scholars program, which "provides a weekly tutoring session taught by a 3L who had the same professor in the same course when he/she was a 1L."

"I've discussed classes and theories with friends at top 25 schools and they are consistently amazed at the depth of the subject matter we've covered," says a 2L. Thoroughness is made possible by the frequent "opportunities for clinical and practical experience," which many here feel is the school's "greatest strength." "Because we are a smaller school, it sometimes feels like we have greater opportunities because we are not likely to get 'closed out' of a class or clinic or an externship," a 2L reports. Environmental and international law are the stand-out programs at Pace, and the school "regularly receives visiting scholars and lecturers who are tops in these fields." Students in the environmental law program are fêted with "outstanding professors," "numerous" course offerings, and "a wide variety of useful resources," including a "tremendous environmental law collection" in the school library. Students in the international law program appreciate their "miraculous" professors who create "many opportunities" for them, "such as summer internships and moot courts." Pace also hosts "the CISG database on international contracts" and students here "started the first ever 'International Criminal Court Moot Competition.'" With all the activity surrounding these two programs, a 2L remarks that "sometimes those of us with different concentrations (mine is constitutional law) get left behind." Similar students note that they have found their choices "limited" since "The basics are offered, but the choices are very difficult to schedule around."

On the job front, Pace's location "only 30 minutes from NYC" is a mixed blessing. The city boasts a large number of law firms, but it's also home to several "'big NYC' [law] schools" with stronger reputations than that of Pace. While all here agree that the school's Center for Career Development "offers a great deal of information," opinions of it are mixed. Some say its staffers "are readily available to students and are more than willing to spend extra time and effort to assist students seeking help." Others believe that "when it comes down to working hard for the individual student to assist in post-graduation employment opportunities, it falls way short." Fortunately, "faculty and alumni" "all seem to sincerely want to see everyone succeed, and so they are accessible for advice and job-hunting" help.

CATHY M. ALEXANDER, ASSISTANT DEAN FOR ADMISSIONS
78 NORTH BROADWAY, WHITE PLAINS, NY 10603
TEL: 914-422-4210 FAX: 914-989-8714
EMAIL: ADMISSIONS@LAW.PACE.EDU • WEBSITE: WWW.LAW.PACE.EDU

Life

As Pace "give[s] students with lower LSAT scores a chance," it "doesn't seem to attract a lot of cutthroat types." By and large, students here are "down to earth and not too image conscious." "Most students commute, so campus clears out in the evenings and on the weekends," a 1L writes. Even if students did stick around, many are the type who "tends to study, even on the weekends." When students take a break from the books, they head to "the local pub" which "receives plenty of its business from Pace Law students." Pace does boast "many student groups, including ethnic and religious ones, various legal interests such as animal law, the environment, and international law, and also the Student Bar Association," and these groups sponsor "many events on campus throughout the semester." Unfortunately, these events are not always well attended, which leads a 1L to suggest that "club events should be more widely communicated" to the student body.

"It is nice that there is a campus as opposed to one building like most law schools," a 1L reflects. Boosters of Pace Law's White Plains location point out that the school is within "walking distance [of] a growing city center that has every amenity imaginable (including shopping, bars, and restaurants)" and "a short train ride away from Manhattan, yet, because it's in Westchester, we also have a great outdoor life, green grass, and trees!" However, other less-satisfied students say White Plains is "overpriced" and lacks a sense of "culture" and "community" unless "you already reside there."

Getting In

For a quick look to see if you've got the right stuff for Pace Law, consider this: admitted students at the 25th percentile had an LSAT score of 153 and a GPA of 3.1, and admitted students at the 75th percentile had an LSAT score of 157 and a GPA of 3.5. Make sure to put a human face to your application as interviews are strongly encouraged.

Legal research course requirement	No
Moot court requirement	Yes
Public interest law requirement	No

ADMISSIONS

Selectivity Rating	**73**
# applications received	3,107
% applicants accepted	39
% acceptees attending	21
Average LSAT	155
LSAT Range	153–157
Average undergrad GPA	3.4
Application fee	$65
Regular application	Rolling
Regular notification	Rolling
Early application program	Yes
Early application deadline	11/5
Early application notification	12/15
Transfer students accepted	Yes
Evening division offered	Yes
Part-time accepted	Yes
LSDAS accepted	Yes

Applicants Also Look At

Seton Hall University, Fordham University, Hofstra University, Rutgers University—Newark, St. John's University, Touro College, Albany Law School of Union University, Brooklyn Law School, New York Law School

International Students

TOEFL required of international students	Yes
Minimum TOEFL (paper/computer)	600/100

FINANCIAL FACTS

Annual tuition	$39,546
Books and supplies	$1,120
Fees	$248
Tuition per credit	$1,333
Room & board (on/off-campus)	$12,020/$19,790
Financial aid application deadline	2/1
% first-year students receiving some sort of aid	90
% receiving some sort of aid	88
% of aid that is merit based	58
% receiving scholarships	54
Average grant	$12,000
Average loan	$26,000
Average total aid package	$36,000
Average debt	$78,000

EMPLOYMENT INFORMATION

Career Rating	**74**	**Grads Employed by Field (%)**
Rate of placement (nine months out)	92	Academic (7)
Average starting salary	$88,693	Business/Industry (17)
State for bar exam	NY	Government (17)
Pass rate for first-time bar	85	Judicial Clerkships (5)
Employers Who Frequently Hire Grads		Private Practice (44)
Small and medium sized law firms, corporations, and government employers like local District Attorney's offices.		Public Interest (6)

Prominent Alumni

John Cahill, Chief of Staff, Former NY Governor George Pataki; Robert F. Kennedy Jr., Co-Director, Pace Environmental Litigation Clinic; Gerry Comizio, Partner, Paul, Hastings, Janofsky & Walker, LLP.

PEPPERDINE UNIVERSITY
SCHOOL OF LAW

INSTITUTIONAL INFORMATION

Public/private	Private
Student-faculty ratio	17:1
% faculty part-time	61
% faculty female	25
% faculty minority	16
Total faculty	113

SURVEY SAYS...

Beautiful campus
Students love Malibu, CA

STUDENTS

Enrollment of law school	633
% male/female	50/50
% out-of-state	45
% full-time	100
% minority	17
# of countries represented	2
Average age of entering class	24

ACADEMICS

Academic Experience Rating	89
Profs interesting rating	90
Profs accessible rating	99
Hours of study per day	4.61

Academic Specialties

Commercial law, corporation securities, international law, taxation, intellectual property law, dispute resolution, entrepreneurship

Advanced Degrees Offered

LL.M. in Dispute Resolution

Combined Degrees Offered

JD/MBA, 4 years; JD/MDR, 3–4 years; JD/MPP, 4 years; JD/MDiv, 5 years.

Clinical program required	Yes
Legal writing course requirement	Yes
Legal methods course requirement	No
Legal research course requirement	Yes
Moot court requirement	Yes
Public interest law requirement	No

Academics

Students looking to be surrounded by "incredible" faculty and staff on possibly "the most beautiful campus in the country," at a school that retains the services of Kenneth Starr—a man who obviously "has a lot of great connections"—as dean, and regularly features "impressive speakers, symposiums, and opportunities to learn outside of the classroom" would be wise to check out Pepperdine. Students agree that Dean Starr is one of "several luminaries in the fields of constitutional and human rights law" on the faculty at Pepperdine and appreciate "how accessible he is to students." "He routinely hosts events at his house for students and will start up a conversation with a student like he is an old friend," explains one student. "He takes so much time making people feel comfortable...The same is true for each and every professor I have had [here]." But don't let the picturesque location "mere yards away from the beach" and the dedicated faculty mislead you—"At best, you may see the beach from a library window. You certainly will not...be out surfing. Pepperdine is very demanding and our professors expect a lot from us," says a 1L.

Pepperdine boasts several stand-out programs, including "the internationally renowned Straus Institute for Dispute Resolution," which students feel "is the best program for learning negotiation, mediation, and arbitration techniques in the country." Students report that "the school also has amazing constitutional law professors and appears to be acquiring great additions to the faculty in the area of property law." Furthermore, its Palmer Center for Entrepreneurship and the Law "is completely unique and opens up a lot of doors for students to understand how the law can be used in many other careers." Students say "classes focus not just on theoretical concepts, but on the actual practice of law." A 3L opines: "I am convinced [that Pepperdine] is the equal or better of many 'top' law schools, including the other LA schools. Pepperdine students routinely outperform 'top school' students in summer clerkships because Pepperdine prepares you 'how to be a lawyer' while many of the 'top schools' focus more on theory. Pepperdine students have an excellent bar-passage rate and are very well prepared for the actual practice of law."

Pepperdine Law is "located next to a great legal market." "The only drawback," a 3L reports, "is fewer job opportunities than the 'top schools,' which is highly related to [Pepperdine's] ranking." By and large, however, students here are satisfied that "the school is working harder than any school in California to move up in the rankings, through getting current Supreme Court Justices and Chief Justices to teach and recruiting the best, brightest, and hardest-working students and professors." "In my interviews at big firms, Pepperdine seemed to be the new buzz," a sanguine 2L reports. "I found it easy to get a job with a big firm!" Helping matters, Pepperdine's "Career Services Center has been recently revamped, and is (thankfully) gaining momentum regarding on-campus interviews and networking." Also receiving attention are "the interior aesthetics of the law school"—"Pepperdine is in the process of refurbishing everything," a 1L reports—which seems to be a good move as one 3L reports that "the library carpet has a path in it." All these improvements cost money, however, and students here gripe about "financial aid and cost" of the school, as the latter is among the highest for U.S. law schools.

Life

Pepperdine students may describe themselves as "California casual," but they're also hard workers. "We're across the street from the beach, but we hardly go," a 1L reports. Regarding the student body's "conservative, religious" reputation, a 1L urges: "Don't let that deter you—no one forces [their opinions] down your throat," though she adds that

SHANNON PHILLIPS, EXECUTIVE DIRECTOR, ADMISSIONS
24255 PACIFIC COAST HIGHWAY, MALIBU, CA 90263
TEL: 310-506-4631 FAX: 310-506-7668
EMAIL: SOLADMIS@PEPPERDINE.EDU • WEBSITE: LAW.PEPPERDINE.EDU

students "have to be somewhat tolerant of other views than [their] own." While the school is "making an effort to take more students who aren't straight in from undergrad," some would like to see "more diversity in minority and religion."

When you have "a lot of smart people competing for a limited number of good grades," "Competition is a fact." Some find this competition is "not palpable in student relations," while others discern a "level of tension." Under these conditions, Pepperdine "does an excellent job of creating a community in its law school." It divides first-year sections into three groups, "so you take the same classes with the same people and bond with them." In addition, the school "provides a great deal of social programming" to foster interaction. "There are Bar Reviews every Thursday," usually "in Santa Monica, where most of the college-aged students hang out." Other events include a "Barrister's Ball," "the Law Dinner," "an annual dodgeball tournament," and, for the service-minded, "humanitarian projects like hurricane relief trips to New Orleans [and] student mentoring for 1Ls."

Pepperdine is "located in a hillside canyon with 180-degree views of the Pacific Ocean, Los Angeles, and Catalina Island...It is paradise compared to every other law school out there," a 1L reports. While Pepperdine law students receive on-campus housing, many here wish there was "more affordable housing available in Malibu."

Getting In

Admitted students at the 25th percentile have an LSAT score of 157 and a GPA of 3.3. Admitted students at the 75th percentile have an LSAT score of 161 and a GPA of 3.7. According to the school, other factors that can play heavily in your favor come admissions time include "work or service experience," "a history of overcoming disadvantage," "unusual life experiences," and "racial and ethnic origin."

ADMISSIONS

Selectivity Rating	85
# applications received	2,655
% applicants accepted	32
% acceptees attending	26
Average LSAT	160
LSAT Range	158–162
Average undergrad GPA	3.55
Application fee	$50
Regular application	Rolling, up to 4/1
Regular notification	Rolling
Early application program	No
Transfer students accepted	Yes
Evening division offered	No
Part-time accepted	No
LSDAS accepted	Yes

Applicants Also Look At
Loyola Marymount University,
University of San Diego

FINANCIAL FACTS

Annual tuition	$35,460
Books and supplies	$800
Fees	$60
Tuition per credit	$1,300
Room & board	$15,110
% first-year students receiving some sort of aid	87
% receiving some sort of aid	87
% of aid that is merit based	30
% receiving scholarships	75
Average grant	$9,950
Average loan	$35,155
Average total aid package	$45,105
Average debt	$111,163

EMPLOYMENT INFORMATION

Career Rating	88	**Grads Employed by Field (%)**
Rate of placement (nine months out)	97	Academic (3)
State for bar exam	CA	Business/Industry (20)
Pass rate for first-time bar	74	Government (13)
Prominent Alumni		Judicial Clerkships (1)
Pierre Prosper, Ambassador-at-Large for		Private Practice (44)
War Crime Issues; Todd Platts,		Public Interest (3)
Congressman—Pennsylvania; Lisa Stern,		
International Holocaust Survivor Advocate;		
Rick Caruso, Real Estate Development;		
Public Service.		

PHOENIX SCHOOL OF LAW*

INSTITUTIONAL INFORMATION

Public/private	Private
Student-faculty ratio	14:1
% part-time	36
% female	42
% minority	18
Total faculty	33

SURVEY SAYS...

Diverse opinions accepted
in classrooms
Great research resources
Great library staff

STUDENTS

Enrollment of law school	146
% male/female	53/47
% full-time	84
Average age of entering class	28

ACADEMICS

Academic Experience Rating	65
Profs interesting rating	72
Profs accesible rating	91
Clinical program required	No
Legal writing	
course requirement	Yes
Legal methods	
course requirement	No
Legal research	
court requirement	No
Moot court requirement	No
Public interest	
law requirement	No

Academics

Located "right in the middle of Phoenix," the Phoenix School of Law is a "franchise in the InfiLaw for-profit law school empire" and many students call it a "little jewel of a law school in the midst of the big metropolitan area." It's basically "a new school" and it has provisional approval by the American Bar Association, which means that graduates can take any bar exam in any U.S. jurisdiction. It's also "the only law school in the state that offers part-time evening classes" in addition to a full-time day program. Students have access to a growing number of internships and judicial externships, however the curriculum is largely geared toward practical skills. "The school does an excellent job of helping students become practice-ready," says a 3L.

Classes here are reportedly "small" and attendance is mandatory. "The school means this and strictly enforces its attendance policy," advises a 3L. Professors are "very demanding" yet, at the same time, they treat students "like adult human beings" and the academic environment is unthreatening. "Because many of the students are working professionals, they bring a wealth of experience to the classroom, which adds to the discussion of legal theory by tempering it with the experiences of those for whom the theory is translated into practical applications in their workplace." PhoenixLaw's "wide range of law professors" includes "practicing attorneys, experienced professors," and "many retired local judges." "Having so many former judges as professors gives students an amazing insight into the practical application of law in the Arizona courts," reflects a 3L. "Their wealth of knowledge about the local courts and all-around legal experience is invaluable." "Access to faculty is outstanding" as well. They "seem to be available for the students for any reason." "My criminal law professor gave the class her home telephone number and even the phone number to her relatives' home where she would be over the holiday break," notes a 1L. Others note however that "extensive practical experience" doesn't translate into excellent professors in every case.

Student opinion concerning the administration is deeply split. Some students tell us that management is "attentive and genuinely interested in helping students succeed academically and professionally." Others say administrators are "still working out the kinks." Some others are dissatisfied with the top brass. "If you agree with the administration, your views are golden," adds a 3L. "If you disagree, you will be ignored." Pretty much everyone agrees that more elective courses need to be added. Also, though PhoenixLaw trumpets "multiple start times" as one of its benefits, students complain that "there are not very many options in terms of class times." As far as job prospects go, "the school goes out of its way to ensure that students have access to help in preparing to find a job upon graduation" but, if you'll forgive a legal pun, the jury is still out. This school is just too young to have much of a track record.

* Provisionally approved by the ABA.

The facilities here are new and "very clean." There are "excellent resources for electronic research as well as traditional library research." The classrooms are "state-of-the-art" and "all have wireless internet." However, "lighting and acoustics are poor and it is often difficult to hear the professor and other students." Classrooms "need better temperature controls," too, and the elevator banks are "a bit crowded and slow at times."

Life

"A diverse group of students" is enrolled here. There are some full-time, traditional students but there is also a large population of older students who are "making a career change later in life." Some students say the academic atmosphere is "relaxed" and "non-adversarial." "Because the school is so new, everyone (professors, students, etc.) is working together to make sure Phoenix School of Law is successful," relates a 1L. "Your success is not my failure because your success means better opportunities and chances for me." Others suggest that the environment "can get very competitive" because the grading curve means that "getting an A is next to impossible."

PhoenixLaw doesn't boast much in the way of a campus. Frankly, "it is not really a law school or campus-type atmosphere" at all. Socially, "there is somewhat of a separation between the nighttime students and the daytime students." Some students "find time to interact academically and socially outside class and on weekends." However, "the part-time nature of the program and the older average age of the student body make social events difficult." It doesn't help that students tend to live all over Phoenix and its myriad suburbs. For the "tired" evening students, "it is a mad dash to the parking garage to try and get home to spend time with family" once class is over.

Getting In

Admitted students at the 25th percentile have LSAT scores in the low 150s and GPAs in the 3.0 range. Admitted students at the 75th percentile have LSAT scores in the mid 150s and GPAs of approximately 3.6.

ADMISSIONS

Selectivity Rating	60*
# applications received	1,423
# applicants accepted	794
# acceptees attending	146
Average LSAT	151
LSAT Range	149–153
Average undergrad GPA	3.09
Application fee	$50
Rolling notification	No
Early application program	No
Transfer students accepted	Yes
Evening division offered	Yes
Part-time accepted	Yes
LSDAS accepted	Yes

International Students

TOEFL required of international students	No
TOEFL recommended of international students	No

FINANCIAL FACTS

Annual tuition	$30,184
Books and supplies	$2,185
Fees	$1,378
Room & board	$11,592
% first-year students receiving some sort of aid	45
% receiving some sort of aid	45
% of aid that is merit based	45
% receiving scholarships	45
Average loan	$41,156
Average debt	$123,468

EMPLOYMENT INFORMATION

Career Rating	60*	Grads Employed by Field (%)
Rate of placement (nine months out)	93	Private Practice (56)
Average starting salary	$63,000	Public Interest (10
State for bar exam	AZ	Government (6)
Pass rate for first-time bar	97	

QUINNIPIAC UNIVERSITY
SCHOOL OF LAW

INSTITUTIONAL INFORMATION

Public/private	Private
Student-faculty ratio	10:1
% faculty part-time	49
% faculty female	39
% faculty minority	6
Total faculty	69

SURVEY SAYS...

Great research resources
Beautiful campus

STUDENTS

Enrollment of law school	387
% male/female	49/51
% out-of-state	41
% full-time	64
% minority	15
% international	2
# of countries represented	5
Average age of entering class	25

ACADEMICS

Academic Experience Rating	**86**
Profs interesting rating	82
Profs accessible rating	87
Hours of study per day	4.52

Academic Specialties

Criminal law, taxation, intellectual property law, health law, family & juvenile law, civil advocacy & dispute resolution

Advanced Degrees Offered

JD, 3 years full-time, 4 years part-time; LLM in Health Law

Combined Degrees Offered

JD/MBA, 4 years; JD/MBA in Health Care Management

Clinical program required	No
Legal writing	
course requirement	Yes
Legal methods	
course requirement	Yes
Legal research	
course requirement	Yes
Moot court requirement	No
Public interest	
law requirement	No

Academics

Students tell us that the Quinnipiac University School of Law has quite a lot going for it. The "wide variety of courses" includes six concentrations, which means that "There are ample opportunities to study any legal subject which interests you." Classes are intimate and "the small size of the academic universe here at QUSL makes it nearly impossible for a student to be lost in the mix." Several "outstanding" clinics and externship programs provide "plenty of hands-on practical learning." Also, moot court teams "consistently rank high in competition" around the country.

The "innovative" and "forward-looking" administration at Quinnipiac is "super-approachable" and "each dean seems to take a genuine interest in the students." "They are always willing to help you if you have a problem," says a 1L. "They always stop you in the hallway to ask how things are going." "Some of the teachers who have been around forever need to retire," but students are generally very pleased with their "student-oriented," "very engaging," and "hysterically" funny professors. The faculty is "a mix of supportive and frighteningly Socratic" professors, but they all "place emphasis on both theory and practical skills." "Everything we learn has a practical approach and isn't purely academic," asserts a 1L. Profs are also "eager to invest in each student" and "always available for questions and to provide whatever academic guidance necessary." "To be able to sit down, one on one, with some of these people is mind-blowing," says an awed 3L.

When the time comes to find a job, Quinnipiac has "a great reputation" in Connecticut and a steadily-growing roster of helpful alums. Firms throughout the state participate in on-campus interviews and the headquarters of several gigantic corporations and financial institutions are located nearby. "However, very few larger and more prestigious firms conduct on-campus interviewing," advises a 3L. "As a result, it is nearly impossible for even the most highly-ranked student to obtain a summer associate position." Also, students who want to leave the state are reportedly left to fend for themselves. "The school could improve by trying to do more for the people who do not want to work in Connecticut after graduation," suggests a 3L.

The "structurally-awesome" law school itself is "practically new" and "absolutely beautiful." The lobby is "flooded with light" and a state park across the street lends "an additional visual appeal to the campus." "Classrooms are well-equipped for students using laptops." Technology is abundant. "Wireless service is perfect." "Research resources are top notch" as well, and the "really comfortable" library is "conducive to long hours of studying."

EDWIN WILKES, EXECUTIVE DEAN OF LAW SCHOOL ADMISSIONS
275 MOUNT CARMEL AVENUE, (LW-ADM), HAMDEN, CT 06518-1908
TEL: 203-582-3400 FAX: 203-582-3339
EMAIL: LADM@QUINNIPIAC.EDU • WEBSITE: LAW.QUINNIPIAC.EDU

Life

Students at Quinnipiac tend to hail from the Northeast. "It's a New England school with the requisite swamp of Yankee social attitudes toward outsiders." That said, students are "extremely capable and motivated," not to mention full of "good and genuine character." Most people here tell us that the academic environment is "very friendly and encouraging." "I expected a very cutthroat environment but was pleasantly surprised to find some of the nicest and most helpful people I have met since elementary school," beams a 1L. Others note that "grading curves can be difficult" and observe some competition, especially "when exam time rolls around and scholarship money is on the line." "You have a small number of students who might actually sell their firstborn to gain some sort of advantage over the rest of the students in their class," says a 3L. "However, I would say that those wackjobs are the minority."

Outside of class, due to Quinnipiac's smaller size, "most students develop lasting friendships." Students who choose to get involved have a wealth of options including "great clubs which do some fabulous public service work." Socially, "Hamden, Connecticut is a beautifully boring town which makes it the perfect place to go to law school." "The evening students tend to be and less interested" in the social scene but, for students who are not too far removed from the glory of their undergraduate years, Quinnipiac is "kind of a party school." Downtown New Haven is not very far at all and "often, a great number of law students will all go out to the same bar" on the weekends. When students need a taste of serious city life, both New York City and Boston are reasonably close.

Getting In

Competition is moderate at Quinnipiac. Admitted students at the 25th percentile have LSAT scores of 158 and GPAs around 3.0. Admitted students at the 75th percentile have LSAT scores of 160 and GPAs around 3.5.

ADMISSIONS

Selectivity Rating	82
# applications received	2,560
# applicants accepted	787
# acceptees attending	134
Average LSAT	159
LSAT Range	158–160
Average undergrad GPA	3.33
Application fee	$40
Regular application	Rolling, up to 7/1
Regular notification	Rolling
Early application program	No
Transfer students accepted	Yes
Evening division offered	Yes
Part-time accepted	Yes
LSDAS accepted	Yes

International Students

TOEFL recommended of international students	Yes

FINANCIAL FACTS

Annual tuition	$40,000
Books and supplies	$1,200
Fees	$780
Fees per credit	$35
Tuition per credit	$1,400
Room & board (off-campus)	$14,794
% first-year students receiving some sort of aid	97
% receiving some sort of aid	98
% of aid that is merit based	79
% receiving scholarships	79
Average grant	$18,325
Average loan	$36,638
Average total aid package	$45,802
Average debt	$75,016

EMPLOYMENT INFORMATION

Career Rating	77
Rate of placement (nine months out)	95
Average starting salary	$63,675
State for bar exam	CT, NY, NJ, MA, RI
Pass rate for first-time bar	82

Employers Who Frequently Hire Grads

QUSL Graduates are hired by law firms, corporations, public defender offices, prosecutor offices, and various government and public interest organizations.

Grads Employed by Field (%)

Academic (2)
Business/Industry (28)
Government (11)
Judicial Clerkships (10)
Private Practice (41)
Public Interest (5)
Other (3)

REGENT UNIVERSITY
SCHOOL OF LAW

INSTITUTIONAL INFORMATION

Public/private	Private
Student-faculty ratio	14:1
% faculty part-time	55
% faculty female	20
% faculty minority	9
Total faculty	64

SURVEY SAYS...

Conservative students
Beautiful campus

STUDENTS

Enrollment of law school	410
% male/female	48/52
% out-of-state	73
% full-time	96
% minority	14
% international	2
# of countries represented	3
Average age of entering class	26

ACADEMICS

Academic Experience Rating	**85**
Profs interesting rating	95
Profs accessible rating	96
Hours of study per day	4.86

Advanced Degrees Offered

LL.M. in American Legal Studies-1 year

Combined Degrees Offered

1.JD/MBA, 4 years; JD/MA in Management, 4 years; JD/MA in Communication, 4 years; JD/MA in Journalism, 4 years; JD/MA in Counseling, 4 years; JD/MA in Divinity, 4 years; JD/M.Div., 4–5 years; JD/MA in Government, 4 years

Clinical program required	No
Legal writing course requirement	Yes
Legal methods course requirement	Yes
Legal research course requirement	Yes
Moot court requirement	Yes
Public interest law requirement	No

Academics

Founded 30 years ago by Christian heavyweight Pat Robertson, Regent University School of Law boasts a campus-wide emphasis on cooperation and support, offering its students an education that is "stressful, engaging, and even entertaining—a great balance for studying law." Regent's "community atmosphere" sets it apart from the vast field of "cutthroat competition . . . at other law schools." However, students say Regent's "academic rigor and challenge is not compromised by the motivation that we all have to see each other succeed."

"Who could imagine a law school where the professors actually wanted to see their students succeed?" Many of Regent's attorneys-in-training, apparently. These students gush over the accessibility of their professors, noting that they "are not only highly qualified, but extremely supportive and available for help when we need them." Professors are easy to track down "during and in between office hours. Not only that, but they respond to e-mails promptly—even on the weekends!" Students also appreciate the wealth of practical experience that faculty members bring to the classroom: "Since most of them were lawyers and judges, they teach you the law in realistic ways that you will be able to use in your practice, not just for law school exams or the bar exam." Other students wish the professors would take a slightly more hands-off approach to mentoring. In the words of one such student, "The *en loco parentis* model of instructing gets old quickly."

Regent engages "law from a Christian perspective." A glowing first-year tells us that the law school's greatest asset is "that God is at the forefront of the classes." Among the opportunities available are the Christian Legal Society and the Institute for Christian Legal Studies. There's also a law library, which earns high marks for its staff and resources, and it's right next door to Robertson Hall, the home turf of the law school. In Robertson Hall, students find classrooms that are "up to date with the latest technology, including adequate places to plug in computers and Internet." In addition, "We have access to multiple full-size court rooms with the latest technology to practice our skills."

Regent's students tell us that all this adds up to a law school on the move. In 2009, students won the Spong Moot Court Competition as well as the Mehrige National Environmental Law Competition (both national championship wins). These successes can be attributed, in part, to a student body that sees law as more than just a career. As the school's motto says, "Law is more than a profession. It's a calling."

Life

Though most students at Regent are very focused on getting their law degree, they're not blind to the fact that RU is just "minutes from the beach and many other cultural and social activities." The campus itself, located in the Hampton Roads area of coastal Virginia, "is beautiful, with plenty of trees, fabulous architecture, and a fountain." Beyond the classroom, students discover "so many opportunities to be involved that no one should go through here without finding something they want to be involved in." When it comes to socializing, "Lots of people meet outside of school for fun."

BONNIE CREEF, DIRECTOR OF ADMISSIONS & FIN. AID
1000 REGENT UNIVERSITY DRIVE, ROBERTSON HALL, VIRGINIA BEACH, VA 23464
TEL: 757-352-4584 FAX: 757-352-4139
EMAIL: LAWSCHOOL@REGENT.EDU • WEBSITE: WWW.REGENT.EDU/LAW

The law school's student body is made up of "an interesting mix of young, out-of-college students who are always ready to socialize and have fun on the weekends mixed with a sizable population of older students who often have families waiting for them at the end of the day." The one thing that most of these students have in common is "a Christian worldview." Many students praise the "strong sense of community." One says "those looking for genuine Christian fellowship will find it here," but also warns, "secular students may find some constraint on dating norms. The balance sits a bit right of center, favoring conservative biblical values." But most students agree that Regent is "a great place for those who want to get a legal education and also mature in their relationship with the Lord."

Getting In

The average LSAT score earned by an incoming law student was 154, and the average undergrad GPA was 3.3, but numbers are only part of the story at Regent. As the law school's Admissions Office states, "Strong academic credentials are crucial, but Regent Law also places significant importance on the personal statement and letters of recommendation." Application materials should not only reflect a clear desire to practice law, but also a personal and professional dedication to Christian principles.

ADMISSIONS

Selectivity Rating	**74**
# applications received	584
# applicants accepted	282
# acceptees attending	135
Average LSAT	154
LSAT Range	150–157
Average undergrad GPA	3.32
Application fee	$50
Regular application	Rolling, up to 6/1
Regular notification	Rolling
Early application program	No
Transfer students accepted	Yes
Evening division offered	No
Part-time accepted	Yes
LSDAS accepted	Yes

Applicants Also Look At
George Mason University, The College of William & Mary in Virginia, Valparaiso University, University of Richmond, Florida Costal School of Law, Appalachian

International Students

TOEFL required of international students	Yes
Minimum TOEFL (paper/computer)	600/250

FINANCIAL FACTS

Annual tuition	$27,450
Books and supplies	$1,336
Fees	$450
Fees per credit	$21
Tuition per credit	$915
Room & board	$8,667
Financial aid application deadline	6/1
% receiving some sort of aid	95
% of aid that is merit based	62
% receiving scholarships	75
Average grant	$8,453
Average loan	$33,895
Average total aid package	$42,348
Average debt	$98,086

EMPLOYMENT INFORMATION

Career Rating	**65**
Rate of placement (nine months out)	90.9
Average starting salary	$49,439
State for bar exam	VA, NC, GA, IN, PA
Pass rate for first-time bar	77.4

Prominent Alumni

Robert F. McDonnell, Attorney General for Virginia; April Wood Berg, North Carolina District Court Judge; Ron Pahl, Oregon Circuit Court Judge; Teresa McCrimmon, Virginia Beach General District Court Judge; Earl Mobley, Portsmouth Commonwealth's Attorney.

Grads Employed by Field (%)

Academic (5)
Private practice (43)
Government (13)
Business/Industry (11)
Judicial Clerkships (11)
Public Interest (9)
Military (6)
Academic (5)

ROGER WILLIAMS UNIVERSITY
SCHOOL OF LAW

INSTITUTIONAL INFORMATION

Public/private	Private
% faculty part-time	32.5
% faculty female	31.5
% faculty minority	7.4
Total faculty	57

SURVEY SAYS...

Diverse opinions accepted
in classrooms
Great research resources

STUDENTS

Enrollment of law school	550
% male/female	50/50
% out-of-state	77
% full-time	100
% minority	11
# of countries represented	4
Average age of entering class	24

ACADEMICS

Academic Experience Rating	**74**
Profs interesting rating	87
Profs accessible rating	85
Hours of study per day	5.35

Academic Specialties

Commercial law, constitutional law,
corporation securities, criminal law,
environmental law, human rights,
international law, labor law, property, intellectual property law, marine
affairs, public enterest law

Advanced Degrees Offered

JD, 3 years full-time

Combined Degrees Offered

JD/MMA Masters Marine Affairs, 3
1/2 years; JD/MS Masters of
Science in Labor Relations &
Human Resources, 4 years;
JD/MSCJ Masters of Criminal
Justice, 3 1/2 years.

Clinical program required	No
Legal writing course requirement	Yes
Legal methods course requirement	Yes
Legal research course requirement	Yes

Academics

Roger Williams University School of Law, founded in 1993, is the only law school in Rhode Island which gives it "incredible contacts in the Rhode Island legal community." Opportunities to visit the state Supreme Court, to obtain judicial clerkships, and to attend networking events are plentiful. Other perks here include "a lot of scholarships," tons of public service options, and an abundance of internships. The Marine Affairs Institute gives students "a full program in admiralty and maritime law." There's also a unique honors program that provides qualified students with three years of seminars, clinics, international training, and externships.

The "great mix" of adjunct and full-time professors at RWU offer "interesting insight into real-world legal issues" in the classroom and are "incredibly available" once class ends. "The faculty excels at scaring the crap out of you for your first year," explains a 3L, "but after class, when their masks come off, they are genuine, caring, normal human beings devoted to the school and its students." Some students tell us that the administrators are "fantastic." "While there are members of the administration who can be curmudgeonly, they are generally a charming and capable bunch," says one student. Others call management "a bit disorganized and agitated." Several students also gripe about the "awful" legal writing program at RWU. Other complaints include the shortage of clinical programs and, especially, the meager course selection after the first year, though the school has increased elective course offerings. "It is difficult to get into classes you want because so few sections are offered," laments a 3L. "Professors take their sweet time turning grades," too.

Some students call Career Services "helpful and welcoming." Others call it "a mess." However, pretty much everyone agrees that the job situation for graduates is mixed. On the one hand, "students at the top here have an honest shot at the lucrative jobs" and "RWU basically has a monopoly on the resources and opportunities in the state." "Opportunities to meet powerful and successful people are high," says a 2L. "Anybody looking to practice law in Rhode Island would be a fool to go elsewhere." Rhode Island is tiny, though, and students caution that their school's brand doesn't get much mileage beyond the state line. "If you want to practice in another state...be prepared to have to sell both yourself and your school," cautions a 2L.

The exterior of the law school building here is "not very attractive." However, the facility is located on a wonderful little piece of "waterfront property" and it's "always clean and comfortable." The library offers "seemingly unlimited resources" and the reference staff is "undoubtedly one of the jewels of the law school." RWU is "very modern" as well. The entire building is wireless, even if it "could be stronger in a few areas."

MICHAEL BOYLEN, ASSISTANT DEAN OF ADMISSIONS
10 METACOM AVENUE, BRISTOL, RI 02809-5171
TEL: 401-254-4555 FAX: 401-254-4516
EMAIL: ADMISSIONS@LAW.RWU.EDU • WEBSITE: LAW.RWU.EDU

Life

"The lack of diversity is noticeable" here despite the persistent efforts of the administration "to involve and recruit minorities." Student opinion concerning the academic environment is divided. Some students say that their peers exhibit "genuine support and goodwill." "The atmosphere is very much one of 'we're all in this together,'" they say. Other students tell us that "the school is competitive, especially among the top students, but not cutthroat." Still others assert that competition is widespread. "I would not agree that the students are cooperative in any way, shape, or form," asserts a 2L.

RWU is located "in one of the most beautiful areas of the country" and most students love the "charming little New England town" of Bristol. Sunsets are "breathtaking" and the ocean views are "great." Extracurricular activities include "a lot of clubs" and "amazing guest speakers." Also, "there are many groups on campus that organize social events and facilitate social interactions." Some students call the atmosphere almost too social. They point out that there is "a rampant rumor mill" and "10 times the drama of high school." "The undergraduate institution is known as a party school and this seems to have spilled over to the law school," complains a 3L. However, most students enjoy the environment and tell us that you can have "a real, fulfilling social life" at Roger Williams. "There's typically one night a week where you could find everyone out on the town—either in Bristol, Newport, or nearby Providence—getting along and having a well-deserved drink," says a 1L.

Getting In

The acceptance rate here is pretty high. Admitted students at the 25th percentile have LSAT scores in the low 150s and GPAs just below 3.0. Admitted students at the 75th percentile have LSAT scores in the mid 150s and GPAs of around 3.5.

Moot court requirement	No
Public interest law requirement	Yes

ADMISSIONS

Selectivity Rating	66
# applications received	1,233
% applicants accepted	58
% acceptees attending	25
Average LSAT	152
LSAT Range	149–155
Average undergrad GPA	3.22
Application fee	$60
Regular application	Rolling, up to 3/15
Regular notification	Rolling
Early application program	No
Transfer students accepted	Yes
Evening division offered	No
Part-time accepted	No
LSDAS accepted	Yes

Applicants Also Look At
Northeastern University, Pace University, Suffolk University, Quinnipiac University, Western New England College, New England Law|Boston, Vermont Law School

International Students

TOEFL required of international students	Yes
Minimum TOEFL (paper/computer/web)	600/250/100

FINANCIAL FACTS

Annual tuition	$31,900
Books and supplies	$1,680
Fees	$600
Room & board	$9,560
Financial aid application deadline	2/15
% first-year students receiving some sort of aid	91
% receiving some sort of aid	92
% of aid that is merit based	15
% receiving scholarships	43
Average grant	$16,716
Average loan	$42,009
Average total aid package	$54,418
Average debt	$106,892

EMPLOYMENT INFORMATION

Career Rating	71
Rate of placement (nine months out)	86.2
Average starting salary	$59,115
State for bar exam	RI, CT, MA
Pass rate for first-time bar	80

Grads Employed by Field (%)
Business/Industry (21)
Judicial Clerkships (13)
Public Interest (8)

Employers Who Frequently Hire Grads
New England judges (state and local) and small New England firms.

Prominent Alumni
Kenneth McKay, Chief of Staff, Republican National Committee; Brent Canning, Partner w/ Hinckley, Allen & Snyder, LLP; Judge Alberto Cardono, Judge, RI Municipal Court; John Sutherland, III, VP Finance/CFO, Women & Infants Hospital.

RUTGERS, THE STATE UNIVERSITY OF NEW JERSEY—CAMDEN
SCHOOL OF LAW

INSTITUTIONAL INFORMATION
Public/private	Public
Student-faculty ratio	5:1
% faculty part-time	58
% faculty female	31
% faculty minority	9
Total faculty	116

SURVEY SAYS...
Diverse opinions accepted
in classrooms
Great library staff
Abundant externship/internship/
clerkship opportunities

STUDENTS
Enrollment of law school	747
% male/female	58/42
% out-of-state	23
% full-time	73
% minority	21
Average age of entering class	25

ACADEMICS
Academic Experience Rating	**88**
Profs interesting rating	88
Profs accessible rating	86

Academic Specialties
Commercial law, constitutional law, corporation securities, criminal law, environmental law, human rights, international law, labor law, taxation, intellectual property law, health law, family law/DV, litigation

Advanced Degrees Offered
JD, 3 year FT or 4 year PT.

Combined Degrees Offered
JD/MBA; JD/MPA-Public Administration; JD/MSW-Social Work; JD/MS-Public Policy; JD/MCRP-City and Regional Planning; JD/MD and JD/DO—University of Medicine and Dentistry of New Jersey; and JD/MPA-Public Administration in Health Care Management and Policy.

Clinical program required	No
Legal writing course requirement	Yes

Academics

If going to law school gives you the jitters, your fears will quickly be assuaged at Rutgers, The State University of New Jersey—Camden School of Law. Sure, just like other prestigious JD programs, Rutgers will treat you to a dose of the "Socratic thunderstorm approach," and there is the typical "never-ending workload" throughout the first year. However, Rutgers maintains a remarkably friendly and supportive academic environment. Students insist that "first-year classes don't intimidate you, as there's no fear of speaking your mind in class, and diversity in thinking is highly encouraged." Outside the classroom, Rutgers professors are personable, to say the least: "Every Wednesday afternoon, there's a veritable party in our torts professor's office during his office hours. So many students go to discuss both academic and non-textbook-related topics that there aren't enough chairs and people sit on the floor," recalls one 2L. In fact, "It's common for professors to take students out to lunch, to conferences, and even to show up at student-sponsored pub crawls." The administration draws similar praise from students, who believe it "tries to be very open door and available for anything we could possibly need." A 1L jokes, "I came to Rutgers expecting to witness students getting 'burned' by professors every day in class. Instead the only burn I got was on the roof of my mouth while eating pizza with the dean."

Students are impressed with the caliber of the Rutgers faculty, describing them as "knowledgeable and passionate about their subjects" and able pedagogues to boot. In the lecture hall, "The faculty is as intelligent as they are witty. Anecdotes from the real-world experiences are common in the classroom and make some of the drudgery more interesting." Many also point out the strength of the adjunct staff, who "come from varied fields, providing a unique and practical perspective to current topics." Indeed, a practical approach is emphasized at Rutgers, and classes may even include "spontaneous field-trips to the federal court house across the street from the campus just so we can view real-world motions to dismiss, jury selection, and final arguments." The school's active alumni network is also called upon to contribute to the JD experience, and students tell us that "in many courses, alumni return to give lectures on the practical aspects of the subject, and they have been willing to assist any student [who] has a question."

Among the greatest perks of Rutgers—Camden is its low tuition, offering a "fantastic and highly respected education at a very reasonable price." As a result, students do not experience the financial anxiety common to law students today. "Due to a scholarship and a summer internship at a Philadelphia law firm," reports one 2L, "I will graduate with a top-rate legal education and virtually no debt. That combination is hard to beat, and I expect it will free up my career options considerably." The downside to a low-cost education is that "because of prior decreases in state funds, the law school's physical facilities are limited," and many complain that the classrooms lack ample outlets for laptops.

The school takes advantage of the resources in the surrounding community to instruct students in the playing out of law in the real world. "The federal courthouse is literally around the corner, the county courthouse a couple of blocks," and Rutgers students "have tremendous access to the judges in the area and several teach as adjuncts." Students also praise the fact that "the law school is very involved in the community through its pro bono clinics."

Rutgers is "located close to Philly, Trenton, and New York, so there are plenty of job opportunities." On that note, "Career Services are always on the job helping students get placed for both summer and permanent positions. They also expose students to the different options available to attorneys by having guests come to the law school to provide

Ass. Director Maureen O'Boyle, Ass't Director of Admissions
406 Penn Street, 3rd floor, Camden, NJ 08102
Tel: 800-466-7561 Fax: 856-225-6537
Email: admissions@camlaw.rutgers.edu • Website: www.camden.rutgers.edu

experiences in different areas." Rutgers is somewhat unique among law schools in that almost half of the graduating class takes judicial clerkship positions, more students than those who take positions in private practice.

Life

Attracting students from all across the nation and the world, the Rutgers student body is "extremely diverse in all aspects, including gender, socioeconomics, age, and interests." On this multicultural campus "There is an organization for just about any interest a person may have, [and] the SBA and other clubs do a great job of providing numerous social functions nearly every week." A 2L explains that "the environment is positive and students are involved with the school. Whether it be moot court, law journals, or politics, students are engaged in society and provide for a very strong sense of community." Off-campus "People are always looking to get together to study or to just go out socially," though most prefer hanging out in Philly to hitting the bars in the surrounding town of Camden. While some describe Camden as "the pit of despair," others tell us that "the waterfront on both sides of the Delaware River is beautiful." In addition, many appreciate the fact that "Philadelphia is exactly a mile away and provides for plenty of social opportunities."

Students warn that there are "a handful of students who are hell bent on getting a certain GPA." Most, however, value kindness and cooperation over competition. A 3L explains, "My school is both cooperative and competitive. Students here care deeply about being successful, but everyone is quick to lend a hand to bring someone else along for the ride." Indeed, many students praise the fact that "you can always find a good conversation outside after class."

Getting In

Rutgers—Camden recently began an experimental recruitment program, soliciting prospective law students based on their performance on the GRE or GMAT, rather than the LSAT. Therefore, there are a number of current law students who were previously pursuing advanced degrees in other subject areas. For all other prospective students, the admissions process is standard fare: Rutgers admits students who have demonstrated a high level of academic achievement, as well as strong standardized test scores.

Legal methods	
course requirement	Yes
Legal research	
course requirement	No
Moot court requirement	Yes
Public interest	
law requirement	No

ADMISSIONS

Selectivity Rating	**85**
# applications received	2,119
% applicants accepted	32
% acceptees attending	32
Average LSAT	160
LSAT Range	159–162
Average undergrad GPA	3.5
Application fee	$60
Regular application	Rolling,
	up to 6/7
Regular notification	Rolling
Early application program	No
Transfer students accepted	Yes
Evening division offered	Yes
Part-time accepted	Yes
LSDAS accepted	Yes

Applicants Also Look At

Temple University, University of California—Los Angeles, University of Pennsylvania, Fordham University, The George Washington University

International Students

TOEFL required	
of international students	Yes
Minimum TOEFL	
(paper/computer)	600/250

FINANCIAL FACTS

Annual tuition (in-state/	
out-of-state)	$20,860/$31,054
Books and supplies	$1,000
Fees	$2,262
Fees per credit	$1,224
Tuition per credit	
(in-state/out-of-state)	$864/$1,294
Room & board	
(on/off-campus)	$7,494/$12,830
Financial aid application	
deadline	4/1
% first-year students	
receiving some sort of aid	92
% receiving some sort of aid	92
% of aid that is merit based	25
% receiving scholarships	40
Average grant	$7,000
Average loan	$37,750
Average total aid package	$37,750
Average debt	$113,250

EMPLOYMENT INFORMATION

		Grads Employed by Field (%)	
Career Rating	**82**		
Rate of placement (nine months out)	92	Business/Industry (10)	
Average starting salary	$81,000	Government (7)	
State for bar exam	NJ, NY, PA, CA, TX	Judicial Clerkships (38)	
Pass rate for first-time bar	81	Military (1)	

Employers Who Frequently Hire Grads

Private Practice (38)

All major Philadelphia, New Jersey, and Delaware law firms hire from Rutgers-Camden, as do numerous prestigious firms from New York City.

Public Interest (2)

Other (4)

Prominent Alumni

Hon. James Florio, Former Governor/U.S. Congressman; Hon. Joseph Rodriguez, U.S. Federal District Judge; Hon. Stephen Orlofsky, U.S.Federal District Judge.

RUTGERS, THE STATE UNIVERSITY OF NEW JERSEY—NEWARK
SCHOOL OF LAW

INSTITUTIONAL INFORMATION

Public/private	Public
Student-faculty ratio	18:1
% faculty part-time	34
% faculty female	34
% faculty minority	26
Total faculty	62

SURVEY SAYS...

Diverse opinions accepted
in classrooms
Great library staff
Liberal students

STUDENTS

Enrollment of law school	818
% male/female	56/44
% out-of-state	29
% full-time	68
% minority	38
# of countries represented	26
Average age of entering class	25

ACADEMICS

Academic Experience Rating	**77**
Profs interesting rating	77
Profs accessible rating	67
Hours of study per day	3.59

Academic Specialties

Civil procedure, commercial law, constitutional law, corporation securities, criminal law, environmental law, government services, human rights, international law, labor law, legal history, legal philosophy, property, taxation, intellectual property law, international business, global affairs

Combined Degrees Offered

JD/ MBA, 4 years; JD/MD, 6 years; JD/PhD (Jurisprudence), 5 years; JD/MA (Criminal Justice), 4 years; JD/MCRP (City, Regional Planning), 4 years; JD/MSW, 4 years

Clinical program required	No
Legal writing	
course requirement	Yes
Legal methods	
course requirement	Yes

Academics

A "gem located in a very unexpected place," Rutgers, The State University of New Jersey—Newark, School of Law attracts a "top-notch" faculty who is "generally very invested in students that are interested or seek them out." Students commend their professors for being "witty and engaging" while simultaneously preparing them for the real legal world. One point of view suggests that the faculty is comprised of an "intriguing mix of academics and practitioners," enabling "students to engage with the material in both an intellectual and practical way." Another speaks to a shared sentiment of a "hands-on feel to the experience." As aptly summed up by one student, "none of [the] professors simply lecture, they all teach by making you work."

Students seem largely in favor of the administration, noting that it "is accessible and quick to respond to student concerns." One 2L attributes rebounding from a "rough start" and "disappointing grades" during the first semester of the program to the "extremely supportive, encouraging and helpful" attitude of the faculty and administration. However, others state that the "administration's efficiency is somewhat lacking" with regard to the red-tape entrenched registration process as well as grade dissemination. While some believe the administration "does not do enough to answer problems posed by the student body," others vouch for its commitment "to student success." Despite varied opinion, a common perception regarding Rutgers—Newark Law is that "it is truly a professional, graduate program"—students "get from it what [they] put in."

Some students call for an increase in course variety "to provide more theory and more specialty courses." Evening students in particular express dissatisfaction with limited course offerings "after 6:00 P.M." On the other hand, "Since patent law is a rapidly growing area, Rutgers—Newark has been actively adding more and more classes in this field" that are "taught by adjuncts who are partners in large patent law firms" imparting upon students their "vast practical knowledge."

For Rutgers—Newark's graduates, its proximity to New York City is considered to be its greatest strength. According to one student, "The vastness of opportunities that the New York City metro area holds is an immeasurable benefit to both the school and the students." While some feel "The students who do well often get jobs at the very best New York firms," the law school's Career Service Center itself receives mixed reviews. Students praise the current "dedicated" and "helpful" staff, but in the same breath remark that "Career Services could use some serious injection of resources," and that "the general glossing over" of the highly competitive job hunt "does not serve students well."

Virtually unanimous in opinion, students rave about the merits of the law library. The "excellent" and "never overcrowded" library "contains an extensive tax alcove" and a "brilliant" staff that is "amazing" and "very willing to help confused students through every stage of the research process." In general "facilities are worth mentioning," especially the law school building described as "a work of art" and the "universal wireless access" is a draw despite being "occasionally plagued with connection issues." "The six year young building makes for a very good learning environment" and students gladly report that "every three seats you can find an outlet for a laptop."

ANITA WALTON, ASSISTANT DEAN FOR ADMISSIONS
CENTER FOR LAW AND JUSTICE, 123 WASHINGTON STREET, NEWARK, NJ 07102
TEL: 973-353-5554 FAX: 973-353-3459
EMAIL: LAWINFO@ANDROMEDA.RUTGERS.EDU • WEBSITE: LAW.NEWARK.RUTGERS.EDU

Life

"There is a real camaraderie among the students" at Rutgers—Newark. The "non-competitive atmosphere, congenial student body and caring professors" "makes it a wonderful place to be." It seems as if "Everyone is very willing to help each other out." One student exclaims, "I asked a stranger for a class outline three days before the final, and she e-mailed it to me in 15 minutes." Another observes, "Competition between students is not noticeable but it does exist once interviewing for second-year jobs begins."

"It's law school; clearly the students aren't going to go out every night and party, but the school provides a vast array of different activities (quite a few that include open bar)." Students agree that "Thursday-afternoon happy hours are something to look forward to every week." Thankfully, "McGovern's (the Irish pub located across the street from the school)" provides a location for "a tradition that allows students to "let loose" and form lasting friendships." According to some, "While weekends in Newark leave everything to be desired, a student can always meet up with a classmate for dinner and drinks in nearby Hoboken (where many students choose to live)." Otherwise you can stay close to campus, as one student diplomatically explains, "Newark takes getting used to, but it grows on you very quickly."

Getting In

A unitary admissions system in place at Rutgers—Newark allows applicants to choose to compete for admissions with primary importance placed either on numerical values of their application, such as the LSAT and undergraduate GPA, or on non-numerical values, such as life experiences and achievements. Admitted students at the 25th percentile have an LSAT score of 154 and a GPA of 3.1. Admitted students at the 75th percentile have an LSAT score of 162 and a GPA of 3.6.

Legal research	
course requirement	Yes
Moot court requirement	Yes
Public interest	
law requirement	No

ADMISSIONS

Selectivity Rating	**83**
# applications received	3,519
% applicants accepted	26
% acceptees attending	21
Average LSAT	159
LSAT Range	155–161
Average undergrad GPA	3.34
Application fee	$60
Regular application	Rolling, up to 3/15
Regular notification	Rolling
Early application program	No
Transfer students accepted	Yes
Evening division offered	Yes
Part-time accepted	Yes
LSDAS accepted	Yes

Applicants Also Look At
Boston University, Seton Hall University, Yeshiva University, Fordham University, The George Washington University, Rutgers University—Newark

FINANCIAL FACTS

Annual tuition (in-state/ out-of-state)	$17,835/$26,187
Books and supplies	$4,225
Fees	$1,788
Fees per credit	$892
Tuition per credit (in-state/out-of-state)	$738/$1,090
Room & board (on/off-campus)	$13,908/$18,108
Financial aid application deadline	3/1
% receiving some sort of aid	90
% of aid that is merit based	13
% receiving scholarships	53
Average grant	$3,449
Average loan	$19,213
Average total aid package	$21,001
Average debt	$45,286

EMPLOYMENT INFORMATION

Career Rating	63	Grads Employed by Field (%)
Average starting salary	$64,067	Academic (1)
State for bar exam	NJ, NY, PA	Business/Industry (15)
Pass rate for first-time bar	72	Government (5)
Employers Who Frequently Hire Grads		Judicial Clerkships (31)
Federal Judges, New Jersey State Court		Military (1)
Judges, Large NJ and NY law firms,		Private Practice (43)
Medium NJ firms.		Public Interest (2)
Prominent Alumni		Other (2)
Robert Menendez, U.S. Senator; Jaynee		
LaVecchia, NJ State Supreme Court		
Justice; Ronald Chen, NJ Public Advocate.		

SAMFORD UNIVERSITY
CUMBERLAND SCHOOL OF LAW

INSTITUTIONAL INFORMATION

Public/private	Private
Affiliation	Southern Baptist
Student-faculty ratio	18:1
% faculty part-time	44
% faculty female	31
% faculty minority	10
Total faculty	48

SURVEY SAYS...

Great research resources
Great library staff
Beautiful campus

STUDENTS

Enrollment of law school	479
% male/female	55/45
% out-of-state	42
% full-time	100
% minority	7
Average age of entering class	24

ACADEMICS

Academic Experience Rating	86
Profs interesting rating	84
Profs accessible rating	96
Hours of study per day	4.29

Academic Specialties

Corporation securities, environmental law, taxation, intellectual property law, trial advocacy, alternative dispute resolution and public interest law

Advanced Degrees Offered

Master of Comparative Law

Combined Degrees Offered

JD/Master of Accountancy, JD/MBA, JD/Master of Divinity, JD/Master of Public Administration, JD/Master of Public Health, JD/MS in Env. Mgmt., and JD/Master of Theological Studies; all three and a half to four year programs except the JD/MDivinity which is a 5 year program.

Clinical program required	No
Legal writing	
course requirement	Yes
Legal methods	
course requirement	Yes

Academics

Samford University's Cumberland School of Law is, as one student puts it, "in the business of producing top-notch litigators." The school accomplishes this through an "exceptional focus on practical skills such as trial advocacy, negotiation, ADR, mediation, and client counseling." In fact, students quickly note that Cumberland's "trial advocacy program is tops in the nation." These future lawyers also benefit from "the legal writing classes [that] all first-years take"—classes that provide a firm foundation in the sort of communication skills that are incredibly marketable in the workforce. Cumberland offers students the opportunity to develop their lawyering skills in a traditional law school curriculum or through joint-degree programs, such as a JD/Master of Accountancy or a JD/Master of Science in Environmental Management. As one satisfied student says, "I am participating in a joint JD/MBA degree program. [This is the] only joint-degree I found in the country where you can graduate with both degrees in three years."

The students are quick to point out that none of these programs would be worth their salt if it weren't for the school's stellar faculty. A first-year beams, "The professors are masters of their craft. Not only are the professors extremely well-versed in their particular legal specialty, [but] they are terrific instructors." Not to mention accessible. Aside from tracking them down during office hours, "You can stop them in the hallway, corner them in the classroom, and call them on their cell phone if need be." A Cumberland first-year tells us, "I have enjoyed speaking with each of them to share my concerns, discuss a topic in class, or to just shoot the breeze." Even the administration has an "open-door policy" that one student is "willing to bet is unmatched at other schools." As one student explains, "I am on first-name basis with the majority of Career Services, professors, secretaries, and the library staff."

As far as resources go, Cumberland students admit that "the classrooms are older," but they are equipped with "the latest technology to enhance the learning experience." "The library is a stunning building with four floors of comfortable, quality furniture for long nights of study." In addition, "the Career Services Office does a great job matching students with potential job or externship opportunities." As one student assures us, "You constantly hear from recent alumni about how they were able to jump right into their practice upon graduation."

Life

Sure, "There is a competitive nature among the students" at Cumberland, but "They are all friendly and will not try to hide books from you at the library or steal pages from books so that you will not have the answers in class." As one first-year student says: "When I came to law school, I expected the 'survival of the fittest and at any cost' mentality. Instead, I found a group of highly supportive, incredibly enthusiastic people." All in all, "Cumberland is a close-knit community," and newcomers are absorbed into this community as soon as they arrive on campus, when they're placed into subgroups. As a 1L explains, "Each section consists of roughly 55 students, and during your first year you stay with those students throughout both semesters. It is a really great opportunity to form some close friendships." Cumberland students are hard workers, but they do not lose their civility and respect towards others in the pursuit of their goals. "Law school is stressful enough—it's nice that we do not have to worry about fellow classmates trying to undercut one another at every turn." The entire student body gets to mingle at the Thursday-night "social functions that anyone at Cumberland can attend." If you're look-

JENNIFER Y. SIMS, ASSISTANT DEAN FOR ADMISSIONS
800 LAKESHORE DRIVE, BIRMINGHAM, AL 35229
TEL: 205-726-2702 FAX: 205-726-2057
EMAIL: LAW.ADMISSIONS@SAMFORD.EDU • WEBSITE: CUMBERLAND.SAMFORD.EDU

ing for something a little more lively, though, you may have to "escape the conservative Baptist bubble that surrounds the university."

Students rave about Cumberland's physical setting. Picture "a beautiful campus full of cherry blossom trees, beautiful green spaces, and pristinely blue fountains." Located in the foothills of the Appalachians, Cumberland offers "a wonderful view of statuesque mountainsides and views of the city sitting below in the valley." That city, of course, is Birmingham—an old Southern metropolis boasting "a wonderful combination of nightlife, culinary variations, and cultural inspirations," and let's not forget the weather. As one student raves, "I'm writing this in February, and the temperature is 68 degrees outside."

Getting In

While Cumberland accepts applications on a rolling basis from September 1 through February 28, the Admissions Committee encourages prospective students to submit their materials by the December 31 priority deadline (when spots and scholarships begin to dwindle). In 2006, incomers arrived with an average undergrad GPA of 3.27 and an average LSAT score of 157. The school's application includes an open-ended personal essay. Take advantage of this opportunity to describe leadership and "other maturing experiences" that will set you apart from the field of applicants.

Legal research course requirement	Yes
Moot court requirement	No
Public interest law requirement	No

ADMISSIONS

Selectivity Rating	**79**
# applications received	1,105
# applicants accepted	519
# acceptees attending	162
Average LSAT	157
LSAT Range	155–159
Average undergrad GPA	3.27
Application fee	$50
Regular application	Rolling, up to 2/28
Regular notification	Rolling
Early application program	No
Early application deadline	No
Early application notification	No
Transfer students accepted	Yes
Evening division offered	No
Part-time accepted	No
LSDAS accepted	Yes

Applicants Also Look At

Florida State University, University of Georgia, The University of Alabama, University of Tennessee—Knoxville, Mercer University

International Students

TOEFL required of international students	Yes
Minimum TOEFL (paper/computer)	550/213

FINANCIAL FACTS

Annual tuition	$29,556
Books and supplies	$1,800
Fees	$110
Tuition per credit	$970
Room & board (off-campus)	$13,500
Financial aid application deadline	3/1
% first-year students receiving some sort of aid	83
% receiving some sort of aid	87
% of aid that is merit based	98
% receiving scholarships	36
Average grant	$20,000
Average loan	$38,772
Average total aid package	$42,360
Average debt	$96,980

EMPLOYMENT INFORMATION

Career Rating	**79**
Rate of placement (nine months out)	94
Average starting salary	$71,931
State for bar exam	AL, FL, TN, GA, NC, SC
Pass rate for first-time bar	94

Employers Who Frequently Hire Grads

Bradley Arant Boult; Burr & Forman; Balch & Bingham; Adam and Reese; Cabaniss, Johnston, Gardner, Dumas & O'Neal; Sirote & Permutt; Alabama Attorney General's Office; Hand Arendall, Stumes & Atchinson.

Prominent Alumni

Charles J. Crist, Jr., Governor of Florida; Joel Dubina, Chief Justice of 11th Circuit Court of Appeals; Anne Pope, Federal Cahir of Appalachian Regional Commision.

Grads Employed by Field (%)

Business/Industry (9)
Government (15)
Judicial Clerkships (12)
Private Practice (62)
Public Interest (2)

SANTA CLARA UNIVERSITY
SCHOOL OF LAW

INSTITUTIONAL INFORMATION

Public/private	Private
Affiliation	Roman Catholic
Student-faculty ratio	16:1
% faculty part-time	41
% faculty female	46
% faculty minority	21
Total faculty	76

SURVEY SAYS...

Diverse opinions accepted
in classrooms
Beautiful campus

STUDENTS

Enrollment of law school	963
% male/female	54/46
% out-of-state	39
% full-time	76
% minority	45
# of countries represented	13
Average age of entering class	26

ACADEMICS

Academic Experience Rating	**67**
Profs interesting rating	65
Profs accessible rating	71
Hours of study per day	4.36

Academic Specialties

Constitutional law, criminal law, environmental law, human rights, international law, labor law, taxation, intellectual property law. We offer certificates in Public Interest Law, Intellectual Property Law, and International Law.

Advanced Degrees Offered

LL.M. in U.S. Law for Foreign Lawyers, 1 year; LL.M. in International and Comparative Law, 1 year; LL.M. in Intellectual Property Law, 1–3 years.

Combined Degrees Offered

JD/MBA, 3.5 to 4 years; JD/MSIS, 3.5 to 4 years

Clinical program required	No
Legal writing course requirement	Yes

Academics

Many students at Santa Clara University School of Law are attracted by its "excellent regional reputation for high-tech law." "Since SCU is based in Silicon Valley, the opportunities for technology-based academia are profound." Specific programs that draw heaping praise include the "great IP [intellectual property] program, social justice program," and the "amazing study abroad options." SCU also "has an excellent part-time program" that brings lots of nontraditional students to the campus. Whatever track a student takes, she'll find an emphasis on "practical excellence and community service. SCU has a more genuine commitment to diversity and social justice than other, 'higher ranked' schools." With this solid selection of quality academic offerings in front of them, the students at SCU are able to enjoy a "small-school feeling" with "big-school opportunities."

Students across the board reserved the highest praise for their professors. At SCU, "The professors are the bright spot. Most are approachable and readily accessible. Most are teaching and practicing so their lectures are a good combination of theory and practical application." The professors are so dedicated that, as one student tells us, "At least one professor will sleep in his office during finals so that he is always available for students." SCU students don't have such nice things to say about the administration, however. While some students say the administration is "extremely helpful" and "genuinely wants students to succeed," many claim the it's "ineffective, unprofessional, [and] can only seem to get it together for the initial seduction of incoming students."

In addition to a "wide range of guest lectures and events for networking," SCU students also enjoy plenty of good old-fashioned career counseling. The school "has a professional Career Services staff that puts on weekly events with alumni. The events help students figure out what area of law they'd like to practice in, mixers help them meet SCU alums, and they're great with intern/externships because there are so many SCU alumni out there." Plus, "The law school is very well respected, especially in the Bay Area. The location is amazing for anyone interested in high tech—this is the heart of Silicon Valley!"

Students say "The campus itself is indeed the highlight of the Santa Clara experience—the grounds are impeccable with peaceful gardens and perfectly manicured lawns." However, students gripe about the "woefully inadequate" classrooms and the "dim and dreary" library that is so "outdated" that studying becomes "harder than it already is." Also, "A lot of students would be happy if the school got rid of the mandatory grade curve and the additional upper-division writing requirement."

Life

"One of the greatest strengths of SCU Law is the collaborative attitude held by the students, faculty, and staff." "There is absolutely none of the cutthroat back-biting that you hear of at other schools," a current student says. "Aside from the usual stress at exam time, students are genuinely happy to be here." "Lots of the students [at SCU] are local residents," and "few live near or on campus." They "come from a variety of life and work backgrounds," which students find "especially enriching." The school's "collaborative atmosphere" helps to ensure that everyone gets along, though students "tend to form cliches with their own section." "Because of the part-time program, the student population is one of the most diverse anywhere (lots of engineers studying to be patent lawyers)."

JEANETTE J. LEACH, ASSISTANT DEAN FOR ADMISSIONS & FINANCIAL AID
500 EL CAMINO REAL, SANTA CLARA, CA 95053
TEL: 408-554-5048 FAX: 408-554-7897
EMAIL: LAWADMISSIONS@SCU.EDU • WEBSITE: LAW.SCU.EDU

Legal methods course requirement	Yes
Legal research course requirement	Yes
Moot court requirement	Yes
Public interest law requirement	No

Academic life at SCU is supplemented by "many extracurricular activities from law journals to basketball leagues," all with "tremendous law student participation." There are "monthly bar nights" and "one or two lunches" every week where students can enjoy "speakers and food." Also, "March is banquet month, and every student organization puts on a party." Students say the Student Bar Association "does its best to put on social events for the law school. Some of the events have been a real success. But to say that any law student really has a social life is a joke. For three years, law school is your life."

"The immediate area around the campus is not really a 'college town' atmosphere. There are not a lot of areas for graduate students to go to hang out other than one or two places." "Your social life is what you make of it"—even if it sometimes "takes a little creativity and exploration of the neighboring towns." On the upside, SCU's location offers "easy access to downtown San Jose" and the true socialites among the student body "drive to San Francisco for fun."

Getting In

SCU's entering students earn an average score of 160 on the LSAT and a 3.32 undergraduate GPA. But the Admissions Committee strives to avoid "a mechanical approach to admissions." In other words, smart undergraduate course selection, improved academic record, and impressive life or professional experience can give a candidate the edge.

ADMISSIONS

Selectivity Rating	**78**
# applications received	3,984
# applicants accepted	1,638
# acceptees attending	310
Average LSAT	160
LSAT Range	157–162
Average undergrad GPA	3.32
Application fee	$75
Regular application	Rolling
Regular notification	Rolling
Early application program	Yes
Early application deadline	11/1
Early application notification	12/20
Transfer students accepted	Yes
Evening division offered	Yes
Part-time accepted	Yes
LSDAS accepted	Yes

Applicants Also Look At

University of California—Davis;
Loyola Marymount University;
University of San Francisco;
Pepperdine University; University of
San Diego; University of California,
Hastings

FINANCIAL FACTS

Annual tuition	$36,750
Books and supplies	$1,102
Tuition per credit	$1,225
Room & board	$13,500
Financial aid application deadline	2/1
% first-year students receiving some sort of aid	84
% receiving some sort of aid	81
% of aid that is merit based	77
% receiving scholarships	33
Average grant	$13,876
Average loan	$37,419
Average total aid package	$39,556
Average debt	$104,258

EMPLOYMENT INFORMATION

Career Rating 88
Rate of placement (nine months out) 82
Average starting salary $114,679
State for bar exam CA, WA, OR, AZ, NY
Pass rate for first-time bar 82

Employers Who Frequently Hire Grads
Bingham McCutchen LLP; Blakely, Sokoloff, Taylor and Zafman LLP; Cooley Godward LLP; Dewey Ballantine LLP; DLA Piper; Fenwick & West LLP.

Prominent Alumni
Leon Panetta, Current C.I.A. Director and Former Chief of Staff under President Bill Clinton; Zoe Lofgren, Congresswoman, U.S. House of Representatives.

Grads Employed by Field (%)
Academic (1)
Government (8)
Military (1)
Private Practice (57)
Public Interest (4)
Other (1)

SEATTLE UNIVERSITY
SCHOOL OF LAW

INSTITUTIONAL INFORMATION

Public/private	Private
% faculty part-time	44
% faculty female	39
% faculty minority	17
Total faculty	124

SURVEY SAYS...
Great research resources
Great library staff

STUDENTS

Enrollment of law school	1,043
% male/female	48/52
% out-of-state	25
% full-time	77
% minority	27
% international	2
# of countries represented	6
Average age of entering class	27

ACADEMICS

Academic Experience Rating	**74**
Profs interesting rating	65
Profs accessible rating	61
Hours of study per day	4.5

Academic Specialties
Commercial law, constitutional law, corporation securities, criminal law, environmental law, human rights, international law, labor law, property, taxation, intellectual property law, estate planning, health law and real estate, poverty law, legal writing

Combined Degrees Offered
It is possible to obtain a joint JD/MBA; JD/Master of International Business; JD/MS in Finance; JD/Master of Professional Accounting; JD/Master of Public Administration and JD/Master of Sports Leadership and JD/Master of Criminal Justice. The programs can be complete in 4 years.

Clinical program required	No
Legal writing course requirement	Yes
Legal methods course requirement	No

Academics

"A fairly large school," the Seattle University School of Law offers an "outstanding," "very flexible, evening, part-time program" in addition to full-time day enrollment. "Course options are diverse and offered consistently." No fewer than 14 specializations include criminal practice, environmental law, and international law. The "tough but very good" legal writing curriculum is far and away the biggest point of pride here. It's "the class that you will despise while you are in it, but will be utterly grateful for when you are through." "This school has the best legal writing program and advocacy programs in the country," brags one student. "It is the best and most useful course I've ever taken at a school," adds a 3L. "The legal writing program really does prepare you for the real world and to a level of detail and precision I did not expect." A throng of externships and clerkships gives students the opportunity to "develop practical skills" "in all different areas of law." Seattle U's location "less than a mile from downtown Seattle businesses and law firms" allows students to walk to many courthouses and downtown law firms. Seattle U Law is also a Jesuit institution, and many students note that many organizations "are devoted to social justice." Other students tell us that "any mention of the Jesuit influence is off base." "If asked [about] the Jesuit tradition," jokes a 2L, many students would ask, "'Is that a type of mocha latte at Starbucks?'" The biggest gripe among students concerns the need to "reduce the size of the incoming classes" Also, warns a 3L, "The grading curve here is very tough. It can get daunting."

Professors "emphasize the practical side" of law and are "generally extremely capable, intelligent, and knowledgeable." It's the "really hit-and-miss" visiting professors whom "you have to watch out for." Outside of class, some faculty members are "extremely helpful and available." However, other professors are "very hard to access." "I wish that the professors were a bit more accessible," complains a 2L. "They are supposed to have set office hours, but none of the professors are held to that." Thoughts about the administration are similarly mixed. Some students say that the SU administration "is a distant, bureaucratic entity" that manifests "a seeming sense of apathy towards the individual student." Others assert that the deans "work hard to eliminate obstacles so that all you have to worry about is learning."

The Center for Professional Development "makes extraordinary efforts to find job placements for students." Also, "The alumni network is broad and very helpful." "The top 10 percent do great and get into private firms with the snap of a finger." Some students complain that SU "should be doing more to market students to regional and national employers." "Seattle University is a regional school," explains a 2L. "It is hard for students to find jobs outside of the Pacific Northwest."

Depending on which students you talk to, the facilities here are either "bordering on beautiful" or "stark and bleak." Whatever the case, the law school is in "a new building with wireless technology" throughout and "very high-tech" gadgetry everywhere. "Superhumanly helpful and friendly research librarians" staff the law library, though "the lack of study space is a serious concern."

Life

"You can always get notes when you need them" at Seattle U Law; "However, there is still a healthy amount of competitiveness among students," who comprise "an interesting mix." "The right-out-of-undergrad students are obviously more competitive, but much more social too." Older students are "considerably more laid-back and have a com-

CAROL COCHRAN, ASSISTANT DEAN FOR ADMISSION
901 12TH AVENUE, SULLIVAN HALL, P.O. BOX 222000, SEATTLE, WA 98122-1090
TEL: 206-398-4200 FAX: 206-398-4058
EMAIL: LAWADMIS@SEATTLEU.EDU • WEBSITE: WWW.LAW.SEATTLEU.EDU

Legal research course requirement	Yes
Moot court requirement	No
Public interest law requirement	No

pletely different attitude." Students (and faculty) tend to lean to the left politically, though "the Federalist Society has a strong presence on campus." Few are particularly religious. "About the most religious this school gets is the Christmas tree and menorah that get put up during the holidays."

"Anyone with minimal social skills can make lifelong friends here," claims one student. "Nobody here is pretentious." "People at the school are tight-knit and supportive of one another." A host of on-campus events "promotes community interaction." However, there isn't much communication between the evening and the day programs. "For the night students who work full-time there aren't many opportunities to socialize with other students. Any socializing is done within the evening section and rarely are any day students involved."

"The school building itself is located just outside of downtown Seattle" in a lively neighborhood called Capitol Hill. "The school is in paradise," brags a 2L. "Seattle really is the greatest city in the world," beams another student. The Emerald City "is a great place to live for a variety of reasons, most notably the climate and the plethora of places to engage in outdoor activities."

Getting In

Admitted students at the 25th percentile have LSAT scores of 155 and GPAs of 3.2. Admitted students at the 75th percentile have LSAT scores of 161 and GPAs of 3.6. If you take the LSAT more than once, Seattle U Law "gives greater weight" to your highest score but also advises you to contextualize the difference in your scores in an addendum.

ADMISSIONS

Selectivity Rating	**80**
# applications received	2,907
# applicants accepted	1,011
# acceptees attending	328
Average LSAT	157
LSAT Range	154–160
Average undergrad GPA	3.3
Application fee	$60
Regular application	Rolling
Regular notification	Rolling
Early application program	No
Transfer students accepted	Yes
Evening division offered	Yes
Part-time accepted	Yes
LSDAS accepted	Yes

Applicants Also Look At
University of Oregon, University of San Francisco, University of Washington, Gonzaga University, Lewis & Clark College

International Students

Minimum TOEFL (computer)	250

FINANCIAL FACTS

Annual tuition	$35,340
Books and supplies	$903
Fees	$66
Tuition per credit	$1,178
Room & board (off-campus)	$16,488
% first-year students receiving some sort of aid	94
% receiving some sort of aid	97
% of aid that is merit based	50
% receiving scholarships	54
Average grant	$4,817
Average loan	$31,875
Average total aid package	$39,935
Average debt	$95,925

EMPLOYMENT INFORMATION

Career Rating	**75**
Rate of placement (nine months out)	95
Average starting salary	$65,000
State for bar exam	WA, CA, OR, TX, IL
Pass rate for first-time bar	84

Employers Who Frequently Hire Grads
Perkins Coie, Lane Powell Spears Lubersky, King County Prosecuting Attorney, Washington State Attorney Gen., Williams Kastner & Gibbs, Foster Pepper Shefelman, Preston Gates & Ellis.

Prominent Alumni
Judge Ralph Beistline, Federal District Court Judge; Judge Charles Johnson, Judge Charles Johnson; Tom Galligan, Dean, University of TN School of Law.

Grads Employed by Field (%)
Academic (1)
Business/Industry (27)
Government (13)
Judicial Clerkships (3)
Military (1)
Private Practice (40)
Public Interest (10)

SETON HALL UNIVERSITY
SCHOOL OF LAW

INSTITUTIONAL INFORMATION

Public/private	Private
Affiliation	Roman Catholic
Student-faculty ratio	15:1
% faculty part-time	51
% faculty female	43
% faculty minority	12
Total faculty	164

SURVEY SAYS...

Diverse opinions accepted
in classrooms
Great research resources
Great library staff
Abundant externship/internship/
clerkship opportunities

STUDENTS

Enrollment of law school	368
% male/female	55/45
% out-of-state	33
% full-time	65
% minority	10
# of countries represented	12

ACADEMICS

Academic Experience Rating	**81**
Profs interesting rating	78
Profs accessible rating	76
Hours of study per day	4.63

Academic Specialties

intellectual property law, Health Law

Advanced Degrees Offered

JD, 3 years full-time, 4 years part-time; LLM, 1 year full-time, two years part-time; MSJ, 1 year full-time, 2 years part-time

Combined Degrees Offered

JD/MD, 6 years; MD/MSJ, 5 years; JD/MBA, 4 years; JD/MADIR (Int'l Relations), 4 years; BS/JD, 3+3

Clinical program required	No
Legal writing course requirement	Yes
Legal methods course requirement	No
Legal research course requirement	Yes

Academics

Seton Hall University School of Law "embraces the theoretical and practical sides of the law." It's also "loaded with scholarship money" and its bar passage rate is typically a handful of points higher than New Jersey's overall rate. Notable programs include "an extremely well-regarded health law concentration," an "excellent entertainment law program," and three very cool opportunities to study abroad. The intellectual property program really enables students "to connect with the pharmaceutical world that is central to New Jersey." "The onsite Center for Social Justice is a fulltime clinic providing direct links to the community of Newark and real opportunity for students to see justice work in people's lives." The moot court program is "absolutely outstanding" as well.

"Professors are generally very accessible" at SHU. "They will make time with you based on your schedule," promises a 1L. In the classroom, the faculty is either "amazing or amazingly awful and rarely in between." The good professors are of "the absolute highest caliber" and "quite impressive in terms of practical experience, intellect, and teaching ability." "With the exception of a select few, the younger faculty members are much better classroom teachers than the older, tenured members," reflects a seasoned 3L. "They are tougher on you in class and tend to give harder exams but they have a more relevant way of making sure you understand the information." As for the bad professors, "there are some serious duds." "Seton Hall Law School has some of the most inept professors I have ever had the misfortune to endure," grumbles a 3L. Also, there are "too many" adjuncts. Some students call the administration "remarkably accessible and responsive, all the way to the top" and say that the deans have "a pragmatic grasp on what a law school should be." "Their doors are always open and they really live to serve the students," gushes a happy 1L. Others charge that management ranges from "very aloof" to "surly and rude."

SHU is a "great school if you want to practice in New Jersey" and students in the top 15 percent have "zero difficulty finding six-figure employment." Also, "Seton Hall emphasizes judicial clerkships" and many grads are able to go that route. However, "there is a huge gap between the haves and the have nots" and students with mediocre grades are "pretty much left to fend for themselves." Also, SHU students who want to work in Manhattan have only moderate success. "Don't expect to receive a job in New York," advises a 2L.

"The research facilities are great" here and "the library staff is exceedingly knowledgeable and friendly." Student opinion is very split concerning the facilities, though. Happy students argue that the law school itself is "stylish," "very modern," and "gorgeous on the inside." They say the library offers "plenty of space" and a "wonderful study environment." They tell us that technology is "state of the art." They also note that federal and state courthouses are "within walking distance." Critics call the building "hideous" and say that the "bland" classrooms are "overcrowded and uncomfortable." They complain that the "library lighting is reminiscent of a monastery in the Middle Ages." Also, they gripe, the wireless connection can be problematic and "the cafeteria is often quite bad and terribly overpriced."

Ms. Gisele Joachim, Asst. Dean of Admissions and Financial Aid
One Newark Center, Newark, NJ 07102
Tel: 888-415-7271 Fax: 973-642-8876
Email: ADMITME@SHU.EDU • Website: LAW.SHU.EDU

Life

We've seen worse cases when it comes to minority enrollment. Nevertheless, students here say that "Seton Hall lacks a diverse student body." They also think there are "too many people from Jersey." Academically, "there is some competition." For the most part, though, the atmosphere is "affable," "collegial" and "genuinely friendly." Outside of class, there are "many interesting seminars" and "tons of organizations and activities." "Just about everyone is involved in something," says a 2L.

The law school is located near the Prudential Center—a new multi-purpose indoor arena—and, "from time to time," students are able to score "free tickets" for events. Otherwise, though, the "dilapidated, post-industrial, and downright dangerous" surrounding town of Newark is "one of the worst cities in America" and "pretty much a forbidden zone after dark." A good chunk of students "lives in apartments only a couple of blocks away," but everyone else commutes. "The students who live in Hoboken seem to have a blast." While some SHU students suggest that "there is not as much a sense of community outside of the standard weekday," the majority tells us that "there is a strong sense of community" and "a bustling social scene." SBA-sponsored social events usually take place someplace besides Newark and "there is always a large turnout."

Getting In

Admission at SHU is moderately competitive. Admitted students at the 25th percentile have LSAT scores in the high 150s and GPAs not too far above 3.0. Admitted students at the 75th percentile have LSAT scores in the very low 160s and GPAs of roughly 3.6.

Moot court requirement	Yes
Public interest law requirement	– No

ADMISSIONS

Selectivity Rating	**83**
# applications received	2,871
% applicants accepted	35
% acceptees attending	21
Average LSAT	160
LSAT Range	158–162
Average undergrad GPA	3.53
Application fee	$65
Regular application	Rolling
Regular notification	Rolling
Early application program	No
Transfer students accepted	Yes
Evening division offered	Yes
Part-time accepted	Yes
LSDAS accepted	Yes

Applicants Also Look At
Hofstra University, Rutgers University—Camden, St. John's University, Brooklyn Law School, New York Law School

International Students
TOEFL recommended of international students	Yes

FINANCIAL FACTS

Annual tuition	$40,380
Books and supplies	$1,000
Fees	$780
Tuition per credit	$1,346
Room & board (off-campus)	$12,150
Financial aid application deadline	4/1
% first-year students receiving some sort of aid	95
% receiving some sort of aid	91
% of aid that is merit based	16
% receiving scholarships	52
Average grant	$24,000
Average loan	$40,000
Average total aid package	$59,750
Average debt	$91,500

EMPLOYMENT INFORMATION

Career Rating	**77**
Rate of placement (nine months out)	94.74
Average starting salary	$76,778
State for bar exam	NJ, NY
Pass rate for first-time bar	89

Employers Who Frequently Hire Grads
Graduates are frequently hired by the nation's most prestigious firms, all national and state government agencies, and public interest organizations.

Prominent Alumni
Michael Chagares, Judge on 3rd U.S. Circuit Court of Appeals; Christopher Christie, Former U.S. Attorney for the State of New Jersey.

Grads Employed by Field (%)
Academic (1)
Business/Industry (13)
Government (5)
Judicial Clerkships (39)
Military (1)
Private Practice (40)
Public Interest (1)

SOUTH TEXAS COLLEGE OF LAW

INSTITUTIONAL INFORMATION

Public/private	Private
Student-faculty ratio	19:1
% faculty part-time	52
% faculty female	32
% faculty minority	11
Total faculty	124

SURVEY SAYS...

Diverse opinions accepted
in classrooms
Great research resources
Great library staff
Students love Houston, TX

STUDENTS

Enrollment of law school	1,267
% male/female	54/46
% out-of-state	9.7
% full-time	75
% minority	21
# of countries represented	3
Average age of entering class	26

ACADEMICS

Academic Experience Rating	**75**
Profs interesting rating	77
Profs accessible rating	72
Hours of study per day	3.85

Academic Specialties

Advocacy, Transactional Skills,
Corporate Compliance, Alternative
Dispute Resolution

Combined Degrees Offered

Through a special cooperative program, students in the JD program at South Texas College of Law are eligible to apply for admission to the MBA program at Mays Business School, Texas A&M University. Upon acceptance into the MBA program, students are granted a leave of absence after their second year of law studies to attain their MBA and then return to South Texas to complete their JD degree.

Clinical program required	No
Legal writing course requirement	Yes

Academics

Centrally located in the heart of downtown Houston, students at South Texas College of Law can take full advantage of the school's proximity to surrounding courtrooms and law firms, not to mention a "very strong network of alumni in practice." Second to none with 100 National Titles, "the pièce de résistance of STCL is its trial advocacy program." Students tell us that STCL "is a great school for practical lawyering skills and is a great choice for those students who wish to practice law in Texas." In addition, South Texas requires four hours of legal research and writing over the first two semesters and students cannot say enough about the legal research and writing program. According to one 2L, "It is the reason we continually win 'Best Brief' in the moot court competitions, and it will leave you well prepared for your summer clerkships." Another student concludes, "If you want to learn how to practice law instead of just learning theory, South Texas is a great place to be."

"The excellent and accessible faculty makes it a great school, even for part-time students who mainly attend evenings and weekends," says one student. Approachable both in and out of the classroom, the faculty's "love" of teaching, "sense of humor," and support is clearly felt by students who claim that "it is not difficult to excel in class given the great learning environment." Students agree that practical teaching is an aspect of STCL that distinguishes it from other law schools. STCL's professors hail from a variety of backgrounds, and the vast majority of the adjunct faculty are sitting judges or practicing attorneys. According to students, "This gives us a great sense of what is 'really' happening in the legal field versus the theoretical or purely academic focus of other schools." A 3L adds that practical learning, "builds the best practicing lawyers of tomorrow," while another boldly attests, "Our school will teach you how to litigate the day after you pass the bar."

Students note that "the Admissions Office is very professional, knowledgeable, and helpful." Though in the past students have noted, "the offices of the Registrar, Financial Aid, and Business Office are in three locations and don't seem to communicate well." Fortunately, students report that past headaches surrounding registration have been remedied due to the implementation of a campus-wide integrated database, resulting in a "smoother" process overall. While students admit that the administration has "streamlined many things lately which goes to show that they listen to students," others argue that "they need to be more responsive to the feedback of their customers—the students."

With regard to facilities at South Texas, students unanimously agree that the "state-of-the-art library is beautiful [and] includes an extensive collection of sources." "It's superior in every respect, and there is never a wait in one of its many computer labs," adds one student. One of its most valued features is the "amazing terrace on the sixth floor," which "provides a relaxing setting in downtown Houston" and can also be utilized for "reading, eating, sunbathing—whatever your pleasure." The only complaint about the library is that it "closes too early!" However, the same enthusiasm doesn't extend to the subject of "deplorable" parking. Due to its downtown location, parking at STCL continues to be the most widely cited grievance.

ALICIA K. CRAMER, ASSISTANT DEAN OF ADMISSIONS
1303 SAN JACINTO STREET, HOUSTON, TX 77002-7006
TEL: 713-646-1810 FAX: 713-646-2906
EMAIL: ADMISSIONS@STCL.EDU • WEBSITE: WWW.STCL.EDU

Life

"The students in the part-time program are a great mix of experienced and right-out-of-college students, so class discussions are rich and varied," says one student. Diversity is reflected through classes that "explore all sides in a professional manner" and foster "creative and stimulating after class conversations with people that you may never have spoken to without the class discussion."

According to students, "While there is an inevitable degree of competition, [this] is not a cutthroat environment." Most here agree that "students work together and rely on each other for assistance." While there is no shortage of studying at South Texas, "Students looking for a social atmosphere can definitely find it here." In fact, one student reports, "The students at my school like to party. I have no idea where everyone finds the time, but we do."

In addition, students declare they "have more student interest organizations than you can count—this provides an opportunity to learn about practice areas that aren't covered in the classroom...fantastic!" "Each month, at least one student organization throws a shindig on the terrace of the library," states one student. Usually well attended, this type of event "breeds camaraderie among the student body. As a result, the law school atmosphere remains upbeat as we all move along the continuum together." Echoing this sentiment, one 2L muses, "I get a big sense of 'we're all in this together.' I only wish this prevailed post-graduation."

Getting In

Although LSAT scores and cumulative undergraduate GPA determine admission for many students applying to STCL, a significant portion of each class is admitted based on other factors including, but not limited to, exceptional personal or academic accomplishment, recommendation letters, and leadership potential. Admitted students at the 25th percentile have an LSAT score of 150 and a GPA of 3.0. Admitted students at the 75th percentile have an LSAT score of 156 and a GPA of 3.5.

Legal methods course requirement	Yes
Legal research course requirement	Yes
Moot court requirement	No
Public interest law requirement	No

ADMISSIONS

Selectivity Rating	**72**
# applications received	2,360
% applicants accepted	45
% acceptees attending	38
Average LSAT	153
LSAT Range	150–156
Average undergrad GPA	3.27
Application fee	$55
Regular application	2/15
Regular notification	5/25
Early application program	No
Transfer students accepted	Yes
Evening division offered	Yes
Part-time accepted	Yes
LSDAS accepted	Yes

Applicants Also Look At
University of Texas at Austin, University of Houston, Texas Tech University, St. Mary's University, Texas Wesleyan University

FINANCIAL FACTS

Annual tuition	$24,390
Books and supplies	$2,000
Fees	$600
Room & board (off-campus)	$9,500
Financial aid application deadline	5/1
% first-year students receiving some sort of aid	85
% receiving some sort of aid	86
% of aid that is merit based	3
% receiving scholarships	49
Average grant	$4,125
Average loan	$28,536
Average total aid package	$29,673
Average debt	$85,859

EMPLOYMENT INFORMATION

Career Rating	**80**	**Grads Employed by Field (%)**
Rate of placement (nine months out)	85	Academic (1)
Average starting salary	$80,000	Business/Industry (23)
State for bar exam	TX	Government (10)
Pass rate for first-time bar	90.4	Judicial Clerkships (2)
Employers Who Frequently Hire Grads		Private Practice (61)
Large to mid-sized law firms, corporations, and state and federal government entities.		Public Interest (2)
		Other (1)

SOUTHERN ILLINOIS UNIVERSITY
SCHOOL OF LAW

INSTITUTIONAL INFORMATION

Public/private	Public
Student-faculty ratio	12:1
% faculty part-time	21
% faculty female	40
% faculty minority	9
Total faculty	42

SURVEY SAYS...
Great research resources
Great library staff

STUDENTS

Enrollment of law school	361
% male/female	63/37
% out-of-state	25
% full-time	100
% minority	9
Average age of entering class	25

ACADEMICS

Academic Experience Rating	**74**
Profs interesting rating	78
Profs accessible rating	89
Hours of study per day	4.48

Academic Specialties
Health Law

Advanced Degrees Offered
JD, 3 years; MLS, two years; LLM, two years

Combined Degrees Offered
JD/MD, 6 years; JD/MBA, 4 years; JD/MPA, 4 years; JD/M.Acc., 4 years; JD/MSW varies; JD/M.S.Ed., varies; JD/PhD, varies

Clinical program required	No
Legal writing course requirement	Yes
Legal methods course requirement	Yes
Legal research course requirement	Yes
Moot court requirement	No
Public interest law requirement	No

Academics

Southern Illinois University's School of Law serves up a legal education that's "excellent for the price." A 3L says, "Because SIU is very inexpensive and has many grants and scholarships, I have been able to study abroad, and my debt after law school will still be way under the average [for] law school grads. Freedom from debt allows me to pick my field of practice after law school instead of being forced into doing something I don't want to do because of student loans." Low cost doesn't equal inferior legal training; SIU places a "strong emphasis on becoming a lawyer with both academic and practical skills," granting its students a well-rounded apprenticeship in the profession. "I think one of the school's greatest strengths is that it offers a lot of real world experience," avers an attorney-to-be. "We have an excellent clinic program as well as an externship program. We also have a 'writing across the curriculum' requirement for each class, so students really have a lot of opportunities to practice their writing skills and get feedback."

Students across the board give their professors high marks. A 1L interested in labor laws explains, "The professors doors are always open. They are always willing to discuss legal theory or current events. Numerous professors have gone out of their way to give advice which has been particularly beneficial to shaping my career aspirations and goals." A similarly chuffed student continues, "Many of them aren't simply professors, they're teachers—some of the best I've ever had. Most of them have had real world experiences which they share in order to better prepare you for the bar and for practice." Even more, these dedicated professors are so accessible that they "often sit in the lunch area and discuss topics of interest to the students." A first-year promises, "You need only show a modicum of enthusiasm and aptitude in order to have lots of people willing to mentor you and foster your skills."

Due in part to its small size, the law school "has a familial feel." Students rave about the school's "warm and friendly atmosphere," which "encourages cooperation and friendship." However, there is a downside to studying law in such a quaint setting, including "limited classrooms" and "many classes that conflict with either required courses or courses that are strongly recommended for passing the bar exam." Additionally, there's "a general lack of support for students wishing to take a nontraditional approach to legal education. The model of three years of law school, graduate, pass the bar, and practice law is rigidly held onto by the administration."

By and large, the school's facilities receive high marks. "Each seat in the classrooms has its own outlet which is very helpful since 99 percent of students here use laptops." In addition, "The library provides ample private study areas and there are two student lounges." One resource that's lacking, however, is the Office of Career Services. "There are not enough summer clerkship opportunities for law students," perhaps due to the school's relative lack of reputation as compared to other law schools. "Many people don't even know we exist!" exclaims one student.

Life

Life at the SIU School of Law begins with "orientation and study group programs" that give students "an opportunity to socialize and meet new people." Typically, everyone gets along with ease. A 2L tells us, "I'd be lying if I said we weren't competitive with each other, but that often takes a back seat to helping each other survive law school." In general, "The student body is very young. Most students came right out of undergrad, or took one year off, two at most." This youthful presence, combined with the small size of

Akami Marik, Director of Admissions & Financial Aid
SIU School of Law Welcome Center, 1209 W. Chautauqua, Mailcode 6811,
Carbondale, IL 62901
Tel: 618-453-8858 Fax: 618-453-8921
Email: lawadmit@siu.edu • Website: www.law.siu.edu

the school, sometimes makes SIU feel "like a high school." A 2L warns, "If you go here, don't expect to have a private life. People will usually find out everything about you."

The school is located in Carbondale, a city of 26,000 that's tucked among the hills of Illinois's southern corridor. The "beautiful wooded campus" and "the campus lake" allow students to enjoy the restorative powers of nature "on a tough day" without exiting SIU's gates. "If you like small-town living, this is a great place to be," says a first-year. "If you want big-city living, what the heck are you doing in Carbondale?" Nonetheless, a student promises that "Carbondale offers a wide variety of social opportunities. Whether it is the nightlife, wineries, or outdoor recreation, there is always something to take your mind off the books." One such distraction is local watering hole where, "on any given Thursday through Saturday night, one can go and find many law students (including those who do not drink)." On university grounds, "There are a lot of student organizations" that "do some cool things like visit immigration detention centers, philanthropic projects, etc."

Getting In

In recent years, approximately one in every three applicants was accepted to the SIU School of Law. Admitted candidates have an average undergrad GPA of 3.26 and a median LSAT score of 154. While these numbers are important, SIU also pays close attention to the "Admissions Committee memorandum" (personal statement). This is an opportunity for candidates to distinguish themselves as multidimensional individuals. Edit well.

ADMISSIONS

Selectivity Rating	75
# applications received	802
# applicants accepted	316
# acceptees attending	111
Average LSAT	154
LSAT Range	151–156
Average undergrad GPA	3.26
Application fee	$50
Regular application	Rolling, up to 3/1
Regular notification	Rolling
Early application program	No
Transfer students accepted	Yes
Evening division offered	No
Part-time accepted	No
LSDAS accepted	Yes

Applicants Also Look At
Northern Illinois University

International Students

TOEFL required of international students	Yes
Minimum TOEFL (paper)	600

FINANCIAL FACTS

Annual tuition (in-state/ out-of-state)	$10,206/$28,500
Books and supplies	$1,150
Fees	$2,832
Room & board	$9,650
Financial aid application deadline	4/1
% of aid that is merit based	0
Average grant	$6,206
Average loan	$16,875
Average total aid package	$20,469
Average debt	$55,486

EMPLOYMENT INFORMATION

Career Rating	71	**Grads Employed by Field (%)**
Rate of placement (nine months out)	81	Business/Industry (9)
Average starting salary	$53,703	Government (20)
State for bar exam	IL	Judicial clerkships (1)
Pass rate for first-time bar	95	Private practice (61)

Employers Who Frequently Hire Grads
Private practice (61)
Public Interest (9)

Various Illinois State's Attorney's Offices, Various large and many small law firms, various public interest organizations

Prominent Alumni
William Enyart, State Adjutant General, IL Dept. of Military Affai; Tim Eaton, Partner, Shefsky & Froelich, Ltd., Hon. Sue Myerscough, Appellate Judge, 4th District Appellate Court, IL

SOUTHERN METHODIST UNIVERSITY
DEDMAN SCHOOL OF LAW

INSTITUTIONAL INFORMATION

Public/private	Private
Affiliation	Methodist
Student-faculty ratio	15:1
% faculty part-time	22
% faculty female	38
Total faculty	50

SURVEY SAYS...
Beautiful campus
Students love Dallas, TX
Good social life

STUDENTS

% male/female	49/51
% full-time	57
% minority	20
# of countries represented	17
Average age of entering class	23

ACADEMICS

Academic Experience Rating	**72**
Profs interesting rating	62
Profs accessible rating	61
Hours of study per day	3.83

Advanced Degrees Offered
LL.M (Taxation), 1 year; LL.M
(General), 1 year; LL.M. (for Foreign
Law School Graduates), 1 year;
S.JD

Combined Degrees Offered
JD/MBA, 4 years; JD/MA
(Economics), 4 years

Clinical program required	No
Legal writing course requirement	Yes
Legal methods course requirement	No
Legal research course requirement	Yes
Moot court requirement	Yes
Public interest law requirement	Yes

Academics

Students say the Dedman School of Law at Southern Methodist University has "a great reputation in Texas" and gives out "an incredible amount of scholarship money." (Roughly 50 percent of each class receives scholarship assistance.) "Diverse course offerings" in "everything from the philosophical to the tediously practical" define the curriculum here, and "The legal clinics are absolutely amazing." Externships and scholarly journals are abundant. Students say there are plenty of opportunities to get involved: "We have consistently won national moot court and mock trial competitions over the past two years and the school has a great Trial Advocacy program co-taught by practitioners and judges." A unique JD/MA program allows students to study economics as well as law, and students have the opportunity to study abroad in Oxford each summer. Academic complaints often revolve around the legal writing program, which "needs a massive overhaul" and "while informational, [can] feel more like fifth grade English in the way [it is] approached."

The "very distinguished" yet "easily approachable" professors "are very receptive to students and concerned with [their] learning" and "make an effort to be available." They are "demanding of their students," but "interesting and entertaining in the classroom." "There are a few who are quite reminiscent of *The Paper Chase* and make you stand to answer questions in class even if it is for the entire class period." Professors "make the classroom experience fun," gushes one student. "My civil procedure exam was one of the funniest things I have ever read, with witty undercurrents and subtle political satire." Opinions of the administration vary considerably. Some students say the deans seem "distant at times, but whenever you need them, they're available and helpful." Others tell us that the administration "does not care about the students" and gripe about "bureaucratic inefficiencies."

Job prospects are very promising for SMU grads. Career Services is "actually concerned with helping you find a job." "Dallas is a wonderful market that pays salaries on par with New York, but the quality of life is so much better," according to students here. "If you want to stay and practice in Dallas, you could not go to a better school." SMU's "exceptionally strong relationship with the Dallas legal market" provides an "extensive network of attorneys" "in every field imaginable." "The alums are very supportive and willing to help out." "A lot of doors are opened by attending the SMU Dedman School of Law, regardless of your class rank." "I was able to secure a six-figure job without being on law review or moot court," says a 3L. "There is definitely a huge hurdle" for students to face who do not want to practice in Texas, though.

The "gorgeous" campus is full of "very pretty, collegiate-looking brick buildings" and "nestled in one of the nicest, most affluent neighborhoods in the Dallas area." "The law school itself is further cloistered away from the rest of the university and, once inside, it is easy to forget you are sitting in the middle of a bustling metropolis." "Large oak trees provide shady walkways and outdoor study places are ample." "I always joke that our tuition goes straight toward landscaping," says a witty 3L. The majority of classrooms are "very comfortable and accommodating," and the "nearly flawless" wireless signal is "strong in every corner of the law school." The library is "amazing," "both with regard to holdings and ease of use."

Virginia Keehan, Assistant Dean and Director of Admissions
P.O. Box 750110, Dallas, TX 75275-0110
Tel: 214-768-2550 Fax: 214-768-2549
Email: lawadmit@smu.edu • Website: www.law.smu.edu

Life

"Most of the students are Texas natives," and "Overall, the people are young, fun, attractive, and smart." Some students are "cooperative, collegial, and very supportive of one another." Others are "very competitive." "There are a lot of married students, though not necessarily a lot older." SMU has its fair share of "obnoxious frat boys and catty, cliquey sorority girls." "There are definitely a few trust fund kids, but a lot of us are living off student loans as well," says one student. "The parking garage does boast an unusual concentration of BMWs and Hummers," agrees a 2L. "But as a non-Texan who shares a beat-up Honda with my wife, I've never felt out of place." "Political views run the gamut, but the large majority of students are tolerant of opposing views." SMU is also "remarkably GLBT-friendly."

Regarding social events on campus, students say "There's a club for everyone, whether you're a gun-toting Second Amendment crusader or a die-hard liberal." "The students put together a lot of fun activities," ranging from happy hours to baseball games to tailgating events. "The highlight of everyone's week is Bar Review where the Student Bar Association gets drink specials at a different local bar every Friday." There's also "a picnic/sports spectacular every semester." SMU's ritzy location is "great" in terms of safety but "can make finding student housing right next to school virtually impossible." Beyond the neighborhood surrounding campus, "Big D" is one of the liveliest cities in the South and "a fun place to live." "You get a great all-around legal education and have the resources of the Dallas-Fort Worth Metroplex right at your doorstep."

Getting In

At SMU, admitted students at the 25th percentile have LSAT scores in the range of about 157 and GPAs in the range of 3.3. Admitted students at the 75th percentile have LSAT scores of about 165 and GPAs approaching 3.8.

ADMISSIONS

Selectivity Rating	96
# applications received	2,571
# applicants accepted	622
# acceptees attending	258
Median LSAT	164
LSAT Range	157–165
Median undergrad GPA	3.78
Application fee	$75
Regular application	Rolling, up to 4/1
Regular notification	Rolling
Early application program	Yes
Early application deadline	12/1
Early application notification	1/31
Transfer students accepted	Yes
Evening division offered	Yes
Part-time accepted	Yes
LSDAS accepted	Yes

Applicants Also Look At
University of Texas at Austin, University of Houston, Baylor University

International Students

TOEFL required of international students	No
TOEFL recommended of international students	No

FINANCIAL FACTS

Annual tuition	$32,806
Books and supplies	$1,800
Fees	$3,960
Fees per credit	$140
Tuition per credit	$1,263
Financial aid application deadline	6/1
% of aid that is merit based	100
Average grant	$15,000
Average loan	$28,508

EMPLOYMENT INFORMATION

		Grads Employed by Field (%)
Career Rating	86	Academic (2)
Rate of placement (nine months out)	98	Business/Industry (23)
Average starting salary	$102,264	Government (5)
State for bar exam	TX	Judicial Clerkships (2)
Pass rate for first-time bar	94	Military (1)
Prominent Alumni		Private Practice (66)
Michael Boone, Founding partner, Haynes		Public Interest (1)
& Boone; Bill Hutchison, President,		
Hutchison Oil & Gas; Angela Braly, CEO,		
WellPoint; Edward B. Rust Jr., Chairman &		
CEO, State Farm Insurance; David B.		
Dillon, CEO and Chairman, The Kroger		
Company.		

SOUTHERN UNIVERSITY
LAW CENTER

INSTITUTIONAL INFORMATION

Public/private	Public
Student-faculty ratio	14:1
% faculty part-time	4
% faculty female	37
% faculty minority	61
Total faculty	41

SURVEY SAYS...

Diverse opinions accepted
in classrooms
Great research resources
Great library staff
Good social life

STUDENTS

Enrollment of law school	480
% male/female	45/55
% out-of-state	15
% full-time	82
% minority	60
# of countries represented	3
Average age of entering class	27

ACADEMICS

Academic Experience Rating	**61**
Profs interesting rating	62
Profs accessible rating	61
Hours of study per day	4.55

Academic Specialties

Civil procedure, commercial law,
criminal law, environmental law,
government services, taxation, intellectual property law

Combined Degrees Offered

JD/MPA, 4 Years

Clinical program required	No
Legal writing	
course requirement	Yes
Legal methods	
course requirement	No
Legal research	
course requirement	Yes
Moot court requirement	No
Public interest	
law requirement	No

Academics

With roughly 500 full-time and part-time students, Southern University Law Center is "small and personable." "I don't feel like just another number at my school," says a 1L. "You feel that the people around you want you to be successful." SULC is also "ridicu-lously affordable." "While others will be coming out of law school hundred of thousands of dollars in debt, Southern grads will have debt that is approximately one fifth of the cost." Additional perks here include a decently broad selection of courses and six clinics that provide hands-on experience with the realities of practicing law for a very good per-centage of students. If you want to pursue both a JD and MPA, the school offers a joint-degree program in cooperation with Southern's Nelson Mandela School of Public Policy and Urban Affairs. There's also a study-abroad program in London, in which students take courses in international law.

Louisiana is a civil law jurisdiction (in the tradition of France and Continental Europe), while law in every other state is based on the common law tradition (of England). While SULC students learn both, the required curriculum focuses on civil law both substan-tively and procedurally. If you plan to practice in the Pelican State, Southern is a great choice. The "wealth of alums" doesn't hurt when it comes to finding a job, either. However, if you want to practice in another state, learning Louisiana's unique system of law and trying to apply it to another state's bar exam won't be the easiest thing in the world.

"Some profs can be very intimidating," but the full-time faculty is full of "sincere, chal-lenging, intelligent people" who are "downright awesome." The faculty is notoriously approachable as well. Most professors are "always willing to help." "I have a great amount of respect for 90 percent of my professors," explains a 2L. "I feel that all of them have been knowledgeable in the subject matter." The "generally excellent" part-time program tends to have more adjunct professors. They're more of a mixed bag. "Some of the evening pro-fessors are practicing attorneys during the day and are not as accessible, or as devoted as the full-time day professors." Students offer considerable praise for the "very profession-al" administration. Deans are "approachable and available," and they "work diligently in their efforts to help the students succeed" and to "know who their students are." Some stu-dents tell us that the financial aid process can be a "nightmare," though. The legal writing program is another complaint. Students say that it "could use a lot of improvement." SULC's "somewhat new facilities" are "very poorly maintained." Otherwise, they are "really good" and "very hospitable." Classrooms have wireless Internet and plenty of elec-trical outlets. The library is "stocked with great resource materials."

Life

"This school is probably the most diverse school in the country in terms of the student body," gushes a 2L. SULC is a historically black institution, and some 60 percent of the students are African-American. Students come here "from all over the country," and they "have very interesting backgrounds." The range of ages is vast as well.

VELMA E. WILKERSON, COORDINATOR OF ADMISSION
A.A. LENOIR HALL, P.O. BOX 9294, 2 ROOSEVELT STEPTOE STREET, BATON ROUGE, LA 70813
TEL: 225-771-4976 FAX: 225-771-2121
EMAIL: ADMISSION@SULC.EDU • WEBSITE: WWW.SULC.EDU

"Southern charm is alive and well at SULC." A "kind and friendly" "family atmosphere" reigns supreme, and "a strong sense of camaraderie and support is evident in every aspect." "Some people are competitive," says a 1L, "but I don't get that extremely competitive vibe from Southern." "It's a smaller law school," explains a 2L, "which allows students to work more cooperatively, instead of against each other as at most law schools." Most everyone "goes out of their way to help." The biggest social divide is probably between the day program, which is generally composed of younger students, and the evening program, which is "mostly older professionals."

During the school day, "the school regularly has speakers and attorneys come in during the noon hour to give practical advice on the practice of law." Students are split when it comes to life beyond the confines of campus. Some tell us that Baton Rouge—the state capital and the second largest city in Louisiana—is a student's Shangri-la, especially if you like music and food. Baton Rouge is home to unique art and culture, tons of festivals, and mouthwatering cuisine of every kind. When students take a break from hitting the books, a good number of bars and clubs and a raging live music scene keep life interesting. Other students aren't feeling the cultural love, though. "The main chances for socialization seem to be at a bar or a church," suggests a 2L. "What if you don't drink or believe?"

Getting In

Admitted students at the 25th percentile have LSAT scores around 143 and GPAs in the 2.6 range. Admitted students at the 75th percentile have LSAT scores of 149 or so and GPAs of around 3.2.

ADMISSIONS

Selectivity Rating	**68**
# applications received	994
% applicants accepted	31
% acceptees attending	58
Average LSAT	147
LSAT Range	144–151
Average undergrad GPA	2.84
Application fee	$25
Regular application	2/28
Regular notification	Rolling
Early application program	Yes
Early application notification	6/1
Transfer students accepted	Yes
Evening division offered	Yes
Part-time accepted	Yes
LSDAS accepted	Yes

Applicants Also Look At
Louisiana State University, Loyola University—New Orleans, Texas Southern University, Thomas M. Cooley Law School

International Students
TOEFL recommended of international students	Yes

FINANCIAL FACTS

Annual tuition (in-state/ out-of-state)	$6,676/$11,276
Books and supplies	$5,581
Tuition per credit (in-state/ out-of-state)	$5,494/$10,094
Room & board	$8,727
Financial aid application deadline	4/15
% first-year students receiving some sort of aid	86
% of aid that is merit based	20
% receiving scholarships	20
Average grant	$7,000
Average total aid package	$18,500

EMPLOYMENT INFORMATION

Career Rating	**60***	
State for bar exam	LA, FL, GA, IL, TX	
Pass rate for first-time bar	61	

Grads Employed by Field (%)
Academic (1)
Business/Industry (5)
Government (15)
Judicial Clerkships (6)
Private Practice (37)
Public Interest (7)
Other (29)

SOUTHWESTERN LAW SCHOOL

INSTITUTIONAL INFORMATION

Public/private	Private
Student-faculty ratio	14:1
% faculty part-time	36
% faculty female	38
% faculty minority	19
Total faculty	96

SURVEY SAYS...

Diverse opinions accepted
in classrooms
Great research resources
Great library staff
Beautiful campus

STUDENTS

Enrollment of law school	1,011
% male/female	50/50
% out-of-state	15
% full-time	69
% minority	35
# of countries represented	10
Average age of entering class	26

ACADEMICS

Academic Experience Rating	**74**
Profs interesting rating	67
Profs accessible rating	75
Hours of study per day	3.67

Academic Specialties

Civil procedure, commercial law, constitutional law, corporation securities, criminal law, environmental law, government services, human rights, international law, labor law, legal history, legal philosophy, property, taxation, intellectual property law, entertainment & media law

Advanced Degrees Offered

LLM, Entertainment and Media Law; LLM, Individual Studies

Combined Degrees Offered

JD/M.B.A; JD/M.A.M. (Master of Arts in Management); JD/M.A. in Conflict Resolution, Negotiation and Peacebuilding.

Clinical program required	No
Legal writing course requirement	Yes

Academics

A "hidden gem" located in Los Angeles within easy commuting distance to the downtown district, Hollywood, and the Valley, Southwestern Law School is known for its flexibility and progressiveness. In addition to the traditional day and evening programs, the school offers a unique SCALE program, which gives students the ability to obtain a JD within two years, and the PLEAS program, a part-time day program that helps nontraditional students juggle the demands of work, family, and school, making for "an awesome way to get a great education and have a life too." The school recently saw a rise in the average GPA of entering students, which reflects its increasingly competitive applicant pool. With the increased local recognition comes "a better chance at competing for jobs with other local law schools," which students here appreciate.

SW's "eclectic" professors "don't just give lip service to an open-door policy, they encourage it," and they "seem to genuinely enjoy interaction with students." With an average of 7 years of law practice experience, many professors place an "emphasis on real-world experience" inside the classroom. As one student explains, "The feelings of most SW students go from being completely overwhelmed upon entry (that's probably the same for all 1Ls), to feeling slightly inferior to other law schools in the area, then to the realization that you will have all the tools necessary to be a successful attorney when you leave and that earning a JD at SW is actually a fun and rewarding experience." Professor accessibility is "fantastic," as one appreciative student can attest: "One professor has gone out of his way to get me three internships in an area of law that is tough to get into." Though the school's program in entertainment law receives rave reviews, many think it would be great "if a wider array of courses were taught—especially in the business area."

The historic restored Bullocks Wilshire building is "particularly gorgeous," "enormous," and situated on a "very clean and comfortable campus." Students cite Southwestern's "beautiful" library as one of the school's greatest strengths, and the research librarians are "very helpful." After just four years in office, the well-received Dean "is leading the school in all the right directions." The "administration has really come alive and is totally committed to helping students to make the best of their experience at Southwestern." The externship program at Southwestern is lauded by students, even if they tend to feel that their hard work is "underappreciated in the job force"; many here often feel that they live in the shadow of other local area law schools. Students also bemoan a lack of "alumni support" and help from the Career Services Office. "After my first year, I had an internship with a bunch of students from USC and UCLA and I was able to rattle all kinds of law off the top of my head while they all had to look it up. But I'm sure they all got a job and I couldn't," complains one critic. On the whole, though, students are satisfied with what they take away from their Southwestern experience. "Southwestern may not be perfect now, but it's definitely moving in an upward direction," says a third-year student. "It's a great time to be at Southwestern."

LISA GEAR, DIRECTOR OF ADMISSIONS
3050 WILSHIRE BOULEVARD, LOS ANGELES, CA 90010-1106
TEL: 213-738-6717 FAX: 213-383-1688
EMAIL: ADMISSIONS@SWLAW.EDU • WEBSITE: WWW.SWLAW.EDU

Life

Because SW is a stand-alone law school, it "definitely has a small-school feel and a good sense of community." Students say this is an admirable trait for a school located in such a large and spread-out city, and they appreciate "the way the main promenade is open to the local community," which "helps to integrate the school within the surrounding neighborhoods." The school itself offers a wide variety of organizations and events for students to take part in, and many of these activities garner enthusiastic participation from students; why wouldn't they, when "Everyone gets along with everyone else." One first-year student says, "The environment is light hearted when it calls for it, and serious when it calls for it." While there is a "competitive edge" to students, for the most part "Everyone is very friendly and supportive of each other." "To my surprise, I have made so many new friends. Being from LA, I wouldn't have thought that I'd be interested in making new friends, because I already have a social network, but the people [at Southwestern] are great," says a 1L.

Getting In

Recently admitted students at the 25th percentile had an average LSAT score of 153 and GPA of 3.1. Students admitted at the 75th percentile had an average LSAT score of 158 and GPA of 3.6. Though undergrad GPA and LSAT scores count, Southwestern pays more attention to undergraduate activities and work experience than a lot of other institutions. The school looks at the difficulty level of the student's undergraduate course of study, as well as extracurricular activities and leadership examples. Up to three letters of recommendation may be submitted by the student; we recommend utilizing all of these.

Legal methods course requirement	Yes
Legal research course requirement	Yes
Moot court requirement	Yes
Public interest law requirement	No

ADMISSIONS

Selectivity Rating	**78**
# applications received	3,545
# applicants accepted	1,082
# acceptees attending	358
Average LSAT	155
LSAT Range	153–157
Average undergrad GPA	3.28
Application fee	$60
Regular application	Rolling, up to 6/30
Regular notification	Rolling
Early application program	No
Transfer students accepted	Yes
Evening division offered	Yes
Part-time accepted	Yes
LSDAS accepted	Yes

Applicants Also Look At

University of Southern California; University of California—Los Angeles; Chapman University; Loyola Marymount University; Pepperdine University; University of San Diego; University of California—Hastings

FINANCIAL FACTS

Annual tuition	$35,070
Books and supplies	$1,250
Fees	$200
Fees per credit	$200
Tuition per credit	$1,169
Room & board (off-campus)	$14,220
Financial aid application deadline	6/1
% receiving some sort of aid	90
Average grant	$11,000
Average loan	$22,800
Average debt	$105,000

EMPLOYMENT INFORMATION

Career Rating	**80**
Rate of placement (nine months out)	94
Average starting salary	$80,000
State for bar exam	CA, NY, NV, OR, AZ
Pass rate for first-time bar	73

Employers Who Frequently Hire Grads

Gibson, Dunn & Crutcher; Lewis Brisbois Bisgaard & Smith; O'Melveny & Meyers; Sedgwick, Detert, Moran & Arnold; Waller, Lansden; Bonne, Bridges.

Prominent Alumni

Tom Bradley, LA Mayor for 20 years; Stanley Mosk, Longest serving Cal. Sup. Ct. Justice; Hon. Vaino Spencer, 1st African American woman judge in Calif. & 3rd in the U.S.

Grads Employed by Field (%)

Academic (2)
Business/Industry (23)
Government (10)
Judicial Clerkships (2)
Military (1)
Private Practice (53)
Public Interest (4)
Other (5)

ST. JOHN'S UNIVERSITY
SCHOOL OF LAW

Academics

Students at St. John's University School of Law brag that their school has "a tremendous reputation for producing excellent attorneys." The bar passage rate is usually significantly higher than the Empire State's overall rate and the JD program here affords students "the opportunity to gain hands-on, practical experience" in a wealth of different practice areas. The "numerous" and "excellent" clinical and externship opportunities are too exhaustive to list but highlights include an immigration rights clinic, a securities arbitration clinic, and an international human rights externship. St. John's is also "a great place for trial lawyers." "Our trial advocacy programs are incredibly beneficial because they provide students with practical lawyering experiences outside of the classroom and allow us to improve on our advocacy skills," attests a 2L. Some students call the legal writing program here "second to none" as well. However, others assert that it is "not very constructive." Also, night students complain that there are "too few evening courses."

Some students tell us that the administration at St. John's is "helpful and accommodating." They emphasize that the deans "treat students with respect." Other students contend that management "is not particularly responsive to student needs." According to critics, the top brass "avoids students in the halls." The "dedicated and highly accomplished faculty" is full of "a fascinating bunch of people." Access isn't a problem. Professors are "approachable" and "always willing to meet with students, oftentimes staying long past office hours to go over old exams before the final." In the classroom, though, not every faculty member is stellar. The good profs are "brilliant" and "full of corny law humor." "Their passion for their field of law really comes through in the classroom." The bad ones simply "do not know how to teach." "Professors range from quality intellectuals who will challenge every person in class to just plain boring individuals who don't know how to keep their students' attention," sums up a 1L.

"St. John's is stuck in the middle in terms of prestige" in New York City's competitive legal job market and some students gripe that Career Services does very little to help students with average GPAs. Most students seem optimistic about their employment prospects, though. "This is a wonderful place to be if you want to practice in New York," promises a 3L. A considerable number of big Manhattan firms participate in on-campus interviews and the "excellent alumni network" is reportedly a notable strength. "St. John's grads really watch out for each other," notes a 2L. Also, alumni are "ubiquitous" at school events so "contacts are easy to come by."

The facilities here aren't terrifically popular. "The building design is weird." In theory, "the entire school is wireless," but service can be spotty. "The classrooms are very modern," but they sometimes get "very hot." The library is comfortable, clean, and well-lit," says a 1L. "Even during finals, there is plenty of space to work." However, it's "much too loud." Students also complain that the "the bathrooms are disgusting."

ROBERT M. HARRISON, ASSISTANT DEAN FOR ADMISSIONS
8000 UTOPIA PARKWAY, QUEENS, NY 11439
TEL: 718-990-6474 FAX: 718-990-2526
EMAIL: LAWINFO@STJOHNS.EDU • WEBSITE: WWW.LAW.STJOHNS.EDU

Life

Ethnic diversity is fabulous at St. John's and students describe themselves as "smart, engaged, motivated, ambitious," and hardworking. "The students all have an inferiority complex despite the fact that everyone here is extremely intelligent and very capable," explains a 2L. "As a result, the students all work hard and, surprisingly, work well together." Some students suggest that the academic environment here is "fairly laid-back." "My fellow classmates are friendly and we try to help each other," says a 1L. "If you miss a class, everyone is willing to share their notes," adds a 2L. "The students at St. John's want each other to succeed." Other students point out that "everything is on a strict curve" and tell us that the atmosphere is "actually very competitive." "There is a lot of tension and secrecy when grades come out," they say.

St. John's is located in "a pretty typical, quiet," and "basically suburban" neighborhood in the nether reaches of Queens. The parking situation is reportedly "atrocious." Otherwise, "there is a variety of clubs and activities for everyone to find their niche." The SBA "hosts some fantastic events" and "there are a few options for bars within a short walking distance." Otherwise, there is "not much of a social setting." "We are mostly commuters so there is little to no social life and school spirit," laments a 3L. However, students admit that that they really have little to complain about socially. "Go up to the atrium on the fourth floor; open your eyes; and look west to the city lights," suggests a 2L. Indeed, the hurly-burly of Manhattan isn't far at all.

Getting In

Admitted students at the 25th percentile have LSAT scores somewhere in the mid to high 150s and GPAs around 3.1. Admitted students at the 75th percentile have LSAT scores in the low 160s and GPAs of roughly 3.6.

ADMISSIONS

Selectivity Rating	82
# applications received	3,886
% applicants accepted	38
% acceptees attending	20
Average LSAT	160
LSAT Range	156–162
Average undergrad GPA	3.6
Application fee	$60
Regular application	Rolling
Regular notification	Rolling
Early application program	No
Transfer students accepted	Yes
Evening division offered	Yes
Part-time accepted	Yes
LSDAS accepted	Yes

International Students

TOEFL recommended	
of international students	Yes
Minimum TOEFL	
(paper/computer)	600/250

FINANCIAL FACTS

Annual tuition	$38,400
Books and supplies	$1,000
Tuition per credit	$1,375
Room & board	$13,670
Financial aid application	
deadline	2/1
% first-year students	
receiving some sort of aid	86
% receiving some sort of aid	85
% of aid that is merit based	22
% receiving scholarships	44
Average grant	$19,548
Average loan	$37,414
Average total aid package	$50,235
Average debt	$96,640

EMPLOYMENT INFORMATION

Career Rating	87	Grads Employed by Field (%)
Rate of placement (nine months out)	96	Academic (3)
Average starting salary	$96,110	Business/Industry (15)
State for bar exam	NY	Government (17)
Pass rate for first-time bar	92	Judicial Clerkships (4)
Employers Who Frequently Hire Grads		Private Practice (58)
Many private law firms, corporations, governmental agencies and judges hire St. John's graduates.		Public Interest (3)

ST. MARY'S UNIVERSITY
SCHOOL OF LAW

INSTITUTIONAL INFORMATION

Public/private	Private
Affiliation	Roman Catholic
Student-faculty ratio	22:1
% faculty part-time	43
% faculty female	31
% faculty minority	13
Total faculty	78

SURVEY SAYS...

Diverse opinions accepted
in classrooms
Great research resources
Great library staff

STUDENTS

Enrollment of law school	742
% male/female	56/44
% out-of-state	10
% full-time	84
% minority	35
Average age of entering class	26

ACADEMICS

Academic Experience Rating	**61**
Profs interesting rating	62
Profs accessible rating	73
Hours of study per day	4.18

Academic Specialties

constitutional law, criminal law, human rights, international lawAdvocacy

Advanced Degrees Offered

LLM in International and Comparative Law for U.S. educated graduates. LLM in American Legal Studies for foreign educated graduates. (Each 1 year)

Combined Degrees Offered

JD/MA Accounting; JD/MA International Relations; JD/MPA Public Administration; JD/MA English Language and Literature; JD/MA Theology; JD/MS Computer Science; JD/MS Industrial Engineering; JD/MBA Business Administration; JD/MA Communication Studies (all 3.5–4 years total)

Academics

Despite an obviously smaller pool of resources than many larger schools, the School of Law at St. Mary's University is doing its best to reach up into the leagues of schools like UT. The overall academic experience is gaining in the race, but a tough curve makes it "challenging and competitive" for students, and the reputation of St. Mary's has yet to have reached outside of the region. Still, there is a strong sense of community, and the law school "won't allow your professor or fellow students to devour you alive in the classroom. Generally, if you prepare, you will succeed." The school takes care of its students, and the past few years have shown a positive trend in bar passage rates, as well as a balance between the clinical and community involvement strengths that make St. Mary's a respected institution in San Antonio and the public sector. The St. Mary's Civil Justice Clinic, which is part of the School of Law, is an excellent way to gain experience in myriad fields of different civil law subjects. In addition, "You are able to help many grateful members of the San Antonio community while earning course credit along the way!" The largest entering class to date (around 300 students) just matriculated, and yet "it doesn't feel like there are that many students. It really feels like a big family everyday at school."

The small school atmosphere really lends itself to the close relationship between students and faculty, and professors "are always willing to meet with students and love to share their insight and love of their particular subject matter." Teaching-wise, some professors here are "fabulous"; others are not. Adjuncts and some of the older, tenured professors seem to be particularly hit-or-miss, but "a motivated student who picks the best professors can still get a good basic legal education." Legal writing and moot court are strong points of the school (right down to the top-notch mock courtroom), but students would like to see a wider course selection (such as computer law, white collar law things). Though most students find the administration to be supportive on the whole, and are excited about the new dean (a former torts professor), there are widespread complaints that the arcane methods of completing some of the more bureaucratic tasks can cause problems in the long run. "Everything works great until you run into a problem—say, a lost grade or incorrectly recorded grade. When faced with those problems, it seems like the school is all over the place," testifies a student. Many wish there was more energy channeled into helping students find employment outside of San Antonio, but "if you want to practice in San Antonio or the surrounding area, the alumni network practically owns the SA Bar Association, and boy do they love to give current students work." The library here is "second to none" and the new classroom building is much loved by students, but the law faculty building where some classes are held is "horribly out of date," and the school's infrastructure needs vast improvements.

Ms. Carolyn Meegan, Director of Recruitment
One Camino Santa Maria, San Antonio, TX 78228-8601
Tel: 866-639-5831 Fax: 210-431-4202
Email: lawadmissions@stmarytx.edu • Website: law.stmarytx.edu

Life

As the neighborhood of the school isn't so hot (and not necessarily so safe), many of the students live in a common area that is a fair distance from campus. However, the campus itself is nicely landscaped, and students love San Antonio, nicknamed "Military City USA." "If the 'Wizard of Oz' was filmed today, Dorothy would be saying 'There's no place like... South Texas.'," says a 3L. There is little political strife, and "most people are very laid back and live and let live." Student organizations are very active, and the school is constantly looking for ways to get students involved with their classmates. Everyone is very friendly, and hence, "the social life is well-developed and very inclusive." "I have found it to be a very rare occasion that I don't get along with someone at my school," says a student. Like many small schools, cliques develop, and there are comparisons drawn to high school. Although the grading is competitive, students "don't feel pressured to resort to ethically questionable practices to succeed," and most are willing to share notes and outlines.

Getting In

Falling well below the mean LSAT score (154) or GPA (3.11) doesn't necessarily result in rejection at St. Mary's. The committee carefully considers intangibles, such as maturity derived from previous career experience, the ability to overcome challenges, and cultural competence. They are looking for rigorous undergraduate course work and an inclination toward public service. It is best to get applications in soon after the Admissions Office starts accepting them in November.

Clinical program required	No
Legal writing course requirement	Yes
Legal methods course requirement	Yes
Legal research course requirement	Yes
Moot court requirement	Yes
Public interest law requirement	No

ADMISSIONS

Selectivity Rating	**70**
# applications received	1,754
% applicants accepted	51
% acceptees attending	36
Average LSAT	153
LSAT Range	149–155
Average undergrad GPA	3.11
Application fee	$55
Regular application	Rolling, up to 3/1
Regular notification	Rolling
Early application program	No
Transfer students accepted	Yes
Evening division offered	Yes
Part-time accepted	Yes
LSDAS accepted	Yes

Applicants Also Look At
University of Texas at Austin, University of Houston, Texas Tech University, Baylor University, Southern Methodist University, Texas Wesleyan University, South Texas College of Law

International Students

TOEFL recommended of international students	Yes

FINANCIAL FACTS

Annual tuition	$26,350
Books and supplies	$1,300
Fees	$500
Tuition per credit	$850
Room & board (on/off-campus)	$7,730/$7,230
Financial aid application deadline	3/31
% first-year students receiving some sort of aid	85
% receiving some sort of aid	85
% of aid that is merit based	6
% receiving scholarships	28
Average grant	$4,270
Average loan	$29,303
Average total aid package	$32,047
Average debt	$91,841

EMPLOYMENT INFORMATION

Career Rating	**72**
Rate of placement (nine months out)	95
Average starting salary	$65,431
State for bar exam	TX, FL, MO, OK, NM
Pass rate for first-time bar	80

Employers Who Frequently Hire Grads
Bexar County District Attorney's Office; Fourth Court of Appeals; Cox Smith Matthew LLP.

Prominent Alumni
John Cornyn, U.S. Senator from Texas; Charles Gonzalez, Congressman; Alma L. Lopez, Former Chief Justice of the Texas Court of Appeals.

Grads Employed by Field (%)
Academic (2)
Business/Industry (16)
Government (12)
Judicial Clerkships (5)
Military (2)
Private Practice (57)
Public Interest (2)
Other (4)

St. Thomas University
School of Law

Academics

Relatively small, relatively new, and markedly Catholic, St. Thomas University School of Law offers "small class sizes" and a consistent emphasis on ethics. "The practical experience is really good here." "A wide range" of opportunities to gain lawyering skills includes "very good" clinical programs for criminal and immigration law. "There are plenty of externship opportunities in both Miami-Dade and Broward counties" as well. A 40-hour pro-bono work requirement "provides a wide array of opportunities" to work in a variety of nonprofit offices, government agencies, and law firms. The tax law program is well respected. Joint-degree programs are available in—among other things—sports administration and accounting. There's a "cool Summer in Spain program" too. Without question, the biggest academic complaint among students here involves the bar-passage rate, which annually hovers below the state average.

"At St. Thomas, the professors make you work hard, and most students coming out of the school have a good work ethic as a result," says one student. The "extremely dynamic" faculty includes "many judges and prominent lawyers" from the area. Professors are "easily accessible" and "willing to spend as many hours on a subject that the student is willing to invest." "Their willingness to help students pass the bar and become successful, ethical attorneys is at its maximum," beams a 2L. Professors are "very experienced and very involved in the local community." There are some bad apples, though, who "shouldn't teach at a high school." "I had some professors who I felt were the best I'd ever had and others who didn't teach me anything," relates a 3L.

Student reviews of their administrators are decidedly mixed. Some students call the administration "helpful and caring" and tell us that the top brass is "genuinely striving to improve the overall experience at the school." Others counter that the administration is "unresponsive to students' issues" and "the pinnacle of bureaucratic inefficiency." "I have yet to see a final-exam day where the campus isn't pure pandemonium," says one student. "It seems, in all fairness, that many of the problems are associated with the parent university," notes a 1L. Nevertheless, Financial Aid is generally regarded as a mess and "Registering for classes is a disaster."

The facilities at St. Thomas are "nice, especially compared to other law schools around the Miami area." "Study areas abound" on the "very nice and open" campus, though students caution that it's "not in the best neighborhood." "Classrooms are great because of the wireless Internet. However, the air conditioning works too well. The classrooms are like igloos." Research resources are "quite extensive for such a small school, and there is an abundance of access to online resources through the library website." The library itself isn't much, though. "We need a bigger library," says a 2L.

Life

The student population "reflects the multicultural canvas of contemporary American society." "The international distinction of Miami as a gateway to all of the Americas results in professors and students that embody true diversity." "People from every part of the country" and all manner of every religions and ethnicities are studying law here. Politically, students describe a very good mix of liberals, conservatives, and everyone in between. There is a huge population of Hispanic students, and "a lot" of foreign students as well. Students are mostly single. "Miami is a great area to go to law school if you're straight out of undergrad, but it is not the most fun if you're over 25, have kids, or are married." Most students "are focused on making it through school, enjoying Miami while they're here, and then going back to wherever they're from to settle down."

"The breezeway of the law school is the social hub" at STU—"a year-round outdoor gathering place that engenders social interaction on the way to and from classes." From early morning until late at night, people can be found sitting at the tables surrounded by their books and laptops or with their study groups, or sometimes just chatting with whoever happens to walk by. The Student Bar Association "sponsors many happy hours and picnics that a majority of students attend." Of course, "Miami is Miami." There is "great weather for most of the year" and finding something to do instead of reading case law is way too easy. Many students take "full advantage of South Beach on a nightly basis yet, surprisingly, still [find] time to study."

The social atmosphere at St. Thomas is "highly supportive." "Students are very friendly and cooperative with each other." "There is little or no cutthroat competitiveness." "Students get to know each other really quickly and are there right away to help each other out." While "Everybody knows everyone else," "There are a lot of cliques," but "You are able to develop great friendships while you study." "You learn; you compete; but you make friends," sums up a 3L. "At the end of the road, having some kind of social life, being able to make friends, and being happy overall is even more important than a law degree."

Getting In

At St. Thomas, admitted students at the 25th percentile have LSAT scores in the range of 148 and GPAs of about 2.6. Admitted students at the 75th percentile have LSAT scores of about 152 and GPAs of about 3.3. If you take the LSAT more than once, St. Thomas will average your scores.

Clinical program required	Yes
Legal writing course requirement	Yes
Legal methods course requirement	Yes
Legal research course requirement	Yes
Moot court requirement	Yes
Public interest law requirement	Yes

ADMISSIONS

Selectivity Rating	**65**
# applications received	2,628
% applicants accepted	40
% acceptees attending	22
Average LSAT	149
LSAT Range	147–151
Average undergrad GPA	3.08
Application fee	$60
Regular application	Rolling, up to 6/1
Regular notification	Rolling
Early application program	No
Transfer students accepted	Yes
Evening division offered	No
Part-time accepted	No
LSDAS accepted	Yes

Applicants Also Look At

Nova Southeastern University, University of Miami, New England Law|Boston, Florida Costal School of Law

International Students

TOEFL recommended of international students	Yes
Minimum TOEFL (paper/computer)	550/213

FINANCIAL FACTS

Annual tuition	$25,340
Books and supplies	$1,000
Fees	$1,240
Room & board (on/off-campus)	$10,341/$10,575
Financial aid application deadline	4/1
% first-year students receiving some sort of aid	95
% receiving some sort of aid	98
% of aid that is merit based	30
% receiving scholarships	39
Average grant	$14,000
Average loan	$20,500
Average total aid package	$31,250
Average debt	$82,000

EMPLOYMENT INFORMATION

Career Rating	**66**
Rate of placement (nine months out)	71
Average starting salary	$54,292
State for bar exam	FL, NY, GA, CA
Pass rate for first-time bar	73

Employers Who Frequently Hire Grads

Private law firms of all sizes; government agencies, including the U.S. Department of Justice, the Florida State Attorney's Office, Prosecutors and Public Defender's Offices.

Prominent Alumni

Brett Barfield, Partner, Holland & Knight; Mark Romance, Partner, Richman Greer; Representative J.C. Planas, Florida House of Representatives.

Grads Employed by Field (%)

Academic (2)
Business/Industry (15)
Government (17)
Judicial Clerkships (3)
Private Practice (53)
Public Interest (10)

STANFORD UNIVERSITY
SCHOOL OF LAW

INSTITUTIONAL INFORMATION

Public/private	Private
Student-faculty ratio	9:1
% faculty female	31
% faculty minority	18
Total faculty	49

SURVEY SAYS...
Great research resources
Great library staff
Abundant externship/internship/
clerkship opportunities

STUDENTS

Enrollment of law school	539
% male/female	53/47
% full-time	100
% minority	35
Average age of entering class	25

ACADEMICS

Academic Experience Rating	**99**
Profs interesting rating	98
Profs accessible rating	96
Hours of study per day	4.24

Academic Specialties
Civil procedure, commercial law, constitutional law, corporation securities, criminal law, environmental law, government services, human rights, international law, labor law, legal history, legal philosophy, property, taxation, intellectual property law, We offer courses on the above topics, but no specializations/concentrations

Advanced Degrees Offered
M.L.S. 1 year; J.S.M. 1 year; LLM 1 year; J.S.D. 4 years.

Combined Degrees Offered
JD/MBA 4 years; JD/MA 4 years; JD/PhD 7 years.

Clinical program required	No
Legal writing course requirement	Yes
Legal methods course requirement	No

Academics

Students are emphatic that Stanford Law School "delivers on its claim of being a law school in paradise." "The facilities are top-notch" (even if they do look a bit "like corrugated cardboard"). Classrooms are "posh." The "newly redone" library is "luxurious." "You could sit in the chairs all day and, in fact, some people do." "The academic experience at SLS is wonderful." For some students, it "could not possibly be better." "Resources are deep, especially because the class is so small." The small class size "leads to countless opportunities to participate" in and out of the classroom. "There is a lot of freedom to chart your own academic course after your first semester." ("It's like a liberal arts college, only it's a law school," submits one student.) SLS has poured tons of resources into its clinical and public interest programs in the past five years. "Stanford now offers many courses geared towards public interest–minded individuals and the Public Interest Center offers much help in job placement." The "fast-expanding" clinical program provides "very practical and very profound pro-bono experience" and allows students to "work closely" and "on a daily basis" with "top lawyers in the country." "Academically, classes are often exceptionally interesting." Students can "learn about securities from a former SEC chair, [or] learn about Supreme Court opinions from the people who argued them."

The "first-rate" faculty is "less intellectually diverse" than some students would like, but there's no doubt that professors are "at the top of their fields." The "highly attentive" and "incredibly accessible" professors at Stanford "truly care about teaching" and are "desperate for student collaboration." "Whether you take them up on it is another thing, but they are there and willing to help," says another 1L. "Some are kind of quirky, but I have yet to meet a professor who isn't completely available to students." Stanford's administration "really cares about each and every one of its students" and the deans seek student input "on virtually everything." The administration often "proceeds at a California pace," though. "Everything always gets done, but not always as quickly as you might like."

"Jobs are very easy to get" for Stanford graduates. "You come here; you get a great job." "Grades are more important in relation to clerkships and public interest fellowships." "You can work really hard and achieve great things" or "You can coast through and have a great time while still getting the job you want upon graduation." Pickings are so sweet that one student told us, "You can fall out of bed and land a job for $145,000 if you want one." Career Services is "very helpful and proactive." There's a focus on jobs in California and large cities on the East Coast (particularly New York City), but "That may simply be because 90 percent of students here want to work in one of those two places, so the Career Services people are just filling demand." While "People who graduate from Stanford don't generally make less than $100,000 dollars a year unless they choose to," "The staff in public interest law is amazingly accessible and helpful" for students who do choose to pursue public interest careers. "SLS also boasts one of the most generous loan repayment programs in the country."

Life

Students at Stanford Law are "remarkably and uniformly intelligent" and "very supportive of one another." They are "intensely hardworking and super-motivated, but they're by no means outwardly competitive." "The place is full of closet studiers, the kind who say, 'Oh, man, I haven't even looked at that,' even though you saw them in the library until midnight the night before," reports a 3L. Politically, "All of the people in power at the school are exceptionally liberal," but "It's no problem to be a conservative."

"Stanford is tiny." Social life here "is designed for the 22-to-25 set" and resembles undergraduate social life in many ways. "We sometimes have a fraternity-like culture," observes one student. "It's easy to feel excluded from the social scene" "for someone who's older," or "already has a partner and a life outside of school." "There is some drama and gossip." "It can get a bit incestuous at times," but "People are generally very social and friendly." "Everyone knows everyone else" and the intimate atmosphere "allows everyone the opportunity to do something cool, like run an organization, edit a journal, conduct independent research, or start a club."

"The weather is most definitely a plus." "The campus is gorgeous" and "huge and full of life." There is "hiking, biking, running, golf, and pickup soccer" year-round. "From yoga to horseback riding to bike clubs and ski clubs, athletic activities for low or no cost abound." "Sunny Palo Alto" is "a cultural vacuum" and "a crowded suburban hell" for some students, but "The Bay Area is really amazing" and "There is plenty to do in the surrounding area and in San Francisco." "Gorgeous destinations within a few hours' drive" include Tahoe, Napa, and Half Moon Bay. "Plan on bringing a car or else spending a lot of time bumming rides or waiting for the bus," though, because "You can't walk anywhere."

Getting In

Fewer than 10 percent of all applicants to SLS are admitted. The 25th percentile of admitted students has LSAT scores of 166 and GPAs in the 3.7 range. Admitted students at the 75th percentile have LSAT scores of 171 and GPAs approaching 4.0.

Legal research course requirement	Yes
Moot court requirement	Yes
Public interest law requirement	No

ADMISSIONS

Selectivity Rating	**99**
# applications received	3,943
# applicants accepted	364
# acceptees attending	170
Average LSAT	170
LSAT Range	168–172
Average undergrad GPA	3.81
Application fee	$75
Regular application	Rolling, up to 2/1
Regular notification	Rolling
Early application program	No
Transfer students accepted	Yes
Evening division offered	No
Part-time accepted	No
LSDAS accepted	Yes

FINANCIAL FACTS

Annual tuition	$40,880
Books and supplies	$1,770
Fees	$1,200
Room & board (on/off-campus)	$17,100/$18,720
Financial aid application deadline	3/15
% first-year students receiving some sort of aid	88
% receiving some sort of aid	81
% of aid that is merit based	0
% receiving scholarships	52
Average grant	$20,725
Average loan	$34,603
Average debt	$97,552

EMPLOYMENT INFORMATION

Career Rating	**98**
Rate of placement (nine months out)	99
State for bar exam	CA, NY
Pass rate for first-time bar	97.5

Prominent Alumni

Sandra Day O'Connor, First female Supreme Court Justice (1981 to 2006); Warren Christopher, Former Secretary of State (1993 to 1997); Josh Bolten, Former White House Chief of Staff (2006 to 2009); Max Baucus, U.S. Senator (1979 to Present); Jeff Bingaman, U.S. Senator (1983 to Present).

Grads Employed by Field (%)

Academic (2)
Business/Industry (9)
Government (5)
Judicial Clerkships (24)
Private Practice (56)
Public Interest (4)

STATE UNIVERSITY OF NEW YORK—UNIVERSITY AT BUFFALO
LAW SCHOOL

INSTITUTIONAL INFORMATION

Public/private	Public
Student-faculty ratio	15:1
% faculty part-time	54
% faculty female	43.6
% faculty minority	10
Total faculty	110

SURVEY SAYS...

Diverse opinions accepted
in classrooms
Great research resources
Great library staff
Abundant externship/internship/
clerkship opportunities

STUDENTS

Enrollment of law school	737
% male/female	54/46
% out-of-state	9
% full-time	98
% minority	15
% international	5
# of countries represented	13
Average age of entering class	25

ACADEMICS

Academic Experience Rating	77
Profs interesting rating	76
Profs accessible rating	63

Academic Specialties

corporation securities, criminal law, environmental law, human rights, international law, labor law, intellectual property law, Affordable Housing and Community Development Law, Civil Litigation, Family Law, Finance Transactions, Health Law

Advanced Degrees Offered

LL.M. in Criminal Law, 1 year; LL.M General, 1 year.

Combined Degrees Offered

JD/MSW; JD/MBA; JD/MPH; JD/MLS; JD/MA Appplied Economics; JD/MA; JD/Ph.D.; JD/MUP; JD/Pharm.D.

Clinical program required	No
Legal writing course requirement	Yes

Academics

Offering an "outstanding range of resources, excellent faculty, and top-notch research facilities," "you get more than what you pay for" at the University at Buffalo Law School. What's more, you don't pay much, as this public law program is one of the most affordable options in New York State. Educationally, Buffalo emphasizes a comprehensive approach to the study of law, and academics take place in "a well-balanced environment that promotes learning real-world lawyering and legal theory." Throughout the curriculum, you'll have access to "some of the top scholars in their field" and, in the classroom, "creative legal thinking is highly encouraged." The JD kicks off with a full course load in traditional legal subjects like contracts, torts, and civil procedure. In the second year, students may begin taking elective courses, while further tailoring their academic experience through extracurricular activities and research centers. Buffalo emphasizes "civic engagement and becoming a lawyer through experiences outside of the classroom." In fact, "there is a clinic or concentration offered for almost every area of law." Drawing on the city's legal talent to augment the academic staff, "most of the local practitioners and judges who teach at the school are outstanding."

Perhaps University at Buffalo's most distinctive characteristic is its incredibly supportive, non-competitive, and "family oriented" atmosphere. "At UB, you feel like you are part of the law school team," one student says. "Professors are respectful, and value student insight. Their doors are always open." Mutual respect is clearly an effective approach, as Buffalo professors "expect the best from their students, and you feel compelled to rise to their expectations." At the same time, professors "want you to succeed and will do everything in their power to assist you in doing that." If you need a little extra instruction outside the lecture hall, professors "are always available to meet with you, and are willing to meet at 10:30 at night or even on weekends." Between students, the atmosphere is likewise collegial, as "the school steers away from creating the usual competitive, cutthroat environment amongst law students, fostering a more cooperative and supportive relationship amongst the students." A case in point, listen to this third-year student's noteworthy anecdote: "I commute over an hour to school and have to contend with the weather. Once, when I missed class because of snow, I came to class the next day to find three different outlines from that class sitting on my chair."

Currently, the lack of modern classroom facilities might be one area where Buffalo is sorely deficient, and students lament the hours spent in "unsightly lecture halls with hideous brick patterned walls." Future students, however, will have things much better as "the classrooms are currently being refurbished." Fortunately, even today, the library is excellent, and "the school is completely wireless and offers teachers the ability to teach using a broad range of technology."

After graduation, job prospects look good for Buffalo's well-trained young lawyers. In particular, many appreciate the low-stress decision-making they enjoy thanks to minimal educational debt. A first year student shares, "I'm not sure exactly what type of legal job I'll be looking for, but with the low cost of tuition and minimal loans, I'll have the option to take a job that I'm passionate about—not just the one that pays the most." However, those who'd like to practice outside the immediate region feel "the career services office needs to reach out to more private firms in areas other than Buffalo, New York City, and Washington, D.C."

LILLIE V. WILEY-UPSHAW, VICE DEAN FOR ADMISSIONS AND FINANCIAL AID
309 O'BRIAN HALL, BUFFALO, NY 14260
TEL: 716-645-2907 FAX: 716-645-6676
EMAIL: LAW-ADMISSIONS@BUFFALO.EDU • WEBSITE: WWW.LAW.BUFFALO.EDU

Life

The school's stimulating academic atmosphere is augmented by its gifted student body, which encompasses "lots of diversity in age, ethnicity, gender and background in general." Despite differences, everyone gets along fabulously, and "no GPAs and no curves make for an awesome, laidback environment where students not only tolerate and help each other out, but also become best friends." The camaraderie easily spills out of the classroom. "The social life at UB is tops," one student explains. "There is always something to do, and the 1Ls, particularly in each section, are very close." You don't have to wait until Friday to have some fun, as "most Thursday nights during the semester, one group or another sponsors a bar night, and many of the students attend with relative regularity to socialize."

While the classrooms need a little TLC, the university grounds, facilities, and resources are excellent, boasting "at least three libraries, easily more than 20 places to eat (both dining services and chains), any number of different student services (including free massages at the Wellness Center), a CVS, and a speaker on most any topic at some point every week." Students warn us, however, that unless you were born and raised in upstate New York, "you've never experienced weather like this! An average winter day is 20 degrees with a 30 mph wind."

Getting In

UB enrolls about 250 new students each year, evaluating applicants based on both qualitative and quantitative factors. In particular, the Admissions Committee seeks students whose academic backgrounds suggest a high probability for scholastic achievement in law school, who have demonstrated excellence in work or community activities, or who display potential for substantial contribution to the law after graduation.

Legal methods course requirement	No
Legal research course requirement	Yes
Moot court requirement	No
Public interest law requirement	No

ADMISSIONS

Selectivity Rating	81
# applications received	2,304
% applicants accepted	31
% acceptees attending	31
Average LSAT	157
LSAT Range	154–160
Average undergrad GPA	3.48
Application fee	$50
Regular application	Rolling, up to 3/1
Regular notification	Rolling
Early application program	No
Transfer students accepted	Yes
Evening division offered	No
Part-time accepted	No
LSDAS accepted	Yes

Applicants Also Look At

Syracuse University, The Catholic University of America, Case Western Reserve University, Hofstra University, Albany Law School of Union University, Brooklyn Law School, New York Law School,

International Students

TOEFL required of international students	Yes
Minimum TOEFL (paper/computer/web)	650/280/114

FINANCIAL FACTS

Annual tuition (in-state/ out-of-state)	$14,135/$22,130
Books and supplies	$1,627
Fees	$1,485
Fees per credit	$60
Tuition per credit (in-state/out-of-state)	$628/$1,011
Room & board	$10,980
Financial aid application deadline	3/1
% first-year students receiving some sort of aid	95
% receiving some sort of aid	90
% of aid that is merit based	52
% receiving scholarships	61
Average grant	$1,837
Average loan	$20,500
Average total aid package	$21,550
Average debt	$55,771

EMPLOYMENT INFORMATION

Career Rating	**78**
Rate of placement (nine months out)	99
Average starting salary	$69,042
State for bar exam	NY, NJ, MA, FL, TX
Pass rate for first-time bar	85

Employers Who Frequently Hire Grads
Ropes & Gray; Hodgson Russ; Phillips Lytle; NYS Court of Appeals; NYS App. Div. 4th Dept.; Dewey LeBoeuf; DLA Piper; Nixon Peabody; New York County District Attorney; Kings County District Attorney.

Prominent Alumni
Hon. Julio Fuentes, U.S. Court of Appeal for the 3rd Circuit; Julia Hall, Sr. Counsel, Human Rights Watch; Nicole Lee, Executive Director, TransAfrica.

Grads Employed by Field (%)
Academic (2)
Business/Industry (11)
Government (11)
Judicial clerkships (6)
Military (2)
Other (5)
Private practice (52)
Public Interest (11)

SUFFOLK UNIVERSITY
LAW SCHOOL

INSTITUTIONAL INFORMATION

Public/private	Private
Student-faculty ratio	17:1
% faculty part-time	45
% faculty female	32
% faculty minority	11
Total faculty	132

SURVEY SAYS...

Great research resources
Beautiful campus
Students love Boston, MA

STUDENTS

Enrollment of law school	1,657
% male/female	50/50
% out-of-state	43
% full-time	62
% minority	17
% international	2
# of countries represented	30
Average age of entering class	25

ACADEMICS

Academic Experience Rating	81
Profs interesting rating	80
Profs accessible rating	70
Hours of study per day	4.45

Academic Specialties

International law, intellectual property law, health and biomedical law; business law and financial services, civil litigation

Advanced Degrees Offered

JD, 3 years full-time, 4 years part-time. LLM in Global Technology, 1 year, full-time, 3 years, part-time. LLM in U.S. Law for International Business Lawyers, completed in 3 years of study in Budapest, Hungary.

Combined Degrees Offered

Economics, JD/MS in Finance, JD/MS in Criminal Justice. Each program can be completed in 4 years of full-time study or 5 years of part-time study.

Clinical program required	No

Academics

The Suffolk University Law School "provides a wonderful mix of strong academics and opportunities for the practical application of law." Academics are enhanced by the "new, beautiful law school," which some call "the envy of all others in the Boston area." The school touts the "state-of-the-art technology" in its new building, but some students claim that "this is over-hyped," especially the wireless Internet system, which one student said "cuts out constantly." That said, other facets of the technologies upgrade are working quite well. "The library is also totally wired, and the print volumes are more than you will ever need."

Suffolk also affords its future lawyers access to professors that "are amazing. All of them are accessible and quirky, on top of being incredibly challenging." A second-year tells us, "Whether students want to be in public interest," take classes "in Suffolk's excellent IP program," study to "be tax attorneys," or work "in corporate law," Suffolk "has the professors and talent to guide students and prepare them for lives in the law." The faculty typically takes "a more practical approach rather than a theoretical focus in the classroom, which enables students to become more engaged in discussion and debate." This practical emphasis has given way to the nine clinical experience programs for which Suffolk students are eligible. "I am currently in the Juvenile Justice Clinic, and my law school experience would not have been the same without it," says a 2L. "I am in court as a student attorney at least once a week and handle all of my own cases and clients. My experiences in the clinic have also given me an advantage in the job market."

The fiercely proud students at Suffolk are adamant that the law school deserves a stronger national reputation, even declaring that "the academics are comparable to" cross-town rival Harvard, but "without the fierce competition." One of the reasons its name is not so widely known, they suggest, is that the "Career Development Office needs a kickstart—especially for those students seeking work "outside of the Boston area." It should be noted, though, that among the school's "greatest strengths" is its "alumni network." A first-year says, "Over 22,000 strong, Suffolk alums are always willing to give both personal and professional advice to students, frequently offering to put in a good word on the behalf of students or make introductions to important networking contacts." Students also benefit from on-campus "speakers such as George H. W. Bush and Justice Ginsburg. . . There are plenty of school- and student-sponsored events to keep you in the know."

Students note that the school's evening program lends significant weight to SULS's regional acclaim. One participant tells us, "As evening students, we have more of the adjunct faculty. They are all practitioners in the field and have practical and up-to-date information. The student body in the evening school is very diverse and brings a great deal of variety in viewpoints and life experience." "Overall, the school provides a quality, cohesive learning environment within the heart of one of nation's greatest cities," says a law student. A classmate adds, "After you get over the initial shock of the price and the ridiculous underrating that the school seems to have, you realize that the faculty, administration, and student body cannot be beat."

Life

In a way, the tenor of life at Suffolk comes down to circumstance. A 1L explains, "Some first-year sections are very friendly and social outside of the classroom, and others are not." The same can be said inside the classroom. While "Most people seem to understand

GAIL ELLIS, DEAN OF ADMISSIONS
120 TREMONT STREET, BOSTON, MA 02108-4977
TEL: 617-573-8144 FAX: 617-523-1367
EMAIL: LAWADM@SUFFOLK.EDU • WEBSITE: WWW.LAW.SUFFOLK.EDU

the concept of 'we're not just classmates, but future colleagues' and want the respect of their peers," the typical stories about "ultra-competitive" law school students sometimes do play out at Suffolk. As one SULS first-year relays: "Everybody is quite competitive, but not in a way that is destructive to the community."

At Suffolk, "The students tend to be quite active in a plethora of activities and clubs, as well as competitions and Law Reviews and journals." Also, the SBA—or Student Bar Association—"is very active and responsive to the large student body." But Suffolk's law students don't always think about studying the law. "People want to party a lot," nods a student. Others like to shop, exercise, or just wander around Beantown. Students across the board agree that the location is "a boon" because SULS "is close to everything. Suffolk is right across from beautiful Boston Common, mere hundreds of yards away from the State House, and near several bars for after-class unwinding." "Midday shopping, errands, and part-time jobs in the heart of the city are even made possible by the great location."

Getting In

Suffolk's Admissions Committee seeks candidates who are poised to contribute to the life of the campus community as well as to the future of the legal profession. Prospective students can demonstrate their potential in these areas by getting involved in community service, extracurricular undergraduate organizations, and pre-professional societies. The 2008 incoming class scored a median 157 on the LSAT and boasted a 3.3 median undergraduate GPA.

Legal writing	
course requirement	Yes
Legal methods	
course requirement	Yes
Legal research	
course requirement	Yes
Moot court requirement	Yes
Public interest	
law requirement	No

ADMISSIONS

Selectivity Rating	**77**
# applications received	2,666
% applicants accepted	47
% acceptees attending	26
Average LSAT	157
LSAT Range	155–159
Average undergrad GPA	3.3
Application fee	$60
Regular application	Rolling, up to 3/1
Regular notification	Rolling
Early application program	No
Transfer students accepted	Yes
Evening division offered	Yes
Part-time accepted	Yes
LSDAS accepted	Yes

Applicants Also Look At

Boston University, Northeastern University, Boston College, New England Law|Boston, New York Law School

International Students

TOEFL required	
of international students	Yes
TOEFL recommended	
of international students	Yes
Minimum TOEFL	
(paper/computer/web)	600/250/100

FINANCIAL FACTS

Annual tuition	$39,550
Books and supplies	$900
Fees	$120
Tuition per credit	$1,325
Room & board	
(off-campus)	$18,264
Financial aid application	
deadline	3/1
% first-year students	
receiving some sort of aid	84
% receiving some sort of aid	84
% of aid that is merit based	45
% receiving scholarships	39
Average grant	$12,148
Average loan	$35,528
Average total aid package	$39,864
Average debt	$102,150

EMPLOYMENT INFORMATION

Career Rating	**75**
Rate of placement (nine months out)	88
Average starting salary	$76,633
State for bar exam	MA, NY, FL
Pass rate for first-time bar	94

Employers Who Frequently Hire Grads

Suffolk alumni practice in numerous large, medium and small law firms in Boston. Many practice in the Public Sector, work in all levels of Government Service, and serve on the Judiciary.

Prominent Alumni

John Joseph Moakley, U.S. Congressman; James Bamford, Author; Kristen Kuliga, Principal, K Sports and Entertainment; Patrick Lynch, Rhode Island Attorney General.

Grads Employed by Field (%)

Academic (3)
Business/Industry (28)
Government (13)
Judicial Clerkships (12)
Military (1)
Private Practice (39)
Public Interest (3)
Other (1)

Syracuse University

College of Law

Academics

Syracuse University's name holds plenty of weight in the world of academia, and the law school comes up relatively close behind. Everyone at the College of Law is encouraged to be well-rounded, and students can tell that a conscious effort is being made to make sure that equal emphasis and support is given to each area of student involvement. The administration tries very hard to listen to the students through its annual survey, and Office of Student Life which opens communication between the students, faculty, staff, and administration. As at most schools given the economic climate, getting a job is "a big worry" at SUCOL, and following massive complaints, the school recently overhauled its Office of Professional and Career Development, whose focus is on engaging students, employers and alumni. The bar passage rate isn't so hot here, possibly because many students "focus too much on dual degree programs," so it would be beneficial if the law school had more required and bar-focused classes. There are lots of opportunities to join law journals, participate in moot court and trial competitions, and students have the ability to specialize in a variety of fields through seven clinical programs, multiple certificate programs, several specialized institutes connected with the school, joint degree opportunities with most of the other graduate schools at Syracuse University, a vast array of student organizations, and opportunities to do externships. The Legal Writing program at SU is also excellent, and "the professors in the department go out of their way to help students and make the material interesting, even if it takes jokes and top ten lists." The best thing about the Legal Writing classes? They end a few weeks before finals "so students have time to focus solely on studying for their other classes."

The school's academic reputation shines through in the professors, who are as geographically diverse as the students. Most have written books or articles on their area of expertise, and "others are quoted regularly." They "all have a unique way of bringing their life and practice experiences into the classroom to teach more than just the black letter law," adding excitement to their courses through realistic hypotheticals and issues they've confronted in the past. "Learning here at SUCOL definitely goes beyond the textbook. Knowing the rule of law isn't good enough—it's how those rules apply in the field, and that's what our professors strive towards," says a student. Teachers are also interested in extending that application toward their students as people, as well, and "take time out of their evenings to sit down with a group of students just to discuss life outside of law school." Most professors use the Socratic Method, so "it is a good idea to be prepared for every class." There are space issues at the SUCOL building; double booking of classrooms isn't unheard of, students are clamoring for more study areas, and the library could use some serious updating.

NIKKI S. LAUBENSTEIN, DIRECTOR OF ADMISSIONS
OFFICE OF ADMISSIONS; SUITE 340, SYEARACUSE, NY 13244
TEL: 315-443-1962 FAX: 315-443-9568
EMAIL: ADMISSIONS@LAW.SYR.EDU • WEBSITE: WWW.LAW.SYR.EDU

Life

The law students are frequently isolated from the many activities going on throughout the rest of the campus, but within the College of Law, they're very close, and "there is very little division amongst the classes." Most students here believe that having a social life is important, and often gather on weekends and after exam periods in a social context. There "is a student organization for everyone to join," organized social events every Friday night, and during the fall, over half of the student body plays in the "intense" law school flag football league (those who don't play watch). While the population is by no means homogenous (there are a fair number of international students), "there is opportunity in terms of cultural diversity." Amongst the student body, there is "a higher degree of competitiveness to get those few good jobs that are available," but nothing too cut-throat; on the whole, there's a "close sense of community," and people are "generous and helpful to others" and "push each other in class to make appropriate and intelligent comments." Though Syracuse itself isn't the prettiest of cities, and the building for the school itself "is no architectural wonder," the cost of living is cheap, and central New York is "a beautiful area for outdoor enthusiasts, including hikers, runners, bikers, skiers, and nature photographers."

Getting In

In addition to the numbers that go into your admissions index, the Admissions Committee closely analyzes a student's undergraduate transcript, considering difficulty of the course of study, caliber of the school attended, and course selection. Academic letters of recommendation are weighed heavily. Syracuse may also consider other subjective information about you, like graduate study or work experience, as well as commitment to the study of law. A B-plus undergraduate average and a LSAT score in the mid-150s makes you competitive at Syracuse.

Legal methods	
course requirement	Yes
Legal research	
course requirement	Yes
Moot court requirement	No
Public interest	
law requirement	No

ADMISSIONS

Selectivity Rating	**60***
# applications received	1,842
Average LSAT	154
LSAT Range	152–156
Average undergrad GPA	3.26
Application fee	$70
Regular application	Rolling, up to 4/1
Regular notification	Rolling
Early application program	No
Transfer students accepted	Yes
Evening division offered	No
Part-time accepted	No
LSDAS accepted	Yes

Applicants Also Look At
American University, SUNY at Buffalo, Hofstra University, University of Miami, Pace University, Rutgers University—Newark, Suffolk University, St. John's University, Albany Law School, New York Law, Villanova University, University of the Pacific

International Students
TOEFL required	
of international students	Yes
Minimum TOEFL	
(paper/computer/web)	600/250/100

FINANCIAL FACTS

Annual tuition	$43,000
Books and supplies	$1,270
Fees	$722
Fees per credit	$188
Tuition per credit	$1,888
Room & board	$11,270
Financial aid application deadline	2/15
% first-year students receiving some sort of aid	73
% receiving some sort of aid	88
% of aid that is merit based	60
% receiving scholarships	25
Average grant	$10,105
Average loan	$40,120
Average total aid package	$47,682
Average debt	$47,566

EMPLOYMENT INFORMATION

Career Rating	**73**
Rate of placement (nine months out)	92
Average starting salary	$75,000
State for bar exam	NY, NJ, CA, PA, CT
Pass rate for first-time bar	82

Employers Who Frequently Hire Grads
Medium sized law firms, Federal and State Government

Prominent Alumni
Joseph R. Biden, Jr., Vice President of the United States; Theodore A. McKee, Federal Appeals Court Judge; David Gordon, Managing Partner, Latham & Watkins; Melanie Gray, Ptr & Lit Co-Chair, Weil, Gotshal & Manges LLP.

Grads Employed by Field (%)
Academic (1)
Business/Industry (24)
Government (10)
Judicial Clerkships (9)
Military (4)
Private Practice (46)
Public Interest (6)

TEMPLE UNIVERSITY

JAMES E. BEASLEY SCHOOL OF LAW

INSTITUTIONAL INFORMATION

Public/private	Public
Student-faculty ratio	13:1
% faculty female	46
% faculty minority	26
Total faculty	70

SURVEY SAYS...

Diverse opinions accepted in classrooms
Great research resources
Great library staff
Liberal students

STUDENTS

Enrollment of law school	974
% male/female	52/48
% out-of-state	38
% full-time	79
% minority	21
# of countries represented	9
Average age of entering class	25

ACADEMICS

Academic Experience Rating	**85**
Profs interesting rating	88
Profs accessible rating	84
Hours of study per day	4.33

Academic Specialties

Commercial law, constitutional law, corporation securities, criminal law, environmental law, government services, human rights, international law, taxation, intellectual property law, trial advocacy, public interest

Advanced Degrees Offered

JD; LLM in Trial Advocacy; LLM in Taxation; LLM in Transnational Law; Graduate Teaching Fellowships; LLM for Graduates of Foreign law schools; S.J.D

Combined Degrees Offered

JD/MBA, (3–4 years); JD/LLM degree programs in Taxation and Transnational Law, (3.5 years); JD/Individually designed joint degrees

Clinical program required	No

Academics

Students here tell us that Temple University's James E. Beasley School of Law offers "the best value in a legal education, hands down." "It really is such a deal," affirms a 3L. Temple's "very approachable" professors are "passionate about their fields" and "genuinely interested in the success of their students." "Professors are not brutal with their use of the Socratic Method," says one student. "Every professor I've had has been unbelievably supportive." The adjunct faculty is "quite uneven" though. Though students once noted the stiff grading system. "Temple used to curve to a lower grade,". due to a recent review of the grading policy, effective spring 2009, the faculty voted to raise the suggested mean grade in all exam classes and the first year Legal Research and Writing classes from 2.85 to 3.05. Temple's administration "does what it needs to" and sometimes even provides "awesome support." "Temple Law is a big school and, like any big school, there is opportunity if you seek it out," explains a 3L.

"Temple really emphasizes the practical skills required for legal work" and has a "strong reputation for producing litigators." The focus here is manifestly on "real-world law." The "year-long" trial advocacy program is "beyond amazing." "If you want to learn how to try a case—and win—you'll fit right in at Temple," guarantees a 3L. "You'll learn from some of the top prosecutors and trial lawyers in the country." Students also think the legal writing program "is the best in the nation" and appreciate that it "stresses the fundamentals and really teaches you what you need for success as a junior associate."

One of the law-school buildings here "is a great example of fortress-like architecture that gripped inner-city universities during the 1960s and 1970s." That said, Temple's interiors are "completely renovated." Also, "The other building, Barrack Hall, is one of the original buildings of the university and is gorgeous." Classrooms here are "all equipped with top-of-the-line technology," including wireless Internet that "is accessible everywhere." The library has a "helpful and knowledgeable" staff and contains "many nooks and crannies to hide out and study." Its major flaw is that it is "open to other floors and professors' offices, which sounds good in theory but is loud in fact."

The Career Planning Office is "excellent and extremely helpful." "Temple is deeply entrenched in the Philadelphia legal community, and that is invaluable" for students seeking "internships, externships, and jobs after graduation." "If you want to practice law in Philadelphia, Temple is the best choice," advises a 3L. "It's Temple grads who dominate the Philadelphia legal community." "Career opportunities are great" throughout other "Mid-Atlantic" states as well. A few students say that Temple "needs to do a better job of getting firms to interview on campus from areas outside the Delaware Valley."

Life

"There are students of all ages, walks of life, races, ethnicities, religions, etc.," reports a student. There is also a great deal of "diversity of student experiences prior to law school." Another student explains, "The students at Temple come from all different economic, professional, and ethnic backgrounds, which makes for great conversation and debate in class." Ultimately, "Nothing contributes more to the quality of the education than the diverse points of view provided by classmates."

Though the school prides itself on providing opportunities to day and evening students, some students note, "Day students have more time for community and studying. Evening students rely more on real experience to inform their studying, making up

Johanne L. Johnston, Assistant Dean for Admissions & Financial Aid
1719 North Broad Street, Philadelphia, PA 19122
Tel: 800-560-1428 Fax: 215-204-9319
Email: lawadmis@temple.edu • Website: www.law.temple.edu

(somewhat) for less time." "There is less competition and more civility" in the evening program as well.

Many find that "most" students are "friendly and supportive" and the overall environment "is one of 'we-are-in-this-together.'" "There are many student organizations, and they are always holding meetings, social events," and "happy hours." "We study together, go to lunch together, and most of us have formed lasting friendships with people in our classes," relates a 2L. "Students and faculty are very involved in law school life," reports a student. Others take into account the fact that many "students live throughout Philadelphia" and it can be "hard for students to get together and socialize."

Temple's law school is located in "one of the seedier areas" of Philadelphia, though "The campus itself is pretty safe." "It really can't be denied that the school is bounded on three sides with grinding poverty," admits a 2L. Nevertheless, many students think the area "has gotten a bad rap." There are always "many security guards around." A 2L explains, "Yes, you have to keep your eyes open. Yes, you shouldn't leave jewelry lying on your front seat. But these are things that could be said of any urban area." Beyond this, "The quality and cost of life in Philadelphia is remarkable." And "center city Philly" is only "five minutes away" on the subway.

Getting In

The 25th percentile of admitted students has LSAT scores of 161 and GPAs of 3.25. Admitted students at the 75th percentile have LSAT scores of 165 and GPAs of 3.7. Temple says that it doesn't average multiple LSAT score, however "all scores from the LSAT will be considered."

Legal writing	
course requirement	Yes
Legal methods	
course requirement	No
Legal research	
course requirement	Yes
Moot court requirement	No
Public interest	
law requirement	No

ADMISSIONS

Selectivity Rating	**82**
# applications received	4,541
% applicants accepted	40
% acceptees attending	18
Average LSAT	162
LSAT Range	159–164
Average undergrad GPA	3.44
Application fee	$60
Regular application	Rolling, up to 3/1
Regular notification	Rolling
Early application program	No
Transfer students accepted	Yes
Evening division offered	Yes
Part-time accepted	Yes
LSDAS accepted	Yes

Applicants Also Look At
American University, Villanova University, Fordham University, The George Washington University, Georgetown University

International Students
TOEFL recommended	
of international students	Yes

FINANCIAL FACTS

Annual tuition (in-state/ out-of-state)	$16,118/$28,062
Books and supplies	$1,500
Fees	$625
Tuition per credit (in-state/out-of-state)	$624/$1,147
Room & board	$11,385
Financial aid application deadline	3/1
% receiving some sort of aid	87
% of aid that is merit based	95
% receiving scholarships	41
Average grant	$8,574
Average loan	$25,233
Average total aid package	$29,293
Average debt	$74,941

EMPLOYMENT INFORMATION

Career Rating	**83**
Rate of placement (nine months out)	89
Average starting salary	$80,670
State for bar exam	PA
Pass rate for first-time bar	90.3

Employers Who Frequently Hire Grads
District Attorney, Public Defender, national law firms, state and federal judges, non-profit legal organizations.

Grads Employed by Field (%)
Academic (3)
Business/Industry (14)
Government (12)
Judicial Clerkships (17)
Military (2)
Private Practice (45)
Public Interest (7)

TEXAS TECH UNIVERSITY
SCHOOL OF LAW

INSTITUTIONAL INFORMATION

Public/private	Public
Student-faculty ratio	15:1
% faculty part-time	30
% faculty female	33
% faculty minority	23
Total faculty	53

SURVEY SAYS...

Diverse opinions accepted
in classrooms
Great research resources
Great library staff

STUDENTS

Enrollment of law school	647
% male/female	57/43
% out-of-state	15
% full-time	100
% minority	24
Average age of entering class	24

ACADEMICS

Academic Experience Rating	**86**
Profs interesting rating	87
Profs accessible rating	98
Hours of study per day	4.88

Academic Specialties

Commercial law, constitutional law, corporation securities, environmental law, international law, property, taxation, intellectual property law, water law, law & bioterrorism, law & science, health care law, military law

Combined Degrees Offered

JD/MBA, 3 years; JD/MPA, 3.5 years; JD/MS-Agricultural Economics, 3–3.5 years; JD/MS-Accounting (Taxation), 3–3.5 years; JD/MS-Environmental Toxicology, 3–4 years; JD/PFP-Personal Financial Planning, 3–3.5 years; JD/MS-Biotechnology, 3–4 years; JD/MS-Crop Science/Horticulture/Soil Science/Entomology, 3–4 years; JD/MD-Doctor of Medicine, 7 years

Clinical program required	No

Academics

Students dole out praises for Texas Tech's rigorous and practical JD program, which really "teaches you what you need to know to be a good lawyer." From day one, real-world principles are incorporated into the learning experience, and throughout the program "the instruction [features] a good balance of the Socratic Method with practical advice." During the 1L curriculum, "emphasis is put on legal writing and research so that we are able to go straight into practice during the summer of our first year." 1Ls also participate in a "year-long legal practice requirement," which "gives you a fantastic foundation before you step your foot in the real world." In addition to curricular offerings, the school offers an incredible breadth of "opportunities to gain practical experience through procedure classes, barrister competitions, clinics, and national competitions."

While the JD curriculum is "rigorous and demanding," it would be very difficult to slip through the cracks at Texas Tech. When they start the program, students are grouped into sections that serve as a support network during 1L, and "all of the first-year classes have upper-level students as tutors to supplement your classroom hours." The teaching staff is also committed to student success, and maintains consistent office hours so that students "can stop by and talk to professors at any time." A totally user-friendly experience, "the resources provided by the school are top-notch and they've designed everything to revolve around the student and their schedule." To top it all off, the school has completed the construction of the Lanier Professional Development Center building, which added 34,000 square feet to the law school building. The school is already equipped with a first-rate library, and "the library staff is amazing and always available."

When its time to start looking for a job or clerkship, Texas Tech maintains "a great reputation in the Texas legal markets as producing hard-working, effective lawyers." Students choose Tech precisely for this reputation and are proud of the results. A third-year student asserts, "I've been told on several occasions that a firm would rather pick up a Tech Law graduate who knows what to do when he steps foot in the office than some Ivy League grad who knows more about theory and less about how to get the job done." While career placement is highly successful in Texas, many students feel that the school could improve its national reputation and help "out-of-state students find jobs in their home states." In general, students would like their top school to take a more leading role in the national legal community, urging the administration to "spend more money to attract more nationally-known, rather than regionally-known, guest speakers and employers."

Life

The surprisingly friendly and open atmosphere at Texas Tech is all due to students who aren't afraid to "help one another, encourage one another, and be kind to one another." No need for first-year jitters. You'll quickly feel at home at Texas Tech, thanks to a "tremendous student-run mentoring program for incoming students." Within the law school, there are a number of students clubs and organizations—plus many more in the larger university—and if you're married, there are "resources and social networking opportunities for students with spouses and their families." Conservative politics predominate, but students reassure us that "you can survive as a liberal." In fact, "the Tech democrats are more active than the republicans," and everyone listens to and respects different opinions.

DONNA WILLIAMS, ADMISSIONS COUNSELOR
TEXAS TECH UNIVERSITY SCHOOL OF LAW 1802 HARTFORD AVENUE, LUBBOCK, TX 79409
TEL: 806-742-3990 FAX: 806-742-4617
EMAIL: DONNA.WILLIAMS@TTU.EDU • WEBSITE: WWW.LAW.TTU.EDU

If you've never been to West Texas, a student dryly describes it for us as "a vast, tree-less, invariably flat expanse of dirt...They even have tumbleweeds here—like out of a John Wayne movie or Looney Tunes." Although it sounds a bit inhospitable, students say the advantage to Lubbock's small city environment and arid landscape is that there are fewer distractions, which makes it easier to focus on your homework. More importantly, "Lubbock is a great environment for law students to partner with local lawyers and learn the ropes." "The Lubbock legal community is extremely strong and polite, and the rela-tionship is emphasized over the case," one student says.

If you are looking for nightlife and social outlets, "Lubbock is not the most exciting town on the universe." However, students guarantee us that the lively campus commu-nity can make life surprisingly entertaining. For sports fans, "there is a very good football team on the field," and the basketball team isn't too shabby either. On top of that, the law school's friendly students "have managed to carve out a pretty decent social life. The bars here are okay, but the law students will sponsor various events and they are typically very fun."

Getting In

Texas Tech evaluates students based on their previous academic performance, LSAT scores, letters of recommendation, and personal statements. While no specific pre-law cur-riculum is required, the admissions committee favors students who have a background in public speaking, reading and writing skills, an understanding of public institutions and government, and the ability to think both creatively and critically.

Legal writing	
course requirement	Yes
Legal methods	
course requirement	Yes
Legal research	
course requirement	Yes
Moot court requirement	No
Public interest	
law requirement	No

ADMISSIONS

Selectivity Rating	**80**
# applications received	1,576
% applicants accepted	34
% acceptees attending	38
Average LSAT	156
LSAT Range	154–159
Average undergrad GPA	3.44
Application fee	$50
Regular application	Rolling, up to 3/15
Regular notification	Rolling
Early application program	Yes
Early application deadline	11/1
Early application notification	1/15
Transfer students accepted	Yes
Evening division offered	No
Part-time accepted	No
LSDAS accepted	Yes

Applicants Also Look At
University of Texas at Austin, University of Houston, University of New Mexico, University of Oklahoma, Baylor University, Southern Methodist University, South Texas College of Law

International Students
TOEFL required	
of international students	Yes
Minimum TOEFL	
(paper/computer)	550/213

FINANCIAL FACTS

Annual tuition (in-state/ out-of-state)	$11,660/$19,100
Books and supplies	$1,000
Fees	$2,878
Room & board	$12,957
% first-year students	
receiving some sort of aid	90
% receiving some sort of aid	90
% of aid that is merit based	47
% receiving scholarships	65
Average grant	$2,481
Average loan	$17,866
Average total aid package	$18,098
Average debt	$57,362

EMPLOYMENT INFORMATION

Career Rating	**71**	**Grads Employed by Field (%)**
Rate of placement (nine months out) 90.45		Business/Industry (17)
Average starting salary	$66,881	Government (17)
State for bar exam	TX, NM, FL, AZ, MD	Judicial Clerkships (5)
Pass rate for first-time bar		Other (1)

Employers Who Frequently Hire Grads
Jones, Day Reavis & Pogue; Thompson & Knight; Haynes & Boone; Thompson & Coe; Cousins & Irons; Strasburger & Price; Cooper & Scully.

Prominent Alumni
Karen Tandy, Senior Vice President, Motorola, Inc.; Brian Quinn, Chief Justice, 7th Court of Appeals for Texas; Philip Johnson, Texas Supreme Court Justice.

TEXAS WESLEYAN UNIVERSITY
SCHOOL OF LAW

INSTITUTIONAL INFORMATION

Public/private	Private
Affiliation	Methodist
Student-faculty ratio	26:1
% faculty part-time	35
% faculty female	46
% faculty minority	10
Total faculty	29

SURVEY SAYS...
Diverse opinions accepted
in classrooms
Great research resources
Great library staff

STUDENTS

Enrollment of law school	273
% male/female	46/54
% full-time	68
% minority	20
# of countries represented	4
Average age of entering class	28

ACADEMICS

Academic Experience Rating	**80**
Profs interesting rating	87
Profs accessible rating	94
Hours of study per day	4.17

Advanced Degrees Offered
JD, full-time, 3 years to complete;
part-time, 4 years to complete.

Clinical program required	No
Legal writing	
course requirement	Yes
Legal methods	
course requirement	Yes
Legal research	
course requirement	Yes
Moot court requirement	Yes
Public interest	
law requirement	Yes

Academics

Established in 1989, the School of Law at Texas Wesleyan University is an up-and-comer that offers a solid education, an excellent price tag, and a good bar passage rate (a main focus of the curriculum and pride of the school). "It's really nice to feel a part of a young school that is one the rise!" says a 1L. The school takes extraordinary effort to not only teach legal theory, but to "prepare students for the bar and for employment in the legal community." There are many opportunities to gain real-world experience, as well as many practicum courses designed to simulate what an attorney will be faced with on a daily basis once admitted to the bar. The legal writing program is rigorous (three semesters required) and "the writing professors emphasize real-world legal writing skills to impress a busy judge." Facilities are essentially brand-new, classrooms are state-of-the-art with interactive AV components, the building is equipped with wireless internet access, and the school itself "is always clean and secure with controlled keycard access." "Thankfully," the location is away from the main campus right in the middle of downtown Fort Worth, which is a "great town to live in."

The administration "will bend over backward to help you" and "seem to have an uncanny knack for remembering first names." "My first impression as a 1L-returning student was that everyone on the staff, from the dean of the law school to the maintenance staff, was committed to the students' success. Now, as a jaded 3L, I still believe that," says a student. School name recognition could use some work here, however, "Texas Wesleyan is a newer school and "it is sometimes difficult to get your foot in the door with the bigger firms." "Right now it seems we are the only Texas law school that can't get the big firms to conduct on campus interviews... doesn't make sense when our bar passage rate is better than a good portion of those schools!" says a 2L. However, some students are so proud of the education they're receiving that they see this as a strength for the school, as they gladly feel up to the task of "forcing those in the legal community to recognize that there is another great legal education being established in this state."

The professors at the school are "exceptional" and "make every effort to be available for students." They ensure students "really feel as though we are part of a bigger calling, and not just corralled through classes." Classes are smaller here, so if you are not prepared, you are "going to be humiliated and the professors will not be happy with you." There's great flexibility in scheduling, so students that can only attend classes in the evening are taken care of, though night students would like more options in their classes, and day students would like more specializations. The school has a public service message running throughout its curriculum, and things like the Pro Bono Family Law Clinic "make a difference in people's lives every day."

SHEROLYN HURST, ASSISTANT DEAN OF ADMISSIONS AND SCHOLARSHIPS
1515 COMMERCE STREET, OFFICE OF ADMISSIONS, FORT WORTH, TX 76102
TEL: 817-212-4040 FAX: 817-212-4141
EMAIL: LAWADMISSIONS@LAW.TXWES.EDU • WEBSITE: LAW.TXWES.EDU

Life

The school has a fair number of night students in relation to its day students, and "they are two different worlds." Both have close bonds within, but "there is some resentment between the groups." Usually there are several events every week sponsored by student organizations, and it is "not a stuffy environment," as there is always something to do. The school's downtown location across from the water gardens "allows for easy access to the courthouses and allows attorneys easy access to our building," and there are lots of programs to get students acquainted with local attorneys in a variety of fields. All facilities are in one building and walking distance from dining and entertainment. There are a lot of students that commute to school, so parking is tight, and "you have to get here early, or you may be circling for a while looking for a spot." For students that live close to the school there is a lot of social interaction on the weekends, but for commuters, "the interaction is largely confined to the campus during the week." The building itself looks rather boring on the outside, but once inside, "you can feel the community spirit," and "the student body overall is cooperative." There is no traditional cafeteria to speak of, which means "getting food at odd hours occurs via vending machine."

Getting In

Admission to the school becomes slightly more competitive every year. In addition to a completed application and LSAT scores, applicants are required to submit two letters of recommendation and a personal statement. Texas Wesleyan welcomes students of different ages and backgrounds, and the school looks beyond test scores and grades when making admissions decisions.

ADMISSIONS

Selectivity Rating	**70**
# applications received	1,970
% applicants accepted	48
% acceptees attending	29
Average LSAT	153
LSAT Range	150–155
Average undergrad GPA	3.15
Application fee	$55
Regular application	Rolling, up to 5/15
Regular notification	Rolling
Early application program	No
Transfer students accepted	Yes
Evening division offered	Yes
Part-time accepted	Yes
LSDAS accepted	Yes

Applicants Also Look At
University of Texas at Austin, University of Houston, Texas Tech University, University of Oklahoma, University of Arkansas at Little Rock, Baylor University, Oklahoma City University, Southern Methodist University, University of Tulsa, St. Mary's University, South Texas College of Law, Thomas Jefferson School of Law, Florida Costal School of Law

International Students

TOEFL required of international students	Yes
TOEFL recommended of international students	
Minimum TOEFL (paper/computer/web)	600/250/100

FINANCIAL FACTS

Annual tuition	$23,960
Books and supplies	$1,300
Fees	$750
Fees per credit	$750
Tuition per credit	$800
Room & board (off-campus)	$10,521
Average grant	$7,500
Average loan	$22,000
Average debt	$72,576

EMPLOYMENT INFORMATION

Career Rating	**70**	
Rate of placement (nine months out)	76	
Average starting salary	$70,381	
State for bar exam	TX, OK, CT, GA, NC	
Pass rate for first-time bar	85	

Grads Employed by Field (%)
Business/Industry (28)
Government (9)
Judicial Clerkships (2)
Military (1)
Private Practice (59)
Public Interest (1)

Employers Who Frequently Hire Grads
Mid to small size private practice firms, District Attorney's Offices, Government Agencies, various corporations and businesses.

Prominent Alumni
Craig Watkins, Dallas County District Attorney; Carlos Cortez, Judge, 44th District of Dallas County; Susan Hawk, Judge, 291st Criminal District Court; Nancy Berger, Judge, 322nd District Family Court of Tarrant County.

THOMAS M. COOLEY LAW SCHOOL

INSTITUTIONAL INFORMATION

Public/private	Private
Affiliation	Independent
Student-faculty ratio	20:1
% faculty part-time	65
% faculty female	37
% faculty minority	7
Total faculty	283

SURVEY SAYS...

Diverse opinions accepted
in classrooms
Great research resources
Great library staff

STUDENTS

Enrollment of law school	3,733
% male/female	52/48
% out-of-state	64
% full-time	12
% minority	33
% international	4
# of countries represented	11
Average age of entering class	27

ACADEMICS

Academic Experience Rating	**72**
Profs interesting rating	81
Profs accessible rating	75
Hours of study per day	5.17

Academic Specialties

Constitutional law, environmental
law, government services, human
rights, international law, taxation,
intellectual property law, business
transactions, general practice, litigation, administrative law

Advanced Degrees Offered

Juris Doctor, 2 to 5 years; LL.M.
(Taxation), LL.M. (Intellectual
Property), LL.M. (U.S. Legal Studies
for Foreign Lawyers), LL.M.
(Corporate Law and Finance.)

Combined Degrees Offered

JD/MPA, JD/MBA, 3–6 years with
Western Michigan University or
Oakland University; JD/LLM, 3–6
years

Academics

The Thomas M. Cooley Law School in Michigan is the "the largest law school" in the United States in terms of enrollment. There are four campuses—one in the state capital of Lansing, one in the northern suburbs of Detroit, one in Grand Rapids and its newest location in Ann Arbor. Cooley prides itself on "flexible" and "accommodating" scheduling. There are "daytime, nighttime, and weekend" classes. There are "three terms year round" as well, and you can start in January, May, or September. Some students complain that "the cost is very high." Others tell us the price tag is "very affordable." Either way, Cooley offers "a lot of financial aid and scholarship opportunities." Technology is also "cutting edge," and the law library is one of the most extensive in the country.

Students here describe Cooley as an "underrated" "lawyer-making machine." It's not the place for you if you want to imbibe legal theory, though. "The school promotes practical application so you are ready to jump into your career" immediately upon graduation. Real legal experience "is required." Every student must complete a clinic, internship, externship, or otherwise demonstrate the equivalent in work experience. "Lectures are practical and grounded instead of theoretical." Course selection is broad and specializations are available but the number of mandatory courses is "a little ridiculous," and it "may prevent you from taking many electives and delving deeply into a particular area of interest." Basically, "Cooley's thinking is that if it is tested on the bar, it should be a required class." "This law school prepares you for the bar exam." Period.

Some students love the "hard-working" administration. Others say that the top brass is "frigid." Far and away, the biggest administrative complaint is that Cooley takes its sweet time posting grades. Like, "forever." The faculty is "interesting, entertaining, and knowledgeable," and it's full of professors who have "actually practiced law." There are also "many adjunct professors." They're typically judges, partners at big law firms, or general counsel for major corporations. Outside of class, faculty members are very approachable. "The accessibility of the professors is second to none," beams a 3L.

The "rigorous" academic atmosphere here is "not for the faint hearted." "Class sizes tend to be quite large." Professors generally "employ the Socratic Method and are always seeking to test your knowledge of the material." "The majority of students get c's." "Exams are tough, and an A is well earned." "Cooley lowers the bar for admissions, but after that you are on your own to sink or swim," warns a 1L. "Cooley is very hard to stay in." "Few students here have above a 3.0." Although the school has a fully-staffed academic support resouce center, students uniformly promise that "you will struggle to survive through all three of your years here." "You better know the law," they say. "If you slack off, you'll fail out."

Life

Cooley "accepts just about anyone and everyone." The student population is "a mixture of students who didn't get in any place else and students who are on full scholarships because their LSAT and GPA were so high." An overwhelming majority of students is enrolled part time. Diversity of all kinds is a fabulous strength. Well more than half the future attorneys here come from some state other than Michigan. More than one third represent an ethnic minority. There are "nontraditional students from many different professions." "Age, background, and socioeconomic status" really run the gamut. "Cooley is so diverse that one could not even attempt to discriminate without confusing himself," declares a 3L. On the one hand, the vast assortment of students "makes for excellent class discussions." On the other hand, "people divide into cliques easily" outside the classroom.

STEPHANIE GREGG, ASSISTANT DEAN OF ADMISSIONS
PO BOX 13038, 300 SOUTH CAPITOL AVENUE, LANSING, MI 48901
TEL: 517-371-5140 FAX: 517-334-5718
EMAIL: ADMISSIONS@COOLEY.EDU • WEBSITE: WWW.COOLEY.EDU

The three campuses each have their own identity. In Lansing, students have a "beautiful" building downtown "by the capitol." However, the surrounding area is largely "bleak" and "depressing." The Grand Rapids campus is similarly located in "a refurbished old building in the heart of downtown," and it's not in the greatest neighborhood, either. The decidedly suburban Auburn Hills campus is a nice and new facility "tucked away in a wooded compound" that feels like "a generic corporate headquarters."

Social life can be hit or miss. Cooley is home to a tremendous number of student organizations," and "most students are nice people." However, there isn't much of a community. "A lot of people come to class and then leave immediately after," explains a 1L. "Building a social life takes effort." The fact that "grades are impossible during the first few terms" certainly doesn't help. "Those who are social butterflies mostly ended up failing out after one or two semesters," cautions a 2L. "People get along, but it's best to focus on studying."

Getting In

Cooley is one of the easiest law schools to get admitted to in the country. The acceptance rate hovers at about 60 percent annually. Admitted students at the 25th percentile have LSAT scores around 145 and GPAs of roughly 2.75. Admitted students at the 75th percentile have LSAT scores of 152 or so and their undergraduate GPA is about 3.3. Be warned, though: Cooley also has an extremely high attrition rate. The philosophy here is to give students with lesser credentials a chance but throw them out if they can't cut the demanding academics.

Clinical program required	Yes
Legal writing course requirement	Yes
Legal methods course requirement	Yes
Legal research course requirement	Yes
Moot court requirement	No
Public interest law requirement	No

ADMISSIONS

Selectivity Rating	**61**
# applications received	6,094
% applicants accepted	3,736
% acceptees attending	1,533
Average LSAT	147
LSAT Range	144–149
Average undergrad GPA	2.99
Regular application	Rolling, up to 9/1
Regular notification	Rolling
Early application program	No
Transfer students accepted	Yes
Evening division offered	Yes
Weekend division offered	Yes
Part-time accepted	Yes
LSDAS accepted	Yes

Applicants Also Look At
Michigan State University, Widener University, University of Detroit Mercy, St. Thomas University, Valparaiso, Florida Costal School of Law, University of Dayton

International Students
TOEFL recommended of international students	Yes

FINANCIAL FACTS

Annual tuition	$28,710 (FT)
Books and supplies	$1,200
Fees	$40
Tuition per credit	$957
Room & board (off-campus)	$7,800
Financial aid application deadline	9/6
% first-year students receiving some sort of aid	89
% receiving some sort of aid	92
% receiving scholarships	63
Average grant	
Average loan	$7,256
Average total aid package	$20,500
Average debt	$90,800

EMPLOYMENT INFORMATION

Career Rating	**61**
Rate of placement (nine months out)	82
Average starting salary	$52,422
State for bar exam	MI, NY, FL, IN, CA, OH, PA, TX.
Pass rate for first-time bar	86

Employers Who Frequently Hire Grads
Michigan Court of Appeals Prosecutors
Legal Services programs Michigan law firms

Prominent Alumni
John Engler, Former Governor; Bart R. Stupak, U. S. Representative; Jane Markey, Michigan Court of Appeals; Chris Chocola, U.S. Representative

Grads Employed by Field (%)
Academic (4)
Business/Industry (17)
Government (14)
Judicial Clerkships (5)
Military (1)
Private Practice (53)
Public Interest (4)
Other (2)

TOURO COLLEGE
JACOB D. FUCHSBERG LAW CENTER

Academics

Located on suburban Long Island, Touro Law Center boasts "many clinics on site." Five in-house clinics give full-time and part-time students the opportunity to serve real clients in civil rights litigation, immigration litigation, elder law, family law, and not-for-profit corporation law. Off-campus clinics include business, law and technology, civil practice, judicial clerkship, and criminal law. The school also offers an intensive, 20-hour-a-week rotation program with the United States Attorney's office. Touro's "focus on internships and externships" and its unique location, "only a five-iron shot" from federal and state courthouses, draws many students to the school. "Being located next to district, family, supreme, and federal courthouses gives Touro students a unique real-life look at what attorneys do while in court," explains one student. "I've randomly visited the court in the morning and observed attorneys conduct direct and cross-examinations in a $150 million court case." "We have a court [observation] program for the 1Ls, which is the first of its kind in law school academia," describes a 1Ls,. "This program allows us access to more than just viewing a proceeding. With the hard work of the school staff, we have been given extra privileges at the court house including visits to chambers, personal audiences with both prosecutors, defense counsel, and all levels of court officers." "The direct contact with judges and attorneys and their input helps to [provide] insight into different areas of law." Also, "Having a better perspective on the various areas of law helps with deciding which area of law one may want to practice."

The course work at Touro "emphasizes legal writing and analysis." "Class sizes are pretty small, so it's not so intimidating to speak in front of everyone." The "smart, friendly, and approachable" professors are "excited to educate" (though there are a few "pretty boring ones"). "Plenty of judges and practitioners also teach classes." Accessibility is not a problem. "There is a high level of morale, and the daily interaction between student and professor is priceless." Faculty members are "always willing to meet with and talk to the students outside the classroom," "no matter how long—or how many times—they have to go over a given concept." "Professors can be seen dining with students in the school's cafeteria while casually discussing the law," adds a 1L.

Some students call the Career Services Office "exceptional." "They will do their absolute best to make sure you are prepared for interviews and aware of upcoming opportunities," says one happy customer. Other students gripe that Career Services is "not at all helpful." Also, though Touro offers very flexible full-time and part-time programs, course scheduling is a huge problem. "There is not a lot of flexibility with regard to course selection" and "There are too many required courses after the first year." The administration, though "very accessible," seems "out of touch with the student body," "and they never seem to know what is going on."

The facilities here are "brand new," and students love them. Touro has a "state-of-the-art building" in which "Everything is high-tech and top-of-the-line." The "layout of the classrooms is odd," and "There are some problems with acoustics," but the "roomy" library has ample study space. There is a ton of free parking as well. The Law Center "follows a Jewish calendar," and one student notes that Touro "could improve by staying open on Saturday."

SUSAN THOMPSON, DIRECTOR OF ENROLLMENT
225 EASTVIEW DRIVE, CENTRAL ISLIP, NY 11722
TEL: 631-761-7010 FAX: 631-761-7019
EMAIL: ADMISSIONS@TOUROLAW.EDU • WEBSITE: WWW.TOUROLAW.EDU

Life

"Generally people get along very well" at Touro. "There is a good mix of both young and older, more experienced students." "The greatest strength of my law school is the sense of community that begins from the moment you enter the school," waxes a 3L. "In the full-time program you spend a full year with your incoming section and then half your classes the second year," adds a 2L. "This enables you to form strong bonds for study groups and lifelong friendships. Also, even though everyone studies a lot during the week, students find time to be social on Thursday or Friday nights."

"The location of the school is perfect from an educational standpoint because of the proximity to the courthouse." There's "an on-campus lecture-luncheon series with state and federal judges." The downside to life here is the "almost nonexistent social atmosphere." "The majority of the students commute from great distances which doesn't facilitate social opportunities." "People try to get involved and sponsor extracurricular social activities" and there are "plenty of opportunities to party and have fun," but you have to seek them out. "We need more social activities that cater to more students and bring us together as a community," suggests a 2L. The inescapable fact that "Central Islip is not exactly the party capital of the world" doesn't help. Fortunately, the culture and nightlife of New York City is only about an hour away.

Getting In

At Touro Law Center, recently admitted students at the 25th percentile have LSAT scores of approximately 150 and GPAs of approximately 2.8. Admitted students at the 75th percentile have LSAT scores of 153 and GPAs of roughly 3.4.

Moot court requirement	No
Public interest law requirement	Yes

ADMISSIONS

Selectivity Rating	60*
# applications received	2,057
% applicants accepted	44
% acceptees attending	30
Average LSAT	150
LSAT Range	149–153
Average undergrad GPA	3.10
Application fee	$60
Regular application	Rolling, up to 8/1
Regular notification	Rolling
Early application program	No
Transfer students accepted	Yes
Evening division offered	Yes
Part-time accepted	Yes
LSDAS accepted	Yes

Applicants Also Look At
Hofstra University, New York Law School

International Students

TOEFL recommended of international students	Yes
Minimum TOEFL (paper/computer/web)	600/250/100

FINANCIAL FACTS

Annual tuition	$36,490
Books and supplies	$1,900
Fees	$120
Fees per credit	$100
Tuition per credit	$1,150
Room & board (off-campus)	$17,500
Financial aid application deadline	5/1
% first-year students receiving some sort of aid	89
% receiving some sort of aid	89
% of aid that is merit based	66
% receiving scholarships	61
Average grant	$3,500
Average loan	$32,000
Average total aid package	$35,000
Average debt	$92,249

EMPLOYMENT INFORMATION

Career Rating	**69**	**Grads Employed by Field (%)**
Rate of placement (nine months out)	72	Academic (1)
Average starting salary	$58,910	Business/Industry (14)
State for bar exam	NY	Government (19)
Pass rate for first-time bar	81.2	Judicial Clerkships (5)
Employers Who Frequently Hire Grads		Military (1)
mid-size and small law firms; D.A. Offices,		Private Practice (57)
Legal Aid Offices and County Attorney		Public Interest (3)
Offices.		
Prominent Alumni		
Lewis Lubell, Justice, NYS Supreme Court;		
Kathleen Rice, Nassau County District		
Attorney.		

TULANE UNIVERSITY
LAW SCHOOL

INSTITUTIONAL INFORMATION

Public/private	Private
Student-faculty ratio	16:1
% faculty part-time	0
% faculty female	24
% faculty minority	12
Total faculty	40

SURVEY SAYS...
Students love New Orleans, LA
Good social life

STUDENTS

Enrollment of law school	750
% male/female	55/45
% out-of-state	84
% full-time	100
% minority	21
% international	3
# of countries represented	20
Average age of entering class	24

ACADEMICS

Academic Experience Rating	**88**
Profs interesting rating	86
Profs accessible rating	82
Hours of study per day	4.28

Academic Specialties
environmental law, international law, intellectual property law, admiralty & maritime law, sports law, civil law, public interest law

Advanced Degrees Offered
S.J.D, 2–3 years depending on length of time to complete dissertation; Master of Laws, 1 year full-time; Master of Laws in Admiralty, 1 year full-time, 2 years part-time; Master of Laws in Energy and Environment, 1 year full-time, 2 years part-time; Master of Laws in Int'l and Comparative Law, 1 year full-time; Master of Laws in American Business Law, 1 year full-time; Master of Laws in American Law, 1 year full-time.

Combined Degrees Offered
JD/MBA; JD/MHA; JD/MSPH; JD/MSW; JD/MS in International Development; JD/MA in Latin American Studies; JD/MACCT; JD/MA in other fields on an ad hoc basis.

Academics

Tulane University Law School is "extremely enjoyable because it provides you with the same resources as all the top law schools, with a more laid-back atmosphere." "The quality of teaching is superb." The "world-renowned faculty" here is full of "experts and kick-ass attorneys" who are "funny, extremely smart, and extremely approachable." "They are highly qualified and accomplished but remain accessible and down-to-earth." Some students call the administration "ridiculously awesome," too. The deans are "nice and helpful," they say, "and most of them teach a 1L or 2L class, which gives you the opportunity to be exposed to them early on in your career." More critical students call the management merely "vaguely competent."

Tulane is home to "quite a few unique programs and strengths." In addition to "exceptional clinical opportunities" and a host of dual-degree programs, students edit no fewer than eight journals. Tulane also offers certificates in international and comparative law, admiralty law, environmental law, sports law, and civil law. Also, Louisiana is a civil law state (whereas every other state is a common law state), so students are exposed to two very different legal systems. "The ability to follow a common law or civil law track not only opens up opportunities in Louisiana, but it also makes an international law career more feasible." The big academic complaint here is the research and writing program. "I am not sure whoever designed it has ever heard the term 'best practices,'" speculates a 1L. "If you came as a strong technical writer, you will leave with no new skills. If you did not, you are on your own."

"The mandatory curve and class ranking systems mean that 70 to 80 percent of the graduating class will not even be considered by most employers hiring new law school grads," gripes a 3L. Others contend that Tulane is "extremely active in helping everyone secure summer employment and beyond." Students also note that their school's brand name is often a real advantage on a resume. "We're the best law school in Louisiana, and the firms know it," brags a 2L. "We are not all competing for the same 30 spots at the top law firm in our city because our goals are incredibly diverse," adds a 2L.

Facilities wise, Tulane has "a wonderful library." Some students say that "classrooms are nice." Others disagree. "The actual building and classrooms are forgettable," they tell us. "The horrid ergonomics of it all!" bemoans a 2L. "To plug in your laptop can take two minutes and can set the stage for an awkward encounter with the person sitting next to you while you fumble around under the table like a teenager on a first date."

Life

New Orleans is definitely located in "the American South, and many students come from the South." Geographic diversity is pretty abundant, though. Some 85 percent of the students come from a state other than Louisiana. More than 20 percent of the students represent an ethnic minority. There's a "wide range of international students" and plenty of "diversity of opinion and background." Some students insist that "there's no cut-throat competition here." They say that the typical student is as "friendly, cooperative, and as laid-back as a stressed law student could possibly be." Others tell us that competition exists "but it's not as prevalent until exam time."

Outside of class, Tulane students are an "extremely social," "fun-loving bunch." There are "plenty of cliques, largely organized according to special interests areas of law, ethnicity, and age." At the same time, the environment is "very collegial." "The community atmosphere is a definite plus." Quite a few students "enjoy a good party." There are "a lot of the smart kids who had fun in undergrad" here, and their good times continue unabated in law school. "Socializing is in overdrive at TLS," cautions a 2L, "which can be a distraction from your studies if you let it." "Most people go out at least once or twice a week." "Whether it's a run-of-the-mill bar review or renting out a restaurant on the Mardi Gras parade route, there's always a social event on the horizon."

Off campus, the Big Easy is reportedly "the most relaxed city in the USA" and "a perfect place to unwind on weekends or after finals." Students love the food, the nightlife, and the "warm winter weather." There's the debauchery of Bourbon Street, of course, but there's also an array of "incredible" streets and neighborhoods. "The sidewalk bistros and beautiful, lush scenery add significant character to your day-to-day experience as a law student." Beyond the city of New Orleans, "there are lots of good places for weekend trips in the area" as well.

Getting In

Tulane has a fabulous regional reputation and a very good national reputation. Admitted students at the 25th percentile have LSAT scores around 158 and GPAs not much less than 3.4. Admitted students at the 75th percentile have LSAT scores of 163 or so and GPAs around 3.7.

Clinical program required	No
Legal writing course requirement	Yes
Legal methods course requirement	No
Legal research course requirement	Yes
Moot court requirement	Yes
Public interest law requirement	Yes

ADMISSIONS

Selectivity Rating	**85**
# applications received	2,600
# applicants accepted	900
# acceptees attending	242
Average LSAT	162
LSAT Range	159–163
Average undergrad GPA	3.59
Application fee	$60
Regular application	Rolling, up to 6/1
Regular notification	Rolling
Early application program	No
Transfer students accepted	Yes
Evening division offered	No
Part-time accepted	No
LSDAS accepted	Yes

Applicants Also Look At

American University, Boston College, The George Washington University, Emory University, University of Miami, Georgetown University

FINANCIAL FACTS

Annual tuition	$35,500
Books and supplies	$1,500
Fees	$3,200
Room & board	$11,690
Financial aid application deadline	3/15
% first-year students receiving some sort of aid	87
% receiving some sort of aid	87
% of aid that is merit based	95
% receiving scholarships	65
Average grant	$15,000
Average loan	$27,337
Average total aid package	$31,000
Average debt	$87,000

EMPLOYMENT INFORMATION

Career Rating	**87**	**Grads Employed by Field (%)**
Rate of placement (nine months out)	95	Academic (1)
Average starting salary	$88,500	Business/Industry (10)
State for bar exam	NY, LA, TX, FL, DC	Government (12)
Pass rate for first-time bar	93	Judicial Clerkships (10)

Employers Who Frequently Hire Grads

Fulbright & Jaworski; Skadden Arps; Arnold & Porter; White & Case; Mayer Brown & Platt; Cleary Gottlieb; Schulte Roth; McGlinchey; Adams&Reese.

Military (2)
Private Practice (57)
Public Interest (4)

Prominent Alumni

Edith Clement, U.S. Ct of Appeals judge; William Suter, U.S. Supreme Court clerk; William Pryor, US Court of Appeals judge; Rod West, CEO of Entergy; Michael Tannenbaum, General Manager of the Jets; Gail Agrawal, Dean Kansas Law.

THE UNIVERSITY OF AKRON
SCHOOL OF LAW

INSTITUTIONAL INFORMATION

Public/private	Public
Student-faculty ratio	13:1
% faculty part-time	48
% faculty female	24
% faculty minority	8
Total faculty	34

SURVEY SAYS...

Diverse opinions accepted
in classrooms
Great research resources
Abundant externship/internship/
clerkship opportunities

STUDENTS

Enrollment of law school	451
% male/female	57/43
% out-of-state	26
% full-time	52
% minority	14
Average age of entering class	26

ACADEMICS

Academic Experience Rating	**70**
Profs interesting rating	67
Profs accessible rating	62
Hours of study per day	4.34

Academic Specialties

Corporation securities, criminal law,
international law, taxation, intellectual property law, litigation

Advanced Degrees Offered

LL.M. in Intellectual Property, 1 year
full-time or 2 or 3 years part-time

Combined Degrees Offered

JD/Master in Business
Administration; JD/Master of
Science and Management in Human
Resources; JD/Master in Taxation;
JD/Master in Public Administration;
JD/Master in Applied Politics

Clinical program required	No
Legal writing	
course requirement	Yes
Legal methods	
course requirement	Yes
Legal research	
course requirement	Yes

Academics

Far away from the world of academic pretension and staggering student loans, The University of Akron is a laid-back and engaging place to earn a JD at a very reasonable price. One of the most inexpensive programs in the United States, Akron students ask us, "Where else can you get a well-respected law degree for less than $15,000 a year?" While Akron doesn't provide the posh classrooms and high-tech facilities you might find at a pricier program, the school delivers on every point that really matters. As one student explains, "Akron cuts out some of the unnecessary frills of law school but keeps the essential quality of faculty and passes on the savings to the student." In fact, students describe the teaching staff as no less than a "fleet of hard-core Ivy League pedagogues" who "genuinely care about our academic and professional success." But there are a few who seem "more worried about sticking to the Socratic Method...than ensuring that their students comprehend class materials."

Akron attracts a high-energy and accomplished student body and staff. One student elaborates, "The administration excels at recruiting high-caliber young professors and attracting students who are intelligent, skilled, and capable. In these areas Akron is accomplished and improving." The evening program draws a particularly interesting mix of students, including "physicians, teachers, paralegals, social workers, mid-level managers for *Fortune* 1000 companies, engineers of all sorts, police officers, business owners, amongst the usual part-time types." However, the professional diversity isn't limited to moonlighters; "Second and third year students often take a night class or two, and the two sections become intermixed after that first year."

Discussion, interaction, and practical applications of legal theory take precedence at Akron. "Many of the classrooms are set up like courtrooms, which give students the opportunity to have a courtroom experience, or meeting rooms, which provides the students with an excellent opportunity to discuss and engage in academic debate with the professor and one another," says one student. The school also employs a team of adjunct faculty who "teach the skills that will actually be needed to practice law." In addition, Akron offers a large number of courses that prepare you for the bar (the school boasts a very high bar-passage rate), as well as placing "a strong emphasis on legal research and writing." On top of that, students praise the school's "opportunities for practical experience via internships, clinic placements, trial team, trial practice, and pleading practice classes." For example, students may gain experience through the New Business Legal Clinic that "gives students hands-on transactional business law experience with real clients in the area."

When it comes to job and internship placement, Akron is competitive, especially in the local community. A current student elaborates, "It seems like the students who want big-firm summer associate positions fight for them and get them, just like at any 'higher ranked' school. I have not suffered from any shortage of opportunities here." However, students also complain that the school's "hard" grading policies negatively affect their job opportunities and create unnecessary competition amongst the student body. Plus, lower academic performance can negatively effect or cancel a student's scholarship package, which "the majority of students lose after the first year" due to the steep grading curve.

Life

While course work keeps them busy, "students at Akron are generally social and participate in community activities and student organizations." The school's "very active

LAURI S. THORPE, ASST. DEAN OF ADMISSION, FIN. AID, STUDENT SVCS.
THE UNIVERSITY OF AKRON SCHOOL OF LAW, 302 BUCHTEL COMMON, AKRON, OH 44325-2901
TEL: 800-425-7668 FAX: 330-258-2343
EMAIL: LAWADMISSIONS@UAKRON.EDU • WEBSITE: WWW.UAKRON.EDU/LAW

SBA," coordinates events with the SBA's at neighboring law schools." Students also like the fact that "professors are also present at most school/organizational functions supporting their students in their free time." As is the case for students in most professional programs, the evening division at Akron is less involved in the campus community, since they are usually balancing full-time work with school, and sometimes family. "Among evening students there is not a real sense of community because most of them have full-time jobs and families, and they just don't have time to 'hang out' outside of class," explains a current moonlighter.

Day students warn us that you'll see your share of "drama and gossip" amongst some members of the student body, many of whom are recent college graduates. However, students reassure us that the vibe is generally "very friendly and helpful" amongst their fellow students. One explains, "We attempt to help one another learn, because in the end the future clients are what matters most, and we want all clients, whether they are our own or not, to be represented in the best way possible." Whether of not they study or party together, "All students—evening students included—bond during their first year" thanks to the demanding workload. Don't discount the fact that despite all this work, students here "know how to have fun."

Getting In

The University of Akron's full-time day program and evening program had roughly a 30 percent acceptance rate. The median LSAT score was 158 and 152 for the day and evening programs, respectively. The median undergraduate GPA for all entering students was 3.32. Non-Ohio residents made up approximately 25 percent of the entering class, and 24 different states were represented.

Moot court requirement	No
Public interest law requirement	No

ADMISSIONS

Selectivity Rating	**77**
# applications received	1,670
% applicants accepted	26
% acceptees attending	15
Average LSAT	154
LSAT Range	150–158
Average undergrad GPA	3.38
Regular application	Rolling, up to 8/1
Regular notification	Rolling
Early application program	No
Transfer students accepted	Yes
Evening division offered	Yes
Part-time accepted	Yes
LSDAS accepted	Yes

Applicants Also Look At

The Ohio State University—Columbus, Case Western Reserve University, Cleveland State University, University of Dayton, University of Toledo, Thomas M. Cooley Law School

International Students

TOEFL required of international students	Yes
Minimum TOEFL (paper/computer/web)	600/250/110

FINANCIAL FACTS

Annual tuition (in-state/out-of-state)	$15,007/$25,079
Books and supplies	$900
Fees	$2,436
Fees per credit	$91
Tuition per credit (in-state/out-of-state)	$500/$836
Room & board	$10,100
Financial aid application deadline	3/1
% first-year students receiving some sort of aid	94
% receiving some sort of aid	89
% of aid that is merit based	98
% receiving scholarships	35
Average grant	$14,139
Average loan	$19,336
Average total aid package	$23,694
Average debt	$57,305

EMPLOYMENT INFORMATION

Career Rating	**70**	**Grads Employed by Field (%)**
Rate of placement (nine months out)	82	Academic (1)
Average starting salary	$63,808	Business/Industry (23)
State for bar exam	OH	Government (17)
Pass rate for first-time bar	78	Judicial Clerkships (4)

Employers Who Frequently Hire Grads
Military (2)

Buckingham, Doolittle,& Burroughs; Private Practice (48)
Brouse & McDowell; Roetzel & Andress; Public Interest (5)
Vorys, Sater, Seymour and Pease; Squire, Sanders & Dempsey; Sughrue Mion; Jones Day; 9th District Court of Appeals.

Prominent Alumni
Deborah Cook, Judge, U.S. Court of Appeals-Sixth Circuit; Rochelle Seide, Partner, Schwegman Lundberg Woessner; John Vasuta, VP, Gen. Counsel & Sec., Bridgestone Firestone.

THE UNIVERSITY OF ALABAMA—TUSCALOOSA
SCHOOL OF LAW

INSTITUTIONAL INFORMATION
Public/private	Public
Student-faculty ratio	10:1
% faculty part-time	48
% faculty female	21
% faculty minority	9
Total faculty	99

SURVEY SAYS...
Great research resources
Great library staff
Abundant externship/internship/
clerkship opportunities

STUDENTS
% male/female	60/40
% out-of-state	23
% full-time	97
% minority	13
Average age of entering class	25

ACADEMICS
Academic Experience Rating	71
Profs interesting rating	84
Profs accessible rating	95
Hours of study per day	4.62

Advanced Degrees Offered
LL.M In Taxation, 2 years part-time;
International Graduate Program
(LL.M.), 1 year full-time

Combined Degrees Offered
JD/MBA, 3 or 4 years. Dual enrollment with various University graduate programs

Clinical program required	No
Legal writing	
course requirement	Yes
Legal methods	
course requirement	No
Legal research	
course requirement	Yes
Moot court requirement	Yes
Public interest	
law requirement	No

Academics

Students seeking a very good and very affordable legal education might want to check out The University of Alabama School of Law. "It is unlikely that you will receive a better legal education for the amount of tuition anywhere in the country," ventures a 3L. "The bang for the buck can't be beat." UA offers "small" class sections, a "broad range of courses," and "a wide variety of clinical opportunities" which allow students to get practical experience at the school in exchange for academic credit. "Great study abroad and exchange programs" send students to Switzerland and Australia. In a word, the "overall academic experience is excellent."

"The administration and faculty are friendly and seem to genuinely care about the students." "Alabama professors integrate theory with real-world practicality." "The faculty's mission is not to turn out legal academics, but rather to prepare capable attorneys for real-world situations." In terms of teaching, professors are either "excellent in the classroom" or "deplorable." "There aren't a whole lot of middle-of-the-road professors," explains one student. "I've had the best professors in my life at this school—and the worst." Outside of class, "Professors get to know their students" and "welcome the opportunity to help students in a variety of endeavors." The administration is "top-notch" and "extremely accessible to students." The deans are much beloved and "ready, able, and willing to help you out." In general, staff members "request, listen to, and act on feedback from students," though they "can lag in response time."

"Career Services is still a work in progress, but it is improving." "Because the school is so inexpensive," "Alabama is a no-brainer" for students who are interested in public interest careers. For students interested in private-sector work, UA's reputation is "still regional." Students are "confident" that their degrees "will open doors" throughout the Southeast, but they admit that Career Services tends to "focus on the big regional firms and because of that, most of the attention goes to the students at the very top of the class." "Attracting more out-of-state firms to on-campus recruiting" would be a big improvement.

The facilities here are mostly excellent. The library "screams 1970s," but "has more than sufficient resources." "The new building is terrific." UA "just completed a new wing that has two large, very high-tech seminar classrooms; several high-tech courtrooms; a new dining area and lounge area for students; a new bookstore; and new rooms and offices for all of the law clinics."

Life

The UA law student population is "not very diverse." "There is a small group of Black students and very few Hispanic and Asian students. There are just a couple of older students." "The average student is young and direct from college," and "usually" from Alabama "or from a neighboring state." Students describe themselves as "very smart" and "down-to-earth." Politically, it's a pretty conservative atmosphere, and "expressing a more liberal viewpoint can sometimes be intimidating.'"

Academically, some students are "very grade-oriented" ("bordering on obsession") but, overall, "The competition appears healthy." "Civility among students is paramount," and "The atmosphere at Alabama is extremely collegial." "People at the top are very competitive with each other. But there is also a sort of community with those people as well." "We don't have too many gunners or too many of the socially inept," says

Ms. Claude Reeves Arrington, Associate Dean
Box 870382, Tuscaloosa, AL 35487
Tel: 205-348-5440 Fax: 205-348-5439
Email: admissions@law.ua.edu • Website: www.law.ua.edu

a 2L. "It's friendly competition, because we know we'll all be working together throughout our careers." "Students share course outlines freely."

Socially, UA is "really a great place to study the law." "Students are overwhelmingly friendly and very cooperative." "It has been very easy for me to make several good friends among very diverse individuals with differing interests," says a 2L. "While we study a great deal, we also find time to hit up the bars in large groups." "The Student Bar Association throws parties every other week, and the students all socialize together." Tuscaloosa offers "great weather" and it's "a great college town." If you're not "super-interested" in football, though, "That's sacrilegious down here." Alabama's social scene generally "revolves around sports," and "Football is a near-religious experience." Devotion to the Crimson Tide definitely extends to the law school. Students have their own cheering section, "right there with the fraternities." "We schedule our work so that we can attend Crimson Tide ball games," says a 1L. If you "don't like football, you'll probably have a harder time finding your niche." "However, it is possible to escape that and do your own thing." "Birmingham is an awesome city a mere 45 minutes away from Tuscaloosa and it offers everything an urbanite could need," including "fantastic shopping, excellent restaurants, lots of young singles, a sense of community, and even a little bit of the hipster scene (somewhat of a rarity in Alabama)."

Getting In

At the University of Alabama, matriculated students at the 25th percentile have LSAT scores of 158 and GPAs of nearly 3.3. Enrolled students at the 75th percentile have LSAT scores of 165 and GPAs just over 3.8.

ADMISSIONS

Selectivity Rating	**60***
# applications received	1,276
# applicants accepted	424
# acceptees attending	154
LSAT Range	160–165
Application fee	$40
Regular application	Rolling, up to 3/31
Regular notification	Rolling
Early application program	No
Transfer students accepted	Yes
Evening division offered	No
Part-time accepted	No
LSDAS accepted	Yes

International Students

TOEFL required of international students	Yes

FINANCIAL FACTS

Annual tuition (in-state/ out-of-state)	$12,564/$24,158
Books and supplies	$1,350
Room & board	$9,842

EMPLOYMENT INFORMATION

Career Rating	**79**
Rate of placement (nine months out)	97.4
Average starting salary	$72,527
State for bar exam	AL, GA, FL, TN, VA
Pass rate for first-time bar	90.44

Employers Who Frequently Hire Grads
Bradley Arant Rose & White LLP; Maynard Cooper & Gale, P.C.; Balch & Bingham LLP; Burr & Forman LLP; Lightfoot, Franklin & White, L.L.C.; Kilpatrick Stockton LLP; Alston & Bird LLP; Sirote & Permutt, P.C.; Baker, Donelson, Bearman, Caldwell & Berkowitz, PC; Adams and Reese LLP; Cabaniss, Johnston, Gardner, Dumas & OÂ'Neal LLP.

Grads Employed by Field (%)
Academic (2)
Business/Industry (12)
Government (12)
Judicial Clerkships (12)
Military (4)
Private Practice (54)
Public Interest (4)

UNIVERSITY OF ARIZONA
JAMES E. ROGERS COLLEGE OF LAW

INSTITUTIONAL INFORMATION
Public/private	Public
Student-faculty ratio	12:1
% faculty part-time	42
% faculty female	40
% faculty minority	20
Total faculty	83

SURVEY SAYS...
Diverse opinions accepted
in classrooms
Abundant externship/internship/
clerkship opportunities
Students love Tucson, AZ

STUDENTS
Enrollment of law school	460
% male/female	50/50
% out-of-state	30
% full-time	100
% minority	28
# of countries represented	3
Average age of entering class	26

ACADEMICS
Academic Experience Rating	**89**
Profs interesting rating	87
Profs accessible rating	93
Hours of study per day	4.23

Academic Specialties
Commercial law, constitutional law,
corporation securities, criminal law,
environmental law, human rights,
international law, legal history, legal
philosophy, property, taxation, intellectual property law, indian law, international indigenous peoples rights
and policy, international trade law

Advanced Degrees Offered
JD, 85 units, 3 years; LLM in
International Trade Law, 24 units, 1
year; LLM in Indigenous Peoples
Law and Policy, 24 units, 1 year;
SJD, 3 years.

Clinical program required	No
Legal writing course requirement	Yes
Legal methods course requirement	No

Academics

The University of Arizona James E. Rogers College of Law offers "small class sizes"; "a very friendly, welcoming environment"; and "a price tag that lets students pursue careers in public service and nonprofit organizations" without racking up a gargantuan debt. Opportunities to gain practical experience are plentiful. The "strong" judicial externship program "can accommodate students interested in everything from bankruptcy court to superior court to district court." Clinics offer "hands-on experience" in six areas including immigration, child advocacy, and indigenous peoples' law.

"This school is the most student-focused academic institution I have ever attended," says a happy 3L. The small size "limits the number of advanced classes" available but students tell us that the personal attention they receive more than compensates. Faculty members "truly care about their students" and "are available constantly." In the classroom, professors "make every effort to make the classes interesting and enjoyable" and "The small-section format during first year allows students to build a relationship with at least one professor." "They encourage discussion before and after class and are more than willing to provide letters of recommendation and reference." "They are approachable, friendly, and most even greet you by name as they pass you in the lobby or going to and from class." "Most are around campus all day and not just available during their office hours." "I e-mailed my property professor on a Sunday at roughly 10:30 P.M., with a pretty lengthy question," describes a 2L. "The question was answered at length by 10:45 P.M." "The administration is great too," enthuses a 1L. "Everyone is very helpful and interested in you getting a good education." "The dean is fantastic." "She's approachable" and "will bend over backwards for you." Ideological diversity among the "very left-wing" faculty and administration is limited, though. "The professors do not hide the fact that they are liberal; the student body is liberal; and if you are conservative, you are made to feel like a two-headed monkey monster."

Some students tell us that the "very helpful" Career and Professional Development Office at the U of A is "active in helping students connect with amazing internship and job opportunities in both the public sector and in law firms" in Arizona, California, and other Western states. Other students complain that the Career Office "is less than helpful" and "does not bring in that many employers compared to other law schools." "Their attitude seems to be that they don't care what job you get, as long as you get one somewhere and they can mark you on their statistic sheet," complains a 3L.

Life

There is a "relaxed Arizonan attitude" among the "amazingly friendly, smart" students at the U of A. "There is definitely competition here, as is unavoidable, but the school has a very laid-back atmosphere that allows you to keep things in perspective." "The second- and third-year students are very active in assisting the first-years adapt to law school through tutorials for all first-year classes," and teaching assistants "help with briefing and outlining." "Despite the curve, grades are not a big issue among students, and we tend to be excited for others' successes," declares a 1L. "This place is the opposite of cutthroat." Small sections for first-year students "are really conducive to forming lasting friendships." "I became very close with the other 26 students in my small section and continue to be good friends with several of them," says a 2L. "There is an overriding sense that everyone, from faculty to administration to students, really wants to be at the school and wants to see the school succeed."

The social atmosphere is "very vibrant." "I have had so much fun in law school," gushes a 1L. "There are dozens of student groups and lots of social events." "Almost every day, there are informative and thought-provoking guest speakers, panel discussions, or film screenings, especially during the lunch hour." Intramural sports are also popular. Social tends to be "polarized between younger people coming straight out of college and older students with families." "The crowd divides into three groups," elaborates a 3L, "the married/serious relationship/older crowd, the nerds who rarely go out, and those who are trying to extend their undergraduate experience by going to law school." Without question, if you are "interested in partying, you cannot beat the University of Arizona bar scene."

The U of A campus itself is "beautiful, complete with palm trees and a gigantic, ideal student union." "The weather is ideal." The low cost of living is "fabulous, especially from a student's perspective," but "Tucson itself does not offer much for a social life outside of the undergraduate Greek life scene." If you like outdoor activity, there are "myriad" activities within minutes of campus, including hiking, biking, swimming, and rock climbing.

Getting In

Admitted students at the 25th percentile have LSAT scores in the range of about 158 and GPAs in the range of 3.3 or so. Admitted students at the 75th percentile have LSAT scores of about 164 and GPAs approaching 3.8.

Legal research	
course requirement	Yes
Moot court requirement	No
Public interest	
law requirement	No

ADMISSIONS

Selectivity Rating	**86**
# applications received	2,242
# applicants accepted	756
# acceptees attending	160
Average LSAT	161
LSAT Range	159–164
Average undergrad GPA	3.56
Application fee	$50
Regular application	Rolling, up to 2/15
Regular notification	Rolling
Early application program	Yes
Early application deadline	11/15
Early application notification	12/23
Transfer students accepted	Yes
Evening division offered	No
Part-time accepted	No
LSDAS accepted	Yes

Applicants Also Look At
University of Texas at Austin; University of Southern California; University of California—Los Angeles; Arizona State University; University of California, Davis; University of San Diego; University of California—Hastings

International Students

TOEFL required	
of international students	Yes

FINANCIAL FACTS

Annual tuition (in-state/ out-of-state)	$19,500/$32,200
Books and supplies	$1,000
Room & board	
(on/off-campus)	$8,864/$12,688
Financial aid application	
deadline	3/1
% first-year students	
receiving some sort of aid	80
% receiving some sort of aid	82
% of aid that is merit based	50
% receiving scholarships	75
Average grant	$5,000
Average loan	$13,500
Average total aid package	$18,000
Average debt	$50,000

EMPLOYMENT INFORMATION

		Grads Employed by Field (%)
Career Rating	**79**	**Grads Employed by Field (%)**
Rate of placement (nine months out)	95	Academic (4)
Average starting salary	$76,483	Business/Industry (8)
State for bar exam	AZ, CA, WA, NV, DC	Government (20)
Pass rate for first-time bar	93	Judicial Clerkships (19)
Employers Who Frequently Hire Grads		Military (2)
Firms:Snell & Wilmer; Perkins Coie; Lewis		Private Practice (45)
& Roca; Kirkland & Ellis; Heller Erhman;		Public Interest (2)
Quarles & Brady; Bryan Cave; Greenberg		
Traurig; Squire Sanders; Gibson Dunn.		
Prominent Alumni		
Morris K. Udall, Former Congressman;		
Stewart Udall, Former Congressman &		
Sec'y of Interior; Dennis DeConcini,		
Former Senator.		

UNIVERSITY OF ARKANSAS—FAYETTEVILLE
SCHOOL OF LAW

INSTITUTIONAL INFORMATION
Public/private	Public
Student-faculty ratio	14:1
% faculty part-time	31
% faculty female	14
% faculty minority	6
Total faculty	33

SURVEY SAYS...
Diverse opinions accepted
in classrooms
Great research resources
Beautiful campus
Students love Fayetteville, AR
Good social life

STUDENTS
Enrollment of law school	403
% male/female	59/41
% out-of-state	35
% full-time	100
% minority	20
Average age of entering class	25

ACADEMICS
Academic Experience Rating	**71**
Profs interesting rating	67
Profs accessible rating	68
Hours of study per day	3.92

Advanced Degrees Offered
LL.M in Agricultural Law, one academic year.

Combined Degrees Offered
JD/MBA, 3 years; JD/MPA, 3 years; JD/MA; LLM/MS, 1 years.

Clinical program required	No
Legal writing	
course requirement	Yes
Legal methods	
course requirement	No
Legal research	
course requirement	No
Moot court requirement	No
Public interest	
law requirement	No

Academics

The very affordable University of Arkansas School of Law in Fayetteville provides "some of the best opportunities in the nation to develop real-world skills in trial advocacy." "This campus is the primary source in the state for legal information and is a huge asset to students, as well as local and visiting practitioners and scholars." Clinical opportunities "are few," a new Immigration Law Clinic was just added this past year. Further skills-based courses are ample. There are "many competitions" which "let students put their skills to practice." "Several ongoing collaborative community projects" involve externships and pro bono work. The school offers a traditional JD/MBA program and a unique JD/MA in international law and politics. In addition, students can pursue summer study-abroad programs in Cambridge, England and St. Petersburg, Russia.

You'll find "a diverse range of professors" here, "from the weathered courtroom practitioner to the young vibrant scholar." "While the Socratic Method employed in the classroom is stressful by nature, all of my professors seem to truly care about whether students understand the material," relates a 1L. "They will challenge you, mentor you, and teach you how to be the best advocate possible." "All of my professors have relevant experience that allows them to relate the cases in the book to something they have done in the real world, making those concepts easier to remember in the long run," adds another 1L. Outside the classroom, "All the professors have open-door policies, so you can stop in at anytime to ask anything." Reviews of the administration are mixed. Some students "can't stand the administration." Others call the administration "warm, welcoming, and personable." "They know the majority of the students on a first-name basis" and the deans are "truly helpful in any pursuit you may have, such as disseminating student organization information, providing general and tailored advice about internship searching, and providing pragmatic feedback."

Employment prospects following graduation are fair. "The school seems to have very good clout within the state and pretty good clout around the region." Plenty of students find employment in Little Rock and in smaller communities across the state. Other students don't find jobs in Arkansas because, they say, "There are no jobs available in this state." Northwest Arkansas in particular "is saturated with lawyers and so the starting salaries are depressed."

Facilities at the school "consist of a really ugly old building merged with a really ugly new building." The new building is "high-tech, comfortable, [and] beautiful" on the inside. "The library is now large and very modern. The new classrooms are extremely nice and are very technologically advanced." "With several study rooms, a coffee shop, a brand-new computer lab, a beautiful new courtroom, and many other additions, the U of A Law School facilities rival any other in the nation." Naturally, the new building is now "overrun with undergraduate students who are drawn to the coffee shop and study space." "Ironically, I often go to the campus' main library to study," says a 2L.

Life

The "vibrant and interesting" student population here is seriously diverse. This is either really great or a source of tension, depending on whom you talk to. Some students say that "too much emphasis is placed on diversity," "There is no sense of community," and "There are lots of cliques." "Social circles divide on the basis of race and ethnicity," adds one student. "The student chapter of BLSA (Black Law Student Association), of which I am a member, is strong and active but not overly inclusive of non-Black students,"

JAMES K. MILLER, ASSOCIATE DEAN FOR STUDENTS
UNIVERSITY OF ARKANSAS SCHOOL OF LAW, FAYETTEVILLE, AR 72701
TEL: 479-575-3102 FAX: 479-575-3937
EMAIL: JKMILLER@UARK.EDU • WEBSITE: LAW.UARK.EDU

observes a 3L. "It's a great support [network] but also a segregating factor." Other students disagree entirely. "I am amazed at the diversity in the law school, both among students and faculty," beams a 1L. "I've never noticed a racial divide." "Social circles seem to be quite diverse." "The majority of the campus and classes aren't divided or walking on eggshells about this issue." "I am originally from Los Angeles and I had some concerns that such a divide would exist in a Southern law school," explains a 3L. "I was pleasantly surprised with the racial interaction and harmony among the law students."

With only about 150 students per class, "everyone knows everybody." "Competitiveness among the student body varies widely by groups. Some are very competitive, others not so much." Mostly, "Students are courteous and friendly" and "generally willing to help each other study." When students put away their casebooks, there are "many social events to attend coordinated by the law school." "The social life is quite good," and it's really good if you like "drinking at different locations." The surrounding college town of Fayetteville oozes with "hometown charm" and is "a great place to be." According to one student, "Northwest Arkansas is the most beautiful part of the country."

Getting In

Recently admitted students at the 25th percentile have LSAT scores of about 153 and GPAs in the 3.25 range. Admitted students at the 75th percentile have LSAT scores of about 159 and GPAs approaching 3.73.

ADMISSIONS

Selectivity Rating	80
# applications received	1,239
# applicants accepted	381
# acceptees attending	137
Average LSAT	155
LSAT Range	153–159
Average undergrad GPA	3.53
Regular application	Rolling, up to 4/1
Regular notification	Rolling
Early application program	No
Transfer students accepted	Yes
Evening division offered	No
Part-time accepted	No
LSDAS accepted	Yes

International Students

TOEFL required of international students	Yes
Minimum TOEFL (paper/computer)	550/213

FINANCIAL FACTS

Annual tuition (in-state/ out-of-state)	$10,712/$21,379
Books and supplies	$1,000
Fees	$1,433
Financial aid application deadline	4/1
% first-year students receiving some sort of aid	82
% receiving some sort of aid	82
% of aid that is merit based	66
% receiving scholarships	66
Average grant	$6,000
Average loan	$18,500
Average debt	$51,336

EMPLOYMENT INFORMATION

Career Rating	70
Rate of placement (nine months out)	91
Average starting salary	$53,505
State for bar exam	AR, GA, MO, OK, TX

Employers Who Frequently Hire Grads
Wright, Lindsey & Jennings LLP; Friday, Eldredge & Clark LLP; Mitchell Williams; Kutak Rock LLP.

Prominent Alumni
George W. Haley, Former Ambassador to Gambia; Mark Pryor, U.S. Senator from Arkansas; Mike Beebe, Governor of Arkansas; Rodney Slater, Former U.S. Secretary of Transportation.

Grads Employed by Field (%)
Academic (2)
Business/Industry (17)
Government (15)
Judicial Clerkships (3)
Private Practice (62)
Public Interest (1)

UNIVERSITY OF ARKANSAS—LITTLE ROCK
WILLIAM H. BOWEN SCHOOL OF LAW

INSTITUTIONAL INFORMATION

Public/private	Public
Student-faculty ratio	14:1
% faculty part-time	68
% faculty female	41
% faculty minority	14
Total faculty	107

SURVEY SAYS...
Diverse opinions accepted
in classrooms
Great research resources
Great library staff

STUDENTS

Enrollment of law school	456
% male/female	52/48
% out-of-state	20
% full-time	68
% minority	20
% international	2
# of countries represented	3
Average age of entering class	26

ACADEMICS

Academic Experience Rating	**70**
Profs interesting rating	64
Profs accessible rating	71
Hours of study per day	4.31

Academic Specialties
Civil procedure, commercial law, constitutional law, corporation securities, criminal law, environmental law, government services, international law, labor law, legal history, property, taxation, health law

Combined Degrees Offered
JD/MBA, JD/MPA, JD/MPH; 3.5–4 years, JD/MD, 7 years

Clinical program required	No
Legal writing course requirement	Yes
Legal methods course requirement	Yes
Legal research course requirement	Yes
Moot court requirement	No
Public interest law requirement	No

Academics

For the prospective law student interested in practicing in the state of Arkansas or regionally, it's hard to beat the "location" and "quality of instruction for your dollar" that the William H. Bowen School of Law offers. Because the school "is in the capital of the state, there are many opportunities for practical experience" such as "externships . . . for justices in the Arkansas Supreme Court, Federal District Court, and the U.S. Court of Appeals for the Eighth Circuit." The location also likely has something to do with the sizable part-time JD program offered here. Many say that "it is great for part-time students" and that the "school does not push off adjunct professors on the part-time students; instead full-time faculty members are required to also teach in the part-time division." In terms of price, tuition and fees clock in at just over $10,000 a year for in-state students—what you might call a legal steal.

The school has reportedly "spent $1 million . . . in renovations" in recent years. Results include "wireless and plugs for laptops at every seat" and "high-tech teaching workstations with projectors and cameras to video capture the class for students that are not there. They also have high-tech sound systems with microphones throughout the room so everybody can be heard." The "incredible" library has "an abundance of private study areas and more than adequate [research] resources." Most students agree that the school should focus its next round of capital improvements on dining facilities. "The lunch room and general access to food is terrible. There is no place within walking distance to get a cup of coffee!" says one student. The solution? "Build a cafeteria."

Professors at Bowen "are not in any shape, form, or fashion second-rate: They all have some pretty impressive resumes and most of them have practical experience" to inform the theories they teach. "They all seem genuinely engaged in teaching law" and "really care about your health [and] your well-being" as a student. They are "knowledgeable," "not haughty," and "demand high effort from students." This faculty is complemented by a "very helpful and approachable" administration.

The school promotes a "friendly" and "supportive" environment that fosters "an atmosphere of cooperation" rather than "abound[ing]" competition. But expect a challenge. "Everyone wants you to do the best that you possibly can with the best resources and the most thorough understanding, and then they want to beat you," explains one student. However students would like to see the grading curve "raised" or see the school "get rid" of it since many find that though they enjoy "being challenged on the level of graduates from across the country," "Our grades make us look inferior" to students from law schools with more forgiving curves.

AARON N. TAYLOR, ASSISTANT DEAN FOR ADMISSIONS
1201 MCMATH AVENUE, LITTLE ROCK, AR 72202-5142
TEL: 501-324-9903 FAX: 501-324-9433
EMAIL: LAWADM@UALR.EDU • WEBSITE: WWW.LAW.UALR.EDU

Life

The relatively small Bowen School of Law has a very solid mix of full-time and part-time students and "there are a lot of opportunities for students to meet each other and mix." "If you want a social life, there is always someone who wants to go out with you," says one student. "The hard part is actually refusing temptation."

The part-timers, who represent the other third of the student population, apparently have an easier time resisting the lure than the full-timers do. One typical member of this cohort indicates that he has been "invited to social functions by other students, but have mostly declined. Any time I have outside of class and studying I want to spend with my wife, the law school widow." That said, "The social life among the part-timers is pretty good considering we all have a lot of things going on; we still find time to occasionally go out for some drinks or whatever." Like most part-timers at most law schools, those here think they are "less competitive than the full-timers, for a variety of reasons—most of us work, most have other life priorities, [and] most realize grades aren't everything."

Students happily note that "there are a ton of meetings with free food every week." As one explains, "You can manage a free lunch at least twice a week just by going to lectures and meetings." Students "love the location," though a few mention that the school sits "in a pretty gnarly part of town."

Getting In

Bowen's admissions standards are comparable to its sister school in Fayetteville, so if you get in there, you have a very good shot at getting in here, too (and vice versa). A B-plus/A-minus undergraduate grade point average and an LSAT score in the mid-150s makes you a competitive candidate here, if not a shoo-in. For those with marks below these, note that the Admissions Office considers the personal statement the most important factor in its admissions decision-making process, so a compelling argument can go a long way in getting you through the door.

ADMISSIONS

Selectivity Rating	81
# applications received	1,589
# applicants accepted	409
# acceptees attending	154
Average LSAT	154
LSAT Range	150–157
Average undergrad GPA	3.28
Regular application	Rolling, up to 04/15
Regular notification	Rolling
Early application program	Yes
Early application deadline	01/01
Early application notification	01/15
Transfer students accepted	Yes
Evening division offered	Yes
Part-time accepted	Yes
LSDAS accepted	Yes

Applicants Also Look At
University of Arkansas—Fayetteville,
University of Missouri—Columbia,
University of Tulsa

International Students
TOEFL recommended of international students	Yes

FINANCIAL FACTS

Annual tuition (in-state/ out-of-state)	$9,486/$29,812
Books and supplies	$1,250
Fees	$1,321
Tuition per credi (in-state/ out-of-state)	$316/$693
Room & board (off-campus)	$7,454
Financial aid application deadline	3/1
% first-year students receiving some sort of aid	74
% receiving some sort of aid	79
% of aid that is merit based	50
% receiving scholarships	30
Average grant	$4,557
Average loan	$19,500
Average total aid package	$19,500
Average debt	$51,000

EMPLOYMENT INFORMATION

Career Rating	61	
Rate of placement (nine months out)	98	
Average starting salary		$53,000
State for bar exam	AR, TN, TX, GA, FL	
Pass rate for first-time bar	77	

Employers Who Frequently Hire Grads
Wright, Lindsey & Jennings Law Firm;
Friday, Eldredge & Clark Law Firm;
Prosecuting Attorney;

Prominent Alumni
Vic Snyder, Member, U.S. Congress;
Annabelle Clinton-Imber, State Supreme
Court; Dustin McDaniel, Arkansas Attorney
General; Beth Deere, U.S. Magistrate
Judge for the Eastern District of Arkansas

Grads Employed by Field (%)
Academic (3)
Business/Industry (19)
Government (18)
Judicial Clerkships (4)
Private Practice (56)
Public Interest (4)

UNIVERSITY OF CALIFORNIA
HASTINGS COLLEGE OF THE LAW

INSTITUTIONAL INFORMATION

Public/private	Public
Student-faculty ratio	15:1
% faculty part-time	57
% faculty female	38
% faculty minority	20
Total faculty	168

SURVEY SAYS...

Diverse opinions accepted in classrooms
Abundant externship/internship/ clerkship opportunities
Students never sleep
Liberal students

STUDENTS

Enrollment of law school	1,251
% male/female	46/54
% full-time	100
% minority	33
# of countries represented	13
Average age of entering class	24

ACADEMICS

Academic Experience Rating	**79**
Profs interesting rating	80
Profs accessible rating	61
Hours of study per day	4.22

Academic Specialties

Criminal law, international law, taxation, intellectual property law, civil litigation, Public interest law

Advanced Degrees Offered

JD, 3 years; LL.M., 1 year

Combined Degrees Offered

JD and LLM degrees offered at Hastings; may combine JD with other institutions' masters' degrees, with some cross-crediting (e.g. JD/MBA can be completed together in 4 rather than 5 years separately).

Clinical program required	No
Legal writing course requirement	Yes
Legal methods course requirement	No
Legal research Course requirement	Yes

Academics

The University of California's Hastings College of the Law "is like the redheaded stepchild among public law schools in California." While Hastings offers a "great commitment to legal education, an ambitious student body, and a wonderful alumni reputation," it's often underrated. Plus, there are "way too many students." (1L sections have "about 85 people.") Some students tell us that the grading curve is "ruthless"; others note that "most students get B's." Hastings has "a number of notable legal scholars," many whom have "written their own casebooks." "The problem is that there are not enough of them." Faculty accessibility can be sparse, too, though "Some of the professors genuinely care about students' learning and even their well-being." Administratively, "Hastings is a great school for making you feel wanted and treating you like an adult." "There's not a lot of hand-holding here, but the support is there (in ample supply) when you need it."

At Hastings, "If you walk away without practical experience, it's your own fault," admonishes a 2L. "The focus is on getting students to actually practice the law, rather than just study it." "Theories are taught when necessary." "Hastings is right next to practically every courtroom in Northern California," so "There are unparalleled opportunities to extern." Clinics are abundant. The "invaluable" moot court program is "one of the best in the country." Other highlights include the Legal Education Opportunity Program, an academic support program for students who have had to face a lot of educational obstacles.

Career Services "is very helpful," offering "tons of forums and panels pertaining to different types of law." Students appreciate that the "responsive" staff is "honestly interested in helping students find the right job for them." Others are highly critical. "They focus way too much on the top 25 percent of the class," leaving the rest to "just fend for [them]selves," charges a 3L. A happy contingent of students brags about the "huge" alumni network, particularly in the area. "Just about every big law firm comes to interview," enthuses a 2L. Hastings is also "very good at pointing out alternatives to a traditional law firm." "The school does a good job of encouraging public interest work." Hastings is also "a big feeder" for district attorney and public defender offices.

Hasting's "busy, urban campus" is in "the worst neighborhood in an otherwise beautiful city." "A seismic retrofit renovation" of the facilities is pretty much completed. However, student say it's still "an ugly school" (and "the lack of working copy machines and printers" can be annoying). On the upside, "Classrooms are spacious and modern," "with comfortable chairs." There is "wireless everywhere" and "The library is completely brand new."

Life

Students here are "intelligent and hardworking." Though Hastings students are a left-leaning, liberal bunch, "Everyone is welcome, even conservatives." "Contrary to popular myth," claims a 1L, "Hastings is not competitive." Other students tell us that "there are definitely some very competitive students." "You will have at least one time when you're slapped in the face with the fact that people are trying to outdo you." Still others describe a more nuanced situation. "Hastings gets a bad rap from young students who should have been out in the world for a while before coming here, and who have a chip on their shoulders because they didn't get into Boalt." Ultimately, "Hastings is designed for people with thick skin." "I am now thoroughly calloused," explains a 3L. "If you want to be known as a tough lawyer, go to Hastings."

GREG CANADA, DIRECTOR OF ADMISSIONS
200 McALLISTER STREET, SAN FRANCISCO, CA 94102
TEL: 415-565-4623 FAX: 415-581-8946
EMAIL: ADMISS@UCHASTINGS.EDU • WEBSITE: WWW.UCHASTINGS.EDU

"Hastings is basically a commuter school," and it can be "hard to feel connected" here. On the other hand, there are "lots of ways for students to get involved and pursue their own interests." "There are micro-communities if you join a student organization like the public interest group or a journal," and "If you want to participate in something that interests you, this is a place that will definitely support and encourage it." "Most of the social life is centered on the students living in the campus housing." "There's free beer every other Thursday on the concrete patio affectionately called 'The Beach.'"

Hastings is "right in the heart of San Francisco," "a world-class city" with "good public transportation" and teeming with cultural activity. On the downside, Hastings is located in a "homeless Mecca" called The Tenderloin, "the epicenter of drugged-out craziness on the West Coast." "This is humanity at its lowest, at its down-and-outest," warns a 2L. "For some, it's an opportunity to engage with a community in need." "For others, it's a source of annoyance, hassle, and fear." "I would be dumbfounded to hear that an alumnus ever came back to campus for nostalgic purposes," suggests one student. "I recommend everyone interested in attending Hastings at least come and check out the neighborhood so they know what it's like."

Getting In

Students admitted to Hastings at the 25th percentile have LSAT scores of 160 and GPAs of about 3.4. Admitted students at the 75th percentile have LSAT scores of 165 and GPAs of about 3.75. If you feel like you've faced a lot of cultural or economic obstacles in your academic career, check out the Legal Education Opportunity Program, which accepts students with lower numbers but requires a more complex application.

Moot court requirement	Yes
Public interest law requirement	No

ADMISSIONS

Selectivity Rating	90
# applications received	5,982
% applicants accepted	24
% acceptees attending	30
Average LSAT	163
LSAT Range	161–165
Average undergrad GPA	3.57
Application fee	$75
Regular application	Rolling, up to 3/1
Regular notification	Rolling
Early application program	Yes
Early application deadline	11/15
Early application notification	12/15
Transfer students accepted	Yes
Evening division offered	No
Part-time accepted	No
LSDAS accepted	Yes

Applicants Also Look At
University of Southern California. University of California—Berkeley. University of California—Los Angeles. Boston University. Boston College. University of California—Davis. Fordham University. University of San Francisco

FINANCIAL FACTS

Annual tuition (in-state/out-of-state)	$28,864/$40,089
Books and supplies	$1,150
Fees	$2,861
Room & board	$14,040
Financial aid application deadline	3/1
% first-year students receiving some sort of aid	90
% receiving some sort of aid	90
% of aid that is merit based	1
% receiving scholarships	78
Average grant	$8,989
Average loan	$32,727
Average total aid package	$39,617
Average debt	$85,421

EMPLOYMENT INFORMATION

		Grads Employed by Field (%)
Career Rating	91	Business/Industry (8)
Rate of placement (nine months out)	93	Government (8)
Average starting salary	$114,853	Judicial Clerkships (6)
State for bar exam	CA, NY	Private Practice (63)
Pass rate for first-time bar	81.5	Public Interest (6)

Employers Who Frequently Hire Grads
Major San Francisco and Los Angeles large and medium-size law firms.

Prominent Alumni
Marvin Baxter, Associate Justice, CA Supreme Court; Willie Brown, Former Mayor, San Francisco; Carol Corrigan, Associate Justice, CA Supreme Court; Joseph Cotchett, Founding Partner, Cotchett Pitre & Simon.

UNIVERSITY OF CALIFORNIA—BERKELEY
BERKELEY LAW

INSTITUTIONAL INFORMATION

Public/private	Public
Student-faculty ratio	12:1
% faculty part-time	37
% faculty female	41
% faculty minority	11
Total faculty	140

SURVEY SAYS...
Great library staff
Liberal students
Students love Berkeley, CA

STUDENTS

Enrollment of law school	874
% male/female	46/54
% out-of-state	40
% full-time	100
% minority	34
# of countries represented	27
Average age of entering class	24

ACADEMICS

Academic Experience Rating	**94**
Profs interesting rating	85
Profs accessible rating	82
Hours of study per day	3.74

Academic Specialties
Corporation securities, environmental law, international law, intellectual property law, law & technology, comparative legal studies, business law & economics, social justice.

Advanced Degrees Offered
LL.M., (1 year); J.S.D., (number of years to completion varies); Ph.D. in Jurisprudence and Social Policy, (6 years).

Combined Degrees Offered
JD/M.A. and JD/Ph.D. Economics; JD/M.B.A. School of Business; JD/M.A. Asian Studies; JD/M.A. International Area Studies; JD/M.C.P. Department of City and Regional Planning; JD/M.J. Graduate School of Journalism; JD/M.P.P. School of Public Policy; JD/M.S.W. School of Social Welfare; JD/M.A. and JD/Ph.D. Information Management Systems; JD/Ph.D. History (Legal History); JD/M.S. J.D./Ph.D.

Academics

UC—Berkeley Boalt School of Law gives its happy students a "rigorous and yet collegial" academic environment surrounded by beautiful scenery and ripe opportunities. The "ingeniously" laid-back grading scale (described as an "all-or-nothing curve") is a "blessing," as it takes much of the pressure off, and "there is almost no feeling that students are competing with one another." "It allows you to focus on the courses you really like and found engaging and not stress out about the ones that you ended up not hitting it off with so well," says a 3L. As one might expect, the job opportunities for a Berkeley Law grad are pretty plum, as the strong reputation facilitates landing summer associate jobs at prestigious firms all around the world, but there are fantastic opportunities for pro-bono clinical involvement as well. Berkeley also has "a huge network of alums," who can be called upon for advice and advancement, especially in the west. The LRAP (debt repayment) program for students who choose to go work in the public interest is also one of the best in the nation, and it "definitely helps those who are dedicated to public interest work actually feasibly enter it."

Classes fill up quickly, which, coupled with the "disorganized" registrar's office, means that some core classes can have a wait list, but there is a "breadth of specialized courses" also available, and "small section classes make the 1L year a little more inviting." "It is wonderful to be able to pick electives your second semester, and very fulfilling to be a member of a journal from your very first week," says a student. A "great mix" of legal theory and practicum courses are offered, and in any given semester, you can likely find a prof looking for a student to help with research, as well as a variety of clinics and centers doing both practical and academic legal research, although there's still no environmental law clinic ("grrrr," says one student). The top-notch professors "take pride in teaching at Berkeley" and most "are engaging and luminaries in their fields," no question about it. But some students get the feeling that a few can be more focused on their research and sabbaticals, and there are a large number of visiting professors. Liberalism is present not just in the students but in the faculty, and "freedom of speech is a protected value in the classroom."

Students speak highly of the dean, claiming he "has a vision for the school" that will vault Berkeley Law even higher in people's eyes, and "he cuts an accessible and friendly figure in his suits and tennis shoes, getting himself coffee at the student cafe." Students partake in most of the major decisions made at Boalt, and students say one of the biggest pluses of Boalt life is, well, themselves. "Everyone has a story and interesting background... the student groups are the backbone of student life," says one. However, nobody comes to Boalt for the architecture or the furniture, they come "because it can stand toe-to-toe with the best law schools DESPITE its facilities"; the law building looks like it hasn't been updated "since the 70s," though there have been some improvements made and more renovations are in full swing.

EDWARD TOM, ASSISTANT DEAN OF ADMISSIONS
2850 TELEGRAPH AVENUE, SUITE 500, BERKELEY, CA 94720-7200
TEL: 510-642-2274 FAX: 510-643-6222
EMAIL: ADMISSIONS@LAW.BERKELEY.EDU • WEBSITE: WWW.LAW.BERKELEY.EDU

Life

The Admissions team does "a great job of admitting a very diverse class with varied career goals," and everyone is "astonishingly smart but also sane, kind, and interesting." Students "are thrilled to be here" and cannot stress the lack of cutthroatism enough, and everyone here benefits from their classmates' intelligence and experiences while very rarely having to directly compete with them for job opportunities. "Everyone is ambitious, and yet we have very few gunners," says a student. "There is a deep-seated sense that we are all in this together," says another. Berkeley Law is located in the San Francisco Bay Area, a great place to live at all times of year, and the small "mod" groups the first year enable a manageable community right off the bat. Every Thursday night there is the classic law school "bar review" where everyone goes to a pre-specified bar ("whose location is mysteriously posted early Thursday mornings") and gets to know their fellow classmates, plus there are tons of student organizations. Unlike a lot of law schools, all of the journals (except for the Law Review) are open membership and students are allowed to participate "from the second you start." Much like the professors, students are very liberal, so if you are anywhere near the center or, God forbid, right of the political scale, "be prepared to endure lots of super liberal comments about race and politics, with little tolerance for other points of view."

Getting In

Good luck. Berkeley Law receives approximately 8,000 applications annually for fewer than 300 first-year spots. The average GPA for enrolled students is 3.84, and the average LSAT score is 167, but the LSAT range is quite broad. Berkeley Law also prides itself on considering more than just an applicant's grades and test scores, reviewing extracurricular activities, achievements, and the overcoming of obstacles when making an admissions decision.

Clinical program required	No
Legal writing course requirement	Yes
Legal methods course requirement	Yes
Legal research course requirement	Yes
Moot court requirement	Yes
Public interest law requirement	No

ADMISSIONS

Selectivity Rating	98
# applications received	7,957
# applicants accepted	791
# acceptees attending	273
Average LSAT	167
LSAT Range	150–180
Average undergrad GPA	3.84
Application fee	$75
Regular application	Rolling, up to 2/1
Regular notification	Rolling
Early application program	No
Transfer students accepted	Yes
Evening division offered	No
Part-time accepted	No
LSDAS accepted	Yes

Applicants Also Look At

University of Southern California; Columbia University; University of California—Los Angeles; New York University; Stanford University; Georgetown University; University of California—Hastings, University of Chicago, Michigan State University

International Students

TOEFL required of international students	Yes
Minimum TOEFL (paper/computer/web)	600/250/100

FINANCIAL FACTS

Annual tuition	$12,245
Books and supplies	$1,495
Fees	$30,943
Room & board	$15,485
Financial aid application deadline	3/2
% first-year students receiving some sort of aid	90
% receiving some sort of aid	89
% of aid that is merit based	9
% receiving scholarships	64
Average grant	$10,260
Average loan	$30,832
Average total aid package	$37,895
Average debt	$74,802

EMPLOYMENT INFORMATION

		Grads Employed by Field (%)
Career Rating	92	Business/Industry (4)
Rate of placement (nine months out)	97	Government (5)
Average starting salary	$135,000	Judicial Clerkships (9)
State for bar exam	CA	Private Practice (72)
Pass rate for first-time bar	88	Public Interest (10)

Employers Who Frequently Hire Grads

Roughly 450 employers recruit at Berkeley Law each fall including national firms, multi-national corporations, public interest groups, and governmental agencies.

UNIVERSITY OF CALIFORNIA—DAVIS
SCHOOL OF LAW

INSTITUTIONAL INFORMATION

Public/private	Public
Student-faculty ratio	12:1
% faculty part-time	26
% faculty female	37
% faculty minority	34
Total faculty	62

SURVEY SAYS...
Diverse opinions accepted
in classrooms
Great library staff

STUDENTS

Enrollment of law school	578
% male/female	47/53
% full-time	100
% minority	38
# of countries represented	12
Average age of entering class	25

ACADEMICS

Academic Experience Rating	**85**
Profs interesting rating	82
Profs accessible rating	85
Hours of study per day	4.32

Academic Specialties
Criminal law, environmental law,
human rights, international law, taxation, intellectual property law, business, social justice

Advanced Degrees Offered
LL.M, 1 year

Combined Degrees Offered
JD/MBA, 4 years; JD/MA, JD/MS, 4
years

Clinical program required	No
Legal writing	
course requirement	Yes
Legal methods	
course requirement	Yes
Legal research	
course requirement	Yes
Moot court requirement	No
Public interest	
law requirement	No

Academics

The "cozy" University of California—Davis, School of Law is "one of the smallest law schools in California." The "dynamic" professors here "know what they're talking about" and are "passionate about teaching." Sure, some are "mean and unhappy," but overall, "The faculty is the best part of King Hall." "Most use some form or other of the Socratic Method." "My professors have at least added humor to my life, ranging from role play (like arresting people in class) and poking fun at our being stumped over rela- tively simple questions just because it's sometimes terrifying to be called on," relates a 2L. These "incredibly approachable" professors are also "willing to help in anyway they can to enhance your education or career goals." Tutors in the highly praised teaching assistant program "hold office hours and review sessions to solidify big-picture concepts" for 1Ls. The UCD administration is good at "seeking student involvement in decision-making."

The whopping 11 clinics at UCD "are a great way to really understand how to practice law." The prison law clinic in particular "has enjoyed a great deal of success and acclaim." There are certificate programs in public service law and environmental law, and students say they are "truly are committed to public interest work." "We take the fact that we are named after Martin Luther King Jr. very seriously," asserts a 2L. "It's great to be in an environment where people truly care about cause lawyering." However, many students pine for more of a course selection. "About one-fourth of a class has the oppor- tunity to take Pre-trial Skills, but there are so many classes like Latinos and the Law and Disability Rights with classrooms that sit half empty."

As for employment, alumni are "supportive," and with San Francisco and Sacramento nearby, "Davis is conveniently connected to two powerful cities that are full of federal, state, and local agencies as well as important judicial offices." Students complain that the "inept" Career Services staff "needs to get its act together," though the school is working to increase student satisfaction in this department. "'Big-law' possibilities are fairly good," and "approximately 25 percent of the student body will work in a large law firm after graduation." There is "an awesome loan forgiveness program" for graduates who pursue public interest careers.

The "depressing" King Law building is "run down and showing its age." "There's not a lot of windows," and "Space is a big issue." The "ancient" chairs are "very uncomfort- able." The library is an "exceptional" research facility, but it's "grungy," "with a little bit of a 1960s industrial feel." "Fortunately the school is about to undergo a dramatic facelift." "Future classes should have newer and more spacious facilities."

Life

Student diversity is comparatively strong on campus, with a visible "Asian and Pacific Islander" presence and a "decent" Hispanic student population. "There are active Jewish, Muslim, and Catholic student groups in the law school, as well as a feminist forum, a pro-choice group, a GLBT group, and a Federalist society." Politically, "Students are often very liberal or very conservative" and "Moderates aren't very vocal."

"There is certainly competition" among students, but "the King Hall Spirit" "keeps it from getting dirty or uncomfortable." "A laid-back atmosphere" permeates. "People loan notes and books without a qualm." "Not that we all hold hands in the hallway and sing Kumbaya," elaborates a 3L, "but everybody is very respectful and has a good time together." Socially, "Most people find a niche," and events and parties occur "pretty

SHARON L. PINKNEY, DIRECTOR OF ADMISSION
SCHOOL OF LAW-KING HALL, 400 MRAK HALL DRIVE, DAVIS, CA 95616-5201
TEL: 530-752-6477
EMAIL: ADMISSIONS@LAW.UCDAVIS.EDU • WEBSITE: WWW.LAW.UCDAVIS.EDU

much every weekend." "There are a large number of traditions at King Hall that students really get into" as well, including "softball and bowling leagues, the law school talent show, and a law school prom." "While these may seem lame and tacky, they are actually really fun, and the large majority of students get involved," explains a 3L. There's also "a co-op nursery, so students with children can drop their kids off while in class."

"The city of Davis is a delightful college town." "You don't have to fight traffic, and people are just downright friendly." "Armies of students ride bicycles to classes, and the fun downtown area is a short walk from campus." There is a "dearth of interesting restaurants," but "The weather is nice." "You can focus," notes a 3L, because "It's quiet." "Davis is a fantastic place to spend three years of graduate school," adds another 3L.

"Sacramento is 15 minutes away and the Bay Area is only an hour [away]." "Great skiing" and "wine country" are not far. Davis is also "a town where hippies settle down after . . . making high salaries." As a result, apartments aren't cheap. "The housing crunch cannot be overstated enough," warns a 2L. "Students considering Davis should immediately check Craigslist and do everything in their power to get housing secured as soon as they accept."

Getting In

Admitted students at the 25th percentile have LSAT scores of 161 and GPAs of nearly 3.5. Admitted students at the 75th percentile have LSAT scores of 166 and GPAs of 3.8. UC Davis will consider all LSAT scores and asks that applicants add an addendum explaining increases of 5 points or more for multiple LSAT scores.

ADMISSIONS

Selectivity Rating	87
# applications received	3,310
# applicants accepted	1,005
# acceptees attending	200
Average LSAT	160
LSAT Range	143–172
Average undergrad GPA	3.57
Application fee	$75
Regular application	Rolling, up to 2/1
Regular notification	Rolling
Early application program	No
Transfer students accepted	Yes
Evening division offered	No
Part-time accepted	No
LSDAS accepted	Yes

Applicants Also Look At

University of California—Berkeley, University of California—Los Angeles, University of California, Hastings

International Students

TMinimum TOEFL (paper/computer)	600/250

FINANCIAL FACTS

Annual tuition	$12,245
Books and supplies	$1,014
Fees	$25,515
Room & board (off-campus)	$11,584
Financial aid application deadline	3/2
% first-year students receiving some sort of aid	89
% receiving some sort of aid	89
% of aid that is merit based	3
% receiving scholarships	75
Average grant	$11,500
Average loan	$25,380
Average total aid package	$36,880
Average debt	$66,620

EMPLOYMENT INFORMATION

Career Rating	83	**Grads Employed by Field (%)**
Rate of placement (nine months out)	96	Academic (2)
Average starting salary	$96,807	Business/Industry (7)
State for bar exam	CA	Government (11)
Pass rate for first-time bar	84	Judicial Clerkships (5)
		Military (1)
		Private Practice (60)
		Public Interest (13)

UNIVERSITY OF CALIFORNIA—LOS ANGELES
SCHOOL OF LAW

INSTITUTIONAL INFORMATION

Public/private	Public
Student-faculty ratio	12:1
% faculty part-time	32
% faculty female	33
% faculty minority	10
Total faculty	165

SURVEY SAYS...

Great research resources
Great library staff
Students love Los Angeles, CA

STUDENTS

Enrollment of law school	1,012
% male/female	53/47
% out-of-state	32
% full-time	100
% minority	15
% international	2
# of countries represented	12
Average age of entering class	25

ACADEMICS

Academic Experience Rating	**95**
Profs interesting rating	89
Profs accessible rating	75
Hours of study per day	3.58

Academic Specialties

Constitutional law, corporation securities, criminal law, environmental law, human rights, international law, labor law, legal philosophy, property, taxation, intellectual property law, public interest law and policy, business law and policy program, critical race studies, entertainment and media law and policy program

Advanced Degrees Offered

In addition to the JD degree, we offer a one-year Master of Laws (LL.M.)

Combined Degrees Offered

JD/M.A. (African American Studies), JD/M.A. (American Indian Studies), JD/M.B.A, JD/Ph.D. (Philosophy), JD/M.P.H, JD/M.A. (Public Policy), JD/M.S.W. (Social Welfare), and JD/M.A. (Urban Planning)

Academics

"If you are looking for professors who encourage you, want you to do well, and want to interact with you outside of school, UCLA School of Law is ideal," proclaims a satisfied 1L. Though in the past students have noted that class sizes "are probably larger than they are at most schools," the first year curriculum has been changed. Students have 3 small sections of 40 students or less. "UCLA has a very positive academic atmosphere." "The resources are boundless," and students brag that they are receiving "a world-class legal education in a beautiful city." "Superstar professors" regularly teach 1L courses and the faculty as a whole is full of "amazing and dedicated teachers" who are "quite witty and entertaining." They "will cold-call students, but if you're not able to answer the question, saying 'I don't know' is fine, and they'll leave you alone." The administration is hit-or-miss. Some administrators are "amazingly accessible." "One particular time I went in to get an extension on an independent study paper and wound up playing Barrel of Monkeys for 20 minutes with the Dean of Students," relates a 3L. "I won and she wants a rematch." "The Financial Aid Office seems to get very little right," though, and the bureaucracy can be "horribly inefficient and a pain to wade through." "I don't know how much of that is the law school's fault as opposed to the UC system's," offers a 1L.

"The grading curve is not particularly brutal." "About 60 percent get B's," estimates one student. The curriculum stresses theory as well as practical skills (though one student calls the legal writing curriculum "completely impractical"). The "incredibly valuable" clinical program "is truly the institution's crown jewel." "Trial advocacy is the best class that I have taken at any level," attests a 3L, and the "incredible" public interest program "can turn out lawyers who want to make the world better." Still, many wish that there was less focus placed upon gearing students towards corporate law.

Graduates don't have much of a problem finding jobs. "It is completely standard to leave here and earn $130,000" in your first year as an attorney. UCLA has an "excellent reputation among the big firms in Los Angeles" and is "highly regarded nationally." "Many students also go to work in New York and Washington, DC." "Those who, for some absurd reason, want to leave behind the fantastically high quality of life offered here and instead earn the same money but for more hours in Manhattan seem to have no problem doing so," notes a 1L.

The UCLA campus as a whole is "stunning." "The school is located on the most beautiful part of the generally gorgeous UCLA campus, in one of the most upscale parts of Los Angeles." "The law school building looks great on the outside, but is outdated on the inside." "Classes, bathrooms, and the library are all overcrowded." The "cramped" classrooms "are equipped for laptops," but "need some aesthetic upgrading." On the upside, the "luxurious and modern law library" has "big windows," making it "a pleasing place to study."

Life

Students describe themselves as "very smart." A lot of students complain about the lack of ethnic diversity on campus; "It bears no resemblance to the demographics of the population of the United States, much less that of California." Whatever the case, students "interact well with each other." "Different backgrounds and opinions are not merely tolerated, they are encouraged and respected." "UCLA has a large and active GLBT community, with a think tank and an academic journal both housed at the law school dedicated to sexual orientation law and policy." Politically, "students seem predominantly liberal but there are definitely conservatives too."

KARMAN HSU, DIRECTOR OF ADMISSIONS
71 DODD HALL, BOX 951445, LOS ANGELES, CA 90095-1445
TEL: 310-825-2080 FAX: 310-206-7227
EMAIL: ADMISSIONS@LAW.UCLA.EDU • WEBSITE: WWW.LAW.UCLA.EDU

"People get quite stressed and preoccupied with grades and jobs" and "There is a serious spirit of competition" at UCLA. It's "not personal," though. "Students generally root for each other, rooting for themselves just a bit more." Also, you can easily "find your own space away from the gunners." At the end of the day, it's hard to be stressed out "when you study so close to the beach" (in "shorts and flip-flops"), and "It's 80 degrees in January." "The sunny weather compromises students' ability to stay indoors and study," admits a 1L.

"Lunch in the courtyard is probably the best part of being at UCLA." "People are always outside, reading or eating lunch, with the sun beaming down and the giant redwoods providing shade." "People study hard" but social activities are very prevalent (particularly early in each semester). There is "no shortage of people going out on a random Thursday night." "Rent is fairly expensive" in the surrounding area, but "UCLA offers pretty good, convenient housing to many law students." "If you can deal with a commute, there are many cheaper areas to live that are not too far" as well. Overall, UCLA students are among the more satisfied groups of law students in the country. "After my brother asked me how law school was going, he listened patiently to my answer and then told me that it sounded like Club Med with some required reading," says a 3L. "I couldn't be happier with my experience."

Getting In

Recently admitted students at UCLA at the 25th percentile have LSAT scores of 163 and GPAs in the 3.54 range. Admitted students at the 75th percentile have LSAT scores of 169 and GPAs of roughly 3.85.

Clinical program required	No
Legal writing course requirement	Yes
Legal methods course requirement	Yes
Legal research course requirement	Yes
Moot court requirement	No
Public interest law requirement	No

ADMISSIONS

Selectivity Rating	**96**
# applications received	8,009
% applicants accepted	17
% acceptees attending	23
Average LSAT	168
LSAT Range	164–169
Average undergrad GPA	3.74
Application fee	$75
Regular application	Rolling, up to 2/1
Regular notification	Rolling
Early application program	Yes
Early application deadline	11/15
Early application notification	12/31
Transfer students accepted	Yes
Evening division offered	No
Part-time accepted	No
LSDAS accepted	Yes

Applicants Also Look At
University of Southern California, Columbia University, University of California—Berkeley, New York University, Georgetown University

FINANCIAL FACTS

Annual tuition (in-state/out-of-state)	$31,103/$41,624
Books and supplies	$1,881
Room & board	$20,292
Financial aid application deadline	3/2
% first-year students receiving some sort of aid	92.8
% receiving some sort of aid	87.2
% receiving scholarships	55.8
Average grant	$12,611
Average loan	$35,309
Average total aid package	$40,624
Average debt	$83,220

EMPLOYMENT INFORMATION

Career Rating	95
Rate of placement (nine months out)	99
Average starting salary	$125,467
State for bar exam	CA
Pass rate for first-time bar	90

Employers Who Frequently Hire Grads
Leading employers from law firms, corporations, government agencies, and public interest organizations.

Prominent Alumni
Hon. Kirsten Gillibrand '92, U.S. Senator; Hon. Henry Waxman '64, U.S. House of Representatives (29th District); Nelson Rising '67, President and CEO, Rising Realty Partners, LLC.

Grads Employed by Field (%)
Academic (4)
Business/Industry (9)
Government (8)
Judicial clerkships (11)
Other (1)
Private practice (59)
Public Interest (8)

THE UNIVERSITY OF CHICAGO
THE LAW SCHOOL

INSTITUTIONAL INFORMATION

Public/private	Private
Student-faculty ratio	10:1
% faculty part-time	45
% faculty female	21
% faculty minority	10
Total faculty	110

SURVEY SAYS...

Diverse opinions accepted in classrooms
Great library staff
Abundant externship/internship/ clerkship opportunities

STUDENTS

Enrollment of law school	593
% male/female	55/45
% full-time	100
% minority	28
% international	2
Average age of entering class	24

ACADEMICS

Academic Experience Rating	**99**
Profs interesting rating	99
Profs accessible rating	92
Hours of study per day	4.48

Academic Specialties

Civil procedure, commercial law, constitutional law, corporation securities, criminal law, environmental law, government services, human rights, international law, labor law, legal history, legal philosophy, property, taxation, intellectual property law

Advanced Degrees Offered

JD, 3 years; LLM, 1 year; JSD, Depends on Dissertation (up to 5 years)

Combined Degrees Offered

JD/MBA, 4 years; JD/PhD in conjunction with Graduate School of Business, depends on dissertation; JD/AM Public Polcy, 4 years; JD/AM International Relations, 4 years

Clinical program required	No

Academics

The rigorous and ultra-prestigious Law School at The University of Chicago offers "an incredibly dynamic educational environment full of quirky but brilliant professors and an eclectic mix of students." "Expectations are high" and a unique trimester system means "There is little rest for the weary." Even so, students report that "there is no other place like The University of Chicago when it comes to intellectual curiosity." Course work is cerebral and highly analytical. Classes "have a strong theoretical bent" and are "geared to those who like thinking about the law." Chicago is virtually synonymous with the interdisciplinary combination of law and economics. The humanities, the social sciences, and the natural sciences are all integrated into the curriculum as well.

Students swear that their school has, "without a doubt, the best faculty in the country." The professors are "unquestionably the greatest part of this school." Somehow "they manage to produce brilliant work" while maintaining "a real emphasis on teaching" and making students "feel like top priority." "It's incredible to take classes from Cass Sunstein, Richard Epstein, and numerous others as a 1L, and to find out how accessible they are," beams one satisfied student. These "rock stars of legal academia" "treat students with respect," "are often in the common areas, and readily have lunch with students." "I have been amazed by the accessibility of my professors, particularly considering who they are," says a 3L. "They are always available for office hours." "The professors can help you get amazing jobs, can impart unparalleled wisdom, and are the people who write the books you use," explains another student. "I don't know where they find the time."

The administration "makes the experience seamless" and is quite popular with most students. "I would call the administration extremely overqualified if it weren't for the negative implications of that label," says a 1L. "I can't imagine a more enthusiastic and at-your-service administration." "The law school tries harder than any other school I've heard of to make its students happy," declares another student. Career Services does a good job too. There are "no worries about jobs." "Over 600 employers compete for only 190 students in each class," so "everyone will get a great job (public or private) making top dollar." There are some complaints, though. "The grading system is a little bizarre. It's tough on the ego because nearly everyone gets the same grade." Students must "lottery" into many seminars and clinical programs. Consequently, while the nine clinics are "great" for real-world experience, only the best get into the clinics they want. "You are very lucky if you are able to obtain practical experience through credited work." Though the recent introduction of a summer public interest program has guaranteed funding for public interest jobs, the majority of students become corporate lawyers.

"The facilities are state of the art" at the U of C, though the "boringly modern" architecture won't exactly elevate your soul—unless, of course, a floating-cube-of-glass design is your idea of beautiful. Inside the law school, "The 1L classrooms are gorgeous but cramped." The library has undergone extensive renovation recently and boasts "a great number of resources and a willing and helpful staff."

Life

Chicago is "small" and home to "an intense intellectual environment." "It's quite an experience to know that some of my friends will clerk for the Supreme Court and work at the highest level in the field," relates one student. Debates are "constant and vibrant." "Our faculty and student body has many liberals, libertarians, moderates, and conservatives," explains a 2L. "The political views...range from ultra-liberal to ultra-conservative, but all

ANN PERRY, ASSISTANT DEAN FOR ADMISSIONS
1111 EAST 60TH STREET, CHICAGO, IL 60637
TEL: 773-702-9484 FAX: 773-834-0942
EMAIL: ADMISSIONS@LAW.UCHICAGO.EDU • WEBSITE: WWW.LAW.UCHICAGO.EDU

viewpoints are respected. Great weight is placed on academic inquiry and discussion, as opposed to vacuous politicking." "People are very interested in learning and maturing as legal thinkers."

Many students tell us that the academic environment is "easygoing" and "mostly non-competitive." "It is an extremely friendly school with a low degree of competition," they say, where "2L and 3L students frequently offer their assistance to the 1L class." However, other students tell us "The competition is tough." "Students are definitely not laid-back about getting jobs," observes a 3L. "Even though everyone ends up with plenty of great job offers, students are intense and cutthroat."

Socially, there is "community atmosphere" and "a great attitude on campus." People are "interesting and cool" and "genuinely excited to be a part of the law school." "Lots of people . . . participate in social events." Because many people hail from outside the Midwest, everyone arrives looking for friends. "The 1L class bonds quickly." "The small class size is a phenomenal advantage because I feel as if I get to know everyone," comments a 1L. Also, "weekly events such as Wine Mess and Coffee Mess" are perennial social institutions where students mingle with classmates and professors. "Nearly every day there is free food for some political or legal guest speaker," which is great if you like "sandwiches, pizza, or Thai food." The biggest complaint about life here appears to be the law school's affordable but "inconvenient" Hyde Park location. When students need to get away for work or any other reason though, downtown Chicago is "easy enough to live in and get to school" by car, bike, or public transportation.

Getting In

If you can get admitted here, you can get admitted to virtually any law school in the country. Admitted students at 25th percentile have LSAT scores of about 169 and GPAs of about 3.5. Admitted students at 75th percentile have LSAT scores of 172 and GPAs of about 3.8. If you take the LSAT a second time, Chicago will consider your higher score.

Legal writing course requirement	Yes
Legal methods course requirement	Yes
Legal research course requirement	Yes
Moot court requirement	Yes
Public interest law requirement	No

ADMISSIONS

Selectivity Rating	**97**
# applications received	5,032
# applicants accepted	887
# acceptees attending	187
Average LSAT	171
LSAT Range	169–173
Average undergrad GPA	3.68
Application fee	$75
Regular application	Rolling, up to 2/1
Regular notification	Rolling
Early application program	Yes
Early application deadline	12/1
Early application notification	12/31
Transfer students accepted	Yes
Evening division offered	No
Part-time accepted	No
LSDAS accepted	Yes

Applicants Also Look At

Harvard University, Yale University, Columbia University, New York University, University of Pennsylvania, University of Virginia, Stanford University

International Students

TOEFL required of international students	Yes
Minimum TOEFL (paper/computer/web)	600/250/104

FINANCIAL FACTS

Annual tuition	$41,157
Books and supplies	$1,650
Fees	$678
Room & board	$13,455
Financial aid application deadline	3/1
% first-year students receiving some sort of aid	90
% receiving some sort of aid	82
% of aid that is merit based	50
% receiving scholarships	52
Average grant	$13,482
Average loan	$42,564
Average debt	$119,000

EMPLOYMENT INFORMATION

Career Rating	98	Grads Employed by Field (%)	
Rate of placement (nine months out)	99	Academic	(1)
Average starting salary	$160,000	Business/Industry	(3)
State for bar exam	IL, NY	Judicial Clerkships	(13)
Pass rate for first-time bar	99	Private Practice	(82)

Employers Who Frequently Hire Grads

Cravath Swain & Moore, Latham & Watkins, Gibson Dunn & Crutcher, Sidley & Austin, Kirkland & Ellis, Skadden Arps Slate Meagher & Flom.

UNIVERSITY OF CINCINNATI
COLLEGE OF LAW

INSTITUTIONAL INFORMATION

Public/private	Public
% faculty part-time	15
% faculty female	52
% faculty minority	10
Total faculty	31

SURVEY SAYS...

Diverse opinions accepted
in classrooms
Great library staff
Good social life

STUDENTS

Enrollment of law school	123
% male/female	57/43
% out-of-state	44
% full-time	100
% minority	16
% international	2
# of countries represented	4
Average age of entering class	25

ACADEMICS

Academic Experience Rating	**76**
Profs interesting rating	73
Profs accessible rating	76
Hours of study per day	4.42

Academic Specialties

Criminal law, environmental law,
human rights, international law,
labor law, taxation, intellectual
property law

Advanced Degrees Offered

JD, 3 years

Combined Degrees Offered

JD/Master's Business
Administration, 4 years; JD/Master's
Community Planning, 4.5 years;
JD/MA in Women's Studies, 4
years; JD/Master's Social Work, 4
years; JD/MA-PhD in Political
Science, 4–6 years

Clinical program required	No
Legal writing	
course requirement	Yes
Legal methods	
course requirement	No

Academics

Students at the University of Cincinnati get the "small class sizes" and "intimate environment" typical of a private college while paying the comfortable, low tuition you would expect from a public institution. With roughly 125 students in each entering class, the school strikes an "excellent" balance with "its affordability, reputation, small class size, and excellent faculty. Students agree that UC professors are an "amazing and diverse group of people who care just as much for teaching and students as they do about publishing their own work." UC is particularly noted for its focus on "public interest" and "international" law; however, "There is no shortage of brilliant legal minds in a broad range of subjects—that goes for students as well as the professors." In addition to the accomplished tenured faculty, students rave about the school's recent acquisition of "exceptional young faculty members that have great teaching skills to match their great scholarship." A 2L sums it up, "As one of the smallest public law schools in the country, I feel my educational experience has been fantastic, and yet, at very little cost. Because our class consists of only 128 people, all of my professors know my name."

University of Cincinnati runs several "amazing" legal institutes and research centers focused on unique topics such as domestic violence, law and psychiatry, and corporate law. Through these centers, students can earn credit hours while doing fulfilling and useful work in the community. Many students make particular note of the Ohio Innocence Project, an institute at the University of Cincinnati through which students research and write reports, and work on real criminal cases. The institute also brings notable speakers to campus. Students also have the opportunity to research and write for the school's renowned publications, including the Human Rights Quarterly and Tenant Information Project. While students at other schools might scramble for spots on the school's law review or clinic programs, "Since the school is small, each student can participate in get involved in a number of organizations."

Thanks to an "ambitious but not overly competitive student body," the learning environment is charged, but not cutthroat, at University of Cincinnati. A 3L attests, "While academic achievement is always a numbers game in law school, the atmosphere at UC is nonpretentious and noncontentious." When it comes to the job and internship placements, University of Cincinnati maintains a "deep and well-regarded history as a legal educational institution" both locally and nationally. As a result, most students say the school "is a great place for students with all different kinds of career aspirations, and especially has a public interest/human rights orientation that I think is unparalleled in the Midwest." In fact, "Public interest students can actually obtain funding for their summer jobs through the school's Public Interest Group." Most UC grads stay in the Cincinnati area and meet with good results while those looking outside the region must do a little extra legwork to find a good placement. "While plenty of our grads go on to excellent careers in major firms, federal clerkships, and other government positions, I don't feel like our school does enough PR work to get out-of-town employers interested in our students," says one student.

AL WATSON, ASSISTANT DEAN AND DIRECTOR OF ADMISSION AND FINAN
PO BOX 210040, CINCINNATI, OH 45221
TEL: 513-556-6805 FAX: 513-556-2391
EMAIL: ADMISSIONS@LAW.UC.EDU • WEBSITE: WWW.LAW.UC.EDU

Life

For starving students/aspiring lawyers, Cincinnati is an excellent home base offering the unbeatable combination of "small town prices (housing, dining, entertainment) with big city amenities." For both professional and recreational pursuits, the UC campus is pleasantly located "close to downtown so it's easy to get to work, ballgames, and entertainment." While Cincinnati has its charms, students complain that the law school "building looks like a 1950s bomb shelter" and could use "more outlets and better lighting." "Windows would be nice," adds another. However, students are optimistic that the school will consider remodeling the law school along with other campus projects. The good news is that "the new parking garage has been built, and there are brand-new (and attractive) living units pretty much right across the street." Not to mention that a few "Ice cream shops have opened within a short walk from school."

Despite the rigors of the academic curriculum, "The students that are here create a suitable balance between academic and social life. There are plenty of opportunities to go out and have fun and not be completely overwhelmed with school." On and off campus, "There are frequently SBA social events for students, such as happy hours at local bars." In fact, the SBA is very active and "most of the students are friends and spend time together outside of the law school." On the other hand, students remind us that Cincinnati also attracts "a large contingent of commuter students who spend little if no time involved in the school outside of actual class."

Getting In

To apply to the University of Cincinnati College of Law, students must submit LSAT scores and register with the Law School Data Assembly Service Report. If the LSAT was taken more than once, the highest score will be considered by the Admissions Committee. Almost 1,200 hopefuls applied for 135 spots in the JD program. Students in the 25th percentile had LSAT scores of 157 and GPAs of 3.31, while those in the 75th percentile had LSAT scores of 161 and GPAs of 3.80.

Legal research	
course requirement	Yes
Moot court requirement	No
Public interest	
law requirement	No

ADMISSIONS

Selectivity Rating	82
# applications received	1,198
% applicants accepted	40
% acceptees attending	25
Average LSAT	160
LSAT Range	156–162
Average undergrad GPA	3.64
Application fee	$35
Regular application	Rolling, up to 3/1
Regular notification	Rolling
Early application program	Yes
Early application deadline	12/1
Early application notification	1/15
Transfer students accepted	Yes
Evening division offered	No
Part-time accepted	No
LSDAS accepted	Yes

Applicants Also Look At
University of Illinois at Urbana-Champaign, University of Kentucky, Indiana University—Bloomington, The Ohio State University—Columbus, The University of Akron, Case Western Reserve University, University of Dayton, Northern Kentucky University

International Students

TOEFL required	
of international students	Yes

FINANCIAL FACTS

Annual tuition (in-state/ out-of-state)	$19,362/$33,764
Books and supplies	$1,227
Room & board (off-campus)	$14,713
Financial aid application deadline	3/1
% first-year students receiving some sort of aid	84
% receiving some sort of aid	84
% of aid that is merit based	99
% receiving scholarships	66
Average grant	$6,500
Average debt	$60,558

EMPLOYMENT INFORMATION

Career Rating	72
Rate of placement (nine months out)	96
Average starting salary	$75,704
State for bar exam	OH, KY, NY, IN, IL

Employers Who Frequently Hire Grads
All major law firms in Cincinnati and other Ohio cities as well as other Midwestern cities.

Prominent Alumni
Stan Chesley, Class Action; Cris Collinsworth, Journalist; Billy Martin, Wash, DC based high profile case attorney; Andrew Savage, IP Guru; Survivor Contestant.

Grads Employed by Field (%)
Academic (4)
Business/Industry (10)
Government (13)
Judicial clerkships (6)
Other (2)
Private practice (47)
Public Interest (18)

UNIVERSITY OF COLORADO
LAW SCHOOL

INSTITUTIONAL INFORMATION

Public/private	Public
Student-faculty ratio	13:1
% faculty part-time	39
% faculty female	37
% faculty minority	12
Total faculty	59

SURVEY SAYS...
Beautiful campus
Students love Boulder, CO

STUDENTS

Enrollment of law school	520
% male/female	52/48
% out-of-state	14
% full-time	100
% minority	19
# of countries represented	2
Average age of entering class	24

ACADEMICS

Academic Experience Rating	**69**
Profs interesting rating	82
Profs accessible rating	74
Hours of study per day	4.89

Academic Specialties
Environmental law, taxation, American indian law, juvenile and family law, telecommunications law

Advanced Degrees Offered
JD, 3 years.

Combined Degrees Offered
JD/MBA, 4 years; JD/MPA, 4 years; JD/Master of Science and Telecommunications, 4 years; JD/LLB 4 years, JD/Master of Environmental Science, 4 years; JD/MD; JD/MURP

Clinical program required	No
Legal writing course requirement	Yes
Legal methods course requirement	Yes
Legal research course requirement	Yes
Moot court requirement	No

Academics

The University of Colorado Law School has much coming by way of recommendations. The faculty and the small student population are "eclectic and diverse." Colorado Law's "solid and growing" clinical programs boast "fantastic" facilities that help in "spreading its practical wings." Students in the Indian Law Clinic, for example, represent low-income Native American clients with specific Indian law-related problems. There are three law journals and seven joint-degree programs. Though the international law program is "seriously lacking," there is a "particularly strong" specialization in environmental law, and CU has strong connections "within the environmental law community." Students here can participate in "cutting-edge climate change and renewable energy work" through the law school's Center for Energy and Environmental Security. CU is also a "very affordable school" and, if you come from another state, it is reportedly "easy to get in-state tuition your second year."

The "whip-smart" and "amazingly accomplished" professors here "could teach anywhere but choose the lifestyle that Colorado affords." While "The curriculum is rigorous," professors "use the Socratic Method in a friendly way that makes students feel comfortable in the classroom." Somehow, "It isn't very intimidating." Outside of class, the faculty is "accessible," "frequently attending student events and very willing to talk with students." Bureaucracy does exist, but the "very chill" administration is generally "polite, service-oriented, and very responsive to student needs." "They treat you like one of their own from the first day," claims a 1L.

Student opinion on the Office of Career Development is mixed. Some students tell us that job prospects are "excellent" thanks to the "hard work" of the "great" staff "coupled with a good local and regional job market." "I feel confident that I will get a great job," declares a 1L. Other students complain that CU "provides virtually no assistance" to those "looking for a job outside of Colorado or the surrounding states," and feel that special attention is paid to the top 10 percent of the class. Still, the office is working to remedy this, travelling out-of-state to conduct employer and alumni outreach and increase networking opportunities for students.

Colorado Law's "brand-spanking-new" and otherwise "stunning" building "has the latest and greatest bells and whistles" (including "three plugs for every law student"). "The layout of the building is not very conducive to socializing," but "It's a great place to spend most of your time." "Breathtaking" views are everywhere. "The cafeteria has an entire wall of glass windows looking out onto the flatirons." Classrooms are "comfortable and designed for discussion" and have "the latest modern technology" as well as "good old-fashioned chalk boards." The "inviting" library is "huge and has everything."

Life

"There is a good mix" of "traditional" and "older students" here. Colorado Law students describe themselves as "genuinely kind and cooperative" and "diligent but laid-back." They also hasten to add that "a lot of the stereotypes about Boulder (yuppies, hippies, liberals, potheads, etc.) do not apply to the law school." There are "ski bums and outdoorsy people who are in the mountains every weekend," but "very few students are actually Teva-wearing, beard-growing sorts of people," explains one student. "Most are completely ordinary, and dress professionally if not casually." Politically, "While this is a generally liberal town and school, there are a surprising number of conservatives at the law school, balancing the diehard liberals out and making the atmosphere very middle-of-the-

KRISTINE JACKSON, ASSISTANT DEAN FOR ADMISSIONS & FINANCIAL AID
403 UCB, BOULDER, CO 80309-0403
TEL: 303-492-7203 FAX: 303-492-2542
EMAIL: LAWADMIN@COLORADO.EDU • WEBSITE: WWW.COLORADO.EDU/LAW

road." If anything, "The student body overall seems slightly apathetic" when it comes to "political or philosophic issues."

Life outside the classroom here is reportedly awesome. "There have been dozens of occasions where someone has uncontrollably muttered, 'I'm so glad I'm here,'" observes a 1L. "It's just such a great place." "Everyone knows everyone," and Colorado Law "can be gossipy," but it's "a friendly place with a serious work ethic." "Sharing notes" is common. "Competition between students is barely noticeable." In fact, "Competitions such as mock trial are friendly and in fun." You may even "find legal writing answers underlined in reference books for research exercises." The "very active" student government "is fantastic at addressing student concerns" and "contributes a lot to a relatively low-stress atmosphere." "Free beer . . . almost every Friday" is another great perk and, while the party scene isn't raging, "There is something going on almost every weekend."

The surrounding college town of Boulder is "outrageously expensive." If you can find the means, though, "Boulder is a unique and interesting place" that "offers a broad variety of experiences ranging from the cultural to the bizarre." With "300 days of sunshine a year" and an "absolutely gorgeous physical environment," it's "an outdoor rec haven" as well. "Skiing is fantastic during the winter, and you can't beat a Boulder summer." The law school is "perfectly situated at the base of the Front Range to allow for ample ways to relieve stress by being physically active all year long," explains one student. "Ski trips happen regularly" and "You can leave class and go for a hike in the mountains without having to get in your car." In the odd event that students would want to leave the Boulder area, "Denver's less than an hour away."

Getting In

The 25th percentile of admitted students has LSAT scores of about 160 and GPAs of about 3.33. Admitted students at the 75th percentile have LSAT scores of roughly 165 and GPAs of about 3.79. CU Law will consider all of your scores if you take the LSAT multiple times.

Public interest law requirement	No

ADMISSIONS

Selectivity Rating	**60***
# applications received	3,000
# applicants accepted	665
# acceptees attending	171
LSAT Range	160–165
Application fee	$65
Regular application	Rolling, up to 3/15
Regular notification	Rolling
Early application program	Yes
Early application deadline	11/1
Early application notification	12/23
Transfer students accepted	Yes
Evening division offered	No
Part-time accepted	No
LSDAS accepted	Yes

Applicants Also Look At
University of Texas at Austin, American University, University of Arizona, University of Denver, University of Georgia, University of California—Berkeley, University of California—Los Angeles, Cornell University, Boston College, The George Washington University, Georgetown University, Lewis & Clark College

International Students

TOEFL required of international students	Yes

FINANCIAL FACTS

Annual tuition (in-state/ out-of-state)	$20,340/$30,852
Books and supplies	$1,749
Fees	$1,708
Room & board (on/off-campus)	$15,983/$14,601
Financial aid application deadline	4/1
% first-year students receiving some sort of aid	99
% receiving some sort of aid	93
% of aid that is merit based	24
% receiving scholarships	50
Average grant	$12,484
Average loan	$23,331
Average total aid package	$28,431
Average debt	$65,846

EMPLOYMENT INFORMATION

Career Rating	**73**
Rate of placement (nine months out)	88
Average starting salary	$66,657
State for bar exam	CO
Pass rate for first-time bar	94

Employers Who Frequently Hire Grads
Ballard Spahr Andrews & Ingersoll; Brownstein Hyatt Farber Schreck; Gibson Dunn & Crutcher; Hogan & Hartson; Patton Boggs; Arnold & Porter.

Prominent Alumni
Wiley B. Rutledge, Former Associate Justice, U.S. Supreme Court; Bill Ritter, Jr., Governor of Colorado; Roy Romer, former Governor of Colorado.

Grads Employed by Field (%)
Private practice (42)
Government (14)
Judicial clerkship (25)
Business (6)
Public interest (7)
Academic (4)

UNIVERSITY OF CONNECTICUT
SCHOOL OF LAW

Academics

University of Connecticut's undergraduate campus is located in the town of Storrs, whereas the law school makes its home on a "small" and "pretty" campus in the state's capital of Hartford. Without suffering from the distractions of a larger university but retaining the strength of the UConn name and reputation, students benefit from a close-knit academic atmosphere in which "You really get to know everyone within the law school community." While many UConn professors are "big names in law," students reassure us that "the faculty feel more like allies than oppressors," taking an active interest in professional and academic development of their students. Academically, UConn emphasizes both practical and theoretical aspects of the law, drawing a faculty comprised of "practicing lawyers, superior and appellate court judges, the chief disciplinary counsel and many other practicing professionals with real life experience who have not learned what they teach from a book." Catering to students interested in many legal fields, UConn operates "20-plus clinics for practical skills, even though they only reference 3 or 4 on our website, and the course selection is quite varied for a school of our size."

Like 1Ls across the nation, you'll have your fill of late-night cram sessions at UConn. However, students assure us that the "academic experience is challenging but fun." A student relates, "As a 1L, you will stress out over the workloads, but you will also get everything done without killing yourself." While competition doesn't reach cutthroat levels, it's still a legal pressure cooker because "Professors grade on a B-median scale, meaning that...you end up competing against the other people in your classes for the best grades, since most of you will receive B's." However, students also reassure us that,"Traditional academic rigor and competition are very well balanced with a very friendly, collegial environment. Students are smart, hardworking, and friendly."

In addition to the teaching staff, "Administration really supports the student, both academically, personally, and professionally. They attend and participate in all student organized events, help students think about different jobs, and counsel students about problems at school or home." However, many students at this public school also feel that despite their good intentions, "The administration tends to be out of step with the needs and wishes of the student body." One student explains, "We always joke that any change around here needs a legislative act....sadly, that is true!" On the other hand, students don't overlook the quality of the Career Services Office that helps the school to maintain its "very strong connection to CT firms and lawmakers, which is good if you plan to practice here." A current student shares: "The Career Services Office helped me, as an evening student, find a full-time job working as a law clerk with some of the best lawyers in the country." However, like most schools that are deeply invested in their community, students at UConn feel that "more emphasis needs to be given to acquiring interviewing firms from outside New England."

Life

University of Connecticut's student population is largely comprised of students in their mid-20s but also includes a decent number of recent college grads. As a result, there's an active group of students who are ready to enjoy both work and play during law school. A current student tells us, "UConn's biggest strength is a quality social life. We have a lot of parties, and a lot of sports teams to play on, including soccer, hockey, basketball, and softball."

KAREN DEMEOLA, ASSISTANT DEAN FOR ADMISSIONS AND STUDENT FINANCE
45 ELIZABETH STREET, HARTFORD, CT 06105
TEL: 860-570-5100 FAX: 860-570-5153
EMAIL: ADMISSIONS@LAW.UCONN.EDU • WEBSITE: WWW.LAW.UCONN.EDU

In addition to the traditional program, the school also supports a fairly large evening program, whose students tend to differ from day students in that they are "pretty focused on school and their lives with family and friends outside school, and may have graduated from college some time ago." However, there are some who would like the school to provide "greater access to programs for evening students, as most of the student groups meet during the day, when most of the evening class is working." While they praise the campus as having a "very nice community feel," many students mention a general lack of diversity on campus (both on the faculty and within the student body), admitting to us that "there is not a ton of interaction between students of different races/ethnicities."

While hometown Hartford "won't win any style or fun points," the school is located in "a charming residential neighborhood" on a "pretty, Gothic-style" campus. Plus, Hartford's dicey reputation doesn't match up with reality. One current student assures that "Hartford is...on the way up, offering some surprisingly good cultural opportunities." Another agrees, "I think Hartford is coming out of its shell as a city, and UConn Law students are leading the charge in some of the bars and restaurants downtown."

Getting In

Students are admitted to UConn School of Law once annually, for entry in the fall semester. No numeric index is used to rank applicants to UConn School of Law and each applicant is considered individually. Connecticut residents receive special consideration in an admissions decision, though no absolute preference is given. Of the 282 1Ls accepted the median undergraduate GPA was 3.47 and the median LSAT score was 162.

Legal research	
course requirement	Yes
Moot court requirement	Yes
Public interest	
law requirement	No

ADMISSIONS

Selectivity Rating	**60***
# applications received	1,872
% applicants accepted	23
% acceptees attending	45
Average LSAT	161
LSAT Range	157–163
Average undergrad GPA	3.39
Application fee	$30
Regular application	Rolling, up to 3/1
Regular notification	Rolling
Early application program	No
Transfer students accepted	Yes
Evening division offered	Yes
Part-time accepted	Yes
LSDAS accepted	Yes

Applicants Also Look At
American University; Boston University; Northeastern University; Tulane University; Yeshiva University; Boston College; Fordham University; Brooklyn Law School; University of California, Hastings

International Students

TOEFL required	
of international students	Yes

FINANCIAL FACTS

Annual tuition (in-state/ out-of-state)	$18,840/$38,976
Books and supplies	$1,100
Fees	$742
Fees per credit	$304
Tuition per credit (in-state/ out-of-state)	$770/$1,624
Room & board (off-campus)	$11,490
Financial aid application deadline	3/1
% first-year students receiving some sort of aid	88
% receiving some sort of aid	81
% of aid that is merit based	6
% receiving scholarships	54
Average grant	$10,966
Average loan	$22,990
Average total aid package	$28,278
Average debt	$58,413

EMPLOYMENT INFORMATION

Career Rating	73	Grads Employed by Field (%)
Rate of placement (nine months out)	92	Academic (2)
Average starting salary	$98,800	Business/Industry (14)
State for bar exam	CT, NY, MA	Government (10)
Pass rate for first-time bar	90	Judicial Clerkships (13)

Employers Who Frequently Hire Grads

Private Practice (58)

Adler, Pollock & Sheehan Akin Gump

Public Interest (3)

Strauss Hauer & Feld LLP Alix, Yale & Ristas, LLP Axinn, Veltrop and Harkrider Bernstein, Shur, Sawyer, Nelson Bingham McCutchen LLP Bond, Schoeneck & King, PLLC Bowditch & Dewey Thelen Reid Brown Raysman & Steiner LLP Brown Rudnick & Berlack Israels LLP

UNIVERSITY OF DAYTON
SCHOOL OF LAW

INSTITUTIONAL INFORMATION

Public/private	Private
Affiliation	Roman Catholic
Student-faculty ratio	9:1
% faculty part-time	45
% faculty female	41
% faculty minority	8
Total faculty	51

SURVEY SAYS...

Diverse opinions accepted
in classrooms
Great research resources
Great library staff
Beautiful campus

STUDENTS

Enrollment of law school	479
% male/female	62/38
% out-of-state	39
% full-time	100
% minority	13
# of countries represented	4
Average age of entering class	24

ACADEMICS

Academic Experience Rating	**68**
Profs interesting rating	75
Profs accessible rating	77
Hours of study per day	5

Academic Specialties

Civil procedure, criminal law, property, intellectual property law, computer/cyberspace law, advocacy and dispute resolution, personal and transactional law

Advanced Degrees Offered

JD, 3 years or 2.5 years

Combined Degrees Offered

JD/MBA, 4 years

Clinical program required	Yes
Legal writing course requirement	Yes
Legal methods course requirement	Yes
Legal research course requirement	Yes
Moot court requirement	No

Academics

Students at the University of Dayton School of Law call their school "a diamond in the rough." "The number of elective classes is extremely limited," but class sizes are smaller. There's a notable program in intellectual property law and a "very strong legal writing program." There's an "extremely helpful" bar prep course available for credit, too. You can enroll in either May or August. Probably the most unique thing here is the accelerated program. "UDSL allows summer starters and fall starters but also allows students to graduate in five semesters." If you are really gung-ho, you can squeeze a J.D. into two years here (and still get a summer off). The facilities are still another perk. By all accounts, the "clean, modern, comfortable," "absolutely beautiful," and "totally brand new" building is "a joy." "The classrooms and the courtroom are equipped with the latest technology." Students also laud the "big, comprehensive" library.

Students tell us that they love the "emphasis on applicable skills" throughout the curriculum. Among other things, "UDSL encourages students to learn practical lawyering skills by requiring students take either a clinic or a capstone." Clinical opportunities allow students to work with real, live clients, "preparing all aspects of a case, from the initial client interview to preparing for trial and possibly even participating in a trial." Capstone courses are lot like simulated clinics. Externships, which allow students to work, just for example, at a government agency, or for a judge, or in a law firm, are another big hit. "The externship program is world-class," gloats 2L. "It gives students real-world experience that is invaluable." However, "the externship classroom portion is comprised of a bunch of busy work and touchy-feely exercises that do not belong in a law school." Some students also complain about the fact that specialization is pretty much mandatory here. All 1Ls choose one of three tracks (advocacy, transactional law, or intellectual property). According to some students, the mandatory track choice pigeonholes them, making them choose before they have a real idea of the field of law they would actually like to practice.

"There are a few professors that are difficult to deal with," but students say that, for the most part, faculty members "make classes very enjoyable." "The professors are wonderful," reflects a 3L. "Choosing a favorite would be an impossible task, because it would be a 15-way tie." Outside of class, the faculty is reportedly "open door all the way." "Professors are approachable before class, after class, and almost anytime a student needs." The "professional and cordial" administration is almost universally beloved as well—rare for a law school, we might add, or any kind of school. The dean "knows students by name," and the top brass on the whole is "extremely accommodating." "They really get to know the students and will do whatever they can to help." "They are constantly in communication with us," adds a 1L, "and I like that."

Students are divided when it comes to career prospects. Many say that the school has a "terrific reputation in Ohio." "The school is very connected within the Dayton community and Ohio for jobs, references, and resources," promises a 2L. Other students disagree. "Career Services could be bolstered," counters another 2L. "More lobbying for what UDSL students can provide would be helpful."

Life

The population of soon-to-be attorneys here hails "mainly from the Midwest." They're "generally very welcoming, sincere, and enthusiastic." Academically, "things are competitive." "Many people spend a great deal more time studying than they let on," spec-

JANET L. HEIN, ASST. DEAN, DIR. OF ADMISSIONS AND FINANCIAL AID
UNIVERSITY OF DAYTON SCHOOL OF LAW, 300 COLLEGE PARK, 112 KELLER HALL,
DAYTON, OH 45469-2760 • TEL: 937-229-3555 FAX: 937-229-4194
EMAIL: LAWINFO@NOTES.UDAYTON.EDU • WEBSITE: LAW.UDAYTON.EDU

ulates a 3L. However, students are quick to point out that "the community feel of UDSL is evident from the moment one steps through the doors." "There is a sense of togetherness within each class." "There are jerks, but they are few and far between."

Socially, life can be "very dramatic" at times because of the school's small size. "Like anywhere, there are cliques." Overall, though, it's "a very pleasant environment." "Most students are involved in student organizations." "There are always school and non-school gatherings to attend." "We have organized parties," adds a 1L, "and I don't just mean drinking at a bar, but actual social adult functions that are classy." If you "still have that college mentality in terms of partying," don't worry. You can find a good deal of that here, too. The medium-sized metropolis that surrounds the school has its advantages and disadvantages. On one hand, Dayton is a good place to go to law school because there aren't many distractions. On the other hand, at least according to a 2L here, it's "one of America's top 10 dying cities."

Getting In

The acceptance rate here isn't crazy high, but it's pretty high. Admitted students at the 25th percentile have LSAT scores that hover around 150 and GPAs a little under 3.0. Admitted students at the 75th percentile have LSAT scores of 155 or so and GPAs a little over 3.4.

EMPLOYMENT INFORMATION

Career Rating	75
Rate of placement (nine months out)	93
Average starting salary	$59,241
State for bar exam	OH, FL, GA, KY, IN
Pass rate for first-time bar	92

Employers Who Frequently Hire Grads
Proctor & Gamble, Ohio Attorney General, Thompson Hine, Fronst Brown Todd, LexisNexis, Jackson Kelly PLLC, Dinsmore & Shohl LLP

Prominent Alumni
Barbara Gorman, Judge, Common Pleas Court; Ron Brown, CEO, Milacron Inc.; Honorable Mary Donovan, Justice of 2nd District Court of Appeals.

Grads Employed by Field (%)
Academic (3)
Business/Industry (13)
Government (13)
Judicial Clerkships (9)
Private Practice (58)
Public Interest (4)

Public interest law requirement	No

ADMISSIONS

Selectivity Rating	63
# applications received	2,230
% applicants accepted	55
% acceptees attending	18
Average LSAT	150
LSAT Range	148–153
Average undergrad GPA	3.21
Application fee	$50
Regular application	Rolling, up to 5/1
Regular notification	Rolling
Early application program	No
Transfer students accepted	Yes
Evening division offered	No
Part-time accepted	No
LSDAS accepted	Yes

Applicants Also Look At
Michigan State University, The University of Akron, Cleveland State University, Capital University, University of Toledo, Valparaiso University, Northern Kentucky University, Ohio Northern University, Thomas M. Cooley Law School, Florida Costal School of Law

International Students
TOEFL recommended of international students	Yes
Minimum TOEFL (paper/computer)	600/250

FINANCIAL FACTS

Annual tuition	$32,340
Books and supplies	$1,500
Fees	$288
Tuition per credit	$950
Room & board	$13,000
Financial aid application deadline	5/1
% first-year students receiving some sort of aid	90
% receiving some sort of aid	51
% of aid that is merit based	45
% receiving scholarships	31
Average grant	$10,797
Average loan	$23,213
Average total aid package	$24,607
Average debt	$90,203

UNIVERSITY OF DENVER
STURM COLLEGE OF LAW

INSTITUTIONAL INFORMATION

Public/private	Private
Student-faculty ratio	15:1
% faculty female	44
% faculty minority	10
Total faculty	55

SURVEY SAYS...

Great research resources
Beautiful campus
Students love Denver, CO

STUDENTS

Enrollment of law school	1,003
% male/female	54/46
% out-of-state	47
% full-time	77
% minority	16
# of countries represented	14
Average age of entering class	24

ACADEMICS

Academic Experience Rating	81
Profs interesting rating	73
Profs accessible rating	71
Hours of study per day	4.26

Academic Specialties

Employment law, clinical education, environmental law, human rights, international law, labor law, taxation

Advanced Degrees Offered

LLM Taxation, 1 year; LLM Natural Resources, 1 year

Combined Degrees Offered

Business, Geography, History, International Management, International Studies, Legal Administration, Mass Communications, Professional Psychology, Psychology, Social Work, Sociology.

Clinical program required	No
Legal writing course requirement	Yes
Legal methods course requirement	Yes
Legal research course requirement	Yes

Academics

The luxury liner of law schools, the University of Denver Sturm College of Law boasts "amazing" facilities, "several" journals and clinical experiences, an "increasing" endowment, and a "strong" alumni network in the Denver metropolitan area. This large private school is "great" for its public interest and environmental law programs, though a wider range of interests, such as a Lawyering in Spanish program and "numerous opportunities for those of us that want to work for a corporate law firm" also garner praise. Diverse as the courses they teach, DU's "kind, brilliant, tough, and challenging" faculty is comprised of a "mixture of tenure-track professors and practicing attorneys." Despite the variety, students find that "the scheduling and availability of classes could be a little more diverse," especially when it comes to "basics" and "bar classes." Some students report "concern" over "bar-passage rates," though note that the "new administration is iron-fisted with purpose of bringing [them] up."

A practical perspective is paramount to the academic experience at University of Denver. For those interested, Career Services hosts frequent—almost daily—sessions (many offering free lunch) on "topics in international law, human rights, politics, practical career advice, debates on current issues, etc." Students say that these daily extra talks allow them to gain a better grasp of "life out of law school and after law school, which is a huge help." Through the mentorship program, "All students have regular opportunities to get career advice and direction from lawyers in the Denver community." To top it off, the school operates a large number of clinic programs, five law journals, and, from day one, "1Ls are invited and encouraged to participate in almost every moot court competition, so students develop exceptional trial advocacy skills early on."

Students explain that "as with any large law school there are some administrative problems"; however, one student sums it up this way: "Right now DU is like a teenager whose metaphysical development is just a little behind his or her physical growth. Make no mistake, all indications are that DU's going to be a stunner; however, on occasion administrative clumsiness leads to collective student body headaches." That said, students dole out praise for the new and spacious facilities, housed in an environmentally friendly (aka "green") building. One student explains, "The building is beautiful and well designed. There are lots of commons areas, and it would be nearly impossible to make it through a day without interacting with other people."

Students get a jump start on their career through the school's "outstanding" internship program that offers "internships with sole practitioners, large firms, and judges in legal fields ranging from water law to criminal law to administrative law." Come graduation, satisfied students praise the school's "incredible alumni network in the community and its incredible reputation in Denver and Colorado." Job-seekers are given an additional edge due to the fact that "DU is the only law school in Denver, and one of only two law schools in the state of Colorado, which creates numerous opportunities for DU graduates to find jobs." Plus, the Career Development Center does an "excellent" job introducing students to the local legal community. A current student elaborates, "Between guest speakers, networking events, on-campus interviews, resume and writing sample coaching, and weekly e-mails announcing new job/internship opportunities, if you don't have a job or at least some leads when you graduate, it's because you didn't want it."

SUSAN ERLENBORN, ASSISTANT DIRECTOR OF ADMISSIONS
2255 E. EVANS AVENUE, DENVER, CO 80208
TEL: 303-871-6135 FAX: 303-871-6992
EMAIL: ADMISSIONS@LAW.DU.EDU • WEBSITE: WWW.LAW.DU.EDU

Life

While DU is a large school, the program is structured in a way that creates a more intimate atmosphere. One student says, "Day students are divided into one of three sections comprised of 80 students. I see the same people day in and day out for every class." Many find this "very helpful for forming close friendships" since it allows students to get "to know and become comfortable" with each other while "forming study groups." No matter what your background, you're likely to find a friend or two amongst the large student body. "There's a wide range of social groups, from 'high school' gossiping, partying groups, to academic and career-centered groups," explains one student. In addition, "There's a club for every interest you could think of, which is great."

Not surprisingly, many law students admit that they are "too busy studying to go out and have a social life." However, if you are looking for a good time, "The straight-out-of-college crew is probably the most social, or at least the ones that seem to go out and hang out the most," and "There are lots of informally organized nights at the local restaurant or bar that are open to all." Students agree that "Denver is a great city" with "so much to do." And being only "an hour from the mountains," winter sport fans find that "you can be in court in the morning and on the slopes by afternoon."

Getting In

Applicants to the University of Denver Sturm College of Law must have a bachelor's degree from an accredited college and current LSAT scores. Competition is steep as for the entering class, the school received just less than 3,000 applications for its full-time division and enrolled 259 full-time and 77 part-time students. The median LSAT score for matriculated students was 158 with a median GPA of 3.4.

Moot court requirement	No
Public interest law requirement	Yes

ADMISSIONS

Selectivity Rating	83
# applications received	2,783
# applicants accepted	865
# acceptees attending	219
Average LSAT	159
LSAT Range	156–160
Average undergrad GPA	3.5
Application fee	$60
Regular application	Rolling, up to 5/30
Regular notification	Rolling
Early application program	No
Transfer students accepted	Yes
Evening division offered	Yes
Part-time accepted	Yes
LSDAS accepted	Yes

International Students

TOEFL required of international students	Yes
Minimum TOEFL (paper/web)	550/80

FINANCIAL FACTS

Annual tuition	$33,780
Books and supplies	$1,698
Fees	$124
Tuition per credit	$1,126
Room & board	$9,765
Financial aid application deadline	3/30
% first-year students receiving some sort of aid	94
% receiving some sort of aid	88
% of aid that is merit based	26
% receiving scholarships	43
Average grant	$17,473
Average loan	$31,797
Average total aid package	$41,982
Average debt	$96,771

EMPLOYMENT INFORMATION

Career Rating	72	**Grads Employed by Field (%)**
Rate of placement (nine months out)	85	Academic (1)
Average starting salary	$63,000	Business/Industry (13)
State for bar exam	CO	Government (12)
Pass rate for first-time bar	84	Judicial Clerkships (9)
Employers Who Frequently Hire Grads		Private Practice (46)
Small, medium & large law firms, government agencies (DA's Office, PD's office, etc.), corporations, non-profit organizations, courts		Public Interest (4)
		Other (14)

UNIVERSITY OF THE DISTRICT OF COLUMBIA
DAVID A. CLARKE SCHOOL OF LAW

Academics

The small David A. Clarke School of Law at the University of the District of Columbia is one of a handful of ABA-accredited law schools at Historically Black Colleges and Universities. By all accounts, UDC is "a great bargain." It's "dirt cheap" if you are a resident of Washington, D.C. Even if you aren't, it's still remarkably affordable since "the school now has a scholarship program that offers free tuition to 20 activists." Otherwise, the two pillars that set UDC apart are its "all-consuming" "commitment to public interest law" and its stellar clinical program. This school was founded with the mission to train students from groups underrepresented at the bar and it remains "committed to social justice and advocacy through the law." Students agree that UDC is "a law school with a conscience" and that they will graduate with "a strong sense of public service and how to serve their communities as lawyers." The clinical program goes hand in hand with this ethos. Under the supervision of a practicing attorney, all students must complete 700 hours of "hands-on work" assisting low-income clients with substantive, real legal issues before they graduate. "Our clinical experience is like none other," a 3L boasts. Students gush that they learn skills "that you just cannot learn from casebooks" and they tell us that the clinical requirement provides the expertise necessary "to start practicing law immediately." "You will have experiences that many first-level associates can only dream of having," a 2L promises.

Everyone seems to agree that "the professors want to see you succeed" and that faculty accessibility at UDC "couldn't possibly be any better." However, the professors here are reportedly uneven when it comes to teaching ability. While some professors are "extraordinary," "very brilliant," and "often inspiring" teachers, others are either "stuck in the 60s and 70s" or "have no business being in a classroom at any level." "There are some fantastic teachers and some lousy ones," a 3L says. The administration is similarly hit or miss. On the one hand, the deans are "caring and personal." "They are very approachable to students and will generally remember you when you return for assistance." On the other hand, management as a whole is "very slow and not very efficient." Students also complain that there are "not enough electives" for 2Ls and 3Ls.

The employment situation for UDC graduates is unique, primarily because it stresses public service so much. The administration and a tremendous number of the students who enroll here want to provide access to the legal system to people who don't have much money. A very solid percentage of graduates obtain judicial clerkships. Graduates also find jobs at small law firms, with the federal government, and with nonprofit organizations of all sizes. Older UDC alumni have gone on to become judges in a host of states. Ultimately, if you want to start out as a public defender, or work for a federal agency or a public interest organization, UDC is an ideal law school.

"The actual school facilities leave much to be desired." "The building is horrible" and "there are no amenities on campus for people to meet and spend any time with each other." The library is "comfortable," but "there is not enough room in the school and library for the 1Ls, 2Ls, and 3Ls at one time." The small and generally "awful" classrooms "really need improvement," too. Students complain especially loudly about the heating and cooling system. One student calls UDC "the Sauna School of Law."

VIVIAN CANTY, ASSISTANT DEAN OF ADMISSION
4200 CONNECTICUT AVENUE, NW, BUILDING 38, WASHINGTON, DC 20008
TEL: 202-274-7336 FAX: 202-274-5583
EMAIL: VCANTY@UDC.EDU • WEBSITE: WWW.LAW.UDC.EDU

Life

At UDC Law, "diversity is a big thing." Roughly half the students represent a minority group and it's very likely that you'll fit in fine here regardless of your age or sexual orientation. Students also bring a "wide range of experience." There isn't a ton of political diversity, though, as UDC slants pretty far to the left. There are reportedly "some politically-conservative students," but both students and faculty tend to have "progressive political views about justice."

One student likens the academic atmosphere to "a pit of snakes," but most everyone else tells us that competition is very low. "'Friendly and cooperative' best describes our law school environment and the relationships among students," a 2L says. "The school's noncompetitive nature creates an environment where the hard work is enjoyable and, for the majority, rewarded." A 3L adds, "It's nice to know that if you miss a class other students notice and send you class notes and assignments before the next course begins." Students tend to get along equally well in the social sphere. "The graduating classes are small, so the students leave with lifelong friends and contacts."

Getting In

UDC Law is a very small school. The acceptance rate is low but the raw numbers of admitted applicants are equally low. Applicants possess a broad range of LSAT scores and grade point averages. LSAT scores of admitted students at the 25th percentile are typically a little under 150. GPAs are around 2.8 at the 25th percentile. Admitted students at the 75th percentile have LSAT scores in the mid 150s and GPAs around 3.3.

ADMISSIONS

Selectivity Rating	**72**
# applications received	1,200
# applicants accepted	290
# acceptees attending	90
Average LSAT	152
LSAT Range	144–167
Average undergrad GPA	3.00
Application fee	$35
Regular application	Rolling, up to 3/15
Regular notification	Rolling
Early application program	No
Transfer students accepted	Yes
Evening division offered	No
Part-time accepted	No
LSDAS accepted	Yes

Applicants Also Look At
American University, The Catholic University of America, Howard University, George Mason University, University of Baltimore, University of Maryland—Baltimore, CUNY Law School at Queens College

International Students
TOEFL and PTE Academic required of international students　　Yes

FINANCIAL FACTS

Annual tuition (in-state/ out-of-state)	$7,350/$14,700
Books and supplies	$2,000
Fees	595
Room & board (off-campus)	$19,800
Financial aid application deadline	3/31
% first-year students receiving some sort of aid	92
% receiving some sort of aid	89
% of aid that is merit based	82
% receiving scholarships	60
Average grant	$4,067
Average loan	$35,170
Average total aid package	$40,764
Average debt	$82,970

EMPLOYMENT INFORMATION

Career Rating		**70**
Rate of placement (nine months out)		75
Average starting salary		$55,250
State for bar exam		MD, DC, VA, CA, FL
Pass rate for first-time bar		82

Employers Who Frequently Hire Grads
Local and federal government agencies, legal service providers and public interest advocacy groups, small law firms, judicial clerkships, business, and industry.

Grads Employed by Field (%)
Academic (2)
Business/Industry (29)
Government (24)
Judicial clerkships (15)
Other (2)
Private practice (10)
Public Interest (17)

UNIVERSITY OF FLORIDA
LEVIN COLLEGE OF LAW

INSTITUTIONAL INFORMATION

Public/private	Public
% faculty part-time	0
% faculty female	48
% faculty minority	17.33
Total faculty	75

SURVEY SAYS...
Diverse opinions accepted in classrooms
Great research resources

STUDENTS

Enrollment of law school	1,200
% male/female	52/48
% out-of-state	9
% full-time	100
% minority	21
% international	2
# of countries represented	5
Average age of entering class	24

ACADEMICS

Academic Experience Rating	**79**
Profs interesting rating	74
Profs accessible rating	70
Hours of study per day	4

Academic Specialties
Environmental law, international law, taxation, intellectual property law, family law, estates & trusts practice

Advanced Degrees Offered
LL.M. in Taxation, one year; LL.M. in International Taxation, one year; LL.M. in Comparative Law, one year; LL.M. in Environmental Law, one year; S.JD in Taxation, Multi-Year

Combined Degrees Offered
More than 30 joint degree programs (JD/Masters & Ph.D.); length of program varies.

Clinical program required	No
Legal writing course requirement	Yes
Legal methods course requirement	No

Academics

The University of Florida Levin College of Law is "top dog in Florida," where a vast majority of in-state residents leads to an "amazing" alumni network; plus, the school is a downright bargain for Florida residents. As one of the top law schools in the fourth largest state, firms in Florida view UF pretty highly, and students say that if you do well, you can pretty much "have your pick of jobs in Florida and the southeast." Even if one does wish to practice elsewhere, all of the courses are heavy in theory, allowing students to work anywhere in the United States, and the "the externship programs are extremely valuable and well-organized." However, this doesn't necessarily mean that Career Services is doing a bang-up job, as more than a few students say that those "who are looking for opportunities elsewhere, or who wish to pursue less typical career paths, must seek out their own opportunities," particularly in the non-corporate and public interest arenas.

As a large law school, UF has a broad range of teachers (in regards to teaching style, method, and personal viewpoints), and a "fantastic" legal writing program. As the law school evolves, tenured professors have left their positions, "permitting an influx of witty, experienced, and engagingly diverse modern professors." Teachers here "don't just spoon feed [students] the law," they make them understand the reasoning behind it, though many have an aversion to the Socratic method within the classroom. "All of the professors that I have met so far have been nothing but impressive, caring, and all around great," says a student. Many students would like to see an increased variety in course offerings, as a few feel that they are "forced into classes that aren't in the area we wish to pursue simply because nothing else is offered that fits our schedule." The Office of Student Affairs gets mixed reviews ranging from "unwilling to provide assistance" to "I've never seen a college or graduate institution so concerned for its students before." As one 2L says, "It's a large school with some excellent resources and some great faculty who are more than willing to help out the interested students; if you're self-motivated, you'll do great."

The "sparkling new," first-rate facilities (including the weather-appropriate outside study tables) are universally beloved, and "everything is very modern, tastefully luxurious, professional, spacious, and inviting." The library is often singled out for its appeal, its space, and its peaceful atmosphere "conducive to studying," and students feel it "lends integrity to the law school experience."

NOEMAR CASTRO, ACTING ASSISTANT DEAN FOR ADMISSIONS
BOX 117622, GAINESVILLE, FL 32611
TEL: 352-273-0890 FAX: 352-392-4087
EMAIL: ADMISSIONS@LAW.UFL.EDU • WEBSITE: WWW.LAW.UFL.EDU

Life

Those who worry about the relative seriousness of the program in relation to UF's main campus need not worry, as "the law school has a distinctly separate, but connected, feel to it and it and does not have the same 'Greek' social environment." That means students get to enjoy the attractive campus, the spectacular weather, and the Division I athletics, without the distraction of everyone enjoying them too much. The entire town (including the library) does shut down for Gator Football, though, "which is a good thing or a bad thing, depending on your priorities." Gainesville is "one of the greatest college towns in the country," in both its small size and its offerings of cute restaurants, performing arts, and culture, and for the active students, Lake Wauberg offers wakeboarding, boating, skiing, and sunbathing basically year-round. Perhaps it's the weather or the steal of an education they're getting, but students here are friendly and non-competitive, and on the whole, there are "very little cutthroat or sneaky activities engaged in by students." The "not very diverse" student body is also very friendly, but a lot of the students are right out of college (many of them from UF undergrad), so the social scene can have a bit of a high school/cliquey feel, and "there is a lack of social relationships between those students who are not in one's own section." "It's called Levin High for a reason," says a student, though "people are generally nice and you have the common bond of misery at law school to allow you to talk to one another." While there are student organizations, they "aren't very powerful, and many people join simply as resume-stuffers," though the happy hours do draw good crowds. Students are clamoring for better parking and a new, less-unsightly cafeteria, for both food options and as a central place to hang out in their downtime.

Getting In

Accepting fewer than around one in three candidates, admission to Levin is tough. About 90 percent of the student body are residents of the state of Florida, but there is no cap on the percentage of the student body who can come from out of state, so your non-resident status is not a strike against you in the admissions process.

Legal research	
course requirement	Yes
Moot court requirement	No
Public interest	
law requirement	No

ADMISSIONS

Selectivity Rating	**89**
# applications received	3,373
% applicants accepted	28
% acceptees attending	42
Average LSAT	161
LSAT Range	158–163
Average undergrad GPA	3.65
Application fee	$30
Regular application	Rolling, up to 1/15
Regular notification	Rolling
Early application program	No
Transfer students accepted	Yes
Evening division offered	No
Part-time accepted	No
LSDAS accepted	Yes

Applicants Also Look At

Florida State University, American University, Washington University, Emory University, University of Miami, Stetson University, Florida Costal School of Law

International Students

Minimum TOEFL	
(paper/computer)	550/213

FINANCIAL FACTS

Annual tuition (in-state/ out-of-state)	$10,814/$10,814
Books and supplies	$2,060
Fees (in-state/ out-of-state)	$1,525/$20,890
Room & board (on/off-campus)	$7,900/$8,710
Financial aid application deadline	4/7
% first-year students receiving some sort of aid	82
% receiving some sort of aid	83
% of aid that is merit based	2
% receiving scholarships	22
Average grant	$4,288
Average loan	$21,473
Average total aid package	$21,397
Average debt	$56,053

EMPLOYMENT INFORMATION

Career Rating	**74**
Rate of placement (nine months out)	96.1
Average starting salary	$76,911
State for bar exam	FL, GA, NY, CA
Pass rate for first-time bar	83

Employers Who Frequently Hire Grads

Foley & Lardner; King & Spalding; Holland & Knight; White & Case; Greenberg Traurig; Hunton & Williams; Troutman Sanders; McGuire Woods.

Prominent Alumni

Martha Barnett, Holland & Knight LLP; ABA President 2000; W. Reece Smith Jr., Carlton, Fields; ABA President 1980; Stephen Zack, Boies, Schiller & Flexne.

Grads Employed by Field (%)

Academic (4)
Business/Industry (12)
Government (14)
Judicial clerkships (4)
Military (1)
Private practice (56)
Public Interest (9)

UNIVERSITY OF GEORGIA
SCHOOL OF LAW

INSTITUTIONAL INFORMATION

Public/private	Public
Student-faculty ratio	14:1
% faculty part-time	25
% faculty female	36
% faculty minority	7
Total faculty	73

SURVEY SAYS...

Diverse opinions accepted
in classrooms
Great research resources
Great library staff

STUDENTS

Enrollment of law school	660
% male/female	53/47
% out-of-state	20
% full-time	100
% minority	19
# of countries represented	4
Average age of entering class	24

ACADEMICS

Academic Experience Rating	**92**
Profs interesting rating	84
Profs accessible rating	87
Hours of study per day	4.74

Advanced Degrees Offered
LL.M., 1 year

Combined Degrees Offered
JD/Master of Business
Administration, 4 years; JD/Master
of Historic Preservation, 4 years;
JD/Master of Public Administration,
4 years; JD/Master of Social Work,
4 years; JD/Master of Education in
Sports Studies, 4 years; JD/M.A.,
various fields; JD/Ph.D., various
fields

Clinical program required	No
Legal writing course requirement	Yes
Legal methods course requirement	Yes
Legal research course requirement	Yes
Moot court requirement	No

Academics

The price is right at the University of Georgia School of Law, which holds one of the best international law programs in the nation and enjoys a positive reputation in the Southeast. The high-caliber faculty at UGA run students through "mental boot camp," the unique year-long courses (for first-year students) prepare students for a professional environment, and the grading system is set up in a such a way as to encourage students to stay with courses instead of quitting: Students do not receive grades for the first semester, and at the end of the first year, fall semester performance counts toward the final grade, but it is weighted significantly less than spring exam scores. Most students agree that this system provides a lot of motivation for students who found themselves overloaded in the first semester to increase their effort and grades. The alumni network is pretty useful at UGA, but Career Services has a lot of holes; students feel they need more "contacts for jobs outside the state of Georgia," as well as more internships and public interest opportunities made available to them before and after graduation.

Everyone is happy with their academic experiences in the classroom, where faculty "follow the Socratic method rigorously" and the "talented" and "knowledgeable" professors appear "genuinely interested in their students." Though "not every faculty member is inspiring," there are still "some exceptional professors and a long list of very capable ones," and a few of the deans still teach classes "because they love teaching so much." "The administration and professors invite interaction outside of class, and it is very common to go to lunch or have dinner with professors," says a student. The open-door policy of both the faculty and the administration wins students over, who see their instructors "not as distant and unapproachable figures, but as mentors who genuinely strive to see each student succeed." "They expect a great deal from us and it pays off," says a student. There is also applause for the administration for their accessibility and their work ensuring that students "are aware of everything that goes on in the school, including water main breaks or closings due to inclement weather." The facilities available at the school have "the right mix of modern technology and a historical building," and "whatever resource you need is available when you need it without the hassle of waiting or trying to search for it in some obscure place."

PAUL ROLLINS, DIRECTOR OF LAW ADMISSIONS
225 HERTY DRIVE, ATHENS, GA 30602-6012
TEL: 706-542-7060 FAX: 706-542-5556
EMAIL: UGAJD@UGA.EDU • WEBSITE: WWW.LAW.UGA.EDU

Life

Athens is "one of the greatest college towns in America," with coffee shops and bars downtown that students visit "at least one or two nights a week," but for older students, particularly those with spouses or significant others, the town "may not provide the opportunities found in a more metropolitan area. (Spouses may find it hard to find a good job or friends of the same age or station in life, which is important since you will be devoting so much of your time to school.)" Still, plenty of people do things together outside of school, such as "planning parties, going out to eat, running or going to the gym, or even grocery shopping," and Atlanta is "close enough" for those needing a metropolitan hub. "Students study together, students party together," says a 2L. "We really enjoy each other's company and would do anything within the limits of the honor code to help each other succeed." The moderately-sized school means that "everyone knows each others names," and everyone works to "keep each other sane here." There is a real sense of cohesion among students, and while there is competition (especially amongst 1L's trying to make the curve), "it is more like a gentlemen's game," and "the prevailing mood is 'Let's all get through this together' as opposed to stepping on each other to get ahead." The school is "about as liberal as you can expect in northeast Georgia"; most people here are middle-class and Caucasian, and many wish for more diversity, in terms of both ethnicity and viewpoints.

Getting In

Admission to the University of Georgia is selective. UGA seeks students with a strong academic background who can add diversity of experience to the class. In 2008, the entering class had a median LSAT score of 163 and a median undergraduate GPA of 3.67.

Public interest law requirement	No

ADMISSIONS

Selectivity Rating	**93**
# applications received	2,283
# applicants accepted	556
# acceptees attending	229
Average LSAT	163
LSAT Range	159–164
Median undergrad GPA	3.67
Application fee	$50
Regular application	Rolling, up to 2/10
Regular notification	Rolling
Early application program	No
Transfer students accepted	Yes
Evening division offered	No
Part-time accepted	No
LSDAS accepted	Yes

Applicants Also Look At
Duke University, Mercer University, University of North Carolina at Chapel Hill, Vanderbilt University, University of Virginia, Emory University, Georgia State University

FINANCIAL FACTS

Annual tuition (in-state/ out-of-state)	$13,090/$29,940
Books and supplies	$1,200
Fees	$1,374
Room & board	$11,200
Financial aid application deadline	3/1
% first-year students receiving some sort of aid	91
% receiving some sort of aid	89
% of aid that is merit based	20
% receiving scholarships	52
Average grant	$4,250
Average loan	$18,000
Average debt	$34,000

EMPLOYMENT INFORMATION

Career Rating	**89**	**Grads Employed by Field (%)**
Rate of placement (nine months out)	99	Business/Industry (7)
Average starting salary	$94,000	Government (11)
State for bar exam	GA	Judicial Clerkships (17)
Pass rate for first-time bar	98.7	Private Practice (58)
Employers Who Frequently Hire Grads		Public Interest (6)
Alston & Bird, King & Spalding, Troutman		Academic (1)
Sanders, Jones Day, Greenberg Traurig,		
U.S. Department of Justice, public defenders and prosecutors, Federal District and Circuit Court Judges.		

UNIVERSITY OF HAWAII—MANOA
WILLIAM S. RICHARDSON SCHOOL OF LAW

INSTITUTIONAL INFORMATION

Public/private	Public
% faculty part-time	45
% faculty female	43
% faculty minority	42
Total faculty	84

SURVEY SAYS...

Diverse opinions accepted
in classrooms
Abundant externship/internship/
clerkship opportunities
Students love Honolulu, HI

STUDENTS

Enrollment of law school	300
% male/female	46/54
% out-of-state	16
% full-time	88
% minority	64
% international	2
# of countries represented	6
Average age of entering class	27

ACADEMICS

Academic Experience Rating	**84**
Profs interesting rating	83
Profs accessible rating	86
Hours of study per day	4.92

Academic Specialties

Environmental law, international law, Pacific Asian Legal Studies with Native Hawaiian specialization

Advanced Degrees Offered

JD, 3 years

Combined Degrees Offered

JD/Environmental Law, 3 years, JD/Pacific-Asian Legal Studies, 3 years, JD/Grad. Ocean Policy, JD/MA, JD/MBA, JD/MS, JD/MSW, JD/PhD

Clinical program required	Yes
Legal writing course requirement	Yes
Legal methods course requirement	Yes
Legal research course requirement	Yes

Academics

Nestled at the "crossroads of the Pacific," the University of Hawaii—Manoa William S. Richardson School of Law offers local, national, and international students an equal opportunity to get a law degree while enjoying a little piece of heaven on earth. Don't be fooled by the laid-back nature of the students and faculty—academics here are plenty "rigorous," particularly in the school's strong Pacific Island law and environmental law programs. Fortunately, it's easy to wind down from a long day of hitting the books when you're surrounded by beaches and happy fellow students. As a second-year student eloquently observes: "Just the right mix of *aloha* and Socratic thrashing yields capable, happy lawyers."

Richardson's "first-rate" faculty has a reputation for being "very accessible and easy to work with," and it's obvious to students that "they take pride in teaching." Even the handful of students who aren't raving about their instructors can only offer up the mildest criticism, as one second-year demonstrates: "A few I've encountered are just okay." Abiding by an open-door policy and demonstrating an openness "to discussing topics at most anytime," Richardson professors take the time to make sure that everyone understands the concepts, while at the same time being "very supportive of independent research." "I generally feel that I am able to explore my intellectual pursuits as I deem fit, with guidance and support from the faculty," states a 2L.

The "very friendly" administration is certainly accessible; the Richardson School of Law is "the kind of school where the dean is seen in the halls everyday and says hello to you by name," and administrators are often spotted participating in school activities. In return, they ask for student input on many school matters, such as the hiring of professors, expansion of the school library, and improving student services. Richardson students speak very highly of the regard shown by the entire campus community for the well-being of first-year students, from the "truly concerned" deans to "supportive" upperclassmen. The island is a magnet for a great deal of "very impressive" adjunct faculty and visiting lecturers. "Professors from top law schools are always looking for an excuse to spend a semester or a year in paradise," surmises a 2L. "[During] my 1L year, I had two visiting professors from Georgetown and one from Duke, in addition to the excellent professors tenured at UH." Networking opportunities are "exceptional if you're staying in Hawaii," although some students seeking employment in the continental United States wish they had more assistance in their job search.

Both the facilities and the library are "useful" and sufficient for the typical student's needs, and include "access to up-to-date online sources, as well some print materials." Unsurprisingly, students prefer to congregate outside whenever possible, and a "courtyard where students can relax or talk" is usually where you'll find them. Even so, students clamor for more study and meeting rooms, and complain about the state of the library and the "very cold" air conditioning levels in classrooms. Luckily, the law school facilities are up for renovation within the next few years.

Life

A good mix of students fresh out of undergrad and those with more life experience bring diversity to Richardson' student population. Some students say that the school is "trying too hard to get diversity," which results in the enrollment of "lots of mainland people who will get their degree and bolt back." "Diversity of opinion and views is important, but not at the expense of the community at large," says a student. Still, there's

LAURIE TOCHIKI, ASSOCIATE DEAN
2515 DOLE STREET, HONOLULU, HI 96822
TEL: 808-956-3000 FAX: 808-956-3813
EMAIL: LAWADM@HAWAII.EDU • WEBSITE: WWW.HAWAII.EDU/LAW

Moot court requirement	No
Public interest	
law requirement	Yes

ADMISSIONS

Selectivity Rating	82
# applications received	992
% applicants accepted	28
% acceptees attending	29
Average LSAT	158
LSAT Range	155–169
Average undergrad GPA	3.47
Application fee	$60
Regular application	3/1
Regular notification	4/15
Early application program	No
Transfer students accepted	Yes
Evening division offered	Yes
Part-time accepted	Yes
LSDAS accepted	Yes

Applicants Also Look At

University of California—Berkeley;
University of California—Los
Angeles; Santa Clara University;
University of San Diego; University of
California, Hastings

International Students

TOEFL required	
of international students	Yes
Minimum TOEFL	
(paper/computer/web)	600/250/100

FINANCIAL FACTS

Annual tuition (in-state/	
out-of-state)	$14,424/$26,328
Books and supplies	$1,179
Fees	$317
Tuition per credit	
(in-state/out-of-state)	$601/$1,097
Room & board	
(on/off-campus)	$10,876/$15,805
Financial aid application	
deadline	3/1
Average grant	$6,502
Average loan	$21,943
Average total aid package	$21,976
Average debt	$57,743

not many downsides to life at Richardson. As one can imagine, "It's a very tightly knit community." Most students agree that competition at this "small, intimate" school is present and "healthy," but it takes a back seat to "learning how to be both a zealous advocate for clients and a responsible officer of the court." Classmates definitely "don't claw each other to get to the top of the class." It's hard to imagine all that much back-stabbing going on when "The culture and values of Hawaii permeate the school and administration," and the general happiness of students contributes to a "communal atmosphere" in which students "build ties and form lifelong bonds." "You become *ohana* (family) when you attend the Richardson School of Law," says one student. Still, there's a bit of "Hawaiian/not Hawaiian, *haole*/not *haole* tension" present on the island, but "in general, it's civil." The options of things to do in your downtime are unrivaled. "How many schools have a Surf Club?" asks a first-year. There are a "wide variety" of student clubs and organizations on campus (it's also easy to start one), and these groups do "a nice job" of promoting events such as guest speakers and symposiums.

Getting In

As the only ABA-accredited law school in the Pacific Asia region, the University of Hawaii—Manoa Richardson School of Law can afford to be selective. They've got a lock on the local talent and anyone looking to practice within the area will be competing for a limited number of seats. The school is very strict about its deadlines, and all applications must be received by March 1.

EMPLOYMENT INFORMATION

Career Rating	73	**Grads Employed by Field (%)**
Rate of placement (nine months out)	88	Academic (6)
Average starting salary	$65,483	Business/Industry (7)
State for bar exam	HI	Government (13)
Pass rate for first-time bar	85	Judicial Clerkships (23)
Prominent Alumni		Military (3)
John Waihee, former Governor of Hawaii;		Private Practice (34)
Jack Fritz, Spkr, House of Congress of Fed.		Public Interest (2)
St. of Micrones.; Alexa Fujise, Associate		Other (12)
Judge, Hawai`i Intermediate Court of		
Appeals; James Duke Aiona, Lieutenant		
Governor, State of Hawaii; Junichi		
Yanagihara, Managing Director &		
Producer, Sprite Animation Studios.		

UNIVERSITY OF HOUSTON
LAW CENTER

INSTITUTIONAL INFORMATION

Public/private	Public
Student-faculty ratio	13:1
% faculty part-time	45
% faculty female	37
% faculty minority	1
Total faculty	156

SURVEY SAYS...

Diverse opinions accepted
in classrooms
Great library staff
Abundant externship/internship/
clerkship opportunities

STUDENTS

Enrollment of law school	1,070
% male/female	57/43
% out-of-state	11
% full-time	75
% minority	28
% international	5
# of countries represented	29
Average age of entering class	25

ACADEMICS

Academic Experience Rating	**85**
Profs interesting rating	82
Profs accessible rating	73
Hours of study per day	4.15

Academic Specialties

Commercial law; criminal law; environmental law; international law; labor law; taxation; intellectual property law; health, energy, consumer law; clinical programs; trial advocacy; higher education

Advanced Degrees Offered

LL.M, 24 credit hours: Health, Intellectual Property, Tax, Energy & Natural Resources, International Law, Foreign Scholars (for Foreign Attorneys)

Combined Degrees Offered

JD/MBA, 4 years; JD/MPH, 4 years; JD/MA History, 4 years; JD/Ph.D. in Medical Humanities, 5–6 years; JD/MSW, 4 years; JD/Ph.D. in Criminal Justice, 5–6 years; JD/MD, 6 years.

Academics

As large and lively as the state of Texas, the University of Houston Law Center enrolls more than 1,000 students in its diverse and challenging JD, LLM, and joint-degree programs. Drawing top names from the Houston legal community, professors are "either extremely accomplished attorneys or nationally renowned experts in a particular field of law." Though they represent the top of their field, "There are no 'bigger than Texas' egos with any of the faculty." In fact, "The entire faculty is very accessible and willing to help students learn in any way they can." Students agree that their professors are "not only available during office hours, many professors host lunches or parties in their homes to learn more about their students."

In the classroom, the professors are "very much focused on teaching us to think creatively" and throughout the JD program the "Practical aspects of lawyering are stressed." Things here begin with a bang as "All first-year students are required to take part in a moot court competition and it's a great experience for everyone." In addition, "There are six different law journals in which a student may participate, including the Houston Law Review, which consistently ranks in the top 50 of all Law Reviews in the country." What's more, the school operates a number of clinics and research institutes that augment classroom experiences with hands-on experience. "I have spent three semesters working at the Immigration and Civil Clinic and will always remember this time as the most exciting and rewarding aspect of my law school experience," explains one clinic participant. "We are given enormous responsibility for our clients and the experience has given me an invaluable opportunity to learn actual lawyering skills."

Those looking for great value relative to cost in their education will be extremely satisfied with U of H. Students love that they get a "high-value education for a low cost in a great legal market." If you can manage a "scholarship" or are "a Texas resident" it only sweetens the proverbial deal. Even so, students admit there are some sacrifices associated with a U of H education, particularly with regard to the school's facilities which most agree "need improvement." There are no ivy-lined walls at U of H; instead, think "East-German-bunker school of architecture." However, most students take the environs in stride. "Students who enter with high expectations of facilities will be disappointed," says one student. "But you learn at this school in an environment conducive to learning." On that note, U of H "fosters a community and not a rivalry among students. Fellow students are always willing to answer a question, share notes, and form study groups."

Outside the classroom, "There are lots of opportunities to work with major law firms and other community organizations during the summer and during the school year," and the "Office of Career Services is particularly helpful for summer job opportunities." After graduation, Houston is a well-suited environment for future attorneys, boasting its reputation as one of the "largest legal markets in the country." A current student insists, "If you want to succeed, you can, and you can get a great job when you graduate too—with all the top firms in Texas including all the elite New York satellite offices."

Life

Students say the school is a great place to work on your powers of persuasion as there's lots of debate on the U of H campus. A student explains, "Because the student body is fairly conservative, but, at the same time, lawyers generally exhibit liberal thinking (at least in the social realm), you get a nice balance of liberal and conservative, often

JAMIE WEST, ASSISTANT DEAN FOR ADMISSIONS
100 LAW CENTER, HOUSTON, TX 77204-6060
TEL: 713-743-2280 FAX: 713-743-2194
EMAIL: LAWADMISSIONS@UH.EDU • WEBSITE: WWW.LAW.UH.EDU

leading to lively debate absent from more liberal institutions." Even so, don't expect "any cutthroat type of competitive environment" here since students agree that "even if they have polar opposite views in the classroom, afterwards they hang out."

On campus, the prevailing atmosphere is "friendly" with "an awesome SBA that is very active in helping make UHLC a better place." Students tend to form strong friendships in their first-year sections, and when the weekend arrives "Plenty of people . . . go out on a regular basis." Night students are generally less involved in the campus community, admitting that there is something of a "social divide between part-time and full-time students"; many complain that events and activities take place during the day (while they are working) and that "most of the social events are geared towards single people or those without children."

Unfortunately, the campus isn't much of a social hub because "It is in a part of Houston that nobody really cares to live in, so most people come in for class and then head home." However, the cosmopolitan city of Houston is a great place to live, offering "a standing symphony, opera, and ballet, NFL, NBA, MLB, and MLS sports teams (and minor league ice hockey) a great zoo and museums, and a multitude of golfing opportunities."

Getting In

There is no set minimum LSAT score or undergraduate GPA required for acceptance to the University of Houston Law Center; all applicants are reviewed individually. In 2009, the lowest LSAT score accepted was in the upper-140s, while the median score for accepted applicants was 163. The median GPA was 3.49. Non-Texans comprise approximately 11 percent of the student population and the acceptance rate is equally competitive for out-of-state and in-state residents.

Clinical program required	No
Legal writing course requirement	Yes
Legal methods course requirement	Yes
Legal research course requirement	Yes
Moot court requirement	Yes
Public interest law requirement	No

ADMISSIONS

Selectivity Rating	**86**
# applications received	3,337
# applicants accepted	958
# acceptees attending	313
Average LSAT	161
LSAT Range	157–163
Average undergrad GPA	3.45
Application fee	$70
Regular application	Rolling, up to 2/15 / 5/15
Regular notification	Rolling
Early application program	Yes
Early application deadline	11/1
Early application notification	2/15
Transfer students accepted	Yes
Evening division offered	Yes
Part-time accepted	Yes
LSDAS accepted	Yes

Applicants Also Look At

University of Texas at Austin, Texas Tech University, Baylor University, Southern Methodist University

International Students

TOEFL required of international students	Yes
Minimum TOEFL (paper/computer)	600/250

FINANCIAL FACTS

Annual tuition (in-state/out-of-state)	$13,984/$21,514
Books and supplies	$1,100
Fees	$4,442
Tuition per credit (in-state/out-of-state)	$466/$717
Room & board (on/off-campus)	$12,512/$15,456
Financial aid application deadline	4/1
% receiving some sort of aid	84
% of aid that is merit based	38
% receiving scholarships	45
Average grant	$4,357
Average loan	$18,659
Average total aid package	$23,068
Average debt	$68,939

EMPLOYMENT INFORMATION

		Grads Employed by Field (%)
Career Rating	87	
Rate of placement (nine months out)	97	Academic (2)
Average starting salary	$90,933	Business/Industry (20)
State for bar exam	TX	Government (10)
Pass rate for first-time bar	90.5	Judicial Clerkships (6)

Employers Who Frequently Hire Grads
Baker & Botts; Locke Liddell & Sapp; Fulbright & Jaworski; Vinson & Elkins; Bracewell & Giuliani; Harris Co. D.A.; Weil Gotshal & Manges

Private Practice (58)
Public Interest (4)

Prominent Alumni
Richard Haynes, Litigation; John O'Quinn, Litigation; Charles Matthews, Vice President and General Counsel/ExxonMobil.

UNIVERSITY OF IDAHO
COLLEGE OF LAW

INSTITUTIONAL INFORMATION

Public/private	Public
Student-faculty ratio	16:1
% faculty part-time	25
% faculty female	43
% faculty minority	8
Total faculty	40

SURVEY SAYS...

Diverse opinions accepted
in classrooms
Great library staff
Students never sleep

STUDENTS

Enrollment of law school	306
% male/female	55/45
% out-of-state	32
% full-time	100
% minority	18
# of countries represented	4
Average age of entering class	27

ACADEMICS

Academic Experience Rating	**62**
Profs interesting rating	65
Profs accessible rating	84
Hours of study per day	4.69

Academic Specialties

Commercial law, environmental law,
advocacy and dispute resolution,
business and entrepreneurship,
environmental and natural
resources, Native American law

Combined Degrees Offered

Dual JD/MS/PHD in Water Law,
Management, and Policy Dual
JD/MS in Environmental Science, 8
semesters; Dual JD/Master of
Accountancy, 7 semesters; Dual
JD/Master of Business
Administration (at Washington St.
University), 7 semesters.

Clinical program required	No
Legal writing course requirement	Yes
Legal methods course requirement	No

Academics

"Handwritten on my letter of acceptance were the words 'We would love to have you in the Idaho family,'" beams a 1L at the University of Idaho College of Law. "I didn't think anything of it at the time, but it really does have that kind of feel here." "The low tuition is a bargain," and "The administration is kind, fair, and involved." Plus, "The Dean rocks." "There are a few profs here and there who obviously just want to do their research, and teaching is a bit of a dead weight for them, but they are definitely in the minority." Most "dedicated" professors at this "small public law school" are "unbelievably friendly and accessible" and "genuinely care about the students." The faculty "knows students by name by the end of their first year, even if you do not have a class with them." "I've never seen anything like it, quite frankly," says an impressed 1L. "Sure, one moment they're using the Socratic Method to grill you in class," says a 2L, "but after class they take the time to discuss any topic with you."

Some students complain that "practical legal skills, other than writing, seem to get short shrift." Others contend that there are "ample opportunities for pro bono work" and "other ways to allow students to get some practical experience before they graduate." "Many of these programs are student run, which I think is great," notes a 1L. "The externship, internship, clinic, and semester-in-practice programs are wonderful."

U of I is the only law school in Idaho, "and its graduates are extremely well respected throughout the state and throughout the geographic region in general." "Because Idaho is a small state with a relatively small legal community, alumni are very actively involved at the law school." "During orientation, a group of us were eating lunch on the lawn outside the law school," explains a 1L. "A man approached us and asked to join us. Only after five minutes of casual conversation did he mention that he was the Attorney General for the state of Idaho." "There are quite a few job opportunities in the area surrounding Moscow," but "It is hard to get good placements" for jobs, internships, and externships because of the school's relatively remote location. "You pretty much have to live in Spokane or Boise for the summer to get a really well-paid job with valuable experience."

The "somewhat old" and "small" law school facilities are "functional," but "could be more aesthetically pleasing." The administration is "working to improve aesthetics," and major renovations have just been completed. The study areas are "roomy and nice," and classrooms are "comfortable" and "very large." "There is a beautiful courtroom where the Idaho Supreme Court and Court of Appeals come twice a year and provide the students an opportunity to observe actual proceedings." The library is "pretty good for a small school."

Life

The administration "is striving to increase diversity," but it's not easy because U of I is "somewhat isolated by its location and lack of diversity in the general population." Students do run the gamut in terms of age. "I am enjoying my experience of returning to school as an older student," says a 2L. Also, "There is a sizeable Mormon population." Politically, the student population is "divided between extreme conservatives and extreme liberals," which "creates tension" occasionally.

DIRECTOR OF ADMISSIONS
6TH & RAYBURN STREETS, MOSCOW, ID 83844-2321
TEL: 208-885-2300 FAX: 208-885-5709
EMAIL: LAWADMIT@UIDAHO.EDU • WEBSITE: WWW.LAW.UIDAHO.EDU

"This is a tremendously friendly law school." Students describe themselves as "cooperative and accepting." "The 1Ls, though competitive," demonstrate a "strong camaraderie." Cliques do tend to form, though, and gossip runs "rampant." Outside of class, there is "a lot of student involvement." "Because of the limited number of students [at the law school], there are countless opportunities for involvement in extracurricular activities, legal aid clinics, positions in student groups, and for membership on administration committees." "About half of the students socialize on a regular basis," and there are "some pretty hard partiers."

Moscow is "a fairly remote," "beautiful," rural hamlet "in northern Idaho," "closer to Seattle than Boise," and "two hours from a city of any size (Spokane, Washington)." Idaho boasts "many recreational opportunities." "If you love hiking, biking, skiing, and the outdoors, then it is heaven," counsels a 2L. "If you need constant activity and entertainment, U of I is not for you, but if you're serious about getting a good-quality, inexpensive education, you'll get both here." "The cost of living is affordable," and "There is a large food co-op" and "an impressive farmer's market." There are "great parks" and "many festivals" as well. It's "easy to walk anywhere." "There isn't an apartment in town that isn't five minutes from the school."

Getting In

Enrolled students at the 25th percentile have LSAT scores of 151 and GPAs a little over 3.1. Admitted students at the 75th percentile have LSAT scores of 157 and GPAs of nearly 3.6. If you take the LSAT more than once, the U of I "may put more weight on the most recent score, especially when there is several years between scores."

Legal research course requirement	Yes
Moot court requirement	Yes
Public interest law requirement	Yes

ADMISSIONS

Selectivity Rating	**73**
# applications received	759
% applicants accepted	45
% acceptees attending	30
Average LSAT	154
LSAT Range	151–157
Average undergrad GPA	3.29
Application fee	$50
Regular application	Rolling, up to 7/1
Regular notification	Rolling
Early application program	No
Transfer students accepted	Yes
Evening division offered	No
Part-time accepted	No
LSDAS accepted	Yes

Applicants Also Look At
Seattle University, University of Oregon, Gonzaga University, Willamette University

International Students

Minimum TOEFL (paper/computer)	560/280

FINANCIAL FACTS

Annual tuition (in-state/ out-of-state)	$10,882/$20,962
Books and supplies	$5,296
Room & board	$8,784
Financial aid application deadline	2/15
% receiving some sort of aid	100
% of aid that is merit based	100
% receiving scholarships	47
Average grant	$6,030
Average loan	$22,080
Average debt	$55,326

EMPLOYMENT INFORMATION

Career Rating	**62**	**Grads Employed by Field (%)**
Rate of placement (nine months out)	85	Academic (4)
Average starting salary	$51,079	Business/Industry (8)
State for bar exam	ID, WA, UT, AZ, CO	Government (13)
Pass rate for first-time bar	81.2	Judicial clerkships (24)

Employers Who Frequently Hire Grads
Military (4)

Employers w/offices in Idaho, Washington, Oregon, Utah, Nevada, Montana.
Other (3)

Prominent Alumni
Private practice (34)

Linda Copple Trout, Justice & past Chief Justice, Idaho Supreme Court; Frank A. Shrontz, Former CEO Boeing Co.; Dennis E. Wheeler, President, Coeur: The Precious Metals Co.; James A. McClure, Former United States Senator.

Public Interest (10)

UNIVERSITY OF ILLINOIS
COLLEGE OF LAW

Academics

"You'll definitely get the bang for your buck" at the University of Illinois College of Law, "a jewel amid the cornfields [that boasts] the best mix of academic excellence, social interaction, and human decency for the best price available." Tuition is especially affordable for in-state students. The "tireless [administration] is also very accessible" and extraordinarily popular among students. "The new dean is extremely supportive of the students and does a wonderful job of building community."

Students at the U of I tell us emphatically that "the faculty is the school's greatest strength." The "tough but not unreasonable" professors are "prolific writers [who are] clearly brilliant and accomplished." Students say the professors "are, for the most part fantastic, both in and out of the classroom [and] always able to clarify concepts that are confusing. More significant, they are completely available [and] genuinely interested in teaching and working with students." The professors make an effort to be reached in that they "have open-door policies and are available for discussions with students about class, a job, or just life in general." Students also note that the school "employs a nice mix of tenured and adjunct faculty, which makes for a perfect balance of legal theory and real-world experience. The primary complaint that students have with regard to the faculty is "keeping the good professors around. "One student explains, "There's not much reason for them to stay in central Illinois. The school really needs to make an effort to not let the good ones get away."

Graduates enjoy "a great employment rate" thanks to an aggressive Career Services Office. As one transfer student attests, "I'm in a unique position in that I've seen how two different law schools operate. I was blown away by the quality of the Career Services Department at the University of Illinois. The administration goes to great lengths to make sure that not only do all University of Illinois College of Law graduates get jobs, but that they get the jobs they want." "If you do well here, nothing in Chicago will be off limits." However, students complain that the college "needs to broaden its resources [and] expand beyond the Midwestern market." Until that happens, "It is difficult to get much traction" on either coast "when searching for jobs in Champaign."

The facilities at the U of I "are good" in that large chunks "are wired," and the research resources of the library are as abundant as you'll find anywhere. Overall, though, the "rather Spartan [College of Law] could use some serious help." Suffice it to say, the "incredibly ugly and cheap-looking [building] does not give anyone goose bumps for the grand study of the law." One student writes, "There are no windows in any of the rooms." It's like going to school in a casino." Students note, "Sometimes seats are scarce [in the] crowded" classrooms, as well as in the "cramped" library, though now that the school has reduced the size of the incoming class, this should help to alleviate the problem. Also, wear layers because "There also seems to be a bit of a temperature control problem" no matter what the season.

Life

If they do say so themselves, the students at the U of I are "very amiable, noncompetitive, [and] very intellectually minded, yet not stuck on themselves." These are the "brightest [and] most fun" people—"all the cool, smart kids." Students at the U of I are also "a bit neurotic [and] love to hear their own voices." The student population "has a wonderful mix of student ethnicities, religions, sexual orientation, and gender." There is also a laid-back atmosphere on campus. "Everybody really cares about you. They want you to succeed, and it's almost difficult not to."

PAUL D. PLESS, ASSISTANT DEAN FOR ADMISSIONS AND FINANCIAL AID
504 EAST PENNSYLVANIA AVENUE, ROOM 201, MC-594, CHAMPAIGN, IL 61820
TEL: 217-244-6415 FAX: 217-244-1478
EMAIL: ADMISSIONS@LAW.UIUC.EDU • WEBSITE: WWW.LAW.UIUC.EDU

"The school truly is a community because of its manageable size. Lunches with the dean" are common, and there are "endless other ways to connect with the other students and, more important, the faculty." One content student writes, "The cafeteria has good food and, best of all, they carry Starbucks coffee." Students also say, "Although U of I is located in the corn fields of Illinois, it is impossible to feel isolated" because the administration "is constantly bringing in lecturers, symposiums, and guest speakers." In addition, the College of Law sponsors "a weekly happy hour, [at which] professors and administrators act as the celebrity bartenders."

Life outside the classroom has many positive aspects. Students are very "sports-oriented" and say "It is great to be on a Big Ten campus and be able to devote yourself to the study of law full-time," and surprising though it seems, "There is actually a lot to do in Urbana-Champaign." There are "great bars, coffee houses, [and] centers for the arts." There is also "a progressive music scene." Some students gripe that "social life can seem dominated by a frat/sorority type atmosphere," even at the law school level. "The town is basically designed for college students, so it gets a little dullsville at times." Many students would "prefer to be in a larger city," with Chicago being the example of choice. "Socially, we do the best we can with the town we're in," asserts one student. "That means we drink a lot [and] go en masse to football and basketball games."

Getting In

The average LSAT score for admitted students is 166. The median GPA is 3.5. Those numbers are serious but not forbidding. Note also that, while it's substantially cheaper for Illinois residents to attend the college, residency in the Land of Lincoln will not get you one iota of special treatment from the admissions office.

ADMISSIONS

Selectivity Rating	92
# applications received	3,221
% applicants accepted	23
% acceptees attending	25
Average LSAT	166
LSAT Range	160–167
Average undergrad GPA	3.5
Application fee	$50
Regular application	Rolling, up to 3/15
Regular notification	Rolling
Early application program	Yes
Early application deadline	10/31
Early application notification	12/15
Transfer students accepted	Yes
Evening division offered	No
Part-time accepted	No
LSDAS accepted	Yes

Applicants Also Look At

University of Wisconsin—Madison, University of Michigan—Ann Arbor, Northwestern University, Indiana University—Bloomington, Washington University, Illinois Institute of Technology, University of Iowa

International Students

TOEFL required of international students	Yes
Minimum TOEFL (paper/computer)	600/250

FINANCIAL FACTS

Annual tuition (in-state/ out-of-state)	$18,102/$29,100
Books and supplies	$3,020
Fees	$1,824
Room & board	$8,532
Financial aid application deadline	3/15
% first-year students receiving some sort of aid	99
% receiving some sort of aid	99
% of aid that is merit based	90
% receiving scholarships	58
Average grant	$8,000
Average loan	$21,556
Average total aid package	$35,000
Average debt	$62,223

EMPLOYMENT INFORMATION

Career Rating	79
Rate of placement (nine months out)	99
Average starting salary	$75,072
State for bar exam	IL, CA, DC, NY, MO
Pass rate for first-time bar	93

Employers Who Frequently Hire Grads

Baker & McKenzie; Brinks Hofer Gilson & Lione; Bell Boyd & Lloyd; Foley & Lardner; Sidley Austin Brown & Wood, McGuire & Woods, McAndrews Held & Malloy; Deloitte Touche; Gardner Carton & Douglas; Husch & Eppenberger; Jenner & Block; Jones Day; Kirkland & Ellis; KMZ Rosenman; U.S. Securities and Exchange Commission: and Winston & Strawn.

Grads Employed by Field (%)

Academic (3)
Business/Industry (12)
Government (9)
Judicial Clerkships (13)
Military (2)
Private Practice (58)
Public Interest (3)

THE UNIVERSITY OF IOWA
COLLEGE OF LAW

INSTITUTIONAL INFORMATION

Public/private	Public
Student-faculty ratio	14:1
% faculty part-time	26
% faculty female	37
% faculty minority	13
Total faculty	52

SURVEY SAYS...

Diverse opinions accepted
in classrooms
Great research resources
Great library staff

STUDENTS

Enrollment of law school	627
% male/female	55/45
% out-of-state	49
% full-time	100
% minority	18
# of countries represented	10
Average age of entering class	24

ACADEMICS

Academic Experience Rating	**88**
Profs interesting rating	88
Profs accessible rating	83
Hours of study per day	4.74

Academic Specialties

Commercial law, constitutional law,
corporation securities, international
law, property, intellectual property law

Advanced Degrees Offered

LL.M in International and
Comparative Law, 24 hours of academic credit and a thesis, 1 year

Combined Degrees Offered

JD/MBA, 4 years; JD/MA, 4 years;
JD/MHA, 4 years; JD/MSW, 4 years;
JD/MPH, 4 years; JD/MS, 4 years;
JD/MD, 6 years

Clinical program required	No
Legal writing course requirement	Yes
Legal methods course requirement	Yes
Legal research course requirement	Yes

Academics

Students at the affordable University of Iowa College of Law are unanimous on one point: Iowa is "the most underrated school in the country." "If you want to learn from the best without giving an arm and a leg for tuition," they say, "come to this school." The "sympathetic" faculty at Iowa is "very concerned with providing the best academic experience." "Professors are demanding in a way that I know will make me a better lawyer," relates 2L. "They are brilliant yet not egomaniacs." "Some scare the crap out of you, and some create a warm classroom environment." Outside of class, "The professors are, for the most part, interesting and cool people," and interaction between students and professors is exceedingly common. Sure, they are "awkward socially," but "Even the most distinguished professors welcome you into their offices, and it's not uncommon to go out to dinner with your professor and a few classmates."

Classes here "tend toward the theoretical." "Iowa presents kind of a contradiction," proffers a 2L. "It is a theory-driven program that produces mostly practicing attorneys." Iowa's 10 practice clinics are "very strong," "and there are plenty of slots available" (though you do have to lottery into them). "The Iowa City/Cedar Rapids area has opportunities to practice while in law school, but those opportunities are somewhat limited." The legal writing program garners mixed reviews. "We are learning to write legal briefs and memos from the best," contends a satisfied 1L. Others feel "cheated." "We could use a lot more hands-on training with writing and research," says one student. Pretty much everyone who mentions the moot court program is unhappy with it. "The faculty can't be bothered to provide meaningful coaching or instruction," laments one student.

The Career Services staff here "is a group of all-stars" that provides "all of the assistance you need." "The top 25 to 30 percent of students don't seem to have any trouble finding work in cities across the country, including New York, San Francisco, Los Angeles, and Boston." By and large, though, students end up practicing in one of "several large markets" throughout the Midwest. Some students complain that "Iowa could do better in attracting and encouraging employers outside of the Midwest." "If you want to work in the Midwest, this school is considered good, and employers are eager to interview you," advises a 2L. "If you want to work anywhere else, go to law school in that region."

The "really space-constrained" law school building is "functional, though it looks pretty awful." "It was built in the early '80s, and I think at that time people thought it was cool and futuristic," adds a 2L, "but now it just looks like something out of Star Trek IV." "Classrooms are pretty typical," though students "appreciate the plentiful outlets and wireless Internet." "There is no shortage of PCs available in the computer labs," and "The school also has very friendly tech gurus." The "extensive" law library is "a little bubble of greatness." It's "open late" and "always staffed by friendly librarians who know more about the law than anyone ever should."

Life

Students are "mostly White and from Iowa or Illinois," but there is also "a surprisingly large number of kids from the coasts." "I was actually surprised by how many non-Midwestern students are currently at the school," admits a 1L. Overall, it's "a good mix of people from all walks of life." There are "some very conservative points of view" but "young crazy liberals" predominate. There are "a lot of do-gooders who are very socially conscious and commit a tremendous amount of time to community and national issues."

JAN BARNES, ADMISSIONS COORDINATOR
320 MELROSE, IOWA CITY, IA 52242
TEL: 319-335-9095 FAX: 319-335-9646
EMAIL: LAW-ADMISSIONS@UIOWA.EDU • WEBSITE: WWW.LAW.UIOWA.EDU

"U of I law students and most of the professors have a definite liberal slant," says a 2L. "If you're conservative and not articulate and able to defend your opinions, you'll never survive classroom discussion."

"Students at Iowa are competitive, certainly." "I was surprised by how many gunners there actually are," relates a 3L. It's "friendly" gunning, though. Iowa students are "a group of people who have their priorities in order, who are willing to lend a hand, and who are remarkably grounded in reality." "There's an earnestness and commitment to integrity and excellence that Iowa students, faculty, and staff all share," enthuses a 3L. "It makes Iowa a unique place, and it makes me hopeful for the legal profession as a whole. As a jaded California native and East Coast private college graduate, I never cease to be surprised by the quality and professionalism I've found here in the heartland."

Socially, though "People tend to buckle down when it is demanded," "You can be sure to find friends out at a bar" on virtually any given weekend night. "Everyone is very good friends with each other," and Iowa City is "a fun town." Coffee shops, libraries, bookstores, and great restaurants abound. There are "weekly Law Nights held at a local drinking establishment." "There's no such thing as a grad student bar in Iowa City," and there is "a pretty big divide between people who took time off and people who came straight from undergrad."

Getting In

Admitted students at the 25th percentile have LSAT scores of 158 and GPAs in the range of 3.3. Admitted students at the 75th percentile have LSAT scores of 163 and GPAs of around 3.8.

Moot court requirement	Yes
Public interest law requirement	No

ADMISSIONS

Selectivity Rating	85
# applications received	1,502
% applicants accepted	38
% acceptees attending	34
Average LSAT	161
LSAT Range	158–164
Average undergrad GPA	3.56
Application fee	$60
Regular application	Rolling, up to 3/1
Regular notification	Rolling
Early application program	No
Transfer students accepted	Yes
Evening division offered	No
Part-time accepted	No
LSDAS accepted	Yes

Applicants Also Look At

University of Wisconsin—Madison, University of Illinois at Urbana-Champaign, Indiana University—Bloomington, Washington University, University of Minnesota—Twin Cities, Boston College, University of Notre Dame

International Students

TOEFL required of international students	Yes
Minimum TOEFL (paper/computer/web)	620/260/105

FINANCIAL FACTS

Annual tuition (in-state/ out-of-state)	$16,758/$33,526
Books and supplies	$2,300
Fees	$1,158
Room & board (off-campus)	$9,630
Financial aid application deadline	1/1
% first-year students receiving some sort of aid	94
% receiving some sort of aid	94
% of aid that is merit based	8.7
% receiving scholarships	32
Average grant	$16,758
Average loan	$27,438
Average total aid package	$34,294
Average debt	$76,353

EMPLOYMENT INFORMATION

Career Rating	87	Grads Employed by Field (%)
Rate of placement (nine months out)	99	Academic (5)
Average starting salary	$86,196	Business/Industry (13)
State for bar exam	IA, IL, MN, MO, NY	Government (7)
Pass rate for first-time bar	93.1	Judicial clerkships (13)

Employers Who Frequently Hire Grads
Business/Industry, National Law Firms, Government Agencies, State and Federal Judges

Military (2)
Private practice (55)
Public Interest (5)

Prominent Alumni
Justice Rita Garman, Illinois Supreme Court; Victor Alvarez, Partner, White & Case, Miami; John J. Bouma, Chairman, Snell & Wilmer, Phoenix.

UNIVERSITY OF KANSAS
SCHOOL OF LAW

Academics

The "extremely affordable" University of Kansas School of Law "produces good attorneys and loyal alumni." "If you like the Midwest, you can't get better than KU," declares a 1L. "If you don't like the Midwest but ended up here anyway, you really can't get any better than KU." There are "a lot of different kinds of clinical opportunities available" for students looking to gain practical experience. Certificate programs at KU include elder law, environmental law, media law, tax law, tribal law, advocacy law, and business and commercial law. There is also a program in international trade and finance. Another nifty feature here is a Summer Start program which allows first-year students to enroll in 1L courses during the summer before the traditional first semester begins. It was "a big help in getting plugged in to the social aspect of law school," reports a student. Career Services "does an excellent job of bringing potential employers from all over the country for on-campus interviews." However, students do note that the legal research and writing program could use some "improvement."

KU's "sharp" and "funny" professors are "highly qualified, both academically and professionally." "The faculty seems genuinely interested in seeing the students happy and successful at the end of the day," explains a student. "We have a good balance between the more 'scholarly' professors—the ones who do lots of research and writing and are known in their field for these activities but maybe only practiced a few years— and professors who have lots of real-world experience," says a 2L. The Socratic Method, though "scary at first," "really helps students to learn." Outside of class, KU professors are notoriously "approachable" and "friendly." "I feel comfortable walking into any professor's office, whether I'm currently taking a class from them or not," claims a 3L.

Many students tell us that KU's "very student-oriented" administration maintains "an open-door policy" and is "available to help students in a variety of ways." "You can tell the administration is truly concerned about student satisfaction and preparation," gushes a 1L. Other students see room for improvement, citing the "outdated" law building.

KU Law is located on "one of the prettiest campuses in the country." Though "There have recently been renovations" to the law building, students complain that the facilities are "far too small" and could use "an interior designer." That said, the "state-of-the-art classrooms" are "laptop friendly," and Internet access is "anywhere and everywhere." However, the library "needs more printers and computers." "The long and ridiculous lines at the restrooms are a serious consideration" as well. On the bright side, common areas are "aesthetically pleasing" and offer "a comfortable place to spend the time between classes."

Life

KU is "generally a young school, so if you are coming just out of undergrad you will be pretty happy," says one student. The "dynamic student body" also includes students "who have worked for a few years" and "those who have lived and worked throughout their lives and are now returning in their 40s and 50s." Students here come primarily from Kansas and its neighboring states and exhibit plenty of "Midwestern charm." Though students would like to see KU "encouraging diversity," members of ethnic minorities feel quite at home. "Everyone knows me and treats me with respect," says one minority student. Politics are "rarely discussed in classes," though that isn't to say that people don't "have opinions and vote." Ultimately, "There are just as many conservative students as there are liberal." "I wouldn't say that students are obnoxious in their liberality, it is just part of the package at a university like KU," explains a 2L.

JACQLENE NANCE, DIRECTOR OF ADMISSIONS
1535 W. 15TH STREET, LAWRENCE, KS 66045-7577
TEL: 785-864-4378 FAX: 785-864-5054
EMAIL: ADMITLAW@KU.EDU • WEBSITE: WWW.LAW.KU.EDU

Students report that "there is some competition," but this is mostly a "cooperative and friendly" group. By and large, KU Law has a "very collegial" and "laid-back" atmosphere. "Students tend to get along pretty well" and, "as a whole, do not tolerate rudeness." "There are some cliques," says one student, but, by and large, "Camaraderie and good will" are the rule. "We regularly trade outlines, discuss cases, and help each other out," says a happy 1L.

"The social life is pretty great at KU," and "Most students find a good balance between school and personal life." Student-organized activities are popular. "If you attend student organization meetings, you can enjoy several free pizza lunches each week and learn more about different areas of law," explains a student. "The student body has numerous pub crawls and other events" as well. The surrounding college town of Lawrence provides for off-campus fun, and when students want to escape to the plains, Kansas City is only a short drive away.

Getting In

Admitted students at the 25th percentile have LSAT scores of roughly 154 and GPAs of roughly 3.3. Admitted students at the 75th percentile have LSAT scores of about 160 and GPAs of just under 3.8. If you are coming to KU from another state, note that it is very tough to become recognized as a resident of Kansas for tuition purposes if you aren't one already.

Public interest
law requirement — No

ADMISSIONS

Selectivity Rating	**82**
# applications received	1,101
# applicants accepted	395
# acceptees attending	162
Average LSAT	158
LSAT Range	154–160
Average undergrad GPA	3.5
Application fee	$55
Regular application	Rolling, up to 3/15
Regular notification	Rolling
Early application program	No
Transfer students accepted	Yes
Evening division offered	No
Part-time accepted	No
LSDAS accepted	Yes

Applicants Also Look At
University of Wisconsin—Madison, University of Illinois at Urbana-Champaign, American University, University of Colorado at Boulder, University of Denver, Indiana University—Bloomington, University of Nebraska—Lincoln, Arizona State University

International Students
TOEFL required
of international students — Yes
Minimum TOEFL
(paper/computer) — 600/250

FINANCIAL FACTS

Annual tuition (in-state/ out-of-state)	$13,301/$23,934
Books and supplies	$900
Fees	$847
Room & board	$9,616
Financial aid application deadline	3/1
% first-year students receiving some sort of aid	84
% receiving some sort of aid	87
% of aid that is merit based	13
% receiving scholarships	76
Average grant	$5,376
Average loan	$8,732
Average total aid package	$12,218
Average debt	$31,585

EMPLOYMENT INFORMATION

Career Rating	**77**
Rate of placement (nine months out)	94
Average starting salary	$67,650
State for bar exam	KS, MO, CA, CO, TX
Pass rate for first-time bar	90

Employers Who Frequently Hire Grads
Baker Sterchi Cowden & Rice, Husch Blackwell Sanders, Bryan Cave, Fleeson Gooing, Foulston Siefkin, Hinkle Elkouri, Lathrop & Gage, Lewis Rice & Fingersh, Martin Pringle, Polsinelli Shughart, Shook Hardy & Bacon, Snell & Wilmer.

Prominent Alumni
Stephen Six, Attorney General of Kansas; SaMary Beck Briscoe, 10th Circuit Judge; Sheila Bair, Chair, FDIC.

Grads Employed by Field (%)
Academic (7)
Business/Industry (14)
Government (16)
Judicial Clerkships (7)
Military (1)
Private Practice (52)
Public Interest (3)

UNIVERSITY OF KENTUCKY
COLLEGE OF LAW

INSTITUTIONAL INFORMATION

Public/private	Public
Student-faculty ratio	15:1
% faculty part-time	0
% faculty female	48
% faculty minority	15
Total faculty	33

SURVEY SAYS...

Heavy use of Socratic Method
Diverse opinions accepted
in classrooms
Great library staff

STUDENTS

Enrollment of law school	395
% male/female	55/45
% out-of-state	22
% full-time	100
% minority	10
# of countries represented	6
Average age of entering class	23

ACADEMICS

Academic Experience Rating	**71**
Profs interesting rating	71
Profs accessible rating	78
Hours of study per day	4.09

Advanced Degrees Offered
JD only: No LLM or Masters of Law programs offered

Combined Degrees Offered
JD/MPA, 4 years; JD/MBA, 4 years; JD/Masters in Diplomacy and International Commerce, 4 years

Clinical program required	No
Legal writing	
course requirement	Yes
Legal methods	
course requirement	No
Legal research	
course requirement	Yes
Moot court requirement	Yes
Public interest	
law requirement	No

Academics

A personable public school with strong regional ties, University of Kentucky offers a challenging JD program in the context of a super-student-friendly environment. Professors here "maintain an appropriate level of publication and research, but focus primarily on teaching the students." In fact, when it comes to their personal pursuits, professors "are always eager to include students in their research outside the classroom." While students admit that there are a few professors "who are not up to typical UK standards," most agree that the school remains "a great place to get a classical legal education." The program is nonetheless difficult, requiring a major time commitment and willingness to put yourself on the line. But that doesn't mean you won't get a little help from the "engaging" faculty who are "concerned with helping you do the best can—if you're willing to do the work to do so."

Though students find their "academic training rigorous," they do note that "practical experience is seriously lacking." Most here would like to feel better prepared "upon graduation...to enter a courtroom." Others mention they'd like to see more "clinical opportunities" since there is only "one legal clinic and roughly 20 3Ls may participate" though "There are over 130 3Ls." On the other hand, "Steps are being taken to increase the diversity of classes being offered." Indeed, UK will begin offering 18 professional skills courses, including three new externship courses with local government and public interest agencies, added to the five existing externship courses and the legal clinic. In addition to its traditional strength in corporate law, UK is now "a great place to study equine law, and a number of health law courses have proven quite popular this year."

From professors and students to staff and administrators, a friendly and hospitable vibe permeates the UK campus. When it comes to the higher ups, students say "The Dean is one of the most personable deans one could have." On top of that, "The librarians are the best. They help on completely unrelated topics besides legal research." Unfortunately, the pleasantness of UK community is not reflected in its shabby facilities. Students warn us that "the building is outdated and desperately needs work." Fortunately, UK Law is "scheduled to break ground on the new building in the next few years," so future students will be sitting pretty. In the meantime, most UK students are willing to forgo the frills in exchange for a "personalized" and "very thorough" education. Plus, the school manages to uphold high standards in the most important arenas. For example, students rave that their "Research facilities couldn't be better" and classrooms (though in need of sprucing up) are "technologically updated and super wired."

The immitigable goal of any law student is to get a job after graduation, and UK grads say their school amply prepares them for a competitive position. A current 3L enthuses, "Overall, my experience has been excellent. I got a job at a top-five national firm, and felt like I was competitive with my peers during my summer clerking experience." On the other hand, "Many students are frustrated with the level of service provided by the Career Services Office"—in particular, complaints arise from those students who hail from out of state and would like to consider jobs in geographical regions other than Kentucky.

DRUSILLA V. BAKERT, ASSOCIATE DEAN
209 LAW BUILDING, LEXINGTON, KY 40506-0048
TEL: 859-257-6770 FAX: 859-323-1061
EMAIL: DBAKERT@EMAIL.UKY.EDU • WEBSITE: WWW.UKY.EDU/LAW

Life

Expect a dose of Southern hospitality in the amiable state of Kentucky, a place filled with "nothing but friendly people." In and out of the classroom, "Students get along well, helping one another out, and no one attempts to sabotage the success of another student." One 1L explains, "There is such a familial feeling here . . . [with] instant camaraderie and friendship." However, as the school tends to draw students of similar backgrounds from the surrounding community, students also admit that "there could stand to be more diversity among the student body." A student agrees, "It may be more diverse than many Kentuckians are accustomed to, but I think if it were compared to national law school demographics, UK would not fare very well."

Though there isn't a lot of extra time for socializing in law school, students are pleased to report that "the student government here is amazing in keeping social activities going so that there are always chances to meet more people." In particular, "The Student Bar Association is very active in providing frequent, enjoyable social events." However, those who do not enjoy a typical night of partying and carousing won't be alone. "There has recently been a movement among nontraditional, nonalcoholic students to create more low-key and family-friendly social activities," says one student. "I think they've succeeded. It seems everyone who wants to be socially active among their colleagues has a way to do that."

Getting In

The University of Kentucky starts with a prospective student's LSAT scores and GPA when making an admissions decision. However, all applications are reviewed in full and other academic factors (such as writing ability, grade trends, and letters of recommendation) are also considered. Last year, the school extended just 408 offers of admission to over 1,200 candidates. The median LSAT score for the entering class was 160 and their median GPA was 3.63.

ADMISSIONS

Selectivity Rating	86
# applications received	1,202
# applicants accepted	408
# acceptees attending	138
Average LSAT	160
LSAT Range	157–162
Average undergrad GPA	3.63
Application fee	$50
Regular application	Rolling, up to 3/1
Regular notification	Rolling
Early application program	No
Transfer students accepted	Yes
Evening division offered	No
Part-time accepted	No
LSDAS accepted	Yes

Applicants Also Look At

University of Georgia, University of Tennessee—Knoxville, Indiana University—Bloomington, University of Louisville, University of Cincinnati, University of Florida, The Ohio State University—Columbus, Vanderbilt University, University of Dayton, Northern Kentucky University

International Students

TOEFL required of international students	Yes
Minimum TOEFL (paper/computer)	650/280

FINANCIAL FACTS

Annual tuition (in-state/ out-of-state)	$14,392/$25,570
Books and supplies	$900
Fees	$866
Room & board	$10,900
Financial aid application deadline	4/1
% first-year students receiving some sort of aid	85
% receiving some sort of aid	75
% of aid that is merit based	0
% receiving scholarships	64
Average grant	$5,000
Average loan	$20,500
Average total aid package	$25,500
Average debt	$50,000

EMPLOYMENT INFORMATION

Career Rating	**77**	**Grads Employed by Field (%)**
Rate of placement (nine months out)	99	Academic (2)
Average starting salary	$53,942	Business/Industry (7)
State for bar exam	KY	Government (6)
Pass rate for first-time bar	95	Judicial Clerkships (25)
Employers Who Frequently Hire Grads		Military (2)
All KY legal employers; major firms in		Private Practice (53)
Cincinnati, Nashville, West Virginia, D.C.,		Public Interest (5)
NYC, and Atlanta.		
Prominent Alumni		
Mitch McConnell, U.S. Senator; Hal		
Rogers, U.S. Representative; Ben		
Chandler, U.S. Representative; Steve		
Bright, National Public Interest Attorney;		
Jennifer Coffman, Federal Judge.		

UNIVERSITY OF LA VERNE*
COLLEGE OF LAW

INSTITUTIONAL INFORMATION

Public/private	Private
Student-faculty ratio	16:1
% faculty part-time	34
% faculty female	34
% faculty minority	31
Total faculty	29

SURVEY SAYS...

Heavy use of Socratic Method
Diverse opinions accepted
in classrooms
Great research resources
Great library staff

STUDENTS

Enrollment of law school	356
% male/female	62/38
% out-of-state	17
% full-time	66
% minority	20
# of countries represented	3
Average age of entering class	26

ACADEMICS

Academic Experience Rating	**66**
Profs interesting rating	71
Profs accessible rating	79
Hours of study per day	4.99

Advanced Degrees Offered

JD, full-time 3 years, part-time 4 years

Combined Degrees Offered

JD/MBA, 4 years; JD/MPA, 4 years

Clinical program required	No
Legal writing	
course requirement	Yes
Legal methods	
course requirement	Yes
Legal research	
course requirement	Yes
Moot court requirement	Yes
Public interest	
law requirement	No

Academics

It's a satisfying time to be a student at University of La Verne College of Law. Having recently received provisional accreditation from the ABA, "there is a sense of excitement and a feeling that the school is on the rise." Offering a grounded and practical legal education, "La Verne seems to be a 'meat and potatoes' school interested in preparing future lawyers" rather than dallying over theory and concepts. In the classroom, professors draw heavily on real world examples, and "While the theoretical side of law is covered to some extent, the emphasis seems to be on the practical application of law." A student elaborates, "Professors usually incorporate their personal legal experiences into the lecture; this could range from having a federal judge give his legal perspective on civil rights to a cutting-edge professor speaking about gaming law and how the ever-changing laws have affected the legal games he has created." As the school grows its reputation, it has likewise expanded the diversity of coursework and extracurricular offerings. For example, "La Verne Law was the first ABA school in the country to offer a course devoted to the computer game industry and its applicable laws. Other interesting/specialized electives include: terrorism and the law, white-collar crime, entertainment law, immigration law and patent law." In addition, the school operates "a great externship program with ties to many of the local governmental and nonprofit offices/organizations."

Getting a JD from La Verne Law is no walk in the park. The school's uniformly small class sizes "force you to prepare for each class because you will be called on," and the "harsh grading curve" has students struggling to keep up with academic standards. Fortunately, "The school does a great job at supporting the 1Ls and helping prepare them for the rigors of the first-year law school exams." For example, "The school holds ungraded practice exam sessions in formal conditions," as well as the opportunity to enroll in "great optional workshops on briefing, outlining, and exam preparation." On top of that, stress is soothed by the school's supportive academic atmosphere. One student shares, "I love that when I have a question regarding material discussed in class I can go straight to my professor rather than having to go through a TA." Another student adds, "The school is very small, so you have an opportunity to get one-on-one instruction and help in almost every class."

Once they've got their JD in hand, prospects are good for La Verne grads. Thanks to strong bar preparation courses, "Students who earn GPAs higher than 2.6 have a 97 percent chance of passing on the first attempt!" On top of that, La Verne lawyers have a corner on a significant job market. One student explains, "Since La Verne Law is the only law school in the Inland Empire region of California, which is growing rapidly, there are ample opportunities for not only great externships, but employment." Even so, students fret over the school's tough grading policies, saying it puts them at a professional disadvantage. A student elaborates, "Grading system is not on par with schools in the local area, which makes it harder for graduates from La Verne to match up without having to explain why GPAs are traditionally lower."

* Provisionally approved by the ABA.

ALEXIS THOMPSON, ASSISTANT DEAN OF ADMISSIONS
320 EAST D STREET, ONTARIO, CA 91764
TEL: (909) 460-2001 FAX: (909) 460-2082
EMAIL: LAWADM@ULV.EDU • WEBSITE: LAW.ULV.EDU

Life

La Verne is law school on a first-name basis. On this personable campus, "Class sizes are small, so we have the opportunity to get to know each other," and the program structure fosters personal relationships among the students. A student elaborates, "Since the one 1Ls are split into two groups, it is as if the 30 or so students grouped together learn how to read each other and understand how others think and relate to the law." Despite the school's tough grading policies, students insist that competition is minimal, and "A majority of the students are very willing to help one another in comparing class notes or answering questions." However, students also warn us, "Since this is such a small school, it has a junior high atmosphere where everyone knows and gossips about your personal life like it's a sitcom on MTV."

Socially, there is a noticeable rift between day and evening students, who don't have much overlap in their schedules or interests. Evening students also say it's harder for them to participate in campus clubs and activities, since most are held during the day. For full-timers, there are plenty of ways to get involved in campus life through "activities like softball, membership in the SBA, Delta Theta Phi, and Sports and Entertainment Law Society that bring together the three years of students."

About 10 miles away from the main university campus, "The school is located in the city center close to the main library, city hall, [and] restaurants." However, students say Ontario "isn't exactly paradise," and the school itself is situated in a dicey part of town. On the upside, "It's only 45 minutes from LA and 30 minutes from OC [Orange County]."

Getting In

University of La Verne College of Law is committed to admitting students from diverse educational and professional backgrounds. The school admits students with a strong academic background and competitive LSAT scores. The school also considers qualitative factors, such as an applicant's verbal skills, letters of recommendation, community service work, leadership, and maturity.

ADMISSIONS

Selectivity Rating	**66**
# applications received	1,640
% applicants accepted	39
% acceptees attending	22
Average LSAT	150
LSAT Range	148–153
Average undergrad GPA	2.94
Application fee	$60
Regular application	Rolling, up to 7/1
Regular notification	Rolling
Early application program	Yes
Early application deadline	12/20
Early application notification	1/31
Transfer students accepted	Yes
Evening division offered	Yes
Part-time accepted	Yes
LSDAS accepted	Yes

Applicants Also Look At
Chapman University, Whittier College, Western State University College of Law, Southwestern College

International Students
TOEFL recommended
of international students   Yes
Minimum TOEFL
(paper/computer/web) 600/250/100

FINANCIAL FACTS

Annual tuition	$35,500
Books and supplies	$1,638
Fees	$826
Tuition per credit	$26,630
Room & board (on/off-campus)	$11,110/$17,100
Financial aid application deadline	3/2
% first-year students receiving some sort of aid	99
% receiving some sort of aid	97
% of aid that is merit based	33
% receiving scholarships	87
Average grant	$11,292
Average loan	$31,629
Average total aid package	$42,921
Average debt	$88,102

EMPLOYMENT INFORMATION

Career Rating	**63**
Rate of placement (nine months out)	77
Average starting salary	$64,643
State for bar exam	CA, TX, NY, NJ
Pass rate for first-time bar	60.56

Employers Who Frequently Hire Grads
Private Law Firms Business/Industry
Government

Prominent Alumni
Thomas M. Finn, HSC Regional Director (S.Region), Dublin, Ireland; Hon. Dennis Aichroth, Judge, Superior Court, Los Angeles, CA; Hon. Jean Pfeiffer Leonard, Judge, Juvenile Court, Riverside, CA.

Grads Employed by Field (%)
Academic (2)
Business/Industry (17)
Government (59)
Private Practice (72)
Public Interest (4)

UNIVERSITY OF MAINE
SCHOOL OF LAW

Academics

The quality of the education is so high and the cost of tuition is so low that the University of Maine School of Law often flies under the radar, but the character of the school hasn't changed much over the years. As the only law school in the state, all of the 270 students enrolled are able to become closely acquainted with the legal system, and students have "extraordinary access to decision makers, judges at all levels, and lawyers in all fields and types of practice." The Maine Supreme Judicial Court takes many Maine Law grads as clerks and interns, and there "are lots of opportunities for students to get clinical experience in diverse fields from Prisoner Assistance to Intellectual Property."

The administration here is lauded for its "positive attitude" and responsiveness to student needs, and the new dean and his staff "seem really intent on making improvements where the school needs them." Professors here are "not only great teachers but personally intriguing," and the school is "very responsive" to student requests for particular courses, bringing in tons of practicing lawyers to teach short courses and "very high powered visiting faculty." Some of the adjuncts cause grumbling with their work assignments and teaching skills, but most students appreciate the variety. There's a nice balance of academic legal subjects and practical lawyering skills, and depending on their choices, a student here "could fade wholly into academia, eschew the impractical entirely, or graduate with a mix of practical and theoretical skills." One thing's for sure, though: The professors' first priority is teaching, and "they do a truly exceptional job."

On the facilities front, "a new law building is desperately needed." The library collection "is adequate but not huge," and the staff works very hard to obtain any requested sources from other collections. All complain about the infrastructure of the building, primarily the heating system, parking, lack of power sources, and the poorly ventilated and windowless classrooms, and students are downright miserable about the "1970s spaceship" décor of the place, but in a great testament to the school, students are happy enough otherwise that they forgive the surface flaws. "Our professors make up for any shortfalls with the facility. Even Plato's students listened to lectures from a grassy knoll," says a student.

Class scheduling is a sore spot, and some wish they received the next semester's class schedule in a timely manner so they could better plan their schedules and ensure that prerequisite courses are taken; also, "the number of core faculty is extremely small, so the same professors teach the same courses year after year," which can be an issue if you don't like a particular one. Still, students appreciate this "hidden gem" for what it offers them academically, plus the sterling reputation within the state and the fact that "alums are always willing to lend an ear and a hand to students" helps. "Maine Law continues to impress me with the depth and breadth of its educational experience," says a student.

DAVID PALLOZZI, ASSISTANT DEAN FOR ADMISSIONS
246 DEERING AVE, PORTLAND, ME 04102
TEL: 207-780-4341 FAX: 207-780-4239
EMAIL: MAINELAW@USM.MAINE.EDU • WEBSITE: MAINELAW.MAINE.EDU

Life

Maine Law is tiny, so "it is easy to make friends and become close to a large group of people quickly," but "if you step out line or are different expect to be in a fishbowl." "We work hard, but one virtue of being part of a very small bar is that we will all have to be colleagues for the remainder of our careers," points out a 2L. "Being such a small school, it really gives an opportunity to get to know your classmates well, which will help later on in practice." The school welcomes older students and treats them equally, but otherwise there is "zero diversity and almost no minorities (students or faculty)." However, the atmosphere is quite liberal, and "tree-huggers are in full force." The sense of community is strong, but "not in an annoying, Kumbaya, kind of way," and people socialize within their classes a great deal. "You'll see 20-somethings hanging out together a bit more, while 30-somethings also are drawn together, too, while the 3rd group, 30-somethings who are married and commute and hang out with everyone, naturally are a little less a part of the community." Everyone is sociable and willing to help others, so "you'll rarely find any crazy competitive hoaxes like ripping pages out of books or hiding books altogether." Portland is no metropolis but is a fantastic little city for living and working, and "every week there is an opportunity to gather at a different bar."

Getting In

Though the deadline doesn't come until March 1, decisions are already being made in January: Get in early. Students applying from Massachusetts, New Hampshire, Rhode Island, Vermont, or Canada pay slightly less tuition than normal out-of-state rates.

ADMISSIONS

Selectivity Rating	**76**
# applications received	697
% applicants accepted	49
% acceptees attending	27
Average LSAT	157
LSAT Range	155–159
Average undergrad GPA	3.28
Application fee	$50
Regular application	Rolling, up to 3/1
Regular notification	Rolling
Early application program	Yes
Early application deadline	11/15
Early application notification	12/31
Transfer students accepted	Yes
Evening division offered	No
Part-time accepted	No
LSDAS accepted	Yes

Applicants Also Look At

Boston University, Northeastern University, Boston College, Hofstra University, Suffolk University, Western New England College, Franklin Pierce Law Center, New England Law|Boston, Roger Williams University, Vermont Law School

International Students

TOEFL recommended of international students	Yes

FINANCIAL FACTS

Annual tuition (in-state/ out-of-state)	$18,360/$28,860
Books and supplies	$1,500
Fees	$1,020
Fees per credit	$1,020
Tuition per credit (in-state/out-of-state)	$612/$962
Room & board (on/off-campus)	$14,434/$14,434
Financial aid application deadline	2/15
% first-year students receiving some sort of aid	90
% receiving some sort of aid	89
% of aid that is merit based	
% receiving scholarships	44
Average debt	$64,235

EMPLOYMENT INFORMATION

Career Rating	**76**
Rate of placement (nine months out)	92
Average starting salary	$54,194
State for bar exam	ME, MA, NY, FL, NH
Pass rate for first-time bar	91

Employers Who Frequently Hire Grads

Maine law firms Maine courts (judicial clerkships)

Prominent Alumni

Hon. John A. Woodcock, Chief District Judge; United States District Court of Maine; Hon. Leigh I. Saufley, Chief Justice of the Maine Supreme Judicial Court; Janet Mills, Attorney General of Maine.

Grads Employed by Field (%)

Business/Industry (10)
Government (11)
Judicial Clerkships (16)
Private Practice (54)
Public Interest (7)
Other (2)

UNIVERSITY OF MARYLAND
SCHOOL OF LAW

INSTITUTIONAL INFORMATION

Public/private	Public
Student-faculty ratio	12:1
% faculty part-time	37
% faculty female	46
% faculty minority	18
Total faculty	117

SURVEY SAYS...

Great research resources
Great library staff

STUDENTS

Enrollment of law school	897
% male/female	47/53
% out-of-state	39
% full-time	80
% minority	33
% international	2
# of countries represented	5
Average age of entering class	24

ACADEMICS

Academic Experience Rating	**89**
Profs interesting rating	78
Profs accessible rating	76
Hours of study per day	4.4

Academic Specialties

Commercial law, constitutional law, corporation securities, criminal law, environmental law, human rights, international law, labor law, taxation, intellectual property law, health care law, public interest/policy, clinical law, litigation/advocacy

Advanced Degrees Offered

JD

Combined Degrees Offered

JD/Ph.D. Public Policy; JD/MA Public Policy; JD/MBA; JD/MA Public Management; JD/MA Criminal Justice; JD/MSW; JD/MA Liberal Arts; JD/MA Community Planning; JD/Pharm.D. Pharmacy; JD/MPH; JD/MS Risk Assessment & Environmental Law; JD/MS Nursing

Clinical program required	Yes
Legal writing course requirement	Yes

Academics

"Considering the price and the quality of education," you can't beat the "fun, interesting, and hard" University of Maryland School of Law. Boasting a notable "commitment to public service," Maryland Law "has one of the best environmental and health law programs in the country" further abetted by a "terrific alumni network." The "mandatory clinical program" offers two-dozen courses and is "excellent." The legal writing program "is a strength, though very demanding," say some students to which it was taught "by full professors and not adjuncts."

Maryland Law's "mix of professors" ranges from "lively and Socratic" to "quiet lecturers." "Eighty percent of the professors are good," says one 2L, "though some don't have a clue how to teach." "Some professors stand out as excellent and some are the worst teachers I have ever had in my academic career." "All but one of four of my professors were extremely intelligent, enthusiastic, and passionate about the material they were teaching," adds a 1L. The "not-too-bad" administration is "always available," though too much "hand-holding" can be a bit of a problem. "They think that a long informational session needs to be had on everything" when an e-mail would "be a better use of everyone's time." Administrators are "extremely dedicated to racial and economic diversity" both in the student body and faculty. Sometimes, "They overstress diversity," suggests a 2L.

"The Career Development Office, which has continued to improve both years I've attended, needs to continue getting better," says a 2L. Maryland Law has a "solid reputation in the Mid-Atlantic region," and many students "have landed jobs at some of the best firms in DC." There is "little competition for 'big law' positions" locally, while students compete nationally in the school's regional interview programs in other cities. "The opportunities for practical experience with law firms, political organizations, and judges in Baltimore and DC are really impressive," adds a 3L. "Even if you don't achieve the traditional law school honors (top 10 percent, Law Review, moot court, etc.) you can get a lot out of your law school experience and establish an impressive resume record that will help you find a job after school."

The "absolutely beautiful" facilities at Maryland Law are "new, with all the amenities you expect of a top-flight law school." An enclosed, private patio area next to the library allows students "to study or eat outside." There are "comfortable chairs all over." Maryland Law is "well equipped technologically with wireless internet around campus." The library needs "longer hours." There is no cafeteria on campus, although there a coffee bar that services sandwiches and salads made on location (often with locally grown, organic produce). The school's location isn't ideal according to many students. "It is in the inner city," cautions a 1L, "but I think that is important for the clinical program to work."

Life

Maryland Law's "very capable and motivated" student population "is composed of a diverse group of students with different interests and academic backgrounds." "The small sections in the first year give you a real chance to get to know classmates and at least one professor well." "It helps you to not feel lost in the shuffle." "The competition at the school is invigorating and healthy, and almost everyone gets along well," says a 2L. Maryland Law's day students and evening students often have wildly different law school experiences. The "vibrant evening program" has "no social life but is less competitive." "There is a strong sense among the students that we are in this together," relates one happy evening student. Day students are "moderate-to-cutthroat competitive with a

CONNIE BEALS, EXECUTIVE DIRECTOR OF ADMISSIONS & STUDENT RECRUIT
500 WEST BALTIMORE STREET, BALTIMORE, MD 21201
TEL: 410-706-3492 FAX: 410-706-1793
EMAIL: ADMISSIONS@LAW.UMARYLAND.EDU • WEBSITE: WWW.LAW.UMARYLAND.EDU

more active social life." Politically, students (and faculty) are "pretty heavily weighted to the left." Some students at Maryland Law "have a chip on their shoulder because they feel they should have gotten into Georgetown or George Washington." "We have a bit of an inferiority complex, but we seem to be getting over it," notes a 3L.

"One thing that can be improved is the neighborhood" surrounding Maryland Law. The law school is located downtown, "which is not quite the safest area." "Going out alone at night around the law school is scary." There are a lot of security guards and "a free door-to-door shuttle service after 5:00 P.M." "A lot of money has been pumped into redeveloping the entire area. Each year, newly converted loft apartments and restaurants open up, and many plans are continually coming to life." UMD is also "next to other graduate schools and in great proximity to" Baltimore's iconic Inner Harbor and many "stylish bars." Oriole Park at Camden Yards is "within easy walking distance." The absence of undergraduates "in the near vicinity" creates "a unique vibe." "Socializing with other students consists of the traditional Thursday- or Friday-night Bar Reviews." "There is a decent amount of social activities, but students will only participate the first half of the semester; after that they are in crazy-study mode." "Housing near campus is cramped and overpriced," but "local neighborhoods, such as Fells Point, Federal Hill, and Canton offer the charm that makes Baltimore so terrific."

Getting In

Admitted students at the 25th percentile have LSAT scores of approximately 160 and GPAs around 3.5. Admitted students at the 75th percentile have LSAT scores of 166 and GPAs in the 3.8 range.

EMPLOYMENT INFORMATION

Career Rating	**74**
Rate of placement (nine months out)	93
Average starting salary	$79,015
State for bar exam	MD
Pass rate for first-time bar	84

Employers Who Frequently Hire Grads

Skadden Arps et. al.; DLA Piper; Arnold & Porter; Venable; Covington & Burling; Dickstein, Shapiro & Morin, L.L.P.; U. S. Department of Justice; Securities Exchange Commission (SEC); Environmental Protection Agency; Maryland Office of the State's Attorney; U.S. Dept. of Health & Human Services; State of Maryland Office of the Attorney General; Maryland Office of the Public Defender.

Prominent Alumni

Christine A. Edwards, Partner, Winston & Strawn; Benjamin R. Civiletti, former U.S. Attorney General; Partner, Venable; Francis B. Burch, Jr., Joint Chief Executive Officer, DLA Piper; Benjamin L. Cardin, U.S. Senator for MD.

Grads Employed by Field (%)

Academic (6)
Business/Industry (11)
Government (15)
Judicial Clerkships (20)
Military (1)
Private Practice (41)
Public Interest (6)

Legal methods course requirement	Yes
Legal research course requirement	Yes
Moot court requirement	Yes
Public interest law requirement	Yes

ADMISSIONS

Selectivity Rating	**95**
# applications received	3,225
# applicants accepted	469
# acceptees attending	232
Average LSAT	161
LSAT Range	160–165
Average undergrad GPA	3.6
Application fee	$65
Regular application	Rolling, up to 4/1
Regular notification	Rolling
Early application program	No
Transfer students accepted	Yes
Evening division offered	Yes
Part-time accepted	Yes
LSDAS accepted	Yes

Applicants Also Look At

American University, George Mason University, University of Baltimore, The George Washington University, Georgetown University

International Students

TOEFL required of international students	Yes
Minimum TOEFL (paper/computer)	600/250

FINANCIAL FACTS

Annual tuition (in-state/ out-of-state)	$21,139/$32,418
Books and supplies	$1,725
Fees	$905
Fees per credit	$561
Tuition per credit (in-state/out-of-state)	$673/$1,138
Room & board (on/off-campus)	$14,229/$19,440
Financial aid application deadline	3/1
% first-year students receiving some sort of aid	82
% receiving some sort of aid	84
% of aid that is merit based	28
% receiving scholarships	58
Average grant	$7,435
Average loan	$34,006
Average total aid package	$55,430
Average debt	$81,187

UNIVERSITY OF MEMPHIS
CECIL C. HUMPHREYS SCHOOL OF LAW

INSTITUTIONAL INFORMATION

Public/private	Public
Student-faculty ratio	16:1
% faculty part-time	49
% faculty female	36
% faculty minority	11
Total faculty	45

SURVEY SAYS...
Heavy use of Socratic Method
Diverse opinions accepted
in classrooms

STUDENTS

Enrollment of law school	414
% male/female	57/43
% out-of-state	4
% full-time	95
% minority	11
# of countries represented	1
Average age of entering class	26

ACADEMICS

Academic Experience Rating	**65**
Profs interesting rating	71
Profs accessible rating	70
Hours of study per day	4.26

Academic Specialties
Civil procedure, commercial law, constitutional law, criminal law, international law, labor law, property, taxation, intellectual property law, corporate law

Advanced Degrees Offered
JD, 6 semesters

Combined Degrees Offered
JD/MBA, 4 years (8 semesters); JD/MA (Political Science), 4 years(8 semesters).

Clinical program required	No
Legal writing	
course requirement	No
Legal methods	
course requirement	Yes
Legal research	
course requirement	Yes
Moot court requirement	No
Public interest	
law requirement	No

Academics

An affordable, practical-minded, and utterly personable law school program, the University of Memphis is the ideal training ground for future attorneys in the mid-South. Through course work and extracurricular activities, this friendly public school distinguishes itself through its "emphasis on training you to be a lawyer and not just a student of the law." Throughout the curriculum, professors place a "strong emphasis on oral argument abilities," and required course work includes instruction in many of the practical skills you'll need in the real world. For example, "Course work required for the legal methods class is incredibly helpful in learning good writing, oral communication, and other lawyering skills." Students further appreciate the inclusion of Tennessee law into the curriculum—a facet that is particularly useful to those planning to practice in the state.

Offering an intimate academic atmosphere at a friendly price, "U of M Law is one of the best values available." Unlike programs at larger public schools, Memphis students don't have to clamor for attention from their brilliant professors; with an enrollment of about 150 students per class, "The school is small enough that personal attention is readily available, and professors are always willing to talk." With little exception, students say the school's accomplished faculty is its greatest strength. A 1L agrees: "I have never before been taught by so many excellent professors at one time." Outside the classroom, students can augment course work through participation in one of two legal clinics, the Elder Law Clinic, or the Child and Family Litigation Clinic, through which they can represent elderly and indigent clients in the Memphis area. For those who want practice in the courtroom, the school operates a competitive moot court program. In a very lawyerly fashion, a current student attests: "Our moot court people kick ass."

If there is one thing University of Memphis students unanimously criticize, it's the school's ramshackle facilities. From the shabby library to the hot and under-equipped computer lab, students say the facilities certainly don't reflect the quality of the U of M law experience. At times, the building even has adverse effects on academics. A case in point: "In some of the classrooms, the professors have to use microphones because you cannot hear anything but the air conditioner." The good news for prospective students is that the school recently bought a historic building in downtown Memphis, which will serve as the law school's new home in 2010. Optimistic students are sure that their educational experience will "dramatically improve once we move to the new building." In fact, they reassure us, "Once the school moves downtown into the Customs House, this school is likely to become one of the premier public law schools in the South."

The school's excellent bar-passage rate is among its major selling points. At 95 percent for first-time test-takers, it's "unusually high for a small state school." Another appealing facet of a U of M degree is the school's "very high job-placement rate" and its strong "ties with the Memphis community." Deeply entwined in the local legal market, "For a person looking to practice in Memphis, or anywhere else in Tennessee, the school's reputation is outstanding." Of course, there are always a handful of students who are looking for jobs in other regions; given the school's regional strength, its not surprising that these students complain Career Services isn't "much help outside of the Memphis area."

Life

This urban law school attracts all types of students, the range of which includes "college athletes, war veterans, people in their second careers, mothers re-entering the workforce." While they are all scrambling to score the best grades, there is surprisingly little friction between students at U of M. One student explains, "The environment, despite the building, is very positive and upbeat. You don't get the feeling that the guy or girl next to you is looking to stab you in the back." Because the school comprises "a much smaller community than most of us are used to after undergraduate at large schools" and the curriculum requires an incredible time commitment, Memphis students get to know each other well. A student elaborates: "We spend an unbelievable amount of time around each other, so it is to be expected that people will date, people will bicker, people will complain, and people will make up."

University of Memphis is a commuter school, so most "Students attend class and then go their separate ways." However, for those who'd like to participate in campus culture, there are plenty of opportunities and a "fairly small group who consistently attend the law school's social functions." A current student shares, "All in all, we have a lot of fun when we aren't studying, and we are able to find a common bond with pretty much everyone with whom we go to school."

Getting In

Of more than 1,000 students who applied to the University of Memphis JD and joint-degree programs, only about 30 percent were successful. The entering class had a median undergraduate GPA of 3.37 and median LSAT scores of 156. Students range in age from 20–56, but the median age is 26.

ADMISSIONS

Selectivity Rating	81
# applications received	1,026
# applicants accepted	303
# acceptees attending	147
Average LSAT	156
Average undergrad GPA	3.34
Application fee	$25
Regular application	Rolling, up to 3/1
Regular notification	Rolling
Early application program	No
Transfer students accepted	Yes
Evening division offered	No
Part-time accepted	Yes
LSDAS accepted	Yes

Applicants Also Look At
The University of Alabama, University of Tennessee—Knoxville, Mercer University, Southern Illinois University Carbondale, Tulane University, Georgia State University, Mississippi College, University of Mississippi, Samford University, Florida Costal School of Law

International Students

TOEFL required of international students	Yes
Minimum TOEFL (computer/web)	600/283

FINANCIAL FACTS

Annual tuition (in-state/ out-of-state)	$11,168/$33,040
Books and supplies	$1,600
Fees	$1,756
Fees per credit	$88
Tuition per credit (in-state/ out-of-state)	$526/$1,528
Room & board	$8,355
Financial aid application deadline	4/1
% first-year students receiving some sort of aid	83
% receiving some sort of aid	83
% of aid that is merit based	9
% receiving scholarships	28
Average grant	$3,900
Average loan	$22,267
Average total aid package	$22,725
Average debt	$52,104

EMPLOYMENT INFORMATION

Career Rating	76
Rate of placement (nine months out)	95
Average starting salary	$59,000
State for bar exam	TN, MS, AR, OH, NY
Pass rate for first-time bar	94.1

Employers Who Frequently Hire Grads
Major area and regional law firms, Tennessee Attorney General, Public Defenders office, TN Supreme Court & Court of Appeals, major area corporate legal depts., City & County Government.

Prominent Alumni
Honorable John Wilder, Former Lt. Governor, State of Tennessee; Honorable Bernice Donald, Judge, U.S. District Court, Memphis, TN; Jere Glover, Chief Counsel, U.S. Small Business Administration; Honorable David S. Kennedy, Chief Bankruptcy Judge, Memphis, TN, U.S. Bankruptcy Court.

Grads Employed by Field (%)
Academic (3)
Business/Industry (9)
Government (9)
Judicial Clerkships (6)
Private Practice (69)
Public Interest (4)
Other (6)

UNIVERSITY OF MIAMI
SCHOOL OF LAW

INSTITUTIONAL
INFORMATION
Public/private   Private
Student-faculty ratio   17:1
% faculty part-time   34
% faculty female   32
% faculty minority   23
Total faculty   174

SURVEY SAYS...
Great library staff
Students love Coral Gables, FL

STUDENTS
Enrollment of law school   1,216
Average age of entering class   24

ACADEMICS
Academic Experience Rating   73
Profs interesting rating   71
Profs accessible rating   66
Hours of study per day   4.43

Academic Specialties
Civil procedure, commercial law, constitutional law, corporation securities, criminal law, environmental law, government services, human rights, international law, labor law, property, taxation, intellectual property law

Advanced Degrees Offered
LL.M. degrees offered are: International Law with specializations in International Arbitration, U.S. Transnational Law for Foreign Lawyers, Inter-American Law and International Law in general; Ocean and Coastal Law; Real Property Development, Estate Planning, and Taxation. The Real Property program is launching a part-time distance learning program in the fall.

Combined Degrees Offered
JD/MBA; JD/MPH Masters in Public Health; JD/MS, Masters in Marine Affairs, J.D./LL.M. in Taxation, Real Property Development and the International Law programs.

Clinical program required   No
Legal writing
   course requirement   Yes

Academics

The University of Miami School of Law offers a "wide range of courses" and a host of fantastic programs. Business and tax law are especially notable. Trial advocacy is "excellent," too. Another perk here is the opportunity to get both a J.D. and an LL.M. in just seven semesters in three specialties: international law, inter-American Law, and ocean law. Summer study-abroad programs are available all over Europe. One of them includes a four-day cruise on the Aegean Sea. Additionally, there are "extensive practical experience offerings" "that, for example, help the many immigrants of Miami." However, many students complain that the number of available clinical opportunities is seriously "lacking."

"Class sizes are nightmarishly large" at UM. "During the first and second years, use of the Socratic method is heavy." The faculty is "jam packed with leaders in their respective fields." "Intelligent, engaging, and interesting" professors abound. "Almost all of them are passionate about teaching, and it shows," relates a 2L. "There are certainly a handful of" "windbag profs" to avoid, though. "Our professors are similar to a bag of jelly beans," analogizes a 1L. "For the most part they are great, but there are a couple crappy ones." Outside of class, most professors are "extremely accessible and willing to answer any questions." Some students tell us that the administration is "very student oriented." "The administrators, registrars, and even the financial aid people genuinely seem to care and are willing to help in any way they can," they say. Others gripe that management is "inaccessible" as well as "a step behind and unorganized."

Career-wise, "if you are at the top of the class, you are virtually guaranteed a job at a national firm in Miami." If your grades are less than stellar, prospects are still pretty good. While not everybody is happy with the Career Development Office, the general sentiment seems to be that the staff "works hard to place students." It doesn't hurt that UM is "the biggest fish in the Miami legal community" and "king in South Florida." "There are a lot of networking events held both at the school and around Miami" and the presence of "prominent" alumni all over town definitely helps when the time comes to get a job.

Everyone agrees that "the law library is superb" here and that "parking sucks." Students are otherwise divided about the facilities. Many tell us that "the law school campus itself isn't impressive." Critics call the "overcrowded" classrooms "dated." "The law school building and classrooms look like a California high school with cream-painted concrete walls and exterior walkways into large windowless classrooms," observes a 3L. Other students disagree. "The UM campus is absolutely beautiful," they boast. "It is like going to school at a country club."

Life

UM is located "in the plush suburbs of Miami." By all accounts, the weather is "great," and the location is "wonderful." "I look at the palm trees and sunny sky and feel bad for virtually everyone else in the country," sympathizes a 2L. "I smugly study for finals in December on the beach," adds another 2L. The city is "amazing." "People are just beautiful." "If you are going to suffer through law school, it may as well be in Miami," recommends a 1L. However, "Miami is not a college town, and there's no cheap student housing in this area." The cost of living is generally high as well. "Be prepared to throw down some cash" when you come here.

THERESE LAMBERT, DIRECTOR OF STUDENT RECRUITING
PO BOX 248087, CORAL GABLES, FL 33124-8087
TEL: 305-284-6746 FAX: 305-284-3084
EMAIL: ADMISSIONS@LAW.MIAMI.EDU • WEBSITE: WWW.LAW.MIAMI.EDU

Life outside of class is fabulous. Clubs and organizations are "numerous." "There are too many social activities to ever do." There is "a large outdoor quad in the middle of the law school" known as the "Bricks." This common area facilitates interaction and it's the locale for frequent social events. Off campus, nightlife is spectacular. The club scene of South Beach is "only 15 minutes away," and "there is quite a bit of partying that goes on at UM Law among the younger students." If you aren't a partier, don't worry. "You can live a low-profile life and focus on your studies."

Diversity is tremendous—ethnically, geographically, and otherwise. There's definitely some money floating around. "Upon arrival, I could not believe the amount of Beemers, Porsches, Mercedes, and Maseratis in the law school parking lot," recalls a 1L. At the same time, plenty of students come from more modest circumstances. "The students at University of Miami come from all different backgrounds," beams a 1L. "The diverse community creates an excellent atmosphere for sharing ideas and perspectives." The academic atmosphere is reasonable. "The harsh curve" creates some strife but "students really have fun together." "I would not classify this school as being cut-throat, nor would I classify it as being laid-back in terms of academic competitiveness," explains a 3L.

Getting In

UM reigns supreme in the legal culture of South Florida. If you want to practice in this region, you can't do much better than this school. Admitted students at the 25th percentile have LSAT scores around 155 and GPAs of about 3.4. Admitted students at the 75th percentile have LSAT scores of 160 or so and GPAs of around 3.6.

EMPLOYMENT INFORMATION

Career Rating	84	**Grads Employed by Field (%)**
Rate of placement (nine months out)	97	Academic (1)
Average starting salary	$81,000	Business/Industry (8)
State for bar exam	FL, NY, IL, GA, CA	Government (11)
Pass rate for first-time bar	85	Judicial Clerkships (4)

Employers Who Frequently Hire Grads
Private Practice (67)
Law Firms: Holland & Knight; Greenberg
Public Interest (8)
Traurig; Hunton & Williams; White & Case;
Other (1)
Weil, Gotshal & Manges; Morgan Lewis &
Bockius; Squires Sanders
Prominent Alumni
Congressman Thomas J. Rooney, representing Florida's 16th District; Sue M. Cobb, State of Florida Secretary of State, 2005-2007, Ambassador to Jamaica, 2001-200; Carolyn Lamm, Partner at White & Case, Washington D.C. and President of the American Bar Association, 2009-2010; Dennis Curran, the NFL's Senior Vice President in charge of labor litigation and policy, New York, New York 5. Karyn Smith, Director of Programming for Fox Television Studios.

Legal methods course requirement	Yes
Legal research course requirement	Yes
Moot court requirement	No
Public interest law requirement	No

ADMISSIONS

Selectivity Rating	75
# applications received	4,246
% applicants accepted	52
% acceptees attending	17
Average LSAT	157
LSAT Range	155–160
Average undergrad GPA	3.43
Application fee	$60
Regular application	Rolling, up to 7/31
Regular notification	Rolling
Early application program	No
Transfer students accepted	Yes
Evening division offered	No
Part-time accepted	No
LSDAS accepted	Yes

Applicants Also Look At
Florida State University, American University, Tulane University, University of Florida, Nova Southeastern University, Fordham University, The George Washington University, University of San Diego, Stetson University, Georgetown University, Brooklyn Law School

International Students

TOEFL required of international students	Yes
Minimum TOEFL (paper/computer)	600/250

FINANCIAL FACTS

Annual tuition	$37,418
Books and supplies	$1,200
Fees	$594
Room & board (off-campus)	$13,302
Financial aid application deadline	3/31
% first-year students receiving some sort of aid	80
% receiving some sort of aid	84
% of aid that is merit based	28
% receiving scholarships	33
Average grant	$15,232
Average loan	$29,374
Average total aid package	$38,739
Average debt	$95,087

UNIVERSITY OF MICHIGAN
LAW SCHOOL

INSTITUTIONAL INFORMATION

Public/private	Public
Student-faculty ratio	12:1
% faculty part-time	24
% faculty female	35
% faculty minority	9
Total faculty	121

SURVEY SAYS...

Great research resources
Beautiful campus

STUDENTS

Enrollment of law school	1,151
% male/female	57/43
% out-of-state	78
% full-time	100
% minority	24
% international	4
# of countries represented	24
Average age of entering class	25

ACADEMICS

Academic Experience Rating	**98**
Profs interesting rating	93
Profs accessible rating	81
Hours of study per day	4.46

Academic Specialties

Civil procedure, commercial law, constitutional law, corporation securities, criminal law, environmental law, government services, human rights, international law, labor law, legal history, legal philosophy, property, taxation, intellectual property law, asylum and refugee law

Advanced Degrees Offered

LL.M. Master of Laws, International Tax LL.M., M.C.L. Master of Comparative Law, and S.JD Doctor of the Science of Law

Clinical program required	No
Legal writing course requirement	Yes
Legal methods course requirement	Yes
Legal research course requirement	Yes
Moot court requirement	No

Academics

The University of Michigan Law School "is definitely a special place." "Just entering the Law Quad puts into perspective the good fortune students have in attending this great institution," says a 3L. A faculty features "a good mix of 'institutions' and up-and-comers," making for "an interesting and unique educational experience." The "engaging" and "hilarious" professors here are "academic rock stars" who "challenge you and help you think about the law in novel ways." "Our professors are definitely brain ninjas," declares a 2L. Professors "have open-door policies" and are "truly available to meet with you and help you in any way they can." The administration is "very approachable." "Michigan students adore their school, and the school adores them right back," says one student. "I've e-mailed various deans and had my e-mails returned within minutes." Such first-class treatment comes at a hefty price, though. Students wish that tuition were more "affordable."

The "massive course selection" provides "an interdisciplinary perspective to the law and promotes interdisciplinary learning." "Cutting-edge legal theory" is the norm, and course work tends to focus more on "policy implications of the law," meaning that the campus doesn't function as "a factory of corporate lawyers." Several clinics including the Environmental Law Clinic and the Urban Communities Clinic provide "options that allow you to get real experience in the courtroom." Nevertheless, many students insist that there should be more of an emphasis on "practical skills for lawyering."

"Career Services is incredibly well organized" and "the Michigan reputation" is an "asset" since "Employers fall all over themselves for you." "About 700 employers" come to campus to interview, and they "can't screen by GPA," which many students find allows them to "interview with top firms even if [they] are at the bottom of the class." "My successful job hunts on the West Coast and in the South showed me that a Michigan degree opens doors all over the country," boasts a 3L. "I have friends who will be practicing everywhere from New York to Phoenix." For graduates wishing to pursue careers in public interest, there is "a generous loan repayment program."

Michigan's "Gothic" and "beautiful" Law Quad is "definitely what you imagine when you think about what 'law school' should look like." "The stone buildings are covered in climbing ivy" and the "somewhat dauntingly quiet and eerie" Reading Room ("open until 2:00 A.M.") is "like a cathedral to learning." While "No one...wants to lose the feel" of such impressive sights, many lament that "modern amenities sometimes take a back seat" on campus. Some buildings "lack plug space", though the school and Quad are totally wireless. The most pressing problem at Michigan Law appears to be a severe bathroom shortage. "More toilets! Working toilets!" demands a 3L.

Life

Students state that "Michigan is more diverse than any other law school out there." "A range of geographic, ideological, religious, and ethnic backgrounds" is represented. Michigan is also a "very tolerant" place for gay students. "The Admissions Office does an amazing job of selecting individuals who are talented, diverse, friendly, and normal," says one student. "The student body is a hotbed of intellectual discussion, but then we all play flip-cup on the weekends." "Michigan draws not only incredible smart individuals but also individuals with personality."

SARAH C. ZEARFOSS, ASSISTANT DEAN AND DIRECTOR OF ADMISSIONS
726 OAKLAND AVENUE, ANN ARBOR, MI 48104
TEL: 734-764-0537 FAX: 734-647-3218
EMAIL: LAW.JD.ADMISSIONS@UMICH.EDU • WEBSITE: WWW.LAW.UMICH.EDU

"The atmosphere is highly conducive to learning the law with an absolute minimum of stress." Generally, "Everyone wants everyone to do well." "The theory is, 'We're all smart; we all deserve to be here; if we all help out each other then we can get the most out of law school.'" However, some students disagree with this view. Students are "always sizing others up," they say. "People are secretly competitive."

"Michigan's social scene is one of its greatest strengths." The law school's dorm ("Lawyers Club") is very popular, and many students eat "lunch and dinner" together on campus. ("The food is not too bad either.") "Finals are stressful," of course, but "The rest of the year is very laid-back, and there are plenty of opportunities to engage in social activities." "In some respects," Michigan Law "still has a college feel to it." "Many law students attend the home football games" and "Going out to the local watering holes happens almost every night (even first year)." "If your social life doesn't involve drinking, there aren't many organized activities for you," gripe some students. Others say that "there is a great deal to do in Ann Arbor besides [going] to the bar." "There is a downtown area that is geared more towards adults." There is "a show, symphony, or concert somewhere in Ann Arbor at any point in time." Most here "love" Ann Arbor, though several students long for "a more hip area."

Getting In

Michigan Law is a tough nut to crack. Admitted students at 25th percentile have LSAT scores of 167 and GPAs of about 3.5. Admitted students at 75th percentile have LSAT scores of 170 and GPAs of about 3.8. If you take the LSAT multiple times, Michigan will give the most weight to the highest scores but will consider the average score as well.

Public interest law requirement	No

ADMISSIONS

Selectivity Rating	**97**
# applications received	5,577
# applicants accepted	1,181
# acceptees attending	361
Average LSAT	169
LSAT Range	166–170
Average undergrad GPA	3.70
Application fee	$60
Regular application	Rolling, up to 2/15
Regular notification	Rolling
Early application program	Yes
Early application deadline	11/15
Early application notification	12/15
Transfer students accepted	Yes
Evening division offered	No
Part-time accepted	No
LSDAS accepted	Yes

Applicants Also Look At
Harvard University, Columbia University, University of California—Berkeley, New York University, University of Chicago, University of Pennsylvania, Georgetown University

FINANCIAL FACTS

Annual tuition (in-state/ out-of-state)	$41,311/$44,311
Books and supplies	$5,250
Fees	$189
Room & board	$10,400
% first-year students receiving some sort of aid	87
% receiving some sort of aid	91
% of aid that is merit based	37
% receiving scholarships	30
Average grant	$14,370
Average loan	$39,622
Average total aid package	$46,109
Average debt	$92,000

EMPLOYMENT INFORMATION

Career Rating	99	Grads Employed by Field (%)
Rate of placement (nine months out)	99	Academic (1)
Average starting salary	$151,319	Business/Industry (5)
State for bar exam	NY, IL	Government (3)
Pass rate for first-time bar	96/98	Judicial Clerkships (14)
		Private Practice (73)
		Public Interest (5)

UNIVERSITY OF MISSISSIPPI
SCHOOL OF LAW

INSTITUTIONAL
INFORMATION

Public/private	Public
Student-faculty ratio	16:1
% faculty part-time	30
% faculty female	34
% faculty minority	13
Total faculty	53

SURVEY SAYS...
Diverse opinions accepted
in classrooms
Good social life

STUDENTS

Enrollment of law school	517
% male/female	55/45
% out-of-state	13
% full-time	100
% minority	14
# of countries represented	2
Average age of entering class	24

ACADEMICS

Academic Experience Rating	**75**
Profs interesting rating	75
Profs accessible rating	83
Hours of study per day	3.53

Academic Specialties
Commercial law, corporation securities, criminal law, environmental law, international law, taxation, remote sensing and space law

Advanced Degrees Offered
None

Combined Degrees Offered
JD/MBA, 4 years; JD/MA-Tax, 4 years; JD/MA-Accounting, 4 years

Clinical program required	No
Legal writing course requirement	Yes
Legal methods course requirement	Yes
Legal research course requirement	Yes
Moot court requirement	No
Public interest law requirement	No

Academics

Students at Ole Miss love the combination of "a down-home, small-town atmosphere where everyone knows your name" and a law degree that is "given much credit within the state." Though "academically strenuous," the school's "laid-back atmosphere" prevails, and students praise the "easily accessible" staff, the "large student mall with plenty of couches and chairs for discussions between classes," and the "professors with awesome senses of humor." By all accounts, Ole Miss is not a school that "makes you feel like they are trying to weed you out." As one student explains, "I love the dynamics of the classes and the size of the student body. It is nice to be friends with 2Ls and 3Ls and not feel like a freshman again." "Everyone in the administration is incredibly friendly and helpful," a classmate adds. "If you have any question, even if it has nothing to do with their particular job, they will do everything they can to get you the right answer." Professors here hail from "a broad diversity of backgrounds" and "are all extremely knowledgeable and very experienced." Not only do they "present the material in an entertaining way," they "take a special interest" in students, "which can help build up [students'] confidence and help them to excel."

The professors at Ole Miss are a major reason why its students say the school is a "great value." "It is not nearly as expensive to go to school here as the other schools to which I applied or was accepted," says one student. "I can still get pretty much any job I want coming out of Ole Miss, yet I have zero debt." Other students, however, temper such expectations, noting that while Ole Miss' "Career Services Office is always there to help with a resume or to provide Tylenol during exams," securing a job outside of Mississippi can be an uphill battle. That said, this situation seems to be on the upswing thanks to the school's "great relationship with alumni" and also in that "Ole Miss changed their grading curve [a few years ago] and that has significantly helped those who are looking to get a job out of state."

Students consistently report that the faculty is one of the school's "greatest strengths." "They take away the mundane, stereotypical experience of law school and present the material in an entertaining way without compromising the integrity of the institution," says one student. Many feel that "there is a lot of potential in the legal writing and research classes"; however, they are damaged by "the lack of communication between...departments." Others would like "more classes to choose from," particularly in the area of entertainment law. Students are divided on the school's aesthetics, finding that the "great library" is "extremely up to date with the latest technology" while the building itself is "not very pretty" and "somewhat outdated." A 1L provides some perspective, explaining that "the law school building would be aesthetically pleasing at most major schools, but when compared to the columned architecture and tree-lined walkways of the rest of the campus, you can immediately tell it is a relic of the early 70s...Instead of being 'postmodern,' it simply looks out of place." However, "a new state-of-the-art building" "will soon be under construction."

Life

Ole Miss students emphasize that theirs is a "relaxed learning environment," one that "promotes collaboration between students instead of the cutthroat competition that you hear about at other law schools." The school divides 1Ls into sections of "about 60 students." While this can be "good for making friends" and forming "study groups and TV nights," it can at times seem "like high school all over again with the distinct social circles." "In true Southern form," law students at Ole Miss "like to work hard and play

BARBARA VINSON, DIRECTOR OF ADMISSIONS
OFFICE OF ADMISSIONS, P.O. BOX 1848, LAMAR LAW CENTER, UNIVERSITY, MS 38677
TEL: 662-915-6910 FAX: 662-915-1289
EMAIL: LAWMISS@OLEMISS.EDU • WEBSITE: WWW.LAW.OLEMISS.EDU

hard," and "There is a huge effort to make sure that students do more than study." "There is a great Law School Social Board (LSSB) that throws parties, organizes intramural teams, and puts together community-service projects so that students have a way to get to know each other and put the books down for a few hours," a 1L reports. When they do take a break, Ole Miss students find themselves in a pleasant location. The university's campus is "beautiful," and hometown Oxford is "a unique place" with "a healthy social scene." Though most will tell you that "drinking is a big part of social life" here, popular opinion states that "you can absolutely have a good time without drinking." "There are two great new movie theaters, and there are plans to open a 'New Square,'" says one student. "Oxford is constantly growing, and hopefully there will be a lot more for students to do soon." One thing that students agree could be improved a more "diverse student body."

Getting In

The early bird gets the worm at Ole Miss since admitted first-year students can begin their studies during the summer. Certain factors, such as "residency, undergraduate institution, difficulty of major, job experience, social, personal or economic circumstances, non-academic achievement, letters of recommendation and grade patterns and progression," can impact your application favorably, according to the school. Admitted students at the 25th percentile have an LSAT score of 152 and a GPA of 3.25. Admitted students at the 75th percentile have an LSAT score of 158 and a GPA of 3.76.

ADMISSIONS

Selectivity Rating	79
# applications received	1,550
% applicants accepted	32
% acceptees attending	36
Average LSAT	155
LSAT Range	152–157
Average undergrad GPA	3.52
Application fee	$40
Regular application	Rolling, up to 3/1
Regular notification	Rolling
Early application program	No
Transfer students accepted	Yes
Evening division offered	No
Part-time accepted	No
LSDAS accepted	Yes

Applicants Also Look At
The University of Alabama, University of Tennessee—Knoxville, Mississippi College

International Students

TOEFL required of international students	Yes
Minimum TOEFL (paper/computer)	625/263

FINANCIAL FACTS

Annual tuition (in-state/ out-of-state)	$9,277/$18,997
Books and supplies	$1,300
Room & board (on/off-campus)	$16,752/$1,300
% of aid that is merit based	90
Average grant	$5,788
Average loan	$15,334
Average debt	$41,632

EMPLOYMENT INFORMATION

Career Rating	73	
Rate of placement (nine months out)	88	
Average starting salary	$64,025	
State for bar exam	MS, TN, GA, FL, TX	
Pass rate for first-time bar	92	

Employers Who Frequently Hire Grads
Top regional employers from across the South and Southeast.

Prominent Alumni
C. Trent Lott, Former U.S. Senator; Thad Cochran, U.S. Senator; John Grisham, Author; Robert C. Khayat, Chancellor, The University of Mississippi

Grads Employed by Field (%)
Business/Industry (17)
Government (7)
Judicial Clerkships (19)
Military (2)
Private Practice (50)
Public Interest (5)

UNIVERSITY OF MISSOURI—COLUMBIA

SCHOOL OF LAW

INSTITUTIONAL INFORMATION

Public/private	Public
Student-faculty ratio	16:1
% faculty part-time	15
% faculty female	36
% faculty minority	8
Total faculty	42

SURVEY SAYS...

Diverse opinions accepted in classrooms

STUDENTS

Enrollment of law school	451
% male/female	63/37
% out-of-state	20
% full-time	99
% minority	10
# of countries represented	5
Average age of entering class	23

ACADEMICS

Academic Experience Rating	**78**
Profs interesting rating	79
Profs accessible rating	79
Hours of study per day	4.02

Academic Specialties

criminal law, government services, alternative dispute resolution

Advanced Degrees Offered

LLM in Dispute Resolution Began Fall 1999. This is a one-year program.

Combined Degrees Offered

JD/MBA, 4 years; JD/MPA, 4 years; JD/MA (Economics), 4 years; JD/MA (Human Development and Family Studies), 4 years; JD/MA (Educational Leadership & Policy Analysis), 4 years; JD/MA (Journalism), 4 years; JD/PhD (Journalism), 6 years; JD/MLS (Library and Information Science), 4 years; JD/MS (Consumer & Family Economics), 4 years.

Clinical program required	No
Legal writing course requirement	Yes

Academics

The University of Missouri—Columbia School of Law, "provides a high-quality legal education at an affordable price." Its small size, collegial atmosphere and "absolutely outstanding" faculty make Mizzou a "place where you can find all the challenge you want in a law school, without unnecessary stress on top of it." In the words of one student, "If you want to practice in the state of Missouri, there's no better place. Our law school consistently produces the future leaders of Missouri."

Students offer nothing but the utmost praise for their faculty. "The professors are intelligent yet not intimidating; they really care about the students." They "are leading scholars in their field yet available outside the classroom." "Although the Socratic Method is used throughout the first year, and often in other classes, it is used effectively, to help teach students to think like lawyers, but not to embarrass them." Of particular note, one student expresses pleasure in discovering that "classes integrate well with each other, in that professors seem aware of the other classes students are taking, and they draw connections between various fields of the law, thus helping students see how the law comes together." In the words of one particularly enthusiastic student, "The university is the reason I chose MU School of Law, but the faculty is why I would recommend it to any future students. Go Tigers!"

Similar feelings resonate over the administration. One student shares, "The dean of the law school teaches one of my classes. That's probably one of the coolest things about the law school—everyone is so attainable. The administration knows me, and probably every other student in the school, and they genuinely do have our best interests in sight." An older student returning to school after having a family, remarks, "The administration and professors are willing to work with students when those pesky issues of life come along and interfere with the school schedule." Another fan declares, "Law school is hard, MU made it easier."

Academically, students are challenged "within the comfort of a community." Students appreciate "the rigor and intensity of the curriculum" and especially call attention to Mizzou's noteworthy program in alternative dispute resolution. However, of greatest frustration to students are course offerings that conflict with scheduling. One student explains, "Although the course catalog offers a nice variety, students sometimes will have only one opportunity to take a particular class during their student careers, since some 2L/3L classes are offered only every other year." Unfortunately, the wait for in-demand classes can range from a semester to a year, depending on availability.

Career services receive mixed reviews. One student feels that "Career Services does an excellent job with the top 25 percent of the class, but the other three-fourths could use more attention, in my opinion." Another agrees, remarking that "the career development services are probably the most deserving of attention." Specifically, some feel that "the Career Office could do a better job attracting employers from more geographical areas." Fortunately, it appears that Career Services is addressing some of these issues; as one student reports, due to recent changes, "Career Services has done a much better job at providing job and internship opportunities for the students."

Mizzou's facilities—specifically the lack of technology in classrooms—seem to be one of its few weaknesses. "The classrooms do not have electrical outlets, which makes it difficult to take notes on a computer when you have class for four hours straight." As a result, "students are commonly seen lugging around extension cords" with them on campus.

DONNA L. PAVLICK, ASSISTANT DEAN
103 HULSTON HALL, COLUMBIA, MO 65211
TEL: 573-882-6042 FAX: 573-882-9625
EMAIL: UMCLAWADMISSIONS@MISSOURI.EDU • WEBSITE: WWW.LAW.MISSOURI.EDU

Additionally, students feel that "physical facilities are starting to show their age and need to be remodeled."

Life

"Mizzou is a great place for law school, the vast majority of people get along well with everyone else, and we all socialize together as well." "As [for] social life—you can get exactly what you want out of it. If you want to be involved, you got it. If you want to be a hermit and just come in for class," go ahead. "It is an environment that allows people to be flexible with their time, but it is also demanding in a sense that it has the proper time constraints to get people motivated." "Furthermore, Columbia is a great city, and the law school is right in the heart of campus with easy access to the recreation center as well as all of the amenities of downtown."

The degree of competition varies depending on who you ask. One student notes, "The thing I like best about this school is that very few individuals are worried about hiding books from each other in the library in order to get that cutthroat best grade." Another explains, "Students are friendly, but not shy about competition. We are here to learn how to be good lawyers, not to tear each other up." "MU is not a love fest though; people are here because they want to succeed."

Getting In

While application decisions are made on a rolling basis as long as the entering class has openings (class size is 150), the school recommends early application, preferably in the fall of the year prior to enrollment. Admitted students at the 25th percentile have an LSAT score of 156 and a GPA of 3.2. Admitted students at the 75th percentile have an LSAT score of 160 and a GPA of 3.7.

Legal methods course requirement	Yes
Legal research course requirement	Yes
Moot court requirement	Yes
Public interest law requirement	No

ADMISSIONS

Selectivity Rating	**80**
# applications received	875
% applicants accepted	44
% acceptees attending	40
Average LSAT	158
LSAT Range	156–160
Average undergrad GPA	3.49
Application fee	$50
Regular application	Rolling, up to 3/1
Regular notification	Rolling
Early application program	Yes
Early application deadline	11/15
Early application notification	12/31
Transfer students accepted	Yes
Evening division offered	No
Part-time accepted	Yes
LSDAS accepted	Yes

Applicants Also Look At

Washington University, University of Missouri—Kansas City, Saint Louis University

International Students

TOEFL required of international students	Yes
Minimum TOEFL (paper/computer)	600/250

FINANCIAL FACTS

Annual tuition (in-state/out-of-state)	$14,752/$28,176
Books and supplies	$1,372
Fees per credit	$476
Tuition per credit	$433
Room & board	$7,590
Financial aid application deadline	3/1
% first-year students receiving some sort of aid	90
% receiving some sort of aid	90
% of aid that is merit based	22
% receiving scholarships	52
Average grant	$4,000
Average loan	$16,500
Average total aid package	$18,500
Average debt	$57,889

EMPLOYMENT INFORMATION

Career Rating	**66**
Rate of placement (nine months out)	93
Average starting salary	$52,022
State for bar exam	MO, IL, TX, KS, CA
Pass rate for first-time bar	89

Employers Who Frequently Hire Grads

Missouri law firms of all sizes; Missouri, federal & governmental agencies; business, accounting & insurance industries; and federal & state judges, both inside and outside the state of Missouri.

Prominent Alumni

Claire McCaskill, U.S. Senator; Ted Kulongowski, Governor of Oregon; John R. Gibson, U.S. Ct of Appeals—8th Cir;

Grads Employed by Field (%)

Business/Industry (4)
Government (15)
Judicial Clerkships (12)
Military (4)
Private Practice (49)
Public Interest (5)
Other (4)

UNIVERSITY OF MISSOURI—KANSAS CITY
SCHOOL OF LAW

INSTITUTIONAL INFORMATION

Public/private	Public
Student-faculty ratio	13:1
% faculty part-time	21
% faculty female	33
% faculty minority	10
Total faculty	52

SURVEY SAYS...

Diverse opinions accepted
in classrooms
Students love Kansas City, MO

STUDENTS

Enrollment of law school	475
% male/female	64/36
% out-of-state	32
% full-time	94
% minority	12
# of countries represented	5
Average age of entering class	26

ACADEMICS

Academic Experience Rating	**71**
Profs interesting rating	71
Profs accessible rating	84
Hours of study per day	4.52

Academic Specialties

International law; taxation; intellectual property law; business & entrepreneurial law; urban, land use & environmental law; litigation; child & family law

Advanced Degrees Offered

LL.M, 1–3 years

Combined Degrees Offered

JD/MBA, 3–4 years; JD/MPA, 3–4 years; JD/LLM, 3.5–4 years.

Clinical program required	No
Legal writing course requirement	Yes
Legal methods course requirement	No
Legal research course requirement	Yes
Moot court requirement	Yes
Public interest law requirement	No

Academics

A small public law school that brings a personal touch to the academic experience, the University of Missouri—Kansas City is a great place to get a solid legal education and develop ties within the local bar. The school prides itself on maintaining a small student body and "the faculty and staff take a genuine interest in helping every student to succeed in school, on the bar exam, and in their professional career." In the classroom, the Socratic Method is widely used. Fortunately, at UMKC, it isn't as terrifying as you might fear since "Most teachers will ask you questions but allow others to help you out if you get stumped." A current student insists, "The faculty here is extraordinarily supportive, always available for individual and group meetings, and never vindictive in class when a student is ill-prepared. Faculty uses the Socratic Method to encourage students, rather than degrade them." While academics are challenging, "for the most part, professors are accessible" and willing to help struggling students outside of class. In fact, "2L and 3L offices are located in the same areas with professors' offices so that the faculty is very accessible to students for advice and counsel."

The curriculum is designed to prepare students for government posts and general practice of law; however, you can tailor your education through coursework in specific areas of interest, including child and family law, business law, and litigation. One particular strength are the school's "extensive taxation courses, including the option to get an LL.M in Taxation by applying tax courses to your JD and LL.M requirements, allowing you to earn the degree quicker.... [Also], the tax and estate planning faculty are excellent." In addition, the extracurricular offerings allow students to add dimension and breadth to their degree. If you'd like to get some experience in international law, "the school's two main study abroad programs, China and Ireland, are very well established and popular among students at UMKC and even from other schools. Internship and academic writing credit are both available with these programs." In addition, the school's mentorship program, or Inns Program, "provides students with valuable opportunities to build relationships with the local practitioners." On that note, the school has deep ties in the local community, and there are "countless firms, county, state, and federal government courthouses and offices in the area, which provide students with the opportunity for excellent clerkship, internship, and work experience."

While the school's tough grading policies could certainly lead to unwelcome competition between students, the academic atmosphere is nonetheless collegial. At UMKC, "fellow students are very supportive of one another and smaller social groups will form immediately." A 3L explains, "Everyone understands and appreciates that we are all in this together and it's much easier to get through three years of law school if we all work together and help one another out." The cooperative atmosphere is partially a by-product of the school's academic organization: "The school divides each incoming class into three sections of about 60–70 students in each section. You take your first year core classes together and hence get to know the students in your section very well."

After graduation, most UMKC students go on to positions in Kansas City, and "the job market is relatively good, if you don't want to get rich right out of school." A current student writes, "If you want to practice in Kansas City, UMKC is a great choice because of its location and because so many Kansas City attorneys have graduated from UMKC."

DEBBIE BROOKS, ASSISTANT DEAN
UMKC SCHOOL OF LAW, 5100 ROCKHILL ROAD, KANSAS CITY, MO 64110
TEL: 816-235-1644 FAX: 816-235-5276
EMAIL: LAW@UMKC.EDU • WEBSITE: WWW.LAW.UMKC.EDU

Life

From the Public Interest Law Group and the Association of Women Law Students, to SBA events and overseas programs, there are plenty of ways to fill up your free time at UMKC. "Many students seem to come to this law school right out of college," so there is a common bond, and "strong personal friendships among its students developed within class and throughout the school's numerous social avenues." Students connect through unique activities like the annual theatrical "$1.98 Law Review," as well as "lots of drinking and happy hours." Striking a balance between work and relaxation, "the students are always working on ways to get out and enjoy life," and students assure us that "if you want to have an active social life here, it is very accessible and welcoming."

The school's Kansas City location is excellent, affording plenty of opportunities to get out in the local community. Unfortunately, the school's physical plant tends to draw myriad complaints. "Some of the facilities are admittedly dated and need improvements" (in particular, students note that there are not enough laptop outlets in the classrooms), and a number of students express concern about safety issues in the evening, when campus security is lax.

Getting In

Students who don't quite have the numbers to get into Mizzou's Columbia campus still have a shot at Kansas City. Applicants who can't commit to the full-time program may want to consider the part-time "flex" program, which allows students up to five years to complete a JD. Applications are accepted any time after September 1, but procrastinators beware—most seats are filled by the end of February.

ADMISSIONS

Selectivity Rating	76
# applications received	928
# applicants accepted	404
# acceptees attending	155
Average LSAT	155
LSAT Range	153–157
Average undergrad GPA	3.33
Application fee	$50
Regular application	Rolling
Regular notification	Rolling
Early application program	No
Transfer students accepted	Yes
Evening division offered	No
Part-time accepted	Yes
LSDAS accepted	Yes

Applicants Also Look At
University of Kansas, University of Missouri—Columbia

International Students
TOEFL required of international students	Yes
Minimum TOEFL (paper/computer/web)	650/280/114

FINANCIAL FACTS

Annual tuition (in-state/ out-of-state)	$14,316/$28,266
Books and supplies	$4,500
Fees	$904
Fees per credit	$65
Tuition per credit (in-state/out-of-state)	$477/$942
Room & board (on/off-campus)	$10,467/$8,443
Financial aid application deadline	3/1
% first-year students receiving some sort of aid	92
% receiving some sort of aid	84
% of aid that is merit based	99
% receiving scholarships	37
Average grant	$9,660
Average loan	$27,937
Average total aid package	$30,121
Average debt	$72,475

EMPLOYMENT INFORMATION

Career Rating	74
Rate of placement (nine months out)	88.7
Average starting salary	$60,954
State for bar exam	MO, KS
Pass rate for first-time bar	95.56

Employers Who Frequently Hire Grads
Bryan Cave LLP; Husch Blackwell Sanders, LLP; Jackson County Circuit Court; Lathrop & Gage L.C.; Legal Aid of Western Missouri.

Prominent Alumni
Harry S. Truman, President of the United States; Charles E. Whittaker, U.S. Supreme Court Justice; Clarence Kelley, FBI Director.

Grads Employed by Field (%)
Business/Industry (6)
Private Practice (57)
Government (16)
Judicial Clerkship (11)
Public Interest (5)
Academic (1)
Other (5)

University of Nebraska—Lincoln
College of Law

Academics

The University of Nebraska—Lincoln College of Law offers a high-quality education at an unbeatable price. One student incredulously declares, "I pay about $9,000 a semester for books and tuition. Where else can you get a top-rate legal education for that cheap?" Students say that UNL offers a first-rate education with a "brilliant and very approachable" staff. "Not only are the professors walking through the library, talking to the students and answering questions, but the staff throughout the college is amazing."

The administration, faculty and research staff undoubtedly serve as UNL's greatest assets. One student remarks, "Honestly, I don't think that one could find a better school administration or research librarians. They always meet you with a helpful smile," and are willing to do all that they can to assist students. Another notes, "The faculty and staff at Nebraska law care about the success of each student," and help "student[s] find their place within the law." According to many, professors are "extremely engaging" and "are able to connect the subject matter to practical experience and real-life cases, which makes class more interesting."

Students warn that "the first year is extremely demanding, especially spring semester [since] our classes are a year long and most of the tests in the spring are cumulative." While April and May in the first year might be "almost unbearable," one seasoned 3L reassures us that "during my three years at UNL, most of my classes have been very interesting. Some of them have changed my life and outlook on the world." Students rave about UNL's prosecutorial clinic, as it is one of the few of its kind amongst an array of defense clinics. One student emphatically declares it "the best class that I took at UNL. Another student is of the opinion that though "there are a lot of classes in varying subjects, [UNL] is lacking in public interest/pro bono–type classes or topics for students wanting a different type of experience."

Students are divided when it comes to the subject of employment after graduation. One student expresses an appreciation for "how UNL is trying to branch out and help students land jobs outside of Nebraska." Another argues that while "The school is great for finding jobs for students with higher grades that want to stay in Nebraska," "There is not enough emphasis on employment after law school if a student wants to work in public interest." One 3L would like "employers more involved in recruiting for clerkships," but in the same breath concedes that "most [students] were able to get clerkships if they wanted them as a 2L."

"The renovation of the school is almost complete," students gladly report. "It's great having brand new classrooms and facilities, as well as complete access to technology anywhere in the building." The almost fully renovated classrooms are "extremely comfortable" and "all have wireless access and plugs for laptops." Additionally, the "auditorium is set for renovation, and [the school is] adding on to accommodate larger class sizes." Overall, students seem content with the refurbished facilities and as one satisfied 1L affirms, "After six years on the East Cost, the beautiful library and outstanding professors made returning to the Midwest an easy decision."

Environment

"UNL recruits some very intelligent and exceptionally talented students," and students agree that "the law school does a really good job of creating community among the students." Specifically, the small class size creates a "close-knit group mentality" and particularly helpful is the practice of scheduling first years "so they have at least one

SARAH GLODEN, ASSISTANT DEAN OF ADMISSIONS
PO BOX 830902, LINCOLN, NE 68583-0902
TEL: 402-472-2161 FAX: 402-472-5185
EMAIL: LAWADM@UNL.EDU • WEBSITE: LAW.UNL.EDU

class with most of the students" in their cohort. One reassured student remarks from experience, "I know that if I need any help, albeit from a librarian, administrator, faculty member, or fellow law student, that I will receive it."

There is no shortage of social opportunities at UNL. "People take the initiative to organize mixers and activities to help people get to know one another and to keep law school stress at bay as much as possible." One student observes, "The social life at Nebraska is great if you like to drink. Many of the students like to go to the bars on the weekends (or on Mondays or Tuesdays), and there's almost always alcohol at Student Bar Association events. Heck, even our Civil Procedure professor took our class out to the bar after a particularly tough week." The bottom line remains clear as expressed in one student's words, "students aren't just classmates—we're friends."

Getting In

LSAT scores and undergraduate GPA are the main factors that UNL's Admissions Committee consider when evaluating applications. Admitted students at the 25th percentile have an LSAT score of 154 and a GPA of 3.2. Admitted students at the 75th percentile have an LSAT score of 160 and a GPA of 3.8. UNL pays particular attention in reviewing applications from members of minority groups that historically have been under-represented in the legal profession.

Moot court requirement	No
Public interest law requirement	No

ADMISSIONS

Selectivity Rating	**79**
# applications received	877
% applicants accepted	42
% acceptees attending	39
Average LSAT	156
LSAT Range	154–160
Average undergrad GPA	3.64
Application fee	$25
Regular application	Rolling
Regular notification	Rolling
Early application program	No
Transfer students accepted	Yes
Evening division offered	No
Part-time accepted	No
LSDAS accepted	Yes

Applicants Also Look At

University of Denver, University of Kansas, Arizona State University, Drake University, Creighton University, University of Iowa, Washburn University

International Students

TOEFL required of international students	Yes
Minimum TOEFL (paper/computer)	600/250

FINANCIAL FACTS

Annual tuition (in-state/ out-of-state)	$6,856/$19,223
Books and supplies	$1,230
Fees	$2,357
Tuition per credit (in-state/out-of-state)	$208/$583
Room & board (on/off-campus)	$7,106/$6,846
Financial aid application deadline	5/1
% first-year students receiving some sort of aid	46
% receiving some sort of aid	44
% of aid that is merit based	38
% receiving scholarships	44
Average grant	$7,000
Average loan	$15,880
Average total aid package	$20,428
Average debt	$44,910

EMPLOYMENT INFORMATION

Career Rating	**76**
Rate of placement (nine months out)	95
Average starting salary	$52,589
State for bar exam	NE, IA, MO, SD, WA
Pass rate for first-time bar	90

Employers Who Frequently Hire Grads
Very Small Law Firms, 2–10 attorneys, Small Law Firms, 11–25 attorneys, State Government

Prominent Alumni
Ted Sorensen, Special Counsel to President John F. Kennedy; Harvey Perlman, Chancellor, University of Nebraska-Lincoln; Ben Nelson, U.S. Senator and former Governor of Nebraska.

Grads Employed by Field (%)
Academic (5)
Business/Industry (13)
Government (11)
Judicial Clerkships (6)
Military (2)
Private Practice (55)
Public Interest (7)
Other (1)

UNIVERSITY OF NEVADA—LAS VEGAS

WILLIAM S. BOYD SCHOOL OF LAW

INSTITUTIONAL INFORMATION

Public/private	Public
Student-faculty ratio	17:1
% faculty part-time	5
% faculty female	41
% faculty minority	19
Total faculty	58

SURVEY SAYS...

Diverse opinions accepted
in classrooms
Great research resources

STUDENTS

Enrollment of law school	487
% male/female	53/47
% full-time	76
% minority	29
# of countries represented	3
Average age of entering class	25

ACADEMICS

Academic Experience Rating	**84**
Profs interesting rating	80
Profs accessible rating	89

Combined Degrees Offered

JD/MBA, 4 years; JD/MSW, 4 years;
JD/PhD in Education, 4 years

Clinical program required	No
Legal writing course requirement	Yes
Legal methods course requirement	Yes
Legal research course requirement	Yes
Moot court requirement	No
Public interest law requirement	Yes

Academics

ABA-accredited in 2003, many students feel "The greatest strength of Boyd is its newness," which lends a sense of optimism, excitement, and challenge to the campus. Because it's not "steeped in tradition, there's an entrepreneurial spirit here. Everyone senses we're building something special." With a quality teaching staff, top-notch facilities, a talented student body, and reasonable tuition costs, students are confident that their school will continue to climb in the ranks. In fact, this sense of excitement extends throughout the city and state. Boyd is the only law school in Nevada; students report that "the legal community and the community in general are excited to have us here and the whole city is invested in all of us succeeding."

Professors boast impressive educational and professional backgrounds and are known to be both "intelligent and well respected in their fields." More important, they are "stimulating individuals who are skilled teachers." Students are "consistently amazed by the ease with which the faculty so effectively employs the Socratic Method, such that the student body...is able to break down even the most complex legal scenarios and digest them as fully understandable rules and concepts." Outside the classroom, "Professors are extremely approachable, even for a shy student."

The administration is generally regarded as "accessible and very pro-student." A 2L affirms, "The administrators I deal with on any sort of regular basis are fantastic. Not only do they know their stuff; they are anxious to help and are just all-around fabulous people." Students particularly applaud the efforts the administration has made to help new students make the transition into law school, citing the "optional 30-minute classes once a week where we are taught exam skills, note-taking, and outlining tips."

Classrooms at Boyd are "new and clean" and very high-tech. The "top quality facilities" include "wireless Internet and cable Internet hook-ups throughout the building," as well as "a state-of-the-art library." Off campus, students say that "being the only law school in Nevada, in the middle of one of the fastest-growing economies in the United States, opportunities abound." For example, UNLV students "have opportunities for something close to 85 judicial externships each year (out of a class of 150)" and additionally "have extraordinary access to the local, regional, and state governments." When it comes to landing a job after graduation, UNLV is extremely well located. In the city of Las Vegas "The local law firms are eager to hire graduates, and the private sector opportunities in gaming, hospitality, real estate, corporate, entertainment and litigation are abundant and highly lucrative."

ELIZABETH KARL, ADMISSIONS & RECORDS ASSISTANT
4505 MARYLAND PARKWAY, BOX 451003, LAS VEGAS, NV 89154-1003
TEL: (702) 895-2440 FAX: (702) 895-2414
EMAIL: REQUEST@LAW.UNLV.EDU • WEBSITE: WWW.LAW.UNLV.EDU

Life

While located in the heart of Las Vegas, "Most of the students commute into campus ...and that can put a strain on the nearby social scene." In lieu of a hopping campus life, "Student organizations are great and have become central to social events at the school." Students have no trouble making friends among their interesting and talented classmates since "The people make the school." One student writes, "I love coming to school because I've made really great friends and don't mind seeing them everyday."

Commuter student or not, "Being in the center of Las Vegas, there is always something to do and somewhere new to go." You may be surprised to learn, however, that law school in Sin City is actually quite serious. Some students feel the competitiveness is a product of the high caliber of the student body. A 1L explains particularly in the school's early years many "of the students in the entering class are in their 40s, and several of them are doctors and dentists, so the bar is set quite high." Though the level of commitment remains the same, the profile of the average entrant may have changed over time as the school's applicant pool has widened in terms of age and experience. In addition to their diligence, UNLV students are a fairly homogenous and quite conservative group. One student points out that some of "The faculty is comprised of very liberal individuals from a diverse background, whereas a majority of the students are very conservative and tend to have similar life experiences."

Getting In

When selecting applicants, the Admissions Committee looks for students with demonstrated academic capability, including depth and breadth of undergraduate course work, grades, concurrent work experience, and extracurricular activities. The school also considers non-academic factors, such as community service and work experience. Older students should feel particularly welcomed at Boyd.

ADMISSIONS

Selectivity Rating	86
# applications received	1,755
# applicants accepted	407
# acceptees attending	157
Average LSAT	158
LSAT Range	155–160
Average undergrad GPA	3.44
Application fee	$50
Regular application	3/15
Regular notification	Rolling
Early application program	No
Transfer students accepted	Yes
Evening division offered	Yes
Part-time accepted	Yes
LSDAS accepted	Yes

Applicants Also Look At

University of Arizona, University of Utah, Arizona State University, Brigham Young University, University of the Pacific, University of San Diego, California Western School of Law, Southwestern University School of Law, Thomas Jefferson School of Law

FINANCIAL FACTS

Annual tuition (in-state/ out-of-state)	$18,000/$30,000
Books and supplies	$1,080
Tuition per credit (in-state/ out-of-state)	$643/$1,071
Room & board (off-campus)	$8,370
Financial aid application deadline	2/1
% first-year students receiving some sort of aid	88
% receiving some sort of aid	86
% of aid that is merit based	90
% receiving scholarships	33
Average grant	$7,400
Average loan	$26,200
Average total aid package	$28,000
Average debt	$55,700

EMPLOYMENT INFORMATION

Career Rating	73
Rate of placement (nine months out)	93.6
Average starting salary	$75,532
State for bar exam	NV, AZ, UT, CA
Pass rate for first-time bar	75

Employers Who Frequently Hire Grads
State, Regional, and National private firms
Local and State governmental agencies
State and Federal judiciary

Grads Employed by Field (%)
Business/Industry (18)
Government (9)
Judicial clerkships (15)
Private practice (55)
Public Interest (2)

UNIVERSITY OF NEW MEXICO
SCHOOL OF LAW

INSTITUTIONAL INFORMATION
Public/private	Public
Student-faculty ratio	10:1
% faculty female	51
% faculty minority	40
Total faculty	35

SURVEY SAYS...
Great research resources
Great library staff
Liberal students

STUDENTS
Enrollment of law school	346
% male/female	47/53
% out-of-state	13
% full-time	100
% minority	47
Average age of entering class	29

ACADEMICS
Academic Experience Rating	**78**
Profs interesting rating	79
Profs accessible rating	92
Hours of study per day	3.73

Academic Specialties
Environmental law, Indian Law

Advanced Degrees Offered
JD, 3 years (full-time program).

Combined Degrees Offered
JD/MBA, JD/MA in Latin American Studies, JD/MA in Public Administration, 4 years.

Clinical program required	Yes
Legal writing course requirement	Yes
Legal methods course requirement	Yes
Legal research course requirement	Yes
Moot court requirement	No
Public interest law requirement	No

Academics

The University of New Mexico School of Law "offers [students] an absolutely amazing experience." By all accounts, it's "a very affordable, friendly, ideal place to study law." Highlights include "a small community"—there are only about 350 law students—"and a really encouraging faculty." "The small size limits the number of classes that are offered," but they also "give a greater opportunity to connect with professors and students alike, not just academically but on a personal level as well." The Family Law curriculum is popular, and certificates are available in Natural Resources Law and in the "superb" Native American Law program. Dual-degree programs include a JD/MA in Latin American Studies. There's also study abroad opportunities in Mexico, Canada, and Tasmania. "The other great thing about UNMSOL is the clinical program." "Participating in clinic has been one of the most rewarding and useful experiences of my law school career," gushes one student. "I've had the opportunity to personally represent actual clients in actual cases with help from an experienced attorney." Also, "The trial practice classes give you real trial experience in front of current judges and real jurors."

The administration is "very accessible and open to student input." "Law students in general always have complaints about everything, but this administration seems to be fairly responsive to student concerns," notes a 2L. Students tell us that teaching is "the focus of the law school." "While some teachers are better than others, the overall experience has been great so far," says a 2L. The faculty "includes some brilliant legal minds" and "could not be more knowledgeable." "Our professors are the best lawyers in the state in their given fields," asserts a 2L. Many "have literally written the book on a given area of New Mexico law." Professors are "accessible" and "student friendly" as well. "Most of my professors know who I am, and I can easily get in contact with most—if not all—of them," declares a 3L.

UNM does a pretty good job of helping students fulfill "a broad array of career goals." There is "great access to externships and clerkships both during and after law school." "Any student can set up an externship with any lawyer in the state." Though in the past students have noted Career Services "is sometimes disorganized." Recent changes have been made to address this concern. "As there's no other law school in the state," UNM graduates ae well positioned to find jobs in The Land of Enchantment.

The facility here is something like "a concrete bungalow surrounded by parking lots." (By the way, "Parking is, and always will be, a hassle.") "The newer wing of the school is beautiful and bright." Though in the past students had noted "the older building could use some aesthetic improvements," recent rennovations have been made. The best feature is probably the library, which is "open and bright with plenty of private spots for intense study."

Life

The diversity of the student population is a tremendous strength at this school. UNM "works hard to ensure that the student population is diverse and reflects the actual demographics" of the state. There is a "strong Mexican American and Native American presence." Students here are "cool, interesting, admirable, energetic, fun people of different ages." They are often "prone to open, heated debate" and "very open to discussion whenever a point of contention might arise." Politically, it's an "overwhelmingly leftist student body," which makes some students uncomfortable. "As a Hispanic who is a moderate Democrat, I cannot believe how . . . intolerant this institution is," gripes a 3L.

Susan Mitchell, Assistant Dean for Admissions & Financial Aid
MSC 11-6070, 1 University of New Mexico, Albuquerque, NM 87131-0001
Tel: 505-277-0958 Fax: 505-277-9958
Email: admissions@law.unm.edu • Website: lawschool.unm.edu

Other students disagree. "I (as a conservative student) still feel that I have a voice that is heard and considered whenever there is a debate, whether it's in class or in the parking lot." There isn't a ton of academic competition. "Most everyone is very friendly; the only serious, cutthroat competition takes place at the Ping-Pong table in the Student Forum."

"Students all know each other, and there is an active social scene" on campus. "It is a tight community." "I have made a lot of really great friends," proclaims a 2L. There are a very high number of student organizations on campus, but "Some of those organizations tend to have a low level of activity due to the small number of students at the school." The surrounding city of Albuquerque (population: about 700,000) is "an extremely affordable place to live with low crime and moderate traffic which makes it great for students." "Albuquerque is just a great place to live, especially for people who like the outdoors." Summers are relatively hot, and it does snow during the mild winters, making it possible to ski in the nearby mountains in the morning and play a comfortable round of golf in the afternoon. "Lots of students are athletic and run or bike; there are extensive trail systems around campus."

Getting In

Admitted students at the 25th percentile have LSAT scores in the range of 152 and GPAs of a little over 3.0. Admitted students at the 75th percentile have LSAT scores of 158 and GPAs just over 3.7.

ADMISSIONS

Selectivity Rating	80
# applications received	1,070
% applicants accepted	25
% acceptees attending	43
Average LSAT	154
LSAT Range	150–157
Average undergrad GPA	3.32
Application fee	$50
Regular application	Rolling, up to 2/15
Regular notification	Rolling
Early application program	No
Transfer students accepted	Yes
Evening division offered	No
Part-time accepted	No
LSDAS accepted	Yes

International Students

TOEFL required of international students	Yes
Minimum TOEFL (paper/ computer/web)	600/250/100

FINANCIAL FACTS

Annual tuition (in-state/ out-of-state)	$11,543/$25,643
Books and supplies	$1,082
Room & board (on/off-campus)	$7,080/$8,180
Financial aid application deadline	3/1

EMPLOYMENT INFORMATION

Career Rating	79	**Grads Employed by Field (%)**
Rate of placement (nine months out)	94	Business/Industry (14)
Average starting salary	$53,675	Government (18)
State for bar exam	NM, CA, PA, TX	Judicial Clerkships (13)
Pass rate for first-time bar	95	Private Practice (35)

Employers Who Frequently Hire Grads
Private firms, government agencies, Federal and State Judges and public interest organizations

Public Interest (17)

Prominent Alumni
Honorable Edward L. Chavez, Chief Justice New Mexico Supreme Court; The Honorable Tom Udall, United States Senate; Gary King, New Mexico Attorney General.

THE UNIVERSITY OF NORTH CAROLINA AT CHAPEL HILL
SCHOOL OF LAW

INSTITUTIONAL INFORMATION

Public/private	Public
Student-faculty ratio	15:1
% faculty part-time	0
% faculty female	50
% faculty minority	18
Total faculty	55

SURVEY SAYS...

Great research resources
Great library staff
Students love Chapel Hill, NC

STUDENTS

Enrollment of law school	735
% male/female	50/50
% out-of-state	30
% full-time	100
% minority	31
# of countries represented	7
Average age of entering class	23

ACADEMICS

Academic Experience Rating	**83**
Profs interesting rating	66
Profs accessible rating	77
Hours of study per day	4.12

Academic Specialties

Civil procedure, commercial law, constitutional law, corporation securities, criminal law, environmental law, government services, human rights, international law, labor law, legal history, legal philosophy, property, taxation, intellectual property law

Combined Degrees Offered

JD/MBA, 4 years; JD/MPA, 4 years; JD/MPPS, 4 years; JD/MPH, 4 years; JD/MRP, 4 years; JD/MSW, 4 years; JD/M.A S.A., 4 years; JD/MALS or MSIS, 4 years; JD/M.A.M.C., 4 years

Clinical program required	No
Legal writing	
course requirement	Yes
Legal methods	
course requirement	No
Moot court requirement	Yes

Academics

The School of Law at The University of North Carolina at Chapel Hill is, according to students, "one of the best public law schools in the country." Many claim that "the faculty here couldn't be more down to earth and accessible." They have "a literal 'my-door-is-open-all-the-time policy' and never hesitate to "[take] the time to talk to every single student before class." Still, some students feel that "there is a strong liberal bias at the school" and that professors sometimes "bring their political views with them into the classroom." To correct this, they are calling for the law school to "improve on fostering a more diverse political atmosphere." UNC Law's "excellent" and "accessible" administration is "unparalleled" in its efforts to promote a "positive and supportive environment for the study of law." Everyone here seems to practice "the 'We're all family at UNC' motto to a fault."

Most UNC survey respondents are pretty pleased about their employment prospects. One student credits the Career Services Office as being "the greatest strength of UNC. Even when they are too busy for a brief meeting about resumes or cover letters, you can just leave your stuff under the door, and someone will get it back to you by the next day with recommendations about what you should fix." However, some feel that it could "stand to improve, particularly with communicating jobs to 1Ls." However, jobs in North Carolina and neighboring states are fairly abundant, though, in large part because the law school maintains "strong connections" with in-state employers.

Student organizations and learning opportunities are aplenty. According to one student, "There are lots of organizations to get involved in, and the pro bono program is one of the best." About one-third of all students do some kind of pro bono work—many during the summer or during winter or spring breaks. Students who have performed more than 75 hours of pro bono service receive certificates of acknowledgment from the state bar association, and those who perform more than 100 hours of pro bono service get special shout-outs at graduation. Other notables include UNC's clinical programs, in which students handle more than 350 civil and criminal cases every year and "really get a lot of hands-on experience" along with "solid academic[s]" in the process. Joint-degree programs include the standard JD/MBA as well as master's of public policy science and a handful of others. UNC also offers a summer program down under in Sydney, Australia, that concentrates on Pacific Rim issues and semester-long programs in Europe and Mexico.

The general consensus is that facilities at UNC are middling, but in terms of the availability of information, "The resources are outstanding." Also, "The school is improving the technology of each classroom every year." It's a pretty slow process, though. As of now, "Half the facilities are brand-new. Once they get around to renovating the other half, they'll be golden." In the meantime, a cry of "More parking!" can be heard throughout campus.

MICHAEL J. STATES, ASSISTANT DEAN FOR ADMISSIONS
CB# 3380, VAN HECKE-WETTACH HALL, UNC SCHOOL OF LAW-ADMISSIONS, CHAPEL HILL, NC
27599-3380
TEL: 919-962-5109 FAX: 919-843-7939
EMAIL: LAW_ADMISSION@UNC.EDU • WEBSITE: WWW.LAW.UNC.EDU

Life

"Carolina offers a healthy balance between academic and student life." UNC is home to "diverse, interesting, charming, and intelligent people." One student exclaims, "I am constantly amazed by how interesting my classmates are." Most agree that "everyone gets along" in this "very friendly" and "very cooperative" academic atmosphere. "It is competitive but not necessarily with each other. It seems we all want to see everyone do well," explains one student.

Students insist that "there is no better college town in the United States than Chapel Hill," a Southern hamlet of about 44,000 souls that offers a good supply of part-time jobs, affordable housing, and a mild climate. These fine qualities have not gone unnoticed: *Money* magazine has before named the Raleigh-Durham-Chapel Hill area the "Best Place to Live in the South," in 2000, and *Sports Illustrated* named Chapel Hill "the Best College Town in America" a few years earlier. "It's a great place to live," says one student. "The people are amazing" and the "campus and city are breathtaking." As one student puts it, "While you don't go to law school for the social life, it makes a big difference to have something to do when you actually do find free time."

"Social life is good" at Chapel Hill because "On the whole, students are very social outside of class." There are always a multitude of "school-sponsored social events in town" and "parties being thrown by law students to celebrate a wide array of milestones" (for instance, there is a "we just took our second practice exam" party). However, some students lament that there is little to do "for someone who does not drink."

Getting In

While perhaps easier than you might think, admissions here is no cakewalk. Admitted students at the 25th percentile have an LSAT score of 158 and a GPA of 3.4. Admitted students at the 75th percentile have an LSAT score of 164 and a GPA of 3.8. If applying as a nonresident, keep in mind that you'll want to be ready to dazzle with your academic prowess as around 75 percent of each admitted year at Chapel Hill are residents of North Carolina, and competition for the remaining quarter of the class is stiff.

Public interest	
law requirement	No

ADMISSIONS

Selectivity Rating	**92**
# applications received	3,063
% applicants accepted	19
% acceptees attending	44
Average LSAT	161
LSAT Range	157–163
Average undergrad GPA	3.6
Application fee	$70
Regular application	Rolling, up to 3/1
Regular notification	Rolling
Early application program	No
Transfer students accepted	Yes
Evening division offered	No
Part-time accepted	No
LSDAS accepted	Yes

Applicants Also Look At
University of Illinois at Urbana-Champaign, American University, Duke University, University of Minnesota—Twin Cities, The Ohio State University—Columbus, University of Virginia, Boston College, The George Washington University, Emory University, Wake Forest University

International Students
TOEFL required of international students	Yes
Minimum TOEFL (paper/computer)	650/250

FINANCIAL FACTS

Annual tuition (in-state/ out-of-state)	$13,212/$26,530
Books and supplies	$1,000
Fees	$2,802
Room & board (on/off-campus)	$13,920
Financial aid application deadline	3/1
% first-year students receiving some sort of aid	86
% receiving some sort of aid	78
% of aid that is merit based	66
% receiving scholarships	53
Average grant	$4,665
Average loan	$18,748
Average total aid package	$22,803
Average debt	$59,329

EMPLOYMENT INFORMATION

		Grads Employed by Field (%)
Career Rating	**86**	Academic (3)
Rate of placement (nine months out)	94	Business/Industry (9)
Average starting salary	$95,000	Government (6)
State for bar exam	NC, NY, FL, GA, VA	Judicial Clerkships (8)
Pass rate for first-time bar	93	Private Practice (65)
Prominent Alumni		Public Interest (9)

Prominent Alumni
John Edwards, Senator; Jim Delany, Big 10 Conference Commissioner; Julius Chambers, Civil Rights Attorney; Sarah Parker, Chief Justice NC Sct.

UNIVERSITY OF NORTH DAKOTA
SCHOOL OF LAW

INSTITUTIONAL INFORMATION

Public/private	Public
Student-faculty ratio	14:1
% faculty part-time	25
% faculty female	44
% faculty minority	7
Total faculty	27

SURVEY SAYS...

Diverse opinions accepted
in classrooms
Great research resources
Great library staff
Abundant externship/internship/
clerkship opportunities

STUDENTS

Enrollment of law school	244
% male/female	52/48
% out-of-state	54
% full-time	100
% minority	11
% international	7
# of countries represented	7
Average age of entering class	27

ACADEMICS

Academic Experience Rating	**70**
Profs interesting rating	72
Profs accessible rating	86
Hours of study per day	3.63

Advanced Degrees Offered
JD, 3 years

Combined Degrees Offered
JD/MPA, 4 years; JD/MBA, 4 years

Clinical program required	No
Legal writing	
course requirement	Yes
Legal methods	
course requirement	Yes
Legal research	
course requirement	Yes
Moot court requirement	No
Public interest	
law requirement	No

Academics

The School of Law at the University of North Dakota benefits from low costs, a helpful administration, and a dedicated faculty, helping propel an already well-respected reputation in the region. While UND Law is a small school, it's the only law school in a relatively unpopulated state, so there are "more exclusive opportunities for clerkships and externships" than most public law schools, better chances of participating in moot court and law reviews, and the school brings in great speakers (even the ND Supreme Court every year). Many of the state's lawyers also came out of this school, which helps boost employment prospects.

With "some of the brightest and hardest working legal minds in the country hiding here in North Dakota," UND Law professors "always have open-door policies," and many are published, some even with their own casebooks. "I feel privileged to have been allowed to learn from some of the best legal scholars in the United States. They almost made me forget how cold it was outside in the winter," muses a student. The one-on-one relationships between professors and students here "is like nothing you'd expect out of a law school." Class sizes are capped at about 75 students, and 2L and 3L classes have significantly less students, so classes are with relatively small groups a lot of the time. Faculty "seem to keep up with the latest news and incorporate it into the lectures." In order to add some more practical flavor into the curriculum, many courses are offered by adjunct faculty. The attorneys, some with 35 or more years of legal practice, "offer a lot of insight and practical advice that academic professors just can't bring to the table." This results in a diverse group of professors who teach very different courses ranging from general to specialized, allowing students some opportunity to pick and choose, although there is plenty of clamoring for stronger specialization programs, especially in the areas of business and tax law. Administration-wise, the school has three dedicated deans who work to keep the tuition affordable while still managing to offer a broad range of academic and practical experiences, and a helpful staff to boot. Faculty and administration have made great strides in getting student feedback, and there are always student question-and-answer sessions with new and prospective faculty members.

UND Law has the biggest law library in the state, including full and free access to WestLaw, LexisNexis, CALI, and Audio Case Files, as well as a section in the library dedicated to "academic success" that includes study aids and treatises. Beyond that, "the audiovisual technology and seating arrangement are great, however that greatness ends at the door. More bathrooms are needed just about everywhere, and as far as the classrooms go, there's one state-of-the-art classroom (used almost exclusively by 1Ls), and the rest are "straight out of *The Paper Chase*, wooden chairs and all."

BEN HOFFMAN, DIRECTOR OF ADMISSIONS & RECORDS
CENTENNIAL DRIVE PO BOX 9003, GRAND FORKS, ND 58202
TEL: 701-777-2260 FAX: 701-777-2217
EMAIL: HOFFMAN@LAW.UND.EDU • WEBSITE: WWW.LAW.UND.NODAK.EDU

Life

For most UND Law students, "law school is about everyone getting to the end, not who can get there first," and there's very little competition amongst classmates, fostering an "amicable environment with level-minded people." There are many extra and co-curricular activities at UND, ranging from special interest organizations to art auctions, formals, football games between the UND Law and Med students, student-run plays, and "hundreds of fun—but wallet-blasting—fundraisers"; student social events, "whether 'official' or not, are very well attended." Every year the Student Association throws a party for the students

to celebrate the half way point for the 2Ls. There's a sense that everybody knows everybody, along with the idea that "you're going to have to work with these people when you get out, so be nice while you're here." There are a surprising number of out-of-state attendees, and although diversity is incredibly low, the small size of the school eliminates any different treatment of minorities. The school's Norway exchange program "is one of the coolest things this school does, both from a diversity standpoint (read: fresh blonde females each year for a semester) and from an educational one, with respect to international law." UND Law is in the small town community of Grand Forks, so the nightlife is not so much centered on the town, but "there are always parties of one kind or another going on, and for the most part everyone is always invited."

Getting In

While there is no specific pre-law course work required for admission, demonstrated oral and written communication skills are paramount to an admissions decision at University of North Dakota. The applicant's undergraduate record, LSAT scores, and letters of recommendation are the most heavily weighted factors in an admissions decision; however, the school will consider all factors that may suggest a student is capable of completing a rigorous legal curriculum.

ADMISSIONS

Selectivity Rating	**71**
# applications received	484
% applicants accepted	42
% acceptees attending	41
Average LSAT	151
LSAT Range	148–153
Average undergrad GPA	3.36
Application fee	$35
Regular application	Rolling, up to 7/31
Regular notification	Rolling
Early application program	No
Transfer students accepted	Yes
Evening division offered	No
Part-time accepted	No
LSDAS accepted	Yes

FINANCIAL FACTS

Annual tuition (in-state/ out-of-state)	$6,373/$15,880
Books and supplies	$900
Fees	$2,837
Room & board	$8,600
Financial aid application deadline	4/15
% first-year students receiving some sort of aid	95
% receiving some sort of aid	92
% of aid that is merit based	1
% receiving scholarships	26
Average grant	$500
Average loan	$21,286
Average total aid package	$20,500
Average debt	$57,665

EMPLOYMENT INFORMATION

Career Rating	78	**Grads Employed by Field (%)**
Rate of placement (nine months out)	97	Academic (1)
Average starting salary	$53,100	Business/Industry (17)
State for bar exam	ND, MN, WI, NV, MO	Government (10)
Pass rate for first-time bar	90	Judicial Clerkships (22)
Employers Who Frequently Hire Grads		Private Practice (44)
Judicial systems of ND & MN; Private firms in ND and MN		Public Interest (6)
Prominent Alumni		
Earl Pomeroy, Congressman, ND; H.F. Gierke, Chief Justice, U.S. Armed Forces Court of Appeals; Kermit Bye, Judge, 8th Circuit Court of Appeals; Peter Pantaleo, DLA Piper, NY Managing Partner; Mary Maring, Justice, ND Supreme Court.		

UNIVERSITY OF NOTRE DAME

LAW SCHOOL

Academics

Notre Dame Law School provides "a sense of community that doesn't exist elsewhere," "strong traditions," and a "large network throughout the United States." Arguably its greatest asset, the alumni connection allows students to "go anywhere in the country and find someone who has a link to the school and, more importantly, who is willing to go out of his or her way to help out a fellow Domer." "The school takes its Catholic faith and heritage seriously, and a majority of the student body does as well. Don't come here expecting a watered-down Catholicism."

"Uniformly personable and approachable," "The professors are one of the best things about Notre Dame." "They've ranged from rising stars who have clerked in the Supreme Court, to veteran public officials who came to teaching after years in the Justice Department or White House." "Some of the professors here have a reputation of using the Socratic Method so efficiently [that] they often leave students arguing the opposite of their original point within seconds." However, one 2L observes, "'Conservative' jurisprudential views are more common among the faculty here than at other law schools, and they actually predominate in the student body, but this hasn't kept me from being exposed to a broad range of legal perspectives."

There is general consensus that the administration is disconnected from its students. Categorized by students as "infamously inflexible and unresponsive," "The higher up the administration chain, the less interested they seem to be in the welfare of the students," though in recent years, this has led the administration to make a commitment to improving responsiveness. A new dean took office in the summer of 2009.

Students say that their overall academic experience has been first rate but warn prospective students of the "very conservative nature of the student body." Others note that "there is a surprisingly large percentage of students who hold moderate to liberal views on socially divisive issues which is very refreshing and leads to great discussion in classes such as Con Law."

Although students previously registered significant complaints about the law school building, it is no longer in use. A new 85,000 square foot law building opened in January of 2009. The classrooms contain updated technology and more comfortable seats, with room for textbooks and laptops. The new building also contains a courtroom and a commons area. The renovation of the old law building will be completed in time for the start of the 2010-11 academic year, with a library and additional classroom space.

MELISSA FRUSCIONE, ACTING DIRECTOR OF ADMISSIONS AND FINANCIAL AID
NOTRE DAME LAW SCHOOL, 2180 ECK HALL OF LAW, NOTRE DAME, IN 46556
TEL: 574-631-6626 FAX: 574-631-5474
EMAIL: LAWADMIT@ND.EDU • WEBSITE: LAW.ND.EDU

Life

Students agree that "there isn't any of the unsavory competitiveness you might find in other places." In fact, "Most schools only say their students are non-cutthroat; here, the administration practically makes it mandatory. NDLS doesn't rank students, there is no forced curve, and OCI interviews are based off of a lottery system rather than class rank." "Plus the relatively small class size ensures that you know almost everyone in your class (if not the whole law school!) and that makes the whole experience very enjoyable."

"Thanks to Fightin' Irish football, Notre Dame may be the one law school where even a 1L can forget the pain of first year, if only for a few hours on Saturdays in the fall." "Most students participate in intramural sports like flag football and softball. Nearly all students participate in the springtime bowling league, which promises kegs of beer and tons of laughs." One student describes the makeup of the study body very simply: "There are two predominate social groups at NDLS: (1) single and fun loving, who frequent the handful of bars in South Bend and have fun doing so, and (2) married with children who have a great community of fellowship, babysitting arrangements, Bible studies, and general fun neighborhood-type activities." All in all, students are very close. One 3L concludes, "South Bend is not a particularly nice city, so Notre Dame students have to make their own fun [and] we do a pretty good job."

Getting In

Applicants are encouraged to take the LSAT in June, September/October or December in the year preceding enrollment, as doing so provides the advantage of receiving full consideration for fellowship assistance. Admitted students at the 25th percentile have an LSAT score of 163 and a GPA of 3.42. Admitted students at the 75th percentile have an LSAT score of 166 and a GPA of 3.78. It is NDLS policy to review the highest LSAT score when an applicant has taken the LSAT more than once within a five-year period.

Legal research course requirement	Yes
Moot court requirement	Yes
Public interest law requirement	No

ADMISSIONS

Selectivity Rating	**93**
# applications received	3,319
# applicants accepted	765
# acceptees attending	179
Average LSAT	166
LSAT Range	163–166
Average undergrad GPA	3.62
Application fee	$60
Regular application	Rolling, up to 3/15
Regular notification	Rolling
Early application program	Yes
Early application deadline	11/1
Early application notification	12/15
Transfer students accepted	Yes
Evening division offered	No
Part-time accepted	No
LSDAS accepted	Yes

Applicants Also Look At
Harvard University, Columbia University, University of Michigan—Ann Arbor, University of California—Berkeley, University of California—Los Angeles, Washington University, Boston University, Duke University

International Students

TOEFL required of international students	Yes

FINANCIAL FACTS

Annual tuition	$37,190
Books and supplies	$7,950
Fees	$460
Room & board (on/off-campus)	$8,300/$8,300
Financial aid application deadline	2/15
% of aid that is merit based	95
Average debt	$83,200

EMPLOYMENT INFORMATION

Career Rating	**94**	**Grads Employed by Field (%)**
Rate of placement (9 months out)	98.7	Private Practice (5)
Average starting salary	$127,919	Judicial Clerkships (14)
State for bar exam	IL, NY, IN, CA, VA	Government (7)
Pass rate for first-time bar	91.28	Public Interest (6)
Employers Who Frequently Hire Grads		Business/Industry (5)
Major law firms in locations throughout the country and abroad: federal circuit and district judges; state judges at all levels, government agencies, corporations and public interest organizations.		Military (4)
		Other (2)
		Academic (1)

UNIVERSITY OF OKLAHOMA
COLLEGE OF LAW

INSTITUTIONAL INFORMATION

Public/private	Public
Student-faculty ratio	8:1
% faculty part-time	19
% faculty female	23
% faculty minority	10
Total faculty	66

SURVEY SAYS...

Great research resources
Great library staff
Beautiful campus

STUDENTS

Enrollment of law school	517
% male/female	56/44
% out-of-state	25
% full-time	100
% minority	22
# of countries represented	3
Average age of entering class	24

ACADEMICS

Academic Experience Rating	**83**
Profs interesting rating	73
Profs accessible rating	80
Hours of study per day	3.5

Academic Specialties

Civil procedure, commercial law, constitutional law, corporation securities, criminal law, environmental law, international law, labor law, property, taxation, intellectual property law, Native American law, oil and gas law

Advanced Degrees Offered

None

Combined Degrees Offered

JD/MBA, 4 years; JD/MPH, 4 years; JD/Generic Dual Degree, 4 years

Clinical program required	No
Legal writing	
course requirement	Yes
Legal methods	
course requirement	No
Legal research	
course requirement	Yes
Moot court requirement	Yes

Academics

"An incredible, first-class facility" is one of the most appealing aspects of the University of Oklahoma College of Law. Chief new features of the remodeled law school building include: "A new library and a new state-of-the-art courtroom, which has brought several appellate courts, including the *en banc* Tenth Circuit, to hold hearings at OU, video conferencing capabilities in the classrooms [that] make distance learning from specialized lawyers possible, in-house clinical facilities, and a designated lab for writing and research." The recent expansion and renovation is just the tip of the iceberg. According to one student, "The administration is committed to shaking down the alumni to continue to build up OU's facilities as well as its scholarship fund."

Posh surroundings might make the school a comfortable place to study, but its professors are what garner the most unequivocal student praise. These dedicated professionals are both knowledgeable and accessible: they're "always wandering the halls talking to students outside of class." It's worth noting that OU students describe their law professors in terms seldom (if ever) uttered about any law professor anywhere: Namely, "Our professors are so cool." One first-year student reports that his professors for constitutional law and torts "both play in bands"—one "actually invited our section to come and hear his jazz band play, and they were good." Savvy recruitment has something to do with the presence of such uncommon law professors. "As far as the professors go we have some hidden gems at our law school, which in large part is due to our Dean, Andrew Coats. We have brought in some incredible professors, especially bright and engaging women," a contingent one student sees missing at other schools. The addition of these "new, young professors in the past few years has been an invaluable addition to the school, providing instruction from varied backgrounds from throughout the country." Students can easily get to know these brilliant young minds because "Small sections provide very good access to faculty." The administration earns equally high marks: administrators are "open to suggestions by students who wish to begin new programs or expand the curriculum in a new direction. Innovation, enthusiasm, and activism by the student body is both encouraged and appreciated."

As far as career planning goes, student opinion is divided. While some think that "our Career Services Office could be better funded in order to assist the students in finding the best career, not just a job," others contend that the "College of Law offers outstanding career opportunities within the Midwest and Southwest, but...is only slowly gaining the national prominence needed to place well outside of these regions."

The administration has responded to these student concerns by replacing the prior career services director, doubling the size of the placement staff, developing new support services, and changing the name to the office of Professional Career Development.

KATHIE G. MADDEN, ADMISSIONS COORDINATOR
ANDREW M. COATS HALL, 300 TIMBERDELL ROAD, NORMAN, OK 73019
TEL: 405-325-4728 FAX: 405-325-0502
EMAIL: KMADDEN@OU.EDU • WEBSITE: WWW.LAW.OU.EDU

Life

While small size might be a boon to students in the classroom, it can be a bit of a problem outside of it. At OU "The student body is so small and spends so much time around each other that we often morph into high school students, including the rumor mill." This cliquishness "can be disappointing to see in aspiring professionals, but also teaches you to watch your step and remember that your colleagues are going to be observing your actions [when] forming their opinions of you." Unlike many law school student bodies, "OU's student community encourages us to work hard and excel, but doesn't have the issues with 'gunner' students who will do anything to succeed." Most students agree that "the student body on the whole possesses the proper balance between commitment to academic excellence and being a normal well-rounded person with a life outside of law school." Politically, "The student population is somewhat conservative," but "The classrooms are full of debate, and everyone is treated fairly."

There are "lots of clubs" at OU and "student organization participation is excellent." "There is never a shortage of social events hosted by someone affiliated with the law school," and the "Halloween party" and "Law School Prom" are popular events. Off-campus entertainment options are also plentiful, as the school is within easy reach of Oklahoma City.

Getting In

Admission to OU is "highly competitive," with just over a quarter of applicants accepted. The average GPA of accepted students last year was 3.51, and the average LSAT score was 157. Both GPA and LSAT score are large factors in admissions, but so are personal statements and letters of recommendation. The school's website states that "in addition to giving considerable weight to the LSAT and undergraduate grade point average, the Admissions Committee also examines the other more personal variables of motivation, character, and capability. Insight into these variables can be derived from a careful examination of your resume, personal statement, and other contents in the file."

Public interest law requirement	No

ADMISSIONS

Selectivity Rating	84
# applications received	1,137
% applicants accepted	29
% acceptees attending	54
Average LSAT	157
LSAT Range	154–160
Average undergrad GPA	3.54
Application fee	$50
Regular application	Rolling, up to 3/15
Regular notification	Rolling
Early application program	No
Transfer students accepted	Yes
Evening division offered	No
Part-time accepted	No
LSDAS accepted	Yes

Applicants Also Look At

University of Texas at Austin, Texas Tech University, Baylor University, Oklahoma City University, Southern Methodist University, University of Tulsa, Texas Wesleyan University

FINANCIAL FACTS

Annual tuition (in-state/ out-of-state)	$17,218/$22,147
Books and supplies	$950
Fees	$4,459
Room & board	$16,724
Financial aid application deadline	3/1
% first-year students receiving some sort of aid	88
% receiving some sort of aid	84
% of aid that is merit based	60
% receiving scholarships	68
Average loan	$23,757
Average total aid package	$20,500
Average debt	$71,271

EMPLOYMENT INFORMATION

Career Rating	77	Grads Employed by Field (%)
Rate of placement (nine months out)	96	Academic (3)
Average starting salary	$60,500	Business/Industry (14)
State for bar exam	OK, TX, CO, MO, KS	Government (20)
Pass rate for first-time bar	97	Judicial Clerkships (3)

Employers Who Frequently Hire Grads

Military (1)

McAfee & Taft; Crowe & Dunlevy; Conner & Winters; Gable & Gotwals; Hall, Estill, Hardwick, Gable & Nelson; Phillips & Murrah.

Private Practice (57)

Public Interest (2)

Prominent Alumni

Frank Keating, Former Gov. of Oklahoma; David L. Boren, Pres. of OU (Former U. S. Senator); William T. Comfort, Pres. CitiCorp Venture Capital.

UNIVERSITY OF OREGON
SCHOOL OF LAW

INSTITUTIONAL INFORMATION

Public/private	Public
Student-faculty ratio	9:1
% faculty part-time	42
% faculty female	53
% faculty minority	5.3
Total faculty	57

SURVEY SAYS...

Great research resources
Liberal students
Beautiful campus

STUDENTS

Enrollment of law school	531
% male/female	57/43
% out-of-state	60
% full-time	100
% minority	19
# of countries represented	2
Average age of entering class	25

ACADEMICS

Academic Experience Rating	**83**
Profs interesting rating	81
Profs accessible rating	89
Hours of study per day	4.85

Academic Specialties

Civil procedure, commercial law, constitutional law, corporation securities, criminal law, environmental law, government services, human rights, international law, property, taxation, intellectual property law

Advanced Degrees Offered

JD/MS (conflict and dispute resolution), LLM (Environmental and Natural Resources)

Combined Degrees Offered

JD/MBA Business & Law; JD/MA or JD/MS Environmental Studies; JD/MA International Studies; JD/MA or JD/MS Conflict & Dispute Resolution.

Clinical program required	No
Legal writing	
course requirement	Yes
Legal methods	
course requirement	No

Academics

The University of Oregon School of Law offers a "diverse" and "amazing" array of opportunities "to see what practice is like before getting out into the field." The school has "a strong pro bono and public interest program." It's also a "great school" for ocean and coastal or environmental law. Students in the "fantastic" clinics get a chance to help to advance cutting-edge and previously untested legal theories. Every year, the Public Interest Environmental Law Conference is "an unbelievable mash-up of activists and public interest attorneys." The Center for Law and Entrepreneurship works to "integrate the Portland campus into business law study." A litany of other clinics is available as well. Despite the breadth of hands-on opportunities, students gripe that UO Law could "offer a few more practical courses" and "use a bit more diversity in the classes offered."

"The course work is challenging" but the "intelligent and often quirky" professors are "supportive and enthusiastic." "They have high expectations while demonstrating genuine interest in students," reports one student. "The business law professors are fantastic," although "A couple of professors are extremely confusing and hard to follow." Nearly all professors here are "excellent teachers." "Overall, I'd say B-plus," assesses a 3L. "Stimulating class discussions about a wide variety of topics" are the norm. Also, "the entire faculty" is "very approachable outside of class" and "willing to help." "Oregon is probably one of the most liberal schools" anywhere and some note that "the liberal bias in the faculty is rather extreme"—a good or bad thing depending on your perspective. The "friendly" and "helpful" administration is also "very approachable" and "singularly focused on making law school the smoothest experience possible for the students." However, registration "is a work in progress." "The course scheduling" is "routinely disappointing," and "popular classes" are "too small."

UO grads face a highly competitive local job market. Some students find that "it is harder to find a job in Oregon than elsewhere" since Portland is "a desirable place to live," and the big Portland firms can "easily" import new attorneys from other states. Also, "A lot of students come here thinking they will return to their home state, but end up wanting to stay." "Opportunities for jobs and externships are particularly limited" in the surrounding college town of Eugene. "Our removed location makes it more difficult to network in other areas of Oregon," advises a 3L. "Many students need to relocate during the summers or commute during the school year for the better jobs."

The "new" building here is "gorgeous" and "very well designed," "allow[ing] for lots of light." "Students enjoy spending time at the school and the common area acts as a social meeting place," says one student. The facility is "super wired" and generally "a great place to have classes." "State-of-the-art" classrooms provide "the ability to do multimedia presentations." A student explains, "Many faculty members have added multimedia aspects to class to enhance lessons, aid understanding, and even entertain. (One professor shows clips of *The Simpsons* and *Saturday Night Live* to illustrate the rules of evidence)."

Life

UO Law is "small," and students appreciate the "congenial atmosphere." "The school has the feel of a small community within the larger UO campus," notes one student. The student body is "fun but serious, and many are committed to making positive social change through the law." There are "lots of very active minority student groups," and "Lots of students are California transplants." "There certainly is a competitive environment but in a good way" due to the "strong feeling of getting through this together rather

LAWRENCE SENO, JR., ASSISTANT DEAN OF ADMISSIONS
1221 UNIVERSITY OF OREGON, EUGENE, OR 97403-1221
TEL: 541-346-3846 FAX: 541-346-3984
EMAIL: ADMISSIONS@LAW.UOREGON.EDU • WEBSITE: WWW.LAW.UOREGON.EDU

than competing against one another." What's more is that "even the most alpha and turbo students can't help but be calmed by the surrounding community's hippie culture." "The cooperative spirit among the students is pretty amazing," says an awed 2L. "When you need to miss class, students are very happy to provide notes or to pass along outlines or answer questions."

"Student groups are very active on campus," but life "behind the Granola Curtain" in "very small" Eugene, Oregon is "laid-back." There are "cultural activities" and "big-name music performances throughout the year," but "Eugene is not a glamorous town." "Don't come here if you are looking for a cosmopolitan experience," warns one student. However, "The great thing about Oregon is there are several ways to disconnect yourself from the inherent stress." While "It would be fair to classify UO as a 'party law school,'" students here "are very outgoing, and there's always something you could do on any night of the week." "Most social events include alcohol, and UO students are serious about fitting in time for social gatherings." Also, the "geographically breathtaking location" affords "biking trails, hills to climb, [and] outdoor activities galore."

Getting In

When applying to a strong law program located in a gorgeous setting, expect some competition. Oregon's admitted students at the 25th percentile have LSAT scores of 157 and GPAs of 3.08. Admitted students at the 75th percentile have LSAT scores of 161 and GPAs of 3.63.

Legal research course requirement	Yes
Moot court requirement	No
Public interest law requirement	No

ADMISSIONS

Selectivity Rating	**79**
# applications received	2,128
# applicants accepted	855
# acceptees attending	183
Average LSAT	158
LSAT Range	157–160
Average undergrad GPA	3.4
Application fee	$50
Regular application	Rolling, up to 3/1
Regular notification	Rolling
Early application program	No
Transfer students accepted	Yes
Evening division offered	No
Part-time accepted	No
LSDAS accepted	Yes

Applicants Also Look At

University of Colorado at Boulder; University of Denver; Seattle University; University of Washington; Lewis & Clark College; Willamette University; University of California, Hastings

International Students

TOEFL required of international students	Yes
Minimum TOEFL (paper/computer)	600/250

FINANCIAL FACTS

Annual tuition (in-state/ out-of-state)	$18,954/$23,994
Books and supplies	$1,600
Fees	$1,616
Room & board (off-campus)	$8,235
Financial aid application deadline	3/1
% first-year students receiving some sort of aid	93
% receiving some sort of aid	92
% of aid that is merit based	10
% receiving scholarships	42.9
Average grant	$6,463
Average loan	$27,871
Average total aid package	$29,932
Average debt	$70,811

EMPLOYMENT INFORMATION

Career Rating	74	**Grads Employed by Field (%)**
Rate of placement (nine months out)	91	Academic (2)
Average starting salary	$60,592	Business/Industry (8)
State for bar exam	OR, CA, WA, NV, UT	Government (15)
Pass rate for first-time bar	85	Judicial Clerkships (16)

Employers Who Frequently Hire Grads
Law firms from Portland, Eugene (OR), Seattle, San Francisco and Los Angeles areas.

Military (1)
Private Practice (49)
Public Interest (9)

Prominent Alumni
Ron Wyden, U.S. Senator; Alfred T. Goodwin, Former Chief Judge, U.S. Ct. of Appeals, Ninth Cir.; Jim Carter, VP & General Counsel, Nike; Mathew McKnown, Acting Asst. Atty. Gen., Environmental & Natural Resources; Katherine Gurun, Former VP of General Counsel, Bechtel.

UNIVERSITY OF THE PACIFIC
MCGEORGE SCHOOL OF LAW

Academics

Students agree that one of the best things about Pacific McGeorge School of Law is the fact that it is a stand-alone law school, meaning "every person and building on the 13-acre campus is dedicated to nothing other than the study of law." Though Pacific McGeorge is part of the University of the Pacific in Stockton, CA, the law school is self-contained in the heart of state capital Sacramento, CA. This "student-centered environment" stresses academics while simultaneously making known the importance of being "well-rounded and not as stressed out." "It's a communal learning experience, which is just what I was hoping for," says a 1L. Though students do wish for a bit more focus on practical lawyering skills within the classroom, the clinics and internship/externship possibilities provide "practical, hands-on experience to what would otherwise be a very expensive bar prep course." The year-long core classes during the first year make the learning experience much more in-depth, and allow students a chance to succeed. "It works out to be great because you get two sets of exams, instead of your grade riding on one set of exams. It takes a little bit of the first year pressure off," says one student. The advocacy program is strong and nearly every course incorporates an international aspect. It should say something that the main grievance here is that the school does not get the recognition it deserves.

"As students, we often feel as if the administration is 'against' us, but this is not necessarily the case here. For example, the administration voluntarily rescheduled a huge summer construction project around [bar] review lectures." says a student. The "efficiency, promptness, accuracy, and student-focus" with which the administration runs the school makes law school more enjoyable for all that go here. Professors make themselves available anytime you need to meet with them ("most even give out their phone numbers allowing them to be reached at anytime"), and will explain concepts to you one-on-one or "just provide moral support." "I cannot imagine going through this traumatic experience anywhere else with less supportive teachers," says a 1L. Furthermore, the professors find interesting and unique ways to help us learn and retain the information needed: "videos, props and costumes are just a few examples." Though many report their first year as being a bit scary, everyone who survived till their second year report that as long as you swim instead of sink, Pacific McGeorge will take care of you after that.

The school has an excellent writing curriculum; while it gets "frustrating" spending the first year in Legal Process writing three memos, then another two memos and a brief in Appellate and International Advocacy, students "are much more confident in their summer jobs and externships, and local firms and government agencies seem to always be pleased with Pacific McGeorge students' research and writing abilities." The campus is small, but "clean and friendly," and the facilities are excellent. The library "has every source imaginable (and some that aren't imaginable)" to help with research and locating the applicable law.

ADAM W. BARRETT, DEAN OF ADMISSIONS
3200 FIFTH AVENUE, SACRAMENTO, CA 95817
TEL: 916-739-7105 FAX: 916-739-7301
EMAIL: ADMISSIONSMCGEORGE@PACIFIC.EDU • WEBSITE: WWW.MCGEORGE.EDU

Life

Although there's some competition, overall the student body is "like a big, stressed-out family," and second, third and fourth year students are "always willing to help and give advice to the first year students." Students are incredibly friendly and get along well with each other, and are happy to help bolster a fellow student in need. Affirmative action is somewhat big Pacific McGeorge, and the diversity of the student body reflects this. The school "encourages students to seek out activities which balance the rigors and stress of study/school life with real life." There are sporadic social events scattered throughout the year, plenty of student organizations, and whole classes get together on Fridays to socialize at a bar in order to get out of the law school environment. But it's the first year classes that are probably the biggest bonding mechanism, and "the friends and connections you make the first year tend to carry through your law school experience." "Usually our camaraderie results from enduring the same intellectual boot camp together," says a student. While the exact location is not considered one of the most appealing areas of Sacramento, the campus itself is beautiful, and security keeps it perfectly safe.

Getting In

At Pacific McGeorge, the most important factors in an admissions decision are a student's previous academic record, LSAT scores, graduate school or post-college career experience, and community service or extracurricular activities. Pacific McGeorge also looks for students who might add a diversity of background or perspective to the campus community.

Legal research course requirement	Yes
Moot court requirement	Yes
Public interest law requirement	No

ADMISSIONS

Selectivity Rating	**78**
# applications received	2,627
# applicants accepted	1,085
# acceptees attending	1227
Average LSAT	158
LSAT Range	156–159
Average undergrad GPA	3.31
Application fee	$50
Regular application	Rolling, up to June
Regular notification	Rolling
Early application program	No
Transfer students accepted	Yes
Evening division offered	Yes
Part-time accepted	Yes
LSDAS accepted	Yes

Applicants Also Look At

University of California—Berkeley; University of California, Davis; Loyola Marymount University; University of San Francisco; Santa Clara University; University of California, Hastings

International Students

TOEFL required of international students	Yes
Minimum TOEFL (paper/computer)	600/250

FINANCIAL FACTS

Annual tuition	$36,544
Books and supplies	$1,300
Fees	$73
Tuition per credit	$1,236
Room & board	$19,094
% first-year students receiving some sort of aid	97
% receiving some sort of aid	96
% of aid that is merit based	68
% receiving scholarships	57
Average grant	$10,000
Average loan	$38,904
Average total aid package	$38,904
Average debt	$115,191

EMPLOYMENT INFORMATION

Career Rating	**72**
Rate of placement (nine months out)	95.5
Average starting salary	$72,181
State for bar exam	CA, NV, HI, OR, DC
Pass rate for first-time bar	81

Employers Who Frequently Hire Grads
National and California law firms, Federal and California State Agencies, Sacramento County DA + PD

Prominent Alumni
Scott Boras, Sports Agent/Baseball; Bill Lockyer, State Treasurer/CA Gvt; Steve Martini, Novelist; Johnnie Rawlinson, U.S. 9th Circuit Court of Appeals; Consuelo M. Callahan, U.S. 9th Circuit Court of Appeals.

Grads Employed by Field (%)
Academic (3)
Business/Industry (9)
Government (25)
Judicial Clerkships (3)
Private Practice (50)
Public Interest (9)

UNIVERSITY OF PENNSYLVANIA
LAW SCHOOL

INSTITUTIONAL INFORMATION

Public/private	Private
Student-faculty ratio	11:1
% faculty part-time	33
% faculty female	28
% faculty minority	14
Total faculty	103

SURVEY SAYS...
Great research resources
Abundant externship/internship/
clerkship opportunities

STUDENTS

Enrollment of law school	786
% male/female	53/47
% out-of-state	89
% full-time	100
% minority	35
% international	3
# of countries represented	20
Average age of entering class	24

ACADEMICS

Academic Experience Rating	**95**
Profs interesting rating	88
Profs accessible rating	80
Hours of study per day	4.33

Academic Specialties
Civil procedure, commercial law,
constitutional law, corporation securities, criminal law, environmental
law, government services, human
rights, international law, labor law,
legal history, legal philosophy, property, taxation, intellectual property
law

Advanced Degrees Offered
JD, 3 years; LL.M., 1 year; S.JD, 1+
year; LL.C.M., 1 year.

Clinical program required	No
Legal writing course requirement	Yes
Legal methods course requirement	Yes
Legal research course requirement	Yes
Moot court requirement	No

Academics

The University of Pennsylvania attracts the big legal names you would expect to find at an Ivy League school; however, it is also a true teaching college, where classroom excellence is taken seriously. You won't sleep through any dry lectures at Penn. The Socratic Method will keep you on your toes, and "Most of the professors are great teachers and make class fun." How fun can law school be? A current student insists, "It feels more like I'm going to see a stand-up comedian than a law professor at some points." Penn's teaching staff excels at being both "ridiculously accomplished and truly happy to have a lot of student interaction." Outside the classroom, "Professors are available to meet with students, and it is tradition for all 1Ls to have lunch with their professors at some point during the semester." Guiding their students professionally, personally, and academically, professors "teach us more than legal scholarship; they elevate us from disorganized, arrogant, first-year students into fine, sophisticated, and yet tough advocates."

In addition to the prestige carried by Penn's well-established name, law students benefit from their association with the university in other ways. Adding uniqueness and depth to their JD, "Most students take law-related classes at some of Penn's other graduate schools." For those with a specific academic interest, the school offers "a series of 'certificate' programs offered in conjunction with other schools, including a certificate from the Wharton School of Business and a certificate in Politics from the Fels Institute of Government." Certificates are also available in environmental studies, Middle East and Islamic Studies, women's studies, and international and business law (with ESADE in Barcelona, Spain). Students further augment traditional legal course work by participating in the school's legal journals and clinics, including the Interdisciplinary Child Advocacy Clinic, the Entrepreneurship Legal Clinic, and the Legislative Clinic. The only gripe that many Penn students express is with the first-year legal writing program. While some report positive experiences, many complain that the program is of poor quality and "instructed by third-year law students that often don't have a lot of real-world experience outside of the summer clerking opportunities."

Penn's administration receives gold stars for friendliness, effectiveness, and accessibility. Highly responsive to student concerns, "If you ever have a problem with anything, relate it to an administrator and expect to have it either fixed or about to be fixed." In particular, "The Associate Dean of Student Affairs is a much-loved character around the law school and is the highly accessible 'point man' for anyone and everyone's problems." This friendly attitude permeates campus, and students likewise promote a supportive and noncompetitive atmosphere. "A common phrase around the law school is 'feel the love,' because you do. The students here are a very cooperative, social bunch," insists a 1L. Students surmise that the non-competitive attitude is partially due to the fact that "there is no ranking and no formal GPA at Penn," so students aren't pitted against each other to win choice jobs. On the contrary, "Students freely share notes and study together for finals." When it's time to consider life after graduation, "The school has an incredible Career Services Program," and "Everyone gets a top-tier job. Everyone." On the other hand, those looking for public interest or judicial internships find their desires slightly suffocated in this "pre-professional wonderland."

RENEE POST, ASSOCIATE DEAN, ADMISSIONS AND FINANCIAL AID
3400 CHESTNUT STREET, PHILADELPHIA, PA 19104-6204
TEL: 215-898-7400 FAX: 215-898-9606
EMAIL: ADMISSIONS@LAW.UPENN.EDU • WEBSITE: WWW.LAW.UPENN.EDU

Life

Penn promotes a well-balanced lifestyle, attracting students who "want to enjoy their time at law school as well as get an excellent education." Campus is a hub of activity, and "The central courtyard really pulls the school together, especially when there are kegs out there." After class, "People spend hours hanging out at school, chatting and doing crossword puzzles." As they spend many hours confined to such close quarters, students admit, "Sometimes it's tiring to hang out with only law students, and a small community of law students at that. Penn Law doesn't do much to encourage mingling with other grad schools at Penn." However, the vast majority of Penn students feel that "law school is a social paradise—there is always plenty to drink and plenty people willing to drink with you!" Indeed, "There is almost always a law school group holding an event or happy hour on any given weekend (except for maybe finals)—the school encourages students to get away from studying and have a real life."

Penn students enjoy the school environment, telling us "Philadelphia can be 'gritty,' but there is a lot to do in the city, and the campus itself is clean and safe." Students also mention, "Philadelphia is now attracting more and more grad students and young professionals. If hanging out with other law students isn't your thing, there are plenty of people around; you just have to find them yourself."

Getting In

Last year, the University of Pennsylvania received more than 5,800 applications for an entering class of 250 students. The entering class had a median LSAT score of 170 and a median GPA of 3.8. Penn evaluates an applicant's entire academic history, including grade trends and rigor of course work. The Admissions Committee also evaluates a candidate's writing ability, as well as leadership experience, personal background, and achievements.

Public interest law requirement	Yes

ADMISSIONS

Selectivity Rating	98
# applications received	5,811
# applicants accepted	957
# acceptees attending	250
Average LSAT	170
LSAT Range	166–171
Average undergrad GPA	3.8
Application fee	$75
Regular application	Rolling
Regular notification	Rolling
Early application program	Yes
Early application deadline	11/1
Early application notification	12/31
Transfer students accepted	Yes
Evening division offered	No
Part-time accepted	No
LSDAS accepted	Yes

Applicants Also Look At
Harvard University, Yale University, Columbia University, University of Michigan—Ann Arbor, University of California, Berkeley, New York University, University of Chicago, Stanford University, Georgetown University

FINANCIAL FACTS

Annual tuition	$43,680
Books and supplies	$6,422
Fees	$2,834
Room & board	$12,090
Financial aid application deadline	3/1
% first-year students receiving some sort of aid	81
% receiving some sort of aid	77
% of aid that is merit based	77
% receiving scholarships	44
Average grant	$15,302
Average loan	$40,334
Average total aid package	$55,636
Average debt	$100,901

EMPLOYMENT INFORMATION

Career Rating	97
Rate of placement (nine months out)	99
Average starting salary	$135,100
State for bar exam	NY
Pass rate for first-time bar	93

Employers Who Frequently Hire Grads
Variety of Major Corporate Law Firms Nationwide; Prestigious National Fellowship Organizations and Public Interest Organizations; Federal and State Judges

Grads Employed by Field (%)
Business/Industry (4)
Government (1)
Judicial clerkships (13)
Other (1)
Private practice (79)
Public Interest (2)

UNIVERSITY OF PITTSBURGH
SCHOOL OF LAW

INSTITUTIONAL INFORMATION
Public/private	Public
Student-faculty ratio	13:1
% faculty part-time	62.16
% faculty female	33.78
% faculty minority	5.41
Total faculty	148

SURVEY SAYS...
Diverse opinions accepted
in classrooms
Great library staff

STUDENTS
Enrollment of law school	710
% male/female	56/44
% out-of-state	40
% full-time	100
% minority	18
% international	2
# of countries represented	5
Average age of entering class	24

ACADEMICS
Academic Experience Rating	**75**
Profs interesting rating	74
Profs accessible rating	77
Hours of study per day	4.08

Academic Specialties
Civil procedure, corporation securities, environmental law, international law, taxation, intellectual property law, health law

Advanced Degrees Offered
Master of Laws LL.M for foreign-trained attorneys.

Combined Degrees Offered
JD/MPA, 4 years; JD/MPIA, 4 years; JD/MBA, 3 1/2 years; JD/MPH, 3 1/2 years; JD/MA, Medical Ethics, 3 1/2 years; JD/MS, Public Management, 4 years; JD/MSW, 4 years.

Clinical program required	No
Legal writing course requirement	Yes
Legal methods course requirement	No

Academics

The "underrated" University of Pittsburgh School of Law has "a very good position in the Pittsburgh community" and features a "very strong" faculty. "Legal theory" is here, of course, and so is "real-world application." But there is also "a great deal of emphasis on practical skills such as legal writing, oral arguments, and externships." "Many strong clinical programs" include a tax clinic and a civil practice clinic that focuses on both health law and elder law. A host of "fantastic" certificate programs includes civil litigation and intellectual property. Students interested in international law will find "a strong and effective emphasis" on this area through study abroad opportunities, internships, and classes." There's also Jurist, a very comprehensive legal news and research online service run exclusively by faculty and staff. Pitt's Laws new program in Law Entrepreneurship will provide a range of opportunities for students in counselling entrepreneurs or in becoming and entrepreneur.

Pitt has "a number of highly energetic, brilliant, [and] helpful" professors. "Some members of the faculty are absolutely astounding," and several adjunct professors "are really impressive." "Many of our professors are active practitioners in the fields that they teach, giving students opportunities to participate in ongoing cases and to hear about the issues that are most pressing in the field at that moment," adds a 2L. However, "There are some truly awful professors here too." One student notes that the "younger ones tend to be better." Ultimately though, "almost all" of the professors are "very friendly" and "exceedingly accessible" outside of class.

Many students say that "aesthetically, Pitt could use an upgrade." The Law School building "sits right in the middle" of Pitt's "urban" campus. While the building "certainly isn't beautiful," one student says, "it isn't as bad as everyone likes to pretend." A 1L offers, "The building as a whole reminds me of a 1970s fort." Classrooms are "laptop friendly" but "can be quite uncomfortable and acoustically flawed."

Students would love to see course registration go "online." Many students tell us that "the administration is incredibly frustrating" and "often seems adrift." They say there is too much "needless bureaucracy." Other students have had a very different experience. They contend that the administration is "open and responsive to student concerns." "The school is small enough that you can get to know someone in the Registrar's Office, Career Services, and the Dean's Office," claims a satisfied 3L. Speaking of Career Services, it "still gets mixed reviews," but students report that "they are working hard at reaching out." Students also say that Pitt is "strong" regionally. If you want to practice law in Pennsylvania or in Washington, D.C., "good job opportunities" are abundant, and the alumni network is solid. Students in their second or third year can also receive a semster's worth of academic credit for working as an extern or government agency or non profit in D.C.

Life

Students confide that Western Pennsylvania is "not the most diverse school in the world"; however, the campus has a "clear liberal bent" politically. Many here say that Pitt is "a warm, friendly place to learn." "Even during the first year," one student says, "Students at the school are generally pretty laid-back, friendly, and non-competitive." On the other hand, some find that "people are normal on the outside and freaking out on the inside." "I was really, really surprised at how friendly other students are," gushes a 1L. "If I miss a class I never have a problem getting notes from someone, and students tend to help each other out with research questions."

CHARMAINE C. McCALL, ASSISTANT DEAN FOR ADMISSIONS AND FINANCIAL AID
3900 FORBES AVENUE, PITTSBURGH, PA 15260
TEL: 412-648-1413 FAX: 412-648-1318
EMAIL: ADMITLAW@PITT.EDU • WEBSITE: WWW.LAW.PITT.EDU

Outside of class, "There is a great social scene," and "Making friends is fairly easy." The Student Bar Association sponsors "a lot of social events." The 'Burgh is "a cheap city with lots of cultural activities" and it is perennially rated among the best cities in the United States in which to live and work. "Pittsburgh is far more beautiful than people who have never been here would imagine," promises a 1L. There are good bars "right across the street from the law school." "There is tons of cheap...housing within walking distance," and "nicer housing" is only "a bus ride away." With your Pitt ID you can ride the buses for free (If you drive, though, students warn that "parking is a nightmare.") "You absolutely need a car," because many places you'll have to go "are all 15 miles away from each other." But for those that are still unsure, one student suggests: "Drive up Mt. Washington and look down on the Pittsburgh skyline and the rivers, and you'll be convinced."

Getting In

Admitted students at the 25th percentile have LSAT scores of roughly 158 and GPAs of 3.1. Admitted students at the 75th percentile have LSAT scores of about 161 and GPAs of just over 3.6. Pitt's administration says that it will consider your highest score if you take the LSAT multiple times. Decisions are based on many factors, and the admissions committee prefers online applications through LSAL starting September 1 through March 1. Applications are considered for only the current year for the Full Semester.

Legal research	
course requirement	Yes
Moot court requirement	No
Public interest	
law requirement	No

ADMISSIONS

Selectivity Rating	**81**
# applications received	2,113
# applicants accepted	781
# acceptees attending	242
Average LSAT	159
LSAT Range	157–161
Average undergrad GPA	3.4
Application fee	$55
Regular application	Rolling, up to 3/1
Regular notification	Rolling
Early application program	Yes
Transfer students accepted	Yes
Evening division offered	No
Part-time accepted	No
LSDAS accepted	Yes

Applicants Also Look At

Temple University, American University, University of Pennsylvania, Villanova University, Case Western Reserve University, The George Washington University, University of Maryland—Baltimore

International Students

TOEFL required	
of international students	Yes
Minimum TOEFL	
(paper/computer)	600/250

FINANCIAL FACTS

Annual tuition (in-state/ out-of-state)	$23,432/$31,576
Books and supplies	$1,500
Fees	$730
Room & board	$14,546
Financial aid application deadline	3/1
% first-year students receiving some sort of aid	85
% receiving some sort of aid	85
% of aid that is merit based	27
% receiving scholarships	46
Average grant	$10,000
Average loan	$22,680
Average debt	$74,738

EMPLOYMENT INFORMATION

Career Rating	**82**	**Grads Employed by Field (%)**
Rate of placement (nine months out)	93.4	Academic (2)
Average starting salary	$85,734	Business/Industry (20)
State for bar exam	PA, VA, MD, NY, CA	Government (5)
Pass rate for first-time bar	91.5	Judicial clerkships (12)

Employers Who Frequently Hire Grads
Buchanan Ingersoll & Rooney; K&L Gates; Reed Smith,; Morgan, Lewis & Bockius; Jones Day; Pepper Hamilton; Eckert Seamans; Vorys Sater Seymour & Pease.

Military (2)
Private practice (56)
Public Interest (3)

Prominent Alumni
Richard Thornburg, Former U.S. Attorney General; Orrin Hatch, Senator,Utah; Joseph Weis, Senior Judge for the Third Circut.

UNIVERSITY OF RICHMOND
SCHOOL OF LAW

INSTITUTIONAL INFORMATION

Public/private	Private
Student-faculty ratio	14:1
% faculty part-time	63
% faculty female	40
% faculty minority	7
Total faculty	124

SURVEY SAYS...
Beautiful campus
Students love Richmond, VA

STUDENTS

Enrollment of law school	477
% male/female	53/47
% out-of-state	53
% full-time	100
% minority	10
# of countries represented	10
Average age of entering class	24

ACADEMICS

Academic Experience Rating	87
Profs interesting rating	80
Profs accessible rating	85
Hours of study per day	4.42

Academic Specialties
Civil procedure, commercial law, constitutional law, corporation securities, criminal law, environmental law, international law, labor law, legal history, property, taxation, intellectual property law

Advanced Degrees Offered
JD, 3 years

Combined Degrees Offered
JD/MBA; JD/MURP (Masters in Urban Planning): JD/MHA (Masters in Health Administration): JD/MSW (Social Work); JD/ MPA (Masters in Public Administration); each 4 years.

Clinical program required	No
Legal writing course requirement	Yes
Legal methods course requirement	Yes

Academics

Those looking to receive a first-rate law education while enjoying "Southern hospitality at its finest" would be wise to look into University of Richmond School of Law, where students say "The open dialogue among students and between students and professors is truly special." By all accounts, a "very friendly," "almost family-like" atmosphere prevails at this small school. "It amazes me that I'm able to walk down the hallway and have even professors whose classes I have not taken greet me by name," a satisfied 3L writes. The "well-educated, well-published" faculty members here are "dedicated to bettering their students and compassionate to their needs as individuals." The majority of professors "offer their home numbers and cell phone numbers so that we can call whenever we need help, or even just a little advice."

Professorial love is of the tough variety in the classroom, where students say "the use of the Socratic Method" "can be a bit intimidating," particularly for first-year students, though "It makes class entertaining and ensures that you are prepared," a 1L offers. All students here go through "an outstanding lawyering skills program. During these courses, our legal writing and actual courtroom skills are emphasized in very precise, methodical ways," a 2L writes. If students run into academic difficulties, they can take advantage of Richmond's Academic Success Program, which provides a full-time faculty member to assist students with their course work. The downside to the school's small size is "limited course selection," and "only one section" of most upper-level classes each semester. To expand its offerings, the School of Law partners with other schools within the University of Richmond—for example, the Robins School of Business and the Jepson School of Leadership Studies—to offer students a "diversity of dual degrees" which allows students "to really focus on particular fields of interest."

Richmond enjoys "a tremendous reputation in the Commonwealth of Virginia" and students believe that "the fact that there are so many opportunities for legal experience in Richmond," the state capital, "is a great strength" of the school. "We have access to county, state, and district courts and often have lectures and course[s] taught by Virginia Supreme Court Justices," a sanguine student writes. Many clerkships and externships are made possible through a "highly involved alumni community" in the area and help students to figure out what type of practice they'd like to enter when they graduate. Because many students "fall in love with the city," the school's Career Services Office (CSO) has historically taken a somewhat provincial approach. However, it "recently hired a new dean and two new staff members," and students are beginning to feel that the CSO "has the resources to help any student find a job anywhere in the world."

Administrators are described as "doting," and most maintain an "open-door policy." While there are a few reports of disorganization—"It did take them four tries within a 5-hour period to get our second semester schedule correct," a 1L reports—the vast majority here believe the "personal approach" and lack of red tape transcend the minor difficulties. The "entire campus has wireless Internet access," which allows students to "study anywhere." In addition, "You are provided your own personal study carrel in the library, which functions as a locker and, most importantly, a nice quiet place to study." If students require more incentive to head to the library, "ample" staffing ensures that all customers "find what they are looking for." The student body's biggest complaint is that Richmond is "very underappreciated." "I have friends at Georgetown, UNC, Wake Forest, Duke, NYU, and UVA law schools, and none of them are as happy as I am at Richmond," a 2L boasts.

MICHELLE RAHMAN, ASSOCIATE DEAN FOR ADMISSIONS
LAW SCHOOL ADMISSIONS OFFICE, 28 WESTHAMPTON WAY, UNIVERSITY OF RICHMOND, VA 23173
TEL: 804-289-8189 FAX: 804-287-6516
EMAIL: LAWADMISSIONS@RICHMOND.EDU • WEBSITE: LAW.RICHMOND.EDU

Life

Not only is the University of Richmond campus "one of the most beautiful in the country," it is "surrounded by a safe and pristine neighborhood that is also easily affordable." Adding to the pleasant environment, "Competition among students is healthy and not overwhelming." "I almost enjoy the daily grind of law school when I can so easily relate to my fellow students," a 2L reports. "Little things, like taking lunch breaks at the dining hall or going through flashcards together during exams, [have] helped me find a comfortable niche here." Richmond is "a very social school," and "numerous events and groups meetings" are held "every week." In addition, "The school sponsors monthly happy hours in order to encourage students and faculty/staff to interact," and "There is always the opportunity for free food." The student body can be cliquey, however, "especially if you don't fit in with the pretty and party-oriented mid-20s crowd." Fortunately, "There's plenty to do in Richmond. I went to the opera with one of my friends and his wife," a 2L writes. Bars in the Fan district, "in the heart of Richmond," are very popular with students of all ages.

Diversity is "a big issue" at Richmond. While the school "is making great strides to diversify its student body and faculty," there currently "aren't very many minorities." "It is a little awkward for us (minorities) to adjust at first," a 1L reports. "The professors and students don't really know how to address or interact with us, oftentimes, without trying to seem as if they're treating us differently." A former bastion of conservatism, Richmond is "middle of the road these days, and there is a definite liberal presence on campus."

Getting In

Students frequently mention "the Admissions Office ladies" as a major resource of Richmond. "Literally, if you need a hug, they are there," a 2L reports. Their "personal acceptance phone call" initiates students to an environment in which "Every student is given plenty of attention." The advice the Associate Dean provides at http://law.richmond.edu/admissions/applyingadvice.php is another way in which the staff here goes above and beyond the call of duty.

Legal research course requirement	Yes
Moot court requirement	No
Public interest law requirement	No

ADMISSIONS

Selectivity Rating	87
# applications received	1,960
% applicants accepted	30
% acceptees attending	27
Average LSAT	161
LSAT Range	160–163
Average undergrad GPA	3.4
Application fee	$35
Regular application	Rolling, up to 7/15
Regular notification	Rolling
Early application program	Yes
Early application deadline	12/1
Early application notification	12/24
Transfer students accepted	Yes
Evening division offered	No
Part-time accepted	No
LSDAS accepted	Yes

Applicants Also Look At

Florida State University, Temple University, American University, The Catholic University of America, Boston University, University of North Carolina at Chapel Hill, George Mason University, Villanova University.

International Students

| TOEFL required of international students | Yes |
| Minimum TOEFL (paper/computer) | 650/280 |

FINANCIAL FACTS

Annual tuition	$31,510
Books and supplies	$5,130
Tuition per credit	$1,450
Room & board (on/off-campus)	$8,580/$9,900
Financial aid application deadline	3/1
% first-year students receiving some sort of aid	78
% receiving some sort of aid	93
% of aid that is merit based	25
% receiving scholarships	73
Average grant	$7,745
Average loan	$33,465
Average total aid package	$35,615
Average debt	$84,155

EMPLOYMENT INFORMATION

Career Rating	78	Grads Employed by Field (%)	
Rate of placement (nine months out)	98	Academic	(1)
Average starting salary	$60,719	Business/Industry	(8)
State for bar exam	NC, NY, FL, VA, DC	Government	(20)
Pass rate for first-time bar	87	Judicial Clerkships	(23)

Prominent Alumni

Lawrence L. Koontz, Justice, VA Supreme Court; Harvey E. Schlesinger, U.S. District Court Judge, Middle Dist. of FL; Frederick P. Stamp, Jr., U.S. District Court Judge, Northern District of WV; James C. Roberts, Rated in 4 categories in Best Lawyers in America.

Military (2)
Private Practice (43)
Public Interest (3)

UNIVERSITY OF SAN DIEGO
SCHOOL OF LAW

INSTITUTIONAL INFORMATION

Public/private	Private
Affiliation	Roman Catholic
Student-faculty ratio	14:1
% faculty part-time	37
% faculty female	36
% faculty minority	16
Total faculty	93

SURVEY SAYS...

Diverse opinions accepted
in classrooms
Beautiful campus
Students love San Diego, CA

STUDENTS

Enrollment of law school	1,025
% male/female	59/41
% out-of-state	29
% full-time	78
% minority	26
Average age of entering class	24

ACADEMICS

Academic Experience Rating	**83**
Profs interesting rating	83
Profs accessible rating	73
Hours of study per day	4.02

Academic Specialties

Commercial law, constitutional law, criminal law, environmental law, international law, taxation, intellectual property law, public interest law, administrative law, children's advocacy

Advanced Degrees Offered

JD, 3 years. Master of Law, General, Taxation, Business and Corporate, International, Comparative Law for Foreign Attorneys; approx. 1 year.

Combined Degrees Offered

JD/MBA, JD/MA (International Relations), JD/IMBA (International Business Administration; 4–4 1/2 years.

Clinical program required	No
Legal writing course requirement	Yes

Academics

A stalwart Southern California institution, the University of San Diego draws rave reviews for its fine faculty, practical programs, and, of course, weather. A large and diverse program, "USD attracts some of the finest professors from across the country, specializing in criminal law, corporate, international law and IP." A current student enthuses, "Each professor is unique in their approach to teaching, and because most of them are the brightest minds in their field, they are able to give you the tools you will need to succeed as a practicing attorney." Academically, the "Socratic Method isn't so big at USD" and, on the whole, the curriculum is "conscious of the practical aspects of lawyering, and doesn't obsess over theory." Even so, course work is challenging, and faculty is "helpful and welcoming, yet not afraid to be blunt and mean business." When considering USD, students remind us of the school's Catholic affiliation, telling us that the professors are "rather conservative in their approach to teaching and the law in general." A current student shares, "It's no secret that the legal profession is a liberal one, so USD Law is a refreshing haven for more moderate and right-thinking students."

Despite the practical emphasis, many feel that USD could offer more courses that directly prepare you for the legal profession. For example, "USD offers no classes whatsoever in drafting or licensing, and what courses are offered in interviewing and negotiations are typically oversubscribed 2:1 [or] 3:1." However, those looking for practical experience will find "a multitude of opportunities outside of the classroom that simultaneously offer course credit." For example, the school operates a "competitive mock trial team, which provides very rigorous and thorough training and preparation for future trial practice." Students may also participate in one of "13 clinics in diverse areas that offer hands-on legal experience with a classroom component." A 3L shares, "I never got law school burnout because I was able to work for credit for a nonprofit, a government agency, and a court, which all kept me focused on my future career as a lawyer instead of the daily grind of a law student."

Students point out that the "USD campus is beautiful." Though in the past students have noted "the law school is outdated and needs a massive facelift," the school has recently major renovations to offices and classrooms. "The library resources are also unparalleled. There are literally floors of books, journals, microfiches, and other legal resources."

Maybe it's the school's hefty tuition that has USD students dreaming of dollar signs; whatever the reason, "Most students that come to USD seem to be far more focused on fields that make money more than anything else, and the culture is very conservative." Lucky for them, "USD Law is considered the preeminent local law school, so networking and job opportunities abound." In fact, students insist, "This is a very 'hometown' area, and is not welcoming to outsiders. To employers here, USD really is a better school than Harvard."

Life

Beachside living and law school aren't necessarily a natural pair. A student bemoans, "There's nothing like spending three years living next to the beach yet never having time to actually go to the beach." However, students unanimously agree that the mellow San Diego atmosphere really reduces the stresses of law school. "Being able to spend a Saturday at the beach or riding your bike or doing something outdoors on a regular basis makes a huge difference in how positive you feel about your life during law school," confesses a current student.

CARL EGING, ASSISTANT DEAN OF ADMISSIONS AND FINANCIAL AID
OFFICE OF ADMISSIONS AND FINANCIAL AID, 5998 ALCALA PARK, SAN DIEGO, CA 92110
TEL: 619-260-4528 FAX: 619-260-2218
EMAIL: JDINFO@SANDIEGO.EDU • WEBSITE: WWW.LAW.SANDIEGO.EDU

You'll bump into quite a few beemers in the USD parking lot, and students admit the school "has the SoCal rich-kid culture one would expect from a conservative, wealthy, private school with a student body drawn primarily from upper-class kids in and around the LA, OC, and San Diego regions." On the whole, however, "Most people are pleasant and friendly, help each other, and have interests beyond studying." If you want to connect with your classmates, "There are more than enough social opportunities including the famed Bar Review every week. There are also more alumni/networking events than anyone could every find time to attend." Around town, "San Diego is full of young people around my age, and there is always something to do whether it is hanging at the beach, going to the bars, or taking in a Chargers or Padres game." When it's time to blow off steam, "San Diego has a great bar scene, and finals aside you'll never be lacking an excuse to go grab a beer."

Getting In

While there are no pre-legal courses required for entry to the USD law program, all applicants must have a bachelor's degree from an accredited college. LSAT scores and GPA are important to an admissions decision, as are the personal qualities and skills demonstrated by your personal statement and letters of recommendation. The 2007–2008 entering class had a median LSAT score of 161 and a median GPA of 3.42.

Legal methods course requirement — No
Legal research course requirement — Yes
Moot court requirement — Yes
Public interest law requirement — No

ADMISSIONS

Selectivity Rating	83
# applications received	4,311
% applicants accepted	35
% acceptees attending	23
Average LSAT	161
LSAT Range	160–164
Average undergrad GPA	3.42
Application fee	$50
Regular application	Rolling, up to 7/1
Regular notification	Rolling
Early application program	No
Transfer students accepted	Yes
Evening division offered	Yes
Part-time accepted	Yes
LSDAS accepted	Yes

Applicants Also Look At
University of Southern California, University of California—Berkeley, University of California—Los Angeles, University of California—Davis, Loyola Marymount University, University of San Francisco

International Students
TOEFL required of international students — Yes
Minimum TOEFL (paper/computer/web) 600/250/100

FINANCIAL FACTS

Annual tuition	$39,060
Books and supplies	$982
Fees	$144
Tuition per credit	$1,350
Room & board	$19,054
Financial aid application deadline	3/1
% first-year students receiving some sort of aid	87
% receiving some sort of aid	84
% of aid that is merit based	55
% receiving scholarships	41
Average grant	$18,000
Average loan	$37,000
Average total aid package	$53,000
Average debt	$105,208

EMPLOYMENT INFORMATION

Career Rating	81
Rate of placement (nine months out)	95
Average starting salary	$88,000
State for bar exam	CA, NV, AZ
Pass rate for first-time bar	81

Prominent Alumni
Shelley Berkley, Congresswoman from Nevada; Frances Townsend, Former Homeland Security Advisor; Hon. Thomas Whelan, U.S. District Court, So. Cal.; Steve Altman, President Qualcomm; Hon. Lynn Schenk, Former San Diego Congresswoman.

Grads Employed by Field (%)
Academic (2)
Business/Industry (18)
Government (11)
Judicial Clerkships (4)
Military (2)
Private Practice (56)
Public Interest (6)
Other (1)

UNIVERSITY OF SAN FRANCISCO
SCHOOL OF LAW

INSTITUTIONAL INFORMATION

Public/private	Private
Affiliation	Roman Catholic
Student-faculty ratio	16:1
% faculty part-time	67
% faculty female	32
% faculty minority	27
Total faculty	101

SURVEY SAYS...
Great research resources
Beautiful campus

STUDENTS

Enrollment of law school	702
% male/female	47/53
% out-of-state	20.8
% full-time	78.1
% minority	35.3
% international	1.5
# of countries represented	24
Average age of entering class	26

ACADEMICS

Academic Experience Rating	**84**
Profs interesting rating	80
Profs accessible rating	81
Hours of study per day	4.3

Academic Specialties
International law, intellectual property law, business law, and public interest.

Advanced Degrees Offered
LL.M in International Transactions and Comparative Law, one year. LL.M in Intellectual Property, one year.

Combined Degrees Offered
JD/MBA, 4 years.

Clinical program required	No
Legal writing course requirement	Yes
Legal methods course requirement	No
Legal research course requirement	Yes
Moot court requirement	Yes

Academics

A fine private law school with a distinctly friendly culture, the University of San Francisco is a great place to pursue a traditional legal education while simultaneously getting an introduction to the practical aspects of the legal profession. The school's attractive Bay Area location helps maintain a fleet of competent faculty, and USF professors are "available and helpful, committed scholars, [and] often personally committed to social causes." In the classroom, the Socratic Method is pervasive, though students benefit from a "diverse range of teaching styles." A current student shares, "We have highly creative professors so exams are always entertaining. For example, we had the author of *The Paper Chase*, Professor Osborn, as our contracts professor, so the fact patterns for his exams read like a hilarious short story." Bar preparation professors are "experts in their fields," and many students agree that the school's "greatest strength, hands-down, is our Legal Research and Writing program." Others point out that "USF has four student law journals that students can work on, including the growing and improving Intellectual Property Law Bulletin, a law journal that is published twice a year." To get your feet wet, the school operates excellent legal clinics, many with a public interest focus. For example, "the international human rights clinic is superb in that students are allowed to partake in advocacy at the United Nations in Geneva and New York."

Students love USF's patently friendly and supportive student atmosphere, praising the accessibility and leadership of Dean Brand. Likewise, USF professors "are extremely accessible and willing to hash out material with students after class and during office hours." A current student shares, "I even had one law professor invite me for Thanksgiving! Now that's something you don't find anywhere." Between students, "USF is unusually collegial—students are very supportive of each other, and there is no sense of mean-spirited competition." On the other hand, non-competitive does not mean that students are lackluster. A 1L explains, "To me, USF students engage in the perfect amount of competition. If there were no competition in law school, students would not be motivated to do their best work!"

With sweeping views of San Francisco, USF's library is so stellar that you'll "often see law students from the other schools studying in our library because of the quality of the library and the resources." In addition, "the law librarians are some of the most knowledgeable and helpful individuals I have ever met." On the whole, USF's pretty and modern campus is a major selling point, boasting great views, comfortable study spaces, and classrooms "equipped with the latest media and set up in such a way a child could navigate them."

Maintaining deep ties within the Bay Area legal community, USF professors "have connections within the city or at least in the Bay Area, so they are a great resource both for classroom questions as well as summer or post-graduation job opportunities." Many students, however, point out the following irony: "While holding itself out as a Public Interest law school, [USF] charges an astronomically high tuition with little financial help to those wishing to pursue this avenue of the law. When graduating $100k in the hole, it's hard to take a job that will only pay you $40k a year even if it is something you believe in vehemently." For those looking for more lucrative positions, the Office of Career Planning is "putting a lot more resources in helping students obtain competitive, private sector jobs."

ALAN GUERRERO, DIRECTOR OF ADMISSIONS
2130 FULTON STREET, SAN FRANCISCO, CA 94117
TEL: 415-422-6586 FAX: 415-422-6433
EMAIL: LAWADMISSIONS@USFCA.EDU • WEBSITE: WWW.LAW.USFCA.EDU

Life

A beautiful urban oasis, USF's "downright luxurious" campus helps offset the stresses of law school. A satisfied student shares, "At the USF law library, you can watch the sun set over the Golden Gate Bridge while reading contracts." Students love the school's bustling campus environment, where there is "an active and vibrant community of extracurricular clubs, journals, groups and programs." Even an evening student expresses, "I did not know how accessible activities would be to me, however I have found that where I want to be involved I can be, and have been able to participate in the Student Bar Association, other student organizations, and school advocacy teams." Reflecting its San Francisco environs, liberal politics predominate, though students say all viewpoints are equally valued and respected. In line with its leftist leanings, USF is generally "very supportive of students' involvement in social justice work and community activism, and provides a lot of support to students interested in these areas."

Starving students take note: San Francisco is pricey, so "living is going to be a bit expensive around the campus and even far away from it!" However, the overall lifestyle might be worth the extra cost. Take it from a second year student, who sums up the USF experience: "Beautiful weather, beautiful location, lots of students from all ethnicities, more than enough clubs, too many noontime lectures and free lunches to count, good friends, and good times."

Getting In

University of San Francisco carefully evaluates each applicant's pre-law transcripts and curriculum, admitting students whose undergraduate course work demonstrates success in a broad set of liberal arts courses, as well as an emphasis on oral and written skills. Last year, the school received more than 3,000 applications for just 250 first-year spots. The biggest five feeder undergraduate schools are all members of the University of California system.

EMPLOYMENT INFORMATION

		Grads Employed by Field (%)
Career Rating	81	Academic (1)
Rate of placement (nine months out)	88	Business/Industry (14)
Average starting salary	$90,000	Government (11)
State for bar exam	CA	Judicial Clerkships (2)
Pass rate for first-time bar	87.4	Private Practice (61)

Employers Who Frequently Hire Grads
Bingham & McCutcheon; Morgan, Lewis & Brockius; Reed Smith; Wilson, Sonsini, Goodrich & Rosati; Legislative Counsel; San Francisco Superior Court.
Public Interest (11)

Prominent Alumni
Justice Ming Chin, CA Supreme Court; Judge Martin Jenkins, U.S. District Court Northern California.

Public interest law requirement — No

ADMISSIONS
Selectivity Rating	81
# applications received	4,162
% applicants accepted	36
% acceptees attending	16
Average LSAT	159
LSAT Range	156–161
Average undergrad GPA	3.32
Application fee	$60
Regular application	Rolling, up to 2/1
Regular notification	Rolling
Early application program	No
Transfer students accepted	Yes
Evening division offered	Yes
Part-time accepted	Yes
LSDAS accepted	Yes

Applicants Also Look At
University of Southern California, University of California—Berkeley, University of California—Los Angeles, University of the Pacific, University of California—Davis, Golden Gate University

International Students
TOEFL required of international students Yes
Minimum TOEFL (paper/computer/web) 600/250/100

FINANCIAL FACTS
Annual tuition	$35,800
Books and supplies	$950
Fees	$80
Fees per credit	$12
Tuition per credit	$1,280
Room & board (on/off-campus)	$14,000/$13,500
Financial aid application deadline	2/15
% first-year students receiving some sort of aid	92
% receiving some sort of aid	90
% of aid that is merit based	15
% receiving scholarships	30
Average grant	$10,950
Average loan	$30,216
Average total aid package	$24,000
Average debt	$92,500

UNIVERSITY OF SOUTH CAROLINA
SCHOOL OF LAW

INSTITUTIONAL INFORMATION

Public/private	Public
Student-faculty ratio	14:1
% faculty part-time	0
% faculty female	40
% faculty minority	10
Total faculty	48

SURVEY SAYS...

Diverse opinions accepted
in classrooms
Great library staff

STUDENTS

Enrollment of law school	680
% male/female	59/41
% out-of-state	40
% full-time	100
% minority	10
% international	11
# of countries represented	6
Average age of entering class	24

ACADEMICS

Academic Experience Rating	**78**
Profs interesting rating	77
Profs accessible rating	73
Hours of study per day	4.04

Advanced Degrees Offered
JD, 3 years

Combined Degrees Offered
4 year programs: (IMBA),
Accountancy (MACC), Criminal
Justice (MCJ), Earth amd
Environmental Resource
Management (MEERM), Health
Administration (MHA), Human
Resources (MHR), Public
Administration (MPA), Science in
Business (MSB), Social Work
(MSW), Environmental Law (MSEL).

Clinical program required	No
Legal writing course requirement	Yes
Legal methods course requirement	No
Legal research course requirement	Yes
Moot court requirement	No

Academics

Deeply enmeshed and dearly loved in the local legal community, the University of South Carolina boasts a prestigious faculty, a well-connected alumni network, and an ultra-friendly staff and student body. At USC, the classroom experience is top of the line, spearheaded by talented professors who are "very accessible and willing to interact with students formally and informally." A student raves, "The faculty really care about teaching and are always available to help explain or give you further enrichment. They are very encouraging, which is very important when you've had a hard day under the Socratic Method!" In addition to the impressive roster of tenured faculty, "The administration has done a great job of recruiting new, more dynamic professors in recent years." The resulting atmosphere is a "welcome mixture of the stuffy old law professors with the young, cutting-edge, recent academics." Even so, the program takes a fairly traditional approach to legal education, and some students say the school should "work on addressing more diverse needs than just the typical needs of the corporate lawyer-to-be."

Students adore the "the collegial, friendly, and open attitude" at USC, assuring us that "the faculty and administration will move mountains to help you make it through to graduation." Fellow students also form an important support network at USC. A 1L elaborates: "We are placed with a group of 12 students that comprise our legal writing class; you are with these students in almost every class your first year. They become like your law school family; everyone watches out for each other." Another adds, "My favorite part about the law school is the collegiality of the students; although there is healthy competition, we truly look out for one another's best interest."

There's no doubt about it: "If you want to be an attorney in South Carolina, this is the best place to be." Smack dab in the middle of the capital, USC is "just blocks away from the state legislature and the state supreme court, as well as to administrative agencies and local government," which offers students "a great opportunity to see the law in action while still in school." When looking for a job or internship, USC students enjoy "a wonderful reputation in the Southeast"; not to mention a corner on the regional market. "Because over 70 percent of the South Carolina Bar attended this law school," the alumni network is beyond compare. If that weren't enough, Career Services does "an excellent job informing us with local and regional opportunities and equipping us with skills to 'land the job' (i.e., interview workshops, resume workshops, and individual evaluations)."

Amidst glowing reviews, students give the school's aging facilities a decisive thumbs-down. Thinking like a future prosecutor, a 2L informs us, "The walls are filled with asbestos. The pipes are filled with lead. Not the smartest place to house a bunch of aspiring lawyers." Another student comments, "Apparently [they] have been planning on building a new one for decades but instead have used duct tape to keep it together. Literally, the window next to me is held up with duct tape." Fortunately, administrators are aware of the duct tape problem, and "The Law School is in the process of fund-raising for its new, top-of-the-line building."

803-777-6605, DIRECTOR OF ADMISSIONS
701 SOUTH MAIN STREET, COLUMBIA, SC 29208
TEL: 803-777-6605 FAX: 803-777-2847
EMAIL: USCLAW@LAW.SC.EDU • WEBSITE: WWW.LAW.SC.EDU

Life

At USC, students enjoy the incomparable combination of an excellent academic program and a stellar social life. Attracting a fun-loving and outgoing student body, "There are very few law students you wouldn't invite to have a beer with after a rough week of classes." When they aren't hitting the books, "There is no shortage of social events at USC." For example, "Students put together tailgates during football season, and SBA puts on great theme parties and a formal [get-together] in the spring." Students also hang out casually, and "It's easy to find law students out every night of the week."

Besides drinking and studying, many students spend their free time participating in clubs, intramural sports, and extracurricular activities. Demonstrating a community-oriented and philanthropic spirit, students organize "massive food-drive competitions with each class donating tens of thousands of pounds of canned goods, and most students donate their study guides and commercial outlines to the Public Interest Law Society's outline bank, which then sells them back to other students at highly discounted rates." Since they end up spending so much time together, students admit that law school is something like "High School II, complete with lockers and gossip, but at least we are old enough to legally drink."

A great mix of cosmopolitan and cozy, hometown Columbia is "small enough to be comfortable but large enough to have opportunities in private and corporate law." Thanks to USC's sizable undergrad and graduate programs, "The area has a 'happenin'' bar scene." More liberal thinkers beware: this Southern school has "a feeling of staunch South Carolina Republicans."

Getting In

At University of South Carolina, the Admissions Committee takes a holistic approach to reviewing applicants. LSAT scores and GPA are important factors among many considered. The Admissions Committee also considers a student's employment and life experiences, residency, letters of recommendation, personal statement, and ability to contribute to a diverse community. USC received 2,068 applications for a class of 227 students (708 applicants were successful). The median LSAT score for the class was 159, and the median GPA was 3.4.

Public interest law requirement	No

ADMISSIONS
Selectivity Rating	84
# applications received	2,068
# applicants accepted	708
# acceptees attending	227
Average LSAT	159
LSAT Range	156–161
Average undergrad GPA	3.39
Application fee	$60
Regular application	Rolling, up to 4/1
Regular notification	Rolling
Early application program	No
Transfer students accepted	Yes
Evening division offered	No
Part-time accepted	No
LSDAS accepted	Yes

International Students
TOEFL required of international students	Yes

FINANCIAL FACTS
Annual tuition (in-state/out-of-state)	$17,448/$35,220
Books and supplies	$936
Room & board (off-campus)	$16,200
Financial aid application deadline	4/1
% receiving some sort of aid	80
% of aid that is merit based	n/a
% receiving scholarships	35
Average grant	$7,600
Average loan	$8,200
Average total aid package	$18,000
Average debt	$56,000

EMPLOYMENT INFORMATION

Career Rating	67
Average starting salary	$63,000
State for bar exam	SC, NC, GA, FL, TX
Pass rate for first-time bar	92

Employers Who Frequently Hire Grads
Nelson, Mullins, Riley & Scarborough; Alston & Bird; Haynsworth, Sinkler, Boyd; Nexsen Pruet.

Prominent Alumni
Richard W. Riley, Former U.S. Secretary of Education; Lindsay Graham, U.S. Senate; Karren J. Williams, 4th Circit Court of Appeals; Joe Wilson, U.S. Congress.

Grads Employed by Field (%)
Business/Industry (10)
Government (14)
Judicial Clerkships (16)
Private Practice (52)
Public Interest (7)

THE UNIVERSITY OF SOUTH DAKOTA

SCHOOL OF LAW

INSTITUTIONAL INFORMATION

Public/private	Public
Student-faculty ratio	16:1
% faculty part-time	29
% faculty female	29
% faculty minority	4
Total faculty	24

SURVEY SAYS...

Diverse opinions accepted
in classrooms
Great library staff

STUDENTS

Enrollment of law school	199
% male/female	55/45
% out-of-state	29
% full-time	99
% minority	4
Average age of entering class	26

ACADEMICS

Academic Experience Rating	**61**
Profs interesting rating	69
Profs accessible rating	72
Hours of study per day	3.83

Academic Specialties

Environmental Law, Indian Law

Advanced Degrees Offered

None

Combined Degrees Offered

JD/MBA, JD/MPA(Professional
Accountancy)

Clinical program required	No
Legal writing	
course requirement	Yes
Legal methods	
course requirement	Yes
Legal research	
course requirement	Yes
Moot court requirement	No
Public interest	
law requirement	No

Academics

Those who attend The University of South Dakota School of Law can expect to get a legal education at a great price. The small-town atmosphere of hometown Vermillion and the small-town background that most of the students come from fosters quite the communal atmosphere amongst students and professors, and there are definitely no worries of feeling like a number. Appropriately, USD has one of the best Native American Law programs available, as well as a strong criminal law program, though some students would like more breadth in both course and concentration selection, the school has widened its curriculum, offering such courses as media and communication law, immigration law, sports law, and military law during the 2008–2009 academic year. "The professors want to make sure their students are prepared to become general practitioners in South Dakota. If that is what you want to do, then that's great, but… in Family Law you'll learn how to file a divorce but you'll never read Roe v. Wade," says a 2L. Because it is the only law school in the state, USD has a very close relationship with the State Bar and the Unified Judicial System in South Dakota, which means great opportunities for students to get involved in the practice of law in the state of South Dakota. "Knowing the members of the Supreme Court of South Dakota is priceless," says a student.

Unfortunately, some students feel that being the only law school in the state has given the deans a "sense of complacency,"and others think that the administration could be better organized. Students also wish Career Services would take more initiative. "I realize that the primary burden of finding employment rests on the law student but I would expect more drive from the administration when 'recruiting' employers," says a 3L. However, it should be noted that the dean directing career services does make it a point to reach out to 3L students and most statewide firms. Luckily, the "well-versed" professors are often "willing to help students plan for their lives after law school" and "have a genuine concern for the students and take time to help out wherever they can." The range of legal thinking within in the faculty is "refreshing and invigorating," and the tiny classes make it so that students have one-on-one time with professors and "no one is ignored." "USD is the type of law school where the professors know you by your first and last name. You see each other at the grocery store and swap dinner ideas," says a student.

The facilities here are functional enough, with a top-notch student lounge and wireless Internet available throughout the entire school, but the actual usage of modern technology and its applications in today's law are definitely behind the times. "Teach [professors] to use Westlaw and Lexis and get rid of expensive code and casebooks destined for doorstop duty or landfill when the exam is over," says a student.

Jean Henriques, Admission Officer/Registrar
414 East Clark Street, Vermillion, SD 57069-2390
Tel: 605-677-5443 Fax: 605-677-5417
Email: Law.School@usd.edu • Website: www.usd.edu/law

Life

As one student puts is, "The good thing about going to law school in Vermillion is you can't complain about too many distractions from your pursuit of the law." There's no real competitive streak at USD, and everyone is "extremely helpful," with upperclassmen always willing to discuss classes and professors and offer any advice they may have to the 1Ls, who in turn are similarly ready to lend a hand to each other. With around 250 students at the school in total, class sizes are small, so everyone "feels like part of a family"; however, the cozy atmosphere can be "somewhat like high school, with the drama and lasting friendships," and there are very defined cliques among students, but most everyone still gets along and there's an overall friendly vibe, as well as several social events every year that give students the opportunity to relax and "get to know their co-counsels." Students see each other all of the time, during the day at class, then again in the afternoon in the library, and then at night at the gym or at other "social establishments."

Getting In

The University of South Dakota School of Law seeks students who demonstrate intelligence, a strong desire to practice law (especially in the state of South Dakota), and commitment to helping others through legal advocacy. You are a competitive applicant with a solid B undergraduate GPA and an LSAT score above 153.

EMPLOYMENT INFORMATION

Career Rating	**64**
Rate of placement (nine months out)	92
Average starting salary	$46,860
State for bar exam	SD, IA, MN, GA, ND
Pass rate for first-time bar	93

Employers Who Frequently Hire Grads
U.S. Eighth Circuit Court of Appeals; U.S. District Court; South Dakota Supreme Court; South Dakota Circuit Court.

Prominent Alumni
Tim Johnson, U.S. Senator; David Gilbertson, Chief Justice, SD Supreme Court; Judith Meierhenry, Justice, SD Supreme Court.

Grads Employed by Field (%)
Academic (4)
Business/Industry (13)
Government (21)
Judicial Clerkships (18)
Private Practice (32)
Public Interest (8)
Other (4)

ADMISSIONS

Selectivity Rating	**68**
# applications received	323
% applicants accepted	53
% acceptees attending	36
Average LSAT	151
LSAT Range	148–155
Average undergrad GPA	3.3
Application fee	$35
Regular application	Rolling, up to 5/1
Regular notification	Rolling
Early application program	No
Transfer students accepted	Yes
Evening division offered	No
Part-time accepted	Yes
LSDAS accepted	Yes

Applicants Also Look At
University of Nebraska—Lincoln, University of Wyoming, Drake University, Creighton University, Hamline University, University of North Dakota

International Students

TOEFL required of international students	Yes
Minimum TOEFL (paper/computer/web)	600/250/100

FINANCIAL FACTS

Annual tuition (in-state/ out-of-state)	$4,844/$14,040
Books and supplies	$1,400
Fees	$4,777
Fees per credit	$159
Tuition per credit (in-state/out-of-state)	$161/$468
Room & board (on/off-campus)	$5,112/$6,715
% first-year students receiving some sort of aid	92
% receiving some sort of aid	91
% of aid that is merit based	90
% receiving scholarships	28
Average grant	$2,326
Average loan	$20,262
Average total aid package	$20,085
Average debt	$60,000

UNIVERSITY OF SOUTHERN CALIFORNIA
GOULD SCHOOL OF LAW

INSTITUTIONAL INFORMATION

Public/private	Private
Student-faculty ratio	12:1
% faculty part-time	36
% faculty female	26
% faculty minority	15
Total faculty	150

SURVEY SAYS...

Diverse opinions accepted
in classrooms
Great research resources
Great library staff
Abundant externship/internship/
clerkship opportunities

STUDENTS

Enrollment of law school	616
% male/female	55/45
% out-of-state	50
% full-time	100
% minority	40
% international	2
# of countries represented	7
Average age of entering class	26

ACADEMICS

Academic Experience Rating	**88**
Profs interesting rating	75
Profs accessible rating	74
Hours of study per day	3.32

Academic Specialties

Civil procedure, commercial law, constitutional law, corporation securities, criminal law, environmental law, government services, human rights, international law, labor law, legal history, legal philosophy, property, taxation, intellectual property law

Advanced Degrees Offered

JD, 3 years; LL.M., 1 year; MCL, 1 year.

Clinical program required	No
Legal writing course requirement	Yes
Legal methods course requirement	No
Legal research course requirement	Yes

Academics

The University of Southern California's Gould School of Law offers students "an excellent legal education on a beautiful campus in the middle of one of the most vibrant, diverse, and exciting cities in the world." "USC seems to cover it all," proclaims a 3L: "a near-perfect climate, affable students, engaging professors, a legal education that readies you for the top ranks of any practice, and a commitment to pro bono legal services that is inspiring." "If you want to be pushed and if you want be rewarded for your hard work, this place is perfect," adds a 2L. "The Public Interest Law Foundation is very large and active." The school's "very wide range" of clinical programs includes a cutting-edge Intellectual Property Clinic. Students say the "intensive" legal writing program at Gould is "amazing." "They are beating us over the head with writing and the importance of writing skills for our future until we are numb," says an exhausted 1L. However, "You really learn to appreciate it when you take your first summer job and realize how impressive a legal writer you are compared with law students from other schools."

Some professors "are very theoretical." "More emphasis on the practical side of things" would be nice, students say. On the whole, though, "Classes are quite good and a few professors are spectacular." They are always "available to have lunch, talk, and give advice." "The professors who go out of their way to make minority students feel welcome are the highlight of the law school," beams a 3L. Most students also seem pleased with the "very available and helpful" administration. "No matter how big or ridiculously small the problem, someone is there to help you," though "We have our share of lackluster profs who couldn't teach a dog to eat," confesses a 2L.

Career prospects are outstanding. "USC Law opens doors nationally" and is "absolutely worth every penny even though it is not cheap." "The USC Law community has amazing clout within Los Angeles," and "The alumni connections are unbelievable." "People may think the Trojan Family is a cheesy notion," but alumni are "crazy about USC, and they are incredibly loyal to the school and its graduates." The administration "formally sets you up with a mentor in the legal path of your interest during your first year," explains a 2L. "Mine is the general counsel to the Los Angeles Lakers." "More than half of the student body has no problem landing top corporate jobs paying $135,000 or more." However, many students are "still jobless in year three because they choose not to settle for a position with compensation less than California's highest market price." Some students worry that USC is "brainwashing students into being corporate peons." Others argue that "the Law School actually puts a huge effort into making it possible for students to pursue public interest work when they graduate."

The law school's "concrete," "late-60s-ugly" building "isn't that bad" but students agree that it "could be more aesthetic." The interior is "relatively pleasant" and "functional," despite a "terrible layout." "Some of the classrooms are dark, grim, and uber-institutional." "I haven't seen a window in three years," laments a 3L. "The wireless network could suck less" too. On the plus side, "The library is new and hi-tech," and "The research librarians are amazing."

Life

"If you're 22 and gorgeous, you'll have a rollicking social life" at USC. "If you're already (gasp!) in your mid-20s, or older, it's tough to find mature, like-minded friends who aren't only interested in hooking up and partying." While "The immediate location of the campus is less than ideal, Southern California itself is a wonderful place to live."

CHLOE REID, ASSOCIATE DEAN
USC LAW SCHOOL, LOS ANGELES, CA 90089-0074
TEL: 213-740-2523 FAX: 213-740-4570
EMAIL: ADMISSIONS@LAW.USC.EDU • WEBSITE: WWW.LAW.USC.EDU

Academically, USC is "tolerant and more laid-back than other law schools." Students are "generally very down-to-earth, helpful, and considerate." "Virtually everyone here is extremely motivated and wants to succeed but not at someone else's expense." As one 2L notes, "Overall, I believe that the University of Southern California really is the family atmosphere that it proclaims itself to be. Although we all operate in a competitive environment, students are in this thing together." It's "an incredibly communal place."

"The Law School is not the trust-fund stomping ground that the undergraduate college is" but "If you're a White person coming from an upper-middle-class or affluent background, you'll fit in perfectly here." Nevertheless, the law school boasts a "richly diverse student body" full of "top students with very interesting backgrounds." This "amazing blend of really different people with different backgrounds and interests mixes together and has a good time while they do it, both in class and out." Students say that "there's a creative energy [on campus] that's infused in everything." "You can see it in the students, on the students (their aesthetic mix), and in the work they do." As one student sums up: "If you want to work or study on the West Coast, you would be crazy to pass on the opportunity to join this community of entrepreneurial, bright, and personable individuals."

Getting In

The range of admitted applicants is pretty narrow. Admitted students at the 25th percentile have LSAT scores of 165 and GPAs of about 3.46. Admitted students at the 75th percentile have LSAT scores of 167 and GPAs of 3.72.

Moot court requirement	Yes
Public interest law requirement	No

ADMISSIONS

Selectivity Rating	**95**
# applications received	5,595
# applicants accepted	1,147
# acceptees attending	204
Average LSAT	166
LSAT Range	165–167
Average undergrad GPA	3.6
Application fee	$75
Regular application	2/1
Regular notification	Rolling
Early application program	No
Transfer students accepted	Yes
Evening division offered	No
Part-time accepted	No
LSDAS accepted	Yes

Applicants Also Look At

University of California—Berkeley, University of California—Los Angeles, New York University, Loyola Marymount University, Georgetown University

International Students

TOEFL recommended of international students	Yes

FINANCIAL FACTS

Annual tuition	$42,968
Books and supplies	$1,664
Fees	$1,542
Room & board	$15,842
Financial aid application deadline	3/1
% first-year students receiving some sort of aid	90
% receiving some sort of aid	90
% of aid that is merit based	20
% receiving scholarships	63
Average grant	$12,556
Average loan	$38,000
Average total aid package	$66,164
Average debt	$104,137

EMPLOYMENT INFORMATION

Career Rating	**93**
Rate of placement (nine months out)	96
Average starting salary	$135,000
State for bar exam	CA, NY, DC, WA, TX
Pass rate for first-time bar	90

Employers Who Frequently Hire Grads

Private firms, corporations, federal judges, government and public interest non profits.

Prominent Alumni

Justice Joyce Kennard, California Supreme Court; Amy Trask, Chief Executive, Oakland Raiders; Judge Dorothy Nelson, Ninth U.S. Circuit Court of Appeals; Walter Zifkin, CEO of William Morris Agency; Carlos Moorehead, U.S. Congressman, Alan Hoffman, Deputy Chief of Staff to Vice President Joseph Biden, Larry Flax,Co-Founder CA Pizza Kitchen

Grads Employed by Field (%)

Academic (2.5)
Business/Industry (4.5)
Government (8)
Judicial Clerkships (7.5)
Private Practice (68)
Public Interest (3.5)
Other (1)

UNIVERSITY OF ST. THOMAS
SCHOOL OF LAW

INSTITUTIONAL INFORMATION

Public/private	Private
Affiliation	Roman Catholic
Student-faculty ratio	17.6:1
% faculty part-time	61
% faculty female	42
% faculty minority	14
Total faculty	83

SURVEY SAYS...
Beautiful campus
Students love Minneapolis, MN

STUDENTS

Enrollment of law school	451
% male/female	55/45
% out-of-state	33
% full-time	100
% minority	13
# of countries represented	8
Average age of entering class	25

ACADEMICS

Academic Experience Rating	**82**
Profs interesting rating	85
Profs accessible rating	94

Combined Degrees Offered
College of Business (JD/MBA),
Catholic Studies (JD/MA); Public
Policy (JD/MA); Professional
Psychology (JD/MA); Social Work
(JD/MSW); all about 4 years.

Clinical program required	No
Legal writing course requirement	Yes
Legal methods course requirement	No
Legal research course requirement	Yes
Moot court requirement	No
Public interest law requirement	Yes

Academics

The University of St. Thomas School of Law is "conveniently located" in downtown Minneapolis. The building here "still has that new car smell" and is "gorgeous in the extreme." "You can see the downtown skyscrapers" through the wall of windows in the marble atrium and "the architecture is open, airy, and inviting." "Because of the openness and general layout of the law school, community necessarily flourishes," a 1L says. "It is impossible to walk from class to class without passing faculty offices or running into professors in the hallways." Technology is "top of the line." Study areas in the library are plentiful. The "fantastic" classrooms "have comfortable chairs and stadium seating." "I think the rest of the law students in Minneapolis are pretty jealous," a 2L says.

There's Catholic mass every weekday in UST Law's chapel and, academically, this place is serious about faith. "They're not kidding when they say 'faith-based,'" a 1L notes. St. Thomas Law "promotes social justice and volunteer work" quite a bit and "requires a minimum number of community service hours prior to graduation." "Most of the professors are extremely knowledgeable and experienced in their practice areas." "I've never had better professors," a 1L gushes. "Although they are tough and expect a lot, they make you want to learn and work hard," a 3L adds. Outside of class, professors are "readily accessible." "In fact, they seem to camp out in their offices at all hours." They "genuinely care for the well-being of the students" and they go "out of their way to have lunch or coffee or interact otherwise" with students.

The "friendly" and "highly effective" administration runs "smoothly" and is "very willing to listen and adapt to student needs and suggestions." "They are concerned with our development as people as well as lawyers," a 1L says. However, UST Law is "still working out kinks" in its curriculum and there aren't a lot of classes to pick from. "There is a scramble to get the upper-level courses" and "many" classes are available only in the evening. "A broader course selection would be an improvement," a 2L suggests. "There could be a greater range of clinic opportunities," too.

It's difficult to assess employment prospects because the first batch of UST graduates only received their diplomas in May 2004. The school is really too young to have much of a track record. Students tell us that "if you're looking to work in Minneapolis, St. Paul or northern Minnesota, there are tons of opportunities." Also, a required three-year mentor externship program "pairs students with a practicing lawyer or judge" and allows every student to gain practical experience. Nevertheless, UST Law "still carries the reputation of the 'new school' and hasn't attained the credibility in the community that it deserves," a 2L says. "That will change with time though."

Cari Haaland, Director of Admissions
1000 LaSalle Av, MSL 124, Minneapolis, MN 55403
Tel: (651) 962-4895 Fax: (651) 962-4876
Email: lawschool@stthomas.edu • Website: www.stthomas.edu/law

Life

Homogeneity generally pervades at UST Law. "My law school needs to improve upon diversity," a 3L says. "The community atmosphere is fantastic," though. "There is healthy competition," a 3L notes, "but it is still a very collaborative environment." "People are so nice you almost forget you're in law school." "Whether you are a 1L and they are a 3L or you are both 2L's, fellow students are some of the best resources." "St. Thomas is in the establishment stage," a 1L adds. "It is in our best interest to hope that other students in our section succeed because they are our reputation. Their reputation reflects on the school, which reflects on us."

Students report that "social life is awesome" here. The law school is small, so students are able to get to know each other. The setting is also great. "We are in the heart of the city which means walking distance to jobs and, more importantly, bars," a 2L explains. "Due to the location, students tend to go out more to unwind and relax." "There is the inter-class football game, a large turn out at bar review every week, a law school hockey league, and a lot of participation in intramural events." There are also "tons of student organizations" and support for student-led activities and groups is abundant. "If what you are interested in isn't available, you can start it yourself."

Getting In

St. Thomas Law has a high acceptance rate. Admitted students at the 25th percentile have LSAT scores around 154 and GPAs around 3.0. Admitted students at the 75th percentile have LSAT scores around 160 and GPAs in the 3.7 range.

ADMISSIONS

Selectivity Rating	74
# applications received	1,713
# applicants accepted	836
# acceptees attending	151
Average LSAT	156
LSAT Range	154–160
Average undergrad GPA	3.36
Regular application	Rolling, up to 7/1
Regular notification	Rolling
Early application program	No
Transfer students accepted	Yes
Evening division offered	No
Part-time accepted	No
LSDAS accepted	Yes

Applicants Also Look At
University of Wisconsin—Madison, University of Minnesota—Twin Cities, Marquette University, Hamline University, William Mitchell College of Law, Loyola University—Chicago

International Students
TOEFL required of international students — Yes
Minimum TOEFL (paper/computer) 600/254

FINANCIAL FACTS

Annual tuition	$32,519
Books and supplies	$1,300
Fees	$275
Room & board (off-campus)	$15,545
Financial aid application deadline	7/1
% first-year students receiving some sort of aid	94
% receiving some sort of aid	95
% of aid that is merit based	100
% receiving scholarships	59
Average grant	$18,803
Average loan	$33,063
Average total aid package	$40,432
Average debt	$87,814

EMPLOYMENT INFORMATION

Career Rating	91
Rate of placement (nine months out)	89
State for bar exam	MN, IL, AL, WI, CA
Pass rate for first-time bar	90

Employers Who Frequently Hire Grads
Dorsey & Whitney LLP, Southern Minnesota Regional Legal Services, Target Corporation, State of Minnesota, Hennepin County

Prominent Alumni
Jake Schunk, United States Department of Justice; Erin Collins, Law Clerk, The Honorable Diana E. Murphy, U.S. Court of Appeals for the Eighth Circuit; Robert Parish, Faegre & Benson, LLP; Lael Robertson, Legal Aid Society of Minnesota.

Grads Employed by Field (%)
Academic (2)
Business/Industry (18)
Government (9)
Judicial Clerkships (12)
Military (2)
Private Practice (38)
Public Interest (5)
Other (1)

THE UNIVERSITY OF TENNESSEE
COLLEGE OF LAW

INSTITUTIONAL INFORMATION

Public/private	Public
Student-faculty ratio	13:1
% faculty part-time	46
% faculty female	40
% faculty minority	4
Total faculty	84

SURVEY SAYS...

Great research resources
Great library staff
Beautiful campus
Good social life

STUDENTS

Enrollment of law school	468
% male/female	53/47
% out-of-state	20
% full-time	100
% minority	19
% international	3
# of countries represented	0
Average age of entering class	24

ACADEMICS

Academic Experience Rating	**86**
Profs interesting rating	80
Profs accessible rating	87
Hours of study per day	4.77

Academic Specialties
Business Transactions, Advocacy and Dispute Resolutions

Advanced Degrees Offered
JD, 3 years

Combined Degrees Offered
JD/MBA, 4 years; JD/MPA, 4 years

Clinical program required	No
Legal writing	
course requirement	Yes
Legal methods	
course requirement	Yes
Legal research	
course requirement	Yes
Moot court requirement	No
Public interest	
law requirement	No

Academics

Affordable, practical, and blessed with a touch of Southern charm, the University of Tennessee is a friendly place to study the law and to learn to be a lawyer. Across the board, UT students praise their school's unequivocal "emphasis on practical and 'real' lawyering instead of just philosophical theory." The school's fleet of faculty is equipped with impressive real-world credentials, and "Several classrooms are laid out exactly like courtrooms" to help students hone their litigation skills. In addition to the tenured staff, the "Adjunct professors for skills-based classes are a wonderful resource." UT students can further augment course work through the school's ample and long-standing clinical programs, which teach lawyering skills through real-world experience, including a pro bono clinic for indigent clients. They can also pursue a specialization in advocacy through the Center for Advocacy and Dispute Resolution. While the practical offerings are outstanding, many students mention that they would like to see more diverse academic specializations. A student clarifies, "Classes in a wide number of specialties are available, but it wouldn't hurt to hire a few more professors to have more options available in a given semester. It would seem the school has taken a "quality-over-quantity" approach in this regard."

Although University of Tennessee is a stalwart Southern institution, "There are numerous professors that cater to a wide range of philosophical beliefs and legal theories ...from the far-left stereotypical 'academics' all the way to the right side with Instapundit.com creator Glenn Reynolds." A stimulating academic atmosphere, "The class discussions that ensue between such a faculty and the geographically and academically diverse student body are most rewarding." The notorious Socratic Method remains a classroom favorite; however, it's never used to torture or embarrass. Rather, it "is a tool to encourage learning, and professors and students are seen as partners in that endeavor, as opposed to adversaries." Outside the classroom, "Teachers are willing to meet you after class and help you in anyway possible," and students reassure us that "there isn't a faculty member I would feel intimidated approaching." A satisfied student sums it up: "The laid-back attitude juxtaposed with expert instruction and the feeling that the UT College of Law, while already well ranked, is one of the most underrated schools and is by all means a rising star among law schools nationwide."

When transitioning to the real world, UT grads are prepared to hit the ground running. A 3L shares: "I worked at a big New York firm last summer with several Ivy Leaguers. Everyone was very smart, but many of them were just as lost when it came to advocacy skills (namely trial practice and negotiation). What I learned at Tennessee gave me an opportunity to shine in these areas." Another 3L chimes in, "I have a great job in Atlanta after graduation. When I was clerking down there this summer, I really enjoyed surprising people with how well prepared I am to practice." On that note, career placement is no problem for UT grads—especially those looking to work in the South; however, generally speaking, "The Career Services Center is geared towards students who want to practice in Tennessee or in big law firms elsewhere. Other career options are usually up to the students to pursue."

Life

The UT campus is a pleasant place for work and play, and students admit, "The beautiful classrooms and library make coming to school a lot easier." In and out of the classroom, "The majority of students are very friendly and cooperative," and most strike a good balance between recreation and study. To burn some calories and blow off steam,

Dr. Karen R. Britton, Director of Admissions and Financial Aid
Director, The Betty B.Lewis Career Center
1505 West Cumberland Avenue, Suite 161, Knoxville, TN 37996-1810
Tel: 865-974-4131 Fax: 865-974-1572
Email: lawadmit@utk.edu • Website: www.law.utk.edu

there are "law school teams in several of the intramural sports leagues on campus." When its time for a study break, there is a social event for almost every night of the week in Knoxville, a first-rate college town, boasting "a good music scene, an independent film theater, and lots of local festivals." Law students get together for "mixers every Thursday, bowling every Monday in the spring semester, and tailgates every Saturday in the fall." In addition to the weekly gatherings at local watering holes, the school sponsors many special events including "the yearly Halloween party called Chilla" and the enticing (or so students assure us) Learned Hand Bowling League. Within this tight-knit community, "Even if you don't go out every night you still develop good friendships with your peers."

Despite the social vibe, a student admits, "We have had some racial tension. We are trying to work on it and have less social segregation." Another student adds this perspective: "There are different social circles, but it is natural that people with common interests will be drawn to one another. On the whole, I feel that we have active and amiable community here."

Getting In

UT received more than 1,400 applications for an entering class of about 150 students. Undergraduate GPA and LSAT scores are important to an admissions decision; however, the school also considers qualitative factors including strength of undergraduate institution, extracurricular activities, and professional experience. The school has no minimum LSAT requirement; however, 75 percent of the 4 entering class had an LSAT score 161 or lower, and 25 percent had an LSAT score of 155 or lower. Tennessee residents made up over 70 percent of entering students.

ADMISSIONS

Selectivity Rating	86
# applications received	1,411
# applicants accepted	412
# acceptees attending	153
Average LSAT	159
LSAT Range	154–161
Average undergrad GPA	3.53
Application fee	$15
Regular application	Rolling
Regular notification	Rolling
Early application program	No
Transfer students accepted	Yes
Evening division offered	No
Part-time accepted	No
LSDAS accepted	Yes

Applicants Also Look At
University of Georgia, University of Kentucky, The University of Memphis, University of North Carolina at Chapel Hill, George Mason University, Vanderbilt University, Samford University

International Students
Minimum TOEFL (paper)	213

FINANCIAL FACTS

Annual tuition (in-state/ out-of-state)	$10,272/$27,192
Books and supplies	$1,560
Fees (in-state/ out-of-state)	$1,812/$2,112
Fees per credit (in-state/ out-of-state)	$36/$52
Tuition per credit (in-state/ out-of-state)	$571/$1,512
Room & board	$16,822
Financial aid application deadline	3/1
% first-year students receiving some sort of aid	92
% receiving some sort of aid	87
% receiving scholarships	52
Average grant	$6,263
Average loan	$21,406
Average total aid package	$25,875
Average debt	$57,064

EMPLOYMENT INFORMATION

Career Rating	79	**Grads Employed by Field (%)**
Rate of placement (nine months out)	97	Academic (2)
Average starting salary	$70,800	Business/Industry (6)
State for bar exam	TN	Government (14)
Pass rate for first-time bar	92	Judicial Clerkships (13)

Employers Who Frequently Hire Grads
Law firms, judges, government agencies, corporations, public interest organizations, and academic institutions.

Military (2)
Private Practice (59)
Public Interest (4)

Prominent Alumni
Howard H. Baker, Jr., Govenment/Public Service; Joel A. Katz, Entertainment Lawyer; Dan Adomitis, President, Firestone Natural Rubber Company; Justices Sharon Lee and Gary Wade, Tennessee Supreme Court.

THE UNIVERSITY OF TEXAS AT AUSTIN
SCHOOL OF LAW

INSTITUTIONAL INFORMATION

Public/private	Public
Student-faculty ratio	13:1
% faculty part-time	42
% faculty female	33
% faculty minority	13
Total faculty	132

SURVEY SAYS...

Diverse opinions accepted
in classrooms
Great research resources
Students love Austin, TX
Good social life

STUDENTS

Enrollment of law school	1,289
% male/female	57/43
% out-of-state	32
% full-time	100
% minority	30
% international	2
# of countries represented	18
Average age of entering class	24

ACADEMICS

Academic Experience Rating	**98**
Profs interesting rating	94
Profs accessible rating	91
Hours of study per day	3.32

Academic Specialties

Commercial law, constitutional law,
corporation securities, criminal law,
environmental law, international law,
labor law, legal philosophy, property, taxation, intellectual property law

Advanced Degrees Offered

LL.M., 1 year

Combined Degrees Offered

JD/MBA; JD/MPA in Public Affairs;
JD/MA in Latin American Studies;
JD/MS in Community and Regional
Planning; JD/MA in Russian, East
European & European studies;
JD/MA in Middle Eastern Studies;
informal combined programs lead-
ing to the JD & PhD in Government,
History, or Philosophy

Academics

Students at the University of Texas at Austin School of Law receive "the most bang for the buck in Texas" and a "great overall education." UT boasts a "huge network of alumni," a "focus on high-level analytical thinking," and a "diverse student body and faculty." Tuition is "relatively low," and graduates rack up very little debt. "I couldn't imagine a better law school as far as the quality of the professors," says one student. Another writes, "What I particularly appreciate is how they encourage us to try new areas of law. They show such enthusiasm and knowledge in the courses they teach that even the most boring or difficult course can be interesting and not so difficult after all." Another student brags, "In my first semester, I had the leading expert in admiralty law teach torts by singing songs on guitar, a contracts professor who could have been the stunt-double-professor in *The Paper Chase*, and a criminal law professor who clerked for Thurgood Marshall." Students praise the "writing program," "Constitutional law instruction," and "great clinics" that include a mental health clinic, a capital punishment clinic, and an actual innocence clinic, in which students screen and investigate claims of innocence from prison inmates. "The legal research and writing program is undervalued and under-funded," reports one student. Others would like to see "bar preparation improved." "Public interest law" could use more "interest" too. Students note smaller classes "would be nice." On the plus side, though, "going to such a large law school [guarantees a] wide range of courses."

When the time comes to get a real job, "The academic reputation enjoyed by Texas is unsurpassed in this part of the country." Thanks to this, students have "many great opportunities for jobs, internships, and clerkships." Being "right in the middle of one of the nation's biggest legal markets," UT maintains a "strong presence in the business and law communit[es]," effectively providing "ample employment opportunities." If you want to get out of the Lone Star State, no problem: More than 60 percent of the employers who interview on campus are from other states. There are differing views on Career Services, with some students seeing them as focusing "too much on students that want to go into a big-firm environment," while others find them "open, helpful, [and] a valuable resource."

"The facilities are generally nice" at UT, though they "could use some updating." "The law school occupies an oddly cobbled together set of interconnected buildings representing a number of architectural styles," says one student. Unfortunately, "the older buildings were not built to accommodate the number of students that attend this law school—it can get quite crowded at times." The "pretty" and "wonderfully comprehensive" law library is one of the "largest in the country," thanks to the "generous donations of alumni." Students are pleased that "the school is complete with wireless Internet throughout."

Life

Is UT competitive? It depends on whom you ask. According to one school of thought, "A lot of kids are really tough, [and] competition among 1Ls can be fierce." Others tell us that UT doesn't have "competitive tension running throughout the student body" and that the school "does a good job of making it seem more like a family and a support network."

MONICA INGRAM, ASSISTANT DEAN FOR ADMISSIONS AND FINANCIAL AID
727 EAST DEAN KEETON STREET, AUSTIN, TX 78705-3299
TEL: 512-232-1200 FAX: 512-471-2765
EMAIL: ADMISSIONS@LAW.UTEXAS.EDU • WEBSITE: WWW.UTEXAS.EDU /LAW

"Many political [and] social viewpoints are represented here," but lots of those viewpoints come from Texas. Most agree that the majority of students here were "born and raised in Texas." A student explains, "The saying that Texas is its own country and culture seems to be pretty accurate...[Yet despite] these negative impressions, I am falling in love with the charm of the area and may even stay here upon graduation." Students do add that the school "could improve by having more students with life and work experience."

Because the school's law student population "is so large, there's not a real feeling of camaraderie." Nevertheless, "The campus is very social" and "There's always something fun to do." "There are a wide variety of student organizations, from political or ethnic groups, to journals or practice-oriented organizations, to a hugely successful variety show written, produced, and performed by law students," a student explains. Students can take advantage of "tons of opportunities to do extracurricular things off campus" as well.

If there's one thing people agree on, it's that "Austin is a truly fascinating city with a bundle of outdoor activities, social life, and dining experiences."

Getting In

Admitted students at the 25th percentile have an LSAT score of 162 and a GPA of 3.3. Admitted students at the 75th percentile have an LSAT score of 168 and a GPA of 3.8. If you take the LSAT more than once, the school will consider all scores—not just the average of them. Note also that nonresident matriculation can only constitute 35 percent of the student body.

Clinical program required	No
Legal writing course requirement	Yes
Legal methods course requirement	No
Legal research course requirement	Yes
Moot court requirement	Yes
Public interest law requirement	No

ADMISSIONS

Selectivity Rating	95
# applications received	4,850
% applicants accepted	25
% acceptees attending	32
Average LSAT	167
LSAT Range	164–168
Average undergrad GPA	3.62
Application fee	$70
Regular application	2/1
Regular notification	4/1
Early application program	Yes
Early application deadline	11/1
Early application notification	1/31
Transfer students accepted	Yes
Evening division offered	No
Part-time accepted	No
LSDAS accepted	Yes

Applicants Also Look At

Boston University, Duke University, Cornell University, Vanderbilt University, The George Washington University

FINANCIAL FACTS

Annual tuition (in-state/ out-of-state)	$23,998/$39,642
Books and supplies	$1,024
Room & board (on/off-campus)	$9,000/$9,500
Financial aid application deadline	3/31
% first-year students receiving some sort of aid	87
% receiving some sort of aid	82
% of aid that is merit based	45
% receiving scholarships	65
Average grant	$9,620
Average loan	$23,760
Average total aid package	$33,250
Average debt	$70,814

EMPLOYMENT INFORMATION

		Grads Employed by Field (%)
Career Rating	96	Academic (2)
Rate of placement (nine months out)	99	Business/Industry (10)
Average starting salary	$113,000	Government (6)
State for bar exam	TX, NY, CA, IL	Judicial Clerkships (14)
Pass rate for first-time bar	90	Military (1)

Employers Who Frequently Hire Grads
Akin Gump Strauss Hauer & Feld LLP; Baker Botts LLP; Bracewell & Guliani LLP; Fulbright & Jaworski LLP; Haynes & Boone LLP; Jones Day LLP.

Private Practice (61)
Public Interest (4)
Other (2)

Prominent Alumni
Joseph D. Jamail, Jr., Owner, Jamail & Kolius Law Firm; Kay Bailey Hutchison, United States Senator; Frederico Pena, Former Secretary of Transportation.

UNIVERSITY OF TOLEDO
COLLEGE OF LAW

Academics

The University of Toledo College of Law offers an affordable, welcoming, yet structured atmosphere designed to "accommodate, relax, and train the student." The school has climbed in stature the last couple of years, yet retains its rather "humble, calm nature," partially due to its "intelligent, caring, involved, and self-regulating" students and decidedly not arrogant, "wonderful" professors. "We are given the chance to learn a very intense academic field, but not lose ourselves in the process," says a 1L. Students speak overwhelmingly of the school's obvious care and concern for their future, and the focus on learning and helping students to succeed "rather than promoting the more Darwinian method of setting 1Ls up for failure" the way that some law schools do. There is some confusion as to the curve policies, in that the school states that there is no curve for classes of less than 30 students, but professors "are quick to disagree with this." If you do want to discuss flagging grades or class issues, all professors have an "open door" policy, and are very accessible whenever you need them; UT Law "is one school that actually follows through on that." "First year students at UT are told upon arrival that the faculty does not keep set office hours because their primary role is to be available for student questions," says a student. Many 1Ls are also allowed to take a smaller course load the first year and catch up during the first summer, though this does not apply to transfer students. The "relatively new" administration is seemingly open to enhancing the law school experience on the terms of the students, and two of the deans have even had "small focus groups with the students to gather feedback on curriculum, teaching methods, facilities, and any other concern that the students feel the need to discuss." Students do wish for a "more formalized joint degree program" and a "broader variety of courses," as well as a less rigid attendance policy.

The research and writing program is "very thorough and puts an emphasis on real-world concerns," and the school furthers each student's practical background through almost-weekly opportunities to attend speakers or lecturers, such as Justice Scalia. Law Career Services "has put a great deal of effort" into the school's Mentorship programs and Public Service Externship programs in order to ensure that students have the opportunity to network while still in school; the office is "always working with students on getting jobs, experience, and training," although the employment rate after graduation leaves something to be desired, and students complain that much of this is focused on the "oversaturated" Toledo and Midwest market, when the school's lack of reputation means that more help is needed in other regions.

Aside from the somewhat archaic building and library, which are "more appropriate to an era of bell bottoms and platform shoes," the law school's facilities are up-to-date (though definitely "not glamorous), with wireless internet access available in "every corner of the building" and Smart Boards in every classroom. "If you can look beyond the bright orange decor, you can see it's a real quality institution," says a student.

CAROL E. FRENDT, ASSISTANT DEAN FOR ADMISSIONS
2801 WEST BANCROFT, TOLEDO, OH 43606
TEL: 419-530-4131 FAX: 419-530-4345
EMAIL: LAW.ADMISSIONS@UTOLEDO.EDU • WEBSITE: WWW.UTLAW.EDU

Life

Racial diversity isn't all that great here, but "that goes along with the area of the country," and the faculty is very sensitive to both racial and gender issues. The political views also "follow a Midwestern range," ranging from liberal to conservative. The student body remains uncompetitive and "gets along great," even though many students (especially 1L's) have GPA-based scholarships, and there's a great camaraderie amongst classes. To further this sense of interconnectedness, intramural sports are big, "there are many organizations to get involved with," and the Student Bar Association does "a very good job at bringing students together through social events (including weekly bar reviews) and volunteer opportunities." "Toledo isn't exactly a party town" and it's "not the most enjoyable place to be," so there aren't too many distractions from school, but for those looking to blow off steam, UT Law us is located within an hour of Detroit and Sandusky, within two hours of Dayton and Cleveland, and within five hours of Chicago, Indianapolis, Columbus, and Cincinnati. Still, when students are on campus, the parking situation "is a nightmare" and "it's difficult to get any kind of food after 11 P.M.," and the law school doesn't have any food options that can accommodate for the late hours students normally spend here.

Getting In

To be accepted by the University of Toledo College of Law for the full-time day program, you should aim for an LSAT score in the high 150s and a B-plus undergraduate GPA. The college enrolls around 90 full-time students in each entering class, for which the college receives approximately 1,000 applications annually. Part-time programs are slightly less competitive in their admissions requirements.

Moot court requirement	No
Public interest law requirement	No

ADMISSIONS

Selectivity Rating	**86**
# applications received	1,023
% applicants accepted	32
% acceptees attending	41
Average LSAT	159
LSAT Range	155–160
Average undergrad GPA	3.6
Regular application	Rolling, up to 8/1
Regular notification	Rolling
Early application program	No
Transfer students accepted	Yes
Evening division offered	Yes
Part-time accepted	Yes
LSDAS accepted	Yes

Applicants Also Look At

Michigan State University, University of Michigan—Ann Arbor, Indiana University—Bloomington, Indiana University—Purdue University Indianapolis, University of Cincinnati, The Ohio State University—Columbus, The University of Akron

FINANCIAL FACTS

Annual tuition (in-state/ out-of-state)	$16,440/$26,184
Books and supplies	$2,802
Fees	$1,452
Fees per credit	$64
Tuition per credit (in-state/out-of-state)	$685/$1,091
Room & board (off-campus)	$9,366
Financial aid application deadline	8/1
% first-year students receiving some sort of aid	93
% receiving some sort of aid	92
% of aid that is merit based	20
% receiving scholarships	42
Average grant	$16,869
Average loan	$26,666
Average total aid package	$32,958
Average debt	$56,898

EMPLOYMENT INFORMATION

Career Rating	**76**
Rate of placement (nine months out)	95
Average starting salary	$72,761
State for bar exam	OH, MI
Pass rate for first-time bar	87

Employers Who Frequently Hire Grads

Robinson Curphey & O'Connell; Eastman & Smith; Marshall & Melhorn; Shumaker,Loop & Kendrick; Reminger & Reminger; Spengler Nathanson.

Prominent Alumni

Honorable Judith Lanzinger, Justice, Ohio Supreme Court; Robert E. Latta, Ohio Fifth Congressional District; Joseph Farnan, U.S. District Court, Wilmington, DE.

Grads Employed by Field (%)

Academic (4)
Business/Industry (13)
Government (24)
Judicial Clerkships (4)
Military (1)
Private Practice (44)
Public Interest (8)
Other (2)

THE UNIVERSITY OF TULSA
COLLEGE OF LAW

Academics

One of only three law schools in the state, the University of Tulsa College of Law works to turn out lawyers who will impact their communities in a positive manner. Noted for its programs in Native American Law and Oil and Gas Law, there are many chances to learn outside the classroom, all of which "are supported by the school." The school does seem to have made good working relationships with the area judges and some other companies, and opportunities for internships, clerkships and other related experience endeavors are "plentiful," and "even students with poor grades are able to secure top clerkships because of the demand." The excellent legal writing and research programs go along with the similarly broad research facilities and staff, especially the absolutely top-notch library, which is new within the last few years—many undergraduate students even go to it to study.

The professors here are tough without being overbearing, "taking a relaxed attitude that is appropriate for Tulsa while still maintaining a highly academic and respectable presence," and most "know the right mix of teaching styles in terms of challenging and helping you." Though there are a few complaints in the mix, those who attend TU appreciate the efforts of the faculty to bring practical experience into their teachings and the use of adjuncts to bring "real world" experience into the classrooms. No one has ever found a time when professors aren't available outside of class to help with questions or difficulties, and "even in large classes, professors tend to know students by name when outside of the classroom." "My contracts professor gave the whole class his personal cell phone number on the first day of class, so that we could call if we had any questions or problems!" says a student. "The communication could be a little more frank and open between administration and students," says a 2L. Though the school has seen some turnover in the Deans position in recent years, the current Dean is committed to facilitating student feedback. Post-graduation concerns are the main issue that students wish to be addressed. Though growing, the school's reputation outside of the region is not well-known. Students not in the top 5–10% of the class may need to be a little more proactive in their job search. Luckily, there are three respected journals on which students can participate, which "really opens up law review for those students whose academic success is not best measured by letter grades."

APRIL M. FOX, ASSISTANT DEAN OF ADMISSIONS
3120 EAST FOURTH PLACE, TULSA, OK 74104-3189
TEL: 918-631-2406 FAX: 918-631-3630
EMAIL: LAWADMISISONS@UTULSA.EDU • WEBSITE: WWW.LAW.UTULSA.EDU

Life

Located in downtown Tulsa, TU Law's campus is "beautiful and continually growing." The city is "the perfect size for those who don't want to live in crowded cities but who also don't want to be in the middle of nowhere." The building itself is aesthetically mixed. This summer, the school plans to massively renovate the "hideous" common area (known as the Pit due to its recessed nature). Further, students note that the straight-out-of-the-70s classrooms offer a distinctly despised juxtaposition with a much beloved library that one 1L claims "is a great place to live for the next 3 years of my life!" While TU might not be a highest tier school, those who chose to attend really do love it. Relations among students are terrific, and "everyone is very friendly and cordial and willing to help one another." Despite the curve, there's no real competitive streak, and "the upperclassmen also take a lot of time to answer your questions or concerns or just sit and talk about school in general." With an enrollment of around 424 law students, students are able to get know a very large percentage of the students in this vaguely high school atmosphere ("right down to the sack lunches and lockers"), and though cliques and gossip do make the rounds, "these cliques intermingle and aren't deeply segregated" and "most everyone gets along really well." The diversity of the student body, both ethnically and socially, is at respectable levels for almost all students. As for time spent not in the awful classrooms, "the social life is what you make of it." "You don't have to go out of your way to make a friend and in most cases that friend leads to many others," says a student. The Student Bar Association is very active, and "there is always something going on, and families are welcome to come together."

Getting In

Tulsa Law, like all law schools, admits students whose test scores and academic background suggest they will be successful in the study of law. It is also a little more welcoming of older students than many of its peers. Tulsa Law admits students from across the nation, and more than half of the student body hails from outside Oklahoma.

Legal methods	
course requirement	Yes
Legal research	
course requirement	Yes
Moot court requirement	No
Public interest	
law requirement	No

ADMISSIONS

Selectivity Rating	74
# applications received	1,293
# applicants accepted	566
# acceptees attending	139
Average LSAT	155
LSAT Range	152–157
Average undergrad GPA	3.27
Application fee	$30
Regular application	Rolling, up to 7/30
Regular notification	Rolling
Early application program	No
Transfer students accepted	Yes
Evening division offered	No
Part-time accepted	Yes
LSDAS accepted	Yes

Applicants Also Look At

University of Missouri—Kansas City, University of Oklahoma, University of Arkansas—Fayetteville, Oklahoma City University, St. Mary's University, Texas Wesleyan University, Washburn University

International Students

TOEFL required	
of international students	Yes
Minimum TOEFL	
(paper/computer/web)	570/230/90

FINANCIAL FACTS

Annual tuition	$27,500
Books and supplies	$1,500
Fees	$134
Tuition per credit	$1,117
Room & board	
(on/off-campus)	$6,100/$7,800
% first-year students	
receiving some sort of aid	95
% receiving some sort of aid	94
% receiving scholarships	47
Average grant	$13,518
Average loan	$29,977
Average total aid package	$33,779
Average debt	$65,847

EMPLOYMENT INFORMATION

Career Rating	75	Grads Employed by Field (%)
Rate of placement (nine months out)	91.6	Academic (3)
Average starting salary	$77,355	Business/Industry (21)
State for bar exam	OK, TX, MO, CO	Government (10)
Pass rate for first-time bar	88.75	Judicial Clerkships (1)

Employers Who Frequently Hire Grads
Law Firms; Energy Companies; State and Federal Government

Military (1)
Private Practice (59)
Public Interest (5)

Prominent Alumni
Layn R. Phillips, Member, Irell & Manella; former U.S. District Judge, Western District of OK; Drew Edmondson, Oklahoma Attorney General; Kayla Paige Shell, Legal Director, Dell, Inc.

UNIVERSITY OF UTAH
S. J. QUINNEY COLLEGE OF LAW

Academics

Students at the S.J. Quinney College of Law at the University of Utah are quite confident that they are receiving the "best law education available in the country for the price." The "extremely approachable" and "very student-oriented" professors "make every effort to meet with students and make sure they understand the material." "I went to an expensive liberal arts school for undergrad that advertised itself as offering available and motivated professors," relates a 3L. "My undergrad experience pales in comparison to the individual attention and encouragement I have received at this state school." "Professors here actually try to minimize stress rather than build it up," agrees a 1L. The standard Socratic Method is not en vogue. Some students tell us that professors' more easygoing approach allows "for a more comfortable environment in which to learn." Other students say it's "just too easy to doze off." "I know this sounds crazy," admits a 1L, "but I wish more of the professors would use the Socratic Method or, at least, engage the students in class more."

The administration at Utah "is always looking for new, creative ways to improve the school." "The new dean has brought a new vision of Dream Big," and administrators "demonstrate a great interest in not only hearing the students' voices, but in improving student experience, academic quality, and transition to real-world practice." "All the deans keep themselves highly available." "Nobody's got an attitude," and "no one is too busy to answer a question."

Students here are "right in the middle of Salt Lake City, surrounded by large and prestigious law firms." The College of Law has "a great relationship with practitioners and judges in the community" and "There are plenty of opportunities to gain practical experience." "It is fairly easy to do judicial clinics and other legal internships." "Terrific outreach programs afford students opportunities to work pro bono with public interest organizations." The "excellent first-year legal writing program" is "rigorous and well thought out." "You'll walk out of here writing better than most lawyers who have been practicing for years," claims a 2L. If you want to specialize, "There are plenty of courses, especially in natural resources law." Professional Development Office is "friendly and helpful," but "A lot of students get jobs from other sources."

"A new [law school] building is in the works," but in the meantime, the current "aging" and "undersized" building is "from the late 60s and reflects that boring architecture." "Our building sucks, in a word," laments a 2L. "The campus seems designed to drive students off campus as soon as classes are over." The computer network is "spotty in some places," and the library gets average reviews.

Life

"People at this school actually seem happy," and "There is a sense of community and connectedness" on campus. "We're small," explains one student. "You'll know most of the school and faculty by the time you're a 2L." "The U fosters a great environment, where everyone helps everyone else." "Individual personalities flourish and the interaction of personalities is like that among family members who have known each other their entire lives." "People here see the whole person. It's a very collaborative environment."

Students report that their peers are "equal parts brilliant, collegial, encouraging, competitive, and just flat-out a joy." It's "probably an older and more mature crowd than at the average law school." Many students "are married with children." "I don't regret for a moment choosing to come here as a 30-something, second-career mom," says a 2L. "I

Susan Baca, Operations Coordinator for Admissions & Finaincial
Admissions, 332 South 1400 East, Room 101, Salt Lake City, UT 84112-0730
Tel: 801-581-7479 Fax: 801-820-9154
Email: admissions@law.utah.edu • Website: www.law.utah.edu

fit in." "The nontraditional demographic allows for an interesting mix and a few extra designated drivers." The Church of Latter-Day Saints is, of course, prevalent everywhere in Utah. "Don't think that because this isn't BYU there won't be plenty of Mormons." Politically, "The school is fairly evenly split between liberals and conservatives." "The divide can be fierce at times," but "Overall there is great acceptance of different viewpoints and lifestyles."

"The social life is not great" here. "Salt Lake culture is fairly conservative," and "The Mormon influence is felt both in the city and in the law school." Though wild parties are few, Utah sponsors "many social events which are geared toward building relationships between the school and the local bar." "Throughout the week there are plenty of opportunities to hang out with students in many different social settings and activities." Off campus, "Salt Lake City is a gorgeous place to live" "The city is clean; the crime rate is low." And It's surrounded by "one of the most scenic and beautiful areas in the country." "Outdoor life is great." "We are six hours away from red-rock desert and half an hour's drive from the greatest snow on earth," declares a 1L. "You can spend all that tuition money you're saving on ski passes and road trips."

Getting In

Recently admitted students at the 25th percentile have LSAT scores of 157 and GPAs of nearly 3.4. Admitted students at the 75th percentile have LSAT scores of 162 and GPAs of about 3.8. If you take the LSAT more than once, Utah will presume to use the highest score.

ADMISSIONS

Selectivity Rating	**86**
# applications received	1,089
# applicants accepted	346
# acceptees attending	123
Average LSAT	160
LSAT Range	157–162
Average undergrad GPA	3.63
Application fee	$60
Regular application	Rolling, up to 7/31
Regular notification	Rolling
Early application program	No
Transfer students accepted	Yes
Evening division offered	No
Part-time accepted	No
LSDAS accepted	Yes

Applicants Also Look At

University of Arizona, University of Colorado at Boulder, University of Denver, Arizona State University, University of Oregon, Brigham Young University, University of Washington, George Washington University

International Students

Minimum TOEFL (paper/computer)	600/250

FINANCIAL FACTS

Annual tuition (in-state/ out-of-state)	$13,625/$29.134
Books and supplies	$1,916
Fees	$708
Room & board	$9,072
Financial aid application deadline	4/1
% first-year students receiving some sort of aid	88
% receiving some sort of aid	83
% of aid that is merit based	30
% receiving scholarships	53
Average grant	$5,010
Average loan	$18,780
Average total aid package	$24,780
Average debt	$54,273

EMPLOYMENT INFORMATION

Career Rating	**70**
Average starting salary	$76,383
State for bar exam	UT, CA, NV, AZ, ID
Pass rate for first-time bar	90

Employers Who Frequently Hire Grads

Utah Attorney General's Office, Parsons, Behle &Latimer(SLC,UT); Ray Quinney & Nebeker(SLC,UT); Jones Waldo Holbrook & Mconough.

Prominent Alumni

Larry EchoHawk, Assistant Secretary of Indian Affairs for U.S. Department of Interior; Robert Bennet, U.S. Senator; Deborah Dugan, President, Disney Publishing World Wide; Kelli Sager, Voted one of the 50 most influential women lawyers by the National Law Journal

Grads Employed by Field (%)

Academic (1)
Business/Industry (11)
Government (12)
Judicial Clerkships (11)
Military (1)
Private Practice (62)
Public Interest (2)

UNIVERSITY OF VIRGINIA
SCHOOL OF LAW

INSTITUTIONAL INFORMATION

Public/private	Public
Student-faculty ratio	13:1
% faculty part-time	54
% faculty female	22
% faculty minority	5
Total faculty	150

SURVEY SAYS...

Great research resources
Great library staff
Abundant externship/internship/
clerkship opportunities
Beautiful campus
Good social life

STUDENTS

Enrollment of law school	1,156
% male/female	59/41
% out-of-state	59
% full-time	100
% minority	16
# of countries represented	16
Average age of entering class	23

ACADEMICS

Academic Experience Rating	**99**
Profs interesting rating	97
Profs accessible rating	99
Hours of study per day	3.76

Academic Specialties
Civil procedure, commercial law, constitutional law, corporation securities, criminal law, environmental law, human rights, international law, labor law, legal history, legal philosophy, taxation, intellectual property law

Advanced Degrees Offered
LL.M., 1 year; S.JD, 2–5 years

Combined Degrees Offered
JD/MA in Economics, English, Government or Foreign Affairs, History, Philosophy, Sociology, 3–4 years; JD/MS in Accounting, 3.5 years; JD/MPH, 3.5 years; JD/MBA, 4 years; JD/Masters in Urban and Environmental Planning, 4 years; JD/MPA, 4 years; JD/MA in Law and Diplomacy, 4 years; JD/MA in International Relations, 4 years

Academics

"You couldn't pay me to go anywhere else," says one of the many thrilled students attending the University of Virginia School of Law. "I don't think there is another law school that strikes such a perfect balance between rigorous academics and genuine fun. People are actually happy to be here and sad to leave." UVA offers a vast array of different concentrations; students can participate in no fewer than nine Law Review journals; and several interdisciplinary programs utilize the strengths of the medical and business schools. "There are many opportunities for independent research" as well.

By all accounts, Virginia Law's "enthusiastic, expert" professors are "tremendous." "Witty and entertaining," they are "teachers in the fullest sense of the word," and take an "extraordinary interest in their students." "They genuinely respect all opinions" and "People from both sides of the political spectrum are welcomed and encouraged to speak," proclaims a 2L. Outside of class, "friendly interactions" are the norm. "I have had lunch with every single professor this semester and so have most of my classmates," declares a 1L. The "totally responsive" administration is also "excellent." The deans and the staff "try their best to help" whenever students identify problems. "I hardly notice the administration, which says wonders," observes a 1L.

Not shy about singing UVA's praises, students rave: The facilities are "gorgeous, fantastic, [and] state of the art," and "The grounds are breathtakingly beautiful." "UVA has more windows than any law school in America," alleges one student. Classrooms with "wood paneling and super-comfy seats" "make it bearable to sit through an hour and 15 minutes of class." The honor code here is a big deal, and "It is not uncommon for students to leave laptops, purses, wallets, cell phones, and textbooks unattended in the library and study areas."

"Employment opportunities abound" for UVA Law graduates. "Professors are not afraid to pull strings to get students jobs, particularly in the public interest sectors." Many students "with middling to low GPAs still get positions with large law firms." The school "tends to channel students into traditional career paths," explains a 2L. "This law school aims to produce law firm lawyers," and most students "expect to graduate and make a salary upwards of $130,000." UVA's "clerkship reputation is phenomenal," and the "dedicated and comprehensive" public service program "offers generous loan repayment" options.

Life

"UVA School of Law is the summer camp of all law schools" and has arguably the "greatest quality of life of any law school." "There is beer on the quad every Thursday afternoon and a law-school-wide party at a local bar every Thursday evening." For many students, "Social life revolves largely around softball and beer," "with some reading on the side." Others say that "the whole 'beer-and-softball thing' is always exaggerated." Pretty much everyone agrees, though, that "UVA Law strikes an ideal balance between work and fun, study and softball, theoretical and practical." "People will go out three to four nights a week, but will still be sitting in torts class the next morning no less brilliant for being hung over," claims an impressed 1L. "The most overwhelming thing about UVA in the first few weeks is not its academics," admits another 1L. "It's the sheer number of social events." Be warned, however: "This is not a slacker school." "There is a lot of pressure" when exams get close.

Jason Trujillo, Senior Assistant Dean
580 Massie Road, Charlottesville, VA 22903-1738
Tel: 434-924-7351 Fax: 434-982-2128
Email: lawadmit@virginia.edu • Website: www.law.virginia.edu

UVA's "easygoing" students describe themselves as "intelligent and insightful," not to mention "industrious and well-rounded." "Students are competitive without being negatively so," says a 3L. "Any competition here is healthy, and the students who choose to perform exceptionally well have an opportunity [to do so]," while "Those who want to just work hard enough to get good (but not great) grades can do so with no pressure or fear that they won't get a desirable job." Some students say that "the school could stand to be a bit more diverse" ethnically, but students definitely display "varying opinions" and "varied interests." "One class of mine has a former Navy fighter pilot, a neurosurgeon, and a top Division I basketball player," says a first-year student. Politically, UVA is home to "a mix of both conservatives and liberals," which "provides for more interesting conversation." "Tolerance for diverse opinions and a general laid-back attitude make this place a real joy to be at day in and day out," says a 2L.

Off campus, the surrounding town of Charlottesville has a "very cool downtown," a thriving "bohemian art scene," and "a surprisingly sophisticated host of restaurants" and "small clubs." The local music scene is fabulous too. "The only people who will be unhappy at UVA Law are those who worship city life," says one student. "Charlottesville can be a very small place for anyone who has ever lived in even a moderately sized city."

Getting In

Admitted students at the 25th percentile have LSAT scores of roughly 167 and GPAs of about 3.5. Admitted students at the 75th percentile have LSAT scores of about 171 and GPAs of just over 3.8. UVA has a policy of not having a policy when it comes to evaluating multiple LSAT scores. It's purely case by case.

Clinical program required	No
Legal writing course requirement	Yes
Legal methods course requirement	Yes
Legal research course requirement	Yes
Moot court requirement	No
Public interest law requirement	No

ADMISSIONS

Selectivity Rating	**98**
# applications received	6,548
% applicants accepted	20
% acceptees attending	29
Average LSAT	170
LSAT Range	167–171
Average undergrad GPA	3.8
Application fee	$75
Regular application	3/1
Regular notification	Rolling
Early application program	Yes
Early application deadline	12/1
Early application notification	12/15
Transfer students accepted	Yes
Evening division offered	No
Part-time accepted	No
LSDAS accepted	Yes

Applicants Also Look At
Harvard University, Columbia University, University of Michigan—Ann Arbor, New York University, Duke University, University of Pennsylvania, Georgetown University

International Students

TOEFL required of international students	Yes
Minimum TOEFL (paper/computer)	600/250

FINANCIAL FACTS

Annual tuition (in-state/ out-of-state)	$34,581/$39,363
Books and supplies	$2,600
Fees	$2,437
Room & board	$15,700
Financial aid application deadline	3/1
% first-year students receiving some sort of aid	87
% receiving some sort of aid	90
% of aid that is merit based	21
% receiving scholarships	57
Average grant	$15,122
Average loan	$38,578
Average total aid package	$47,444
Average debt	$76,150

EMPLOYMENT INFORMATION

Career Rating	**94**	**Grads Employed by Field (%)**
Rate of placement (nine months out)	99	Business/Industry (1)
State for bar exam	NY, VA	Government (3)
Pass rate for first-time bar	95	Judicial Clerkships (14)
Employers Who Frequently Hire Grads		Military (1)
Graduates are employed in every top 100		Private Practice (77)
firm in the country.		Public Interest (4)

UNIVERSITY OF WASHINGTON
SCHOOL OF LAW

Academics

The University of Washington School of Law, one of three law schools in the country on the quarter system, offers great opportunities to control your own legal education and lots of opportunities for learning and experience outside class. The school is well known for its numerous student organizations, many of which have a big public interest/community volunteering aspect; there's also a public service requirement that has "spawned many interesting externship and clinic opportunities for students." Still, students say that despite the touting of public service law, most of the events and funding are driven almost solely by these groups, and the school "doesn't offer much formal curriculum in that area." The Contorts program here is especially "spectacular," as it "allows students to look at a legal problem from a variety of perspectives which you don't get by looking at torts and contracts individually." Small section sizes help make UW seem cozier, and while the forced curve and the newly introduced class rankings system does mean that it can be a competitive place, this competition is "mostly because people want to do well, not because they want others to do well."

The collaborative atmosphere between the students and faculty is a great boon to the school and makes for a great working environment and a very collegiate atmosphere, so that "gunners and ultra-competitive attitudes are frowned on here." Many of the professors are brilliant in their field, and they "bring their own expertise and practical real world experience in the field in ways that really animate and extend the subject matter." Their willingness to discuss almost anything outside of class is deeply appreciated by students, even if there are "a few professors that should never be allowed anywhere near 1Ls." The law building is new and built with a grant from Bill Gates, so classrooms and study areas are "clean and up-to-date," and the building itself is "light and spacious" and has incredible views out over the sound and downtown Seattle. Classes are recorded and podcast for those with parental responsibilities (an accommodation "especially invaluable to student-parents ") and the law library is amazing and gorgeous, with librarians that "are among the best anywhere."

The administration is genuine in their care for students, and one of the deans even hired an on-call psychologist for students to use for free in the interest of helping them to maintain their mental health, but the two hands-down weakest areas are found in Financial Aid and Career Services. The single administrator who runs all of the Financial Aid accounts for the law school is "unable to answer routine questions" and "can tell you the ins and outs of computer solitaire, but wouldn't know where to find a grant or extra loan if it bit him on the butt," and the Career Services office is "great if you want to work in a private law firm" or stay in Washington to practice, but "if you want to work in international human rights/humanitarian law or domestic non-profit law" the institutional resources aren't really there, and "job postings themselves are mostly centered in the Pacific Northwest." "They are more talk than action and somewhat out of touch with what employers are really looking for," says a student.

KATHY SWINEHART, ADMISSIONS SUPERVISOR
WILLIAM H. GATES HALL, BOX 353020, SEATTLE, WA 98195-3020
TEL: 206-543-4078 FAX: 206-543-5671
EMAIL: LAWADM@U.WASHINGTON.EDU • WEBSITE: WWW.LAW.WASHINGTON.EDU

Life

Like any other law-school, UW has their share of type-A's, but the personality clashes are minimal. It's a small and tight-knit community, so naturally gossip can travel at the speed of light, but "it's all good natured and there is rarely, if ever, any rancor or backbiting." Competitiveness is kept to a minimum, and one student says that if he were to miss class, "several people would email and offer to review the material with me." UW's rather long orientation really bonds folks, and many people report having made some of the best friends of their lives in their classes. Located in a neighborhood of Seattle that "is reasonably funky and fun, and not too far from the center of town," there are also a lot of student groups at the law school that are active, as well as intramural sports and school-organized weekly meet-ups at bars, so students can easily find something to match their interests. "There are not parties every weekend, but there are plenty of social events if you make the effort to find out about them and get involved," says a student. The left-leaning school is really committed to diversity and as a result, there's a wide range of age, experience, class, nationality, ethnicity, and disability; the sizeable older crowd "is great in the school environment, but socially non-existent outside the school."

Getting In

It's tough getting admitted to the University of Washington, but the school follows your basic law school admissions policy: It puts heavy weight on applicants' undergraduate records and LSAT scores, also considering letters of recommendation, work and volunteer experience, and personal statements. The vast majority of enrollees (about 70 percent) are residents of Washington State; however, residency is not a major factor in an admissions decision.

Legal writing course requirement	Yes
Legal methods course requirement	Yes
Legal research course requirement	Yes
Moot court requirement	No
Public interest law requirement	Yes

ADMISSIONS

Selectivity Rating	90
# applications received	2,585
% applicants accepted	23
% acceptees attending	31
Average LSAT	162
LSAT Range	159–165
Average undergrad GPA	3.65
Application fee	$50
Regular application	1/15
Regular notification	4/1
Early application program	No
Transfer students accepted	Yes
Evening division offered	No
Part-time accepted	No
LSDAS accepted	Yes

Applicants Also Look At

University of Southern California; Seattle University; University of California—Berkeley; University of California—Los Angeles; The George Washington University; Georgetown University; University of California, Hastings

FINANCIAL FACTS

Annual tuition (in-state/ out-of-state)	$17,846/$26,231
Books and supplies	$1,500
Room & board	$16,626
Financial aid application deadline	2/28
% first-year students receiving some sort of aid	85
% receiving some sort of aid	85
% of aid that is merit based	10
% receiving scholarships	43
Average grant	$7,500
Average loan	$22,500
Average total aid package	$30,000
Average debt	$65,507

EMPLOYMENT INFORMATION

Career Rating		**86**
Rate of placement (nine months out)		97
Average starting salary		$90,000
State for bar exam		WA
Pass rate for first-time bar		90

Employers Who Frequently Hire Grads
Preston Gates & Ellis; Davis Wright Tremaine; Perkins Coie; Stoel Rives; King County Prosecuting Attorney; Garvey Schubert & Barer.

Prominent Alumni
Tom Foley, Former Speaker, U.S. House of Representatives; Gerry Alexander, Chief Justice, Washington Supreme Court.

Grads Employed by Field (%)
Academic (2)
Business/Industry (7)
Government (14)
Judicial Clerkships (16)
Private Practice (54)
Public Interest (6)
Other (1)

UNIVERSITY OF WISCONSIN—MADISON
LAW SCHOOL

Academics

The University of Wisconsin Law School takes its motto "law in action" very seriously. The law in action philosophy is "the notion that the law on the books must be understood in the context of the way the law really works on the ground." To that end, the "school places a big emphasis on clinical programs," with "numerous and varied" opportunities to gain "practical experience with clients—even during 1L year." "The Innocence Project and Consumer Law Clinics," for example, "are busy around the clock" and the latter routinely "wins class actions that help fund itself." What's more, the practical impact of the law is not divorced from the approach to teaching law in the classroom: "Many if not most professors adopt a pragmatic approach to teaching the law, focusing as much on the public policy as the doctrine."

Students say professors here "are very knowledgeable in their fields. Many of them are well-known figures across the state, have a tremendous influence on the state government, and are excellent 'people to know' if you plan to remain in the state of Wisconsin." "Professors employ a modified Socratic Method to make students more comfortable," which "is refreshing at first but can lead to classes that drag if they depend on student participation." Exhibiting a particular "strength in contracts," Wisconsin's "public interest and criminal law classes are world class." However, students say the business law courses "[are] not taught by a strong business law faculty."

"Wisconsin does not have the most attractive law building"—"dark, depressing, stale" is how one student describes it. However, it does have certain features that recommend it. There is, for example, "excellent wireless Internet throughout the building." In addition, "The library is magnificent!" It has "one end composed entirely of glass, overlooking Bascom Hill (the heart of the university)." Inside, you will find "library staff [who] are extremely friendly and willing to go the extra mile to help you find what you are looking for." If they can't do it for you, the "Lexis and Westlaw reps are knowledgeable and accessible."

Cost-conscious and risk-averse students should note that "in-state tuition and automatic bar admission are two of the best deals around." Automatic bar admission? Yes, you read correctly. The University of Wisconsin Law School is only one of two law schools in the Badger State (the other being Marquette) that enjoys a certain "diploma privilege which allows you to be licensed in Wisconsin without taking the bar exam."

Life

One of the signature traits of the Wisconsin law experience is the school's "laid-back atmosphere." "Considering [that] law school is supposed to be some sort of nightmare where everything is like the *The Paper Chase*" students are constantly "surprised [by] how uncompetitive UW is." For example, "If you miss a lecture, it is commonplace for a classmate to e-mail you notes without being asked."

Students across the board say "This is a very left-wing law school, on par with Berkeley and Boulder." A lot of students love the liberal atmosphere on campus, but others complain that the "overall learning environment is hindered by an absence of diversity in thought." "Conservative ideas are not seriously considered in classes while liberal ideas are," observes one student. Despite their pervasive liberal ethos, students note that "there is definitely a degree of de facto segregation within the student body." Students point to "the large number of student orgs designed around different minority groups," which they feel sometimes "creates an 'us against them' mentality."

MICHAEL A. HALL, ASSISTANT DEAN FOR ADMISSIONS AND FINANCIAL AID
975 BASCOM MALL, MADISON, WI 53706
TEL: 608-262-5914 FAX: 608-263-3190
EMAIL: ADMISSIONS@LAW.WISC.EDU • WEBSITE: LAW.WISC.EDU

Socially, "The attitude among students is to work hard and play hard." Lucky for them "The law school is a very active environment. Students who want to be involved have a number of different organizations they can join and the student government offers a number of social events to facilitate interaction not only within classes but from year to year." A little-known fact is that UW was the first university to open a campus pub after passage of the twenty-first amendment, and a proud drinking culture still perseveres in the law school. Some students go so far as to say that there is "too much drinking." Bar Reviews, Dean Mixers, and similar social events "always have a keg."

Hometown "Madison is a fantastic place to be in school—it's a beautiful city with lots to do, but the cost of living is very affordable and the city isn't so distracting that you end up neglecting your studies." Students also "love their proximity to Chicago" for those times when they do crave the distractions that can help them to neglect their studies.

Getting In

Incoming students at the 25th percentile have an LSAT score of 156 and a GPA of 3.2. Incoming students at the 75th percentile have an LSAT score of 163 and a GPA of 3.7. UW Law School excels in minority student recruitment, and minority applicants who meet all the traditional criteria for admission often have a better shot at getting in. If you are in any way a unique or nontraditional student, it could work in your favor here.

Legal research	
course requirement	Yes
Moot court requirement	No
Public interest	
law requirement	No

ADMISSIONS

Selectivity Rating	**87**
# applications received	2,797
# applicants accepted	804
# acceptees attending	249
Average LSAT	160
LSAT Range	157–163
Average undergrad GPA	3.53
Application fee	$56
Regular application	Rolling, up to 3/1
Regular notification	Rolling
Early application program	No
Transfer students accepted	Yes
Evening division offered	No
Part-time accepted	No
LSDAS accepted	Yes

Applicants Also Look At
University of Illinois at Urbana-Champaign, American University, University of Minnesota—Twin Cities, Boston College, Marquette University, DePaul University, Loyola University—Chicago

International Students

TOEFL required	
of international students	Yes

FINANCIAL FACTS

Annual tuition (in-state/ out-of-state)	$14,730/$34,655
Books and supplies	$2,160
Room & board	$8,250
Financial aid application deadline	3/1
% first-year students receiving some sort of aid	90
% receiving some sort of aid	90
% of aid that is merit based	20
% receiving scholarships	23
Average grant	$10,000
Average loan	$23,000
Average debt	$66,300

EMPLOYMENT INFORMATION

Career Rating	**89**	**Grads Employed by Field (%)**
Rate of placement (nine months out)	97	Academic (4)
Average starting salary	$91,014	Business/Industry (9)
State for bar exam	WI	Government (9)
Pass rate for first-time bar	100	Judicial Clerkships (5)

Employers Who Frequently Hire Grads
Military (1)
Foley & Lardner; Quarles & Brady; Godfrey & Kahn; Reinhart Boerner; Michael Best & Friedrich; McDermott Will & Emery; Skadden Arps; Latham & Watkins.

Private Practice (61)
Public Interest (10)
Other (1)

Prominent Alumni
Tommy Thompson, Fmr Sec. of Health & Human Srvc, frmr Gov of WI; Tammy Baldwin, U.S. House of Representatives, Madison, WI.

UNIVERSITY OF WYOMING
COLLEGE OF LAW

INSTITUTIONAL INFORMATION

Public/private	Public
Student-faculty ratio	12:1
% faculty part-time	15
% faculty female	41
% faculty minority	15
Total faculty	27

SURVEY SAYS...

Diverse opinions accepted
in classrooms
Great research resources
Great library staff
Students never sleep

STUDENTS

Enrollment of law school	219
% male/female	54/46
% out-of-state	37
% full-time	100
% minority	10
% international	3
# of countries represented	2
Average age of entering class	26

ACADEMICS

Academic Experience Rating	**70**
Profs interesting rating	69
Profs accessible rating	90
Hours of study per day	4.57

Academic Specialties
environmental law, natural
resources law, energy law

Advanced Degrees Offered
JD, 3 years

Combined Degrees Offered
JD/MPA, 3.5–4 years; JD/MBA,
3.5 –4 years; JD/MA Environment &
Natural Resources

Clinical program required	No
Legal writing	
course requirement	Yes
Legal methods	
course requirement	Yes
Legal research	
course requirement	Yes
Moot court requirement	Yes
Public interest	
law requirement	No

Academics

The University of Wyoming College of Law is one of the smallest law schools in the country and, according to students here, "completely underrated." They tell us that "small class sizes" (roughly 80 in each first-year class), "low cost," "a friendly and unintimidating atmosphere," and a "wonderfully approachable" faculty make UW "a great school." "At the University of Wyoming you can be on a first-name basis with the deans and all the professors," boasts a 1L. "The deans have an open-door policy" and the "extremely supportive" administration "has to be one of the best around."

Legal writing is solid and "Opportunities for practical experience are top-notch." Five real-world legal clinics and a wealth of externships provide "a lot of great practical opportunities" for students. A "huge environmental law contingent" takes advantage of internships and externships associated with the "excellent" environment and natural resources program. There is "great networking within the state" and "plenty of opportunity for employment" reportedly awaits students upon graduation. "Wyoming—including the law school—tends to take care of its own," explains one student. "I am confident, if I want to work outside of Wyoming, I will be able to find a job," adds a fearless 1L.

The "highly qualified" professors at UW "teach a wide variety of course subjects" and "most" are "pretty good at teaching the material." "Some of the professors are the best you could hope for." Others "are less inspiring" and "Some courses they teach might not truly be their expertise." However, "The professors are extremely helpful and will give you all the individual attention that you need and want," explains a 2L. "Of course, this leaves little chance of 'blending' to escape notice." "I have never felt intimidated to approach any of them in order to ask a question or advice," adds a 2L. "I have professors who have offered to look over sample exam answers and who have given their home telephone numbers out."

Students say that the facilities "could use some work," but they are "by no means hideous." Some aspects of the College of Law building are "a relic of the 1970s," including the "limited space" and "dated décor." At least "There are a few nice classrooms that are really updated for the new technology requirements of school." Wireless capabilities and the number of electrical outlets facilities have been "vastly improved" in recent years. "In every carrel in the library, there is a power outlet for a laptop" and "There is no lack of computer stations." Tech support is "very helpful" as well.

Life

Many students say the University of Wyoming "clearly lacks diversity in terms of ethnic minorities" but they also note that geography is a limitation in this regard. "I don't think that the lack of diversity is caused by lack of effort in recruiting," observes a 2L. "I just don't think that many people want to move to Wyoming." There are quite a few nontraditional students here but "Most students are traditional students" just a few years out of undergrad.

Academically, a "competitive yet cooperative spirit" prevails. "Students are very friendly and helpful to each other." They actually "leave their laptops unlocked overnight." The "very small" size of UW "is a great strength of the school" because it fosters "a very strong sense of community" and "a real camaraderie" "regardless of class rank." Students here become lifelong friends and colleagues. "We are able to have a much more intimate relationship with the faculty and staff, administration, and classmates," explains a 2L. "We don't let the competition of getting a high ranking get in

ANTHONY PLEDGER, COORDINATOR OF ADMISSIONS
DEPT. 3035, 1000 E. UNIVERSITY AVE., LARAMIE, WY 82071
TEL: 307-766-6416 FAX: 307-766-6417
EMAIL: LAWADMIS@UWYO.EDU • WEBSITE: WWW.UWYO.EDU/LAW

the way of establishing meaningful relationships." "I transferred in from another law school that was just [an] overly competitive environment," elaborates another 2L. "Students here are much more friendly and helpful toward one another."

"The people of Wyoming are the nicest people in the world," and "no one's complaining about the 'lower cost' of living in Wyoming." However, Laramie—the surrounding town of about 30,000 souls—isn't much in the way of culture and nightlife. At 7,200 feet, Laramie is also home to "the highest elevation law school in the country." "It's bloody cold up here," cautions a 1L. It's also "safe" and "very Western." "You will typically run into other law students no matter where you go." "Everyone congregates at certain bars in town on weekends" like "one big, happy family." "The social life is limited," though. "That is, if you're not particularly fond of the Cowboy Bar." "The rumor mill runs rampant" in the tiny College of Law universe as well. "Everyone is well aware of who is dating who, who broke up with who." When students need a break, outstanding skiing, hiking, hunting, and fishing are easily accessible and "larger towns like Denver and Fort Collins" are a short drive south.

Getting In

The 25th percentile of admitted students has LSAT scores of 156 and GPAs of a little over 3.1. Admitted students at the 75th percentile have LSAT scores of 154 and GPAs of about 3.6. A whopping 79 percent of all the law students at UW receive scholarships of some kind.

ADMISSIONS

Selectivity Rating	76
# applications received	738
# applicants accepted	237
# acceptees attending	78
Average LSAT	153
LSAT Range	150–156
Average undergrad GPA	3.37
Application fee	$50
Regular application	Rolling, up to 3/1
Regular notification	Rolling
Early application program	Yes
Early application deadline	02/01
Early application notification	12/31
Transfer students accepted	Yes
Evening division offered	No
Part-time accepted	No
LSDAS accepted	Yes

Applicants Also Look At
University of Colorado at Boulder, University of Denver, University of Utah, University of Nebraska—Lincoln, University of Idaho; The University of Montana, University of North Dakota

International Students
TOEFL required of international students	Yes
TMinimum TOEFL (paper/computer)	525/195

FINANCIAL FACTS
Annual tuition (in-state/ out-of-state)	$8,640/$19,290
Books and supplies	$1,200
Fees	$901
Room & board	$12,326
Financial aid application deadline	3/1
% first-year students receiving some sort of aid	89
% receiving some sort of aid	85.7
% of aid that is merit based	18
% receiving scholarships	79
Average grant	$2,242
Average loan	$17,438
Average total aid package	$19,680
Average debt	$34,753

EMPLOYMENT INFORMATION

Career Rating	62
Rate of placement (nine months out)	84.1
Average starting salary	$49,915
State for bar exam	WY, CO, AZ, UT, MT
Pass rate for first-time bar	87

Employers Who Frequently Hire Grads
Government (Attorney General, Federal and District courts, Supreme Court, Public Defender, County Attorney); General practice firms

Prominent Alumni
Mike Sullivan, Former Ambassador to Ireland & Governor of Wyoming; Gerry Spence, Trial Lawyer, Author, TV personality.

Grads Employed by Field (%)
Government (10)
Private Practice (42)
Business/Industry (16)
Judicial Clerkships (14)
Public Interest (7)
Academic (2)
Military (5)

VALPARAISO UNIVERSITY
SCHOOL OF LAW

Academics

One of the oldest schools in the nation, the Valparaiso University School of Law (Valparaiso Law) places a great deal of emphasis on practical skills and retains strong ties to the community, which in turn results in numerous clinics and externships that allow student to gain a wide variety of practical experiences. The school also draws excellent participants to its lecture/speaker series, having had the governor of Indiana, the former mayor of Detroit, the president of the ACLU, and Supreme Court Justices visit the school in the past year alone. Located "close enough to Chicago to nurture your social life, and yet far enough to ground you in your studies," the proximity provides world class culture, shopping, and entertainment as well as jobs. The research and writing courses are "definitely challenging," with a two-semester 1L requirement, a 2L requirement, and a 3L seminar requirement, students are aware that it pays off in the long run, as "employers are always impressed by the amount of legal research we know how to conduct." "At Valpo, you will not work in groups to write an appellate brief. You learn to compose yourself," says a 1L. Still, these skills could use more of a forum during the year, as many students bemoan the lack of more than one journal or review.

Professors take an active role in their teaching and their students' lives, making it "a joy to take classes and learn," and absence from class is clearly noticed. Accessibility abounds both in and outside of school, when the "approachable and modest" teachers "mingle with students after hours, and truly inspire you to probe and reach out for more knowledge." They "get students excited about what they can achieve with their future degrees." The administration "always seems happy to engage with students and to constantly solicit feedback" and "advocates [their] interests in the broader University and community," though the Career Planning Center "struggles to place students in big metropolitan areas." The library staff is very helpful with any research questions and "availability is rarely a problem," (says one student: "the smaller the library, the faster you will find the book you are looking for"). The library itself was recently updated including the creation of a new quiet zone reading room that seats 120. As for the building in which Valparaiso Law is housed, it's "not a Cadillac, but if you want a place that has practical and functional facilities with an outstanding faculty" then it will do, and the school is in the process of undergoing a renovation and upgrade. Many here wish that their school's reputation was a few tiers higher, not for lack of academic quality, but for marketability purposes when seeking jobs—others note the poor state of alumni networking.

Diane Lapin, JD Executive Director of Admissions
Wesemann Hall, 6565 Greenwich street, Valparaiso, IN 46383
Tel: 888-825-7652 Fax: 219-465-7808
Email: www.admissions@valpo.edu • Website: www.valpo.edu/law

Life

The students here are smart and helpful—they all want to do their best "but they aren't willing to bring you down to get there," and many are "regularly friends on the outside as well." With a bit more than 500 students enrolled, the size facilitates "a high school-like situation where everyone knows everyone, which is both good and bad." Seniority or "classism" is not a problem, and "1Ls, 2Ls, and 3Ls don't impose a hierarchy on one another." The small town in which Valparaiso Law is located doesn't provide much distraction, so students have to be resourceful when it comes to social outlets. Most pretty much rely on school-based events for fun; there is "healthy inter-class competition at certain sporting and entertainment events" and also plenty of social functions for the entire body. "We as students go out a lot," says a 3L. "The events are very fun and allow the students to interact with faculty and create lasting friendships with their classmates," testifies a student. There's also a forty minute chapel break everyday, when students "have an opportunity to catch up with the news in the lounge, participate in a club meeting, or simply chat and mingle with each other in the atrium."

Getting In

Valparaiso seeks to enroll students who demonstrate a consistently high level of academic achievement as evidenced first by their undergraduate GPA and, secondly, by a competitive LSAT score. Also key to success is a student's record of service and extra-academic experiences. A holistic admissions review process ensures that every applicant's full record of achievement is seriously considered including resumes, personal statements, and letters of recommendation.

Legal methods	
course requirement	Yes
Legal research	
course requirement	Yes
Moot court requirement	No
Public interest	
law requirement	Yes

ADMISSIONS

Selectivity Rating	**72**
# applications received	1,684
# acceptees attending	215
Average LSAT	151
LSAT Range	144–165
Average undergrad GPA	3.35
Application fee	$60
Regular application	Rolling
Regular notification	Rolling
Early application program	No
Transfer students accepted	Yes
Evening division offered	No
Part-time accepted	Yes
LSDAS accepted	Yes

International Students

TOEFL required	
of international students	Yes
Minimum TOEFL	
(paper/computer)	600/95

FINANCIAL FACTS

Annual tuition	$34,430
Books and supplies	$1,200
Fees	$800
Fees per credit	$26
Tuition per credit	$1,147
Room & board	$8,800
Financial aid application	
deadline	4/1
% first-year students	
receiving some sort of aid	90
% receiving some sort of aid	95
% of aid that is merit based	60
% receiving scholarships	30
Average grant	$17,215
Average loan	$20,500
Average total aid package	$47,990
Average debt	$97,135

EMPLOYMENT INFORMATION

		Grads Employed by Field (%)
Career Rating	**67**	Academic (1)
Average starting salary	$56,000	Business/Industry (16)
State for bar exam	IN, IL, MI, WI, GA	Government (12)
Pass rate for first-time bar	84	Judicial Clerkships (4)

Prominent Alumni

Stephan Todd, VP Law & Environment U.S. Steel Corporation; Cornell Boggs, VP & General Counsel, Tyco Plastics & Adhesives; Honorable Nancy Vaidik, Justice, Indiana Court of Appeals; Koreen Ryan, Senior Council, South Asia McDonald's Corporation; Honorable Robert Rucker, Justice, Supreme Court of Indiana.

Grads Employed by Field (%):
Military (1)
Private Practice (63)
Public Interest (2)

Vanderbilt University
Law School

INSTITUTIONAL INFORMATION

Public/private	Private
Student-faculty ratio	13:1
% faculty part-time	58
% faculty female	39
% faculty minority	8
Total faculty	120

SURVEY SAYS...

Diverse opinions accepted
in classrooms
Great research resources
Beautiful campus

STUDENTS

Enrollment of law school	578
% male/female	51/49
% out-of-state	86
% full-time	100
% minority	17
% international	3
# of countries represented	20
Average age of entering class	23

ACADEMICS

Academic Experience Rating	98
Profs interesting rating	97
Profs accessible rating	88
Hours of study per day	4.37

Academic Specialties

Civil procedure, commercial law, constitutional law, corporation securities, criminal law, environmental law, government services, human rights, international law, labor law, legal history, legal philosophy

Advanced Degrees Offered

LLM, 1 year

Combined Degrees Offered

JD/MBA, 4 years; JD/MA, 5 years; JD/PhD, 7 years; JD/MDiv, 5 years; JD/MTS, 4 years; JD/MD, 6 years; JD/MPP, 4 years; LLM/MA of Latin American Studies, 2 years, PhD in Law and Economics, 5–6 years

Clinical program required	No
Legal writing	
course requirement	Yes

Academics

More than a law school, Vanderbilt is "a home away from home," students here tell us. The school is remarkably "student friendly." One 1L elaborates, "Not only does [the Dean of Students] know your name, she knows about you and actually cares about your progress." Impressive facilities are a matter of course. "Our law building is gorgeous," a 3L reports. "It underwent massive renovations a few years ago, so our classrooms are spacious, comfortable, and equipped with all of the latest technology. The building also has a ton of windows to let in natural light, a great asset when you spend every daylight hour inside." Professors, "despite being legal scholars of national fame . . . are approachable people [who] can explain the law in a way that is easy to understand." They are also remarkably helpful. "A week before my torts exam, my professor gave the 100-person class his private cell phone number and told us we could call him with questions between 8:00 A.M. and 11:00 P.M. as long as there was no heavy breathing. That's commitment."

The course selection at Vanderbilt leans to a "general legal education." In recent years, however, many students have called for "more formal specialization programs," and the "responsive" administration is taking action. Already in possession of a "very strong business law program," the school is "currently working on creating . . . a program in technology and entertainment law." In addition, "new concentrations [are] being developed by the faculty" in areas such as "regulatory concerns and litigation." Students here have also called upon the school "to better prepare us for legal practice, rather than engage us in theoretical discussions about how the law should be." The administration, as expected, has heeded their calls. Vanderbilt's "new dean" is "making positive moves towards incorporating more practical experience in the curriculum," and some here believe the school is "on the cusp of a fairly radical curriculum change" that will "make Vandy on the cutting edge of approaching legal education in a more practical way." Recently, the school has also provided "more encouragement for students to pursue careers outside private law firms," such as "public interest work and government work." In particular, "The school is putting a great effort into expanding its public interest profile with the addition of a Public Interest Institute in the coming years." To that end, students say "more clerkships and government opportunities" would also be appreciated as well as "better loan-forgiveness programs for students" who plan to enter those fields.

Students believe "Vandy's Career Cervices Department is top-notch, with motivated and dedicated people running the department." A top-third class rank seems to be key and "can get you a big-firm job in a major city." A 3L writes, "Like many of my classmates, I had a job early on in my third year. I am not at the top of my class (probably top third), but I've had plenty of offers and opportunities. I will be working in the (Midwestern) city of my choice next year and making a little over $100,000." While some students question the reach of Vanderbilt's Career Services Office, it is now "bringing more employers" "from the Northeast and West Coast" to campus. In nearly all areas, "The school's willingness to change to reflect what students need makes it stand out." One notable exception is the legal writing program, which students have long felt "could use some improvement," namely "less emphasis on grades and more opportunities for constructive criticism." In addition, "Registration is needlessly complicated."

Life

"The best thing about Vanderbilt is, by far, the students," a 2L asserts. Students say "Vandy has the types of diversity that count: ideological, experiential, and geographical. Students hail from all over the country; some are Marines, some are hippies; some are Bible

G. TODD MORTON, ASSISTANT DEAN FOR ADMISSIONS
131 21ST AVENUE SOUTH, NASHVILLE, TN 37203
TEL: 615.322.6452 FAX: 615.322.1531
EMAIL: ADMISSIONS@LAW.VANDERBILT.EDU • WEBSITE: WWW.LAW.VANDERBILT.EDU

thumpers, some are atheistic intellectuals; some are conservative, some are liberal; most are somewhere in between." Perhaps most importantly, "Vandy is a law school filled with non-lawyers." A 2L quips: "Unlike every other law school I have encountered, where 75 percent of the people are unfit for human society, only about a quarter of the people [here] are." On the whole, students "provide a lot of support for one another, and keep things in perspective. People are friendly, generally upbeat, and willing to help out." "You'll never have a hard time finding someone to study or eat with you during the day or to go out with you at night," a sanguine 1L adds. Competition here "is low; most people are self-motivated but go out of their way to seem under-motivated. Actually, it can be annoying sometimes how anti-competitive people are; they will profess not to be working, but you know they are spending some extra hours here and there to do their best."

Vanderbilt's "Campus is beautiful and serene, which compensates for the stress of finals." Hometown Nashville "is a fantastic and up-and-coming city," an enthusiastic 1L writes. "I have been extremely impressed by the culture and environment. The town is much more cosmopolitan than [a] New York City girl would expect." In case you haven't heard, "People party" at Vanderbilt. In fact, "The social demands of the school might consume more time than the classwork, depending on who your professors are and what you take." Social options include "Bar Review every Thursday night for students who want to do the bar scene" and "lots of gatherings among friends." In addition, Blackacres, social events for the law school, are held on many Friday afternoons. Both students and professors come together for a drink, a bite to eat, and lively conversation."

Getting In

A plethora of qualified candidates apply to Vanderbilt each year, and the school's rolling selection policy allows it to take the time it needs to carefully consider each application. Applicants who take the LSAT in December or February are at no disadvantage here.

Legal methods	
course requirement	No
Legal research	
course requirement	Yes
Moot court requirement	No
Public interest	
law requirement	No

ADMISSIONS
Selectivity Rating	94
# applications received	4,336
% applicants accepted	25
% acceptees attending	18
Average LSAT	168
LSAT Range	164–169
Average undergrad GPA	3.72
Application fee	$50
Regular application	Rolling, up to 3/15
Regular notification	Rolling
Early application program	No
Transfer students accepted	Yes
Evening division offered	No
Part-time accepted	No
LSDAS accepted	Yes

Applicants Also Look At
University of Southern California, Columbia University, University of Michigan—Ann Arbor, University of California—Los Angeles, Duke University, University of Pennsylvania, Cornell University, University of Virginia, Georgetown University

International Students
| TOEFL required | |
| of international students | Yes |

FINANCIAL FACTS
Annual tuition	$41,850
Books and supplies	$1,668
Fees	$356
Room & board (off-campus)	$12,404
Financial aid application deadline	2/15
% first-year students receiving some sort of aid	90
% receiving some sort of aid	85
% of aid that is merit based	64
% receiving scholarships	69
Average grant	$20,000
Average loan	$40,860
Average total aid package	$63,070
Average debt	$110,080

EMPLOYMENT INFORMATION

Career Rating	97
Rate of placement (nine months out)	98
Average starting salary	$145,000
State for bar exam	NY, TN, IL, TX, CA
Pass rate for first-time bar	96

Employers Who Frequently Hire Grads
King & Spalding LLP; Alston & Bird LLP; Bass, Berry, & Sims PLC; Locke, Lord, Bissell & Liddell; Bryan Cave LLP; Orrick, Herrington & Sutcliff; Paul, Hastings, Janofsky & Walker LLP.

Prominent Alumni
Greg Abbott, Texas Attorney General; Fred Thompson, Senator; Counsel Watergate Committee, Actor; Martha Daughtrey, U.S. Circuit Court Judge.

Grads Employed by Field (%)
Business/Industry (3)
Government (5)
Public Interest (2)
Private Practice (4)
Judicial Clerkships (15)
Academic (1)
Military (2)

VERMONT LAW SCHOOL

INSTITUTIONAL INFORMATION

Public/private	Private
Student-faculty ratio	13:1
% faculty part-time	0
% faculty female	46
% faculty minority	10
Total faculty	63

SURVEY SAYS...

Liberal students
Beautiful campus

STUDENTS

Enrollment of law school	539
% male/female	50/50
% out-of-state	90
% full-time	100
% minority	11
% international	2
# of countries represented	9
Average age of entering class	26

ACADEMICS

Academic Experience Rating	**71**
Profs interesting rating	76
Profs accessible rating	86
Hours of study per day	5.08

Academic Specialties

Civil procedure, commercial law, constitutional law, corporation securities, criminal law, environmental law, government services, human rights, international law, labor law, legal history, legal philosophy

Advanced Degrees Offered

JD, 3 years; M.E.L.P. (Environmental Law and policy), 1 year; LL.M. (environmental law), 1 year

Combined Degrees Offered

JD/Master of Environmental Law and Policy, 3 years

Clinical program required	No
Legal writing course requirement	Yes
Legal methods course requirement	Yes

Academics

"If you are into environmental law, this is the place to be," declares a 3L at Vermont Law School, a "stand-alone law school" in the "picturesque, tranquil, [and] rural" Green Mountains. "Classes are small" and "Environmental law permeates even the traditional core curriculum." There is also "a lot of emphasis on public policy and ethics." Unique summer sessions allow students to analyze dozens of highly specialized aspects of environmental law. In the Semester-in-Practice program, students gain experience working for government agencies, NGOs, and law firms in—among other places—Washington, DC and Montreal. The Environmental and Natural Resources Law Clinic affords students the opportunity to work with leading public-interest attorneys. Other great ways to gain practical experience include the "wonderful" judicial externship program and internships in the Vermont General Assembly.

The "incredibly approachable" faculty members "genuinely care about your success" and are "always available for help." "Some of the top" environmental law professors "in the country" call this school home. "Most professors have a passion for teaching" and "share their enthusiasm." "We have so many top-notch scholars who could be at much higher-ranked law schools but who teach here because they want to live in Vermont, or because they believe in the ethos of the school," brags a 2L. "The Socratic Method isn't used a lot," though, "which sometimes lead to a quiet classroom." Unfortunately, "each first-year section is stuck with exactly one professor who is almost universally dreaded and subject to poor reviews," discloses a 2L. Also, "Some professors are so overly liberal that it impairs their ability to be evenhanded." The administration is "generally fine" but "can sometimes seem unorganized." It also "has its quirks." Students note, for example, that the dean leads "weekly hikes."

Some students call Career Services "decent" while others say that "finding a job after graduating from VLS can be very hard, even in Vermont." Students also gripe about the school's relatively low bar-passage rate. Frustration about school finances is another hardy perennial. "Frankly, VLS alums need to give back to the school," asserts a 2L. While environmental law "will always be" the "bread and butter," a few students feel that "all other areas of the law are ignored."

The "environmentally progressive" facilities here are "very conducive to learning." "Large parts of the school have been either recently built or are newly renovated" providing "plenty of power outlets." The library's environmental collection is "unparalleled" but it's "very limited when it comes to more general topics." Wireless access is not always speedy. The "rudimentary gym on campus" is "pretty pathetic." Many elements of the buildings are "green" and "reflect the school's strong environmental and public policy focus." As such, the heating, cooling, and lighting systems are designed to minimize energy consumption. At mealtime, the "organic cafeteria food" is "unexpectedly tasty." Few other schools can boast that the "freaking awesome" composting toilets—which, somehow, don't involve any water—"are a real treat."

Life

"There is a real mix of students" here—including everyone "from 22-year-olds right out of college who still like to party" to "50-year-olds whose kids are grown." These "smart, fun" students describe themselves as "generally athletic" and "voraciously outdoorsy." Some are "very open and accepting." Others are "judgmental and opinionated." A common bond grows from the fact that students are "passionate" about the environment, social

KATHY HARTMAN, ASSOCIATE DEAN FOR ENROLLMENT MANAGEMENT
CHELSEA STREET, SOUTH ROYALTON, VT 05068-0096
TEL: 888-277-5985 FAX: 802-831-1174
EMAIL: ADMISS@VERMONTLAW.EDU • WEBSITE: WWW.VERMONTLAW.EDU

justice, and human rights. One student finds it all "very refreshing." Another calls it "the personification of the hippy, tree-hugger establishment."

VLS boasts "an unrivaled community." "There really aren't any cutthroat students here," so a "great feeling of camaraderie" prevails. "You can leave your laptop in the library and no one will touch it." "Anyone can send an e-mail to everyone," reports a 2L, "so you are informed about all kinds of things ranging from a lost pair of mittens to the date when the Vermont Supreme Court will next hear oral arguments at the school." There is "absolutely no anonymity," though, and "lots of gossip." "The grapevine is pervasive, but not super vindictive."

"Rural Vermont" has "New England charm" but it's "definitely not for diehard city slickers." The surrounding "natural beauty" "takes your breath away every single day." "It's truly amazing to wake up to," lauds a 1L. "For the nature enthusiast," hiking, rafting, "and all other sorts of outdoor activities" are plentiful. Skiing and snowboarding abound as well. Just "Get used to skiing on ice." ("Builds character," notes a 3L.) Ultimately, though, "You are a long way from anywhere" here. "Vermont Law School is in a 'town' populated by approximately 2,000 permanent residents" called South Royalton where "Rent is extremely high." "SoRo has a bank, a post office, a pizza place, a laundromat, a great co-op, and a "local dive bar." The nearest grocery store is in New Hampshire," which is "25 minutes away." "Students without a car should not come here," advises a 3L. Socially, "the SBA is a little overzealous" and there is "incredible participation in student groups." "There are many student-run conferences and activities—and parties—throughout the school year, which complement those sponsored by the school." Students can join "organized soccer, hockey, softball, and rugby teams" as well. "Though it's a small town, I had a great house to live in, a great housemate to share it with, and have met people here with whom I know I'll be in touch 10 years from now," predicts a 3L. "I actually enjoyed law school."

Getting In

The 25th percentile of admitted students has LSAT scores of 151 and GPAs of just a tad under 3.0. Admitted students at the 75th percentile have LSAT scores of 157 and GPAs of about 3.5.

EMPLOYMENT INFORMATION

		Grads Employed by Field (%)
Career Rating	75	Academic (1)
Rate of placement (nine months out)	91.8	Business/Industry (1)
Average starting salary	$60,000	Government (17)
State for bar exam	NY, VT, MA, NH, NJ	Judicial clerkships (21)
Pass rate for first-time bar	85.2	Military (1)

Employers Who Frequently Hire Grads

Federal & State Judges in the Northeast;
Law firms throughout New England;
Beveridge & Diamond in Washington, DC.

Private practice (31)
Public Interest (15)

Prominent Alumni

Glenn Berger, Partner, Skadden Arps;
Charles diLeva, Lead Environmental
Counsel World Bank; Linda Smiddy,
Professor of Law, Vermont Law School;
Cindy Burns, Sr Representative High UN
Commission on Refugees.

Legal research	
course requirement	Yes
Moot court requirement	Yes
Public interest	
law requirement	No

ADMISSIONS

Selectivity Rating	**72**
# applications received	1,103
# applicants accepted	599
# acceptees attending	193
Average LSAT	155
LSAT Range	152–158
Average undergrad GPA	3.22
Application fee	$60
Regular application	3/1
Regular notification	Rolling
Early application program	No
Transfer students accepted	Yes
Evening division offered	No
Part-time accepted	No
LSDAS accepted	Yes

Applicants Also Look At

University of Colorado at Boulder,
University of Denver, Pace University,
Suffolk University, Lewis & Clark
College, Albany Law School of Union
University, Franklin Pierce Law Center

International Students

TOEFL required	
of international students	Yes
Minimum TOEFL (paper)	600

FINANCIAL FACTS

Annual tuition	$39,995
Books and supplies	$1,000
Fees	$425
Room & board	
(off-campus)	$9,880
Financial aid application	
deadline	3/1
% first-year students	
receiving some sort of aid	91
% receiving some sort of aid	97
% of aid that is merit based	58
% receiving scholarships	57
Average grant	$9,475
Average loan	$32,250
Average total aid package	$48,918
Average debt	$122,951

VILLANOVA UNIVERSITY
SCHOOL OF LAW

INSTITUTIONAL INFORMATION

Public/private	Private
Affiliation	Roman Catholic
Student-faculty ratio	18:1
% faculty part-time	53
% faculty female	39
% faculty minority	17
Total faculty	119

SURVEY SAYS...
Great library staff
Abundant externship/internship/
clerkship opportunities
Students love Villanova, PA

STUDENTS

Enrollment of law school	744
% male/female	57/43
% out-of-state	49
% full-time	100
% minority	17
# of countries represented	5
Average age of entering class	23

ACADEMICS

Academic Experience Rating	**84**
Profs interesting rating	88
Profs accessible rating	79
Hours of study per day	7.5

Advanced Degrees Offered
JD, 3 years; LL.M Taxation, 24 credits

Combined Degrees Offered
JD/MBA, 3–4 years; JD/LLM-Taxation; 3.5 years; JD/LLM in International Studies, 3 years

Clinical program required	No
Legal writing course requirement	Yes
Legal methods course requirement	No
Legal research course requirement	Yes
Moot court requirement	Yes
Public interest law requirement	No

Academics

At Villanova University School of Law, students find "a good balance in an interactive and educational atmosphere" through a blend of lecture, discussion, and serious hands-on experience. Students say the "absolutely wonderful" professors are the heart and soul of the program. "Instructors are all extremely intelligent and have a wealth of real-world experience, yet remain in touch with students," says a 1L. In fact, he tells us, "My law school professors are much more helpful and approachable than my undergrad professors were." Another student agrees that the "Professors' knowledge and experience is fundamental to the Villanova experience." Many here happily report a lack of the "heavy competitive atmosphere that you hear about at other schools," noting that "we all encourage each other to do well."

Villanova takes a fairly traditional approach to introductory course work, and students say "There is still a heavy reliance on the Socratic Method and many classes use a lecture format (especially in the first year)." In the next two years, students continue studying the basic principals of law, while adding elective courses to their schedule. Experiential learning is emphasized throughout the curriculum, and students dole out praise for the school's strong legal writing and research courses, simulation programs, clinics, and externships. The school has a "clear emphasis" on "solidifying students' legal writing skills." In addition, students take on real legal work thanks to the school's "strong commitment to community service and pro bono work."

For a Catholic institution, it should come as no surprise that a "Catholic identity" reigns supreme. However, some students wish opportunities for service were not restricted by the administration's commitment to Catholic values. ("No 'regular hours' in the 40-hour workweek can be spent helping efforts to litigate for women's reproductive freedom, and the participating organization must be aware of the policy.") Ultimately, many wonder "how the administration will balance the school's Catholic mission with its mission as a legal institution."

After bemoaning that the school had "really outgrown its building and parking areas," (many students cite the "severe lack of classrooms, computers, parking spots, hallways, lockers, and space in general") students happily report "a new building is in the works." This new development's plans call for a brand new state-of-the-art law school on a site adjacent to the university's suburban Philadelphia campus. While they may complain that the campus has a "high school atmosphere," students also say they leave Villanova well-prepared for their professional career in the adult world. Students insist that "opportunities for practical experience are abundant," and the "Career Services Department works really hard to help students find jobs in the private and public sectors." They note that the school has "strong professional contacts in Pennsylvania, New Jersey, and Delaware" and that "major firms routinely interview on campus and hire many Villanova graduates."

Life

When they are not hitting the books, Villanova students live the high life at the many bars, clubs, and restaurants in Philadelphia, as well as at campus events. A student assures us, "The Student Bar Association spends a lot of time planning activities to students. There are many active students groups as well." According to another, "Students get along well and the ones that choose to socialize together have a great time."

NOE BERNAL, ASSISTANT DEAN FOR ADMISSIONS
299 NORTH SPRING MILL ROAD, VILLANOVA, PA 19085
TEL: 610-519-7010 FAX: 610-519-6291
EMAIL: ADMISSIONS@LAW.VILLANOVA.EDU • WEBSITE: WWW.LAW.VILLANOVA.EDU

Still, many students choose to maintain a life outside of school, living off-campus with their friends or spouses. Getting to campus is easy since "The train runs literally out the front door of the law school." One student advises, "There is a bar that students usually hang out at which can be fun, but sometimes after seeing these people all day and every day, it's good to do something away from the law school crowd." Luckily, that is easy to accomplish at Villanova thanks to the school's "amazing" location. One student enthuses, "It is 25 minutes from Philadelphia, as well as a short drive to New York City, Washington D.C., Baltimore, the beaches, and skiing!"

Most students say that they get along with their classmates, though some say the student body is pretty "homogenous" and "not exactly diverse." However, "Villanova has openly stated that they feel that diversity is a compelling interest at the institution" and many believe that "in time, Villanova will be one of the more diverse legal institutions."

Getting In

For the admitted class, students in the 25th percentile had an average LSAT score of 160 and a 3.27 GPA. Admitted students in the 75th percentile had an average LSAT score of 163 and a 3.62 GPA. However, Villanova may consider students with a lower GPA if they offer other important qualities, such as commitment to service, volunteer work, or unique professional experience. The majority of students who enter do so within a year or two of college, and the average age of a Villanova student in their first year is 23.

ADMISSIONS

Selectivity Rating	84
# applications received	3,110
% applicants accepted	38
% acceptees attending	21
Average LSAT	162
LSAT Range	160–163
Average undergrad GPA	3.49
Application fee	$75
Regular application	Rolling, up to 3/1
Regular notification	Rolling
Early application program	No
Transfer students accepted	Yes
Evening division offered	No
Part-time accepted	No
LSDAS accepted	Yes

Applicants Also Look At

Temple University, American University, University of Pennsylvania, Seton Hall University, Boston College, Fordham University, The George Washington University, Rutgers University—Newark

FINANCIAL FACTS

Annual tuition	$33,130
Books and supplies	$4,940
Fees	$360
Room & board (off-campus)	$14,400
Financial aid application deadline	3/1
% first-year students receiving some sort of aid	83
% receiving some sort of aid	83
% of aid that is merit based	3
% receiving scholarships	20
Average grant	$14,110
Average loan	$41,312
Average total aid package	$51,095
Average debt	$110,628

EMPLOYMENT INFORMATION

Career Rating	85
Rate of placement (nine months out)	92
Average starting salary	$91,992
State for bar exam	PA, NJ, NY, DE
Pass rate for first-time bar	92

Prominent Alumni

Hon. Edward G. Rendell, Governor, State of Pennsylvania; Hon. Marjorie O. Rendell, Judge, U.S. Court of Appeals for the Third Circuit; Jeffrey S. Moorad, General Partner, Arizona Diamondbacks; Richard L. Trumka, Secretary-Treasurer, AFL CIO; Kelly A. Ayotte, Attorney General, State of New Hampshire.

Grads Employed by Field (%)

Business/Industry (17)
Government (4)
Judicial Clerkships (15)
Military (2)
Private Practice (56)
Public Interest (6)

WAKE FOREST UNIVERSITY
SCHOOL OF LAW

INSTITUTIONAL INFORMATION

Public/private	Private
Student-faculty ratio	10:3
% faculty part-time	26
% faculty female	43
% faculty minority	16
Total faculty	60

SURVEY SAYS...

Diverse opinions accepted
in classrooms
Great research resources

STUDENTS

Enrollment of law school	462
% male/female	58/42
% out-of-state	62
% full-time	98
% minority	12
# of countries represented	11
Average age of entering class	24

ACADEMICS

Academic Experience Rating	**93**
Profs interesting rating	92
Profs accessible rating	97
Hours of study per day	4.61

Academic Specialties

Commercial law, constitutional law, corporation securities, criminal law, international law, labor law, taxation

Advanced Degrees Offered

LL.M in American Law, 1 year. Matriculated candidates are graduates of foreign law schools who plan to return to their native country to practice.

Combined Degrees Offered

JD/MA 4 years; JD/MBA, 4 years; JD/MDIV, 5 years.

Legal writing course requirement	Yes
Legal methods course requirement	No
Legal research course requirement	Yes
Moot court requirement	No
Public interest law requirement	No

Academics

"Litigation-oriented" Wake Forest University School of Law "is an unbelievable experience." "The size of the school is perfect." At Wake Forest, you will not "get swallowed up and just become a number." "There are no more than 40 people in any first-year class," and this "allows you to get to know your professors and your professors to get to know you," exalts one student. An "emphasis on practical applications of the law and on-trial advocacy are two of the greatest strengths" of the curriculum. "Hands-on experience" is available through several clinics. "Structured study groups, practice exams, and one-on-one tutoring" mitigate some of the first-year stress. "I find that there is almost an overwhelming amount of support here," observes an appreciative 1L. The "practical and thorough" three-semester-long legal research and writing curriculum "helps to teach real-world skills." To top it off, "Wake Forest offers a large number of full-tuition scholarships which make it possible to attend law school and take the job you want rather than the job you need in order to pay off debt."

Wake's "approachable, knowledgeable, generous" professors are "invaluable resources." "Learning trial practice from a federal prosecutor and human rights law from someone who negotiated treaties at the U.N. made me feel like I was really getting something useful out of my classroom time," comments one student. Professors are "truly dedicated to excellent teaching," and they "genuinely care about their students." They "also have a great deal of brilliant individual personality, which makes class a lot more fun and makes them kind of like rock stars." Some have "intimidating nicknames" (e.g., "Mad Dog") but they "seem to remember what it was like to be on the other end of the stick and are compassionate." In class, "Discourse is encouraged." "It's not just the loud mouths who chime in." Outside of class, professors "welcome students dropping by their offices at almost any time of the day." The administration here is "available for questions, general help, and crisis situations. "Nothing is ever done in a timely fashion," though.

Some students rave that Career Services "will do just about anything to help you" "if you take the time to actually go in there." They note that Wake "is successfully working to improve its reputation outside the Southeast." A disgruntled faction contends that Career Services is "out of touch with the needs of students." "For on-campus interviews, there aren't as many big New York or DC firms," observes one student.

Wake's facilities are "drab and basically awful." The elevators are "slow [and] small." The bathrooms are "outdated" and "There aren't enough" of them. "Classrooms are always very cold." "The hallways are too narrow. When the bell rings between classes (yes, there's a bell), they fill up with dense mobs of the only thing more obnoxious than middle schoolers: law students." "Wake Forest is at the top of the class when it comes to technological advancement," though. "The wireless Internet and on-call staff make access to all sorts of information easy." The library has "very little study space" and "needs some updating" to accommodate laptops but it contains "a broad range of research materials."

MELANIE E. NUTT, DIRECTOR OF ADMISSIONS AND FINANCIAL AID
PO BOX 7206 REYNOLDA STATION, WINSTON-SALEM, NC 27109
TEL: 336-758-5437 FAX: 336-758-3930
EMAIL: ADMISSIONS@LAW.WFU.EDU • WEBSITE: WWW.LAW.WFU.EDU

Life

"Wake does a good job recruiting students from across the country." In terms of ethnic diversity, though, "The law school could use some work." "They have made steps in the last couple years, but there is still room for improvement." Politically, "Students tend toward the conservative." ("The professors are generally much more liberal.") "Some students are more competitive than others" but "It's not an 'I'm-only-here-to-look-out-for-myself' kind of atmosphere." "People are willing to share their outlines, notes, etc."

A "genuinely friendly atmosphere" makes "going to law school a much more comfortable experience than it might otherwise be." "The welcoming atmosphere at Wake Forest has made the last three years a wonderful experience," reminisces a 3L. "It is really easy to make friends" because "Everyone knows everyone else." Occasionally, "You can get a little too much togetherness": "The gossip mill runs amok. It often feels like high school." However, the student population is "diverse enough socially" that "Everyone can find a niche to fit into." On campus, there is "a fairly strong divide between the 'cool kids'" (who have more of a "throw-down-and-drink mentality") "and the others (who don't)." A large number of older students "tends to have moved past the beer-hazed weekend revelry and, as such, they can do other activities together."

While some students concede that Winston-Salem "isn't the greatest social scene in the world," they "make the best of it." If you are seeking "a good place to buy a home some time this century and raise a family," Winston-Salem is "ideal." "If you want nightclubs open until 4:00 A.M., you should probably consider another city." When students here "need to escape, there is always Charlotte, Greensboro, or Raleigh."

Getting In

Wake Forest is a little bit of a diamond in the rough in the sense that it is nationally recognized as a top law school but not quite as hard to get into as some of its peers. Admitted students at the 25th percentile have LSAT scores of 160 and GPAs of about 3.7. Admitted students at the 75th percentile have LSAT scores of 165 and GPAs of about 3.6.

ADMISSIONS

Selectivity Rating	88
# applications received	2,334
% applicants accepted	28
% acceptees attending	25
Median LSAT	163
LSAT Range	160–165
Average undergrad GPA	3.5
Application fee	$60
Regular application	Rolling
Regular notification	Rolling
Early application program	No
Transfer students accepted	Yes
Evening division offered	No
Part-time accepted	No
LSDAS accepted	Yes

Applicants Also Look At

American University, University of North Carolina at Chapel Hill, Tulane University, Vanderbilt University, The George Washington University, Emory University, The College of William & Mary in Virginia

International Students

TOEFL recommended of international students	Yes
Minimum TOEFL (paper)	650

FINANCIAL FACTS

Annual tuition	$33,950
Books and supplies	$1,000
Room & board (off-campus)	$16,000
Financial aid application deadline	5/15
% first-year students receiving some sort of aid	78
% receiving some sort of aid	78
% of aid that is merit based	74
% receiving scholarships	36
Average grant	$22,125
Average loan	$40,000
Average debt	$86,750

EMPLOYMENT INFORMATION

Career Rating	70
Average starting salary	$110,000 (private)
	$46,333 (public)
State for bar exam	NC, VA, GA, NY, FL
Pass rate for first-time bar	92

Employers Who Frequently Hire Grads
For a representative list see Career Services web site at www.law.wfu.edu

Grads Employed by Field (%)
Business/Industry (9)
Government (13)
Judicial Clerkships (9)
Private Practice (64)
Public Interest (2)
Other (3)

WASHBURN UNIVERSITY
SCHOOL OF LAW

INSTITUTIONAL INFORMATION

Public/private	Public
Student-faculty ratio	14:1
% faculty female	35
% faculty minority	21
Total faculty	31

SURVEY SAYS...

Diverse opinions accepted
in classrooms
Great research resources
Great library staff

STUDENTS

Enrollment of law school	429
% male/female	59/41
% full-time	100
% minority	14
# of countries represented	1
Average age of entering class	26.2

ACADEMICS

Academic Experience Rating	**70**
Profs interesting rating	73
Profs accessible rating	86
Hours of study per day	4.02

Academic Specialties

Corporation securities, environmental law, taxation, family law, advocacy, business and transactional law, estate planning

Advanced Degrees Offered

JD, 3 years

Clinical program required	No
Legal writing course requirement	Yes
Legal methods course requirement	Yes
Legal research course requirement	Yes
Moot court requirement	No
Public interest law requirement	No

Academics

Its "small size" and "close-knit" atmosphere make Washburn University School of Law a popular choice for students. Washburn's "reputation for graduating outstanding trial lawyers" is matched by its "proud historical commitment to public service," not to mention an "exceptional" and "dedicated" faculty. The "family-style setting" makes acclimating to law school an easy process. One student conveys, "I felt very comfortable at Washburn Law the second I entered the school, and that comfort and acceptance has not wavered."

The law school's cozy size allows students to receive one-on-one attention from faculty. Students say the friendly and supportive professors "make law school such a pleasure," and they "are more than willing to help out in any way that they can, as long as you ask." Students rave about the accessibility of the professors and the quality of instruction, saying that "they are tough but compassionate" but most importantly, "really care about your success." According to one student, "They truly want me to be successful and always equal or exceed the effort I put into my education. Here, I feel like I am on a team that wants to win."

Students have mixed feelings about the administration. Some students feel "The administration is fantastic in some respects and completely inept in others. The ones who know what they are doing are wonderful, and the ones who don't unfortunately can make spectacles of themselves at school functions." Others say that the administration is "second to none" and "seems to jump [into action] when a law student asks for something." Overall, there is a feeling that "problems or concerns students have are addressed by the administration promptly."

Students rate their overall academic experience as positive, but many wish that Washburn would offer a wider variety of courses or at least more time slots for required classes. One student observes, "We have great certificate opportunities, but it is very difficult to schedule the necessary classes because class availability is sparse with non-bar classes." On the other hand, students are quick to note that Washburn's legal writing program (one of only eight in the country taught by tenure-track faculty) is excellent and has gained national attention, as is its clinic program. One student remarks, "In addition to a functioning law clinic where third-years can actually practice law under supervision (almost like medical school) there are tons of course offerings that address exactly what lawyers actually do, applying the 'book law' and research and writing skills as you go." "Hitting the real world of law is, of course, scary, but I feel quite confident in both my abilities and familiarity with what to expect thanks to my school."

Students report that "the school itself is well equipped with an amazing legal library, knowledgeable library staff, and great resources at every turn." As a Federal Depository library, Washburn's library has "great access to current government materials," and "The classroom and research facilities at the school are adequate for what every law student would ever need or conceive of needing." On the downside, "Parking is a genuine problem and, though it seems petty, it's a legitimate gripe. Law students should not have to be treated like royalty, but they deserve [better] than to have to park three blocks from the school and walk through snow to class."

KARLA WHITAKER, DIRECTOR OF ADMISSIONS
1700 COLLEGE, TOPEKA, KS 66621-1140
TEL: (785)-670-1185 FAX: 785-670-1120
EMAIL: ADMISSIONS@WASHBURNLAW.EDU • WEBSITE: WASHBURNLAW.EDU

Life

The congenial atmosphere at Washburn has students appreciating its "laid-back, non-competitive tone." Student organizations on campus also work hard to foster student activities and collaboration. Some feel that an air of competition exists, but that this is not necessarily a negative. As one student remarks, Washburn is "competitive, intimate, and tough, but we have all gotten to know each other very well. I have made some wonderful friends. It's weird, like being on a team where we all play the same position." Another satisfied customer reports, "I can honestly say that my choice in going to Washburn was the best I could have made, and I don't think that I would have been happier at another school."

"Truly the only downfall to Washburn is the fact that it is located in Topeka, Kansas, but that downfall may be exactly what provides an ideal location to foster more studying and less partying." One student feels that "Topeka gets a little bit of a bad rap. I think it's fair when students laugh about how *not* hopping Topeka is, but the fact that it is the state capital (with all the jobs and internship opportunities that it provides) far outweighs the fact that it's a dull city." Additionally, students report that Lawrence, a nice college town, is only 25 minutes away, and Kansas City is an hour drive. As one student observes, "If there's not satisfactory action at those two places, law school should probably be postponed."

Getting In

Washburn's Admissions Committee does not base its admissions decisions solely on numerical scores but considers a variety of factors including a sincere interest in the legal profession, a record of excellence, and improvement in grade history. Admitted students at the 25th percentile have an LSAT score of 152 and a GPA of 3.0. Admitted students at the 75th percentile have an LSAT score of 157 and a GPA of 3.7.

ADMISSIONS

Selectivity Rating	67
# applications received	722
% applicants accepted	60
% acceptees attending	35
Average LSAT	152
LSAT Range	150–155
Average undergrad GPA	3.31
Application fee	$40
Regular application	Rolling
Regular notification	Rolling
Early application program	No
Transfer students accepted	Yes
Evening division offered	No
Part-time accepted	No
LSDAS accepted	Yes

Applicants Also Look At
University of Kansas, University of Missouri—Kansas City, Drake University, Creighton University

International Students

TOEFL required of international students	Yes
Minimum TOEFL (paper/computer)	550/213

FINANCIAL FACTS

Annual tuition (in-state/out-of-state)	$15,750/$24,600
Books and supplies	$2,091
Fees	$70
Tuition per credit (in-state/out-of-state)	$525/$820
Room & board	$8,792
Financial aid application deadline	7/1
% first-year students receiving some sort of aid	93
% receiving some sort of aid	94
% of aid that is merit based	9
% receiving scholarships	47
Average grant	$8,285
Average loan	$26,747
Average total aid package	$27,269
Average debt	$64,645

EMPLOYMENT INFORMATION

Career Rating	65
Rate of placement (nine months out)	90
Average starting salary	$52,301
State for bar exam	KS, MO, TX, CO, WA
Pass rate for first-time bar	86.3

Prominent Alumni
Lillian A. Apodaca, Past President Hispanic Bar Association; Robert J. Dole, Former U.S. Senator; William H. Kurtis, Journalist/American Justice; Delano E. Lewis, Former Ambassador to South Africa; Ron Richey, Chair of Exec. Comm. of Torchmark Corp.

Grads Employed by Field (%)
Academic (1)
Business/Industry (13)
Government (20)
Judicial Clerkships (9)
Military (2)
Private Practice (42)
Public Interest (9)
Other (4)

WASHINGTON AND LEE UNIVERSITY
SCHOOL OF LAW

INSTITUTIONAL INFORMATION

Public/private	Private
% faculty part-time	28
% faculty female	28
% faculty minority	14
Total faculty	43

SURVEY SAYS...
Diverse opinions accepted
in classrooms
Great research resources
Great library staff

STUDENTS

Enrollment of law school	394
% male/female	62/38
% out-of-state	79
% full-time	100
% minority	22
% international	3
# of countries represented	16
Average age of entering class	25

ACADEMICS

Academic Experience Rating	**91**
Profs interesting rating	92
Profs accessible rating	97
Hours of study per day	4.62

Advanced Degrees Offered
LL.M.

Combined Degrees Offered
JD/MHA, 6 years

Clinical program required	No
Legal writing	
course requirement	Yes
Legal methods	
course requirement	No
Legal research	
course requirement	Yes
Moot court requirement	No
Public interest	
law requirement	No

Academics

A small student body, a rural location, and a lack of a part-time program combine to create a distinctive academic experience at Washington and Lee University School of Law. "This is not a school where you will go to classes and have a job," a 2L writes. "School is your life; the administration makes that very clear to you when you step on campus." This contributes to a "nurturing and family environment" where students and staff are "on a first-name basis," and "It is not unusual for the deans to stop you in the hall [to] check up on all aspects of your life or for your classmates to send you their notes when you miss a class." Full-time faculty members are "here because they care deeply about teaching." They're also "remarkably good" lawyers—"Several argue before the Supreme Court on a regular basis," a 1L informs—and they "work really hard to get to know you and help you succeed outside the classroom. I interviewed for a federal judicial clerkship, and the judge said that the recommendation that my professor wrote was the best she had ever read. This particular professor was determined that I would get a federal clerkship and went above and beyond the call of duty to ensure that I did," a 3L reports. The school's small size also "allow[s] for significant involvement in a variety of activities, such as moot court and journals." The intimate setting does have its drawbacks, however, as "course selection is limited and the schedule is structured in such a way that you're often prevented from taking a lot of the courses you want to. Many classes are only offered once a year, or once every two years, and it seems that a large portion of classes tend to be offered at the same time." While the school "has a policy of providing any course requested by a minimum number of students, such courses are typically taught by visiting professors" of "varying quality."

Many here believe that Washington and Lee needs "more diversity in its faculty and student body." A 1L explains: "Because there are certain ethnic groups that are still underrepresented, there is a tendency by both the faculty and student body to make assumptions and close their eyes to other important points of view in the world." Compounding the issue, hometown Lexington, Virginia is "in the sticks," so "Students are isolated, with no place to turn but [the school]. This cannot help but narrow their perspective of the world." To broaden perspectives, the school "successfully expends energy and resources" to bring "many notable speakers, including District and Circuit Court judges, political appointees, top international and national lawyers, and policy experts," to campus. Still, a 3L writes: "For me, the hardest part of law school has not been the 'school' aspect, but rather the challenge of doing law school in a very small, very isolated, rural area with a very small group of peers." The upside of this unique experience is that it engenders "a strong alumni base. W&L graduates are always willing to help out fellow alums."

While the active alumni base ensures that Washington and Lee's "reputation among those professionals who are 'in the know'" is strong, students here find it "difficult" to "pursue a legal career outside of the Southeast (especially DC, Virginia, South Carolina, and Alabama)." The school's Office of Career Planning and Professional Development "has made progress helping students break into the New York market," but students say that "if you want to get to the Northeast, the Midwest, or the West, be prepared for a lot of individual legwork." The school's library is "wonderful." "Every student . . . has their own personal study carrel that has a little closet. It is great to have my own space in the law school," a 1L tells us. Classrooms are "state of the art," "well lit, spacious, and comfortable." The new Moot Court Room is "beautiful."

ANDREA HILTON HOWE, DIRECTOR OF ADMISSIONS
SYDNEY LEWIS HALL, LEXINGTON, VA 24450
TEL: 540-458-8503 FAX: 540-458-8586
EMAIL: LAWADM@WLU.EDU • WEBSITE: WWW.LAW.WLU.EDU

Life

Washington and Lee is located in "an extremely isolated, rural area," and law students report "little contact with undergrads, VMI students, and townies." In this potentially "claustrophobic" environment, the school's honor code, now more than 100 years old, is a calming presence. "We can leave our laptops around the school without fear of theft or vandalism," a 1L reports. "There are never any stolen or missing books, and if I have a question I can count on my friends [to give] me an honest answer. There are enough opportunities for everybody, and class rank is not disclosed, so people don't feel a need to compete against anybody but themselves." By all accounts, "Students form very close relationships" with each other. "Law school sports are of paramount importance" here, and students report "a full docket" of them, including "kickball, football, dodgeball, basketball, hockey, and softball." Among these, football is king, and "Every Friday during the fall we play football on the law school lawn and drink kegs of beer." Throw in "cocktail parties" "every other weekend," and some will grouse that "activities held at the school always center [on] alcohol. This focus is less appealing for those who have progressed beyond the drunken days of fraternity and sorority life in undergraduate school." Even if sports and keg beer define fun for you, know that "Almost everyone gets stir crazy to some degree here."

Getting In

Admitted students at the 25th percentile have an LSAT score of 160 and a GPA of 3.2. Admitted students at the 75th percentile have an LSAT score of 166 and a GPA of 3.7.

ADMISSIONS

Selectivity Rating	88
# applications received	2,561
% applicants accepted	33
% acceptees attending	15
Average LSAT	166
LSAT Range	160–166
Average undergrad GPA	3.52
Regular application	Rolling
Regular notification	Rolling
Early application program	No
Transfer students accepted	Yes
Evening division offered	No
Part-time accepted	No
LSDAS accepted	Yes

Applicants Also Look At

Boston University, Vanderbilt University, University of Virginia, Boston College, The George Washington University, University of Notre Dame, The College of William & Mary in Virginia

International Students

TOEFL required of international students	Yes
Minimum TOEFL (paper/computer/web)	600/250/100

FINANCIAL FACTS

Annual tuition	$37,025
Books and supplies	$1,900
Fees	$1,037
Room & board	$14,923
Financial aid application deadline	2/15
% first-year students receiving some sort of aid	93
% receiving some sort of aid	94
% of aid that is merit based	25
% receiving scholarships	62
Average grant	$16,682
Average loan	$38,418
Average total aid package	$45,384
Average debt	$93,725

EMPLOYMENT INFORMATION

Career Rating	81
Rate of placement (nine months out)	91
Average starting salary	$95,526

Grads Employed by Field (%)
Academic (1)
Business/Industry (7)
Government (6)
Judicial Clerkships (21)
Military (2)
Private Practice (57)
Public Interest (6)

WASHINGTON UNIVERSITY
SCHOOL OF LAW

Academics

Washington University School of Law in St. Louis is a "student-centered institution" with "outstanding" clinical programs. One of the biggest draws here is that "all students are guaranteed the opportunity to participate in at least one clinic during law school." Those clinics are stellar. In the Congressional and Administrative Law Clinic, as one example, 3Ls get to spend their spring semester interning in Congress and federal agencies. Notable joint-degree programs include the traditional JD/MBA as well as a unique JD/MA in East Asian studies. "Excellent specializations" include international law, intellectual property, and business law.

WashU's "diverse" and "accomplished" faculty is "available virtually all the time to answer student questions." Many professors here are "great teachers and terrific human beings" who "have a passion for imparting their knowledge upon the students." "Several rank among the best instructors I've had in my educational career," gloats a 2L. However, there are "some mediocre" professors in the mix. Another 2L elaborates: While "a handful of my professors have exceeded my highest expectations as instructors, in a few other classes, I am certain I could teach more effectively than my professors given a month's notice." Administratively, "There is really almost no red tape." The "wonderful," "student-focused" administration "will do anything to help a student survive and flourish." "They do their best to make law school as touchy-feely an experience as possible," describes one student. "From Admissions to the Registrar's Office to various professors' assistants, everyone at WULaw is just great." "Financial aid is lightning fast too."

Students are irreconcilably split when it comes to Career Services. One faction maintains that the staff has a "willingness to get you where you want to go." In addition to St. Louis and other Midwestern metropolises, "Many grads go to DC and New York City." "I think that Career Services does a good job of getting people national exposure," agrees a 2L. "I had callbacks in DC, Orlando, Chicago, Philadelphia, Minneapolis, and New York, and I didn't finish in the top 25 percent." Another faction contends that Career Services is "not very helpful" and "could do more to bring in employers." "The vast majority of students will tell you that CSO is worthless unless you are in the top 15 percent or want to work in the public interest sector in St. Louis," asserts a 2L. "We have some of the best law students in the country, and some employers seem to not recognize this."

The "beautiful" facilities at WashU "seem brand new." Anheuser-Busch Hall "is an amazing place to go to school every day" and "what an undergraduate student dreams of when they think about law school." The law school building is "only a few years old and it has its own cafeteria," an indoor courtyard, and "impressive architectural details." Students do complain a lot about "wireless dead spots," though. Otherwise, the research facilities and technological resources are "nothing short of absolutely satisfactory" and "really enhance the law school experience." "The library is outstanding" and "has lots of study rooms," though it "can be a little congested at times." "The reading room is amazing."

JANET BOLIN, ASSOCIATE DEAN OF ADMISSIONS AND STUDENT SERVICES
1 BROOKINGS DRIVE, CAMPUS BOX 1120, ST. LOUIS, MO 63130-4899
TEL: 314-935-4525 FAX: 314-935-8778
EMAIL: ADMISS@WULAW.WUSTL.EDU • WEBSITE: LAW.WUSTL.EDU

Life

WashU is pretty small, so "You will definitely not be lost in the shuffle." There is a "unique group of talented, intelligent," and "well-rounded" students here and, if these students do say so themselves, they are "the friendliest and funniest people you will ever meet." It tends to be a younger crowd and, while "the paradigmatic law student wearing social blinders" is easily recognizable at WashU, the social scene is very much "a priority." "The students at the law school take its name"—Anheuser-Busch Hall—"very seriously." "We have fun, smart, competitive students who are generally as interested in having a social life as they are in ranking toward the top of our class," explains a 2L. "Every Friday," the school hosts a "well-attended" happy hour in the courtyard. "Students, professors, kegs, and, yes, beer pong," is how one student characterizes the event. "Plenty of organized school activities" also include an annual student-produced comedy called the "Barely Legal Law Revue."

Academically, a few students claim that WashU is "becoming more competitive," but most tell us that "competition is unspoken and left to dark corners of the library." "I have yet to sense any competitiveness among students, even when exams came around," observes a discerning transfer student. "The student population is very laid-back" and students "are always willing to help one another understand the material." Self-scheduled exams for 2Ls and 3Ls help ease some of the tension.

"The WashU campus is located in an upscale suburb of St. Louis with an air of subdued sophistication." The campus is "right by Forest Park, home to the largest free zoo in the country, as well as many other attractions" and not far from bars, restaurants, and things to do. It's a fine place to spend a few years as a student. "St. Louis is not as chic as a lot of cities in the country," admits a 1L, "but it is cheap."

Getting In

The 25th percentile of admitted students has LSAT scores of about 161 and GPAs of about 3.2. Admitted students at the 75th percentile have LSAT scores of roughly 167 and GPAs of about 3.7.

Legal writing course requirement	Yes
Legal methods course requirement	No
Legal research course requirement	Yes
Moot court requirement	No
Public interest law requirement	No

ADMISSIONS

Selectivity Rating	**60***
# applications received	3,700
Average LSAT	167
LSAT Range	162–168
Average undergrad GPA	3.6
Application fee	$70
Regular application	3/1
Regular notification	4/15
Early application program	No
Transfer students accepted	Yes
Evening division offered	No
Part-time accepted	No
LSDAS accepted	Yes

Applicants Also Look At

University of Southern California, Northwestern University, Boston University, Vanderbilt University, Boston College, The George Washington University, Georgetown University

International Students

TOEFL recommended of international students	Yes
Minimum TOEFL (paper)	600

FINANCIAL FACTS

Annual tuition	$39,700
Books and supplies	$2,000
Fees	$796
Room & board (off-campus)	$16,600
Financial aid application deadline	3/1
% first-year students receiving some sort of aid	85
% receiving some sort of aid	82
% of aid that is merit based	100
% receiving scholarships	60
Average grant	$15,000
Average loan	$40,200
Average total aid package	$57,000
Average debt	$102,000

EMPLOYMENT INFORMATION

Career Rating	**60***
State for bar exam	MO, IL, CA, NY

WAYNE STATE UNIVERSITY
LAW SCHOOL

INSTITUTIONAL INFORMATION

Public/private	Public
Student-faculty ratio	15:1
% faculty part-time	44
% faculty female	36
% faculty minority	6
Total faculty	84

SURVEY SAYS...

Diverse opinions accepted
in classrooms
Great research resources
Abundant externship/internship/
clerkship opportunities

STUDENTS

Enrollment of law school	649
% male/female	50/50
% out-of-state	5
% full-time	71
% minority	18
% international	3
# of countries represented	8
Average age of entering class	25

ACADEMICS

Academic Experience Rating	**79**
Profs interesting rating	85
Profs accessible rating	80
Hours of study per day	3.73

Advanced Degrees Offered

JD, 3 years; LL.M., 1 year

Combined Degrees Offered

JD/MBA, 4 years; JD/MA, History,
Political Science or Economics 4
years; JD/MADR, 4 years

Clinical program required	Yes
Legal writing course requirement	Yes
Legal methods course requirement	Yes
Legal research course requirement	Yes
Moot court requirement	No
Public interest law requirement	No

Academics

Wayne State University Law School "in the heart of Detroit" is "a phenomenal value" for both residents of Michigan and out-of-staters. The "very high" bar-passage rate is consistently among the best in the state, and "the part-time evening program allows students to study the law while still maintaining families and other employment." Also, "there is no lack of opportunity to gain professional experience" here. Wayne offers easy access to a host of state and federal courts and "a plethora of resources." There are, for example, five joint-degree programs and six clinics that allow students to represent real clients.

Students here have nary a negative word to say about their "brilliant," "caring," and "world-class" faculty. "The professors at Wayne come from a diverse background of academia, work experience, and beliefs," relates a 3L. "The eclectic mix allows for more robust classroom discussions and brings a 'real-life' component to the theory discussed." Profs are also "real people" who are "accessible and always willing to talk" outside of class about anything "from job search information to current trends in legal theory." "Their dedication and availability to their students is one of a kind," beams a 1L.

The general consensus among students at WSU is that Career Services "needs to be improved," which the new Dean has committed to do. "If you're in the top 10 percent here, you can definitely get into a large firm" through on-campus interviews. If you are in the bottom 90 percent, the small staff is "pretty useless." Also, this school is "strictly regional." "The overwhelming majority of its grads become practicing attorneys in Michigan." Nevertheless, "for those looking to practice in Michigan, WSU remains ideal" and students are pretty optimistic about their employment prospects. "If you want to practice in Michigan upon graduation," they say, "Wayne Law's location in metro Detroit is a major plus." WSU's "amazingly" strong alumni network "dominates the Michigan legal community." Courts and small and midsize firms "all over southeastern Michigan" "respect the school and are confident in hiring Wayne graduates." "It's not the University of Michigan, so employers aren't going to be just handing out jobs," cautions a 3L. "But if you work hard enough, you'll find employment."

Classrooms at Wayne State are "antiquated" and "ridiculously bad," but "there are plans to build new facilities." Other aspects of the facilities are much newer and better, though. A lot of areas within the law school are very computer friendly. The library in particular is "excellent" and "has everything you could ever need."

ERICA M. JACKSON, ASSISTANT DEAN OF ADMISSIONS
471 W. PALMER, DETROIT, MI 48202
TEL: 313-577-3937 FAX: 313-993-8129
EMAIL: LAWINQUIRE@WAYNE.EDU • WEBSITE: WWW.LAW.WAYNE.EDU

Life

"The student body is interesting and diverse and friendly," reports a 2L. "You regularly find a mix of young and old, liberal and conservative, various ethnicities, and work experiences in Wayne State classrooms." A few students observe a good deal of competition here. "Gunners and closet gunners don't make the school inviting to come to every day," they say. However, most students call the atmosphere "congenial." According to the majority, "there is a lot of camaraderie, especially within the sections" and "competitiveness among students is generally low." "If you find that you need help with anything," promises a 1L, "other students are always willing to help you out.

Socially, Wayne Law "isn't a traditional campus environment." This campus is "located in the center of a community that has seen some rough times." Many students tell us that "there isn't as much of a sense of community as at other schools." "Most of the events end by 5 P.M.," they say, and a large segment of the student body "flees back to the suburbs and their respective lives" as soon as class ends. Other students contend that "the school can be very social." "Although most people still think Detroit is a scary place to live, there are several great local bars and restaurants near the school, not to mention Tigers baseball right down the street," notes a 1L. There are also "intramural sports teams as well as competitions between schools within the university, like law vs. med school, where the law students really bond together." And "there are a lot of social outlets within Detroit and its suburbs that are frequented by the law students." "Royal Oak is a big area for law students to live," explains a 2L, "and, generally, we tend to congregate in the downtown Royal Oak area to socialize."

Getting In

The acceptance rate here is pretty high. Admitted students at the 25th percentile tend to have LSAT scores in the low 150s and GPAs in the 3.2 range. Admitted students at the 75th percentile have LSAT scores approaching 160 and GPAs of 3.6 or so.

EMPLOYMENT INFORMATION	
Career Rating 71	**Grads Employed by Field (%)**
Rate of placement (nine months out) 86	Academic (2)
Average starting salary $77,155	Business/Industry (13)
State for bar exam MI, NY, IL, CA, GA	Government (12)
Pass rate for first-time bar 87	Judicial Clerkships (2)
Employers Who Frequently Hire Grads	Private Practice (66)
Dykema, Bodman LLP, Honigan Miller	Public Interest (6)
Schwartz and Cohn LLP, Plunkett	
Cooney, PC	
Prominent Alumni	
John Conyers, U.S. House of	
Representatives; Nancy Edmunds, U.S.	
District Court Judge; Damon J. Keith, U.S.	
Court of Appeals Judge; Marilyn Kelly,	
Chief Justice, Michigan Supreme Court	

ADMISSIONS

Selectivity Rating	**74**
# applications received	1,768
# applicants accepted	777
# acceptees attending	225
Average LSAT	154
LSAT Range	136–169
Average undergrad GPA	3.48
Application fee	$50
Regular application	Rolling, up to 3/15
Regular notification	Rolling
Early application program	No
Transfer students accepted	Yes
Evening division offered	Yes
Part-time accepted	Yes
LSDAS accepted	Yes

Applicants Also Look At

Michigan State University, University of Michigan—Ann Arbor, DePaul University, University of Detroit Mercy, Thomas M. Cooley Law School

FINANCIAL FACTS

Annual tuition (in-state/ out-of-state)	$21,866/$23,280
Books and supplies	$1,214
Fees	$1,487
Fees per credit	$29
Tuition per credit (in-state/out-of-state)	$706/$776
Room & board (on/off-campus)	$7,644/$12,078
Financial aid application deadline	6/30
% first-year students receiving some sort of aid	97
% receiving some sort of aid	91
% of aid that is merit based	11
% receiving scholarships	52
Average grant	$7,562
Average loan	$18,503
Average total aid package	$28,208
Average debt	$68,517

WEST VIRGINIA UNIVERSITY
COLLEGE OF LAW

Academics

The West Virginia University College of Law offers a unique community experience that "fosters intellectual growth and collegiality at the same time." Students say that "WVU can provide a great legal education if you are willing to put in the work." "For the price you can't beat the experiences and the opportunity that WVU Law offers." "If you want to work in West Virginia, or simply get a great 'bang for your buck,' WVU College of Law is a wonderful choice."

Students across the board rave about WVU's personable faculty and note that, while "The school isn't perfect," "Most of the professors are constantly striving to improve." Professors are described as "the type of people you'd like to bump into at a bar and talk [with] for hours." The "phenomenal teaching staff" is "willing to meet with a student anytime, anywhere to discuss topics beyond those addressed in the classroom." "The faculty's greatest strength is their passion," reports one 2L. "Our professors are much more than just our teachers . . . they are our mentors, our confidantes, and our friends."

Students report that "the business law classes are superb and provide an excellent business focus." WVU places a large emphasis on research and writing skills, though the legal research and writing program garners mixed reviews. One self-proclaimed "worst writer in the world" says that WVU's "legal research and writing [curriculum], along with the writing seminars, has improved my writing ability." Other students think the legal writing curriculum "is ridiculously tedious and time consuming." "A lot of time is wasted teaching a legal writing format and citation format not currently utilized in most practices." Some students wish for programs that allow for specialization in various areas of law.

Students find little fault with Career Services, which has reportedly improved significantly over the past three years. Described as "extremely proactive and effective [and] a jewel in the law school's crown," students say that the Career Service Center "offers a great deal of assistance and advice in searching for summer jobs and permanent jobs." While some students complain that "little help is provided outside of [help] obtaining a private law firm job," for those students planning to stay in the area, "The relationship with the state bar is phenomenal and opens up the door to many opportunities in the state." One student confidently tells us, "I can always rest assured that getting my law degree from WVU will [assist] me in finding employment opportunities in West Virginia."

While the majority of students wish for a new, more modern building, one 2L is not overly concerned: "The building may be a box, but it does have everything a student needs to prepare for the practice of law." As one student sums up, "We may not be the highest-ranked school in the nation, but we can go head to head with any other school out there." Recently, the WVU College of Law completed extensive renovations to class and courtroom facilities.

JANET ARMISTEAD, ASSISTANT DEAN FOR ADMISSIONS
PO BOX 6130, MORGANTOWN, WV 26506-6103
TEL: 304-293-5304 FAX: 304-293-6891
EMAIL: WVULAW.ADMISSIONS@MAIL.WVU.EDU • WEBSITE: WWW.LAW.WVU.EDU

Life

Students appreciate that WVU Law offers them a well-rounded experience. "Although it is not a social paradise, the students organize both intellectual and social events on a monthly basis" that are well attended by both students and faculty. Students in general are very supportive of one another. "Most people are willing to share outlines or help you find a certain case. There are always a couple [of] exceptions, but most people laugh at the ultra-competitive people." As one student explains, "We are more than a small school; we're a family . . . sharing shoulders to lean on, sibling rivalry, and a few 'eccentric' relatives included."

"The social scene in Morgantown is one in a million," claims one student. "There are a ton of things to do for fun in our town." "Arts and entertainment, concerts, skiing, hiking, athletics, [and] nights out on the town" are just a few of the options available to WVU students outside of the classroom. Students say it's easy to achieve a balance between life and work: "I make time to exercise, attend church, volunteer in the community, and engage in extracurricular activities at the law school, such as Law Review and mock trial competitions, as well as [find] time to socialize with friends at dinner or athletic events. This type of well-roundedness is evident throughout the student body and contributes to a happy and healthy environment at the school."

Getting In

Admitted students at the 25th percentile have an LSAT score of 151 and a GPA of 3.9. Admitted students at the 75th percentile have an LSAT score of 156 and a GPA of 3.8.

Applicants are required to submit three letters of recommendation from people who have personal knowledge of their character, skills, and aptitude for law study and practice. At least one recommendation must be from a former professor.

Public interest law requirement	No

ADMISSIONS

Selectivity Rating	74
# applications received	884
# applicants accepted	154
# acceptees attending	147
Average LSAT	140–154
LSAT Range	148–155
Average undergrad GPA	3.42
Application fee	$50
Regular application	Rolling, up to 3/1
Regular notification	Rolling
Early application program	No
Transfer students accepted	Yes
Evening division offered	No
Part-time accepted	Yes
LSDAS accepted	Yes

Applicants Also Look At

University of Pennsylvania, University of Pittsburgh, The College of William & Mary in Virginia

International Students

TOEFL required of international students	Yes
Minimum TOEFL (paper/computer)	600/250

FINANCIAL FACTS

Annual tuition (in-state/out-of-state)	$4,926/$14,278
Books and supplies	$1,125
Fees (in-state/out-of-state)	$4,416/$7,432
Fees per credit (in-state/out-of-state)	$492/$826
Tuition per credit (in-state/out-of-state)	$552/$1,592
Room & board	$11,356
Financial aid application deadline	3/1
% first-year students receiving some sort of aid	36
% receiving some sort of aid	91
% of aid that is merit based	1
% receiving scholarships	32
Average grant	$1,822
Average loan	$15,800
Average total aid package	$19,150
Average debt	$54,881

EMPLOYMENT INFORMATION

Career Rating	71	
Rate of placement (nine months out)	97	
Average starting salary	$62,559	
State for bar exam	WV	
Pass rate for first-time bar	79	

Employers Who Frequently Hire Grads
Law Firms, State & Federal Judges/Courts, Business/Corporate, Government Agencies, Public Interest Employers.

Grads Employed by Field (%)
Business/Industry (22)
Government (8)
Judicial Clerkships (16)
Private Practice (46)
Public Interest (5)

WESTERN NEW ENGLAND COLLEGE
SCHOOL OF LAW

Academics

A diverse student body, friendly and competent faculty, and a good location near major cites (not to mention being the only ABA-accredited law school in Massachusetts outside the greater Boston area) make Western New England College School of Law a great school. The facilities are new and clean, and the library is currently undergoing a renovation/move, although the infrastructure is very "outdated." A strong point of the academic experience is the Clason Speaker Series, which brings in lecturers on a wide variety of topics; a weak point is that part-time evening students are not given as many events or class opportunities as day students. Though those who attend WNEC are happy with their education, they wish that the reputation of the school matched. "The problem is not that people have a negative perception of the school. Instead, the issue is that most people haven't heard of it. Though this has improved, much still needs to be done," says a student.

WNEC has a "nice mix" of tenured and adjunct professors with a wide range of experiences, so "there are a lot of 'interesting' stories" told about their respective practices, even if a few tenured professors can be "dead weight." Classes 'offer a "'real law' type of education, with a mix of theory and practical," and the teachers "make learning fun and exciting through their honest enthusiasm and love for their work." They're willing to meet with students outside of the classroom in order to clarify and aid students in the learning process, and often explore creative ways to get the material and principals across. "Professor Leavens, our criminal law professor, never allowed a pronoun in the classroom. Now, you never hear a pronoun in any classroom. At home, I now find myself asking my children, 'Who's 'they'?'" says a student. Students admit that the school could use a broader range of elective courses to allow students to develop a particular area of study, as well as "better exam preparation advice," but the strong writing, moot court, and externship programs help bolster the practice side of the JD program. Massachusetts has an exemption to their bar restrictions that allows 3Ls with the right backgrounds to work with a prosecutor, so "it is possible at WNEC for a 3L to leave the school having actually tried a case." When graduation rolls around, however, the school's contacts don't extend that far past the local area, and "the career networking opportunities available through the career services office are virtually nonexistent," so only the most self-motivated students walk away from the career services office satisfied. Luckily, the rest of the administration takes the time to listen to student input before implementing a new rule, and, much like the faculty, has an open door policy. One 2L arriving from a large undergraduate university expected an uphill battle for simple office requests, but found that "not only did I not have to fight with the offices, they were more than helpful. It was a refreshing and pleasant surprise." This school's size makes it so that at WNEC "you are never a number." It's large enough to provide amazing resources, but at the same time, it's "just small enough to ensure a personal experience."

KAREN ROMANO, ASSISTANT DEAN AND DIRECTOR OF ADMISSIONS
1215 WILBRAHAM ROAD, SPRINGFIELD, MA 01119
TEL: 413-782-1406 FAX: 413-796-2067
EMAIL: ADMISSIONS@LAW.WNEC.EDU • WEBSITE: WWW.LAW.WNEC.EDU

Life

The community aspect of WNEC Law is a strong draw: from an annual basketball tournament and ski trip, to the Federalist Society and Environmental Law Coalition, "there are ways for every student to get involved in something that interests them." Most students have a diverse network of peers, and everyone is "very friendly and open." "There is a great sense of community where all views are accepted and critiqued but not shunned," says a student. Although there is a slight competitive streak throughout the student body, almost all students "are willing to work with each other in order to help understand materials in class," and the 2Ls and 3Ls are "extremely helpful" and "make sure that everyone makes it through the first year and stays on track." Unlike the shining aura surrounding the school itself, Springfield "is a rough city with a depressed economy," something students must know going in, but "it does have both positive and negative effects on your law school experience." Housing is affordable, and public interest internship and clinic opportunities abound, but social opportunities outside of the school "are severely limited by the fact that the city is not terribly safe." The full-time day students and part-time night students "might as well go to two different schools" for all of the social and academic overlap that they experience.

Getting In

WNEC accepts students on a rolling basis for fall admission until March 15 of each year. Among law schools, the admissions process is fairly forgiving, with about three of every five applicants accepted. More than a quarter of students are in the part-time program.

ADMISSIONS

Selectivity Rating	67
# applications received	1,493
# applicants accepted	823
# acceptees attending	131
Average LSAT	153
LSAT Range	151–156
Average undergrad GPA	3.12
Application fee	$50
Regular application	Rolling, up to 6/1
Regular notification	Rolling
Early application program	No
Transfer students accepted	Yes
Evening division offered	Yes
Part-time accepted	Yes
LSDAS accepted	Yes

Applicants Also Look At

Suffolk University, Quinnipiac University, Albany Law School of Union University, New England Law|Boston, New York Law School, Roger Williams University

International Students

TOEFL required of international students	Yes

FINANCIAL FACTS

Annual tuition	$34,378
Books and supplies	$1,528
Fees	$1,234
Room & board (on/off-campus)	$13,400
% first-year students receiving some sort of aid	97
% receiving some sort of aid	93
% receiving scholarships	61
Average grant	$16,732
Average loan	$33,463
Average total aid package	$44,475
Average debt	$79,000

EMPLOYMENT INFORMATION

Career Rating	71
Rate of placement (nine months out)	86.5
Average starting salary	$52,450
State for bar exam	CT, MA, NY, NJ, MD
Pass rate for first-time bar	76

Employers Who Frequently Hire Grads

Midsized law firms, District Attorneys, Police defenders, Corporations, non-profits, state governments, and federal governments

Prominent Alumni

Lois Lerner, Director, IRS; Timothy Murray, Lt. Governor, Massachusetts.

Grads Employed by Field (%)

Academic (6)
Business/Industry (19)
Government (20)
Judicial clerkships (11)
Military (1)
Private practice (37)
Public Interest (6)

WHITTIER COLLEGE
WHITTIER LAW SCHOOL

INSTITUTIONAL INFORMATION

Public/private	Private
Student-faculty ratio	17:1
% faculty part-time	47
% faculty female	48
% faculty minority	14
Total faculty	88

SURVEY SAYS...

Diverse opinions accepted
in classrooms
Students love Costa Mesa, CA

STUDENTS

Enrollment of law school	244
% male/female	67/33
% out-of-state	18
% full-time	55
% minority	20
# of countries represented	10
Average age of entering class	24

ACADEMICS

Academic Experience Rating	**76**
Profs interesting rating	87
Profs accessible rating	72
Hours of study per day	4.75

Academic Specialties

Commercial law, criminal law, international law, intellectual property law, children's rights, health law

Advanced Degrees Offered

JD, 3 years full-time, 4 years part-time; LLM, 1 year

Clinical program required	No
Legal writing course requirement	Yes
Legal methods course requirement	Yes
Legal research course requirement	Yes
Moot court requirement	Yes
Public interest law requirement	No

Academics

Classes are small at Whittier Law School. "This is important because it personalizes the classroom experience," explains a 2L. "The quality of teaching is extremely high" as well. The "amazing" professors at Whittier are "dedicated, smart, funny," and they are "there to teach you the law, not to hide the ball or play games." Faculty members are accessible, too, even though many practice as real attorneys at least part time. "They are always available and attend many of our student events," beams a 2L. Students are split in their views concerning the administration. Enthusiasts note that "everyone who counts knows your name and says hello." They say that the "very responsive" top brass tries "to accommodate all types of students—from the full-time day student who came straight out of undergrad to the part-time evening student who has a full-time job and family." Critics charge that the indifferent management is "a dysfunctional nightmare." "They might find it good to start caring about their students," suggests a disgruntled 3L.

Academic bells and whistles here include a "ridiculously comprehensive legal writing program." There's a specialized certificate in intellectual property and additional concentrations in both business law and criminal law. There are five clinics. There are summer study-abroad opportunities in China, France, Israel, Mexico, and Spain. Whittier is also "a school that is serious about helping with bar prep." "The grading system is particularly harsh," though. The "vicious" curve allows "A" grades for no more than 10 percent of the students in any course. Some 30 percent of all the students in every 1L course will get a "D" or an "F." Students at the bottom of the heap end up getting kicked out after the first year.

Career Services offers "very little" in the way of on-campus interviewing, but Whittier does have more than 4,000 alumni. The immediate region is pretty rich with law firms. It also happens to be the tenth largest economy on the planet. "Career Services makes an effort for motivated students," relates a 2L. "If you don't make an effort, they will not see you out or help you. But if you are motivated, they will provide a strong support structure to help you get jobs."

Whittier Law School is located in "a very office building-heavy section" in the heart of suburban Orange County, "10 minutes from the Orange County and U.S. District courthouses." The library and research facilities are reportedly "excellent" but, otherwise, "the facilities are a bit worn" and merely passable. "The classrooms have no windows. The walls are a sanitized white," observes a 2L. "There's nothing aesthetically pleasing about it at all."

Life

The student population at Whittier is pretty diverse. "Many ethic groups and nationalities" are represented. "There also seems to be socioeconomic diversity," notes a 1L. "There are many stereotypical Orange Countians filling the parking lot with cars that cost more than houses. However, there are also many students getting by on loans and part-time jobs." Students describe themselves as "extremely intelligent." Politics vary widely. "There's a decidedly conservative bent among students who've been out in the world," though, and, on the whole, it's probably safe to say that "the students are more conservative than the teachers."

THOMAS McCOLL, ASSISTANT DIRECTOR OF ADMISSIONS
3333 HARBOR BOULEVARD, COSTA MESA, CA 92626
TEL: 714-444-4141 FAX: 714-444-0250
EMAIL: INFO@LAW.WHITTIER.EDU • WEBSITE: WWW.LAW.WHITTIER.EDU

Some students warn that the academic environment is really intense. "Sabotage" does happen, they claim. First-year students are "crazy competitive and not always nice to each other." Others tell us that a "friendly, familial atmosphere" and a great sense of camaraderie" pervade the campus. "We are silently competitive though against each other academically. In general, we are like a big law school family," says a 3L. "Most students are very friendly and helpful." Either way, there seems to be some consensus that full-time day students are "more competitive" while the "older, working" nontraditional students who attend at night "are more willing to help each other."

The quality of life outside the classroom is pretty high. The cost of living is "reasonable," at least compared to the much higher rents and costs in nearby Los Angeles. Sunshine is constant, and the weather is nice pretty much all the time. Students enjoy "close proximity to Southern California beaches such as Huntington, Newport, and Laguna." "There is an active organization on campus for just about anything a student could think of." "Students who live near the campus are exceedingly social." "There are some cliques and an in crowd." "There are many groups of people who strike me as being very tight," observes a 2L.

Getting In

Whittier has a perennially generous acceptance rate. At the same time, the raw numbers for admitted applicants are pretty high. Admitted students at the 25th percentile have LSAT scores around 150 and GPAs in the B–/C+ range. Admitted students at the 75th percentile have LSAT scores of 155 or so, and their undergraduate GPA is a tad over 3.3.

ADMISSIONS

Selectivity Rating	71
# applications received	2,362
% applicants accepted	41
% acceptees attending	20
Average LSAT	153
LSAT Range	151–155
Average undergrad GPA	3.12
Application fee	$50
Regular application	Rolling, up to 8/15
Regular notification	Rolling
Early application program	No
Transfer students accepted	Yes
Evening division offered	Yes
Part-time accepted	Yes
LSDAS accepted	Yes

Applicants Also Look At

Chapman University, University of the Pacific, University of San Francisco, Pepperdine University, University of San Diego, California Western School of Law

International Students

TOEFL required of international students	Yes
Minimum TOEFL (paper/computer)	600/250

FINANCIAL FACTS

Annual tuition	$30,750
Books and supplies	$6,406
Fees	$40
Tuition per credit	$1,025
Room & board (off-campus)	$10,084
Financial aid application deadline	5/1
% first-year students receiving some sort of aid	83
% receiving some sort of aid	86
% of aid that is merit based	25
% receiving scholarships	57
Average grant	$8,904
Average loan	$34,990
Average total aid package	$34,500
Average debt	$86,000

EMPLOYMENT INFORMATION

Career Rating	70
Rate of placement (nine months out)	93
Average starting salary	$65,000
State for bar exam	CA
Pass rate for first-time bar	59

Employers Who Frequently Hire Grads
Small law firm practices (2–10 attorneys)

Prominent Alumni
Florence Marie Cooper, U.S. District Judge; Garo Mardirossian, Mardirossian and Associates, Personal Injury; Judith Ashmann-Gerst, California Court of Appeal; Mablean Ephraim, Presiding Judge, Divorce Ct. TV Program.

Grads Employed by Field (%)
Academic (3)
Business/Industry (36)
Government (6)
Judicial Clerkships (1)
Private Practice (48)
Public Interest (5)

WIDENER UNIVERSITY
SCHOOL OF LAW—DELAWARE CAMPUS

INSTITUTIONAL INFORMATION

Public/private	Private
Student-faculty ratio	17:1
% faculty part-time	45
% faculty female	44
% faculty minority	9
Total faculty	111

SURVEY SAYS...
Diverse opinions accepted
in classrooms
Great research resources
Great library staff

STUDENTS

Enrollment of law school	977
% male/female	59/41
% out-of-state	85
% full-time	63
% minority	12
# of countries represented	6
Average age of entering class	23

ACADEMICS

Academic Experience Rating	**70**
Profs interesting rating	79
Profs accessible rating	78
Hours of study per day	4.15

Academic Specialties
Civil procedure, commercial law, constitutional law, corporation securities, criminal law, environmental law, international law, Health Law, Trial Advocacy

Advanced Degrees Offered
LLM in health law, LLM in corporate law and finance

Combined Degrees Offered
JD/Psy.D, 6 years; JD/MBA, 4 years; JD/MMP; JD/MPH, 4 years

Clinical program required	No
Legal writing	
course requirement	Yes
Legal methods	
course requirement	Yes
Legal research	
course requirement	Yes
Moot court requirement	No

Academics

Many students at Widener's Delaware campus believe the school's "greatest strength" is "flexibility of scheduling; whether you are a full-time student or working professional, Widener offers the opportunity to study law," and nearly half here are enrolled in the school's four-year evening program. Students tell us the school's Admissions Office is also rather accommodating. "Most of our students, including myself, are students who may not have gotten a chance to pursue a legal career otherwise due to low LSAT scores or [a] low undergrad GPA," a 3L writes. With many at Widener happy just to have a chance to study law, the school could provide students with the bare minimum they need to get a JD. Instead, Widener impresses students at almost every turn. Students say, "The campus and its facilities are improving almost daily," and "The school has upgraded [its] principal classrooms to include SmartBoards and other modern capabilities." While "facilities outside of the main law building" could still use improvement—the "spotty" wireless network is a common complaint—the library—(i.e., "the only law library in Delaware)" is "beautiful and well equipped." In addition, "students get free access to both Westlaw and LexisNexis and receive plenty of opportunities to be trained in both sources." With a campus that is "solely comprised of the law school," students report that "the focus is totally on law and the students. This allows for law students to feel like a major priority here."

Professors at Widener hail from "well-respected schools" and "bring a great real-world perspective to the classes." They're also accessible: "Any professor in this law school will take time out of their day to help a student out with a difficult concept, write a recommendation for employment, or...chat with students who want to hear a war story." There are a few duds, however, "so you have to ask around to find out who people like." Classes "are fast paced and engaging in a way that makes even the driest of subjects comprehensible and interesting." The curriculum here leans more to the practical than the theoretical and includes a "strong" writing program. The school's location in the state of Delaware—where, because of tax laws, "many major banks, credit card companies, etc. are located"—"is a real asset for those students who are focusing on corporate law." Programs in health law and trial advocacy are also top notch. As Widener is "the only law school in Delaware," its students "have almost exclusive access to externships with the Delaware Chancery Court and Delaware Supreme Court. Some of the Justices are our teachers, and many well-recognized judges are also our teachers," a 2L writes. An aspiring trial attorney reports that he has been "trained and taught by successful practicing prosecutors, plaintiff's attorneys, and defense attorneys, both civil and criminal. Now in my last semester of law school here at Widener, I feel like I...have the skills and abilities to win a case. My clinical externship program at the Attorney General's Office in New Castle County, Delaware has placed me in court trying cases against real defense attorneys and their juvenile clients...and the last trial I had resulted in a victory over a respected defense attorney."

Students tell us Widener's Career Development Office "is always creating seminars for [those] seeking job[s]" and regularly organizes "mock interviews with attorneys and judges." However, "most" here currently find work through "sources other than the university." As such, students call for more job leads and on-campus interviews. Many gripe that Widener "does not get much respect from potential employers," and several suggest that the administration "offer tours to prospective employers in the area to show them what a commodity that Widener Law students are." Students believe Widener's "C curve," "meaning that the majority of the class gets a C," also complicates their job search. "Other law schools in the area are all on the 'B curve,' so our average GPA is much lower than [theirs]," a 3L writes. "We constantly have to clarify this at job interviews where we compete against those students because to employers it just seems like

BARBARA AYARS, ASSISTANT DEAN FOR ADMISSIONS
PO BOX 7474, 4601 CONCORD PIKE, WILMINGTON, DE 19803-0474
TEL: 302-477-2162 FAX: 302-477-2224
EMAIL: LAWADMISSIONS@MAIL.WIDENER.EDU • WEBSITE: LAW.WIDENER.EDU

we just have lower grades." Those attending Widener part-time in the school's Extended Division report a trade-off: "I'm an Evening Division student, and, as such, I miss out on certain activities and resources made available for day students," a 3L writes. "However, I believe it is more than compensated for by the wonderfully diverse, real-world experiences the evening division student body brings to the table."

Life

Perception on campus is that "evening and day students are two completely different animals," and they "run in different packs." And while evening students tend to be more mature and don't interact much with their fellow evening students outside of class—day students at least "congregate every Wednesday night at a local bar"—there are more similarities than differences between them. "We are all very intellectual people in the same boat, so we watch out for each other while still being competitive," a 1L writes. "Students are willing to share notes, form study groups, etc."

The school "is located on a major four-lane artery that leads right into Wilmington and is surrounded by a mall, strip malls, fast-food restaurants, and motels." Students say the campus is "more or less aesthetically pleasing—with the exception of Polishook Hall, which should be torn down." The campus has earned the nickname "Camp Widener" for its summer-camp-like amenities: "There are three tennis courts, one basketball court, and a huge gym where yoga [and] other aerobic lessons are available," a 2L writes. There could, however, "be more on-campus apartments. The dorms are adequate but begin to feel cell-like to people who have been out of college for a certain amount of time and are accustomed to a certain amount of living space." The food on campus is reportedly "terrible."

Getting In

While the admissions standards for Widener's part-time (aka evening) program are less stringent than the standards for its full-time program, the program itself can involve some difficult choices. A 2L elaborates: "In order to complete a judicial externship/internship, they suggest 'saving your vacation time at work' and taking it all at once... How many full-time employees get so much vacation time that they could use it for an internship?"

EMPLOYMENT INFORMATION

Career Rating	**73**	**Grads Employed by Field (%)**
Rate of placement (nine months out)	93	Academic (2)
Average starting salary	$69,366	Business/Industry (21)
State for bar exam	PA, NJ, DE, MD	Government (6)
Pass rate for first-time bar	80	Judicial Clerkships (24)
Employers Who Frequently Hire Grads		Military (1)
law firms, judges, corporations and other		Private Practice (43)
government employers.		Public Interest (3)
Prominent Alumni		

Risa Vetri Ferman, Montgomery County District Attorney; Cynthia Rhoades Ryan, Chief Counsel, Natl Geospatial Intell Agency; Brian P. Tierey, CEO, Philadelphia Media Holdings L.L.C.; Marc R. Abrams, Partner, Willkie Farr & Gallagher, LLP.

Public interest	
law requirement	No

ADMISSIONS

Selectivity Rating	**65**
# applications received	1,623
% applicants accepted	58
% acceptees attending	26
Average LSAT	152
LSAT Range	150–154
Average undergrad GPA	3.15
Application fee	$60
Regular application	Rolling, up to 5/15
Regular notification	Rolling
Early application program	No
Transfer students accepted	Yes
Evening division offered	Yes
Part-time accepted	Yes
LSDAS accepted	Yes

Applicants Also Look At
Temple University, University of Pennsylvania, Villanova University, University of Baltimore, Rutgers University—Camden, New York Law School, Thomas M. Cooley Law School

International Students

TOEFL recommended of international students	Yes
Minimum TOEFL (paper/computer)	550/220

FINANCIAL FACTS

Annual tuition	$31,950
Books and supplies	$1,200
Fees	$90
Tuition per credit	$1,065
Room & board	$9,450
Financial aid application deadline	4/1
% first-year students receiving some sort of aid	87
% receiving some sort of aid	88
% of aid that is merit based	11
% receiving scholarships	21
Average grant	$8,921
Average loan	$29,900
Average total aid package	$35,065
Average debt	$95,113

WIDENER UNIVERSITY
SCHOOL OF LAW—HARRISBURG CAMPUS

Academics

At Widener's Harrisburg campus, "small class sizes" and a location "tuck[ed] away from the hustle of a large university setting" ensure that "the focus of the school is completely and totally on the law student." As "the only [law] school in the state capital" of Pennsylvania, Widener is "an excellent place for any student who is interested in a career in politics—from being a politician to researching and drafting legislation," a 3L reports. "Students at Widener have a very easy time getting internships and clinics with local lawyers, Pennsylvania Supreme Court judges, senators, and representatives." Despite Widener's environmental advantages, many students maintain that the school's "biggest asset is its faculty." Professors here are reportedly "very accessible"—"most have an open-door policy"—and are, just as importantly, "approachable." They also possess "unique eccentricities" that "keep the class interested in the material." "You are never quite sure how it is going to be presented to you," a 1L tells us. While a few "can be a bit condescending," "Most try to associate with the students outside of the class" and "sponsor a collegial atmosphere that is emulated by the students." Many professors bring considerable "real-life experience" to the classroom: "Last semester I took Sports Law which was taught by the author of the book, which is used around the country; I often see professors on television or local news giving opinions on cases that affect the local community," a 2L writes. With the school's part-time program attracting "many students with maturity, life experience, and practical insights," a pragmatic approach is ubiquitous here. Most see Widener's "focus on legal writing and lawyering skills" as a major strength. The school offers 3Ls "a bar review class for credit" and provides "numerous electives that focus on the practice of litigation and trial methods. This is invaluable." In some areas, however, the school's practical approach leaves students unsatisfied. Many here would like the school to "open up the first-year curriculum. Taking the same five classes all year long is boring and unnecessary." And with Widener's "nationally ranked concentrations, corporate law and health care law," only available at the school's Delaware campus, students would also like to see more opportunities for specialization: "[Widener's] emphasis is on [a] general educational background in the law, but there are obviously adjuncts with impressive credentials," a 3L writes. "Concentrations...may attract a greater pool of top recruits to the student body." With existing programs, the school could utilize area resources better: "We have access to a lot of state government resources, but our law and government program is not what it should be."

By all accounts, Widener is a school "constantly seeking to improve," and students here report a "great environment" in which they can "speak to the deans just as candidly" as they do to professors. Both conditions are fortunate, as students have numerous complaints. An evenhanded student puts it this way: "Widener is slowly advancing into the twenty-first century." While many of the classrooms have outlets for laptop computers, a small percentage of them do not. The on-campus "wireless network signal is extremely low"—depending on who you talk to, it either works in "some classrooms" or only "a handful of rooms in the library building"—and, while the school has "two computer labs," "the computers [in each] need to be updated." Widener's "reference librarians are excellent" students say, but maintain that the library could use "bigger study areas" and more comfortable classroom facilities. Policy-wise, the school "allows teachers 21 days from the last final to submit their grades for each semester," which means Widener students receive their grades significantly later than most law school students. In addition, students describe the bookstore as problematic because it doesn't release information about required course texts—not to mention that it's only open for seven

BARBARA AYARS, ASSISTANT DEAN OF ADMISSIONS
3800 VARTAN WAY, P.O. BOX 69381, HARRISBURG, PA 17106-9381
TEL: 717-541-3903 FAX: 717-541-3999
EMAIL: LAWADMISSIONS@WIDENER.EDU • WEBSITE: WWW.LAW.WIDENER.EDU

hours a day, four days a week. Part-time, predominantly evening students gripe that they "do not get the same breadth of academic offerings nor the same level of administrative support services as do the day students." A big-picture student puts it all in perspective: "While I'm sure Widener does not have the most lavish research facilities and class-rooms, [the school] nonetheless provides its students with everything they need to be successful in law school."

Life

Students who have a cumulative GPA below 2.0 at the end of the first year are dismissed. Students who have between a 2.0 and a 2.3 are placed in the Academic Support Program, so it makes sense that "students are high strung and competitive the first year. Students become more social at the end of the second year and during the third, after the weak links have been academically dismissed and class ranks have settled." Evening students seem to exist outside these peaks and valleys: "We're much more likely to help each other out and share outlines and notes," a 1L writes. "I've found all the horror stories of people backstabbing you in law school and trying to make you look like a fool in class to be gen-erally untrue. Everyone pretty much respects each other." Overall, the atmosphere at Widener is "competitive but friendly, with many of the 2Ls and 3Ls willing to help the incoming students." However, students warn that it can be "hard to get social groups going," and the ones already in place "are pretty tight." Regarding the facilities, "Most classes are in one building, which makes everything very convenient." Unfortunately, "the nearest ATM is one mile away," and "The school's cafeteria operates on a cash-only basis." Its hours are also limited: "One cannot even purchase a cup of coffee on campus in the evening, let alone a sandwich or anything other than crackers or a candy bar from a vending machine," a 3L writes.

Getting In

Students who apply to both Widener campuses are charged only one application fee by the school. Such students, however, waive their right to choose between locations—the school only grants accepted applicants admission to one campus. It tends to populate each campus with students of roughly equal caliber.

ADMISSIONS

Selectivity Rating	**65**
# applications received	700
% applicants accepted	55
% acceptees attending	39
Average LSAT	150
LSAT Range	149–153
Average undergrad GPA	3.18
Application fee	$60
Regular application	Rolling, up to 5/15
Regular notification	Rolling
Early application program	No
Transfer students accepted	Yes
Evening division offered	Yes
Part-time accepted	Yes
LSDAS accepted	Yes

Applicants Also Look At
Temple University, University of Pennsylvania, Villanova University, University of Baltimore, Rutgers University—Camden, New York Law School, Thomas M. Cooley Law School,

International Students

TOEFL recommended of international students	Yes
Minimum TOEFL (paper/computer)	550/220

FINANCIAL FACTS

Annual tuition	$31,950
Books and supplies	$1,200
Fees	$90
Tuition per credit	$1,065
Room & board (off-campus)	$9,450
Financial aid application deadline	4/1
% first-year students receiving some sort of aid	76
% receiving some sort of aid	96
% of aid that is merit based	11
% receiving scholarships	32
Average grant	$9,492
Average loan	$32,569
Average total aid package	$35,671
Average debt	$96,391

EMPLOYMENT INFORMATION

Career Rating	**78**
Rate of placement (nine months out)	97
Average starting salary	$61,933
State for bar exam	PA, NJ
Pass rate for first-time bar	90

Employers Who Frequently Hire Grads
Law firms, judges, corporations and other government employers.

Prominent Alumni
Michele Henry, Bucks County District Attorney; Michael Aiello, Partner, Weil, Gotshal & Manges; Tom Linzey, CEO, Community Environmental Legal Defense Fund; Rory Ritrieve, President and CEO of Mid Penn Bank.

Grads Employed by Field (%)
Academic (2)
Business/Industry (17)
Government (21)
Judicial Clerkships (14)
Military (1)
Private Practice (39)
Public Interest (6)

WILLAMETTE UNIVERSITY
COLLEGE OF LAW

INSTITUTIONAL INFORMATION

Public/private	Private
Affiliation	Methodist
Student-faculty ratio	13:1
% faculty part-time	34
% faculty female	29
% faculty minority	12
Total faculty	59

SURVEY SAYS...
Great research resources
Great library staff

STUDENTS

Enrollment of law school	428
% male/female	57/43
% out-of-state	54
% full-time	99
% minority	23
Average age of entering class	26

ACADEMICS

Academic Experience Rating	**77**
Profs interesting rating	84
Profs accessible rating	80
Hours of study per day	5.07

Academic Specialties

Government services, dispute resolution, law & business, international and comparative law, sustainability law

Advanced Degrees Offered

LL.M., 1 year

Combined Degrees Offered

JD/MBA, 4 year

Clinical program required	No
Legal writing course requirement	Yes
Legal methods course requirement	No
Legal research course requirement	Yes
Moot court requirement	Yes
Public interest law requirement	No

Academics

Willamette University College of Law is "a smaller school in the Pacific Northwest," "in the state capital city" of Salem, Oregon. Highlights here include an exemplary legal research and writing program. A JD/MBA program allows students to earn both degrees in four years. There are three journals, six specialized clinics, and a broad externship program. Certificates are available in dispute resolution, business law, international and comparative law (reportedly "wonderful"), law and government, and sustainability law. Study-abroad programs in Hamburg, Germany; Quito, Ecuador; and Shanghai, China are another big hit. Students also laud their surroundings. "The facilities at Willamette are, by far, among the best," they say. The "beautiful building" is located on the peaceful and collegiate-looking campus of the larger university. Classrooms are recently renovated and modern. "You have access to the library 24/7," too, which can be an invaluable perk when finals roll around each semester.

Classes are definitely on the smaller side, and they're generally "entertaining." "The greatest strength of Willamette Law has to be the faculty," relates a 2L. "The faculty is knowledgeable, accessible, and seems to generally enjoy teaching students—an extremely valuable trifecta." The "very helpful" top brass gets a lot of love as well. "The school's administration works as effectively as possible," says a 3L. "They are very focused on getting us to pass the bar," agrees a happy 1L, "and very focused on getting us a job post graduation."

Course scheduling is probably the biggest single source of frustration among students. After the first year, it can be hard to get into the classes you want (and occasionally need). The fairly strict grading curve comes in for some grief as well. "Grade deflation" is alive and well, and a handful of 1Ls at the bottom of the class at Willamette are inevitably asked to leave each year. On the one hand, it's an intimidating situation. On the other hand, it "will really help motivate." Computing issues can also be a pain. Willamette has wireless, but the connection can be spotty sometimes. "Perhaps they will employ technology that is commensurate with the decade we are currently in," suggests one student.

When the time comes to get a job as an actual attorney, there's good news and bad news for newly minted Willamette alums. On the minus side, the generally mild climate and the culture of Oregon are both professionally appealing for many people. Competition for jobs (especially in Portland) is fierce because the legal market is not huge and a lot of transplant lawyers want to work in the state. On the plus side, the law school here is "down the street from" the Capitol building and various courts. Consequently, students have "fantastic access" to state legislative bodies, state courts, and state agencies. "Great networking opportunities" and prospects for practical experience outside of school abound. Students can "cooperate with the judicial process" in ways that students at the other two law schools in the state cannot.

Life

Students tell us that ethnic diversity is "increasing" at Willamette. More than 20 percent of the population here represents some minority group. "No longer can you count the number of minority students on one hand." Diversity shows itself in other ways, too. There's a decent-sized contingent of older students who are looking to transition into another, more lucrative career, for example. Also, just more than half the students come from a state other than Oregon. Some students are "very competitive" when it comes to grades. At the same time, "Willamette is a tight-knit community." "People generally

CAROLYN DENNIS, ASSISTANT DIRECTOR OF ADMISSION
245 WINTER STREET SE, SALEM, OR 97301-3922
TEL: 503-370-6282 FAX: 503-370-6087
EMAIL: LAW-ADMISSION@WILLAMETTE.EDU • WEBSITE: WWW.WILLAMETTE.EDU/WUCL

hang out with the same group of friends they made in their first year of law school, but everyone still remains friendly to others."

Views about life outside the classroom vary. Some students consider the "small" surrounding burg of Salem "an inexpensive and livable town in a pleasant state." They call the immediate location "great for serious students." They point out that "Salem is less than an hour's drive from Portland and is in the heart of wine country." They also note that temperatures are mild all year long, and the surrounding area is a paradise for lovers of the outdoors. Opportunities for hiking, skiing, and frolicking at the beach are all within relatively easy reach. Closer to home, students also have access to a fabulous campus recreation center. Other students aren't nearly as happy with the setting. "Salem is awful," they say, and the constantly rainy, "gloomy Oregon weather" can be a real downer.

Getting In

The acceptance rate is high, but Willamette is a small school and the candidates competing for spots tend to have solid credentials. Admitted students at the 25th percentile have LSAT scores that hover in the low 150s and GPAs around 3.0. Admitted students at the 75th percentile have LSAT scores of 158 or so; their GPAs are about 3.5.

ADMISSIONS

Selectivity Rating	75
# applications received	1,329
# applicants accepted	504
# acceptees attending	159
Average LSAT	154
LSAT Range	152–157
Average undergrad GPA	3.26
Application fee	$50
Regular application	Rolling, up to 7/1
Regular notification	Rolling
Early application program	No
Transfer students accepted	Yes
Evening division offered	No
Part-time accepted	No
LSDAS accepted	Yes

Applicants Also Look At
Seattle University, University of Oregon, Brigham Young University, University of the Pacific, Golden Gate University, Gonzaga University, Lewis & Clark College

International Students
Minimum TOEFL (paper/web)	600/100

FINANCIAL FACTS

Annual tuition	$29,600
Books and supplies	$1,460
Fees	$80
Room & board (off-campus)	$14,510
Financial aid application deadline	3/1
% first-year students receiving some sort of aid	98
% receiving some sort of aid	95
% of aid that is merit based	19
% receiving scholarships	55
Average grant	$12,849
Average loan	$33,520
Average total aid package	$38,713
Average debt	$89,679

EMPLOYMENT INFORMATION

Career Rating	77
Rate of placement (nine months out)	94
Average starting salary	$60,684
State for bar exam	OR, WA, CA, ID, NY
Pass rate for first-time bar	89

Employers Who Frequently Hire Grads
Stoel Rives, Schwabe Williamson Wyatt, Washington State Attorney General, Lane County Circuit Court, Lane Powell LLP.

Prominent Alumni
Lisa Murkowski, U.S. Senator from Alaska; Paul De Muniz, Chief Justice Oregon Supreme Court; Lindsay D. Stewart, Vice President of Law and Corporate Affairs, Nike.

Grads Employed by Field (%)
Academic (1)
Business/Industry (19)
Government (17)
Judicial Clerkships (6)
Military (1)
Private Practice (49)
Public Interest (6)
Other (1)

WILLIAM MITCHELL COLLEGE OF LAW

INSTITUTIONAL INFORMATION

Public/private	Private
Student-faculty ratio	22:1
% faculty part-time	38
% faculty female	52
% faculty minority	11
Total faculty	321

SURVEY SAYS...

Great research resources
Great library staff
Students love St. Paul, MN

STUDENTS

Enrollment of law school	1,044
% male/female	49/51
% out-of-state	13
% full-time	62
% minority	11
# of countries represented	16
Average age of entering class	26

ACADEMICS

Academic Experience Rating	**76**
Profs interesting rating	75
Profs accessible rating	71
Hours of study per day	4.62

Academic Specialties

Business law, Civil litigation, Elder law, Estate planning, Family law, Indian law, National security law, Product liability law, Tort law, Public interest law, Real estate law, Tax law, Negotiation and ADR

Advanced Degrees Offered

JD, 3 years full-time, 4 years part-time

Clinical program required	No
Legal writing	
course requirement	Yes
Legal methods	
course requirement	Yes
Legal research	
course requirement	Yes
Moot court requirement	No
Public interest	
law requirement	No

Academics

"There is a huge emphasis on practical experience" at William Mitchell College of Law, an independent in the Twin Cities. "The greatest strength at William Mitchell is the real-life advocacy training which allows students to hit the ground running after graduation," asserts a 3L. A wide array of clinics provides ample opportunities to represent clients. Externships, internships, and clerkships are "good," but they're "hard to get into." While most students call the "intense" and nationally-recognized legal writing program "awesome," a few find it "poorly executed." According to most students, legal writing at WMCL is "extremely worthwhile and prepares you with the confidence and competence to go out into the legal world." It's also worth noting that U.S. judges cite the *William Mitchell Law Review* more than any other legal journal in Minnesota.

"The quality of the faculty is superb" overall. Adjuncts "bring an interesting and valuable perspective." The full-time professors are "polished and professional" and "acutely aware that the law does not exist in a vacuum." "Most all of the professors have an extensive real world experience and it provides the students with insight as to how it really works once we get into practice," notes a 1L. "However, some of them can't teach a lick." Students note that "William Mitchell's commitment to the part-time student—a foundational aspect of the college—is very good" and many administrators are reportedly "very helpful," though some say the administration "can always use improvement." However, many students say that "course scheduling can sometimes be tricky, especially if you are a strict night student."

"There are four law schools churning out graduates" in the area but students at WMCL tell us that they are optimistic about their employment prospects. Students "in the top 10 percent" are able to compete for the plum jobs at big firms. Other newly-minted grads "are readily hired" by small and midsize firms. "The alumni network in the Twin Cities is ruled by William Mitchell alums," swears a 1L. "William Mitchell's greatest strength is its extensive and supportive alumni base in many practice areas including corporate and intellectual property lawyers in large firms, in-house counsel at many large corporations, and judges at every level." "Almost every graduate stays in the Twin Cities and Minnesota," though.

The "gorgeous" building here is "a very pleasant place to be." "The school is clearly investing a great deal of money in maintaining and upgrading the facilities," observes a 2L. Pretty much everything is "state of the art." "The whole building" is wireless. "Classroom technology is above average" and there are "adequate plug-ins for laptop computers." "The library is amazing" as well and "research facilities are fabulous."

KENDRA DANE, ASST. DEAN & DIRECTOR OF ADMISSIONS
875 SUMMIT AVENUE, ST. PAUL, MN 55105
TEL: 651-290-6476 FAX: 651-290-6414
EMAIL: ADMISSIONS@WMITCHELL.EDU • WEBSITE: WWW.WMITCHELL.EDU

Life

Students here are "very active within the school's various organizations" and come from many, many different backgrounds. "There's a place at WMCL for the fresh-out-of-college student who wants to plow through classes in three years as well as the grownup who holds a full-time job during the day and takes part-time classes at night," promises a 3L. Ethnic diversity is minimal, though. The student population here is basically "reflective of the ethnic make-up of Minnesota." Many students assert that the academic atmosphere is "completely cooperative." Others suggest that competition is "pretty fierce," especially during first year. "While it appears students are not competitive to your face," says a 1L, "deep down they are around crunch time."

WMCL is located in a "swanky" area of St. Paul full of "rolling, well-manicured lawns." Students call it "one of the most beautiful neighborhoods in any major American city." "Plenty of bars and restaurants along with an eclectic mix of retail stores provide ample sources for relaxation and distraction." The only real negative about the area is that it "cannot be reached easily by public transportation." Socially, "everyone seems to get along pretty well" but "there is sometimes a tension between the full-time students and the part-time students." The "strong and vibrant" population of day students can be "cliquey," but they are more social. "The full-time students certainly find time to relax" and they "drink like they're undergrads." For the older evening students, "the socializing aspect is definitely not there," though this is likely due to students' outside commitments.

Getting In

The acceptance rate here is high. Admitted students at the 25th percentile have LSAT scores in the low 150s and GPAs just over 3.0. Admitted students at the 75th percentile have LSAT scores in the high 150s and GPAs just over 3.6.

ADMISSIONS

Selectivity Rating	**75**
# applications received	1,325
# applicants accepted	763
# acceptees attending	323
Average LSAT	156
LSAT Range	153–158
Average undergrad GPA	3.53
Application fee	$50
Regular application	Rolling, up to 5/1
Regular notification	Rolling
Early application program	No
Transfer students accepted	Yes
Evening division offered	Yes
Part-time accepted	Yes
LSDAS accepted	Yes

Applicants Also Look At
University of Minnesota—Twin Cities, St. Thomas University, Hamline University

International Students

TOEFL required of international students	Yes
Minimum TOEFL (paper/computer)	600/250

FINANCIAL FACTS

Annual tuition	$32,420
Books and supplies	$1,550
Fees	$50
Room & board (off-campus)	$15,800
Financial aid application deadline	3/15
% first-year students receiving some sort of aid	94
% receiving some sort of aid	96
% of aid that is merit based	37
% receiving scholarships	66
Average grant	$8,856
Average loan	$33,000
Average total aid package	$39,115
Average debt	$85,000

EMPLOYMENT INFORMATION

Career Rating	**77**	**Grads Employed by Field (%)**
Rate of placement (nine months out)	91	Academic (1)
Average starting salary	$63,761	Business/Industry (26)
State for bar exam	MD, MN, WI, NY, CA, KS	Government (6)
		Judicial Clerkships (10)
Pass rate for first-time bar	93	Military (1)

Employers Who Frequently Hire Grads
Briggs & Morgan; Faegre & Benson; Gray Plant Mooty; Robins Kaplan Miller & Ciresi; Leonard Street & Deinard.

Private Practice (52)
Public Interest (3)
Other (1)

Prominent Alumni
Warren E. Burger, Chief Justice of U.S. Supreme Court; Rosalie Wahl, Justice Minnesota Supreme Court (retired); Douglas Amdahl, Chief Justice Minnesota Supreme Court (retired), Eric J. Magnuson, Chief Justice Minnesota Supreme Court.

YALE UNIVERSITY
LAW SCHOOL

INSTITUTIONAL INFORMATION

Public/private	Private
Student-faculty ratio	7:1
% faculty female	15
% faculty minority	10
Total faculty	80

SURVEY SAYS...
Great research resources
Great library staff
Abundant externship/internship/
clerkship opportunities
Beautiful campus

STUDENTS

Enrollment of law school	588
% male/female	51/49
% full-time	100
% minority	27
# of countries represented	31
Average age of entering class	24

ACADEMICS

Academic Experience Rating	**87**
Profs interesting rating	68
Profs accessible rating	61
Hours of study per day	1.5

Advanced Degrees Offered
JD, 3 years; LL.M., 1 year; MSL, 1
year; JSD, up to 5 years.

Combined Degrees Offered
JD/Ph.D. (History), JD/Ph.D.
(Political Science), JD/MS
(Forestry), JD/MS (Sociology),
JD/MS (Statistics), JD/MBA and
JD/Ph.D.

Clinical program required	No
Legal writing	
course requirement	No
Legal methods	
course requirement	No
Legal research	
course requirement	No
Moot court requirement	No
Public interest	
law requirement	No

Academics

It's hard to beat Yale Law School, where the atmosphere is "highly intellectual" and classes are mostly "small" (first-year classes vary in size from 15 to 90 students). One of the many uniquely cool things about Yale is that "there aren't very many required courses." All 1Ls must complete course work in constitutional law, contracts, procedure, and torts. There's also a small, seminar-style legal research and writing course, and that's pretty much it. Best of all, there are "no grades." First semester classes are graded pass/fail. After first semester, there is some semblance of grades but, since Yale doesn't keep track of class rank, it's not a big deal.

Academically, "This is the best place in the world." "It's easy to learn about whatever you're interested in, from medieval European law to helping immigrants in the modern-day United States," says one student. Yale is home to cutting-edge centers and programs galore. Clinical opportunities are vast and available "in your first year," which is a rarity. You can represent family members in juvenile neglect cases, provide legal services for nonprofit organizations, or participate in complicated federal civil rights cases. It's also "easy" to obtain joint-degrees or simply "cross-register for other classes" at Yale. A particularly unique program allows students to get a joint-degree at the Woodrow Wilson School of Public and International Affairs at Princeton.

Student report that the administration is "generally friendly." Word on the faculty is mixed. "I love all my professors," beams a 2L. "They will help me with anything." Nearly all agree that "most professors are delighted to help you." When jobs and clerkships are on the line, it's not uncommon for professors to personally make calls on behalf of students "to high-profile firms or government officials." Other students, however, tell us the faculty isn't all it's cracked up to be. "Quality teaching is not valued enough," gripes a critic. "Professors are hired based on their scholarship rather than their ability to teach or their interest in interacting with students."

Employment prospects are simply awesome. A degree from Yale virtually guarantees "an easy time finding a good job" and a lifetime of financial security. There is "very solid career support" (including "lots of free wine" at recruiting events). But did you know that Yale prolifically produces public interest attorneys? It's true. Every one of Yale's graduates could immediately take the big firm route but, each year, hordes of them don't. Yale "encourages diverse career paths" and "nontraditional routes" ("especially in academia and public interest") and annually awards dozens of public interest fellowships to current students and newly minted grads. There's a "great" loan forgiveness program too.

Facilities are phenomenal. Yale boasts Wireless Internet accessthroughout the Law School, wireless common areas, and perhaps the greatest law library in the history of humanity. "The research facilities are spectacular." Aesthetically, "Everything is beautiful," especially if you are into "wood paneling, stained glass windows, and hand-carved moldings." "If you care about architecture and Ivy League ambiance, come to Yale."

Life

Though the student population "is a bit Ivy heavy," it doesn't necessarily follow that everyone is wealthy. Approximately 80 percent of the lucky souls here receive financial assistance of some kind. It does follow, however, that students are pretty conceited about their intelligence and their privileged educational status. "If egos were light, an astronaut on the moon would have to shade his eyes from the glare of New Haven," analogizes one student. "I'm not sure there's a cure for that, but it might not be wise to tell us in the first week of torts that many of us will wind up on the federal bench."

"There are parties," swears a 1L. However, for many students, the social scene at Yale is simply an extension of academic life. Lectures and cultural events of all kinds are, of course, never-ending. The surrounding city of New Haven is lively in its own way and New York City and Boston are both easily accessible by train. On campus, Yale offers an "encouraging environment" and a "wonderful community." "Because of the small size of each class and the enormous number of activities, it is incredibly easy to get involved with journals (even the *Journal*) and any other student group you might want to try." "Students are very engaged and motivated, but not generally in a way that stresses everyone else out," explains one student. "The no-grades policy for first semester completely eliminates the competition I expect exists at other schools." "People ask me what law school is like, and I can honestly say, 'I work pretty hard, but it's fun,'" says a satisfied student. "Then those people stare at me oddly, and maybe they're right that 'fun' isn't exactly the right word. But I've found it enriching and enjoyable and the people I've met here have been great."

Getting In

Let's not sugarcoat the situation: It's ridiculously hard to get into Yale Law School. Consider: with a stellar grade-point average of 3.75 and a near-perfect LSAT score of, say, 176, you have about a 40 percent chance of getting accepted. With a perfectly good GPA of 3.4 and a perfectly good LSAT score of 168, your shot at getting into Yale is a little more than 1 percent. The folks in admissions at Yale say that they don't use any kind of formula or index. They consider many factors including grades; LSAT scores (including multiple LSAT scores), extracurricular activities, ethnic and socioeconomic diversity, and letters of recommendation.

ADMISSIONS

Selectivity Rating	99
# applications received	3,109
# applicants accepted	238
# acceptees attending	189
Average LSAT	172
LSAT Range	169–177
Average undergrad GPA	3.88
Application fee	$75
Regular application	Rolling, up to 2/15
Regular notification	Rolling
Early application program	No
Transfer students accepted	Yes
Evening division offered	No
Part-time accepted	No
LSDAS accepted	Yes

FINANCIAL FACTS

Annual tuition	$44,000
Books and supplies	$1,100
Fees	$2,000
Room & board (on-campus)	$15,500
Financial aid application deadline	3/15
% first-year students receiving some sort of aid	75
% receiving some sort of aid	74
% of aid that is merit based	0
% receiving scholarships	53
Average grant	$19,354
Average loan	$37,390
Average total aid package	$56,744
Average debt	$95,899

EMPLOYMENT INFORMATION

		Grads Employed by Field (%)
Career Rating	92	Academic (3)
Rate of placement (nine months out)	95	Business/Industry (7)
State for bar exam	NY	Government (5)
Pass rate for first-time bar	97.5	Judicial Clerkships (35)
		Military (1)
		Private Practice (41)
		Public Interest (8)

YESHIVA UNIVERSITY
BENJAMIN N. CARDOZO SCHOOL OF LAW

Academics

Despite having only been around about 30 years, Benjamin N. Cardozo School of Law "has accomplished much" in that time and offers "a top-notch legal education" to its students. Academic life at the "underrated, under-known" law school in New York City is pretty exciting. There are "weekly debates featuring legal experts from around the country." Plus, there are lunches or roundtables "every single day with public officials like the New York City Police Commissioner."

Offering "a strong balance of theory and practice," Cardozo provides "superb" opportunities for practical experience. Students also love the "envied" clinical opportunities available. "I've spent a full semester in the New York DA's office, tried a civil case from pleadings to judgment, and this week will argue an appeal at the NY's Appellate Division First Department," says one student. Likewise, a participant in Cardozo's Innocence Project tells us, "Spending eight straight hours in the library doesn't seem so bad after you meet a guy who spent 18 years in jail for a crime he didn't commit." Cardozo also boasts a strong intellectual property program, a unique Public Service Scholars program, several "great journals," and study-abroad programs.

Student are "continually impressed" by the "high caliber" of Cardozo's professors. "The faculty is composed of nationally recognized scholars who care deeply about their specialized fields of law and their students' progress within it," says one student. They "really care about how you are progressing." Not only are they "smart," but they also make "fantastic teachers, which don't always go hand in hand." However, "Some teachers are clearly experts in their field but are unable to convey their knowledge as effective instructors," claims one student. Another remarks, "Cardozo's faculty is a mix of brilliant young stars who have clerked in high places and old-school Socratic Method actors straight out of *The Paper Chase*. My experiences vary so widely from those of 1Ls in other sections that it's as though we go to different schools."

Students find that "some areas of the administration are very strong and certain administrators are particularly sensitive to the needs of the students." Most students are satisfied with their career prospects. "The school's reputation is growing by leaps and bounds," however, Cardozo graduates "unfortunately have to compete with intense competition from Columbia, NYU, and Fordham grads for jobs."

Students applaud the "great facility face-lift in the last few years" and "amazing" location. One student reports that "it's a pretty aesthetically pleasing place to be these days." Many find the moot court room "impressive" but say that "technology across the board" (especially the "website, online course reviews, e-mail system, [and] online research resources") could be improved. Also, technology is not cutting-edge. Cardozo's library has "great reading rooms," but many students complain because it is "closed every Friday night and Saturday." (Cardozo is a Jewish-affiliated law school.)

Life

Besides the fact that the library is closed on Saturdays, "Cardozo does not feel like a religious law school." There are "exceptionally hardworking and dedicated" students of every "religion, ethnicity, and background." Another student adds, "Law school is not about religion, unless one wishes to specialize in religious law." One student explains, "We feel that the school is consistently underrated." This feeling gives students "a strong bond and sense of community," however the school is "shedding its underdog character every year" as its profile rises and successful alumni base expands. Students are divided when it comes to

DAVID G. MARTINIDEZ, DEAN OF ADMISSIONS
55 FIFTH AVENUE, NEW YORK, NY 10003
TEL: 212-790-0274 FAX: 212-790-0482
EMAIL: LAWINFO@YU.EDU • WEBSITE: WWW.CARDOZO.YU.EDU

the level of competition at Cardozo. Some perceive a "very competitive" atmosphere. Others "would like nothing better then to give you their notes." "The students are more competitive with themselves than with other students," writes a student in the latter camp. "There is generally a very supportive and friendly environment among students."

Cardozo's location in "the heart of New York City is its best asset." Certainly, getting a legal education in the world's capital of business and finance has its perks. If urban life is what you are after, you would be hard-pressed to do better. However, it can be somewhat of a "commuter school," and the location "drives students into the city, not into school to socialize." Also, housing comes at a hefty premium in New York City. Some students find housing in Greenwich Village, Tribeca, SoHo, and other nearby neighborhoods. Others aren't so lucky. The law school also has a residence hall, (but space is limited and priority is given to out-of-towners), although it has been possible to accommodate all students in recent years.

Getting In

Admitted students at the 25th percentile have an LSAT score of 162 and a GPA of 3.29. Admitted students at the 75th percentile have an LSAT score of 166 and a GPA of 3.72. If you take the LSAT more than once, Cardozo will review all scores and may give consideration to the highest LSAT score. If you score significantly better on one LSAT, write an explanatory letter to the Admissions Committee—it can do wonders. Finally, note that you can enter Cardozo in January and May as well as in September.

Legal research course requirement	Yes
Moot court requirement	Yes
Public interest law requirement	No

ADMISSIONS

Selectivity Rating	**89**
# applications received	4,207
# applicants accepted	1,096
# acceptees attending	241
Average LSAT	164
LSAT Range	162–166
Average undergrad GPA	3.55
Application fee	$70
Regular application	Rolling, up to 4/1
Regular notification	Rolling
Early application program	No
Early application deadline	
Early application notification	
Transfer students accepted	Yes
Evening division offered	No
Part-time accepted	Yes
LSDAS accepted	Yes

Applicants Also Look At
Columbia University, New York University, Boston University, Fordham University, The George Washington University, Brooklyn Law School

FINANCIAL FACTS

Annual tuition	$42,200
Books and supplies	$1,500
Fees	$370
Tuition per credit	$1,875
Room & board	$19,350
Financial aid application deadline	4/15
% first-year students receiving some sort of aid	93
% receiving some sort of aid	85
% of aid that is merit based	24
% receiving scholarships	60
Average grant	$19,062
Average loan	$39,687
Average total aid package	$47,031
Average debt	$105,283

EMPLOYMENT INFORMATION

Career Rating	**93**
Rate of placement (nine months out)	94.3
Average starting salary	$107,328
State for bar exam	NY, NJ
Pass rate for first-time bar	93.5

Employers Who Frequently Hire Grads
International and national law firms of all sizes; corporations; federal and state judges nationwide; district attorney's offices and other state and federal government entities; and public interest organizations.

Prominent Alumni
Randi Weingarten, President, United Federation of Teachers; Hon. Sandra J. Feuerstein, Judge, U.S. District Court, Eastern District of NY; David Samson, President, Florida Marlins; Sandra L. Cobden, Head of Litigation, Christie's (Auction House).

Grads Employed by Field (%)
Private Practice (58)
Business/Industry (19)
Government (13)
Judicial Clerkships (5)
Public Interest (10)

LAW SCHOOL DATA LISTINGS

In this section you will find data listings of the ABA-approved schools not appearing in the "Law School Descriptive Profiles" section of the book. Here you will also find listings of the California Bar Accredited, but not ABA-approved law schools, as well as listings of Canadian law schools. Explanations of what each field of data signifies in the listings may be found in the "How to Use This Book" section.

ATLANTA'S JOHN MARSHALL LAW SCHOOL*

Atlanta's John Marshall Law School

1422 W. Peachtree St. NW Atlanta, GA 30309
Admissions Phone: 404-872-3593 • **Admissions Fax:** 404-873-3802
Admissions E-mail: admissions@johnmarshall.edu
Web Address: www.johnmarshall.edu

INSTITUTIONAL INFORMATION
Public/private: Private
Total faculty: 55
% part-time: 20
% female: 48
% minority: 23

STUDENTS
Enrollment of law school: 168
% Male/female: 51/49
% Out of state: 20
% Full time: 67
% Minority: 23
% International: 0
Number of countries represented: 1
Average age of entering class: 26

ACADEMICS
Academic Specializations: N/A
Advanced degrees offered: Juris Doctor, Full-Time, 3 years; Part-Time, 4 years
Combined degrees offered: N/A
Grading system: Students are graded on an objective standard. There is no mandatory mean or curve used.
Clinical program required: No
Clinical program description: N/A
Legal writing course requirements: Yes
Legal writing description: The Legal Writing and Professionalism Program (LSAPP) is an integral part of the overall curriculum. In the first year, students take Legal Writing, Research, and Advocacy I and II (for a total of six credit hours) which focuses on objective writing in the fall semester, and persuasive writing in the spring semester. Student are required to take a writing requirement in their second year and another in their third year, for a total of at least five hours of upper-division writing instruction. Students may select among the following classes to fulfill the upper-division requirements: Advanced Appellate Advocacy, Trial Advocacy and Writing, ADR and Writing, Pretrial Practice, and Transactional Drafting. All courses are taught in small sections (generally approximately 20 students) by full-time, tenure-track professors who teach primarily in the LSAPP.
Legal methods course requirements: No
Legal methods description: N/A
Legal research course requirements: Yes
Legal research description: Legal research is incorporated into LRWA I and LRWA II.
Moot court requirement: Yes
Moot court description: In LRWA II, a required first year second semester course, first year students are required to draft and brief and present oral arguments. The best oralists proceed on competing for positions on the Moot Court Board. Students on the Moot Court Board participate in interschool moot court competitions during their second, third, and fourth years at the law school.
Public interest law requirement: No
Public interest law description: N/A
Academic journals: The John Marshall Law Journal: The Law Review of Atlanta's John Marshall Law School

ADMISSIONS INFORMATION
Admissions Selectivity Rating: 60*
# of applications received: 1,252
% of applicants accepted: 38
% of acceptees attending: 24
Average LSAT: 151
LSAT Range: 149–153
Average undergrad GPA: 2.97
Application fee: $50
Regular application deadline: Rolling, up to 8/15
Regular notification: Rolling
Early application program: No
Transfer students accepted: Yes
Evening division offered: Yes
Part-time accepted: Yes
LSDAS accepted: Yes
Applicants also look at: University of Georgia, Barry University, Mercer University, Emory University, Georgia State University, Campbell University, St. Thomas University, Florida Costal School of Law, Appalachian State University

RESEARCH FACILITIES
% of JD classrooms wired: 100

INTERNATIONAL STUDENTS
TOEFL required of international students? Yes

FINANCIAL FACTS
Annual tuition: $29,280
Books and supplies: $2,360
Fees: $150
Tuition per credit: $976
Room & board (off-campus): $17,100
Financial aid application deadline: 6/9
% First-year students receiving some sort of aid: 86
% Receiving some sort of aid: 90
% of Aid that is merit-based: 1
% Receiving scholarships: 5
Average loan: $48,740
Average total aid package: $48,740
Average debt: $60,688

EMPLOYMENT INFORMATION
Rate of placement (nine months out): 94.3
Average starting salary: $60,069
State(s) for bar exam: GA, TN, FL, VA, WA
Pass rate for first-time bar: 79

Employers who frequently hire grads: Georgia Public Interest Organizations, Georgia District Attorney's, Georgia Public Defender's, Georgia Solicitor General's, small and medium firms. Many John Marshall Grads start their own practice or business.

Prominent alumni: Honorable Alan Blackburn, Presiding Judge, Court of Appeals; Honorable Alvin T. Wong, Judge, State Court of DeKalb County; Honorable James Bodiford, Chief Judge, Cobb Superior Court; Joan Boilen Sasine, Partner, Powell Goldstein; Adam Malone, Attorney, Malone Law Office.

Grads employed by field: %
Academic (2)
Business/Industry (15)
Government (10)
Judicial Clerkships (5)
Private Practice (64)
Public Interest (4)

*Provisionally approved by the ABA.

BARRY UNIVERSITY

Barry University School of Law

6441 E. Colonial Drive, Orlando, FL 32807
Admissions Phone: 321-206-5600 • **Admissions Fax:** 321-206-5620
Admissions E-mail: lawinfo@mail.barry.edu
Web Address: www.barry.edu/law

INSTITUTIONAL INFORMATION

Public/private: Private
Student/faculty ratio: 19:1
Affiliation: Roman Catholic
Total faculty: 29
% part-time: 16
% female: 34
% minority: 17

STUDENTS

Enrollment of law school: 511
% Male/female: 50/50
% Out of state: 40
% Full time: 56
% Minority: 23
% International: 1
Number of countries represented: 1
Average age of entering class: 27

ACADEMICS

Grading system: Barry Law utilizes a 4.0 scale with + and – excluding A+.
Clinical program required: No
Clinical program description: Children and Families Clinic, Mediation Externship, Public Defender Externship, State Attorney Externship, Judicial Externship, Civil Government Externship, Civil Poverty Externship
Legal writing course requirements: Yes
Legal writing description: Legal Research and Writing spans two semesters and introduces essential legal research skills and the development of exceptional legal writing skills. Students complete closed and open memos, appellate briefs, and appellate arguments.

Legal methods course requirements: Yes
Legal methods description: Legal Methods introduces first year students to the conceptual building blocks of law in the American Legal System.
Legal research course requirements: Yes
Legal research description: Legal research is combined with the legal writing program.
Moot court requirement: No
Public interest law requirement: Yes
Public interest law description: Currently, students must complete 30 hours of pro bono work prior to graduation.
Academic journals: Barry University Law Review

ADMISSIONS INFORMATION

Admissions Selectivity Rating: 62
# of applications received: 1,500
% of applicants accepted: 49
% of acceptees attending: 33
Average LSAT: 148
LSAT Range: 145–153
Average undergrad GPA: 2.9
Application fee: $50
Regular application deadline: Rolling, up to 4/1
Regular notification: Rolling
Early application program: No
Transfer students accepted: Yes
Evening division offered: Yes
Part-time accepted: Yes
LSDAS accepted: Yes
Applicants also look at: Nova Southeastern University, University of Miami, St. Thomas University, Stetson University

RESEARCH FACILITIES

Research resources available: Westlaw, Lexis, Loislaw
% of JD classrooms wired: 100

INTERNATIONAL STUDENTS

TOEFL required of international students? Yes
Minimum TOEFL (paper/computer): 600/250

FINANCIAL FACTS

Annual tuition: $26,000
Books and supplies: $1,400
Tuition per credit: $925
Room & board (off-campus): $10,400
Financial aid application deadline: 6/30
% First-year students receiving some sort of aid: 90
% Receiving some sort of aid: 94
% of Aid that is merit-based: 16
% Receiving scholarships: 67
Average grant: $6,779
Average loan: $28,400
Average total aid package: $32,598
Average debt: $70,780

EMPLOYMENT INFORMATION

Average starting salary: $57,275
State(s) for bar exam: FL
Pass rate for first-time bar: 58
Grads employed by field: %
Academic (6)
Business/Industry (26)
Government (23)
Military (2)
Private Practice (41)
Public Interest (2)

CALIFORNIA WESTERN

California Western School of Law

225 Cedar Street San Diego, CA 92101
Admissions Phone: 619-525-1401 • *Admissions Fax:* 619-615-1401
Admissions E-mail: admissions@cwsl.edu
Web Address: www.californiawestern.edu

INSTITUTIONAL INFORMATION
Public/private: Private
Student/faculty ratio: 17:1
Total faculty: 118
% part-time: 22
% female: 35
% minority: 11

STUDENTS
Enrollment of law school: 905
% Male/female: 47/53
% Out of state: 45
% Full time: 88
% Minority: 34
% International: 1
Number of countries represented: 15
Average age of entering class: 25

ACADEMICS
Academic Specializations: Constitutional law, criminal law, human rights, international law, labor law, taxation, intellectual property law, Health Law, Family Law, Biotech Law, Telecomm Law, Creative Problem Solving
Advanced degrees offered: JD, 2 to 3 Years; MCL/LLM (Master of Comparative Law, Master of Laws on Comparative Law), 9 months; LLM-Trial Advocacy, 1 Year
Combined degrees offered: JD/MSW Juris Doctor/Master of Social Work, 4 years; JD/MBA Juris Doctor/Master of Business Administration, 4 years; JD/Ph.D. Juris Doctor/Doctor of Philosophy in Political Science or History, 5 years; Master's in Health Law
Grading system: Grades in all courses are subject to a normalization curve and students must finish their first year with at least a 74 average in their substantive courses (on a scale of 95–50) in order to continue
Clinical program required: No
Clinical program description: Clinical Internship Program available to third year students; internships can be done in or out of state; 80% of students participate
Legal writing course requirements: Yes
Legal writing description: Three course series required
Legal methods course requirements: Yes
Legal methods description: Three course series required
Legal research course requirements: Yes
Legal research description: Three course series required
Moot court requirement: No
Public interest law requirement: No
Academic journals: California Western Law Review. California Western International Law Journal.

ADMISSIONS INFORMATION
Admissions Selectivity Rating: 69
# of applications received: 2,433
% of applicants accepted: 54

% of acceptees attending: 26
Average LSAT: 153
LSAT Range: 150–155
Average undergrad GPA: 3.25
Application fee: $55
Regular application deadline: Rolling, up to 4/1
Regular notification: Rolling
Early application program: No
Transfer students accepted: Yes
Evening division offered: No
Part-time accepted: Yes
LSDAS accepted: Yes
Applicants also look at: Chapman University; University of the Pacific; University of California, Davis; Santa Clara University; University of San Diego; University of California, Hastings; Southwestern University School of Law; Thomas Jefferson School of Law

RESEARCH FACILITIES
%.of JD classrooms wired: 95

INTERNATIONAL STUDENTS
TOEFL required of international students? Yes
Minimum TOEFL (paper/computer/web): 600/250/100

FINANCIAL FACTS
Annual tuition: $38,400
Books and supplies: $1,300
Fees: $100
Tuition per credit: $1,480
Room & board (off-campus): $11,600
Financial aid application deadline: 4/1
% First-year students receiving some sort of aid: 87
% Receiving some sort of aid: 87
% Receiving scholarships: 29
Average grant: $20,918
Average loan: $51,750
Average total aid package: $59,612
Average debt: $96,502

EMPLOYMENT INFORMATION
Rate of placement (nine months out): 86
Average starting salary: $73,999
State(s) for bar exam: CA, NV, AZ, NY
Pass rate for first-time bar: 86
Employers who frequently hire grads: Multiple private, public, and non-profit employers of all sizes from many regions nationally.
Prominent alumni: Lisa Haile, Partner at DLA Piper, Rudnick, Gray, Cary; Garland Burrell, US District Court Judge; Duane Layton, Partner at Mayer, Brown, Rowe and Maw; David Roger, D.A., Clark County, Nevada; James Lorenz, US District Court Judge.
Grads employed by field: %
Academic (1)
Business/Industry (13)
Government (12)
Judicial Clerkships (5)
Military (2)
Private Practice (60)
Public Interest (7)

COLLEGE OF WILLIAM & MARY

William & Mary Law School

Office of Admission, PO Box 8795 Williamsburg, VA 23187-8795
Admissions Phone: 757-221-3785 • **Admissions Fax:** 757-221-3261
Admissions E-mail: lawadm@wm.edu • **Web Address:** www.wm.edu/law/

INSTITUTIONAL INFORMATION
Public/private: Public
Student/faculty ratio: 14:1
Total faculty: 102
% part-time: 60
% female: 29
% minority: 6

STUDENTS
Enrollment of law school: 623
% Male/female: 51/49
% Out of state: 53
% Full time: 100
% Minority: 17
% International: 1
Number of countries represented: 7
Average age of entering class: 24

ACADEMICS
Academic Specializations: Civil procedure, commercial law, constitutional law, corporation securities, criminal law, environmental law, human rights, international law, labor law, legal philosophy, property, taxation, intellectual property law
Advanced degrees offered: LL.M. in the American Legal System
Combined degrees offered: JD/Master of Public Policy, 4 years; JD/Master of Business Administration, 4 years; JD/Master of Arts in American Studies, 4 years.
Grading system: 4.0 scale; A+, A, A–, B+, B, B–, C+, C, C–, D, F
Clinical program required: No
Clinical program description: Clinics: Federal Tax Practice, Domestic Violence, Legal Aid and Innocence Project. Externships: General Practice, Non-Profit Organizations, Dept. of Employment Dispute Resolution, VA Court of Appeals, Attorney General, Supreme Court of Virginia, Judicial Clerk, and Theraputic Justice.
Legal writing course requirements: Yes
Legal writing description: The teaching of Legal Writing or Legal Methods is incorporated within our Legal Skills Program, a mandatory two-year program. In addition, all students are required to work closely with a professor or mentor to produce a paper of publishable quality.
Legal methods course requirements: Yes
Legal methods description: The teaching of Legal Writing or Legal Methods is incorporated within our Legal Skills Program, a mandatory two-year program.
Legal research course requirements: Yes

Legal research description: The teaching of Legal Research is incorporated within the mandatory two-year Legal Skills Program. In addition, Advanced Research Techniques (ART) is a 1 credit course that introduces students to a variety of print and electronic research sources over a three-week period. Students attend four 2-1/2 hour presentations over a two week period and must complete two research assignments. ART 1 focuses on United States law, while ART II teaches skills in researching foreign and international law. Students may enroll in ART I, ART II or both.
Moot court requirement: No
Moot court description: Governed by a student-run board. Students participate in an intra-school competition in spring of first year. Winners form inter-school teams in their second and third years. Moot court participants are required to take Advanced Brief Writing and will earn credit for writing a tournament brief.
Public interest law requirement: No
Public interest law description: None exists.
Academic journals: William & Mary Bill of Rights Journal; William & Mary Environmental Law and Policy Review; William & Mary Journal of Women and the Law; William & Mary Law Review

ADMISSIONS INFORMATION
Admissions Selectivity Rating: 88
# of applications received: 4,250
% of applicants accepted: 27
% of acceptees attending: 19
Average LSAT: 162
LSAT Range: 159–166
Average undergrad GPA: 3.59
Application fee: $50
Regular application deadline: Rolling, up to 3/1
Regular notification: 3/30
Early application program: No
Transfer students accepted: Yes
Evening division offered: No
Part-time accepted: No
LSDAS accepted: Yes
Applicants also look at: American University, University of Virginia, The George Washington University, Georgetown University

RESEARCH FACILITIES
% of JD classrooms wired: 100

FINANCIAL FACTS
Annual tuition (in-state/out-of-state): $14,245/$24,240
Books and supplies: $1,250
Fees (in-state/out-of-state): $4,091/$4,296
Room & board (on/off-campus): $6,470/$6,470
Financial aid application deadline: 2/15
% First-year students receiving some sort of aid: 99
% Receiving some sort of aid: 92
% of Aid that is merit-based: 75
% Receiving scholarships: 58
Average grant: $5,496
Average loan: $22,648
Average total aid package: $28,235
Average debt: $68,401

EMPLOYMENT INFORMATION
Rate of placement (nine months out): 99
Average starting salary: $93,218
State(s) for bar exam: VA, CA, NJ, NY, PA
Pass rate for first-time bar: 89

Grads employed by field: %
Academic (1)
Business/Industry (8)
Government (10)
Judicial Clerkships (19)
Military (4)
Private Practice (54)
Public Interest (4)

DREXEL UNIVERSITY*

Drexel University Earle Mack School of Law

3320 Market Street Philadelphia, PA 19104
Admissions Phone: 215-571-4815 • **Admissions Fax:** 215-571-4769
Admissions E-mail: LawAdmissions@drexel.edu
Web Address: www.drexel.edu/law/

INSTITUTIONAL INFORMATION
Public/private: Private

STUDENTS
Enrollment of law school: 420
% Male/female: 45/55
% Minority: 22
Average age of entering class: 25

ACADEMICS
Academic Specializations: Commercial Law, Intellectual Property Law, Health Law, Business & Entrepreneurship
Legal writing course requirements: No
Legal methods course requirements: No

ADMISSIONS INFORMATION
Admissions Selectivity Rating: 60*
LSAT Range: 155–161
Early application program: No

*Provisionally approved by the ABA.

DUQUESNE UNIVERSITY

School of Law

900 Locust Street Pittsburgh, PA 15282
Admissions Phone: 412-396-6296 • **Admissions Fax:** 412-396-1073
Admissions E-mail: campion@duq.edu • **Web Address:** www.law.duq.edu

INSTITUTIONAL INFORMATION
Public/private: Private
Student/faculty ratio: 23:1
Total faculty: 26
% female: 21
% minority: 16

STUDENTS
Enrollment of law school: 630
% Male/female: 50/50
% Out of state: 38
% Full time: 65
% Minority: 7
% International: 0
Average age of entering class: 23

ACADEMICS
Academic Specializations:
Combined degrees offered: JD/MBA, 4 years; JD/M.Div., 5 years; JD/M Environmental Science and Management, 4 years; JD/MS Taxation, 4 years.
Grading system: Numerical system, 4.0 scale. Minimum 3.0 cumulative GPA required to graduate.
Clinical program required: No
Clinical program description: Development law clinic, criminal justice clinic, family & poverty law clinic.
Legal writing course requirements: Yes
Legal methods course requirements: Yes
Legal research course requirements: Yes
Moot court requirement: No
Public interest law requirement: No

ADMISSIONS INFORMATION
Admissions Selectivity Rating: 60*
# of applications received: 0
Average LSAT: 154
Average undergrad GPA: 3.4
Application fee: $50
Regular application deadline: Rolling
Regular notification: Rolling
Early application program: No
Transfer students accepted: Yes
Evening division offered: Yes
Part-time accepted: Yes
LSDAS accepted: Yes

INTERNATIONAL STUDENTS
TOEFL required of international students? Yes
Minimum TOEFL (paper): 600

FINANCIAL FACTS
Annual tuition: $19,394
Books and supplies: $1,000
Fees: $660

Room & board (off-campus): $8,000
% First-year students receiving some sort of aid: 40
% Receiving some sort of aid: 35
% of Aid that is merit-based: 50
Average grant: $4,500
Average loan: $12,000
Average total aid package: $11,000
Average debt: $35,000

EMPLOYMENT INFORMATION

Average starting salary: $59,693
State(s) for bar exam: PA
Pass rate for first-time bar: 71
Employers who frequently hire grads: Reed Smith, Kirkpatrick & Lockhart, Buchanon Ingersoll, Eckert, Seamans
Grads employed by field: %
Academic (1)
Business/Industry (25)
Government (4)
Judicial Clerkships (6)
Private Practice (61)
Public Interest (3)

Early application notification: 12/30
Evening division offered: No
Part-time accepted: No
LSDAS accepted: Yes

RESEARCH FACILITIES

Research resources available: American Judicature Society's Institute of Forensic Science and Public Policy
School-supported research centers: LAWLEAD/NIELLP; National Institute to Enhance Leadership and Law Practice

INTERNATIONAL STUDENTS

TOEFL required of international students? Yes

FINANCIAL FACTS

Annual tuition: $26,000
Books and supplies: $1,300
Room & board (off-campus): $9,650

*Provisionally approved by the ABA.

ELON UNIVERSITY*

Elon University School of Law

201 N. Greene Street Greensboro, NC 27455
Admissions Phone: 336-279-9200 • Admissions Fax: 336-279-8199
Admissions E-mail: law@elon.edu • Web Address: law.elon.edu

INSTITUTIONAL INFORMATION

Public/private: Private
Affiliation: United Church of Christ

ACADEMICS

Academic Specializations: Business; Litigation; Public Interest; General Practice
Advanced degrees offered: J.D., 3-year full-time program
Legal writing course requirements: Yes
Legal writing description: The introductory legal research and writing course will be taught in the fall semester of the first year.
Legal methods course requirements: Yes
Legal methods description: A legal skills course, covering writing, appellate advocacy, negotiation and other legal skills, will be taught in the spring semester of the first year.
Legal research course requirements: Yes
Legal research description: The introductory legal research and writing course will be taught in the fall semester of the first year.

ADMISSIONS INFORMATION

Admissions Selectivity Rating: 60*
Application fee: $50
Regular application deadline: Rolling, up to 7/1
Regular notification: Rolling
Early application program: Yes
Early application deadline: 11/15

FLORIDA A&M UNIVERSITY*

Florida A&M University College of Law

P.O. Box 3113 Orlando, FL 32802
Admissions Phone: 407-254-3268 • Admissions Fax: 407-254-3213
Admissions E-mail: famulaw.admissions@famu.edu
Web Address: www.famu.edu/law

INSTITUTIONAL INFORMATION

Public/private: Public
Student/faculty ratio: 13:1
Total faculty: 40

STUDENTS

Enrollment of law school: 293
% Male/female: 40/60
% Full time: 69
% Minority: 53
Average age of entering class: 33

ACADEMICS

Academic Specializations:
Advanced degrees offered: J.D. (3-year full-time student; 4-year part-time student)
Clinical program required: Yes
Clinical program description: The law school offers a rigorous traditional curriculum of required and elective courses, complemented by extensive skills training which includes an intensive three-year writing program and a strong clinical program. The College of Law curriculum is designed to provide students with both the intellectual and practical skills necessary to meet the demands of the modern practice of law by combining theoretical coursework with clinical and practical experiences.
Legal writing course requirements: No

Legal methods course requirements: Yes

Legal methods description: The law school will offer a rigorous traditional curriculum of required and elective courses that will be complemented by extensive skills training which includes an intensive three-year writing program and a strong clinical program. The College of Law curriculum is designed to provide students with both the intellectual and practical skills necessary to meet the demands of the modern practice of law by combining theoretical coursework with clinical and practical experiences.

Legal research course requirements: No

Moot court requirement: No

Public interest law requirement: Yes

Public interest law description: Public interest will be an important facet of our educational program. The Florida A&M University College of Law plans to serve the Orlando community by educating lawyers and future leaders to understand the value of helping those in need.

ADMISSIONS INFORMATION

Admissions Selectivity Rating: 69
# of applications received: 540
% of applicants accepted: 36
% of acceptees attending: 62
Average LSAT: 148
LSAT Range: 143–150
Average undergrad GPA: 3.1
Application fee: $20
Regular application deadline: Rolling, up to 5/1
Regular notification: Rolling
Early application program: No
Transfer students accepted: No
Evening division offered: Yes
Part-time accepted: Yes
LSDAS accepted: Yes

FINANCIAL FACTS

Annual tuition (in-state/out-of-state): $7,140/$26,580
Books and supplies: $13,591
Tuition per credit (in-state/out-of-state): $239/$88,600
Financial aid application deadline: 4/1
% First-year students receiving some sort of aid: 88
% Receiving some sort of aid: 92
% Receiving scholarships: 16
Average grant: $1,800
Average loan: $18,500

EMPLOYMENT INFORMATION

Grads employed by field: %

*Provisionally approved by the ABA.

FLORIDA COASTAL SCHOOL OF LAW

Florida Coastal School of Law

8787 Baypine Road Jacksonville, FL 32256
Admissions Phone: 904-680-7710 • Admissions Fax: 904-680-7692
Admissions E-mail: admissions@fcsl.edu • Web Address: www.fcsl.edu

INSTITUTIONAL INFORMATION

Public/private: Private
Student/faculty ratio: 18:1
Total faculty: 122
% part-time: 39
% female: 49
% minority: 16

STUDENTS

Enrollment of law school: 1,308
% Male/female: 54/46
% Out of state: 60
% Full time: 79
% Minority: 26.3
% International: 1
Number of countries represented: 8
Average age of entering class: 26

ACADEMICS

Academic Specializations: Civil procedure, commercial law, constitutional law, corporation securities, criminal law, environmental law, government services, human rights, international law, labor law, legal history, legal philosophy, property, taxation, intellectual property law

Advanced degrees offered: J.D. (2 1/2 to 3 years full-time, 3 1/2 to 4 years part-time)

Combined degrees offered: N/A

Grading system: 4.0 Scale

Clinical program required: Yes

Clinical program description: All students are required to take a skills course or participate in one of the following Clinics: Criminal Law Clinic, Civil Practice Clinic, Domestic Violence Clinic, Municipal Law Clinic, and a International Law Clinic.

Legal writing course requirements: Yes

Legal writing description: All students take Legal Writing in their first full year and they are also required to take an advanced legal writing course in their second or third year. Lawyering Process I focuses on basic research and writing and culminates in the submission of an objective memorandum of law. Lawyering Process II focuses on persuasive writing techniques and culminates in submission of an appellate brief. Students also practice basic oral advocacy skills and participate in appellate arguments.

Legal methods course requirements: Yes

Legal methods description: First year students are required to develop legal problem-solving, research and writing skills and focus upon development and enhancement of lawyering skills in rule related and professional responsibility contexts.

Legal research course requirements: Yes

Legal research description: All students take Legal Research in their first full year and they can elect to take an advanced legal research course in their second or third year.

Moot court requirement: Yes

Moot court description: The Moot Court Program is voluntary. Students compete in a intramural competition after completion of Lawyering Process II. Students that are selected for Moot Court may receive academic credit and may compete in national competitions.

Public interest law requirement: No

Academic journals: Florida Coastal Law Review

ADMISSIONS INFORMATION

Admissions Selectivity Rating: 62

# of applications received: 5,734

% of applicants accepted: 62

% of acceptees attending: 18

Average LSAT: 150

LSAT Range: 149–154

Average undergrad GPA: 3.18

Regular application deadline: Rolling, up to 7/31

Regular notification: Rolling

Early application program: No

Transfer students accepted: Yes

Evening division offered: No

Part-time accepted: Yes

LSDAS accepted: Yes

Applicants also look at: Florida State University, Mercer University, University of Florida, Nova Southeastern University, University of Miami, St. Thomas University, Stetson University

RESEARCH FACILITIES

% of JD classrooms wired: 100

INTERNATIONAL STUDENTS

TOEFL recommended of international students? Yes

Minimum TOEFL (paper/computer): 600/250

FINANCIAL FACTS

Annual tuition: $29,362

Books and supplies: $1,200

Fees: $1,454

Fees per credit: $1,424

Tuition per credit: $23,494

Room & board (off-campus): $16,470

Financial aid application deadline: 8/1

% First-year students receiving some sort of aid: 85

% Receiving some sort of aid: 85

% of Aid that is merit-based: 11

% Receiving scholarships: 25

Average grant: $6,200

Average loan: $18,500

Average total aid package: $23,000

Average debt: $60,000

EMPLOYMENT INFORMATION

Rate of placement (nine months out): 87

Average starting salary: $48,525

State(s) for bar exam: FL

Pass rate for first-time bar: 85

Employers who frequently hire grads: Small to mid-sized Florida firms, Florida prosecutors' and public defenders' offices.

Grads employed by field: %

Academic (1)

Business/Industry (15)

Government (16)

Judicial Clerkships (5)

Military (1)

Private Practice (48)

Public Interest (12)

Other (2)

GOLDEN GATE UNIVERSITY

Golden Gate University School of Law

536 Mission Street, Law Admissions Office San Francisco, CA 94105

Admissions Phone: *415-442-6630* • **Admissions Fax:** *415-442-6631*

Admissions E-mail: *lawadmit@ggu.edu* • **Web Address:** *www.ggu.edu/law*

INSTITUTIONAL INFORMATION

Public/private: Private

Student/faculty ratio: 19:1

Total faculty: 108

% part-time: 62

% female: 43

% minority: 17

STUDENTS

Enrollment of law school: 655

% Male/female: 43/57

% Out of state: 28

% Full time: 79

% Minority: 25

% International: 2

Number of countries represented: 28

Average age of entering class: 27

ACADEMICS

Academic Specializations: Criminal law, environmental law, international law, labor law, property, taxation, intellectual property law, Business Law, Litigation, Public Interest Law

Advanced degrees offered: JD full-time, 3 years; JD part-time, 4 years; LLM, 1 year; SJD, 1 year; JD/LLM in Taxation, 3.5 years.

Combined degrees offered: JD/MBA, 4 years; JD/PhD, 7 years.

Grading system: Letter and numerical system, 4.0 scale.

Clinical program required: No

Clinical program description: Students are not required but are encouraged to participate in the clinical programs. More than half of the students at Golden Gate Law participate in our two on-site legal clinics or 10 field placement clinics.

Legal writing course requirements: Yes

Legal writing description: Two semesters of Writing & Research in the 1st year; Appellate Advocacy in the 2nd year; Practical Legal Writing in the 3rd year.

Legal methods course requirements: No

Legal research course requirements: Yes

Moot court requirement: Yes

Moot court description: As part of the first-year legal research and writing course students conduct a law and motion argument, and in the second-year appellate advocacy class they conduct a moot court argument. Students also compete on moot court teams and attend various national and international contests, including the Jessup Moot Court Competition.

Public interest law requirement: No

Academic journals: Golden Gate University Law Review Annual Survey of International and Comparative Law Environmental Law Journal

ADMISSIONS INFORMATION

Admissions Selectivity Rating: 68
# of applications received: 2,410
% of applicants accepted: 52
% of acceptees attending: 17
Average LSAT: 153
LSAT Range: 151–155
Average undergrad GPA: 3.13
Application fee: $60
Regular application deadline: Rolling, up to 4/1
Regular notification: Rolling
Early application program: No
Transfer students accepted: Yes
Evening division offered: Yes
Part-time accepted: Yes
LSDAS accepted: Yes
Applicants also look at: University of California—Berkeley; Chapman University; University of the Pacific; University of San Francisco; Santa Clara University; Whittier College; California Western School of Law; University of California, Hastings; Southwestern University School of Law, Thomas Jefferson School of Law.

RESEARCH FACILITIES

Research resources available: The Student Bar Association provides discount memberships to 24-Hour Fitness Centers located throughout the San Francisco Bay Area.
% of JD classrooms wired: 70
School-supported research centers: All students have wireless access in the classrooms, library, computer labs, lounges and common areas.

INTERNATIONAL STUDENTS

TOEFL required of international students? Yes
Minimum TOEFL (paper/computer/web): 600/250/N/A

FINANCIAL FACTS

Annual tuition: $32,700
Books and supplies: $1,200
Fees: $255
Fees per credit: $12
Tuition per credit: $1,090
Room & board (off-campus): $13,500
% First-year students receiving some sort of aid: 92
% Receiving some sort of aid: 95
% of Aid that is merit-based: 90
% Receiving scholarships: 40
Average grant: $8,000
Average loan: $30,000
Average total aid package: $49,360
Average debt: $112,477

EMPLOYMENT INFORMATION

Rate of placement (nine months out): 80.3
Average starting salary: $71,977
State(s) for bar exam: CA
Pass rate for first-time bar: 77

Employers who frequently hire grads: Small, medium, and large firms, government agencies, public interest organizations, and businesses and corporations.

Prominent alumni: Justice Jesse Carter (deceased), California Supreme Court Justice; Patrick Coughlin, Partner, Coughlin, Stoia, Steller, Rudman, & Robbins, LLP; Karen Hawkins, Director of Professional Responsibility, IRS; Mark S. Anderson, Vice President and General Counsel, Dolby Labs.; Marjorie Randolph, Senior VP for HR and Admin., Walt Disney Studios.

Grads employed by field: %
Academic (9)
Business/Industry (12)
Government (14)
Judicial Clerkships (4)
Private Practice (52)
Public Interest (8)

HOWARD UNIVERSITY

Howard University School of Law

2900 Van Ness Street, NW, Suite 219 Washington, DC 20008
Admissions Phone: 202-806-8008 • **Admissions Fax:** 202-806-8162
Admissions E-mail: admissions@law.howard.edu
Web Address: www.law.howard.edu

INSTITUTIONAL INFORMATION

Public/private: Private
Student/faculty ratio: 13:1
Total faculty: 67
% part-time: 45
% female: 40
% minority: 78

STUDENTS

Enrollment of law school: 402
% Male/female: 40/60
% Full time: 100
% Minority: 94

ACADEMICS

Academic Specializations: Commercial law, constitutional law, corporation securities, criminal law, environmental law, human rights, international law, labor law, property, taxation, intellectual property law
Advanced degrees offered: LL.M. (foreign lawyers only), 1 to 2 years
Combined degrees offered: JD/MBA, 4 years
Grading system: Numerical. Grading is subject to a normalization system.
Clinical program required: No
Clinical program description: The National Moot Court Team is a one year course (students may participate up to 2 years) and represents the law school in various competitions across the country. The International Moot Court Teeam represents the law school in the Jessup International Moot Court Competition and other moot court competitions in international law. This is a one year course (students may participate up to 2 years). The Huver I. Brown Trial Advocacy Moot Court Team represents the law school in regional and national moot court trial competitions. Students can participate up to 2 years on the team. Students are selected to join any of the moot court teams based on intraschool competitions.

Legal writing course requirements: Yes

Legal writing description: Students are required to take two semesters of Legal Writing in the first year and a one semester Legal Writing course in the second year. Students must also satisy an upper level Legal Writing requirement for a substantial research paper for graduation.

Legal methods course requirements: Yes

Legal methods description: Legal Methods is required in the first semester of the first year. The first two weeks of the course are an intensive 2 week introduction followed by a weekly meeting and regular assignments.

Legal research course requirements: No

Legal research description: Legal Research is integrated in the Legal Writing program. Also, there is an advanced Legal Research course offered as an elective for upperlevel students.

Moot court requirement: No

Moot court description: The Howard Law Journal (students can earn academic credit), The SCROLL (Social Justice) journal

Public interest law requirement: No

ADMISSIONS INFORMATION

Admissions Selectivity Rating: 77
# of applications received: 2,550
% of applicants accepted: 17
% of acceptees attending: 37
Average LSAT: 153
LSAT Range: 148–158
Average undergrad GPA: 25
Application fee: $60
Regular application deadline: Rolling, up to 3/31
Regular notification: Rolling
Early application program: No
Transfer students accepted: Yes
Evening division offered: No
Part-time accepted: No
LSDAS accepted: Yes
Applicants also look at: American University; The Catholic University of America; New York University; The George Washington University; University of Maryland—Baltimore; Texas Southern University, Georgetown University

RESEARCH FACILITIES

% of JD classrooms wired: 85

INTERNATIONAL STUDENTS

TOEFL required of international students? Yes
Minimum TOEFL (paper): 550

FINANCIAL FACTS

Annual tuition: $15,990
Books and supplies: $1,103
Fees: $655
Fees per credit: $655
Tuition per credit: $724
Room & board (on/off-campus): $9,869/$10,169
Financial aid application deadline: 3/1
% First-year students receiving some sort of aid: 90
% Receiving some sort of aid: 95
% of Aid that is merit-based: 58
Average grant: $13,000
Average loan: $18,500
Average total aid package: $29,000
Average debt: $60,000

EMPLOYMENT INFORMATION

Rate of placement (nine months out): 96
Average starting salary: $72,465

Employers who frequently hire grads: Law Firms; Judicial Clerkships; Government
Grads employed by field: %
Academic (3)
Business/Industry (13)
Government (18)
Judicial Clerkships (15)
Military (1)
Private Practice (43)
Public Interest (7)

INDIANA UNIVERSITY— INDIANAPOLIS

School of Law

530 West New York Street Indianapolis, IN 46202-3225
Admissions Phone: *317-274-2459* • **Admissions Fax:** *317-278-4780*
Admissions E-mail: *lawadmit@iupui.edu*
Web Address: *www.indylaw.indiana.edu*

INSTITUTIONAL INFORMATION

Public/private: Public
Student/faculty ratio: 14:1
Total faculty: 90
% part-time: 57
% female: 46
% minority: 6

STUDENTS

Enrollment of law school: 952
% Male/female: 52/48
% Out of state: 32
% Full time: 68
% Minority: 11
% International: 5
Number of countries represented: 15
Average age of entering class: 26

ACADEMICS

Academic Specializations: Constitutional law, criminal law, government services, human rights, international law, taxation, intellectual property law, Health Law

Advanced degrees offered: S.J.D.

Combined degrees offered: JD/MPA, 4 years; JD/MBA, 4 years; JD/MHA, 4 years; JD/MPH, 4 years; JD/M. Phil, 4 years; JD/MLS, 4 years; JD/MSW, 4 years.

Grading system: 4.0 scale with a recommended curve

Clinical program required: No

Clinical program description: Civil, Disability, Criminal Law, and Immigration Law

Legal writing course requirements: Yes

Legal writing description: 3 semesters

Legal methods course requirements: Yes

Legal methods description: text

Legal research course requirements: Yes

Legal research description: 1 year

Moot court requirement: No

Public interest law requirement: No
Academic journals: Indiana Law Review, Indiana International and Comparative Law, Indiana Health Law Review

ADMISSIONS INFORMATION
Admissions Selectivity Rating: 77
# of applications received: 1,575
% of applicants accepted: 40
% of acceptees attending: 48
Average LSAT: 154
LSAT Range: 150–158
Average undergrad GPA: 3.51
Application fee: $50
Regular application deadline: Rolling, up to 3/1
Regular notification: Rolling
Early application program: Yes
Early application deadline: 11/30
Early application notification: 12/31
Transfer students accepted: Yes
Evening division offered: Yes
Part-time accepted: Yes
LSDAS accepted: Yes

RESEARCH FACILITIES
% of JD classrooms wired: 100

INTERNATIONAL STUDENTS
TOEFL required of international students? Yes
Minimum TOEFL (paper/computer): 550/213

FINANCIAL FACTS
Annual tuition (in-state/out-of-state): $14,360/$31,715
Books and supplies: $1,600
Fees (in-state/out-of-state): $1,176/$1,176
Tuition per credit (in-state/out-of-state): $463/$1,023
Room & board (on/off-campus): $21,124/$21,124
% First-year students receiving some sort of aid: 59
% Receiving some sort of aid: 86
% of Aid that is merit-based: 59
% Receiving scholarships: 36
Average grant: $5,000
Average loan: $17,965
Average total aid package: $20,500
Average debt: $51,676

EMPLOYMENT INFORMATION
Rate of placement (nine months out): 95
Average starting salary: $65,000
State(s) for bar exam: IN
Pass rate for first-time bar: 85
Employers who frequently hire grads: Private law firms; Baker & Daniels; Barnes & Thornburg; Ice Miller
Prominent alumni: John Pistole, Deputy Director of the FBI; Ellen Engleman, Chairman of the National Transportation Safety Bd; Mark Roesler, President & CEO, CMG Worldwide, Inc.; Alan Cohen, Chairman, President & CEO, The Finish Line Inc.
Grads employed by field: %
Academic (2)
Business/Industry (20)
Government (21)
Judicial Clerkships (2)
Military (1)
Private Practice (51)
Public Interest (2)
Other (1)

LIBERTY UNIVERSITY*
Liberty University School of Law

1971 University Blvd. Lynchburg, VA 24502
Admissions Phone: (434) 592-5300 • **Admissions Fax:** (434) 592-5400
Admissions E-mail: law@liberty.edu • **Web Address:** law.liberty.edu

INSTITUTIONAL INFORMATION
Public/private: Private
Affiliation: Baptist
Total faculty: 16
% part-time: 6
% female: 31
% minority: 6

STUDENTS
Enrollment of law school: 223
% Male/female: 61/39
% Out of state: 75
% Full time: 100
% Minority: 14
% International: 2
Number of countries represented: 2
Average age of entering class: 25

ACADEMICS
Academic Specializations: Civil procedure, commercial law, constitutional law, criminal law, government services, international law, legal history, legal philosophy
Advanced degrees offered: JD, 3 years
Combined degrees offered: None, but several are being developed
Grading system: A 4.0, A– 3.67, B+ 3.33, B 3.0, B– 2.67, C+ 2.33, C 2.0, C– 1.67, D+ 1.33, D 1.00, D– .67, F
Clinical program required: No
Clinical program description: Constitutional Litigation Clinic in conjunction with Liberty Counsel and Liberty Center for Law and Policy
Legal writing course requirements: Yes
Legal writing description: Part of Lawyering Skills I-VI
Legal methods course requirements: Yes
Legal methods description: Part of Foundations of Law I-II
Legal research course requirements: Yes
Legal research description: Part of Lawyering Skills I-VI
Moot court requirement: Yes
Moot court description: There are several moot court components in Lawyering Skills I-VI, which are required courses for all students.
Public interest law requirement: No
Academic journals: Liberty University Law Review

ADMISSIONS INFORMATION
Admissions Selectivity Rating: 71
# of applications received: 491
% of applicants accepted: 38
% of acceptees attending: 58
Average LSAT: 150
LSAT Range: 148–153
Average undergrad GPA: 3.15
Application fee: $50
Regular application deadline: Rolling, up to 6/1
Regular notification: Rolling

Early application program: No
Transfer students accepted: Yes
Evening division offered: No
Part-time accepted: No
LSDAS accepted: Yes

RESEARCH FACILITIES
% of JD classrooms wired: 100

INTERNATIONAL STUDENTS
TOEFL required of international students? Yes
Minimum TOEFL (paper/computer/web): 650/280/100

FINANCIAL FACTS
Annual tuition: $25,369
Books and supplies: $3,062
Fees: $1,140
Room & board (on-campus): $9,993
Financial aid application deadline: 6/1
% First-year students receiving some sort of aid: 100
% Receiving some sort of aid: 100
% of Aid that is merit-based: 40
% Receiving scholarships: 100
Average grant: $13,995
Average loan: $22,805
Average total aid package: $34,781
Average debt: $60,663

EMPLOYMENT INFORMATION
Rate of placement (nine months out): 72
State(s) for bar exam: VA, FL, AR, CA, GA
Pass rate for first-time bar: 90.9
Employers who frequently hire grads: N/A
Prominent alumni: Jeff Johnson, US Federal Court of Appeals, 6th Circuit; Sarah Seitz, Legislative Assistant, Congressional Prayer Caucus; Sarah Smith, IRS Legislative Affairs, Legislation and Reports Branch; Kevin Qualls, Assistant Professor, Dept. of Journalism and and Mass Communication, Murray State University; Mark Pemberton, Kutak Rock, Kansas.
Grads employed by field: %
Academic (5)
Business/Industry (19)
Government (11)
Judicial Clerkships (5)
Private Practice (27)
Public Interest (5)

*Provisionally approved by the ABA.

MCGILL UNIVERSITY
McGill Faculty of Law

3644 Peel Street, Room #406 Montreal, QC H3A 1W9 Canada
Admissions Phone: (514) 398-6646 • *Admissions Fax:* (514) 398-8453
Admissions E-mail: gradadmissions.law@mcgill.ca
Web Address: www.law.mcgill.ca/graduate/

INSTITUTIONAL INFORMATION
Public/private: Public

STUDENTS
Average age of entering class: 35

ACADEMICS
Legal writing course requirements: No
Legal methods course requirements: No

ADMISSIONS INFORMATION
Admissions Selectivity Rating: 69
# of applications received: 248
% of applicants accepted: 49
% of acceptees attending: 25
Average undergrad GPA: 3
Application fee: $80
Regular application deadline: Rolling, up to 2/1
Regular notification: Rolling
Early application program: No
Transfer students accepted: No
Evening division offered: No
Part-time accepted: No
LSDAS accepted: No

INTERNATIONAL STUDENTS
TOEFL required of international students? Yes
Minimum TOEFL (paper/computer): 600/250

FINANCIAL FACTS
Annual tuition (in-state/out-of-state): $9,876/$19,698
Books and supplies: $800
Fees (in-state/out-of-state): $3,211/$11,919
Room & board (on-campus): $9,600

NORTHERN KENTUCKY UNIVERSITY

Salmon P. Chase College of Law

Nunn Hall, Room 529 Highland Heights, KY 41099
Admissions Phone: 859-572-5490 • *Admissions Fax:* 859-572-6081
Admissions E-mail: folger@nku.edu • *Web Address:* chaselaw.nku.edu

INSTITUTIONAL INFORMATION

Public/private: Public
Student/faculty ratio: 17:1
Total faculty: 41
% part-time: 24
% female: 32
% minority: 10

STUDENTS

Enrollment of law school: 991
% Male/female: 57/43
% Out of state: 49
% Full time: 82
% Minority: 11
% International: 0
Number of countries represented: 0
Average age of entering class: 24

ACADEMICS

Academic Specializations: labor law, taxation
Advanced degrees offered: None
Combined degrees offered: JD/MBA, 4 years full-time
Grading system: Letter system, 4.3 scale. Designations for Incomplete, Satisfactory, Unsatisfactory, Pass, Credit, No Credit, Withdrew, and Audit.
Clinical program required: No
Clinical program description: The Clinical Externship Program offers placements in governmental, judicial, administrative, civil, criminal and non-profit settings. Its purpose is to provide students experience in handling actual cases and learning practical aspects of practicing law in supervised settings.
Legal writing course requirements: Yes
Legal writing description: Skills instruction and exercises in legal research and analysis of common and statutory law, legal writing and reasoning, written and oral advocacy. This is a year long course.
Legal methods course requirements: Yes
Legal methods description: Introduction to Legal Studies is a one-credit hour course. Students focus on case briefing, outlining and exam preparation.
Legal research course requirements: Yes
Legal research description: Skills instruction and exercises in legal research and analysis of common and statutory law, legal writing and reasoning, written and oral advocacy. This is a year long course.
Moot court requirement: No
Moot court description: The Moot Court Program provides opportunities for students to develop various legal skills including research, brief writing and presentation of oral arguments. The Moot Court Board conducts 2 intramural competitions annually and selects students to participate in various competitions throughout the country.
Public interest law requirement: Yes
Public interest law description: Beginning with the entering class of 2008, ALL students will be required to participate in 50 hours of pro bono service.
Academic journals: Northern Kentucky Law Review

ADMISSIONS INFORMATION

Admissions Selectivity Rating: 73
# of applications received: 991
% of applicants accepted: 46
% of acceptees attending: 45
Average LSAT: 154
LSAT Range: 153–157
Average undergrad GPA: 3.23
Application fee: $40
Regular application deadline: Rolling, up to 6/1
Regular notification: Rolling
Early application program: No
Transfer students accepted: Yes
Evening division offered: Yes
Part-time accepted: Yes
LSDAS accepted: Yes
Applicants also look at: University of Kentucky, University of Louisville, University of Cincinnati, University of Dayton

RESEARCH FACILITIES

% of JD classrooms wired: 100

FINANCIAL FACTS

Annual tuition (in-state/out-of-state): $12,168/$26,544
Books and supplies: $1,000
Tuition per credit (in-state/out-of-state): $507/$1,106
Room & board (on/off-campus): $9,278/$14,299
Financial aid application deadline: 3/1
% Receiving some sort of aid: 79
% of Aid that is merit-based: 7
% Receiving scholarships: 35
Average grant: $10,804
Average loan: $22,559
Average total aid package: $32,496
Average debt: $61,178

EMPLOYMENT INFORMATION

Rate of placement (nine months out): 90
Average starting salary: $53,054
State(s) for bar exam: KY, OH
Pass rate for first-time bar: 89
Employers who frequently hire grads: Procter & Gamble; Dinsmore & Shohl; U.S. Department of Labor; Kentucky Department of Public Advocacy; Taft, Stettinius & Hollister; Freund, Freeze & Arnold; Adams, Stepner, Woltermann & Dusing; Keating Muething & Klekamp; Frost Brown Todd; Kentucky Office of Commonwealth's Attorney; Deters, Benzinger & LaVelle; and Fidelity Investments.
Prominent alumni: Steve Chabot, United States Representative, 1st District of Ohio; Patricia L. Herbold, United States Ambassador to Singapore; Danny C. Reeves, Judge, U.S. District Court; Robert P. Ruwe, Judge, U.S. Tax Court, Washington, D.C.; Katie Kratz Stine, President Pro Tempore, Ky. State Senate.
Grads employed by field: %
Academic (1)
Business/Industry (17)
Government (11)
Judicial Clerkships (9)
Military (1)
Private Practice (53)
Public Interest (7)
Other (1)

THE PENNSYLVANIA STATE UNIVERSITY

The Dickinson School of Law

100 Beam Building University Park, PA 16802
Admissions Phone: 717-240-5207 • **Admissions Fax:** 717-241-3503
Admissions E-mail: dsladmit@psu.edu • **Web Address:** www.dsl.psu.edu

INSTITUTIONAL INFORMATION

Public/private: Public
Student/faculty ratio: 11:1
Total faculty: 64
% part-time: 17
% female: 47
% minority: 12

STUDENTS

Enrollment of law school: 655
% Male/female: 57/43
% Full time: 87
% Minority: 22
% International: 3

ACADEMICS

Academic Specializations: Civil procedure, commercial law, constitutional law, corporation securities, criminal law, environmental law, government services, human rights, international law, labor law, legal history, legal philosophy, property, taxation, intellectual property law, Arbitration, Sports Law, Mergers and Acquisitions
Advanced degrees offered: J.D., 3 years; LL.M. in Comparative Law, 1 year.
Combined degrees offered: J.D./M.B.A; J.D./M.P.A.; J.D./three Environmental Pollution Control degrees; J.D./MSIS; J.D./M.S.or Ph.D., Forest Resources; J.D./ M.A. or Ph.D., Educational Theory & Policy; J.D./ M.Ed. or M.S. or D.Ed or Ph.D, Educational Leadership; J.D./ M.Ed. or D.Ed. or Ph.D., Higher Education; J.D./ M.S Human Resources & Employee Relations; J.D./ five counseling degree programs with Shippensburg University.
Grading system: Course grades for J.D. students are reported on a alphabetic basis and signify quality of work.
Clinical program required: No
Clinical program description: Child Advocacy; Refugee; Inmate Assistance; Family Law; Disability Law; Elder Law and Consumer Protection; Art, Sports & Entertainment Law; and externships in judges' chambers, district attorneys' & public defenders' offices, government agencies, legal services offices
Legal writing course requirements: Yes
Legal writing description: Lawyering Skills—First year, two semesters. Involves teaching skills such as research, analysis of cases and statutes, writing of legal memoranda and briefs, and oral argument.
Legal methods course requirements: No
Legal research course requirements: Yes
Legal research description: Lawyering Skills—First year, two semesters. Involves teaching skills such as research, analysis of cases and statutes, writing of legal memoranda and briefs, and oral argument.
Moot court requirement: Yes

Moot court description: Beginning with Class of 2010, all upper-level students must complete and pass one of the following skills courses: Advanced Legal Research; Advocacy I (moot court); Advocacy II (moot court); Business Planning; Client Counseling; Field Placement Clinic; In-House Clinic; Mediation; Negotiation; Writing and Editing for Lawyers; Writing Workshop.
Public interest law requirement: No
Public interest law description: N/A
Academic journals: Penn State Law Review; Penn State Environmental Law Review; Penn State International Law Review; World Arbitration and Mediation Review

ADMISSIONS INFORMATION

Admissions Selectivity Rating: 79
# of applications received: 2,459
% of applicants accepted: 33
% of acceptees attending: 18
Average LSAT: 156
LSAT Range: 151–158
Average undergrad GPA: 3.43
Application fee: $60
Regular application deadline: Rolling, up to 3/1
Regular notification: Rolling
Early application program: No
Transfer students accepted: Yes
Evening division offered: No
Part-time accepted: Yes
LSDAS accepted: Yes
Applicants also look at: Syracuse University, Temple University, American University, University of Pittsburgh, Widener University, Villanova University

RESEARCH FACILITIES

% of JD classrooms wired: 100

INTERNATIONAL STUDENTS

TOEFL recommended of international students? Yes

FINANCIAL FACTS

Annual tuition (in-state/out-of-state): $29,200/$29,200
Books and supplies: $1,200
Fees (in-state/out-of-state): $474/$474
Fees per credit (in-state/out-of-state): $43/$43
Tuition per credit (in-state/out-of-state): $1,217/$1,217
Room & board (on/off-campus): $9,378/$9,378
Financial aid application deadline: 3/1
Average debt: $89,529

EMPLOYMENT INFORMATION

Rate of placement (nine months out): 96
Average starting salary: $71,744
State(s) for bar exam: PA
Pass rate for first-time bar: 83
Employers who frequently hire grads: Dickinson graduates are hired by a variety of employers each year including national law firms, small firms, federal and state judges, government agencies, public interest organizations, and other entities.
Prominent alumni: Hon. Thomas Ridge, Secretary of Homeland Security and PA Governor; Hon. Pedro Cortes, PA Secretary of the Commonwealth; Hon. D. Brooks Smith, Third Circuit Court of Appeals; Hon. Thomas Vanaskie, US District Court, MD PA; Hon. J. Michael Eakin, PA Supreme Court.

Grads employed by field: %
Academic (3)
Business/Industry (11)
Government (18)
Judicial Clerkships (16)
Military (1)
Private Practice (39)
Public Interest (4)

SAINT LOUIS UNIVERSITY

Saint Louis University School of Law

3700 Lindell Boulevard, Morrissey Hall, Suite #120 St. Louis, MO 63108
Admissions Phone: *314-977-2800* • **Admissions Fax:** *314-977-1464*
Admissions E-mail: *admissions@law.slu.edu* • **Web Address:** *law.slu.edu*

INSTITUTIONAL INFORMATION

Public/private: Private
Student/faculty ratio: 17:1
Affiliation: Roman Catholic
Total faculty: 55
% part-time: 0
% female: 43
% minority: 8

STUDENTS

Enrollment of law school: 291
% Male/female: 54/46
% Out of state: 44
% Full time: 71
% Minority: 19
% International: 0
Number of countries represented: 1
Average age of entering class: 25

ACADEMICS

Academic Specializations: Civil procedure, commercial law, constitutional law, corporation securities, criminal law, environmental law, government services, human rights, international law, labor law, legal history, legal philosophy, property, taxation, intellectual property law, Public Law, Urban Planning & Development, Health Law
Advanced degrees offered: LL.M. Health Law, one year full-time, two years part-time; LL.M. for Foreign Lawyers, one year full-time
Combined degrees offered: JD/MBA, 4 years; JD/M.A. in Public Administration, 4 years; JD/M.H.A., 4 years; JD/M.P.H., 4 years, JD/M.A. in Urban Affairs, 4 years; JD/PhD in Health Care Ethics, 4–6 years; JD/M.S.W., 4 years.
Grading system: Letter and numerical system, 4.0 scale.
Clinical program required: No
Clinical program description: Corporate Counsel Practicum, Government and Nonprofit Agency Externships, Judicial clerkships, Mediation, In-House Clinical Supervision.
Legal writing course requirements: Yes
Legal writing description: Legal Research & Writing I (3 credits) Legal Research & Writing II (3 credits) Legal Research & Writing, a course required for all students is taught in a small section of 25–30 students.
Legal methods course requirements: No

Legal research course requirements: Yes
Legal research description: Legal Research & Writing I (3 credits) Legal Research & Writing II (3 credits) Legal Research & Writing, a course required for all students is taught in a small section of 25–30 students.
Moot court requirement: No
Moot court description: Moot Court, Jessup Moot Court (International), Giles Sutherland Rich Moot Court (Intellectual Property/Patent Law), Saul Lefkowitz Moot Court (Intellectual Property/Patent Law), National Health Law Moot Court
Public interest law requirement: No
Public interest law description: Public Interest Careers, Public Interest Law Fellowships, Make a Difference Day-Homeward Bound, Habitat for Humanity, CASA, Stand Down for Homeless Veterans, Tax Assistance Project, PILG (Public Interest Law Group), Public Service Awards (The David Grant Clinic Award, The Legal Service Award and The Community Service Award)
Academic journals: The Saint Louis University Law Journal, Saint Louis University Public Law Review, Journal of Health Law & Policy

ADMISSIONS INFORMATION

Admissions Selectivity Rating: 77
# of applications received: 2,030
% of applicants accepted: 47
% of acceptees attending: 22
Average LSAT: 157
LSAT Range: 154–160
Average undergrad GPA: 3.47
Application fee: $55
Regular application deadline: Rolling, up to 7/1
Regular notification: Rolling
Early application program: No
Transfer students accepted: Yes
Evening division offered: Yes
Part-time accepted: Yes
LSDAS accepted: Yes
Applicants also look at: University of Illinois at Urbana-Champaign, Washington University, University of Missouri—Kansas City, University of Missouri—Columbia, DePaul University, Valparaiso University

RESEARCH FACILITIES

Research resources available: ITS has made arrangements for a Symantec Anti-Virus copy to all law students.
% of JD classrooms wired: 100
School-supported research centers: Saint Louis University campus (including the School of Law) maintains a wireless network.

INTERNATIONAL STUDENTS

TOEFL recommended of international students? Yes
Minimum TOEFL (computer): 232

FINANCIAL FACTS

Annual tuition: $31,600
Books and supplies: $1,300
Fees: $400
Fees per credit: $200
Tuition per credit: $1,575
Room & board (off-campus): $11,988
Financial aid application deadline: 6/1
% First-year students receiving some sort of aid: 92
% Receiving some sort of aid: 92
% of Aid that is merit-based: 44
% Receiving scholarships: 46
Average grant: $14,000
Average loan: $32,500
Average total aid package: $24,000
Average debt: $83,500

EMPLOYMENT INFORMATION

Rate of placement (nine months out): 92
Average starting salary: $58,500
State(s) for bar exam: MO, IL
Pass rate for first-time bar: 93
Employers who frequently hire grads: Bryan Cave, LLP; Husch & Eppenberger; Lewis, Rice & Fingersh; Armstrong Teasdale, LLP; Sonnenschein, Nath & Rosenthal; Greensfelder, Hemker & Gale; Blackwell, Sanders, Peper, Martin; Missouri State Public Defender; Evans & Dixon; Brown & James; King & Spalding; ProsKruer Rose; Thompson Coburn; Shook, Hardy & Bacon; United States Postal Service; Missouri Attorney General
Grads employed by field: %
Military (1)

STETSON UNIVERSITY

Stetson University College of Law

1401 61st Street South Gulfport, FL 33707
Admissions Phone: *727-562-7802 • Admissions Fax: 727-343-0136*
Admissions E-mail: *lawadmit@law.stetson.edu*
Web Address: *www.law.stetson.edu*

INSTITUTIONAL INFORMATION

Public/private: Private
Student/faculty ratio: 18:1
Total faculty: 125
% part-time: 54
% female: 23
% minority: 6

STUDENTS

Enrollment of law school: 1,033
% Male/female: 46/54
% Full time: 77
% Minority: 20
Average age of entering class: 24

ACADEMICS

Academic Specializations: International law Advocacy, Elder Law, Higher Education Law and Policy
Advanced degrees offered: JD: Full-Time, 3 years; Part-Time, 4 years; JD/MBA, 3 years (Full Time); LLM, 1 year (Full Time); JD/MPH and JD/MD with University of South Florida
Combined degrees offered: JD/MBA, 3 years for full time students and 4 years for part time students; JD/MPH, 4 years; JD/MD.
Grading system: 4.00 point scale
Clinical program required: No
Clinical program description: Civil Government Clinic Civil Poverty Clinic, Elder Consumer Protection Clinic, Employment Discrimincation Clinic, Labor Law Clinic, Local Government Clinic, Public Defender Clinic and Prosecution Clinic.
Legal writing course requirements: Yes
Legal writing description: Two-semester, graded course that focuses on legal research, objective and persuasive writing, and oral advocacy.
Legal methods course requirements: No
Legal research course requirements: Yes

Legal research description: Legal research is taught as part of the Research & Writing course. The focus is on print and computer-assisted research.
Moot court requirement: Yes
Moot court description: First-year students are taught oral advocacy in the second semester of Research and Writing. They give three oral arguments. Top oralists compete in a first-year appellate advocacy competition for cash prizes and positions on the Moot Court Board.
Public interest law requirement: Yes
Public interest law description: Students must complete 20 hours of pro bono work before graduation.
Academic journals: 1. Stetson Law Review 2. Journal of International Aging Law and Policy 3. Journal of International Wildlife Law and Policy

ADMISSIONS INFORMATION

Admissions Selectivity Rating: 78
# of applications received: 2,783
% of applicants accepted: 32
% of acceptees attending: 29
Average LSAT: 155
LSAT Range: 153–157
Average undergrad GPA: 3.4
Application fee: $55
Regular application deadline: Rolling, up to 3/15
Regular notification: Rolling
Early application program: No
Transfer students accepted: Yes
Evening division offered: Yes
Part-time accepted: Yes
LSDAS accepted: Yes
Applicants also look at: Florida State University, Barry University, University of Florida, Nova Southeastern University, University of Miami, St. Thomas University, Florida Costal School of Law

RESEARCH FACILITIES

Research resources available: Students may use the law library and other facilities at the Tampa Law Center.
% of JD classrooms wired: 100

INTERNATIONAL STUDENTS

TOEFL required of international students? Yes
Minimum TOEFL (paper/computer): 600/250

FINANCIAL FACTS

Annual tuition: $30,500
Books and supplies: $1,200
Fees: $200
Room & board (on/off-campus): $8,420/$11,828
% First-year students receiving some sort of aid: 89
% Receiving some sort of aid: 91
% of Aid that is merit-based: 9
% Receiving scholarships: 18
Average grant: $17,573
Average loan: $38,747
Average total aid package: $40,706
Average debt: $114,624

EMPLOYMENT INFORMATION

Rate of placement (nine months out): 95.9
Average starting salary: $65,000
State(s) for bar exam: FL, GA, DC, VA, MD
Pass rate for first-time bar: 87.6
Employers who frequently hire grads: State attorney's offices, Public defender's office

Prominent alumni: Justice Carol Hunstein, Supreme Court of Georgia; Hon. Elizabeth Kovachevich, USDC Middle District Florida; Rich McKay, President and GM, Atlanta Falcons; Bruce Jacob, Dean Emeritus and Professor of Law, Argued Gideon v. Wainwright, 372 U.S. 335 (1963); Rhea F. Law, President and CEO, Fowler White.

EMPLOYMENT INFORMATION

State(s) for bar exam: TX
Pass rate for first-time bar: 68
Grads employed by field: %
Government (2)
Judicial Clerkships (4)
Private Practice (87)
Public Interest (5)

TEXAS SOUTHERN UNIVERSITY

Thurgood Marshall School of Law

3100 Cleburne Avenue Houston, TX 77004
Admissions Phone: 713-313-7114 • *Admissions Fax:*
Admissions E-mail: lawadmit@tsulaw.edu • *Web Address:* www.tsulaw.edu

INSTITUTIONAL INFORMATION

Public/private: Public
Student/faculty ratio: 17:1
Total faculty: 35
% female: 20
% minority: 83

STUDENTS

Enrollment of law school: 541
% Male/female: 57/43
% Full time: 100
% Minority: 77

ACADEMICS

Academic Specializations: Commercial law, corporation securities
Clinical program required: No
Legal writing course requirements: No
Legal methods course requirements: No

ADMISSIONS INFORMATION

Admissions Selectivity Rating: 61
# of applications received: 1,460
% of applicants accepted: 37
% of acceptees attending: 49
Average LSAT: 141
LSAT Range: 138–144
Average undergrad GPA: 2.8
Application fee: $50
Regular application deadline: 4/1
Regular notification: Rolling
Early application program: No
Transfer students accepted: Yes
Evening division offered: No
Part-time accepted: No
LSDAS accepted: No

FINANCIAL FACTS

Annual tuition (in-state/out-of-state): $4,466/$7,562
Books and supplies: $700
Room & board (off-campus): $6,000

THOMAS JEFFERSON SCHOOL OF LAW

Thomas Jefferson School of Law

2121 San Diego Avenue San Diego, CA 92110
Admissions Phone: 619-297-9700 • *Admissions Fax:* 619-294-4713
Admissions E-mail: admissions@tjsl.edu • *Web Address:* www.tjsl.edu

INSTITUTIONAL INFORMATION

Public/private: Private
Student/faculty ratio: 21:1
Total faculty: 61
% part-time: 40
% female: 50
% minority: 6

STUDENTS

Enrollment of law school: 838
% Male/female: 58/42
% Out of state: 65
% Full time: 73
% Minority: 17
% International: 1
Number of countries represented: 3
Average age of entering class: 24

ACADEMICS

Academic Specializations: Civil procedure, commercial law, constitutional law, corporation securities, criminal law, environmental law, government services, human rights, international law, labor law, property, taxation, intellectual property law, Sports and Entertainment Law, Family Law, Health Law, Litigation & Dispute Resolution
Advanced degrees offered: JD, 3 years full-time; JD, 4 years part-time
Grading system: 4.0 system
Clinical program required: No
Clinical program description: An extensive externship and Judicial internship program for credit
Legal writing course requirements: Yes
Legal writing description: 2 semesters and an additional semester for an upper level research/writing project.
Legal methods course requirements: No
Legal research course requirements: No
Moot court requirement: No
Moot court description: Students may earn credit for participating in moot court and mock trial

Public interest law requirement: No
Public interest law description: Students can perform public interest law work through our pro bono honors and clinical education programs
Academic journals: Thomas Jefferson Law Review

ADMISSIONS INFORMATION
Admissions Selectivity Rating: 72
# of applications received: 3,300
% of applicants accepted: 37
% of acceptees attending: 24
Average LSAT: 153
LSAT Range: 147–157
Average undergrad GPA: 3
Application fee: $35
Regular application deadline: Rolling
Regular notification: Rolling
Early application program: No
Transfer students accepted: Yes
Evening division offered: Yes
Part-time accepted: Yes
LSDAS accepted: Yes
Applicants also look at: Chapman University, Whittier College, California Western School of Law

RESEARCH FACILITIES
% of JD classrooms wired: 100

INTERNATIONAL STUDENTS
TOEFL required of international students? Yes

FINANCIAL FACTS
Annual tuition: $30,100
Books and supplies: $3,228
Fees: $150
Fees per credit: $150
Tuition per credit: $18,900
Room & board (on/off-campus): $11,500/$11,100
Financial aid application deadline: 4/25
% First-year students receiving some sort of aid: 94
% Receiving some sort of aid: 92
% of Aid that is merit-based: 15
% Receiving scholarships: 40
Average grant: $10,394
Average loan: $27,607
Average total aid package: $30,078
Average debt: $99,000

EMPLOYMENT INFORMATION
Rate of placement (nine months out): 84
Average starting salary: $59,251
State(s) for bar exam: CA, NV, AZ, CO, FL
Pass rate for first-time bar: 67
Employers who frequently hire grads: Various private law firms throughout California, Nevada, Arizona, Florida and Illinois; government agencies, such as Attorney General, District Attorney, City Attorney and Public Defender, national and international corporations.
Prominent alumni: Bonnie Dumanis, San Diego District Attorney; Duncan Hunter, Member of U.S. Congress; Roger Benitez, U.S. District Court, Southern District, CA; Mattias Luukkonen, Baker & McKenzie; Dan Vrechek, Qualcomm.

Grads employed by field: %
Business/Industry (25)
Government (13)
Judicial Clerkships (4)
Military (1)
Private Practice (47)
Public Interest (10)

UNIVERSITY OF BALTIMORE
School of Law

1420 North Charles Street Baltimore, MD 21201
Admissions Phone: *410-837-4459* • **Admissions Fax:** *410-837-4450*
Admissions E-mail: *lwadmiss@ubmail.ubalt.edu*
Web Address: *law.ubalt.edu*

INSTITUTIONAL INFORMATION
Public/private: Public
Student/faculty ratio: 18:1
Total faculty: 146
% part-time: 58
% female: 34
% minority: 14

STUDENTS
Enrollment of law school: 1,077
% Male/female: 48/52
% Out of state: 15
% Full time: 59
% Minority: 12
% International: 1
Average age of entering class: 26

ACADEMICS
Academic Specializations: Criminal law, government services, international law, property, intellectual property law, Business Law, Estate Planning, Litigation and Advocacy, Family Law
Advanced degrees offered: LL.M in Taxation LL.M in Law of the United States
Combined degrees offered: JD/MBA, JD/MS in Criminal Justice, JD/MPA, JD/Ph.D. in Policy Science in conjuction with the University of Maryland—Baltimore, JD/LLM in taxation, JD/MS in Negotiation and conflict Management.. Most Combined degrees add 1 year of study.
Grading system: a 4.0 quality scale from A–F
Clinical program required: No
Clinical program description: Appellate Practice Clinic, Civil Advocacy Clinic, Community Development Clinic, Criminal Practice Clinic, Disability Law Clinic, Famility Law Clinic, Family Mediation Clinic, Immigrant Rights Clinic, Tax Clinic, Innocence Project
Legal writing course requirements: Yes
Legal writing description: Students are required to take two semesters of legal writing, as well as, compete an upper-level writing requirement.
Legal methods course requirements: Yes
Legal methods description: Part of two semester program encompassing legal writing and research.
Legal research course requirements: Yes
Legal research description: Part of two semester program encompassing legal writing and research.

Moot court requirement: No

Moot court description: There are currently 24 moot court teams. Two credits are awarded to each member of a school sanctioned team for successful completion of the regional and/or national competition (except for ABA Client Counseling and ABA Client Negotiation teams, which earn one credit). Students may earn an additional two credits for successful completion of the regional and/or national competition as a member of a second team.

Public interest law requirement: No

Academic journals: Law Review Law Forum Environmental Law Journal Intellectual Property Law Journal

ADMISSIONS INFORMATION

Admissions Selectivity Rating: 80
# of applications received: 1,781
% of applicants accepted: 32
% of acceptees attending: 27
Average LSAT: 156
LSAT Range: 153–159
Average undergrad GPA: 3.52
Application fee: $60
Regular application deadline: Rolling, up to 7/30
Regular notification: Rolling
Early application program: No
Transfer students accepted: Yes
Evening division offered: Yes
Part-time accepted: Yes
LSDAS accepted: Yes
Applicants also look at: American University, The Catholic University of America, University of Maryland—Baltimore, Widener University—Harrisburg Campus

RESEARCH FACILITIES

% of JD classrooms wired: 100

INTERNATIONAL STUDENTS

TOEFL recommended of international students? Yes

FINANCIAL FACTS

Annual tuition (in-state/out-of-state): $20,591/$33,137
Books and supplies: $1,000
Fees (in-state/out-of-state): $1,736/$1,736
Fees per credit (in-state/out-of-state): $70/$70
Tuition per credit (in-state/out-of-state): $853/$1,296
Room & board (off-campus): $10,000
Financial aid application deadline: 4/1
% First-year students receiving some sort of aid: 88
% Receiving some sort of aid: 86
% Receiving scholarships: 36
Average grant: $7,330
Average loan: $19,552
Average total aid package: $28,113
Average debt: $42,961

EMPLOYMENT INFORMATION

Rate of placement (nine months out): 95
Average starting salary: $62,672
State(s) for bar exam: MD
Pass rate for first-time bar: 87
Employers who frequently hire grads: LAW FIRMS, JUDGES, GOVERNMENT AGENCIES, CORPORATIONS, Non-profit Organizations; DLA Piper, Venable LLP, Miles & Stockbridge, Ober Kaler, Gordon Feinblatt, Ballard Spahr, Whiteford Taylor, Saul Ewing, Office of the Public Defender, Office of the State's Attorney, Department of Justice, McGuire Woods, Public Interest Organizations

Prominent alumni: William Donald Schaefer, Former Governor of Maryland; Nancy Forster, Public Defender of Maryland; C.A. Dutch Ruppersberger, US Congress, House of Representatives; Joseph Curran, Former Attorney General of Maryland; Peter Angelos, Owner, Baltimore Orioles.

Grads employed by field: %
Academic (3)
Business/Industry (18)
Government (19)
Judicial Clerkships (21)
Military (1)
Private Practice (31)
Public Interest (7)

UNIVERSITY OF DETROIT—MERCY

School of Law

651 East Jefferson Avenue Detroit, MI 48226
Admissions Phone: 313-596-0264 • Admissions Fax: 313-596-0280
Admissions E-mail: udmlawao@udmercy.edu
Web Address: www.law.udmercy.edu

INSTITUTIONAL INFORMATION

Public/private: Private
Student/faculty ratio: 16:1
Affiliation: Roman Catholic
Total faculty: 67
% part-time: 45
% female: 31
% minority: 6

STUDENTS

Enrollment of law school: 751
% Male/female: 57/43
% Full time: 79
% Minority: 10
% International: 19
Average age of entering class: 25

ACADEMICS

Academic Specializations: Comprehensive legal education with courses in all areas
Advanced degrees offered: JD, three years full-time; JD/MBA, four years full-time; JD/LLB, three years full-time
Combined degrees offered: JD/MBA, four years full-time; JD/LLB, three years full-time; JD/LED, four to five years full-time.
Grading system: 4.0 numerical grading system
Clinical program required: Yes
Clinical program description: Urban Law Clinic, Immigration Law Clinic, Mediation Training and Mediation Clinic, Criminal Law Clinic, Appellate Advocacy Clinic, Veterans Clinic, Environmental Law Clinic, Externship Program
Legal writing course requirements: Yes
Legal writing description: First-year, five-credit, two-semester course that integrates research and writing with theory and practice

Legal methods course requirements: Yes

Legal methods description: First-year, five-credit, two-semester course that integrates research and writing with theory and practice

Legal research course requirements: Yes

Legal research description: First-year, five-credit, two-semester course that integrates research and writing with theory and practice

Moot court requirement: Yes

Moot court description: First-year mandatory moot court program http://www.law.udmercy.edu/academics/index.php

Public interest law requirement: Yes

Public interest law description: A clinic or externship

Academic journals: University of Detroit Mercy School of Law Law Review

ADMISSIONS INFORMATION

Admissions Selectivity Rating: 64

# of applications received: 1,714

% of applicants accepted: 47

% of acceptees attending: 27

Average LSAT: 149

LSAT Range: 146–153

Average undergrad GPA: 3.14

Application fee: $50

Regular application deadline: Rolling, up to 4/15

Regular notification: Rolling

Early application program: No

Transfer students accepted: Yes

Evening division offered: Yes

Part-time accepted: Yes

LSDAS accepted: Yes

Applicants also look at: Michigan State University, Wayne State University, St. Thomas University, Thomas M. Cooley Law School

RESEARCH FACILITIES

Research resources available: Westlaw, Lexis

% of JD classrooms wired: 100

INTERNATIONAL STUDENTS

TOEFL required of international students? Yes

FINANCIAL FACTS

Annual tuition: $28,500

Books and supplies: $7,390

Fees: $80

Tuition per credit: $950

Room & board (on/off-campus): $11,406/$11,166

Financial aid application deadline: 4/1

% First-year students receiving some sort of aid: 74

% Receiving some sort of aid: 81

% Receiving scholarships: 18

Average grant: $6,646

Average loan: $32,898

Average total aid package: $44,236

Average debt: $86,431

EMPLOYMENT INFORMATION

Rate of placement (nine months out): 92

Average starting salary: $71,980

State(s) for bar exam: MI

Pass rate for first-time bar: 81

Employers who frequently hire grads: Private sector employers, including local firms (Dykema Gossett PLLC; Butze Long, Plinkett Cooney PC) and national firms (Shearman & Stearling LLP and Paul, Hastings, Hanofsky & Walker LLP in NY). Public sector employers, including state and deferal judges and county prosecutors' offices.

Grads employed by field: %

Academic (2)

Business/Industry (14)

Government (7)

Judicial Clerkships (1)

Private Practice (70)

Public Interest (5)

Other (1)

UNIVERSITY OF LOUISVILLE

Louis D. Brandeis School of Law

University of Louisville, Wyatt Hall—Room 107 Louisville, KY 40292

Admissions Phone: 502-852-6364 • **Admissions Fax:** 502-852-8971

Admissions E-mail: lawadmissions@louisville.edu

Web Address: www.louisville.edu/brandeislaw/

INSTITUTIONAL INFORMATION

Public/private: Public

Student/faculty ratio: 14:1

Total faculty: 35

% part-time: 17

% female: 34

% minority: 10

STUDENTS

Enrollment of law school: 417

% Male/female: 58/42

% Out of state: 23

% Full time: 76

% Minority: 5

% International: 0

Number of countries represented: 1

Average age of entering class: 24

ACADEMICS

Academic Specializations:

Advanced degrees offered: JD, full-time three years, part-time four years

Combined degrees offered: Dual Degree Programs: JD/MBA, JD/MSSW, JD/M.Div., JD/MA in Humanities, JD/MA in Poli Sci, and a JD/MA in Urban Planning (4 to 5 years)

Grading system: Numerical system on a 4.0 scale.

Clinical program required: Yes

Clinical program description: Public service Program and six externship programs

Legal writing course requirements: Yes

Legal writing description: 3 credits—Basic Legal Skill Writing (1st year)

Legal methods course requirements: Yes

Legal methods description: 3 credits—Basic Legal Skill Writing (1st year)

Legal research course requirements: Yes

Legal research description: 1 credit—Research & Writing (1st semester)

Moot court requirement: Yes

Moot court description: Basic Legal Skills—course requirement, 2nd semester oral arguments.

Public interest law requirement: Yes

Public interest law description: 30 work hour public service requirement.

Academic journals: Brandeis Law Journal, Journal of Law and Education

ADMISSIONS INFORMATION

Admissions Selectivity Rating: 81
# of applications received: 1,065
% of applicants accepted: 33
% of acceptees attending: 29
Average LSAT: 157
LSAT Range: 157–159
Average undergrad GPA: 3.48
Application fee: $50
Regular application deadline: Rolling, up to 5/15
Regular notification: Rolling
Early application program: No
Transfer students accepted: Yes
Evening division offered: Yes
Part-time accepted: Yes
LSDAS accepted: Yes
Applicants also look at: University of Kentucky, University of Tennessee—Knoxville, University of Memphis, University of Cincinnati, Vanderbilt University, University of Dayton, Northern Kentucky University

RESEARCH FACILITIES

% of JD classrooms wired: 100
School-supported research centers: The "Brand" websight at Brandeis School of Law

INTERNATIONAL STUDENTS

TOEFL recommended of international students? Yes

FINANCIAL FACTS

Annual tuition (in-state/out-of-state): $11,410/$23,554
Books and supplies: $1,000
Tuition per credit (in-state/out-of-state): $475/$981
Room & board (on/off-campus): $6,618/$6,618
Financial aid application deadline: 4/15
% First-year students receiving some sort of aid: 85
% Receiving some sort of aid: 85
% of Aid that is merit-based: 100
% Receiving scholarships: 65
Average grant: $5,000
Average loan: $18,500
Average total aid package: $23,500

EMPLOYMENT INFORMATION

Rate of placement (nine months out): 95
Average starting salary: $45,000
State(s) for bar exam: KY, IN, TN, OH
Pass rate for first-time bar: 89
Employers who frequently hire grads: Frost, Brown & Todd; Dinsmore & Shohl; Greenebaum, Doll & McDonald; Wyatt, Tarrant & Combs; Stites & Harbison
Prominent alumni: Chris Dodd, US Senator; Ron Mazzoli, Former US Congressman; Joseph Lambert, Chief Justice of Kentucky; Stanley Chauvin, Former ABA President; Ernie Allen, Director, National Center for Missing & Exploited.
Grads employed by field: %
Academic (2)
Business/Industry (10)
Government (15)
Judicial Clerkships (7)
Military (2)
Private Practice (60)
Public Interest (4)

UNIVERSITY OF MAINE

University of Maine School of Law

246 Deering Avenue Portland, ME 04102
Admissions Phone: 207-780-4341 • **Admissions Fax:** 207-780-4239
Admissions E-mail: mainelaw@usm.maine.edu
Web Address: mainelaw.maine.edu/

INSTITUTIONAL INFORMATION

Public/private: Public
Student/faculty ratio: 16:1
Total faculty: 60
% part-time: 52
% female: 38
% minority: 0

STUDENTS

Enrollment of law school: 259
% Male/female: 47/53
% Out of state: 34
% Full time: 99
% Minority: 4
% International: 1
Number of countries represented: 3
Average age of entering class: 26

ACADEMICS

Academic Specializations:
Advanced degrees offered: JD, three years.
Combined degrees offered: JD/MA in Community Planning & Development, Health Policy Management and Public Policy & Management, JD/MBA
Grading system: Letter system.
Clinical program required: No
Clinical program description: Although no clinical programs are required extensive clinics are offered through the Cumberland Legal Aid Clinic of the University of Maine School of Law. Clinic practice areas include general practice, family law, prisoner assistance (civil), and criminal law. An environmental law clinic, field placement and externships with the Patent Law Program are also available.
Legal writing course requirements: Yes
Legal writing description: First year research and writing course that includes moot court; 3 credits 1st semester, 2 credits second semester
Legal methods course requirements: Yes
Legal research course requirements: No
Moot court requirement: Yes
Moot court description: All students do a moot court brief and oral argument as part of the first year legal writing course.
Public interest law requirement: No
Public interest law description: Students are encouraged to perform 80 hours of voluntary pro-bono while in law school.
Academic journals: Maine Law Review, Ocean and Coastal Law Journal

ADMISSIONS INFORMATION

Admissions Selectivity Rating: 76
# of applications received: 760
% of applicants accepted: 43
% of acceptees attending: 31
Average LSAT: 155
LSAT Range: 153–159

Average undergrad GPA: 3.34
Application fee: $50
Regular application deadline: 3/1
Regular notification: Rolling
Early application program: Yes
Early application deadline: 11/15
Early application notification: 12/31
Transfer students accepted: Yes
Evening division offered: No
Part-time accepted: No
LSDAS accepted: Yes

INTERNATIONAL STUDENTS

TOEFL required of international students? Yes

FINANCIAL FACTS

Annual tuition (in-state/out-of-state): $16,590/$26,280
Books and supplies: $944
Fees (in-state/out-of-state): $625/$625
Fees per credit (in-state/out-of-state): $574/$574
Tuition per credit (in-state/out-of-state): $553/$876
Room & board (on/off-campus): $10,727/$10,727
Financial aid application deadline: 2/15
% Receiving some sort of aid: 87
% of Aid that is merit-based: 20
% Receiving scholarships: 49
Average grant: $3,300
Average loan: $19,636
Average debt: $61,170

EMPLOYMENT INFORMATION

Rate of placement (nine months out): 91
Average starting salary: $49,062
State(s) for bar exam: ME, MA, CA, NH
Pass rate for first-time bar: 84
Employers who frequently hire grads: Maine/New England law firms and corporations; federal/state government; federal/state courts.
Grads employed by field: %
Business/Industry (19)
Government (10)
Judicial Clerkships (12)
Private Practice (48)
Public Interest (11)

UNIVERSITY OF MINNESOTA

University of Minnesota Law School

290 Mondale Hall 229 19th Avenue South Minneapolis, MN 55455
Admissions Phone: 612-625-3487 • Admissions Fax: 612-626-1874
Admissions E-mail: umnlsadm@umn.edu • Web Address: www.law.umn.edu

INSTITUTIONAL INFORMATION

Public/private: Public
Student/faculty ratio: 12:1

Total faculty: 66
% part-time: 25
% female: 42
% minority: 6

STUDENTS

Enrollment of law school: 780
% Male/female: 59/41
% Out of state: 51
% Full time: 100
% Minority: 15
% International: 2
Number of countries represented: 25
Average age of entering class: 25

ACADEMICS

Academic Specializations: human rights, labor lawHealth Law
Advanced degrees offered: J.D. Degree LL.M. for foreign lawyers, 1 year
Combined degrees offered: JD/MBA, 4 years; JD/MPA, 4 years; JD/MA; JD/MD; JD/MPP, 4 years; JD/MURP, 4 years; JD/MS, 4 years; JD/PhD; JD/MBT; JD/MBS; JD/MPH
Grading system: Letter system, A–F.
Clinical program required: No
Clinical program description: 18 separate clinics are offered including: Bankruptcy, Child Advocacy, Civil Practice, Consumer Protection, Criminal Appeals, Domestic Assault Prosecution, Federal Defense, Housing, Immigration, Indian Child Welfare, Innocence Project, Misdemeanor Defense, Misdemeanor Prosecution, Multi-Profession Business Law, Public Interest Law, Special Education, Tax, Workers' Rights
Legal writing course requirements: Yes
Legal writing description: Legal writing begins in the first year where every student is given specific problems to resolve through independent research and study. Analysis, writing and rewriting are closely scrutinized by instructors in conference with each student. During the second and third years students are required to participate in further legal writing instruction, through participation on a journal, a moot court or a seminar.
Legal methods course requirements: No
Legal research course requirements: Yes
Legal research description: Legal Research instruction is an integral part of the first year legal writing curriculum.
Moot court requirement: No
Moot court description: The Law School has an extensive moot court program to help students become effective advocates before appellate courts. Unusual among law schools, the program is an academically supervised and graded upper-level writing course; it is not merely extracurricular. Participants learn advanced skills in research, analysis, oral advocacy, brief writing, and appellate litigation tactics. Moot Courts include: Environmental Law Moot Court, Intellectual Property Moot Court, International Moot Court, Maynard Pirsig Moot Court, National Moot Court, Wagner Labor Law Moot Court, William E. McGee National Civil Rights Moot Court.
Public interest law requirement: No
Public interest law description: Through the Law School Public Service Program each student is asked to perform fifty hours of pro bono legal service for low-income and disadvantaged Minnesotans. Although participation is not required, students who complete at least 50 hours of service are recognized for their dedication with a notation on their transcript and at the graduation ceremony.
Academic journals: Law and Inequality: A Journal of Theory and Practice; Minnesota Journal of International Law; Minnesota Journal of Law, Science & Technology; Minnesota Law Review.

ADMISSIONS INFORMATION

Admissions Selectivity Rating: 91
# of applications received: 2,783

% of applicants accepted: 30
% of acceptees attending: 28
Average LSAT: 166
LSAT Range: 163–167
Average undergrad GPA: 3.61
Application fee: $75
Regular application deadline: Rolling, up to 4/1
Regular notification: Rolling
Early application program: Yes
Early application notification: 1/1
Transfer students accepted: Yes
Evening division offered: No
Part-time accepted: No
LSDAS accepted: Yes

RESEARCH FACILITIES
% of JD classrooms wired: 100

INTERNATIONAL STUDENTS
TOEFL required of international students? Yes

FINANCIAL FACTS
Annual tuition (in-state/out-of-state): $21,900/$32,303
Books and supplies: $1,666
Fees (in-state/out-of-state): $2,728/$2,728
Tuition per credit (in-state/out-of-state): $913/$1,346
Room & board (on/off-campus): $9,356/$9,356
Financial aid application deadline: 3/1
% First-year students receiving some sort of aid: 88
% Receiving some sort of aid: 91
% Receiving scholarships: 63
Average grant: $8,885
Average loan: $32,423
Average total aid package: $34,870
Average debt: $80,764

EMPLOYMENT INFORMATION
Rate of placement (nine months out): 93
Average starting salary: $90,330
State(s) for bar exam: MN
Pass rate for first-time bar: 99
Employers who frequently hire grads: Gibson Dunn, Fried Frank, Dorsey & Whitney, Dewey Ballantine, Sidley & Austin, Mayer Brown, Bryan Cave, Arnold & Porter, Faegre & Benson, Minnesota Supreme Court, Minnesota Court of Appeals, U.S. Department of Justice
Prominent alumni: Walter F. Mondale, Former Vice President of The United States; Keith Ellison, U.S. Representative; Jean E. Hanson, Partner Fried, Frank, Harris, Shriver, & Jacobson; Catharine F. Haukedahl, Deputy Director of Mid-Minnesota Legal Assistance; Joyce A. Hughes, Professor Northwestern School of Law.

Grads employed by field: %
Business/Industry (7)
Government (9)
Judicial Clerkships (17)
Military (1)
Private Practice (61)
Public Interest (4)
Other (1)

UNIVERSITY OF MONTANA
School of Law

Admissions Office Missoula, MT 59812
Admissions Phone: 406-243-2698 • Admissions Fax: 406-243-2576
Admissions E-mail: heidi.fanslow@umontana.edu
Web Address: www.umt.edu/law

INSTITUTIONAL INFORMATION
Public/private: Public
Student/faculty ratio: 19:1
Total faculty: 22
% part-time: 18
% female: 32
% minority: 5

STUDENTS
Enrollment of law school: 241
% Male/female: 56/44
% Out of state: 29
% Full time: 100
% Minority: 3
% International: 0
Average age of entering class: 28

ACADEMICS
Academic Specializations: Environmental law, taxation, Indian Law, and Trial Advocacy
Advanced degrees offered: JD, 3 years
Combined degrees offered: JD/MPA, 3 years; JD/MBA, 3 years JD/MS-EVST, 4 years.
Grading system: Students are not graded on mandatory curve
Clinical program required: Yes
Legal writing course requirements: Yes
Legal writing description: Legal writing and an advanced writing project are required
Legal methods course requirements: Yes
Legal methods description: The University of Montana School of Law devotes special attention to legal writing throughout its curriculum. UM's legal writing program has its foundation in the first year, but extends through all three years. Research and writing experiences at UM are integrated into many courses. The first year begins with the basics of legal research, analysis, and writing. Students complete several legal memoranda, draft contract provisions, legal pleadings, and two briefs to a court, and argue their motions for summary judgment. All second year students enroll in Business Transactions, and negotiate and draft business agreements. All students must fulfill our Advanced Writing Requirement by completing a major written piece (and presenting and defending it orally) during their second or third year. To further underscore the inportance of legal writing, roughly half of our elective courses involve writing papers or legal memoranda.
Legal research course requirements: Yes
Legal research description: one semester course
Moot court requirement: No
Public interest law requirement: Yes
Public interest law description: Participation in Clinical Program
Academic journals: Montana Law Review Public Land and Natural Resource Law Review

ADMISSIONS INFORMATION

Admissions Selectivity Rating: 80
# of applications received: 550
% of applicants accepted: 32
% of acceptees attending: 44
Average LSAT: 155
LSAT Range: 152–157
Average undergrad GPA: 3.4
Application fee: $60
Regular application deadline: Rolling, up to 3/1
Regular notification: Rolling
Early application program: No
Transfer students accepted: Yes
Evening division offered: No
Part-time accepted: No
LSDAS accepted: Yes
Applicants also look at: University of Denver, University of Oregon, University of Wyoming, University of Idaho, Gonzaga University, Lewis & Clark College

RESEARCH FACILITIES

% of JD classrooms wired: 100
School-supported research centers: Westlaw, Lexus, Montlaw

INTERNATIONAL STUDENTS

TOEFL required of international students? Yes
Minimum TOEFL (paper): 600

FINANCIAL FACTS

Annual tuition (in-state/out-of-state): $8,710/$17,475
Books and supplies: $1,010
Room & board (on/off-campus): $9,300/$9,300
Financial aid application deadline: 3/1
% First-year students receiving some sort of aid: 85
% Receiving some sort of aid: 88
% of Aid that is merit-based: 3
% Receiving scholarships: 40
Average grant: $1,457
Average loan: $14,350
Average total aid package: $14,619
Average debt: $48,504

EMPLOYMENT INFORMATION

Average starting salary: $41,063
State(s) for bar exam: MT, WA
Pass rate for first-time bar: 80
Employers who frequently hire grads: Church, Harris, Johnson & Williams; Moulton, Bellingham, Longo and Mather; Crowley, Haughy, Hanson, Toole and Dietrich; Towe, Ball Enright, MacKey and Summerfeld; Smith, Walsh, Clark and Gregoire; Jardine, Stephenson, Blewett and Weaver; MT Sup. Ct.; MT Dist. Cts.; MT Fed. Dist. Cts.
Grads employed by field: %
Academic (11)
Business/Industry (6)
Government (12)
Judicial Clerkships (23)
Private Practice (35)
Public Interest (1)

UNIVERSITY OF NEW BRUNSWICK

University of New Brunswick, Faculty of Law

Law Admissions Office, Faculty of Law, P.O. Box 44271, University of New Brunswick Fredericton, NB E3B 6C2 Canada
Admissions Phone: (506) 453-4693 • **Admissions Fax:** (506) 458-7722
Admissions E-mail: lawadmit@unb.ca • **Web Address:** law.unb.ca

INSTITUTIONAL INFORMATION

Public/private: Public
Student/faculty ratio: 13:1
Total faculty: 20
% part-time: 9
% female: 33

STUDENTS

Average age of entering class: 26

ACADEMICS

Academic Specializations: Civil procedure, commercial law, constitutional law, criminal law, environmental law, human rights, international law, labor law, legal history, legal philosophy, taxation, intellectual property law
Advanced degrees offered: LLB (Bachelor of Law), 3 year degree program
Combined degrees offered: LLB/MBA, 4 year degree program
Grading system: Based on the 4.3 scale, students are given A+ down to F, while D is also considered a failure.
Clinical program required: No
Legal writing course requirements: Yes
Legal writing description: Offered to first year students in the second term.
Legal methods course requirements: Yes
Legal methods description: It is a "mini" course offered the first three weeks of first year law, completing before regular classes begin.
Legal research course requirements: No
Moot court requirement: Yes
Moot court description: First year course required for all first year students.
Public interest law requirement: No
Academic journals: The University of New Brunswick Law Journal

ADMISSIONS INFORMATION

Admissions Selectivity Rating: 88
# of applications received: 992
% of applicants accepted: 22
% of acceptees attending: 39
Average LSAT: 159
LSAT Range: 151-173
Average undergrad GPA: 3.8
Application fee: $50
Regular application deadline: Rolling, up to 3/1
Regular notification: Rolling
Early application program: Yes
Transfer students accepted: Yes
Evening division offered: No
Part-time accepted: No
LSDAS accepted: No
Applicants also look at: Dalhousie Law School

RESEARCH FACILITIES
% of JD classrooms wired: 40

INTERNATIONAL STUDENTS
TOEFL recommended of international students? Yes

FINANCIAL FACTS
Annual tuition (in-state/out-of-state): $9,032/$9,032
Books and supplies: $1,500
Fees (in-state/out-of-state): $663/$663
Room & board (on-campus): $6,000
Financial aid application deadline: 11/15
% First-year students receiving some sort of aid: 51
% of Aid that is merit-based: 82
% Receiving scholarships: 44
Average total aid package: $1,000

EMPLOYMENT INFORMATION
Rate of placement (nine months out): 80
State(s) for bar exam: NB, NS, NL, PE, ON
Grads employed by field: %
Government (6)
Private Practice (72)
Other (22)

WESTERN STATE UNIVERSITY*

Western State University College of Law

1111 North State College Boulevard Fullerton, CA 92831
Admissions Phone: *714-459-1101 •* **Admissions Fax:** *714-441-1748*
Admissions E-mail: *adm@wsulaw.edu •* **Web Address:** *www.wsulaw.edu*

INSTITUTIONAL INFORMATION
Public/private: Private
Student/faculty ratio: 20:1
Total faculty: 45
% part-time: 49
% female: 40
% minority: 16

STUDENTS
Enrollment of law school: 129
% Male/female: 54/46
% Out of state: 40
% Full time: 81
% Minority: 33
% International: 1
Number of countries represented: 0
Average age of entering class: 25

ACADEMICS
Academic Specializations: criminal law, business law
Advanced degrees offered: Juris Doctor, part-time 4 years, full-time 3 years
Grading system: Based on a 4.0 scale

Clinical program required: No
Clinical program description: WSU's on-site Legal Clinic assists low income persons with common legal poroblems such as landlord-tenant and family law disputes. Students represent clients at every stage including court appearances, supervised by an attorney.
Legal writing course requirements: Yes
Legal writing description: Incorporated into Professional Skills I & II courses.
Legal methods course requirements: No
Legal research course requirements: Yes
Legal research description: Incorporated into Professional Skills I & II courses.
Moot court requirement: Yes
Moot court description: Incorporated into the Advocacy course.
Public interest law requirement: No
Academic journals: Law Review

ADMISSIONS INFORMATION
Admissions Selectivity Rating: 66
# of applications received: 1,652
% of applicants accepted: 44
% of acceptees attending: 18
Average LSAT: 150
LSAT Range: 148–153
Average undergrad GPA: 3.14
Application fee: $50
Regular application deadline: Rolling
Regular notification: Rolling
Early application program: No
Transfer students accepted: Yes
Evening division offered: Yes
Part-time accepted: Yes
LSDAS accepted: Yes
Applicants also look at: Chapman University, Golden Gate University, Loyola Marymount University, Whittier College, California Western School of Law, Thomas Jefferson School of Law

RESEARCH FACILITIES
% of JD classrooms wired: 100

INTERNATIONAL STUDENTS
TOEFL required of international students? Yes
Minimum TOEFL (paper/computer): 550/213

FINANCIAL FACTS
Annual tuition: $29,500
Books and supplies: $1,500
Fees: $270
Fees per credit: $270
Tuition per credit: $19,800
Room & board (off-campus): $14,018
Financial aid application deadline: 3/2
% First-year students receiving some sort of aid: 99
% Receiving some sort of aid: 93
% of Aid that is merit-based: 17
% Receiving scholarships: 51
Average grant: $10,069
Average total aid package: $36,163
Average debt: $89,151

EMPLOYMENT INFORMATION
Rate of placement (nine months out): 51
Average starting salary: $77,625
State(s) for bar exam: CA, AZ, TX, OR, FL
Pass rate for first-time bar: 48

Employers who frequently hire grads: medium-sized law firms, district attorneys, public defenders, corporations, state governments, federal governments

Prominent alumni: Pearl Mann, President, California Women Lawyers; Gary Kermott, President, First American Title Co.; Richard Fields, Presiding Judge, Riverside Superior Court; Danni Murphy, Board of Governors, State Bar of California; Larry Allen, Presiding Judge, San Bernardino Superior Court.

Grads employed by field: %
Academic (3)
Business/Industry (17)
Government (3)
Judicial Clerkships (2)
Private Practice (28)
Other (4)

*Provisionally approved by the ABA.

CAL NORTHERN SCHOOL OF LAW

Cal Northern School of Law

1395 Ridgewood Drive, Suite 100 Chico, CA 95973
Admissions Phone: *530-891-6900* • **Admissions Fax:** *530-891-3429*
Admissions E-mail: *info@calnorthern.edu*
Web Address: *www.calnorthern.edu*

INSTITUTIONAL INFORMATION
Public/private: Private
Student/faculty ratio: 4:1
Total faculty: 18
% part-time: 100
% female: 28

STUDENTS
Enrollment of law school: 60
Average age of entering class: 32

ACADEMICS
Academic Specializations:
Advanced degrees offered: J.D. only, 4 year program
Clinical program required: No
Legal writing course requirements: Yes
Legal writing description: Legal Writing is required in the 1st year and Advanced Legal Writing is required in the 4th year.
Legal methods course requirements: Yes
Legal methods description: Legal Writing and Legal Analysis is required in the 1st year and Advanced Legal Writing and Advanced Legal Analysis is offered in the 4th year.
Legal research course requirements: Yes
Legal research description: Legal Research is required in the 1st year.
Moot court requirement: Yes
Moot court description: 4th Year Trial Advocacy/15 weeks
Public interest law requirement: No

ADMISSIONS INFORMATION
Admissions Selectivity Rating: 61
# of applications received: 29
% of applicants accepted: 72
% of acceptees attending: 100
Average LSAT: 145
Average undergrad GPA: 3.03
Application fee: $50
Regular application deadline: 6/1
Regular notification: Rolling
Early application program: No
Transfer students accepted: Yes
Evening division offered: Yes
Part-time accepted: Yes
LSDAS accepted: No

RESEARCH FACILITIES
Research resources available: Students receive individual password access to electronic research.
% of JD classrooms wired: 100

INTERNATIONAL STUDENTS
TOEFL recommended of international students? Yes

FINANCIAL FACTS
Annual tuition: $7,920
Books and supplies: $800
Fees: $115
Tuition per credit: $360
Average grant: $250
Average loan: $8,000

EMPLOYMENT INFORMATION
Rate of placement (nine months out): 100
State(s) for bar exam: CA
Pass rate for first-time bar: 67
Prominent alumni: Rick Keene, California State Assemblyman;
Grads employed by field: %

CALIFORNIA PACIFIC SCHOOL OF LAW

California Pacific School of Law

1600 Truxton Avenue, Suite 100 Bakersfield, CA 93301
Admissions Phone: *805-322-5297* • **Admissions Fax:** *805-322-3409*
Admissions E-mail: *inquiry@calpaclaw.edu*
Web Address: *www.calpaclaw.edu*

INSTITUTIONAL INFORMATION
Public/private: Private
Total faculty: 40
% part-time: 100
% female: 25
% minority: 5

STUDENTS
Enrollment of law school: 32
% Male/female: 100/0
% Full time: 0
% Minority: 0
Average age of entering class: 31

ACADEMICS
Academic Specializations:
Grading system: 0 to 4.0; 2.0 required to graduate.
Clinical program required: No.
Legal writing course requirements: No

Legal methods course requirements: Yes
Legal methods description: 2 quarters, research and writing
Legal research course requirements: No
Moot court requirement: No
Public interest law requirement: No

ADMISSIONS INFORMATION

Admissions Selectivity Rating: 60*
Average LSAT: 140
LSAT Range: 134–150
Average undergrad GPA: 2.8
Application fee: $75
Regular application deadline: 6/1
Regular notification: Rolling
Early application program: Yes
Transfer students accepted: Yes
Evening division offered: Yes
Part-time accepted: Yes
LSDAS accepted: No

RESEARCH FACILITIES

Research resources available: Kern County Law Library is one block away.

INTERNATIONAL STUDENTS

TOEFL required of international students? Yes

FINANCIAL FACTS

Annual tuition: $8,580
Books and supplies: $400
Fees: $40
% First-year students receiving some sort of aid: 30
% Receiving some sort of aid: 30
% of Aid that is merit-based: 0

EMPLOYMENT INFORMATION

Average starting salary: $40,000
State(s) for bar exam: CA
Pass rate for first-time bar: 100

EMPIRE COLLEGE

Empire College School of Law

3035 Cleveland Avenue Santa Rosa, CA 95403
Admissions Phone: 707-546-4000 • Admissions Fax: 707-284-2814
Admissions E-mail: spatel@empirecollege.com
Web Address: www.empcol.edu

INSTITUTIONAL INFORMATION

Public/private: Private
Student/faculty ratio: 3:1
Total faculty: 60
% part-time: 100
% female: 14

STUDENTS

Enrollment of law school: 129
Average age of entering class: 38

ACADEMICS

Academic Specializations: Civil procedure, constitutional law, criminal law, environmental law, property, intellectual property law,
Grading system: 90–100 = A, 80–89 = B, 70–79 = C, 65–69 = D, Below 65 = F
Clinical program required: No
Clinical program description: Third and Fourth-year students may clerk in a variety of settings, including private law offices and public agencies such as the District Attorney's or Public Defender's offices.
Legal writing course requirements: Yes
Legal writing description: One Semester: Legal Research and Writing
Legal methods course requirements: No
Legal research course requirements: Yes
Legal research description: Two Semesters: Legal Research & Writing and Advanced Legal Research
Moot court requirement: Yes
Moot court description: One Semester, requiring a written brief and oral argument.
Public interest law requirement: No
Academic journals: Law Review

ADMISSIONS INFORMATION

Admissions Selectivity Rating: 61
# of applications received: 69
% of applicants accepted: 100
% of acceptees attending: 86
Average LSAT: 35
Average undergrad GPA: 2.95
Application fee: $50
Regular application deadline: Rolling
Regular notification: Rolling
Early application program: No
Transfer students accepted: Yes
Evening division offered: Yes
Part-time accepted: Yes
LSDAS accepted: No

RESEARCH FACILITIES

% of JD classrooms wired: 60

FINANCIAL FACTS

Annual tuition: $11,825
Books and supplies: $400
Fees: $223

EMPLOYMENT INFORMATION

State(s) for bar exam: CA
Pass rate for first-time bar: 54
Employers who frequently hire grads: Office of the District Attorney, Public Defender's office, Private, Business
Prominent alumni: Jeanne Buckley, Superior Court Commissioner (ret.); Raima Ballinger, Judge, Sonoma Co. Superior Court; Francisca Tisher, Judge, Napa Co. Superior Court; Lawrence E. Ornell, Juvenile Superior Court Commissioner; Ron Brown, Judge, Mendocino Co. Superior Court.
Grads employed by field: %
Business/Industry (12)
Government (20)
Private Practice (52)

GLENDALE UNIVERSITY
Glendale University College of Law

220 North Glendale Avenue Glendale, CA 91206
Admissions Phone: 818-247-0770 • **Admissions Fax:** 818-247-0872
Admissions E-mail: admissions@glendalelaw.edu
Web Address: www.glendalelaw.edu

INSTITUTIONAL INFORMATION
Public/private: Private
Student/faculty ratio: 25:1

STUDENTS
Enrollment of law school: 130
Average age of entering class: 32

ACADEMICS
Advanced degrees offered: Juris Doctor, 4 years
Clinical program required: No
Legal writing course requirements: Yes
Legal writing description: Three quarters of Legal Writing and Research (LWR) are required each year of the JD program.
Legal methods course requirements: No
Legal research course requirements: Yes
Legal research description: See information about Legal Writing.
Moot court requirement: Yes
Moot court description: As part of the Legal Writing and Research program, third-year students write an appellate brief and present their case in oral argument before a panel of judges.
Public interest law requirement: No
Academic journals: Glendale Law Review

ADMISSIONS INFORMATION
Admissions Selectivity Rating: 63
# of applications received: 160
% of applicants accepted: 50
% of acceptees attending: 75
Average LSAT: 145
Average undergrad GPA: 3
Application fee: $65
Regular application deadline: Rolling
Regular notification: Rolling
Early application program: No
Transfer students accepted: Yes
Evening division offered: Yes
Part-time accepted: Yes
LSDAS accepted: No

RESEARCH FACILITIES
Research resources available: Lexis-Nexis legal database
% of JD classrooms wired: 100
School-supported research centers: Student-only website with sample exam questions and other study aids

FINANCIAL FACTS
Tuition per credit: $355

EMPLOYMENT INFORMATION
State(s) for bar exam: CA
Pass rate for first-time bar: 50

HUMPHREYS COLLEGE
Humphreys College School of Law

6650 Inglewood Avenue Stockton, CA 95207
Admissions Phone: 209-478-0800 • **Admissions Fax:** 209-478-8721
Admissions E-mail: selopez@humphreys.edu
Web Address: www.humphreys.edu/law/

INSTITUTIONAL INFORMATION
Public/private: Private
Student/faculty ratio: 6:1
Total faculty: 12
% part-time: 83
% female: 17

STUDENTS
Enrollment of law school: 60
Average age of entering class: 33

ACADEMICS
Grading system: 90–100 Excellent, 80–90 Good, 70–79 Satisfactory, 55–69 Unsatisfactory, Below 55 Failure
Clinical program required: No
Legal writing course requirements: No
Legal methods course requirements: Yes
Legal methods description: One quarter in first and fourth years each

ADMISSIONS INFORMATION
Admissions Selectivity Rating: 62
# of applications received: 52
% of applicants accepted: 62
% of acceptees attending: 59
Average LSAT: 149
Average undergrad GPA: 2.8
Application fee: $20
Regular application deadline: 6/1
Regular notification: Rolling
Early application program: No
Transfer students accepted: Yes
Evening division offered: Yes
Part-time accepted: Yes
LSDAS accepted: No

INTERNATIONAL STUDENTS
Minimum TOEFL (paper): 450

FINANCIAL FACTS
Annual tuition: $7,062
Books and supplies: $650
Tuition per credit: $214
% First-year students receiving some sort of aid: 21
% Receiving some sort of aid: 66
Average loan: $14,658
Average total aid package: $14,658
Average debt: $48,000

EMPLOYMENT INFORMATION
State(s) for bar exam: CA
Pass rate for first-time bar: 54

Employers who frequently hire grads: D.A. offices; Police Departments
Grads employed by field: %
Academic (5)
Business/Industry (5)
Government (30)
Private Practice (60)

JOHN F. KENNEDY UNIVERSITY

School of Law

100 Ellinwood Way Pleasant Hill, CA 94523
Admissions Phone: *925-969-3330* • **Admissions Fax:** *925-969-3331*
Admissions E-mail: *law@jfku.edu* • **Web Address:** *www.jfku.edu/law*

INSTITUTIONAL INFORMATION
Public/private: Private
Student/faculty ratio: 30:1
Total faculty: 54
% part-time: 94
% female: 54

STUDENTS
Enrollment of law school: 154
% Male/female: 43/57
% Full time: 94
Number of countries represented: 1
Average age of entering class: 37

ACADEMICS
Grading system: Most required courses are graded on a numerical basis on a scale ranging from 50 to 100.
Clinical program required: No
Legal writing course requirements: Yes
Legal writing description: Three semesters of Legal Writing are required. Emphasis is on mechanics and style in the first two semesters. Advanced legal writing evaluates writing skills to identify and remedy writing deficiencies.
Legal methods course requirements: Yes
Legal methods description: Legal Methods is one semester in duration and focuses on the structure of legal rhetoric.
Legal research course requirements: Yes
Legal research description: Legal Research is one semester in duration and adds a research component to analysis and writing.
Moot court requirement: No
Public interest law requirement: No

ADMISSIONS INFORMATION
Admissions Selectivity Rating: 65
# of applications received: 122
% of applicants accepted: 43
% of acceptees attending: 43
Average LSAT: 148
Average undergrad GPA: 3.03
Application fee: $75
Regular application deadline: Rolling

Regular notification: Rolling
Early application program: No
Transfer students accepted: Yes
Evening division offered: Yes
Part-time accepted: Yes
LSDAS accepted: Yes
Applicants also look at: Golden Gate University, New College of California

RESEARCH FACILITIES
% of JD classrooms wired: 100

INTERNATIONAL STUDENTS
TOEFL required of international students? Yes
Minimum TOEFL (computer): 213

FINANCIAL FACTS
Annual tuition: $9,920
Books and supplies: $1,540
Fees: $198
Tuition per credit: $620
% First-year students receiving some sort of aid: 70
% Receiving some sort of aid: 70
% of Aid that is merit-based: 1
% Receiving scholarships: 0
Average loan: $18,500
Average total aid package: $18,500
Average debt: $70,000

EMPLOYMENT INFORMATION
State(s) for bar exam: CA
Pass rate for first-time bar: 45

LINCOLN LAW SCHOOL OF SACRAMENTO

Lincoln Law School of Sacramento

3140 J Street Sacramento, CA 95816
Admissions Phone: *916-446-1275* • **Admissions Fax:** *916-446-5641*
Admissions E-mail: *info@lincolnlaw.edu* • **Web Address:** *www.lincolnlaw.edu*

INSTITUTIONAL INFORMATION
Public/private: Private
Student/faculty ratio: 40:1
Total faculty: 25
% part-time: 100
% female: 20
% minority: 10

STUDENTS
Enrollment of law school: 275
Average age of entering class: 35

ACADEMICS

Academic Specializations: Civil procedure, commercial law, constitutional law, corporation securities, criminal law, environmental law, government services, labor law, legal history, legal philosophy, property, taxation, intellectual property law, Family Law, Applied Legal Reasoning

Advanced degrees offered: Juris Doctor, 4 year

Grading system: 4.0 Grading System

Clinical program required: No

Legal writing course requirements: Yes

Legal writing description: Two semesters of Legal Writing required for first year students

Legal methods course requirements: Yes

Legal methods description: Writing Law School exams, 2 semesters

Legal research course requirements: Yes

Legal research description: One semester required for second year students

Moot court requirement: Yes

Moot court description: Summer semester required for second year students

Public interest law requirement: No

ADMISSIONS INFORMATION

Admissions Selectivity Rating: 61

# of applications received: 150

% of applicants accepted: 70

% of acceptees attending: 90

Average LSAT: 145

Average undergrad GPA: 2.8

Application fee: $30

Regular application deadline: Rolling, up to 6/15

Regular notification: Rolling

Early application program: No

Transfer students accepted: Yes

Evening division offered: Yes

Part-time accepted: Yes

LSDAS accepted: Yes

Applicants also look at: University of the Pacific, University of California, Davis, Golden Gate University, John F. Kennedy University, Humphreys College

RESEARCH FACILITIES

% of JD classrooms wired: 50

INTERNATIONAL STUDENTS

TOEFL recommended of international students? Yes

FINANCIAL FACTS

Annual tuition: $7,000

Books and supplies: $500

Fees per credit: $55

Tuition per credit: $350

Room & board (off-campus): $6,000

Financial aid application deadline: 6/1

% First-year students receiving some sort of aid: 10

% Receiving some sort of aid: 20

% of Aid that is merit-based: 2

% Receiving scholarships: 20

Average grant: $500

Average loan: $10,000

Average total aid package: $7,000

Average debt: $10,500

EMPLOYMENT INFORMATION

Average starting salary: $40,000

State(s) for bar exam: CA, OR, NV, AZ, CO

Pass rate for first-time bar: 60

Employers who frequently hire grads: District Attorney's Office; Attorney Generals Office; Public Defender's Office; local private firms.

Prominent alumni: Jan Scully, Sacramento County District Attorney; Brad Fenocchio, Placer County District Attorney; Robert Holzapfel, Glenn County District Attorney; Hon. Gerald Bakarich, Sacramento County Superior Court Judge; Hon. Sue Harlan, Amador County Superior Court Judge.

Grads employed by field: %

Business/Industry (10)

Government (30)

Judicial Clerkships (5)

Private Practice (50)

Public Interest (5)

LINCOLN LAW SCHOOL OF SAN JOSE

Lincoln Law School of San Jose

One North First Street San Jose, CA 95113

Admissions Phone: *408-977-7227* • **Admissions Fax:** *408-977-7228*

Admissions E-mail: *admissions@lincolnlawsj.edu*

Web Address: *www.lincolnlawsj.edu/*

INSTITUTIONAL INFORMATION

Public/private: Private

Student/faculty ratio: 1:1

ACADEMICS

Clinical program required: No

Legal writing course requirements: No

Legal methods course requirements: No

ADMISSIONS INFORMATION

Admissions Selectivity Rating: 60*

Application fee: $45

Regular application deadline: Rolling

Regular notification: Rolling

Early application program: No

Transfer students accepted: Yes

Evening division offered: Yes

Part-time accepted: Yes

LSDAS accepted: Yes

INTERNATIONAL STUDENTS

TOEFL recommended of international students? Yes

Minimum TOEFL (paper/computer): 600/60

FINANCIAL FACTS

Fees: $130

Tuition per credit: $499

MONTEREY COLLEGE OF LAW

Monterey College of Law

100 Col. Durham St. Seaside, CA 93955
Admissions Phone: 831-582-4000 • **Admissions Fax:** 831-582-4095
Admissions E-mail: wlariviere@montereylaw.edu
Web Address: www.montereylaw.edu

INSTITUTIONAL INFORMATION
Public/private: Private
Student/faculty ratio: 25:1
Total faculty: 44
% part-time: 100
% female: 23
% minority: 2

STUDENTS
Enrollment of law school: 100
Number of countries represented: 3
Average age of entering class: 30

ACADEMICS
Academic Specializations: Civil procedure, commercial law, constitutional law, corporation securities, criminal law, environmental law, government services, human rights, international law, labor law, property, taxation, intellectual property law
Advanced degrees offered: J.D., 4 year evening program; Master of Legal Studies, 2 year evening program.
Grading system: MCL uses a numerical grading system (0 to 100) to reflect academic performance.
Clinical program required: Yes
Clinical program description: Under the supervision of a Clinical Studies professor, students give legal advice to clients in a pro bono legal clinic focusing on small claims issues. Other clinical opportunites include court and government positions.
Legal writing course requirements: Yes
Legal writing description: Students are required to complete a two-semester Legal Writing course in their first year; a summer semester Legal Writing course in 2L; a summer semester Legal Writing course in 3L; and writing advocacy course in 4L.
Legal methods course requirements: Yes
Legal methods description: This is incorporated into the Legal Writing courses, as well as the Legal Research course.
Legal research course requirements: Yes
Legal research description: Legal Research is a required course for first year students. Computer Assisted Legal Research is an elective course available after the student's second year of study.
Moot court requirement: Yes
Moot court description: The Heisler Moot Court gives students an opportunity to study and write about constitutional issues. Starting with drafting an appellate brief, the semester culminates in a series of hearings, where local judges hear the students' oral arguments on each side of a current civil liberties issue. The public is invited to witness the final round of arguments by four students in front of an appellate panel of judges.
Public interest law requirement: No
Academic journals: Law Review.

ADMISSIONS INFORMATION
Admissions Selectivity Rating: 74
# of applications received: 120
% of applicants accepted: 44
% of acceptees attending: 102
Average LSAT: 153
LSAT Range: 141–169
Average undergrad GPA: 3.17
Application fee: $75
Regular application deadline: Rolling, up to 5/1
Regular notification: Rolling
Early application program: Yes
Early application deadline: 2/15
Early application notification: 3/1
Transfer students accepted: Yes
Evening division offered: Yes
Part-time accepted: Yes
LSDAS accepted: No
Applicants also look at: Santa Clara University, Lincoln Law School of San Jose

RESEARCH FACILITIES
% of JD classrooms wired: 100

INTERNATIONAL STUDENTS
TOEFL recommended of international students? Yes

FINANCIAL FACTS
Books and supplies: $1,000
Fees per credit: $12
Tuition per credit: $450
% First-year students receiving some sort of aid: 26
% Receiving some sort of aid: 55
% of Aid that is merit-based: 30
% Receiving scholarships: 25
Average grant: $750
Average loan: $5,000

EMPLOYMENT INFORMATION
Rate of placement (nine months out): 90
Average starting salary: $35,000
State(s) for bar exam: CA
Pass rate for first-time bar: 40
Employers who frequently hire grads: Governmental Offices, Public Agencies, Private Law Firms, Public Defender's Office, District Attorney's Office.
Prominent alumni: Hon. John Salazar, Judge; Hon. Kim Baskett, Judicial Commissioner; Hon. Denine Guy, Judge; Hon. Russel Scott, Judge; Hon. Sam Lavarato, Jr., Judge.
Grads employed by field: %
Business/Industry (35)
Government (5)
Private Practice (40)
Public Interest (20)

New College of California

New College of California School of Law

50 Fell Street San Francisco, CA 94102
Admissions Phone: 415-241-1374 • **Admissions Fax:** 415-241-9525
Admissions E-mail: Lawadmissions@newcollege.edu
Web Address: www.newcollege.edu

INSTITUTIONAL INFORMATION
Public/private: Private
Student/faculty ratio: 15:1
Total faculty: 36
% female: 50
% minority: 50

STUDENTS
Enrollment of law school: 200
% Male/female: 35/65
% Out of state: 10
% Full time: 75
% Minority: 35
% International: 10
Average age of entering class: 35

ACADEMICS
Academic Specializations: Constitutional law, environmental law, government services, human rights, labor law, property
Advanced degrees offered: J.D. 3 year full-time, 4 year part-time
Grading system: Letter Grading, based upon a bar standard
Clinical program required: No
Legal writing course requirements: Yes
Legal writing description: 1 year Legal research and Writing
Legal methods course requirements: Yes
Legal methods description: 1 semester as necessary
Legal research course requirements: Yes
Legal research description: 1 year Legal research and Writing
Moot court requirement: No
Public interest law requirement: Yes
Public interest law description: 600–800 hours of Public Interest Internship
Academic journals: Journal of Public Interest Law

ADMISSIONS INFORMATION
Admissions Selectivity Rating: 64
# of applications received: 250
% of applicants accepted: 44
% of acceptees attending: 59
Average LSAT: 147
Average undergrad GPA: 3
Application fee: $55
Regular application deadline: Rolling
Regular notification: Rolling
Early application program: Yes
Early application notification: 2/7
Transfer students accepted: Yes
Evening division offered: No
Part-time accepted: Yes
LSDAS accepted: Yes

RESEARCH FACILITIES
% of JD classrooms wired: 100

FINANCIAL FACTS
Annual tuition: $15,214
Books and supplies: $400
Fees: $100
Tuition per credit: $180
Financial aid application deadline: 8/7
% First-year students receiving some sort of aid: 90
Average grant: $500
Average loan: $18,500
Average total aid package: $22,000

EMPLOYMENT INFORMATION
Rate of placement (nine months out): 65
State(s) for bar exam: CA
Pass rate for first-time bar: 25
Employers who frequently hire grads: All non profit agencies and small/solo law firms
Grads employed by field: %
Government (10)
Private Practice (30)
Public Interest (60)

San Francisco Law School

San Francisco Law School

20 Haight Street San Francisco, CA 94102
Admissions Phone: 415-626-5550 • **Admissions Fax:** 415-626-5584
Admissions E-mail: admin@sfls.edu • **Web Address:** www.sfls.edu

INSTITUTIONAL INFORMATION
Public/private: Private
Student/faculty ratio: 25:1
Total faculty: 32
% part-time: 100
% female: 13
% minority: 1

STUDENTS
Enrollment of law school: 115
Average age of entering class: 38

ACADEMICS
Advanced degrees offered: Juris Doctorate 4 Year Program beginning in August. 4 1/2 Year program beginning in January.
Grading system: We use the numerical system up to 100
Clinical program required: No
Clinical program description: Private Practice/Judges
Legal writing course requirements: Yes
Legal writing description: Advanced Legal Writing. One semester.
Legal methods course requirements: No
Legal research course requirements: Yes

Legal research description: Covers the use of law books, as well as, legal research on the Internet. Two semesters.

Moot court requirement: Yes

Moot court description: Teams in a workshop setting. One semester course.

Public interest law requirement: No

Academic journals: San Francisco Law Review

ADMISSIONS INFORMATION

Admissions Selectivity Rating: 60*

# of applications received: 150

% of applicants accepted: 58

Average LSAT: 1.48

Average undergrad GPA: 2.8

Application fee: $50

Regular application deadline: Rolling, up to 6/15

Regular notification: Rolling

Early application program: No

Transfer students accepted: Yes

Evening division offered: Yes

Part-time accepted: Yes

LSDAS accepted: No

FINANCIAL FACTS

Annual tuition: $6,700

Books and supplies: $350

Fees: $170

Tuition per credit: $335

Room & board (off-campus): $25,000

% of Aid that is merit-based: 40

EMPLOYMENT INFORMATION

State(s) for bar exam: CA

Pass rate for first-time bar: 30

Employers who frequently hire grads: SF Public Defender, SFDA, Private Sector

Prominent alumni: Edmund G. Brown (late), Governor of California; Milton Marks, Jr. (late), California State Senator; Leo T. McCarthy, Lt. Governor of California; Hon. Lynn O'Malley Taylor, Judge of the Superior Court; Hon. Henry Needham, Judge of the Superior Court.

Grads employed by field: %

Academic (5)

Business/Industry (5)

Government (20)

Judicial Clerkships (5)

Private Practice (60)

Public Interest (5)

SAN JOAQUIN COLLEGE OF LAW

San Joaquin College of Law

901 Fifth Street Clovis, CA 93612-1312

Admissions Phone: 559-323-2100 • **Admissions Fax:** 559-323-5566

Admissions E-mail: jcanalin@sjcl.org • **Web Address:** www.sjcl.edu

INSTITUTIONAL INFORMATION

Public/private: Private

Student/faculty ratio: 16:1

Total faculty: 36

% part-time: 83

% female: 45

% minority: 14

STUDENTS

Enrollment of law school: 185

% Male/female: 54/46

% Full time: 13

% Minority: 26

Average age of entering class: 33

ACADEMICS

Academic Specializations: Commercial law, corporation securities, criminal law, environmental law, international law, labor law, taxation

Advanced degrees offered: JD 3–5 year program; MS Taxation- 2 years

Grading system: 100–85 A; 84–75 B; 74–65 C; 64–55 D; 54–0 F

Clinical program required: Yes

Clinical program description: Alternative Dispute Resolution, small claims

Legal writing course requirements: No

Legal methods course requirements: Yes

Legal methods description: Legal analysis/research writing

ADMISSIONS INFORMATION

Admissions Selectivity Rating: 61

# of applications received: 135

% of applicants accepted: 80

% of acceptees attending: 84

Average LSAT: 148

LSAT Range: 139–174

Average undergrad GPA: 2.9

Application fee: $40

Regular notification: Rolling

Early application program: No

Transfer students accepted: Yes

Evening division offered: Yes

Part-time accepted: Yes

LSDAS accepted: No

FINANCIAL FACTS

Annual tuition: $10,212

Books and supplies: $550

Fees: $125

Fees per credit: $475

% First-year students receiving some sort of aid: 75

% Receiving some sort of aid: 75

% of Aid that is merit-based: 12

% Receiving scholarships: 14
Average grant: $1,600
Average loan: $14,500
Average total aid package: $18,500
Average debt: $62,500

EMPLOYMENT INFORMATION
State(s) for bar exam: CA
Pass rate for first-time bar: 56
Employers who frequently hire grads: Local DA and DD; various small firms
Grads employed by field: %
Government (23)
Private Practice (70)
Public Interest (5)

THE SANTA BARBARA AND VENTURA COLLEGES OF LAW

Ventura College of Law

4475 Market Street Ventura, CA 93003
Admissions Phone: 805-658-0511 • *Admissions Fax:* 805-658-0529
Admissions E-mail: vcl@venturalaw.edu • *Web Address:* www.venturalaw.edu

INSTITUTIONAL INFORMATION
Public/private: Private
Student/faculty ratio: 7:1
Total faculty: 16
% part-time: 100
% female: 12
% minority: 6

STUDENTS
Enrollment of law school: 108
Average age of entering class: 34

ACADEMICS
Academic Specializations:
Advanced degrees offered: Juris Doctor Degree, 4 year part-time/evening program
Combined degrees offered: None
Grading system: Alpha System (A–F) on a 4.0 scale
Clinical program required: Yes
Clinical program description: Off-campus internships
Legal writing course requirements: Yes
Legal writing description: Two separate two-unit courses are required
Legal methods course requirements: Yes
Legal methods description: One-semester course during the first-year curriculum
Legal research course requirements: Yes
Legal research description: One two-unit course is required
Moot court requirement: No
Public interest law requirement: Yes
Public interest law description: 65 hour (1 unit) internship

ADMISSIONS INFORMATION
Admissions Selectivity Rating: 63
# of applications received: 89
% of applicants accepted: 69
% of acceptees attending: 67
Average LSAT: 149
LSAT Range: 133–163
Average undergrad GPA: 3.15
Application fee: $50
Regular application deadline: Rolling, up to 8/1
Regular notification: Rolling
Early application program: No
Transfer students accepted: Yes
Evening division offered: Yes
Part-time accepted: Yes
LSDAS accepted: Yes

RESEARCH FACILITIES
% of JD classrooms wired: 100

FINANCIAL FACTS
Tuition per credit: $395

EMPLOYMENT INFORMATION
State(s) for bar exam: CA
Pass rate for first-time bar: 42

SANTA BARBARA AND VENTURA COLLEGES OF LAW

Santa Barbara College of Law

20 East Victoria Street Santa Barbara, CA 93101
Admissions Phone: 805-966-0010 • *Admissions Fax:* 805-966-7181
Admissions E-mail: admit@venturalaw.edu
Web Address: www.santabarbaralaw.edu

INSTITUTIONAL INFORMATION
Public/private: Private
Student/faculty ratio: 11:1
Total faculty: 19
% part-time: 100
% female: 26
% minority: 5

STUDENTS
Enrollment of law school: 917
% Male/female: 51/49

ACADEMICS
Academic Specializations: None
Advanced degrees offered: None
Combined degrees offered: None
Grading system: Letter grades A–F
Clinical program required: Yes
Clinical program description: All off-site (government or private probono)

Legal writing course requirements: Yes
Legal writing description: Basic legal writing 30 hours and advanced legal writing 30 hours
Legal methods course requirements: No
Legal methods description: N/A
Legal research course requirements: Yes
Legal research description: 30 hours of instruction
Moot court requirement: No
Moot court description: N/A
Public interest law requirement: No
Academic journals: N/A

ADMISSIONS INFORMATION

Admissions Selectivity Rating: 73
# of applications received: 2,528
% of applicants accepted: 50
% of acceptees attending: 23
Average LSAT: 156
LSAT Range: 153–158
Average undergrad GPA: 3.2
Application fee: $40
Regular notification: Rolling
Early application program: No
Transfer students accepted: No
Evening division offered: Yes
Part-time accepted: Yes
LSDAS accepted: No
Applicants also look at: Syracuse University

RESEARCH FACILITIES

Research resources available: Not applicable
% of JD classrooms wired: 40
School-supported research centers: Not applicable

FINANCIAL FACTS

Annual tuition: $22,000
Books and supplies: $903
Room & board (on/off-campus): $9,787/$9,787
% First-year students receiving some sort of aid: 77
% Receiving some sort of aid: 85
% of Aid that is merit-based: 7
% Receiving scholarships: 31
Average grant: $8,071
Average debt: $60,379

EMPLOYMENT INFORMATION

Average starting salary: $58,000
State(s) for bar exam: CA
Pass rate for first-time bar: 71
Grads employed by field: %
Academic (2)
Business/Industry (24)
Government (8)
Judicial Clerkships (4)
Military (1)
Private Practice (58)
Public Interest (3)

SOUTHERN CALIFORNIA INSTITUTE OF LAW

College of Law

877 South Victoria Avenue Ventura, CA 93003
Admissions Phone: 805-644-2327 • Admissions Fax: 805-644-2367
Admissions E-mail: 1973 scil@msn.com
Web Address: www.lawdegree.com

INSTITUTIONAL INFORMATION

Public/private: Private
Student/faculty ratio: 5:1
% part-time: 75
% female: 50
% minority: 10

STUDENTS

Enrollment of law school: 50
% Male/female: 60/40
% Minority: 15
Average age of entering class: 32

ACADEMICS

Legal writing course requirements: No
Legal methods course requirements: Yes

ADMISSIONS INFORMATION

Admissions Selectivity Rating: 60*
# of applications received: 50
Early application program: No
Transfer students accepted: No
Evening division offered: No
Part-time accepted: No
LSDAS accepted: No

RESEARCH FACILITIES

Research resources available: Local courthouse library

FINANCIAL FACTS

Annual tuition: $6,480
Books and supplies: $500
Fees per credit: $200
Tuition per credit: $200
% of Aid that is merit-based: 100

EMPLOYMENT INFORMATION

Average starting salary: $30,000
State(s) for bar exam: CA
Pass rate for first-time bar: 50
Employers who frequently hire grads: Local Law Firms, Government & State Agencies.

University of West Los Angeles

School of Law

9920 S. La Cienega Blvd. #404 Inglewood, CA 90301
Admissions Phone: 310-342-5210 • **Admissions Fax:** 310-342-5295
Admissions E-mail: tsmith@uwla.edu • **Web Address:** www.uwla.edu

INSTITUTIONAL INFORMATION
Public/private: Private
Student/faculty ratio: 30:1
Total faculty: 36
% part-time: 81
% female: 19
% minority: 17

STUDENTS
Enrollment of law school: 262
% Male/female: 45/55
% Full time: 13
% Minority: 24

ACADEMICS
Academic Specializations:
Advanced degrees offered: Juris Doctor (JD), 3 year (full-time); 4 year (part time)
Grading system: Letter Grade, 4 point scale
Clinical program required: No
Clinical program description: Credit for Judicial and public agencies externships(Clinical Placement), Legal Aid, etc.
Legal writing course requirements: Yes
Legal writing description: Three courses are required, a basic research and writing course after the first year and then an advanced writing class in the second year followed by moot court.
Legal methods course requirements: Yes
Legal methods description: First semester required course for all students.
Legal research course requirements: Yes
Legal research description: Basic course required after completion of the first year. Students learn how to use the print and on-line research tools.
Moot court requirement: No
Moot court description: Moot court—hands on practical experience; students particiapte in Moot Court competitions in various areas testing debate skills, etc.
Public interest law requirement: No

ADMISSIONS INFORMATION
Admissions Selectivity Rating: 66
# of applications received: 59
% of applicants accepted: 47
% of acceptees attending: 61
Average LSAT: 148
Average undergrad GPA: 3.1
Application fee: $55
Regular application deadline: Rolling
Regular notification: Rolling
Early application program: No
Transfer students accepted: Yes
Evening division offered: Yes

Part-time accepted: Yes
LSDAS accepted: Yes

RESEARCH FACILITIES
Research resources available: TWEN, CALI, Westlaw
% of JD classrooms wired: 100

INTERNATIONAL STUDENTS
TOEFL recommended of international students? Yes
Minimum TOEFL (paper/computer): 550/213

FINANCIAL FACTS
Annual tuition: $19,488
Books and supplies: $900
Fees: $1,600
Tuition per credit: $695
% First-year students receiving some sort of aid: 0
% Receiving scholarships: 5

EMPLOYMENT INFORMATION
State(s) for bar exam: CA
Pass rate for first-time bar: 35
Prominent alumni: Paula Zinneman, California Real Estate Commissioner; Gail Margolis, Director, Mental Health Services, State of CA; Hon. Ron Skyers, LA Superior Court Judge; Lael Rubin, District Attorney's Office

DALHOUSIE UNIVERSITY

Dalhousie Law School

Dalhousie Law School, 6061 University Avenue Halifax, NS B3H 4H9 Canada
Admissions Phone: 902-494-2068 • **Admissions Fax:** 902-494-1316
Admissions E-mail: law.admissions@dal.ca • **Web Address:** www.dal.ca/law/

INSTITUTIONAL INFORMATION
Public/private: Public
Student/faculty ratio: 13:1
Total faculty: 35
% female: 45
% minority: 6

STUDENTS
Average age of entering class: 25

ACADEMICS
Academic Specializations: commercial law, corporation securities, environmental law, international law
Advanced degrees offered: LLM, JSD
Combined degrees offered: LLB/MBA, LLB/MLIS, LLB/MPA, LLB/MHSA, 4years
Clinical program required: No
Clinical program description: Legal Aid Clinic
Legal writing course requirements: Yes
Legal writing description: Required Course, First Year
Legal methods course requirements: No
Legal research course requirements: Yes
Legal research description: Required Course, First Year
Moot court requirement: Yes
Moot court description: Mandatory moot, second year
Public interest law requirement: No
Academic journals: Dalhousie Law Journal, Dalhousie Journal of Legal Studies, Canadian Journal of Law and Technology

ADMISSIONS INFORMATION
Admissions Selectivity Rating: 85
# of applications received: 1,285
% of applicants accepted: 30
% of acceptees attending: 42
Average LSAT: 161
Application fee: $70
Regular application deadline: Rolling, up to 2/28
Regular notification: Rolling
Early application program: No
Transfer students accepted: Yes
Evening division offered: No
Part-time accepted: Yes
LSDAS accepted: No

RESEARCH FACILITIES
% of JD classrooms wired: 100

FINANCIAL FACTS
Annual tuition (in-state/out-of-state): $12,475/$12,475
Books and supplies: $1,200

Room & board (on-campus): $3,500
Financial aid application deadline: 10/31
% of Aid that is merit-based: 43
Average grant: $4,212
Average loan: $8,000
Average total aid package: $2,500

EMPLOYMENT INFORMATION
Employers who frequently hire grads: Law firms, government, courts.
Grads employed by field: %
Business/Industry (1)
Government (1)
Judicial Clerkships (1)
Private Practice (97)

NORTHUMBRIA UNIVERSITY

Northumbria University School of Law

School of Law, Northumbria University Newcastle upon Tyne, NE1 8ST
Admissions Phone: + 44 191 227 4513/39 • **Admissions Fax:** + 44 191 227 4557
Admissions E-mail: la.information@northumbria.ac.uk
Web Address: www.northumbria.ac.uk

INSTITUTIONAL INFORMATION
Public/private: Public
Student/faculty ratio: 12:1
Total faculty: 83
% part-time: 8
% female: 56
% minority: 3

ACADEMICS
Academic Specializations: Civil procedure, constitutional law, criminal law, environmental law, human rights, labor law, legal history, legal philosophy, property, intellectual property law
Clinical program required: No
Legal writing course requirements: No
Legal methods course requirements: Yes
Legal methods description: Legal Methods is taught as part of a first year Foundations of Law course which extends over the whole academic year.
Legal research course requirements: No
Moot court requirement: No
Public interest law requirement: No
Academic journals: International Travel Law Journal

ADMISSIONS INFORMATION
Admissions Selectivity Rating: 60*
% of applicants accepted:
Application fee: $40
Regular application deadline: Rolling, up to 8/1
Regular notification: Rolling
Early application program: No
Transfer students accepted: No

Evening division offered: Yes
Part-time accepted: Yes
LSDAS accepted: No

RESEARCH FACILITIES

Research resources available: Public libraries in the area offer access to IT facilities
% of JD classrooms wired: 90
School-supported research centers: The Law School has a dedicated IT Lab with 76 PCs. In addition law students have access to 3 open access labs on the main city campus with 700 PCs available.

INTERNATIONAL STUDENTS

TOEFL required of international students? Yes
Minimum TOEFL (paper): 6

FINANCIAL FACTS

Annual tuition (in-state/out-of-state): $13,000/$13,000
Books and supplies: $500

EMPLOYMENT INFORMATION

Prominent alumni: Gordon Sumner (Sting) CBE, Popular Music; Jonathan Ive, VP, Apple Computers; Steve Cram, MBE, Olympic Athlete and Broadcaster

QUEEN'S UNIVERSITY

Faculty of Law, Queen's University

Macdonald Hall, Rm 200, 128 Union St., Queen's University Kingston, ON K7L 3N6 Canada **Admissions Phone:** *613-533-2220*
Admissions Fax: *613-533-6611* **Admissions E-mail:** *jd@queensu.ca*
Web Address: *law.queensu.ca*

INSTITUTIONAL INFORMATION

Public/private: Public
Student/faculty ratio: 6:1
Total faculty: 78
% part-time: 69
% female: 36

STUDENTS

Enrollment of law school: 462
% Male/female: 50/50
% Full time: 98
Average age of entering class: 24

ACADEMICS

Academic Specializations: Civil procedure, commercial law, constitutional law, corporation securities, criminal law, environmental law, government services, human rights, international law, labor law, legal history, legal philosophy, property, taxation, intellectual property law
Advanced degrees offered: The Master of Laws (LL.M.)
Combined degrees offered: MIR/J.D. We offer the "Master of Industrial Relations/Juris Doctor" combined degree program with Queen's School of Policy Studies, in response to the profession's strong demand for graduates with expertise in employment and labour law. Students complete an MIR degree with prescribed law electives in the first year and an J.D. degree in the latter three years.

Grading system: The current grading system for the Faculty of Law is as follows: A Exceptional, A– Excellent, B+ Very Good, B Good, B– Satisfactory, C+ Fair, C Adequate, D Marginal, F Failure, PA Pass, H Honours, PN Pass no Honours.
Clinical program required: No
Clinical program description: Clinical programs offered: Clinical Correctional Law, Clinical Litigation, and Clinical Family. There is a practice skills degree requirement that can be satisfied by completion of clinical programs and other related courses.
Legal writing course requirements: Yes
Legal writing description: The First Year Legal Foundations Program at Queen's Law provides students with an academic orientation to the study of law, and with an introduction to a number of topics that should be considered and understood by successful law students and lawyers.
Legal methods course requirements: Yes
Legal methods description: Practice Skills Requirement: A Practice Skills Course, is one that gives students significant opportunity to undertake legal research and to develop skills of drafting, client interaction, oral advocacy, negotiation or mediation, or offer students a clinical legal experience.
Legal research course requirements: Yes
Legal research description: 6 weeks for 1 credit in first year
Moot court requirement: Yes
Moot court description: Each student completes our Advocacy requirement in the upper years of the progam. Additional opportunities for oral advocacy are provided through competitive moots.
Public interest law requirement: Yes
Public interest law description: First year curriculum includes innovative First Year Legal Foundations Program with enrichment in areas such as ethics, perspectives, diversity and skills. All professors and students are encouraged to raise and discuss issues of diversity, equality , perspectives, ethics and professional responsibility in all first year and upper year courses.
Academic journals: The Queen's Law Journal is a fully refereed scholarly publication produced by a student editorial board under the direction of a faculty advisor. The Editorial Board consists of 7 senior editors and 10–12 associate editors.

ADMISSIONS INFORMATION

Admissions Selectivity Rating: 89
# of applications received: 2,494
% of applicants accepted: 23
% of acceptees attending: 28
Average LSAT: 161
LSAT Range: 157–170
Average undergrad GPA: 3.8
Application fee: $185
Regular application deadline: 11/1
Regular notification: Rolling
Early application program: No
Transfer students accepted: Yes
Evening division offered: No
Part-time accepted: Yes
LSDAS accepted: No
Applicants also look at: University of British Columbia, University of Calgary, University of Toronto, McGill University, Dalhousie Law School, York University

RESEARCH FACILITIES

% of JD classrooms wired: 95
School-supported research centers: Queen's Centre

INTERNATIONAL STUDENTS

TOEFL required of international students? Yes
Minimum TOEFL (paper/computer): 600/250

FINANCIAL FACTS

Annual tuition (in-state/out-of-state): $11,290/$20,960
Books and supplies: $1,875
Fees (in-state/out-of-state): $1,013/$1,013
Tuition per credit (in-state/out-of-state): $2,258/$4,192
Room & board (on/off-campus): $6,310/$5,190
Financial aid application deadline: 10/31
% First-year students receiving some sort of aid: 75
% Receiving some sort of aid: 91
% of Aid that is merit-based: 15
% Receiving scholarships: 26
Average grant: $1,795
Average loan: $9,212
Average total aid package: $13,178

EMPLOYMENT INFORMATION

Rate of placement (nine months out): 98
Average starting salary: $58,500
Grads employed by field: %
Academic (3)
Business/Industry (11)
Government (2)
Judicial Clerkships (1)
Private Practice (76)
Public Interest (1)
Other (3)

UNIVERSITE DE MONTREAL

Faculte de Droit

P.O. Box 6128, Stn. Centre-Ville, Monteal, Quebec Canada Montreal, Qc H3C 3J7 Canada
Admissions Phone: *514-343-6125* • **Admissions Fax:** *514-343-2030*
Admissions E-mail: *monique.bourbonnais@umontreal.ca*
Web Address: *www.droit.umontreal.ca*

INSTITUTIONAL INFORMATION

Public/private: Public
Student/faculty ratio: 16:1
Total faculty: 60
% female: 28
% minority: 2

STUDENTS

Enrollment of law school: 68
% Male/female: 99/1
% International: 7

ACADEMICS

Academic Specializations: Civil procedure, commercial law, constitutional law, corporation securities, criminal law, environmental law, government services, human rights, international law, labor law, legal history, legal philosophy, property, taxation, intellectual property law

Advanced degrees offered: LLD, 3 years; General LLM, 1–2 years; Specialized LLM or Graduate Studies Degree (DESS), 1 year; in Notarial Law, Tax Law, Business Law, Information Technologies, International and Transational Law, North American Common Law and ecommerce.
Grading system: GPA from 1 to 4.3
Clinical program required: No
Legal writing course requirements: Yes
Legal writing description: A mandatory seminar is devoted to the preparation of an essay.
Legal methods course requirements: No
Legal research description: 3 credits of teaching and assignements during the first year
Moot court requirement: No
Public interest law requirement: No

ADMISSIONS INFORMATION

Admissions Selectivity Rating: 88
# of applications received: 2,072
% of applicants accepted: 21
% of acceptees attending: 78
Average undergrad GPA: 3
Application fee: $40
Regular application deadline: 4/1
Regular notification: Rolling
Early application program: No
Transfer students accepted: Yes
Evening division offered: No
Part-time accepted: No
LSDAS accepted: No

FINANCIAL FACTS

Annual tuition (in-state/out-of-state): $1,400/$4,200
Books and supplies: $600
Average loan: $3,456

EMPLOYMENT INFORMATION

State(s) for bar exam: QC, NY
Pass rate for first-time bar: 79
Prominent alumni: Hon Michel Bastarache, Justice of the Supreme Court of Canada; Hon. Marie Deschamps, Justice of the Supreme Court of Canada; Louise Arbour, U.N. High Commissioner for Refugees, ex- JSCC; Philippe Kirsch, President, International Criminal Court; Morris Rosenberg, Deputy Minister, Health Canada.

UNIVERSITY OF ALBERTA

University of Alberta Faculty of Law

University of Alberta, Law Centre Edmonton, AB T6G 2H5 Canada
Admissions Phone: *(780) 492-3115* • **Admissions Fax:** *(780) 492-4924*
Admissions E-mail: *sgarskey@law.ualberta.ca*
Web Address: *www.law.ualberta.ca/*

INSTITUTIONAL INFORMATION

Public/private: Public
Total faculty: 42

% part-time: 62
% female: 33

STUDENTS

Enrollment of law school: 518
% Male/female: 47/53
% Out of state: 27
% Full time: 99
% Minority: 3
Number of countries represented: 2
Average age of entering class: 25

ACADEMICS

Academic Specializations: Civil procedure, commercial law, constitutional law, corporation securities, criminal law, environmental law, government services, human rights, international law, labor law, legal history, legal philosophy, property, taxation, intellectual property law
Advanced degrees offered: LLM, can be completed in one year, some will take longer; PhD program, newly approved in 2007
Combined degrees offered: LLB/MBA program, 4 years
Grading system: Grading is done on a 4.0 scale. Grade points reflect judgements of student achievement performance in a class. The instructors mark in terms of raw scores, rank the papers in order of merit, and assign an appropriate grade to each paper.
Clinical program required: No
Clinical program description: Student Legal Services provides students the opportunity to work on cases with the poverty community in Edmonton, Health Law Research Internship, Court Clerkships
Legal writing course requirements: Yes
Legal writing description: A legal research and writing class is a mandatory first year class.
Legal methods course requirements: No
Legal research course requirements: Yes
Legal research description: A legal research and writing class is a mandatory first year class.
Moot court requirement: Yes
Moot court description: First year LLB students have a mandatory moot class as part of the full-year legal research and writing class
Public interest law requirement: No
Academic journals: Alberta Law Review

ADMISSIONS INFORMATION

Admissions Selectivity Rating: 89
# of applications received: 1,232
% of applicants accepted: 30
% of acceptees attending: 48
Average LSAT: 161
LSAT Range: 149–178
Average undergrad GPA: 3.7
Application fee: $100
Regular application deadline: 11/1
Regular notification: Rolling
Early application program: No
Transfer students accepted: Yes
Evening division offered: No
Part-time accepted: Yes
LSDAS accepted: No

RESEARCH FACILITIES

% of JD classrooms wired: 100
School-supported research centers: The Health Law Institute, The Centre for Constitutional Studies, The Alberta Law Reform Institute, The International Ombudsman Institute

INTERNATIONAL STUDENTS

TOEFL required of international students? Yes
Minimum TOEFL (paper/computer): 580/237

FINANCIAL FACTS

Annual tuition (in-state/out-of-state): $4,686/$4,686
Books and supplies: $1,500
Fees (in-state/out-of-state): $4,773/$4,773
Fees per credit (in-state/out-of-state): $1,269/$1,269
Tuition per credit (in-state/out-of-state): $469/$469
Room & board (on/off-campus): $6,500/$10,000
Financial aid application deadline: 6/1
% First-year students receiving some sort of aid: 44
% Receiving some sort of aid: 42
% of Aid that is merit-based: 30
% Receiving scholarships: 23
Average grant: $5,000
Average total aid package: $3,159

EMPLOYMENT INFORMATION

Prominent alumni: Hon. Beverley McLachlin, Chief Justice Supreme Court of Canada; Hon. E. Peter Lougheed, Former Premier of the Province of Alberta; Frank MacInnis, CEO/President of EMCOR; David McLean, Chairman of CN Railway; Clarence Campbell, Former National Hockey League Pres/Rhodes Scholar.
Grads employed by field: %
Government (6)
Judicial Clerkships (7)
Private Practice (85)
Public Interest (2)

UNIVERSITY OF BRITISH COLUMBIA

Faculty of Law

1822 East Mall Vancouver, BC V6T 1Z1 Canada
Admissions Phone: *604-822-6303* • **Admissions Fax:** *604-822-8108*
Admissions E-mail: *admissions@law.ubc.ca* • **Web Address:** *www.law.ubc.ca*

INSTITUTIONAL INFORMATION

Public/private: Public
Student/faculty ratio: 14:1
Total faculty: 166
% part-time: 3
% female: 52
% minority: 7

STUDENTS

Enrollment of law school: 638
% Male/female: 50/50
% Out of state: 33
% Full time: 97
% Minority: 5
% International: 1

Number of countries represented: 10
Average age of entering class: 25

ACADEMICS

Academic Specializations: Corporation securities, environmental law, human rights, legal history, intellectual property law

Advanced degrees offered: JD is a 3 year program full-time. The Master of Laws (LL.M.)Degree is a 12 month program. The LL.M. (Common Law) is a 1 year program. The Doctorate (Ph.D. Degree is a 2–4 year program.

Combined degrees offered: The combined J.D./M.B.A. Program is 4 years in length and is administered jointly by the Faculty of Commerce and the Faculty of Law. Students are required to complete 86 credits in law and 45 credits in the M.B.A. program. The combined J.D./M.A.(MAPPS) permits students to obtain the degrees of J.D. and M.A. in Asia Pacific Policy Studies (MAPPS) through combined enrollment in the Faculty of Law and the Institute of Asian Research. The program is 3 years in length and requires students to take 86 Law credits (excluding IAR 500) and 30 MAPPS credits.

Grading system: Grades are given in percentages.

Clinical program required: No

Clinical program description: Although students are not required to participate in the clinical program, many students do participate for the experience. Participation in the program allows students a well-rounded education, where the theory learned in the classroom is applied in a practical setting.

Legal writing course requirements: Yes

Legal writing description: The Legal Research and Writing is integrated into the compulsory curriculum during the first year of study. Students will learn proper legal research and writing formatting, and where to find the legal tools they require to complete memos and serve clients.

Legal methods course requirements: No

Legal research course requirements: Yes

Legal research description: In addition to the Legal Research and Writing Program during the first year of study, students must undertake, in either second or third year, at least one independent research project and submit a substantial paper (or series of papers) embodying the results of this research. This obligation usually will be satisfied by taking a four credit seminar but students may also fulfill this obligation by completing a project, for at least four credits, of Directed Research. Students must also complete, in either second or third year, one course designated as fulfilling the legal research requirement.

Moot court requirement: Yes

Moot court description: All 1st year students are required to participate in a moot court program as part of their 1st year curriculum. They must write an appeal factum and participate as an advocate in the mock appeal in front of a bench of legal practitioners acting as judges. Students will wear robes and receive feedback from the judges.

Public interest law requirement: No

Academic journals: Law Review, Canadian Journal of Family Law, Insolvency Journal

ADMISSIONS INFORMATION

Admissions Selectivity Rating: 94
# of applications received: 1,726
% of applicants accepted: 26
% of acceptees attending: 40
Average LSAT: 164
LSAT Range: 151–176
Average undergrad GPA: 3.8
Application fee: $80
Regular application deadline: Rolling, up to 2/1
Regular notification: Rolling
Early application program: Yes
Early application deadline: 2/1
Early application notification: 11/15
Transfer students accepted: Yes

Evening division offered: No
Part-time accepted: Yes
LSDAS accepted: No
Applicants also look at: University of Calgary, University of Toronto, Queen's University, York University, University of Victoria

RESEARCH FACILITIES

% of JD classrooms wired: 100
School-supported research centers: The Centre for Asian Legal Studies, Centre For Global Environmental and Natural Resource Law, UBC Dispute Resolution Program, Centre for Feminist Legal Studies, First Nations Legal Studies, UBC Law Innocence Project, Intellectual Property Law Program

FINANCIAL FACTS

Annual tuition (in-state/out-of-state): $9,742
Books and supplies: $2,200
Fees (in-state/out-of-state): $840/$840
Tuition per credit (in-state/out-of-state): $325/$644
Room & board (on/off-campus): $9,200/$10,400
% First-year students receiving some sort of aid: 66.67
% Receiving some sort of aid: 64.84
% of Aid that is merit-based: 6.92
% Receiving scholarships: 20.49
Average grant: $2,969
Average loan: $10,811
Average total aid package: $13,042
Average debt: $35,465

EMPLOYMENT INFORMATION

Rate of placement (nine months out): 99
Average starting salary: $40,000
State(s) for bar exam: BC, AB, ON, NY
Pass rate for first-time bar: 99
Employers who frequently hire grads: British Columbia Law Firms and Government Agencies (including Lower Mainland, Vancouver Island and Interior); Ontario Law Firms and Government Agencies; Alberta Law Firms and Government Agencies; Yukon/Northwest Territories Law Firms; New York Law Firms; Canadian Public Interest Organizations; Canadian Courts (both Federal and Provincial); Corporate Legal Departments; Canadian Crown Corporations.

Prominent alumni: Frank Iacobucci, Former Justice Supreme Court of Canada; Lance Finch, Chief Justice of British Columbia; Kim Campbell, Former Prime Minister of Canada; Don Brenner, Chief Justice of British Columbia Supreme Court; Ujjal Dosanjh, Former Premier of British Columbia & Attorney Gen.

Grads employed by field: %
Academic (1)
Government (5)
Judicial Clerkships (9)
Private Practice (83)
Public Interest (2)

UNIVERSITY OF CALGARY

Faculty of Law

Murray Fraser Hall, 2500 University Drive NW Calgary, AB T2N 1N4 Canada
Admissions Phone: 403-220-8154 • **Admissions Fax:** 403-210-9662
Admissions E-mail: law@ucalgary.ca • **Web Address:** www.law.ucalgary.ca/

INSTITUTIONAL INFORMATION
Public/private: Public
Student/faculty ratio: 12:1
Total faculty: 21
% female: 50

STUDENTS
Enrollment of law school: 292
% Male/female: 50/50
% Out of state: 51
Number of countries represented: 5
Average age of entering class: 25

ACADEMICS
Academic Specializations: environmental lawNatural Resource, Law Legal Skills Program
Advanced degrees offered: LLB, 3 years; LLM, 15–18 months
Combined degrees offered: LLB/MBA, 4 years; JD/MBA; LLB/MEDes; JD/MA of Environmental design
Grading system: 11 band grading syster; 4-point scale
Clinical program required: No
Clinical program description: Clinical programs are not required. However, the following are offered: criminal seminar, family seminar, natural resourse seminar, business seminar
Legal writing course requirements: Yes
Legal writing description: Contact school for this information
Legal methods course requirements: Yes
Legal methods description: Contact school for this information
Legal research course requirements: Yes
Legal research description: Contact school for this information
Moot court requirement: Yes
Moot court description: Moots are required during the student's first year. In addition, 2nd and 3rd year students may apply to be selected as a member of 6 mooting and debating team, usually held in the Winter session.

ADMISSIONS INFORMATION
Admissions Selectivity Rating: 96
# of applications received: 710
% of applicants accepted: 14
% of acceptees attending: 100
Average LSAT: 158
Average undergrad GPA: 3.5
Application fee: $100
Regular application deadline: 11/1
Regular notification: Rolling
Early application program: No
Transfer students accepted: Yes
Evening division offered: No
Part-time accepted: Yes
LSDAS accepted: No
Applicants also look at: University of British Columbia

INTERNATIONAL STUDENTS
TOEFL required of international students? Yes
Minimum TOEFL (paper/computer/web): 600/250/100

FINANCIAL FACTS
Annual tuition (in-state/out-of-state): $11,500/$11,500
Books and supplies: $1,800
Fees (in-state/out-of-state): $581/$581
Room & board (on/off-campus): $8,000/$12,000

EMPLOYMENT INFORMATION
State(s) for bar exam: AB

UNIVERSITY OF MANITOBA

University of Manitoba, Faculty of Law

424 University Centre, Enrolment Services/Admissions, University of Manitoba Winnipeg, MB R3T 2N2 Canada
Admissions Phone: (204) 474-8825 • **Admissions Fax:** (204) 474-7554
Admissions E-mail: lawadmissions@umanitoba.ca
Web Address: www.umanitoba.ca/law

INSTITUTIONAL INFORMATION
Public/private: Public
Student/faculty ratio: 15:1
Total faculty: 23
% part-time: 43
% female: 30

STUDENTS
Enrollment of law school: 293
% Male/female: 56/44
% Out of state: 11
% Full time: 97
% Minority: 3.1
Average age of entering class: 25

ACADEMICS
Academic Specializations: Civil procedure, commercial law, constitutional law, corporation securities, criminal law, environmental law, government services, human rights, international law, labor law, legal history, legal philosophy, property, taxation, intellectual property law,
Advanced degrees offered: LLM
Grading system: 4.5 GPA scale; A+ 4.5, A 4.0, B+ 3.5, B 3.0, C+ 2.5, C 2.0, D 1.0, F = 0.0
Clinical program required: No
Clinical program description: Clinical Administrative Law The primary purpose of this course is to train students in lawyering skills. Students will be required to engage in classroom work and participate in simulated exercises. Emphasis will be given to the difference between board and court advocacy.
Legal writing course requirements: Yes
Legal writing description: An introduction to legal research and writing skills and oral advocacy.
Legal methods course requirements: Yes
Legal methods description: An introduction to legal research and writing skills and oral advocacy.

Legal research course requirements: Yes
Legal research description: An introduction to legal research and writing skills and oral advocacy.
Moot court requirement: Yes
Moot court description: In second and third years, students participate in moot courts, fictitious trials and appeals, which provide practice in research, examination of witnesses, and courtroom argument.
Public interest law requirement: No
Academic journals: Manitoba Law Journal Published annually by teachers and studetns of th eFaculty of Law in conjunction with the Mantioba Bar Association. It contains learned legal articles, notes case comments, and book reviews of interest not only to Manitobans.

ADMISSIONS INFORMATION
Admissions Selectivity Rating: 84
# of applications received: 968
% of applicants accepted: 31
% of acceptees attending: 34
Average LSAT: 159
LSAT Range: 153–164
Average undergrad GPA: 3.5
Regular application deadline: 11/1
Regular notification: Rolling
Early application program: No
Transfer students accepted: No
Evening division offered: No
Part-time accepted: Yes
LSDAS accepted: No
Applicants also look at: University of British Columbia, University of Calgary, University of Toronto, McGill University, Dalhousie Law School, Queen's University, University of Windsor, University of Victoria

RESEARCH FACILITIES
% of JD classrooms wired: 80

INTERNATIONAL STUDENTS
TOEFL required of international students? Yes
Minimum TOEFL (web): 100

FINANCIAL FACTS
Annual tuition (in-state/out-of-state): $4,600/
Books and supplies: $3,000
Fees (in-state/out-of-state): $4,000/
Room & board (on/off-campus): $5,520/$11,420
Financial aid application deadline: 10/1
% of Aid that is merit-based: 0
Average loan: $11,900
Average debt: $20,000

UNIVERSITY OF OTTAWA
University of Ottawa, Faculty of Law

P.O. Box 450, Stn. A, 57 Louis Pasteur St. Ottawa, ON K1N 6N5 Canada
Admissions Phone: 613-562-5800 • Admissions Fax: 613-562-5124
Admissions E-mail: comlaw@uottawa.ca
Web Address: www.commonlaw.uottawa.ca

INSTITUTIONAL INFORMATION
Public/private: Public
Student/faculty ratio: 17:1
Total faculty: 53
% part-time: 100
% female: 51
% minority: 15

STUDENTS
Enrollment of law school: 219
% Male/female: 42/58
% Full time: 94
Average age of entering class: 26

ACADEMICS
Academic Specializations: Environmental law, human rights, international law, intellectual property law
Combined degrees offered: LL.B./JD, 4 years; LL.B. /MBA, 4 years; LL.B./MA, 4 years; LL.B./LL.L., 4 years.
Grading system: We are on a 10.0 scale
Clinical program required: No
Legal writing course requirements: No
Legal methods course requirements: No
Legal research course requirements: No
Moot court requirement: Yes
Moot court description: Part of oral advocacy course requirement
Public interest law requirement: Yes
Public interest law description: Introduction to Public Law and Legislation is mandatory in 1st year curriculum
Academic journals: University of Ottawa Law & Technology journal and symposium, Canadian Internet Policy & Public Interest Clinic (CIPPIC), Ottawa Law Review

ADMISSIONS INFORMATION
Admissions Selectivity Rating: 87
# of applications received: 3,391
% of applicants accepted: 18
% of acceptees attending: 35
Average undergrad GPA: 3.53
Application fee: $75
Regular application deadline: 11/1
Regular notification: Rolling
Early application program: No
Transfer students accepted: Yes
Evening division offered: No
LSDAS accepted: No

RESEARCH FACILITIES
% of JD classrooms wired: 90

FINANCIAL FACTS

Annual tuition: $9,180
Books and supplies: $1,100
Fees: $439
Tuition per credit: $356
Room & board: $10,000
Financial aid application deadline: 3/15
% First-year students receiving some sort of aid: 65
% Receiving some sort of aid: 65
% of Aid that is merit-based: 67
% Receiving scholarships: 16
Average grant: $1,815
Average loan: $1,159
Average total aid package: $10,440

EMPLOYMENT INFORMATION

Rate of placement (nine months out): 60
State(s) for bar exam: NY, MA
Pass rate for first-time bar: 95
Grads employed by field: %
Government (1)
Judicial Clerkships (1)
Private Practice (57)
Public Interest (1)
Other (40)

UNIVERSITY OF SASKATCHEWAN

University of Saskatchewan College of Law

College of Law University of Saskatchewan, 15 Campus Drive Saskatoon, SK S7N 5A6 Canada
Admissions Phone: 306-966-5045 • Admissions Fax: 306-966-5900
Admissions E-mail: law_admissions@usask.ca
Web Address: www.usask.ca/law/

INSTITUTIONAL INFORMATION

Public/private: Public
Total faculty: 38
% part-time: 18
% female: 20

STUDENTS

Average age of entering class: 25

ACADEMICS

Legal writing course requirements: No
Legal methods course requirements: No

ADMISSIONS INFORMATION

Admissions Selectivity Rating: 93
# of applications received: 901

% of applicants accepted: 13
% of acceptees attending: 100
Average LSAT: 156
LSAT Range: 150–167
Average undergrad GPA: 3.56
Application fee: $75
Regular application deadline: Rolling, up to 2/1
Regular notification: Rolling
Early application program: No
Transfer students accepted: Yes
Evening division offered: No
Part-time accepted: Yes
LSDAS accepted: No

FINANCIAL FACTS

Annual tuition (in-state/out-of-state): $6,840/$6,840
Books and supplies: $1,000
Fees (in-state/out-of-state): $454/$454
Tuition per credit (in-state/out-of-state): $228/$228

UNIVERSITY OF TORONTO

Faculty of Law

78 Queens Park Toronto, ON M5S 2C5 Canada
Admissions Phone: 416-978-3716 • Admissions Fax: 416-978-0790
Admissions E-mail: law.admissions@utoronto.ca
Web Address: www.law.utoronto.ca

INSTITUTIONAL INFORMATION

Public/private: Public
Student/faculty ratio: 10:1
Total faculty: 64

STUDENTS

Enrollment of law school: 601
% Male/female: 50/50
% Full time: 99
% Minority: 28
Average age of entering class: 25

ACADEMICS

Academic Specializations:
Advanced degrees offered: Master of Laws (LLM), 1 year; Doctor of Juridical Science (SJD), 1 year plus thesis; Master of Studies in Law (MSL), 1 year
Combined degrees offered: J.D./M.B.A., 4 years; J.D./M.S.W., 4 years; J.D./M.A. (Criminology), 3 years; J.D./M.A. (Economics), 3 years; J.D./M.A. (English), 3 years; J.D./Master of Global Affairs, 4 years (pending University approval); J.D./M.A. (European, Russian and Eurasian Studies), 4 years; J.D./M.I.St (Master of Information Studies), 4 years; J.D./Certificate in Environmental Studies, 3 years; J.D./Ph.D (Economics), 4 years plus dissertation; J.D./Ph.D (Philosophy), 4 years plus dissertation; J.D./Ph.D. (Political Science), 4 years plus dissertation.
Grading system: Letter grades A, B+, B, C, C+, D, F. Students who are in the top ten percent of the class each year are awarded "A Honours Standing." Students are not ranked except as disclosed on the prize list.
Clinical program required: No

Clinical program description: The U of T does not require students to participate in a clinic program; however, we offer several vibrant and interesting clinical opportunities and a majority of students take part in at least one clinic program. The following clinics are available: Downtown Legal Services, Advocates for Injured Workers, International Human Rights Clinic, Barbra Schlifer Commemorative Clinic, Health Equity & Law Clinic

Legal writing course requirements: Yes

Legal writing description: Students must complete writing assignments in their first year as part of their first year program in their "small group" (see below).

Legal methods course requirements: Yes

Legal methods description: The cornerstone of the first year curriculum is the "small group" which permits students to study one of the first year subjects with a member of the faculty and fewer than twenty classmates. The "small group" introduces students to the techniques of legal research and writing in a personal and direct setting with a member of the teaching faculty.

Legal research course requirements: Yes

Legal research description: As part of the "small group" in first year, students are introduced to the many elements of legal research.

Moot court requirement: Yes

Moot court description: Every student is required to participate in a moot and its successful completion is an academic requirement. Students complete their moot in second term of second or third year. Students may also fulfill the mooting requirement through participation in a competitive moot.

Public interest law requirement: No

Public interest law description: Students are not required to complete a public interest requirement, however, many of our students participate in our Pro Bono Students Canada program (which offers students volunteer placements with pro bono organizations) and summer internships doing pro bono work abroad or domestically.

Academic journals: University of Toronto Faculty of Law Review; Journal of Law & Equality; Indigenous Law Journal; and Journal of International Law and International Relations.

ADMISSIONS INFORMATION

Admissions Selectivity Rating: 99
# of applications received: 1,818
% of applicants accepted: 15
% of acceptees attending: 70
Average LSAT: 167
LSAT Range: 154–180
Average undergrad GPA: 3.9
Application fee: $75
Regular application deadline: Rolling, up to 8/31
Regular notification: Rolling
Early application program: No
Transfer students accepted: Yes
Evening division offered: No
Part-time accepted: Yes
LSDAS accepted: No
Applicants also look at: Harvard University, Columbia University, University of British Columbia, University of California—Berkeley, New York University, McGill University, Dalhousie Law School, York University

RESEARCH FACILITIES

% of JD classrooms wired: 95
Financial aid application deadline: 7/15
% First-year students receiving some sort of aid: 48.6
% Receiving some sort of aid: 39.3
% of Aid that is merit-based: 4
% Receiving scholarships: 38.9

EMPLOYMENT INFORMATION

State(s) for bar exam: NY, MA, CA
Employers who frequently hire grads: All major Toronto law firms, all provincial and federal government departments, many large New York and Boston law firms, large and midsize Vancouver, Halifax and Calgary law firms.
Prominent alumni: Justice Frank Iacobucci, Former Justice Supreme Court of Canada; Justice Rosalie Abella, Supreme Court of Canada; Bob Rae & David Peterson, Former Premiers of Ontario; The Hon. Paul Martin, Former Prime Minister of Canada; Justice Ian Binnie, Supreme Court of Canada.
Grads employed by field: %
Judicial Clerkships (7)
Private Practice (75)

UNIVERSITY OF VICTORIA

University of Victoria, Faculty of Law

P.O. Box 2400, STN CSC Victoria, BC V8W 3H7 Canada
Admissions Phone: 250-721-8151 • **Admissions Fax:** 250-721-6390
Admissions E-mail: lawadmss@uvic.ca • **Web Address:** www.law.uvic.ca

INSTITUTIONAL INFORMATION

Public/private: Public
Student/faculty ratio: 7:1
Total faculty: 60
% part-time: 43
% female: 30
% minority: 9

STUDENTS

Enrollment of law school: 360
% Male/female: 40/60
% Out of state: 50
% Full time: 98
% Minority: 25
Number of countries represented: 6
Average age of entering class: 26

ACADEMICS

Academic Specializations: Environmental law, international law, intellectual property law, Alternative Dispute Resolution; Aboriginal Law; Asia-Pacific Law
Advanced degrees offered: LL.M., one year, Ph.D.,three years
Combined degrees offered: Bachelor of Laws/Master's of Public Administration (LLB/MPA) 4 years; Bachelor of Laws/Master's of Business Administration (LLB/MBA), 4 years; Bachelor of Common Law/Bachelor of Civil Law (LLB/BCL), 4.5 years; Bachelor of Laws/ Master of Arts in Indigenous Government (LLB/MAIG), 4 years.
Grading system: 9 point system: 9-A+; 8-A;7-A–; 6-B+; 5-B; 4-B–; 3-C+; 2-C; 1-D; 0-F
Clinical program required: No
Clinical program description: Although it is not mandatory that students participate in any clinical programs, there are several that we offer or recommend.
Legal writing course requirements: Yes
Legal writing description: Law 110 - Legal Research and Writing
Legal methods course requirements: Yes

Legal methods description: Law 104 - The Law, Legislation and Policy
Legal research course requirements: Yes
Legal research description: Part of the Law 110 as listed above under the Legal Writing course requirement.
Moot court requirement: Yes
Moot court description: All students in first year must complete a moot court exercise as part of the Legal Research and Writing Course.
Public interest law requirement: No
Academic journals: APPEAL: Review of Current Law and Law Reform

ADMISSIONS INFORMATION

Admissions Selectivity Rating: 91
# of applications received: 949
% of applicants accepted: 30
% of acceptees attending: 38
Average LSAT: 163
LSAT Range: 156–173
Average undergrad GPA: 3.84
Application fee: $75
Regular application deadline: Rolling, up to 2/1
Regular notification: Rolling
Early application program: No
Transfer students accepted: Yes
Evening division offered: No
Part-time accepted: Yes
LSDAS accepted: No
Applicants also look at: University of British Columbia, University of Toronto

RESEARCH FACILITIES

% of JD classrooms wired: 90
School-supported research centers: Centre for Asia-Pacific Initiatives Institute for Dispute Resolution

INTERNATIONAL STUDENTS

TOEFL required of international students? Yes
Minimum TOEFL (paper/computer): 600/250

FINANCIAL FACTS

Annual tuition (in-state/out-of-state): $7,860/$20,903
Books and supplies: $2,000
Fees (in-state/out-of-state): $1,009/$1,009
Tuition per credit (in-state/out-of-state): $524/$1,394
Room & board (on/off-campus): $7,000/$10,000
Financial aid application deadline: 6/1
% of Aid that is merit-based: 35
Average grant: $2,500
Average loan: $10,880
Average debt: $30,000

EMPLOYMENT INFORMATION

Rate of placement (nine months out): 95
Employers who frequently hire grads: Local, provincial and national law firms; federal and provincial government; judicial clerkships; and non-profit organizations.
Prominent alumni: Sheridan Scott, Commissioner, Competition Bureau of Canada; Freya Kristjanson, Partner, Borden, Ladner, Gervais, LLP; Gary Lunn, Federal Government Minister; Andrew Petter, Dean of Law.
Grads employed by field: %
Academic (3)
Government (10)
Judicial Clerkships (11)
Private Practice (55)
Public Interest (2)
Other (8)

UNIVERSITY OF WINDSOR

University of Windsor, Faculty of Law

Faculty of Law, 401 Sunset Avenue Windsor, ON N9B 3P4 Canada
Admissions Phone: 519-253-3000 • Admissions Fax: 519-973-7064
Admissions E-mail: lawadmit@uwindsor.ca
Web Address: www.uwindsor.ca/law

INSTITUTIONAL INFORMATION

Public/private: Public
Student/faculty ratio: 15:1
% part-time: 48

STUDENTS

Enrollment of law school: 212
% Male/female: 39/61
% Out of state: 9.95
% Full time: 99.53
% International: 1.42
Average age of entering class: 24

ACADEMICS

Academic Specializations: Civil procedure, commercial law, constitutional law, corporation securities, criminal law, environmental law, human rights, international law, labor law, legal history, legal philosophy, taxation, intellectual property law, Intellectual Property
Advanced degrees offered: None
Combined degrees offered: M.B.A./LL.B., 3–4 years; J.D./LL.B., 3 years
Grading system: 13 point
Clinical program required: No
Clinical program description: Legal Assistance of Windsor, Community Legal Aid, University of Windsor Mediation Service, ProBono Students of Canada
Legal writing course requirements: Yes
Legal writing description: One academic year (Law I) a series of assignments, culminating in the Moot Court.
Legal methods course requirements: Yes
Legal methods description: Part of the Legal Research and Writing course, see "Legal Writing" above.
Legal research course requirements: Yes
Legal research description: Part of the Legal Resesarch and Writing course, see "Legal Writing" above.
Moot court requirement: Yes
Moot court description: Required component of the Legal Research and Writing Course in Law I.
Public interest law requirement: No
Academic journals: Windsor Review of Legal and Social Issues

ADMISSIONS INFORMATION

Admissions Selectivity Rating: 60*
# of applications received: 2,408
% of applicants accepted: 22
% of acceptees attending: 41
Application fee: $175
Regular application deadline: Rolling, up to 1/11
Regular notification: Rolling
Early application program: No
Transfer students accepted: Yes
Evening division offered: No
Part-time accepted: Yes
LSDAS accepted: No

RESEARCH FACILITIES

% of JD classrooms wired: 100

School-supported research centers: CARC (Canadian-American Research Centre for Law and Policy), IPLI (Intellectual Property Law Institute), IPLIN (Intellectual Property and Innovation Law Legal Information Network), and the JD/LLB Program with the University of Detroit Mercy Law School.

INTERNATIONAL STUDENTS

TOEFL recommended of international students? Yes

FINANCIAL FACTS

Annual tuition (in-state/out-of-state): $11,536/$17,743
Books and supplies: $2,000
Room & board (on-campus): $9,225
% of Aid that is merit-based: 25
Average grant: $4,522
Average loan: $12,900

EMPLOYMENT INFORMATION

State(s) for bar exam: ON, AB, BC, NS, NF
Pass rate for first-time bar: 99
Employers who frequently hire grads: Law Firms
Grads employed by field: %
Business/Industry (1)
Government (8)
Judicial Clerkships (3)
Private Practice (85)
Public Interest (3)

THE UNIVERSITY OF WESTERN ONTARIO

The University of Western Ontario Faculty of Law

Administrative Wing, Faculty of Law London, ON N5X 3T5 Canada
Admissions Phone: *(519) 661-3347* • **Admissions Fax:** *(519) 661-2063*
Admissions E-mail: *lawapp@uwo.ca* • **Web Address:** *www.law.uwo.ca*

INSTITUTIONAL INFORMATION

Public/private: Public
Student/faculty ratio: 7:1
Total faculty: 33
% part-time: 33
% female: 27

STUDENTS

Enrollment of law school: 161
% Male/female: 52/48
% Out of state: 15
% Full time: 98
Number of countries represented: 5
Average age of entering class: 25

ACADEMICS

Academic Specializations: Criminal law, taxation, intellectual property law, business law

Advanced degrees offered: LL.B., 3 years; LL.M., 1 year

Combined degrees offered: HBA/LLB BESc/LLB (four degree programs in Engineering), BSc (Computer Science)/LLB Honors, BA (History)/LLB, BA (Kin)/LLB Honors, BA (MIT)/LLB Honors, BA (Political Science)/LLB, LLB/MBA, PhD Philosophy

Grading system: Students are graded by Letter Grade: A+, Excellent 90–100%; A, Excellent 85–89%; A–, Excellent 80–84%; B+, Good 77–79%; B, Good 73–76%; B–, Good 70–72%; C+, Competent 67–69%; C, Competent 63–66%; C–, Competent 60–62%; D, Marginal Pass 50–59%; F, Fail 1-49%

Clinical program required: No

Clinical program description: Litigation Practice, Advanced Litigation Practice, Arbitration Law & Procedure Case Studies in Business Law Clinic in Criminal Law Practice, Criminal Law Advocacy, Family Law Practice and Procedure, Community Legal Services Clinic, Western Business Law Clinic, The Sport Solution, The Dispute Resolution Centre

Legal writing course requirements: Yes

Legal writing description: As part of the First year course: Legal Research Writing & Advocacy (Sept–Feb)

Legal methods course requirements: Yes

Legal methods description: As part of the First year course: Legal Research Writing & Advocacy (Sept–Feb)

Legal research course requirements: Yes

Legal research description: As part of the First year course: Legal Research Writing & Advocacy (Sept–Feb) Upper year elective: Advanced Legal Research (offered in fall term and in spring term)

Moot court requirement: Yes

Moot court description: As part of the first year small group program, students are required to participate in a moot in the January term. Upper year students can participate in a voluntary moot court program, the winners of which are invited to participate in external moot competitions.

Public interest law requirement: No

Academic journals: The Canadian Journal of Law & Jurisprudence

ADMISSIONS INFORMATION

Admissions Selectivity Rating: 89
# of applications received: 2,374
% of applicants accepted: 21
% of acceptees attending: 32
Average LSAT: 160
LSAT Range: 155–173
Average undergrad GPA: 3.72
Application fee: $75
Regular application deadline: 11/1
Regular notification: Rolling
Early application program: No
Transfer students accepted: Yes
Evening division offered: No
Part-time accepted: Yes
LSDAS accepted: No
Applicants also look at: University of Toronto, Queen's University, University of Windsor, York University

RESEARCH FACILITIES

% of JD classrooms wired: 100

INTERNATIONAL STUDENTS

TOEFL required of international students? Yes
Minimum TOEFL (paper/computer): 600/250

FINANCIAL FACTS

Annual tuition (in-state/out-of-state): $11,372/
Books and supplies: $1,400

Fees: $890
Room & board: $8,000
Financial aid application deadline: 10/7
% First-year students receiving some sort of aid: 60
% Receiving some sort of aid: 50
% of Aid that is merit-based: 80
% Receiving scholarships: 50
Average grant: $5,000
Average total aid package: $3,000

EMPLOYMENT INFORMATION

Rate of placement (nine months out): 99
Average starting salary: $50,000
State(s) for bar exam: NY
Pass rate for first-time bar: 100
Employers who frequently hire grads: Toronto, Canada's largest employers
Grads employed by field: %
Business/Industry (2)
Government (3)
Judicial Clerkships (3)
Private Practice (91)

YORK UNIVERSITY

Osgoode Hall Law School

4700 Keele Street Toronto, ON M3J 1P3 Canada
Admissions Phone: *416-736-5712* • **Admissions Fax:** *416-736-5618*
Admissions E-mail: *admissions@osgoode.yorku.ca*
Web Address: *www.osgoode.yorku.ca*

INSTITUTIONAL INFORMATION

Public/private: Public
Student/faculty ratio: 8:1
Total faculty: 134
% part-time: 40
% female: 40

STUDENTS

Enrollment of law school: 954
% Male/female: 48/52
% Full time: 100
% Minority: 30
Average age of entering class: 24

ACADEMICS

Academic Specializations: international law, taxationLitigation
Advanced degrees offered: LLM; D JUR
Combined degrees offered: JD(NYU)/LLB, 4 years; LLB/LLM (NYU), 3.5 years; LLB/MBA, 4 years; LLB/MES, 4 years.
Grading system: A+, A, B+, B, C+, C, D+, D, F
Clinical program required: Yes
Clinical program description: Immigration and Refugee, Business (Small Business Intensive and Mergers & Acquisitions Intensive), Criminal, Aboriginal, Poverty Law (Parkdale and CLASP - 2 legal aid clinics), Innocence Project
Legal writing course requirements: Yes

Legal writing description: Mandatory course, year-long assessment. Case comments, memos, and factum.
Legal methods course requirements: No
Legal research course requirements: Yes
Legal research description: Combined with legal writing as above
Moot court requirement: Yes
Moot court description: All first year students complete a moot as part of their Legal Research and Writing course. In addition, both first and upper year students participate in Osgoode's excellent competitive mooting program.
Public interest law requirement: Yes
Public interest law description: As of September, 2007, all first year students must complete 40 hours of public interest work by third year.
Academic journals: Osgoode Hall Law Journal German Law Journal

ADMISSIONS INFORMATION

Admissions Selectivity Rating: 90
# of applications received: 2,397
% of applicants accepted: 25
% of acceptees attending: 50
Average LSAT: 84
Average undergrad GPA: 3.97
Application fee: $75
Regular application deadline: 11/1
Regular notification: Rolling
Early application program: No
Transfer students accepted: Yes
Evening division offered: No
Part-time accepted: No
LSDAS accepted: No

RESEARCH FACILITIES

% of JD classrooms wired: 100

INTERNATIONAL STUDENTS

TOEFL required of international students? Yes
Minimum TOEFL (computer): 250

FINANCIAL FACTS

Annual tuition (in-state/out-of-state): $13,996/$13,996
Books and supplies: $1,300
Fees (in-state/out-of-state): $800/$800
Room & board (on/off-campus): $10,000/$10,000
Financial aid application deadline: 9/7
% Receiving some sort of aid: 55
% of Aid that is merit-based: 25
% Receiving scholarships: 20
Average grant: $7,500
Average loan: $10,000
Average total aid package: $7,500

EMPLOYMENT INFORMATION

Average starting salary: $55,000
State(s) for bar exam: ON
Pass rate for first-time bar: 98
Grads employed by field: %
Business/Industry (1)
Government (9)
Judicial Clerkships (6)
Private Practice (77)
Public Interest (4)
Other (3)

SCHOOL SAYS

In this section you'll find schools with extended listings describing admissions, curriculum, internships, and much more. This is your chance to get in-depth information on programs that interest you. The Princeton Review charges each school a small fee to be listed, and the editorial responsibility is solely that of the university.

CHAPMAN UNIVERSITY
School of Law

AT A GLANCE

Chapman University was founded in 1861. The School of Law was established in 1995. The School of Law received ABA accreditation in 2002. In 2006, the School of Law received AALS accreditation.

Programs of study include: Juris Doctor

Certificate Programs: Advocacy and Dispute Resolution; Entertainment Law; Environmental, Land Use, and Real Estate Law; International Law; Tax Law; Joint JD/MBA with Chapman's George L. Argyros School of Business; Joint JD/MFA with Chapman's Dodge College of Film and Media Arts; LLM. Program in Taxation

Clinical programs in Appellate Practice, Constitutional Jurisprudence, Elder Law, Family Violence (Domestic Violence and Immigration issues), and Tax Law.

DEGREES OFFERED

Chapman University School of Law offers the traditional Juris Doctor, the LLM degree in Taxation Law, and two dual degrees. A JD/MBA and JD/MFA (Masters of Fine Arts in Film Producing.

GENERAL ACADEMIC PROGRAMS

The Law School requires 88 academic credits for graduation. First-year courses are required and cover traditional subjects: Contracts, Torts, Civil Procedure, Property, Criminal Law, and Legal Research and Writing. Several upper-level courses are also required in the following areas: Constitutional Law, Corporations, Evidence, Federal Income Taxation and Professional Responsibility.

Students may choose to focus their electives in one of five certificate areas: Advocacy and Dispute Resolution, Environmental, Land Use, and Real Estate Law, Entertainment Law, International Law, Tax Law.

EXPENSES AND FINANCIAL AID

Tuition: $35,950 **Fees:** $283

Estimated room and board per academic year: On and off campus $13,968 Estimated cost of books and other academic expenses per academic year (for full-time JD students only) $1,500 Financial aid application deadline: 3/2 Financial aid decisions are rendered on a rolling basis.

Notification of awards generally begins in March Percent of financial aid that is merit based: 17 Percent of JD students from each of the following categories receiving some form of aid—New JD Students: 98; otal JD Students: 93

Percent of JD students from each of the following categories receiving scholarships or grants—New JD Students: 46; Total JD Students: 51

Percent of JD students from each of the following categories receiving loans—New SJD Students: 83; Total JD Students: 91

Individual aid packages awarded to full time JD students—Average annual total aid pack gage awarded to JD Students: $48,422; Average Annual Scholarship/Grant Aid awarded to JD Students receiving scholarships/grants: $17,393; Average annual loan aid to JD students receiving loans: $40,693; Average dollar amount of outstanding educational law school loans per 2007 graduate: $94,397

FACULTY

There are 36 full-time faculty members; 39 percent of our faculty is women and 11 percent of our faculty is minorities. The part-time faculty represents 40 percent of the total faculty. The 2007 student to faculty ratio was 12.2 to 1.

STUDENT BODY

Chapman University School of Law is an ideal environment for learning. The total student body of the Law School numbers about 550.

The first-year students will be divided into three tracks of 60-65 students each. They will be further divided into considerably smaller sections of 12 to 15 students for the Legal Research and Writing component.

The minority representation of the entering class has been 21 percent. The age range is 20 to 55. With respect to geographic representation, 18 percent of the 2007 entering class was from states other than California. The gender breakdown for the Fall 2007 entering class was 58 percent men and 42 percent women.

ADMISSIONS

Chapman University School of Law has a rolling admissions policy. The application deadline for the Fall 2009 class is April 15. The February LSAT is the last test you can take to be considered for the Fall 2009 class.

The admissions process is highly competitive with over 2,485applications for only 200 seats in the entering class.

Applicants are required to submit a formal application, personal statement, resume, two letters of recommendation, $65 nonrefundable application fee, and the LSDAS report from the Law School Admission Council (LSAC). The LSDAS report generally includes your LSAT score(s), official transcript(s), and letters of recommendation. A resume and addendums or optional essays are also acceptable.

Applicants should be advised that the Law School reviews all LSAT scores and does not accept LSAT scores that are more than five years old.

Applicants, who have graduated from college within the past five years, are strongly encouraged to seek letters of recommendation from professors who have taught them in one or more courses.

Applicants may download a PDF version of the application from our website at www.chapman.edu/law or elect to use the electronic application on the web from www.lsac.org. The electronic application is preferred.

SPECIAL PROGRAMS

In addition to its five certificate programs, clinics and externship programs, Chapman Law School offers two joint degree opportunities. JD/MBA joint-degree opportunity. This program affords students the ability to obtain two separate, accredited professional degrees in a shorter period than would normally be required to obtain the degrees independently. The adequately prepared student may obtain both degrees in four years rather than the typical five years. Chapman's George L. Argyros School of Business and Economics is AACSB accredited.

CAREER SERVICES AND PLACEMENT

Chapman Law students successfully find satisfying employment with the assistance of the professionals in the Career Services and Professional Development Office. The office strives to provide Chapman students with the necessary skills to navigate the legal job market and to market the law school and its students to legal employers. In recent years, over 92 percent of each graduating class has been able to secure employment within nine months of graduation.

Employment statistics for the class of 2007 are as follows:

Employment nine months after graduation: 92.5 %

Percentage of graduates enrolled in a full-time degree program: 2.5%

Percentage of graduates' status unknown: 4%

Average starting salary of all 2007 graduates: $77,122

DREXEL UNIVERSITY
Law School

AT A GLANCE

The Drexel University Earle Mack School of Law welcomed its inaugural J.D. class in August 2006. In the finest traditions of Drexel University, Drexel Law is grounded in experiential learning, seeks a diverse student body, provides a practical education, and encourages its graduates both to be productive members of industry and of their communities, in the fullest sense of citizenship and in the proudest traditions of the Philadelphia Lawyer.

Drexel Law offers a unique educational experience to law students, including its exceptional cooperative education program, innovative legal methods program, and outstanding faculty engaged in both the academic and practice worlds.

CAMPUS AND LOCATION

Located in the University City neighborhood just adjacent to downtown Philadelphia, Drexel is mere blocks from the heart of one of the nation's largest and most vibrant legal communities. University City is so named because within our neighborhood, the campuses of Drexel and the University of Pennsylvania combine to form a community of 40,000 students. Within University City, there is ample affordable student housing available a short walk or trolley ride away and students are able to join together after class at many of the nearby bars, restaurants and trendy shops.

DEGREES OFFERED

Drexel University Earle Mack School of Law offers a full-time Juris Doctor (J.D.) program, as well as these joint degrees: JD/MBA, JD/MPH, and JD/PhD in Psychology

PROGRAMS AND CURRICULUM

The Drexel Law Co-op Program: The core of the Drexel Law program is its focus on experiential learning, particularly the co-op program. By working in the field in a nearly six month externship, law students will benefit from the ability to learn-over a significant period of time-not only the law of the practice area and the skills needed to succeed there, but also the knowledge of the host institution and the industries to which it belongs. For a list of our more than 170 co-op partners, please visit our website at http://www.drexel.edu/law/coop-overview.asp.

Drexel Law Concentrations: Drexel Law's three optional concentrations in Health Law, Intellectual Property Law and Business and Entrepreneurship Law reflect the strengths of Drexel University, key areas of practice in the Philadelphia region, and developing areas of law. Students enrolled in a concentration program will gain access to extensive class offerings and specialized co-op and clinical opportunities. By pursuing a concentration, students will gain a deeper and richer exposure in these cutting-edge areas of law, where the opportunities for employment are expanding.

FACILITIES

As part of Drexel's Academic Strategic Plan, Drexel Law offers state of the art facilities, including "smart" classrooms, ready access to reference materials-both traditional and electronic, ample study space and a location in the heart of Drexel's University City Campus. Drexel Law is also proud to be housed in an environmentally sound building that incorporates architecture, technology and building automation focused on energy conservation, emissions avoidance, and compliance with LEED standards.

EXPENSES AND FINANCIAL AID

All applicants are considered for scholarship at the time of admission and awards are communicated in the accept letter. In addition to scholarships, students use Federal Stafford loans, Graduate PLUS loans, private loans and scholarships to finance their education. Our financial aid office works closely with the students to aid them in finding appropriate funding for the student.

Tuition: $32,200

Fees: $720

ADMISSIONS

Drexel Law utilizes rolling admissions, which means it's never too late to apply to Drexel. Nevertheless, students are encouraged to apply as early in the year as possible, as scholarship and admission decisions are weighted favorably towards early applicants. For applicants' convenience, Drexel provides a fee waiver for all online applications.

When considering applicants, Drexel does not employ cutoffs or numerical formulas. Rather, we look at an applicant's entire application and take into consideration both objective factors like the LSAT and G.P.A., as well as subjective factors like leadership skills, work experience and commitment to service.

CAREER SERVICES AND PLACEMENT

As of May 28, 2008, over 90% of the second-year law students secured legal internships or co-op placements for the summer of 2008 with 56 students employed at law firms, 33 working for government agencies (including 10 at district attorney offices), 15 serving at in house corporate counsel, and the remaining 43 clerking for judges, non-profit organizations, co-op placements and alternative jobs such as research assistant for professors. For complete information on where Drexel students are finding employment, please visit our web site at http://www.drexel.edu/law/career-services-employment-statistics.asp .

FAULKER UNIVERSITY
School of Law

AT A GLANCE

Faulkner University's Thomas Goode Jones School of Law is committed to the education of outstanding lawyers. In keeping with its distinctive Christian mission, the school embraces academic excellence and emphasizes a strong commitment to integrity within a caring Christian environment that sustains and nurtures faith. Students are encouraged to dedicate their lives to the service of others.

CAMPUS AND LOCATION

The School of Law is located in the capital of Alabama. Montgomery is widely known as the birthplace of the Confederacy and the civil rights movement.

The campus is located just a few miles from the Alabama State Capitol Building; the Alabama Judicial Building which houses the Alabama Supreme Court, the State Law Library, the Court of Civil Appeals and the Court of Criminal Appeals; and the Frank M. Johnson United States Courthouse Complex.

DEGREES OFFERED

The School of Law offers the Juris Doctor degree through a full-time program of study.

ACADEMIC PROGRAMS GENERAL

The School of Law's curriculum is comprised of fundamental courses such as Civil Procedure, Constitutional Law, Contracts Law, Criminal Law, Evidence, Professional Responsibility, Property Law, and Torts Law. The school also offers an extensive Legal Research & Writing program and a broad elective curriculum with courses in every area of law. Each student is appointed a faculty advisor who assists with course selection, particularly if a student wishes to pursue a certain area in special depth.

The school offers three clinical programs: the Mediation Clinic, the Family Violence Clinic and the Elder Law Clinic. The Mediation Clinic allows students to mediate cases set for trial at the Montgomery County District Court. The Family Violence Clinic provides pro bono services for clients unable to pay for representation and works in conjunction with Legal Services Corporation of Alabama and the Family Sunshine Center. The Elder Law Clinic allows students to represent low-income, elderly citizens in area counties. It works in cooperation with Legal Services Corporation of Alabama and the Alabama Department of Senior Services.

The School of Law's Advocacy Program is a vibrant program that provides students with the opportunity to hone their courtroom skills. Students can participate in national competitions in appellate advocacy, trial advocacy, and mediation. Also, the school hosts the Greg Allen Intra-School Mock Trial Competition and 1L Moot Court Competition each year.

FACILITIES

The School of Law is housed in a beautiful, neo-federal-style building that accommodates the George H. Jones Jr. Law Library, the Judge Walter B. Jones Moot Court Room, and the Institute for Dispute Resolution. It includes state-of-the-art research and lecture facilities with seven classrooms and two large conference rooms. All classrooms are outfitted for laptop computers and wireless Internet is available throughout the building and library.

EXPENSES AND FINANCIAL AID

Tuition for the academic year of 2009-10 is $30,500 ($15,250 in the fall, $15,250 in the spring) for a full-time student.

Students can seek educational loans through the Federal Stafford Loan program and the Graduate PLUS loan program. The School of Law offers merit-based scholarships to qualified entering students. Admitted applicants are automatically under scholarship consideration. Scholarships are limited in number therefore prospective students are encouraged to apply early in the admissions cycle.

FACULTY

The School of Law's curriculum is taught by a dynamic group of faculty. Professors challenge students, welcome ideas and encourage debate. With a low student-to-faculty ratio and an emphasis on small class sizes and personalized instruction, the school provides a more intimate atmosphere that enhances a student's educational experience. The student-to-faculty to ratio is 10 to 1.

STUDENT BODY

The School of Law hosts fifteen student organizations. Those are: American Constitution Society, American Association for Justice, Animal Law Society, Black Law Students Association, Board of Advocates, Christian Legal Society, Delta Theta Phi, Federalist Society, Honor Court, Jones Public Interest Law Foundation, Jones Law Republicans, Jones Law Review, Phi Alpha Delta, Student Bar Association, and Women Students Association.

ADMISSIONS

The School of Law seeks to enroll a highly qualified and diverse student body. The two primary criteria used to make admissions decisions are an applicant's LSAT score and cumulative undergraduate grade point average. Other factors considered are the applicant's personal statement, undergraduate school, undergraduate and/or graduate courses of study, grade trends, community service/involvement and professional employment history. Letters of recommendation are welcome but not required.

SPECIAL PROGRAMS

The Alternative Dispute Resolution (ADR) Program enables law students to integrate their knowledge of conflict management principles and dispute resolution processes with professional skills. This program allows students to receive training normally available only through on-the-job experience after graduation.

Students can earn a certificate in ADR, which is not a supplemental degree but an opportunity for Juris Doctor candidates to enrich their skills training while still in law school. The certificate in ADR requires completion of the following courses: Arbitration, Dispute Resolution Processes, Interviewing/Counseling & Negotiation, Mediation Clinic, and an elective skills course. All of the certificate courses contain both an academic component and a skills component.

As part of a Christian university, the School of Law seeks not only to provide legal knowledge and practical skills necessary to produce competent and ethical members of the legal community, but also to instill in students an attitude of service. This commitment to serve those who otherwise could not afford such assistance complements the legal profession's rich tradition of service.

The Public Interest Program provides opportunities for students to begin their career of service while utilizing the practical skills obtained in their legal education. This program is voluntary and provides students with opportunities to work for nonprofit organizations, government agencies, and private attorneys or firms conducting pro bono legal work. Students are challenged to perform at least 50 hours of voluntary service during their law school career.

CAREER SERVICES AND PLACEMENT

The School of Law's Career Services Office provides a full range of services to support students and alumni in their job search process. It actively develops relationships with employers, alumni, and professional organizations to assist students in developing a network of professional contacts. The school boasts a 95% placement rate for its graduates.

THE GEORGE WASHINGTON UNIVERSITY
School of Law

CAMPUS AND LOCATION

The Law School is located on the main campus of The George Washington University in the downtown Washington, D.C., area known as Foggy Bottom. GW's urban campus is spread over 18 city blocks, and its architectural details, brick courtyards, and green spaces help it fit seamlessly into the surrounding community. Across the street from the Law School are the World Bank and IMF, and the White House is just four blocks away. The State Department and numerous other governmental and arts organizations are all in the immediate vicinity.

DEGREES OFFERED

In addition to the JD; GW offers several joint and advanced degrees. Joint degrees include: JD/MBA; JD/MPA; and JD/MP; J/MA; and JD/MPH. The Master of Laws (LLM) is an advanced degree program for law school graduates who wish to pursue an academic career or to enhance knowledge for practice in a specialized area. The Law School admits a very limited number of candidates for the Doctor of Juridical Science (SJD) degree.

ACADEMIC PROGRAMS GENERAL

Students have the opportunity to sample a broad array of areas of the law with more than 250 elective courses and seminars. In addition to traditionally taught classes, the Law School offers a number of simulation, drafting, and writing skills courses that require students to translate the study of the law into action, and help to prepare graduates to work effectively in a broad range of practice areas. Many of these courses are taught by judges and practicing attorneys.

The Law School's extensive clinical program gives students the opportunity to work with clients-many of whom might otherwise be without representation-while at the same time honing their counseling, advocacy, research, and negotiating skills. Drawing on surrounding institutions, the Law School also provides unparalleled opportunities for students to pursue externships in government agencies, nonprofit organizations, and courts.

FACILITIES

The Law School's attractive and comfortable classrooms and moot court rooms incorporate technology to support a broad range of teaching methods. In addition, power outlets for notebook computers are provided at each student station in most classrooms, and there are more than 70 wireless access points throughout the facility.

The core of the Jacob Burns Law Library's research collection comprises more than 500,000 volumes. The Library offers a variety of legal and law-related databases and automated indexes to enhance research capabilities. The staff administers and maintains the Library during its liberal hours of operation and offers information, instruction, and other research support services. Students also have full access to the many amenities of the GW campus, including a state-of-the-art fitness complex.

EXPENSES AND FINANCIAL AID

The Law Financial Aid Office counsels and assists applicants and current students in applying for various sources of financial aid: federal and commercial loans at negotiated, competitive terms, need-based tuition grants, and outside scholarships. All applicants are considered for merit-based aid. An estimated 85 percent of GW Law students receive some sort of financial aid. The Law School's Loan Reimbursement Assistance Program (LRAP) is designed to alleviate the financial burdens of graduates who pursue public interest employment.

FACULTY

One of the Law School's greatest assets is an exceptionally talented and accessible faculty whose contributions are not limited to the classroom, but instead reach deeply into the students' academic and professional development. While dedicated to excellence in the teaching, the faculty also remains at the forefront of legal scholarship both at the national and international level. Their practical experience adds an important perspective to their presentation of theoretical principles of the law.

STUDENT BODY

GW is one of the largest law schools in the U.S. In fall 2008, 2,000 degree candidates, from the U.S. and more than 30 foreign countries, were enrolled at the Law School. The student body is one of the most diverse in the country, and this diversity greatly enhances the learning environment. For both full-time and part-time students, participation in the academic and social life of the school beyond the classroom greatly enhances and broadens their educational experience.

ADMISSIONS

In 2008, GW Law's entering JD class was selected from a pool of more than 8,900 applicants. All materials submitted by the applicant (including the personal statement and letters of recommendation, if submitted) are considered before a decision is made. There are no inflexible standards, nor are there minimum grade-point averages or LSAT scores that are required. However, students whose undergraduate records and LSAT scores indicate a high probability of success in law study are more likely to be admitted.

SPECIAL PROGRAMS

GW Law offers two summer programs: the Oxford-GW Summer Program in International Human Rights Law and the Munich Intellectual Property Summer Program; and two exchange programs: North American Consortium on Legal Education (NACLE), a consortium of nine law schools and research institutes from the NAFTA countries, and the GW-University of Augsburg (Germany) Student Exchange Program.

CAREER SERVICES & PLACEMENT

The CDO's mission is to provide effective career advising services to students enabling them to engage in a meaningful job search, to compete as professionals in the employment market, and to make well-informed choices leading to long-term career satisfaction. The CDO fulfills its mission through a broad range of services including individual counseling, group seminars, substantive legal practice area programs, interviewing programs, job & internship fairs, on-line job postings, a Resource Library, the Alumni Career Advisor Network, a biweekly newsletter, and a comprehensive website.

HAMLINE UNIVERSITY
School of Law

AT A GLANCE
Hamline University School of Law is accredited by the American Bar Association (ABA) and a member of the Association of American Law Schools (AALS). It offers a broad curriculum with opportunities to focus within 12 areas of legal specialty, as well as two nationally ranked Centers of Excellence. Hamline receives high marks from students for its passionate faculty, student-centered atmosphere and strong opportunities to develop legal skills-both locally and abroad-while learning the law within a friendly campus community.

CAMPUS & LOCATION
Hamline is located in the heart of the Twin Cities of Saint Paul and Minneapolis, with ample opportunities for outstanding cultural, social and recreational activity. For those who chose to remain after graduation, the Twin Cities is a good place to build a career. Nearly two dozen Fortune 500 companies make their headquarters in the Twin Cities urban area, including 3M, Cargill, Medtronic, Target Corporation and General Mills. The Twin Cities has been ranked the "best metro area for business" by MarketWatch.com (12/08) and Forbes ranks Minneapolis as the "third best city for singles" (2008).

DEGREES OFFERED
Hamline University School of Law students may earn a JD degree through a full-time, three year program and a part-time, four-year weekend program. An LL.M. degree for international lawyers also is offered. Dual degrees are available in Public Administration, Business Management, Non-profit Management, Fine Arts in Creative Writing, and Organizational Leadership.

PROGRAMS & CURRICULUM
Hamline's curriculum also supports twelve organized tracks of study or focus areas, including business and commercial law, child advocacy, criminal law, dispute resolution, government and regulatory affairs, health law, intellectual property, international law, labor law, litigation and trial practice, property law, and public law and human rights.

Hamline's nationally ranked alternative dispute resolution (ADR) program provides a full range of ADR-related programming, including a summer institute, January term courses, certificate programs, and a bi-annual symposium. The Health Law Institute, also nationally ranked, focuses on the growth of health law, federal regulation, tort reform, medical device development and regulation, and ethics.

EXPERIENTIAL LEARNING
Hamline's eleven clinics offer students the opportunity to develop litigation, transactional and alternative dispute resolution skills. The Practicum program combines 114 hours of field experience with a classroom component focused on enhancing a student's lawyering skills. Moot court and similar competitions involve legal research, brief writing, and oral argument. Hamline is home to three scholarly journals. Hamline law students staff the Hamline Law Review and the Hamline Journal of Public Law and Policy, and provide editorial assistance for The Journal of Law and Religion. Hamline School of Law offers unique study abroad opportunities in Norway, Italy, Hungary, England, Israel and Puerto Rico, with new programs being developed in Canada and Sweden.

FACILITIES
Hamline law school's architectural design encourages easy access to faculty and administrative offices. The Annette K. Levine courtroom offers a technologically relevant setting for moot court competitions and for observing actual court proceedings. Hamline's law library provides modern collections of print, electronic and microform resources, and has more than 300,000 volumes and electronic databases. In addition, students have access to the libraries of seven other colleges and universities through a consortium arrangement.

EXPENSES & FINANCIAL AID
Hamline University School of Law is a private institution. Full-time tuition for the 2009-2010 academic year is $31,600. Merit-based and endowed scholarships are available for first-year students.

FACULTY
Hamline law school has 41 full-time faculty members (46% women, 15% minority). Adjunct faculty complements the faculty by teaching upper division courses in specialty areas. The law school has recently invested in expanding its faculty, with nationally recognized experts in bio-ethics, health law, intellectual property, international trade, corporate law, and critical race theory. These faculty members join a faculty nationally recognized for scholarship and academic leadership in dispute resolution, commercial law, constitutional law, and many other fields. The Hamline faculty is committed to an "open door" policy to help students learn and practice the law.

STUDENT BODY
Hamline law school's student body includes approximately 700 students from diverse backgrounds. As a student-centered community, student organizations play a key role in the vitality of the law school environment. More than 25 student organizations focus on students' cultural and professional interests.

ADMISSIONS
The admission selection process emphasizes a rigorous but fair examination of each person's application. In addition to the LSAT and undergraduate GPA, other factors are given significant weight including motivation, personal experiences, employment history, graduate education, maturity, letters of recommendation, and the ability to express one's interest in the study of law. Hamline's admission policy is designed to enhance the academic rigor, professional dedication, social concern, and diversity of the student body, including cultural, economic, sexual orientation, racial, and ethnic composition.

CAREER SERVICES & PLACEMENT
The Career Services Office provides informational programs, mock interviews, one-on-one counseling, networking opportunities, and an online job bank. It also hosts on-campus interviews for interested employers and works extensively with employers to market Hamline law students.

MICHIGAN STATE UNIVERSITY

AT A GLANCE

The Michigan State University College of Law is a dynamic school with a proud reputation for excellence. MSU Law students are challenged by the rigor of our academic program and are prepared to enter the legal profession with tangible, practice-ready skills.

As a college integrated with a world-class university, MSU Law offers students the personal attention often associated with private legal education combined with the opportunities of an internationally known, research university. The academic programming is enhanced by dual degree options, certificates and concentrations; externships/internships, and clinical programs designed to connect theory with practice and provide students with academic knowledge along with hands-on experience.

The MSU Law faculty is composed of first-rate scholars who offer an exciting learning environment and demonstrate a strong commitment to teaching. They strive to ensure that all students are provided with the tools to succeed in any legal environment. Our faculty hails from the ranks of established and accomplished attorneys, widely respected scholars, and the most promising newly credentialed faculty candidates. Our distinguished professors are also very accessible to students. Their offices are located close to lecture halls so after class, professors use what is learned in the classroom as an impetus for further discussion.

CAMPUS AND LOCATION

MSU College of Law was founded in 1891 in Detroit, Michigan (formerly known as the Detroit College of Law (DCL)). In 1995, MSU and DCL aligned their academic reputations and identities, and today the College is fully integrated with the academic life of MSU.

DEGREES OFFERED

MSU Law students engage in a comprehensive, three-year, J.D. program. The program combines in-class instruction and theory with multiple experiential options. In addition, students may pursue joint-degree and dual-degree programs, as well as two Masters of Law programs.

The U.S.-Canadian Joint J.D.-LL.B. Program: MSU Law offers an exciting opportunity with the University of Ottawa Faculty of Law. Both U.S. and Canadian students have an innovative and convenient option to pursue a J.D./LL.B. in just four years. Beyond understanding cross-border legal issues, the program will prepare student for the economic and social consequences of international integration and globalization. This training will make students marketable on either side of the border.

Students must apply and be accepted to both institutions in order to participate in the program. Currently, students may apply to the program in the spring of their first or second year of law school and each student is required to complete two full academic years in residence at each institution. Selection for this program is based on academic qualifications, interest in the program, and additional criteria established by the "home" institution.

Dual Degree Programs: Dual degrees are powerful tools in today's marketplace. The combination of a law degree and an expert-oriented master's or doctorate will provide students with an expanded skill set, which is in demand for today's ever changing careers. The interdisciplinary learning opportunities at MSU Law include established dual degree programs with other MSU graduate programs, which enable students to earn their J.D. and a master's degree in just four years.

The following dual degree options have been established with Michigan State University*: JD-MBA; JD-MA in English; JD-MS in Fisheries & Wildlife; JD-MS in Forestry; JD-MA in Interdisciplinary Programs in Health and Humanities; JD-MA in Labor Relations & Human Resources; JD-MS in Community, Agricultural, Recreation, and Resources Studies; JD-Master in Urban and Regional Planning

*Other dual-degree options can be built around your interdisciplinary interests with other graduate programs at MSU.

Master of Laws Program: Michigan State University College of Law offers two opportunities for individuals interested in pursuing an LL.M. degree, one for foreign-educated attorneys interested in obtaining a U.S. LL.M. and another for lawyers interested in specializing in Intellectual Property and Patent law.

The LL.M. for Foreign-Educated Lawyers offers students the opportunity to expand their knowledge of the American legal system and prepare to take a bar examination in many U.S. jurisdiction.

The Master of Laws (LL.M.) degree is aimed at students who have earned their J.D., LL.B. or comparable law degree. The LL.M. provides advanced coursework in a full range of intellectual property and communications law areas and prepare students for career advancement. Candidates may select from the general category of Intellectual Property Law or one of the following five specialized tracks: Communications Law; Copyright/Trademark Law; Entertainment and Sports Law; International Intellectual Property Law; Patent Law.

The LL.M. program strongly encourages students to design their own courses of study with the assistance of their faculty advisors and includes a wide variety of courses and seminars. Students in the LL.M. Program also will benefit from the close alignment between the Law College and other graduate programs at Michigan State University.

PROGRAMS & CURRICULUM

MSU Law offers a rigorous and intellectually challenging required curriculum enhanced by numerous specialty programs. Students can distinguish themselves by building expertise in a specific area of the law and/or with a certificate program. They may choose from a concentration and/or certificate that offers specialized elective courses in a variety of areas. Not only does this build proficiency in a law specialty, but offers students a way to stand out to prospective employers. Currently, the following concentrations are offered at MSU Law: Alternative Dispute Resolution; Corporate Law; Criminal Law; Environmental & Natural Resource Law; Family Law; Health Law; Intellectual Property & Communications Law; International & Comparative Law; Public Law & Regulation; Taxation Law; Certificate Programs; Indigenous Law Certificate Program; Trial Practice; Child & Family Advocacy

FACILITIES

MSU Law offers style and substance, comfort, and convenience in the most technologically advanced setting. Everything an MSU Law student needs to learn the theory and practice of law is located in the Law College Building.

MISSISSIPPI COLLEGE OF LAW

A dynamic, engaging law school in the capital city of Jackson boasting a dedicated faculty, a collegial environment, and a broad curriculum with opportunities for experiential learning and advocacy.

AT A GLANCE

Mississippi College School of Law (MCSOL) is a private law school founded in 1975. It is accredited by the American Bar Association, a member of the Association of American Law Schools, and a charter member of the International Association of Law Schools. MCSOL has developed as a regional law school with over 65% of its students coming from out of state. The school has acquired a reputation for excellence in advocacy training with the national success of its moot court teams, a strong legal writing and research program, and a spirit of professionalism and service. The curriculum is broad based and provides courses and seminars in all the major areas of the law. The students are part of a collegial, collaborative environment. Professors are dedicated to their teaching, respected in their fields, and accessible to the students. Our strategic location supports numerous and varied internships. Volunteer, public service, and pro bono opportunities abound. Many students work in the legal community during their 2L and 3L years to develop experience, earn money, and begin the networking process. The school has enjoyed great success over the years in job placement and bar examination passage.

CAMPUS AND LOCATION

The law school campus is conveniently located in downtown Jackson, Mississippi-the state capital and the center of law, commerce, and politics. Federal and State courthouses are within walking distance. The school is surrounded by office buildings with a high concentration of law firms.

http://law.mc.edu/admissions/promovideo.html

DEGREES OFFERED

MCSOL operates a group of law centers to permit focused and integrated studies in distinct areas of the law-International Law Center, Business and Tax Center, Family and Children's Law Center, BioEthics and Health Law Center, Litigation and Dispute Resolution Center, and Public Service Law Center. Law students can earn joint JD/MBA degrees.

Programs and Curriculum

MCSOL wants its students to be successful. It offers programs designed to assist students develop study skills, understand legal reasoning, and employ test-taking techniques. Law students enjoy a broad range of recreational and social activities through the Law Student Bar Organization. MCSOL offers a summer study abroad program in Korea with international law and international business courses and a bar examination review course.

FACILITIES

MCSOL has created an attractive law school campus in downtown Jackson with convenient parking, green space, and areas where students can study, collaborate, and socialize. The Administration Building houses administrative offices, faculty offices, small classrooms, seminar rooms, and trial and appellate courtrooms. The new Classroom Building provides comfortable, high-tech classrooms with "clicker" technology and a range of audio-visual capabilities. All classrooms offer wireless connection to the Internet and pop-up electrical outlets for laptop computers. The Law Library is the largest in the state and offers a range of research services. A new Student Center features a Food Court with Starbucks Coffee and the Law School Bookstore.

EXPENSES AND FINANCIAL AID

Tuition at MCSOL is modest for a private law school and remains the same for all three years! MCSOL offers generous merit based scholarships.

FACULTY

The MCSOL faculty is experienced, diverse, and dedicated to student learning. They come from a variety of backgrounds and schools, produce scholarship in their area of expertise, and are actively engaged in student learning. The bios of the full time faculty may be found at: http://law.mc.edu/faculty/index.html. Complementing these faculty are talented adjunct professors to include Federal and State judges.

STUDENTS

MCSOL has a diverse student body representing 30 states and 90 undergraduate schools. About half come directly from an undergraduate program and half come with advanced degrees or work experience. Our students hail from a variety of backgrounds to include teachers, medical personnel, athletes, business people, military service members, and politicians. Students are active participants in our law review, moot court, student government, student newspaper, and a variety of other organizations that are associated with groups in the legal community such as the Federal Bar Association. Students may work in the Law Library, for law professors as research or teaching assistants, or in administrative offices.

ADMISSIONS

MCSOL encourages on-line applications through the LSAC process (application fee waived). Applications are considered on a rolling basis with a deadline of June 1. The Admissions Committee uses a "whole person" concept in evaluating applications and considers the high LSAT score, the undergraduate GPA, graduate work, and personal factors.

SPECIAL PROGRAMS

MCSOL offers a Civil Law Program that is of interest to Louisiana and comparative law students.

ADDITIONAL INFORMATION

MCSOL benefits from its strategic location in the State Capital. We have woven our Law School into the fabric of the local legal and judicial communities. These professional relationships and our downtown location assist our students with networking, job placement, and developmental opportunities. Jackson offers an abundance of recreational, cultural, and dining venues and is a comfortable and pleasant place to live. Housing is affordable and varied. Our weather is mild and temperate throughout the school year.

CAREER SERVICES AND PLACEMENT

Our Career Services Office is active and engaged with the students in assisting them with their job placement. This process begins in the first year and continues with classes and instructional programs on subjects ranging from interview techniques to dining and dress etiquette. We administer a viable on-campus recruiting program. Our placement rate has been consistently high with our students going to large and small firms, government, business, military JAG, and advanced legal study.

PACE UNIVERSITY
Pace Law School

AT A GLANCE
Pace Law School, a division of Pace University is fully accredited by the American Bar Association and is a member of the Association of American Law Schools. Known for an outstanding Environmental Program and excellent clinical opportunities, Pace also offers 70 electives, more than those offered at most comparable law schools. The school offers an outstanding and a student/faculty ratio of 16:1 and over 60% of elective classes have less than 20 students enrolled.

LOCATION
Located just 20 miles north of Manhattan in White Plains, the Pace Law School campus provides convenient access to metropolitan New York, Connecticut, and New Jersey. White Plains is home to some of the nation's largest corporations and a strong legal community with county, state, and federal courts. This concentration of resources and the Law School's proximity to New York City have enabled Pace to attract highly qualified professors, speakers, and advisors, as well as offering excellent opportunities for internships and employment after graduation.

FACILITIES
Pace Law School's campus in White Plains features green space, student housing, recreational facilities and on-site parking. The centerpiece of the campus is a wireless classroom building, which joins four other buildings. The five classrooms in this three-story facility feature horseshoe-shaped seating with raised tiers designed to promote interaction between teachers and students. Each classroom is equipped for audio-visual and computer presentations. Wide corridors on each of the three floors accommodate study areas and lounge stations. Special moot courtrooms for the Trial Advocacy program and a fully connected distance-learning classroom are housed in adjoining Aloysia Hall.

The Pace Law Library contains over 345,000 volumes of law and law-related publications, provides access to materials in libraries throughout the United States, and subscribes to national online research systems such as LEXIS/NEXIS, WESTLAW, and DIALOG.

DEGREES OFFERED
LLM in Comparative Legal Studies; JD/LLM in Real Estate Law; LLM and SJD in Environmental Law; JD/MBA and JD/MPA with Pace University; JD/MEM with Yale University School of Forestry; JD/MS with Bard College's Center for Environmental Policy; and a JD/MA with Sarah Lawrence College in Women's Studies

PROGRAMS AND CURRICULUM
The programs of the law school are national in perspective. They do not emphasize the law in any state, and are based on the concept that rigorous standards and high-quality teaching can coexist with an atmosphere congenial to learning and enjoyment. Students can obtain Certificates in Environmental Law and International Law by completing a sequence of courses with a specified GPA in the applicable area. Pace offers the opportunity to pursue several different joint degrees with partnering institutions. These programs can be completed in four years of full-time study. Part-time evening student is also possible.

EXPENSES AND FINANCIAL AID
Tuition for the 2009–2010 year is $39,974/academic year for full-time students and $28,994/academic year for part-time students. A comprehensive aid program provides scholarships, need-based grants, employment, loans, and a loan forgiveness program for graduates who choose a career in public interest law. In 2008, the average scholarship award totaled $14,500/year. Funds are available based on a variety of criteria, including financial need, academic merit, and diversity considerations.

FACULTY
The faculty consists of 105 members, including 45 full time and 60 adjunct professors. Faculty members are authors of widely circulated legal texts and drafters of ground-breaking state laws. Faculty scholarship covers fundamental areas of law such as Civil Litigation, Civil Procedure, Constitutional Law, Contracts, Evidence, Family Law, Federalism and Separation of Powers, Federal Jurisdiction, Federal Law and Procedure, Property, and Torts.

STUDENTS
The entering class of 2008 is a diverse group, representing 24 states and several other countries. The average age for the full-time class is 24 while the part-time class average was 30. More than 125 undergraduate schools are represented within the class which has a 17 percent minority population.

SPECIAL PROGRAMS
The Women's Justice Center is a direct legal services center which trains thousands of judges, attorneys, and others to eradicate women's injustice. Pace Law students participate in all aspects of the program, including direct representation of clients in family court. The Land Use Law Center teaches students to understand how best to develop and conserve land through research, publications, and community outreach. The Pace London Law program, in affiliation with the University of London, provides both an academic and internship experience during the spring semester for 30 to 40 students from Pace and other law schools.

Clinics structured to facilitate the transition to representing clients or prosecuting charges allow students to take full responsibility for casework while under direct faculty supervision. Externship programs and clinical courses are offered in which fieldwork is conducted with the guidance of practicing attorneys. Simulation courses give students the opportunity to learn specific components of lawyering, including written and oral advocacy, interviewing and counseling clients, negotiation, analyzing a trial record, developing strategy, open and closing arguments, all aspects of jury selection, and witness preparation and examination.

CAREER SERVICES AND PLACEMENT
The Office of Career Development actively solicits part-time, summer, and permanent positions after graduation as well as full-time employment for evening students while they are in school. Respondents to the 2007 graduating class survey reported 90.9% employment within the six months following graduation.

ADDITIONAL INFORMATION
Pace Law Admissions, 78 North Broadway, White Plains, NY 10603, 914-422-4210 admissions@law.pace.edu / www.law.pace.edu

ST. THOMAS UNIVERSITY

AT A GLANCE

St. Thomas University School of Law is a highly regarded student-centered law school where diversity is cherished, a commitment to human rights and international law flourishes, and the Catholic heritage of ethical behavior and public service is paramount.

One of the greatest strengths of our law school is the profound sense of community shared by students, faculty, and administration. St. Thomas is a leader in diversity, boasting one of the most culturally diverse student bodies in the country. This global diversity, within such a close-knit community, facilitates a cosmopolitan learning environment where intellectual discovery thrives.

A hallmark of St. Thomas is our emphasis on social justice and ethical behavior. Our unwavering commitment to public service is manifest in everything we do. Our students and alumni have a deep sense of justice and charity, and are encouraged to fully utilize their education and experience to lead the way in making our legal system one that truly champions the rights of the powerless.

CAMPUS AND LOCATION

St. Thomas University School of Law's location in Miami, Florida, provides an ideal setting for the study of law. Miami is a vibrant, thriving international community. As a hub of domestic and international trade, an innovative center for fine arts, and one of the world's most popular vacation spots, Miami is a dynamic place to live and study. Miami enjoys a rapidly expanding multinational legal community and is home to federal and state trial and appellate courts.

DEGREES OFFERED

St. Thomas University School of Law offers the traditional J.D. degree, several joint degrees, an LL.M. and a J.S.D. degree. Our joint degree program includes:

J.D./M.B.A. or M.S. in Sports Administration;
J.D./M.B.A. in International Business;
J.D./M.B.A. in Accounting; and,
J.D./M.S. in Marriage and Family Counseling

St. Thomas University School of Law also offers advanced degrees: the LL.M. and the J.S.D. in Intercultural Human Rights.

J.D. students are able to enroll in the classes offered through the LL.M. in Intercultural Human Rights as electives and can earn a Certificate in Human Rights.

FACILITIES

The law school is designed to provide our students with an outstanding environment for learning the law.

Computers and printers are in abundant supply throughout the law library. The law library offers Internet access to online databases and has been a leader in applying technology to legal education. Our wireless network allows students to conduct Internet-based research from anywhere on the law school's campus. Our classrooms and Moot Court Room have all been recently renovated.

EXPENSES AND FINANCIAL AID

Tuition and fees for the JD degree for 2009-2010 are $31,616 per year.

St. Thomas University School of Law offers merit-based scholarships to qualified students. St. Thomas also offers financial assistance apart from scholarships to eligible students in the form of loans. Many St. Thomas Law students receive some form of financial assistance.

FACULTY

The faculty at St. Thomas is committed to teaching, research and service. Our exceptional faculty has earned law degrees-many of them hold advanced law degrees-from some of the nation's most prestigious institutions, including Harvard, Yale, Columbia, Michigan, Pennsylvania, Georgetown, and New York University. They are leaders in their field with impressive records of publication in the top law reviews and extensive practical experience.

A hallmark of the St. Thomas experience is the genuinely close relationship between faculty and students. Professors maintain a congenial open-door policy, meeting regularly with students, and providing guidance for students that transcends the classroom, assisting them to be successful in law school and beyond.

STUDENT LIFE

St. Thomas University School of Law offers a rich student life. With more than twenty student organizations to choose from, students easily find activities that appeal to their interests. The Student Bar Association serves as the student government, planning activities and events, as well as working with the administration to communicate the student body's interests. Students also enjoy the wealth of activities, cultural and sporting events, and nightlife offered in Miami.

ADMISSIONS

Admissions decisions are made by the Law School Admissions Committee, which evaluates each applicant's potential for excellence in the study of law. The Law School Admission Test (LSAT) score is a factor; however, consideration will also be given to factors such as the undergraduate record and grade point average, undergraduate institution, course of study, graduate degrees, work experience, community service, and so forth.

St. Thomas also offers an alternative process for admission for a select group of candidates by way of our Summer Conditional Admit Program. The program targets candidates who demonstrate excellent qualitative credentials but lack certain quantitative measurements. Successful candidates in the program are automatically offered admission to the law school for that year's fall entering class.

SPECIAL PROGRAMS

St. Thomas University School of Law is committed to student success both in law school and beyond. Using an interactive and cooperative approach to learning, the Academic Support Programs and the Legal Research and Writing Program assist students in developing the skills required for the successful study and practice of law.

Additionally a series of classes is offered for students preparing for the Florida Bar Exam, focusing on both substance and techniques for success on the Bar Exam.

CAREER SERVICES AND PLACEMENT

St. Thomas provides first-rate career services that result in successful and rewarding employment for our graduates, whether their goals are to enter into private law practice, government, business and industry, or public interest areas of law. St. Thomas graduates are partners in major law firms from Florida to California, and the law school is represented in many of the most prestigious firms in the country.

STETSON UNIVERSITY

AT A GLANCE

Stetson University College of Law, Florida's first law school, offers full- and part-time JD and LLM programs in Tampa Bay. Stetson is ranked first for trial advocacy and fifth for legal writing.

CAMPUS AND LOCATION

Stetson's main law campus is located in Gulfport, a suburb of St. Petersburg. A satellite campus in downtown Tampa hosts some classes, conferences, and the Tampa branch of Florida's Second District Court of Appeal.

DEGREES OFFERED

In addition to the Juris Doctor degree, Stetson offers dual-degree programs for the JD/MBA, JD/MD and JD/MPH. Stetson also offers an on-campus LLM in International Law, an online LLM in Elder Law and an M.J. in Law and Aging.

PROGRAMS AND CURRICULUM

Stetson's curriculum combines a strong foundation of legal doctrine and theory with a nationally ranked program in the practical advocacy, legal research and writing skills required to become a successful attorney.

Stetson allows students to specialize their legal education through a variety of programs. JD students may earn certificates of concentration in advocacy, elder law or international law, and JD/MBA students may pursue a certificate in eco-asset management. High-achieving students may be invited to participate in Stetson's Honors Program. Students interested in intellectual property law may participate in Stetson's semester exchange program with the Franklin Pierce Law Center.

Stetson's extensive international offerings include a fall semester in London, exchange programs with law schools in Mexico and Spain, summer abroad programs in Argentina, China, Germany, the Netherlands and Spain, as well as a winter break course in the Cayman Islands.

Stetson also has centers for excellence and institutes that advance legal and policy issues in the fields of advocacy, biodiversity, the Caribbean, elder issues, higher education, and international law. Stetson is home to the National Clearinghouse for Science, Technology and the Law, Stetson Law Review, Journal for International Aging Law and Policy, and the Journal for International Wildlife Law and Policy.

FACILITIES

Originally built in the 1920s as a luxury resort, Stetson's main law campus now features state-of-the-art classrooms, five courtrooms, library and recreational facilities, culminating in an idyllic environment for the study of law. The main law library contains more than 420,000 volumes, 43 group study rooms and offers wireless access to over 40 online databases. The Tampa Law Center includes two courtroom spaces, fully equipped classrooms and seminar rooms, study rooms, wireless access, and a satellite law library. There is a laptop requirement for all admitted students.

EXPENSES AND FINANCIAL AID

2009-2010 full-time tuition (fall/spring): $31,420

2009-2010 part-time tuition (fall/spring/summer): $27,150

Merit and diversity scholarships are offered on a competitive basis, and need and merit scholarships are offered for continuing students. There is no financial aid deadline, and a completed FAFSA is the only required form.

FACULTY

Stetson's 52 full-time professors are engaged in projects that bring them regional, national, and international prominence, but make teaching and working with students their top priority. Approximately 50 practicing attorneys and judges serve as adjunct professors.

STUDENTS

Stetson offers cultural programs, experiential education trips, community service opportunities, leadership workshops, and nearly 40 diverse and active student organizations. The ABA Law Student Division has recognized Stetson with numerous regional and national awards, and Stetson's Student Leadership Development Program was recently awarded the ABA's prestigious E. Smythe Gambrell Award for excellence in professionalism. Stetson was the first law school in Florida to require student and faculty pro bono service.

ADMISSIONS

Stetson University College of Law admits full-time and part-time students each fall. As a prerequisite to enrollment, applicants are required to have earned a baccalaureate degree from a college or university that is accredited by an accrediting agency recognized by the U.S. Department of Education. A final, official transcript evidencing the conferral of the degree must be submitted before enrollment. All applicants are required to take the LSAT and register with the LSDAS. One letter of recommendation is required, and a maximum of three letters will be accepted. The personal statement is also required. More details are available at www.law.stetson.edu/admissions. An equal opportunity education institution, Stetson is fully accredited by the American Bar Association and has been an Association of American Law Schools member since 1931.

SPECIAL PROGRAMS

Stetson routinely wins international, national, regional, and state competitions for alternative dispute resolution, mock trials and moot court.

Stetson offers upper-level students a wide variety of opportunities to work closely with attorneys and judges, and, in some cases, actually represent clients and try cases. Clinical opportunities include Civil Immigration, Civil Poverty Law, Elder Law, Local Government, Prosecution, and Public Defender. Internships include American/Caribbean Law Internship, Bankruptcy Judicial Internship, Elder Law Internship, Employment Discrimination, Environmental Law Internship, EEOC Internship, Federal and State Judicial Internships, In-House Counsel Internship, Intellectual Property Internship, Labor Law Internship, State and Federal Litigation Internships, and U.S. Court of Appeals for Veterans Claims Internship. Stetson also offers a summer Law and Policy internship program in Washington, DC.

CAREER SERVICES AND PLACEMENT

Stetson's commitment to helping students achieve their goals is reflected in its strong career development program. The Office of Career Development assists students and alumni in securing all types of legal and law-related employment and provides group seminars and individual counseling on subjects ranging from interviewing techniques to résumé writing. More than 96 percent of the 2008 graduating class reported that they found employment within nine months of graduation. Approximately 90 percent of recent Stetson graduates practice within Florida; however, alumni are located in 48 states and 22 countries.

TOURO COLLEGE

AT A GLANCE

Touro Law Center is committed to providing the best in legal education. Touro Law students are encouraged to examine the moral goals of the law while promoting social justice and community service. Touro Law, accredited by the American Bar Association (ABA) and a member of the Association of American Law Schools (AALS), offers students full-time and part-time J.D. programs as well as dual degree and LL.M. programs.

CAMPUS AND LOCATION

Touro Law occupies a new 185,000-square-foot state-of-the-art building in Central Islip on the south shore of Long Island, New York. Touro is at the center of what is arguably the nation's first integrated "law campus," comprised of a United States courthouse and federal building as well as a New York State court center, housing supreme, family and district courts. More than mere physical proximity, Touro students interact with legal professionals daily through classroom instruction, court visits, clinics, externships and other academic and social forums.

DEGREES OFFERED

Touro Law offers full-time and part-time Juris Doctor programs as well as J.D./M.B.A., J.D./M.P.A. and J.D./M.S.W. dual degrees. Touro also offers an LL.M. degree in General Studies to graduates of U.S. law schools and an LL.M. degree in U.S. Legal Studies for foreign law graduates.

PROGRAMS AND CURRICULUM

The cornerstone of Touro Law's curriculum is the Court Observation Program, the only one of its kind in the nation. All students participate in the program, which includes interactive, faculty-supervised small group visits to the state and federal courthouses located adjacent to the law school. The program allows students to witness legal proceedings and gain insight from judges, lawyers and court officials.

Touro offers five in-house clinics: Civil Rights Litigation, Elder Law, Family Law, International Human Rights/Asylum Litigation, and Not-for-Profit Corporation Law. There are four field-placement clinics: Business, Law, and Technology; Civil Practice; Criminal Law; and Judicial Clerkship.

In addition, Touro offers two "rotations," where students work intensively in practice groups at the U.S. Attorney's Office for the Eastern District of New York or in Nassau/Suffolk Law Services (a regional legal services agency). To take full advantage of the synergies of its location within a court complex, the Law Center is also developing a Bankruptcy and Foreclosure Clinic and a Veterans Legal Advocacy Clinic. Touro also provides an unlimited selection of externship placements in private law firms, corporate law departments, government agencies, the courts and public interest organizations.

Touro Law offers vibrant opportunities for work and study abroad in Russia, India, China, Germany and Israel as well as summer internships in law firms, courts, and government offices in Europe and Israel.

FACILITIES

Touro Law Center's new facility was designed to be a student-centered, high-tech learning center. The building houses a clinical wing, a state-of-the-art auditorium, a public advocacy center, as well as mock trial classrooms, computer labs, meeting spaces, cafeteria, bookstore, the Gould Law Library and more. The infrastructure is high-tech, supporting wireless access, smart podiums and new technology throughout.

EXPENSES AND FINANCIAL AID

Generous institutional scholarship aid is available to entering students and to continuing students. Awards include dean's fellowships, merit scholarships, and incentive awards. Touro Law also offers stipends for Public Interest Law Fellowships, judicial clerkships, and summer federal work-study placements. Touro provides access to federal loans and work study, New York State loan and assistance programs, and need-based Touro Grants. Most students receive some form of financial aid, and over 50 percent of entering students receive scholarships.

FACULTY

Touro Law's faculty is comprised of more than 40 full-time faculty members. Every entering student is assigned a faculty advisor, matched by background or interest area, for discussions on any aspect of the law school experience including study strategy, course selection, career goals, etc. With an open-door policy and a student faculty ratio of 15:1, Touro Law students benefit from a personal and dynamic educational experience.

STUDENTS

The Law Center's students, coming from diverse backgrounds and experiences, represent over 125 undergraduate institutions and a broad mix of majors. Women comprise approximately 44 percent of the total enrollment; minorities, 26 percent.

ADMISSIONS

Touro Law Center seeks to identify applicants who show an ability to pursue the study of law successfully and to make an important contribution to the Law Center's educational program and to the legal profession. While significant weight is attached to a student's undergraduate cumulative grade point average and law School Admission Test (LSAT) score(s), the selection process is not strictly mathematical and includes an evaluation of several other factors including professional experiences and achievement, writing ability, rigor of undergraduate institution, letters of recommendation, and more.

SPECIAL PROGRAMS

Touro Law Center is home to the William Randolph Hearst Public Advocacy Center. The first of its kind in the nation, the Center provides furnished offices at no cost to non-profit legal advocacy agencies while providing hands-on working opportunities for students.

ADDITIONAL INFORMATION

Touro Law Center provides a unique program of outside-the-classroom assistance. Teaching assistants (TAs) review material covered in class and conduct small-group sessions on effective study methods and test-taking techniques. The Writing Resources Center offers workshops and tutorials to assist students in producing a professional work product. The Legal Education Access Program (LEAP) enhances the experience of students of color, through a four-week summer program for new students with additional mentoring during the academic year. The Honors Program, beginning in the second year, allows outstanding students to become Faculty Fellows. They receive additional scholarship assistance and access to academic enrichment initiatives.

CAREER SERVICES AND PLACEMENT

The Career Services staff assists students and graduates in securing part-time, full-time and summer employment. In addition to placing students with national, regional and local law firms, there are opportunities in federal, state, and local courts and government agencies, and in the legal departments of corporations and municipalities.

THE UNIVERSITY OF THE DISTRICT OF COLUMBIA

David A. Clarke School of Law

AT A GLANCE

The University of the District of Columbia David A. Clarke School of Law (UDC-DCSL) is the only public law school of the Nation's Capital. The School of Law is unique among law schools, with a service-centered mission of recruiting and enrolling students from underrepresented communities, a nationally-recognized clinical program and one of the most diverse student bodies in the country.

CAMPUS & LOCATION

UDC-DCSL is located on the campus of the University of the District of Columbia, the country's only urban land-grant public university. The University and School of Law is located in the upper Northwest section of the District on one of the city's major thoroughfares. The UDC-Van Ness Metro subway stop is located directly in front of the University, making the campus easily accessible. The campus is surrounded by a quiet residential community, Rock Creek Park, the National Zoo, embassies and small businesses.

DEGREES OFFERED

The School of Law offers the Juris Doctor (J.D.) degree and full-time day and part-time evening divisions.

PROGRAMS & CURRICULUM

The School of Law offers the best of both worlds for the study of law-a traditional legal education supplemented by hands-on clinical training. Students are required to complete 90 credits to graduate, 14 of which resulting from two semesters of clinical work. Clinics include Legislation, Juvenile and Special Education, Small Business and Community Development, Low-Income Tax and the Government Accountability Project. Students are also required to complete 40 hours of community service. They may participate as well in a 10- or 4-credit internship

FACILITIES

The School of Law is located on the campus of the University, which sits on several acres of land on Connecticut Avenue, NW.

The law school is located in Buildings 38 and 39 on Level two. The $1.6 million recently renovated Mason Law Library is located in Building 39, Level B. Every seat in the library is wired and WIFI access is available everywhere in the library. The larger classrooms are wired and the large lecture classroom is wired and high-tech.

EXPENSES AND FINANCIAL AID

The School of Law offers its students an affordable legal education and a comprehensive financial aid program. Tuition for District of Columbia resident students is $7350 a year (2009-10). Tuition for non-DC resident students is about $14,700 a year (2009-10). Non-DC resident students may be eligible for resident tuition after residing in the District for one year. Students may be eligible as well for the following financial assistance: Federal loans; merit scholarships; need-based grants; work-study; Dean's Fellowships; Continuing Student Scholarships; and the full-tuition three-year Advocate For Justice Scholarship. For more information on the law school's financial aid program, you may visit www.law.udc.edu.

ADMISSION

The School of Law considers the entire applicant profile when rendering an admission decision. While the candidate's LSAT and grades play an important role in the admission process, other factors are also considered before making a decision, e.g., the applicant's range of life experiences, the content and mechanics of the applicant's writing, community involvement, family background, and recommendations.

The average and median LSAT for the 2008 entering class is 152.

The Committee on Admission requests TOEFL on a case-by-case basis.

SPECIAL PROGRAMS

Other programs for students include the Equal Justice Works Summer Public Interest Fellowship Program and the Center for Immigration Law and Practice internship or federal work-study opportunities.

ADDITIONAL INFORMATION

Students enjoy an 11-to-1 student-faculty ratio and individualized attention from and access to faculty and administration. The small school also affords students a spirited, committed and collegial setting and community in which to study law.

CAREER SERVICES & PLACEMENT

Career Services includes general career exploration and planning, strategizing, resume and cover letter preparation, development of networking and interviewing skills, as well as how to consider and negotiate offers of employment. Programs include guest speakers from a wide variety of practice areas in the public and private sectors. Resources include extensive web site materials, on-line job databases and an email jobs bulletin, as well as a small library. The small size of the law school permits individualized counseling by the career services staff. For more information on Career Services and Placement, you may visit the school website at www.law.udc.edu or contact dbauman@udc.edu.

WESTERN NEW ENGLAND COLLEGE
School of Law

AT A GLANCE
2008 Full-time Entering Class

LSAT median	153
(25th percentile:	151; 75th percentile: 156)
GPA median	3.2
Average age	25
Age range	20-38
Minorities	14%
States represented	21
Total student enrollment:	575

CAMPUS AND LOCATION
Founded in 1919, the School of Law was originally part of Northeastern University and merged with Western New England College which itself was founded in 1951. Western New England College School of Law is located in Springfield, Massachusetts. Springfield is the third largest city in the Commonwealth, and home to a lively cultural scene. In the heart of the Pioneer Valley, Springfield is conveniently located near Boston, New York City, and Hartford, Connecticut.

DEGREES OFFERED
Western New England College School of Law offers many ways to earn a law degree. In addition to our three-year, full-time program, the School of Law also offers four-year, part-time evening and part-time day programs. Students may earn an advanced law degree in Estate Planning and Elder Law.

ACADEMIC PROGRAMS GENERAL
Western New England College School of Law offers students the opportunity to combine our law degree with three other programs. These programs include the JD/MBA (Master of Business Administration) with Western New England College, the JD/MRP (Master of Regional Planning) with the University of Massachusetts, and the JD/MSW (Master of Social Work) with Springfield College.

To assist students in preparing for their careers, and selecting among electives, WNEC School of Law currently offers six areas of concentration: Business Law, Criminal Law, Estate Planning, International and Comparative Law, Public Interest Law, and Real Estate.

WNEC School of Law affords students the opportunity to merge theory with practice. Students take advantage of clinical course work, a wide variety of simulation courses, and participate in a number of moot court teams in order to hone their lawyering skills. For more information on clinical opportunities, externships, and simulation courses visit our website at www.law.wnec.edu.

At WNEC School of Law, we keep our class size small to promote a collegial learning environment in which students are challenged to actively participate in their legal education.

EXPENSES AND FINANCIAL AID
In 2009, tuition for fulltime students is $34,378; part-time students pay $25,774, which includes both the academic year and five credit hours of summer study. Institutional scholarships, including full-tuition scholarships, are typically awarded to over 50% of each incoming class. Partial Scholarships may range from $5,000 to $30,000 a year and may be renewed provided requirements are met. Scholarships are also given based on background and life experiences.

Western New England College School of Law's support for Public Interest Lawyering includes the establishment of its Public Interest Scholars Program. Public Interest Scholars receive three-year tuition scholarships in values ranging from $16,000 up to the cost of full tuition. In addition to the tuition scholarships, Public Interest Scholars are awarded a one-time public interest stipend of $3,500 for approved public interest work in the summer months after the first or second year of law school. For more information on scholarship and loan opportunities, visit our website at www.law.wnec.edu.

FACULTY
Our 38 full time faculty members have been educated at the nation's most prestigious law schools. All have practiced law before joining our faculty and several hold additional graduate degrees in other disciplines. The School of Law places a strong emphasis on collaborative learning and student-professor interaction. Faculty members foster an open and collegial interaction with the students that provides a positive legal education in a comfortable atmosphere. The School of Law also has more than 30 adjunct faculty members, including practicing attorneys and judges, who bring their current legal practices into the classroom setting.

Student Body

The Student Bar Association (SBA) is the student government of the School of Law. The SBA plays a significant role in the administration of the School of Law with representation at the Faculty Meetings and on the Faculty/Student Committees.

Total enrollment of the law school: 575	
% Female/Male:	51/49
% full-time enrolled	71
Student/Faculty ratio	15.1: 1

ADMISSIONS
Each year, the Admissions Committee assembles a talented, interesting, and diverse class of students. We enroll a class whose members come from various races and ethnicities, ages, academic and professional backgrounds, and geographic areas.

Each completed application is read in its entirety and carefully reviewed to determine whether the applicant possesses the academic preparation and motivation necessary to complete the demanding workload of law school. Committee members attempt to gauge each applicant's prior academic performance, expected academic performance, and writing skills. While LSAT scores and undergraduate GPA are important to the Admissions Committee, they form just one part of the picture. We recognize that the ability to succeed in law school and contribute to our law school community and the legal profession is also demonstrated through the personal statement, letters of recommendation, and supplemental essays provided by the applicant. We therefore review these materials closely.

We encourage you to submit your application early since admissions decisions are made on a rolling basis. The Admissions Committee begins admitting applicants in January and completes the majority of its work by April. It is strongly recommended that applications for fulltime enrollment be completed by March 15. Applications for part-time enrollment should be submitted by June 1.

Please visit our website at www.law.wnec.edu to view more details on admissions.

INDEX

ALPHABETICAL INDEX

T

U

INDEX BY LOCATION

INDEX BY COST

LESS THAN $20,000

ABOUT THE AUTHORS

Eric Owens, Esq., attended Cornell College for his undergraduate degree and Loyola University Chicago for law school. He is now an American diplomat.

John Owens, Esq., earned his undergraduate degree in accountancy at the University of Illinois, Urbana-Champaign. He then matriculated at Loyola University Chicago School of Law, where he earned his JD. John works in the tax department of a Chicago law firm. He is currently working on a book, which he hopes to finish up this year. In his spare time, John likes to rock.

Julie Doherty graduated from Stanford University in 1998 with a degree in English. She currently lives in San Miguel de Allende, Mexico, where she works in an art gallery and printmaking studio. She is the co-author of several Princeton Review titles, including *The Best 368 Colleges* and *Planning a Life in Medicine*. She is working on her first novel.

NOTES

NOTES

More exp... from

Increase your chances of getting into the law school of your choice with The Princeton Review. We can help you get higher test scores, make the most informed choices, and make the most of your experience once you get there. We can also help you make the career move that will let you use your skills and education to their best advantage.

**Cracking the LSAT,
2010 Edition**
978-0-375-42929-3 • $22.99/C$27.99

**Cracking the LSAT with DVD,
2010 Edition**
978-0-375-42930-9 • $37.99/C$46.99

**The Best 172 Law Schools,
2010 Edition**
978-0-375-42958-3 • $22.99/C$27.99

LSAT Workout
978-0-375-76459-2 • $19.95/C$27.95

 Available at Bookstores Everywhere
www.PrincetonReview.com